NEW HAMPSHIRE PRACTICE
Volume 10

PROBATE LAW AND PROCEDURE

by
CHARLES A. DEGRANDPRE
with Foreword by
WILLIAM W. TREAT

Sections 1-1–48-11

LexisNexis™

QUESTIONS ABOUT THIS PUBLICATION?

For questions about the **Editorial Content** appearing in these volumes or reprint permission, please call:

Paulina Korenblum at .... 1-800-252-9257 (ext. 2295)
Internet Address: .... estate.plan@bender.com
Outside the United States and Canada please call .... (973) 820-2000

For assistance with replacement pages, shipments, billing or other customer service matters, please call:

Customer Services Department at .... (800) 833-9844
Outside the United States and Canada, please call .... (518) 487-3000
Fax number .... (518) 487-3584

For information on other Matthew Bender publications, please call
Your account manager or .... (800) 223-1940
Outside the United States and Canada, please call .... (518) 487-3000

Library of Congress Card Number: 96-78920

ISBN#: 0-327-16174-4

Editorial Offices
744 Broad Street, Newark, NJ 07102 (973) 820-2000
201 Mission St., San Francisco, CA 94105-1831 (415) 908-3200
701 East Water Street, Charlottesville, VA 22902-7587 (804) 972-7600
www.lexis.com

(Pub.82061)

DEDICATION

To my grandchildren, Berit and Wills DeGrandpre and Nadia Nargi, who have brightened my life and made me proud of their parents.

I also wish to dedicate this book to Libby Fielding, my stepdaughter who graduates from law school as this manuscript is completed. Watching Libby grow and develop into the fine young person she is and the fine lawyer she will become has been one of the joys of my life.

AUTHOR'S PREFACE

The third edition of this treatise describes the continuing development of New Hampshire probate law and procedure and is founded upon the pioneering 1968 treatise on New Hampshire probate law authored by former Rockingham County Probate Judge, William W. Treat.

The new treatise is designed to complement my earlier work, *Wills, Trusts and Gifts, 3rd Edition* (1997), which is volume 7 of the New Hampshire Practice series. An effort has been made to rearrange chapters and topics between the two works and some areas previously covered in the *Wills* treatise have been moved to these volumes, notably chapters related to trusts, trustees and charitable trusts. More importantly, I have added entirely new chapters on the Tortious Interference With Inheritance (chapter 42), Reformation of Wills (chapter 43), the Uniform Management of Institutional Funds (chapter 61), and the Uniform Trust Code (chapter 62).

My prime goal has been to make the new edition as "user-friendly" as possible so that it can be used as a handy desk reference by attorneys, paralegals, trust officers and others interested in this area of the law. For example, I have attempted to define commonly used words and terms and to simplify the task of the probate practitioners as they navigate the increasingly complex practice and procedures found in our probate courts. New appendices have been added to assist the busy probate practitioner who maintains an active practice in this area.

With the press of the author's legal practice, this third edition would not have been possible without the active assistance of attorney Jean Longfellow of the Minnesota Bar. Jean has extensive skills in editing legal work such as this and she was a very able assistant on the second edition of this work. I want to express my appreciation to her because without her help and advice this work would not have been completed in a timely manner.

I would also like to express my appreciation to Administrative Judge John R. Maher, of the Rockingham County Probate Court, who has always been of assistance to me in keeping current with the many changes in the field of probate law that have occurred over the past few years. Without his friendship, advice and assistance, I would have grown discouraged in this process long before this edition went to press.

Also, the registers of probate of Rockingham County, past register Charles K. Thayer and the present register Andrew Christie, Jr., have often provided me with copies of cases and citations and have been of general assistance to me as I scramble to meet deadlines. I thank each of them for their assistance.

At my firm, I wish to thank our office librarians, Leslie R. Duncan and Jennifer Finch, who have assisted in proofreading the manuscript and providing research assistance at innumerable times and on very short notice.

Also, I wish to acknowledge the constant support of my secretary, Jo Catalino, and her assistant, Joanna Diemer, without whose encouragement and active assistance I would not have been able to get the manuscript completed while still meeting the pressures of my practice.

June, 2001

Charles A. DeGrandpre

FOREWORD

The publication of this three volume treatise on New Hampshire probate law and procedure comes on the centennial anniversary of the single volume by Judge Lewis G. Hoyt published in 1901. After a lapse of 67 years, this writer broadened the scope of the first treatise and brought the work up to date with three volumes published in 1968. Charles A. DeGrandpre, Esq., a leading probate and trust authority in New Hampshire, has now published his third edition.

The evolution of probate law in New Hampshire since Attorney DeGrandpre's last publication in 1996 has been remarkable. As the oldest constitutional court in New Hampshire, the Probate Court's jurisdiction has been expanded by many legislative and judicial enhancements and refinements. In recent years the evolution of probate law in New Hampshire has in part been in response to a national trend toward simplified, and even unsupervised, administration of estates. The Uniform Probate Code proposed in 1979, and now adopted by 18 states (but not New Hampshire), called for a major reformation of probate practice. New Hampshire probate jurists have been respectful of their responsibility to oversee the acts of fiduciaries and protect the rights of those beneficially interested. As stated in the foreword to the last treatise, "The future of probate practice in New Hampshire will be of incremental steps" rather than an instant reformation of probate law.

At the initiative of Administrative Judge John Maher the legislature has taken steps to simplify the administration of estates. The incremental steps toward simplification forecast in the foreword to the treatise of 1996 are now part of the New Hampshire Probate Statutes. Depending on the nature of the estate, the probate practitioner has a choice of voluntary administration, summary administration, or waiver of administration, all of which tend to shorten the time and expense of the transfer of property at the decedent's death. These are salutary improvements in the administration of estates which simplify the procedure without jeopardizing the rights of the beneficiaries.

With its growing jurisdiction over intrafamilial issues the Probate Court's volume of family related cases has increased dramatically. In recent years adoptions of minors, termination of parental rights, and guardianships of minors and the elderly have expanded in part due to national cultural and demographic trends. The gradual breakdown of the traditional family structure and the expansion of life expectancy have called for more curial review. Adoptive parents have shown an increasing desire to transcend traditional racial and international borders. The increased use of nutritional knowledge, drug therapy, and health care has extended the life cycle and multiplied the number of elderly requiring care for dementia and similar illnesses of the aged. The New Hampshire Probate Courts have responded to this trend by adopting a very innovative guardian monitoring program in four counties in order to maintain a review of the status and effectiveness of court appointed guardians and the care of wards under their supervision.

The only thing that is certain for probate law in New Hampshire in the future is the need for adaptation to continuing cultural changes. Between now and 2020 Americans between the ages of 35 and 53 will inherit twelve trillion dollars. Much of the generational transfer of this wealth will occur under the jurisdiction of the Probate Courts. More children will be born to single parents. The divorce rate which is now about half the marriage rate will spawn more litigation regarding the rights of minor children as between separated parents. The number of people now living together as unmarried couples, both straight and gay, skyrocketed 72% during the last decade according to the 2000 census and seems to be increasing. These continuing permutations in the traditional family structure and the transfer of wealth will certainly be transformational and the law must inevitably adjust.

I believe that the common law which has served our legal system well by invoking its genius for adaptability will continue in the future to make the necessary accommodations to changing conditions. The law of succession remains one of the enduring customs of our western civilization. It preserves the continuity of person by deeming the executor as a *persona ficta* of the decedent. Since the appointment of the executor relates back to the date of death, there is no lapse of title. Personal representatives succeed to title *per universitatem* with the personal estate going to the administrator but real estate going directly to the heir unless otherwise disposed of by will.

New Hampshire is fortunate to have an able Probate Bar, but a consistent application of the law and practice before the Probate Court requires appropriate tools of the trade. Today's probate lawyer must have an understanding of the complexities of probate law and be prepared to meet the legitimate needs of his clients and the responsibilities of the Probate Court.

While the law of inheritance has not honored William James' principle that every human institution must be fashioned so that its least capable members can operate it, a competent probate attorney in New Hampshire can dispose of the ordinary estate with a minimum of court appearances for a reasonable cost. I believe that these volumes will go a long way toward satisfying the needs of the probate practitioners in New Hampshire.

The New Hampshire Bar is enormously indebted to Charles DeGrandpre for continuing his charge to keep these volumes on probate law and procedure up to date. Judge Hoyt would have been pleased to know that his first volume of one hundred years ago has been refined and updated by DeGrandpre's most recent volumes. With its ancient traditions and its expanding complexity, probate law requires the continuing contributions of those who honor its traditions. By bringing up to date these probate volumes Charles DeGrandpre has maintained the authority and completeness of a body of probate literature that is an essential part of every law library.

William W. Treat

July 2001

SUMMARY OF CONTENTS

VOLUME 10

PART I. INTRODUCTION

PART II. ORGANIZATION, JURISDICTION AND OPERATION GENERALLY OF PROBATE COURTS

PART III. ADMINISTRATION OF ESTATES

PART VII. INTESTACY: THE LAW OF DESCENT AND DISTRIBUTION

PART VIII. TAXATION OF INHERITANCES AND ESTATES

PART IX. ADMINISTRATION OF TRUSTS

PART X. PROTECTION OF PERSONS WITH DISABILITIES

PART XI. PARENT AND CHILD

TABLE OF CONTENTS

PART I. INTRODUCTION

CHAPTER 45. SUITS BY AND AGAINST ADMINISTRATORS

PART I

INTRODUCTION

CHAPTER 1. SCOPE OF THE PUBLICATION; RESEARCH REFERENCES; TERMINOLOGY

§ 1-1. Scope of the Publication
§ 1-2. Research References
§ 1-3. Terminology

§ 1-1. Scope of the Publication

The subject of this treatise is probate law and its practice and procedure. All relevant areas of this subject are included, with the exception of those areas of substantive law that are treated in the author's other volume in the New Hampshire Practice series entitled *Wills, Trusts and Gifts* (3d ed. 1997). The purpose of this treatise is to create a readable desk-top guide that will be as useful to a secretary or legal assistant as it is to the probate lawyer.

This treatise includes all areas of practice before the probate courts of New Hampshire, but emphasizes the most important area of practice, the law of the administration of estates. The practical aspects of practice and procedure in the probate courts of New Hampshire are stressed. The intent of this book is to give the reader a practical guide to the somewhat arcane procedures of the probate courts, while at the same time providing a detailed analysis of statutory and case law. Little-used areas of probate court jurisdiction, such as the role of the probate court in the distribution of partnership property, are given less attention than more frequently encountered areas, such as claims by or against administrators.

The Appendix includes, where appropriate, examples of approved probate court forms to assist the practitioner in the everyday administration of estates.

§ 1-2. Research References

The foundation of all legal research in the area of probate law and administration in New Hampshire is Chief Justice Jeremiah Smith's *Manuscript Treatise on Probate Law* published at pages 447–520 of Smith's Reports. The manuscript treatise was originally entitled *An Essay on the Law of Descent and of Last Wills and Testaments* and consisted of two manuscript volumes that would total some 500 to 600 pages had they been reduced to print. Judge Smith's qualifications as an author in the probate area of the law included being Chief Justice of the Supreme and Superior Courts and serving as a probate judge for Rockingham County for a short period of time. His treatise was apparently begun while he held the office of probate judge. The manuscript treatise itself was never reduced to print in its entirety but substantial excerpts are printed in Smith's Reports, which precedes Volume 1 of the New Hampshire Reports. The manuscript treatise is an essential starting point for all scholarly research in the area of probate law of New Hampshire.

An excellent discussion of the development of probate law prior to the revolutionary period can be found in the work of Albert Batchellor, editor of State Papers and entitled *Outline of the Development of Probate Law and Probate Jurisdiction in New Hampshire* 1623–1775 (1907). This volume provides an excellent historical study of the development of the law of pre-revolutionary New Hampshire, and, in particular, the probate court system in New Hampshire.

The next development in the form of a complete treatise in this area of the law occurred in 1901, with the publication of Rockingham Probate Judge Louis G. Hoyt's one-volume work entitled *Practice and Proceedings in the Probate Courts of New Hampshire*. Judge Hoyt supplemented his 1901 treatise with a shorter "pamphlet" entitled *The Law of Administration in New Hampshire Together With a Table of Descents* published in 1916. These works remained the standard textual treatment of this area of the law until the 1968 publication of Judge William W. Treat's three-volume work entitled *Probate Law*. Following in the footsteps of Judges Smith and Hoyt, his predecessors in the position of Rockingham County probate judge, Judge Treat set forth in his treatise a comprehensive review of the law of probate administration that remains the authoritative work in this field to the present time. The present treatise is intended to be a complete revision of Judge Treat's 1968 work, modifying it to reflect current probate practice and procedure.

In addition to these full treatments of this area of the law, there are several excellent papers and manuscripts on specific areas of the law that are useful resources for research. Attorney Malcolm McLane of Concord is the author of an article presenting an overview of New Hampshire probate practice that appeared in the New Hampshire Bar Journal in Volume 7, Pages 294–301 (1965). There is also an informative article by former Strafford County Probate Judge Leonard C. Hardwick, entitled *Administration of Small Estates*, which is found at 1 N.H.B.J. 40 (1958). This article focuses on the unique statutory provisions relating to the administration of small estates.

There have also been several publications published by the New Hampshire Bar Association, arising out of various programs dealing with estate planning and estate administration sponsored by the Bar Association. These publications are generally known as CLE Handbooks. Handbooks of current interest include:

Medicaid Planning (2000); *Basic Probate Practice* (1999); *Elder Law* (1999); *Estate Planning & Administration in NH & Vermont: A Comparison for Practitioners* (1999); *Utilizing the Qualified Personal Residence Trust* (1999); *Gifts to Minors* (1998); *Disability Law* (1998); *Advanced Trust & Estate Law* (1997); *Uniform Disclaimer Act* (1997); *NH Death & Inheritance Taxes* (1996); *Preparation & Audit of Federal Estate Tax & Federal Gift Tax Returns* (1996); *Irrevocable Trusts* (1995); *Probate Update: Understanding Recent Changes in Accounting Rules and Attorney Liability* (1995) and *Estate Planning for the Experienced Practitioner* (1993). Other recent seminar publications of interest, published by the National Business Institute, Inc., are *A Practical Guide to Estate Administration in New Hampshire* (1993) and *Administration of the Estate in New Hampshire* (1991).

There are also two publications of some general help to the in-depth research in the area of probate law. One of these, a pamphlet entitled *The Probate Court of New Hampshire*, was published in 1978 and is a layman's introduction to the probate courts of New Hampshire. Unfortunately, that publication has not been updated. A more important publication is the *New Hampshire Probate Court Manual*, William W. Treat, Editor. This two-volume looseleaf manual is intended as a procedural handbook to provide guidance to registers of probate and probate judges in various counties. Unfortunately, very few manuals were published and, although most registers of probate have copies of the manual, some do not.

The two-volume work by Supreme Court clerk Crawford D. Hening, entitled *New Hampshire Digest* and published in 1926, is a definitive and exhaustive annotation of the cases in this area of the law to 1920. Of particular interest are the chapters in this work on Probate Law and the Procedure (Volume 2, Page 1168), Administrators (Volume 1, Page 13), Guardians (Volume 1, Page 746), Husband and Wife (Volume 1, Page 806), Trusts (Volume 2, Page 588) and Wills (Volume 2, Page 1620).

West's *New Hampshire Digest* contains some of the more recent cases but is not a complete compilation of cases. Moreover, there is no single topic providing ready reference to this area of the law; one must consult several headings. Of particular importance to this area of the law are the headings Courts, Descent and Distribution, Executors and Administrators, Husband and Wife, Mental Health, Trusts, Wills, and Taxation.

Of interest to serious researchers is Charles R. Morrison's *New Hampshire Probate Directory*, a slim volume published in 1870 that contains the entire statutory probate law to that date with "full notes of decisions and forms of will petitions, citations, orders and decrees and all other matters relating to probate courts and proceedings therein."

The bulk of the statutory law relating to probate law and its administration is found in New Hampshire Revised Statutes Annotated, Title 56, Probate Courts and Decedents' Estates. Chapters 547–567A contain most of the statutory law relating to this area. However, there are other sections of statutory law scattered throughout the Revised Statutes Annotated that are pertinent to this area of the law. The most important are the inheritance and estate tax statutes found in Title 5, particularly Chapter 86, Taxation of Legacies and Successions; Chapter 87, Taxation of Transfers of Certain Estates; Chapter 88-A, Uniform Estate Tax Apportionment Act; Chapter 89, Transfer Tax Upon the Personal Property of Nonresident Decedents; and Chapter 90, Settlement of Disputes Respecting the Domicile of Decedents for Death Tax Purposes.

§ 1-3. Terminology

Throughout the treatise, except where quotation requires, the term *administrator* is used instead of the term *administrator and administratrix*; the term *executor* instead of the term *executor and executrix*, etc. The term *administrator*, unless used specifically to refer only to the personal representative of non-testate estates, is used in its broadest sense to refer to both administrators and executors. A more appropriate term is *personal representative*, which includes both administrators and executors.

To facilitate conciseness, the male pronoun is used instead of "his or her," "his/her," etc. Similarly, the singular term (e.g., "administrator" for "administrators") is used whenever possible. The forms in the Appendix of Forms follow this usage.

The authors' preference for certain terminology (e.g., *legal assistant* instead of *paralegal*) is indulged.

CHAPTER 2. PROBATE TERMS

§ 2-1. Definitions of Commonly-Used Terms

Listed below are a few of the standard terms frequently encountered by the probate practitioner. This glossary is not intended to be a comprehensive dictionary definition. Its function is to provide the reader with a quick reference or refresher, and to point to appropriate places in the text or in a New Hampshire statute where the reader may find more information on the topic.

Accounting. 1. An itemized statement of all sums received by and paid out by the administrator that identifies the source of the funds or the consideration paid. 2. An annual statement of transactions affecting a trustee's estate filed by a testamentary trustee. See Chapters 39, 63.

—Settling an Account. The hearing procedure in which a probate judge approves or "allows" an administrator's account. See Chapter 39.

Administrator. 1. Any individual authorized by the probate court to administer an estate or execute a will. 2. The court-appointed personal representative of a person who died without a will. See Chapters 24, 25.

—Administrator, d.b.n. (*de bonis non*). A successor administrator appointed by the probate court to take over the administration of an estate only partially settled by a prior administrator. See Chapter 29.

—Administrator, w.w.a. (*with the will annexed*). An administrator appointed by the court when the testator fails to nominate an executor or when the person nominated is unable or unwilling to act as executor. See Chapter 29.

Attorney-in-Fact. A person nominated to act as an agent under a power of attorney. See RSA 506:6, 7 and Chapter 74.

Common Law Marriage. The arrangement between a man and a woman who cohabit together without the legal requisites for a marriage. In New

Hampshire, such a cohabitation arrangement is recognized as a marriage for inheritance purposes in very limited circumstances. See Chapter 52.

Conservator. A person appointed by the probate court to manage the affairs of another who is not necessarily mentally incompetent. The conservator controls the estate of the ward and not his person. A conservator may be appointed in a voluntary guardianship. See Chapter 73.

Descent and Distribution. The law relating to the inheritance rights of relatives of a decedent, also referred to as intestacy. See RSA 561 and Chapters 51, 53.

Devise. The gift or bequest of a decedent's real estate under a will. The term is often used interchangeably with legacy and loosely used to define any testamentary gift, whether of real or personal property. See Chapter 37.

—**Devisees.** A person given an interest in real property under a will. See Chapter 37.

—**General Devise.** A passing of land to another under a will without a particular description of the land. See Chapter 37.

—**Specific Devise.** A gift by will of a specific piece of real property that is so described as to distinguish it from other real property. See Chapter 37.

Elective Share. The right of a surviving spouse to take a statutory share in lieu of the share given under the will of a deceased spouse. See RSA 560:10, 14 and Chapter 52.

Escheat. 1. The accruing to the state of property of a decedent dying without heirs. 2. Any unclaimed property that, after the passage of a specific period of time, is presumed abandoned and accrues to the state. See RSA 471-C; RSA 561:8,10-12b and Chapters 37, 54.

Estate. All of an individual's property, real and personal, including any rights and interests that person may have in any property. See Chapter 18 et seq.

Executor. The personal representative of a person who died leaving a will. See Chapters 24, 25.

—**Executor** *De Son Tort.* (*of his wrong*). A person who wrongfully takes possession and control of a decedent's property and is held to the duties of an administrator. See Chapter 29.

Fraud on the Spouse's Share. A prohibition against a spouse's conveyance of assets to others prior to death so as to decrease his spouse's statutory share, when the conveyance is made with the intent to defraud his spouse. See Chapter 52.

Guardian. A person invested by the probate court with the power and duty of taking care of the person and/or property of another who is considered incapable of managing his affairs due to some defect of understanding. See Chapter 69 et seq.

—Guardian Ad Litem. A special guardian appointed by the court to represent the interests of a minor or incompetent person in a lawsuit to which the minor or incompetent person is a party. See Chapters 69, 70, 77.

—Incapacity. The inability of an individual to take care of himself or his property. RSA 464-A requires evidence of recent acts or occurrences demonstrating this inability. See Chapter 77.

—Public Guardian. Where a mentally ill or developmentally disabled person needs or is statutorily required to have a guardian, but no relative, friend, or other interested party is available, the probate court may appoint the Public Guardianship and Protection Program as guardian. See Chapter 72.

Insolvent Estate. An estate where it appears that the assets are insufficient to pay all debts, expenses and taxes due from the estate. It is not necessary that the estate actually be insolvent to be administered as an insolvent estate. An estate which is insolvent is said to be administered in the insolvency course. See Chapter 49.

Intestacy. The law governing the distribution of property upon the death of a decedent who dies without a will, or who dies with a will but without disposing of all of his property. See Chapter 53.

Inventory. An itemized account or listing of the assets in the decedent's estate filed with the probate court by the administrator. The inventory contains a description of all real estate, a schedule of all goods, chattel, stocks, bonds and other effects of the deceased, all notes, bank deposits, interest owed, and other written evidences of debt. See Chapter 34.

Legacy. 1. A gift or bequest of personal property under a will. 2. Legacy may be applied to include a gift of real estate if the will establishes that as the testator's intent. See Chapter 37.

—**Demonstrative Legacy.** A bequest of a certain sum of money that is paid out of a specific fund in existence at the time of the testator's death. See Chapter 37.

—**General Legacy.** A bequest or gift under a will that comes out of the general assets of the testator's estate. The item or the fund from which it comes is not identified. See Chapter 37.

—**Legatees.** One who takes an interest in personal property under a will. See Chapter 37.

—**Pecuniary Legacy.** A bequest of a sum of money or an annuity. See Chapter 37.

—**Specific Legacy.** A gift by will of a specific thing or of some portion of the testator's estate described so as to distinguish it from other articles of the same nature. See Chapter 37.

Letters of Administration. Formal notice of the probate court's appointment of an administrator to act on behalf of an estate. This notice is also known as a certificate of appointment. See Chapter 24.

License. The permission of a probate court to conduct a sale. See Chapter 35.

Lost Person. A person who has left home, has not been heard of, or from, directly or indirectly for one year, and is believed to be dead. See Chapter 22.

Non-Claim Statute. The law requiring a claimant to present and demand payment before commencing an action against an administrator. See RSA 556:1 and Chapter 41.

Personal Representative. A person to whom the administration of an estate or the execution of a will has been granted by the probate court. The term includes executors and administrators. The Uniform Probate Code favors this term. See Chapter 24 et seq.

Principal. A person who executes a power of attorney delegating specified duties to a known agent. See RSA 506:6, 7 and Chapter 74.

Private Claim. A debt due from the estate to its administrator. See Chapters 39 and 49.

Probate. 1. The process of proving the document offered as a decedent's last will and testament before the court. 2. The entire body of law relating to the distribution of property upon a person's death. See Chapters 3, 23.

Probate Bond. A surety instrument that a fiduciary posts, in a specified amount, with the probate court in a probate proceeding, by which the surety promises to indemnify the estate for improper actions by the fiduciary. See Chapter 28.

Probate Law. The areas of law commonly handled by a probate court, including distributions of estates, conservatorships, guardianships, testamentary trusts, adoptions, termination of parental rights, change of name, and permission to marry. See Chapters 3–5.

Proof in Common Form. A method of proving a will in an uncontested probate proceeding that does not require the testimony of a witness to the will as to its proper execution. See Chapter 23.

Proof in Solemn Form. A method of proving a will that requires public notice and examination of all witnesses to a will. It is a more elaborate procedure than proof in common form. See Chapter 23.

Property. Any interest in property owned by a decedent.

   —Personal Property. A decedent's tangible and intangible property, rights, and interests other than real property. See Chapter 34 et seq.

   —Real Property. A decedent's real estate. See Chapter 35.

   —Tangible Personal Property. A decedent's goods and chattels. The term does not include intangible personal property such as stocks and bonds. See Chapter 39.

Survival of Action. The law relating to when an action, pending or not yet pending, by or against a decedent at his death may be initiated or continued after the decedent's death. See RSA 508, 556 and Chapter 46.

Trusts. A right of property, real or personal, held by one party for the benefit of another.

   —Inter Vivos Trust. A trust that is created and put into effect during the lifetime of the grantor. It is also known as a living trust or a revocable trust. See Chapter 64.

   —Revocable Trust. An inter vivos trust over which the grantor retains the power to revoke or terminate. See Chapter 64.

   —Testamentary Trust. A trust that is created under a will, becomes effective upon the death of the grantor, and is subject to the supervision of the probate court. See Chapter 63.

Voluntary Administration. A simplified form of administration designed for small estates. See Chapter 19.

Ward. A person who, due to some defect of understanding, is considered incapable of administering his own affairs and over whom or over whose property a guardian is appointed. See Chapter 69 et seq.

Will Contest. Litigation challenging the validity of a will for any reason. See Chapter 44.

CHAPTER 3. HISTORY AND DEVELOPMENT
OF PROBATE LAW IN NEW HAMPSHIRE

§ 3-1. Introduction

Modern practitioners of probate law are at a loss to explain to clients the origins of the word which defines this entire body of law. The term *probate* has come down from our English common law antecedents. The probable source of the word is the Latin word *probate* which is defined as to try, to test or to prove.[1] This etymological basis is very interesting and fascinating since it has great relevance to its modern usage. As used in current terminology, the term *probate* refers to the process of proving before a court the document offered as the last will and testament of a decedent.[2] In the broad connotation used in this treatise, the word *probate* refers not only to the law relating to the distribution of property by will, but to the entire body of law relating to the distribution of property upon the death of a person. Furthermore, the term *probate law*, as used in this treatise, is deemed to include all of those areas of the law which are commonly handled by the probate court, including guardianships, testamentary trusts, adoptions, termination of parental rights, change of name, and permission to marry.

Library References

Am Jur 2d Wills § 822

CJS Executors and Administrators § 3

CJS Wills § 307

---

[1] WEBSTER'S THIRD NEW INTERNATIONAL DICTIONARY 1806 (1961).

[2] *Id.*

§ 3-2. Ancient History

The roots of probate law are as old as some of the most ancient records of our civilization.[3] Over two thousand years before the birth of Christ, the Code of Hammurabi (2067-2025) provided that a son might be disinherited for good cause.[4] The idea of testation was germinated much earlier. Documents providing for the disposition of property after one's death, executed thirty centuries before Christ[5] have been found in Egypt.

Instruments having the same qualities as our wills of today existed during the Roman Empire and in the pre-Norman period in England.[6] Following the Norman conquest, William the Conqueror (1066–1087) separated the ecclesiastical and secular courts in England, with the result, probably unintentional, that the ecclesiastical courts acquired jurisdiction of succession to personal property, while the secular courts retained jurisdiction of succession to real property.[7]

The origin of our New Hampshire probate courts is traced to the ecclesiastical courts of England, the jurisdiction of which was practically limited to probating wills, granting administration and suing for legacies. In *Patten v. Patten*,[8] the New Hampshire Supreme Court discussed the history of the development of probate law in New Hampshire from its earliest days:

> An examination of the history and development of statutory probate law in this state shows that there never has been a time when the probate court had exclusive jurisdiction over controversies between co-executors. The origin of our probate courts is traced to the ecclesiastical courts of England, the jurisdiction of which was practically limited to the probate of wills, the granting of administration and suing for legacies. In every other respect the control of estates, executors and administrators was exclusively in the common law and chancery courts. . . .. In this state even the appointment of judges of probate depended upon charters and unwritten law until after the revolutionary war. The

---

[3] 1 BOWE-PARKER: PAGE ON WILLS § 2.4 (1960).

[4] *Id.*

[5] *Id.*

[6] 1 BOWE-PARKER: PAGE ON WILLS § 2.7 (1960).

[7] *Id.*

[8] Patten v. Patten, 79 N.H. 388, 109 A. 416 (1920).

constitutional amendment of 1792-93 conferred exclusive jurisdiction, substantially in accord with the English practice. "All
matters relating to the probate of wills and granting letters of
administration shall be exercised by the judges of probate."[9]

The devise of land, as distinguished from the bequest of personal
property, was formally recognized in the English common law in 1540
with the passage of the Statute of Wills.[10] The right to bequeath personal
property by will was freely recognized under the English common law
from its earliest beginnings, since personal property, as distinguished
from real property, was regarded as of inconsiderable value.[11]

§ 3-3. Provincial and State Procedure

Prior to 1680, the duties now performed by the judge of probate were
discharged by the county courts.[12] Between 1680 and 1694, probate
powers were generally performed by the supreme executive magistrate,
whether Lieutenant-Governor or President of the Council.[13] It was not
until 1694 that the offices of judge of probate and register of probate
were established.[14]

In *Kimball v. Fisk*,[15] the Supreme Court rejected the argument that
the probate courts in New Hampshire were of limited jurisdiction. Rather,
the Court pointed out that

> [T]he powers of courts of probate were conferred in Massa-
> chusetts on the "county courts," and in some cases on special
> commissioners, while New Hampshire was subject to that
> colony, but they were conferred as a body of well known
> principles and rules; a settled and general jurisdiction then
> existing at common law in the ordinary or ecclesiastical courts.
> The statutes of the colony did not attempt to define or prescribe
> the powers of those courts in general, otherwise than by a

---

[9] *Id.* (citations omitted).

[10] 32 Hen. VIII, c. 1, 1540. See 1 BOWE -PARKER: PAGE ON WILLS § 2.7 (1960).

[11] MANUSCRIPT TREATISE ON PROBATE LAW, SMITH'S REPORTS p. 457 (1879).

[12] MANUSCRIPT TREATISE ON PROBATE LAW, SMITH'S REPORTS p. 512 (1879).

[13] MANUSCRIPT TREATISE ON PROBATE LAW, SMITH'S REPORTS p. 513 (1879).

[14] MANUSCRIPT TREATISE ON PROBATE LAW, SMITH'S REPORTS p. 514 (1879).

[15] Kimball v. Fisk, 39 N.H. 110 (1859).

reference to the existing law of the land. The like state of things has continued to the present.[16]

Though the common law courts had probate jurisdiction, probate practice bore little similarity to practice in the common law courts. Rather, it was astonishingly like what is presently followed.[17] There is, for example, an inventory of the estate of one John Phillips, dated 1641, which was recorded in Dover, New Hampshire in 1643, and which bears a great resemblance to a twentieth century inventory.[18]

In New Hampshire, the appointment of judges of probate depended upon the charters and upon unwritten law until after the Revolutionary War.[19] In matters of probate, the Governor and Council were a specialized court of appeal.[20] The organization of the modern probate courts began in New England in 1692, with Lieutenant Governor John Usher usually acting as Supreme Ordinary, and John Hinckes, President of the Council, occasionally substituting.[21] The first judge of probate was appointed in 1693 when Lieutenant Governor Usher commissioned Thomas Packer as judge.[22]

The New Hampshire constitutional amendments of 1792-93 conferred exclusive jurisdiction on the probate courts, substantially in accord with the English practice: "All matters relating to the probate of wills and granting letters of administration shall be exercised by the judges of probate."[23] Part II, Article 80 of the New Hampshire Constitution presently provides that

> All matters relating to the probate of wills, and granting letters
> of administration, shall be exercised by the judges of probate,

---

[16] Kimball v. Fisk, 39 N.H. 110, 119–20 (1859).

[17] Elwin L. Page, *Judicial Beginnings in New Hampshire*, N.H. HISTORICAL SOC. p. 153 (1959).

[18] Elwin L. Page, *Judicial Beginnings in New Hampshire*, N.H. HISTORICAL SOC. p. 152 (1959).

[19] Patten v. Patten, 79 N.H. 388, 109 A. 415 (1920).

[20] Court of Appeals in New Hampshire, 4 N.H.B.J. 54. The requirement of a probate appeal bond apparently dates from the Provincial Statutes of 1718. See Dane v. Dane, 67 N.H. 552, 39 A. 433 (1894).

[21] Elwin L. Page, *Judicial Beginnings in New Hampshire*, N.H. HISTORICAL SOC. p. 161 (1959).

[22] *Id.*

[23] Patten v. Patten, 79 N.H. 388, 109 A. 415 (1920).

in such manner as the legislature have directed, or may hereafter direct: And the judges of probate shall hold their courts at such place or places, on such fixed days, as the conveniency of the people may require; and the legislature from time to time appoint.[24]

In 1775, all of the probate records of the province of New Hampshire were stored in Exeter for their great safety and they remained there until 1889.[25] In 1899, these records were moved to Concord and are still in the official custody of the Secretary of State for the State of New Hampshire.[26]

An excellent history of the development of the law of probate in provincial New Hampshire prior to 1775 can be found in the historical note to Albert Batchellor's *Outline of the Development of Probate Law and Probate Jurisdiction in New Hampshire 1623-1775* (1907). Mr. Batchellor was a man of wide reputation as both an attorney and as editor of the New Hampshire State Papers. This volume is an historical gold mine for any serious student of the early history of our courts and in particular the probate court system.

§ 3-4. Provincial and State Procedure

Partly in response to the consumerist wave of the sixties and spurred on by Norman F. Dacey's book *How to Avoid Probate*,[27] the National Conference of Commissioners on Uniform State Laws in 1969 promulgated a Uniform Act entitled, in short, "The Uniform Probate Code". This code was approved by the American Bar Association the same year and presented to the states for adoption. To date, eighteen states have adopted all or some portion of the Uniform Probate Code.

The Uniform Probate Code has been submitted to the New Hampshire legislature for adoption on at least two occasions. However, there was substantial opposition to the Code because of the sweeping changes it would make in the basic procedures. As a result, registers of probate,

---

[24] N.H. CONST. pt. II, art. 80.

[25] BATCHELLOR, OUTLINE OF THE DEVELOPMENT OF PROBATE LAW AND PROBATE JURISDICTION IN NEW HAMPSHIRE 1623-1775, Preface (1907).

[26] *Id.*

[27] Crown Publishers, Inc. (1965).

among many, have opposed the bills and the Code has not been enacted in New Hampshire.

Despite its limited acceptance in the states, the Code has had a substantial impact on probate law in many states. The Code is considered to be an authoritative statement of what the law in this area should be. It is also useful for drafting purposes and New Hampshire draftsmen have used the law in enacting narrow revisions of the probate statutes.

The complete title of the Uniform Probate Code is "An Act Relating to Affairs of Decedents, Missing Persons, Protected Persons, Minors, Incapacitated Persons and Certain Others." Thus, the Code is designed to be a very broad treatment of this area of the law. The Code is made up of several parts. The basic sections relate to the main purpose as described in its long title, but subsequent amendments have included sections which are designed to be enacted either as part of the Code or as freestanding acts. These other sections include the 1977 "Adoption of Uniform International Wills Act," the 1979 "Adoption of Uniform Durable Power of Attorney Act," the 1982 "Adoption of Uniform Guardianship and Protected Proceedings Act," and the 1982 "Adoption of Provisions Relating to Succession Without Administration." The entire Code is a useful tool in providing alternative approaches to New Hampshire procedure and should be part of any New Hampshire probate practitioner's library.

Library References

Am Jur 2d Executors and Administrators §§ 133–156

Am Jur 2d Wills §§ 841, 842

PART II

ORGANIZATION, JURISDICTION AND OPERATION GENERALLY OF PROBATE COURTS

CHAPTER 4. PROBATE COURTS GENERALLY

---

§ 4-1. Court of Record
§ 4-2. Judge of Probate; Probate Court; Judge; Administrative Judge
§ 4-3. Full-and Part-Time Probate Judges
§ 4-4. Adoption of Probate Rules; Diversity in Practice
§ 4-5. National Probate Court Standards

---

§ 4-1. Court of Record

RSA 547:1 provides that the "court of probate is a court of record for all purposes." RSA 547:17 provides that all records of cases shall be kept in the probate court in the county where the case is pending. As a result, the probate court's "records import the same verity as those of other courts."[1] A judgment by the probate court upon any matter within its jurisdiction which is not appealed from, is as conclusive and binding as a judgment from a court of common law[2] and binds all parties and their privies like any other judgment.[3] Originally, the probate court was not considered to be a court of record. In *H v. H*,[4] the Supreme Court described the original nature of the New Hampshire probate court

---

[1] Tebbets v. Tilton, 24 N.H. 120, 124 (1851).

[2] Morgan v. Dodge, 44 N.H. 255 (1862); Tebbets v. Tilton, 24 N.H. 120 (1851).

[3] Bryant v. Allen, 6 N.H. 116 (1833). See Ham v. Ayers, 22 N.H. 412 (1851). See also Judge of Probate v. Robins, 5 N.H. 246 (1830), where it was held that a decree fixing a distributive share cannot be called into question collaterally in a suit upon the probate bond.

[4] H v. H, 4 N.H. 60, 65 (1827).

as follows: "A court of probate is not technically a court of record, and to be valid its proceedings must be warranted by law. Any order or decree of the court, if repugnant to law, is null, and may be avoided by plea."

Library References

Am Jur 2d Courts §§ 14, 69

CJS Courts § 4

§ 4-2. Judge of Probate; Probate Court; Judge; Administrative Judge

Lawyers, as well as laymen, often use the terms *probate court, probate judge* and *judge* interchangeably. In *Carr v. Corning*, the Supreme Court noted that

> [I]t is a matter of common knowledge that when a person attending to probate business or considering probate matters speaks of referring anything to the judge of probate, he usually intends the probate court and not the person who exercises the function of that office.[5]

The legislature has often confused the usage of these terms and they are sometimes used interchangeably in the Revised Statutes Annotated. RSA 547:2 provides that the word *judge*, as used in Title 56 of the Revised Statutes Annotated shall mean the judge of probate to whom the jurisdiction of the matter belongs.

An administrative judge, appointed by the Supreme Court, is a full-time judge and devotes much of his activities to administrative matters as contrasted with the direct day-to-day operation of the probate court. However, the administrative judge is a sitting probate judge and as such has the usual duties of the probate judge for the county in which he or she sits.

§ 4-3. Full-and Part-Time Probate Judges

RSA 491-A:4 provides that "the supreme court, after reviewing population, caseload, judicial time and efficiency, available judicial resources and other relevant criteria, may determine, with prior approval of the fiscal committee, that any part-time probate judge become full-time, provided that funds have been specifically appropriated for the

---

[5] Carr v. Corning, 73 N.H. 362, 365, 62 A. 168, 169 (1905).

salary and benefits for a full-time probate judge." A second full-time probate judge has been appointed who is also a sitting probate judge from a county, but whose duties have been expanded beyond the probate court to include riding the circuit, primarily to hear contested cases in other jurisdictions.[6] This has greatly reduced the backlog of contested cases.

RSA 547:2-a provides that a probate judge designated to be fulltime is not permitted to engage in the practice of law to any degree.

§ 4-4.   Adoption of Probate Rules; Diversity in Practice

Until 1959, the probate courts of New Hampshire, staffed by part-time judges and elected registers of probate, presented a bewildering diversity of practices and procedures to the probate practitioner. There were no uniform rules or uniform forms and constant consultation was required to determine the local rules and forms of each county probate court.

In 1960, the Supreme Court, exercising the administrative jurisdiction over the probate courts granted by RSA 547:33, promulgated a uniform set of probate court rules that helped to establish a more uniform procedure among the courts. More importantly, a uniform set of forms was adopted by the Supreme Court for use in the probate courts. These measures resulted in a higher degree of uniformity of practice between the probate courts. However, there still remains a greater diversity of practice and procedure in the probate courts than one is accustomed to in the superior courts, and the practitioner must be alert for these differences. It is best for the practitioner who intends to practice in an unfamiliar probate court to check frequently with local attorneys to ascertain whether there are any procedures peculiar to the court. Beware

Furthermore, as probate court decisions are seldom published, there is much more diversity between rulings on substantial probate matters in the probate courts than in the superior courts. Thus, unless an appeal to the Supreme Court establishes a uniform ruling, it is not uncommon to find substantially different approaches to substantive law questions among the probate courts of the state.

As a result of the appointment of an administrative judge of the probate court by the Supreme Court, a marked increase in uniformity of practice has been seen.

---

[6] RSA 547:2-a provides that a full-time judge shall assist the probate court in the other counties whenever a probate judge in such other county is disqualified, disabled, or otherwise unable to sit.

§ 4-5.   National Probate Court Standards

In 1993, the Commission on National Probate Standards, operating out of the National Center for State Courts in Williamsburg, Virginia, promulgated a set of standards known as the National Probate Court Standards.[7] The standards represent the culmination of a two-year project to develop national standards for state courts exercising jurisdiction over probate matters. The standards are a helpful resource for guidance in such areas as guardianships, conservatorship, estate matters, etc.

The standards and goals set forth in the National Probate Court Standards are more aspirational than real, but are a helpful look to what proper practice should be. Also, the standards include a state-by-state statistical summary of workloads in estates, guardianships, etc., and therefore, provide a comparative look at workloads in the various state probate courts.

---

[7] National Center for State Courts, 300 Newport Avenue, P.O. Box 8798, Williamsburg, Virginia 23178-8798, Library of Congress Catalog No. 93-87566 (1993).

CHAPTER 5. JURISDICTION OF THE PROBATE COURT

§ 5-1. Introduction; Family Court Distinguished

The jurisdiction of the probate courts in New Hampshire is often confusing. There are many instances of concurrent and overlapping areas of jurisdiction. In addition, the boundaries between areas of exclusive jurisdiction of different courts can be unclear.

Some areas of jurisdiction, however, are quite clear and precise. The jurisdiction of the probate courts is found both in constitutional provisions[1] and statutory law.[2] Unlike many other states, the probate courts of New Hampshire are primarily concerned with the traditional functions of the probate law: the settling of estates and other closely related matters.

In *Kimball v. Fisk*,[3] it was stated that:

> [T]he jurisdiction of probate courts has been vested in different officers at successive periods in the history of the Province; but, excepting in a few cases, the general system of probate jurisdiction has remained as defined at common law. . . .. The jurisdiction of probate courts was at common law restricted to proceedings relative to the estates of persons deceased. . . .. [B]y statute, many other branches of authority have been added. . . .. Such are the distribution of insolvent estates, the appointment of guardians of minors and insane persons, trusts and trustees, and division of estates, etc. . . .. [T]hat the courts of probate, and this court, which is the Supreme Court of Probate . . . are not to be regarded as courts of special and limited jurisdiction, but as courts of general jurisdiction on these subjects. . . ..[4]

The probate court in New Hampshire is not a family court in the way that term is often used. In 1970, the Judicial Council recommended passage of legislation giving probate courts concurrent jurisdiction with the superior courts over domestic relations matters, but that proposal was not enacted.[5] Although there have since been several legislative proposals to give the probate courts such jurisdiction, all such efforts have failed. The present jurisdiction of the New Hampshire probate courts does not extend to divorce[6] or separation or to issues arising within these actions that relate to child custody.

---

[1] N.H. CONST. pt. II, art. 80.

[2] RSA 547:3.

[3] Kimball v. Fisk, 39 N.H. 110, 120 (1859).

[4] *Id.*

[5] 13th Report Judicial Council, p. 19 (1970).

[6] But see RSA 460:8 and 560:19 which grant jurisdiction to the probate court to make findings determining conduct which constitutes cause for divorce under very limited circumstances.

New Hampshire is experimenting with the concept of a family court by creating family divisions in pilot programs in certain counties. The program is intended "to promote the public interest and to better serve citizens who seek judicial resolution of such family matters as divorce, child custody and visitation, child support, legal separation, paternity, domestic violence, juvenile delinquency, child abuse and neglect, children in need of services, guardianship of minors, termination of parental rights and adoption."[7] Jurisdiction over these matters is to be exclusively exercised through the family division as procedurally jurisdiction was previously exercised in superior, district and municipal and probate courts.[8] The creation of family division courts does not affect the jurisdiction of the probate court over guardianships over the estate of a minor, or guardianships over the person and estate of a minor. The legislature has provided specifically that jurisdiction over these issues remains with the probate court in the counties with family court divisions.[9]

Library References

Am Jur 2d Courts §§ 14, 69
CJS Courts §§ 76, 82, 204

§ 5-2.   Court of General Jurisdiction

Probate courts are regarded as courts of general jurisdiction on the subjects to which they relate.[10] However, as with other courts, where jurisdiction does not exist, the parties cannot by consent or agreement confer such jurisdiction on the probate court.[11]

The Supreme Court has said that "the general line separating probate jurisdiction from that of the superior court is not difficult of ascertainment; the distinction is that between things which are incident to the business of conducting the administration and a settlement with the judge of probate concerning matters already had."[12] In practice, though, as the opinions of the Court disclose, this line has been less than clear. The

---

[7] P.L., 1995 152:1, 2.

[8] P.L., 1995 c. 152. See Family Division Rules, effective July 1, 1996, in Appendix.

[9] P.L., 1996 265:13 amending P.L., 1995 152:2, VIII.

[10] Stearns v. Wright, 51 N.H. 600 (1872).

[11] Burgess v. Burgess, 71 N.H. 293, 51 A. 1074 (1902).

[12] Rockwell v. Dow, 85 N.H. 58, 66, 154 A. 229, 233 (1931).

common law test does not solve every problem, particularly as the legislature has conferred additional powers upon the probate court. Such statutory changes must be taken into account in any situation to which they are pertinent.[13]

The authorities are not unanimous with respect to the scope of the jurisdiction of the probate courts.[14] Formerly it was held that the policy of this state was to confine the jurisdiction of the probate court within narrowly specified limits,[15] and that the probate courts did not have general jurisdiction but were limited to such powers as were conferred upon them by statute.[16] Thus, it was said that probate courts were of "limited and special jurisdiction, restricted, unless enlarged by statute, to the probate of wills, the administration and settlement of estates, and the distribution thereof among the heirs and legatees and other like administrative and ministerial acts."[17] However, the legislature has extended the probate court's jurisdiction over many other matters,[18] such as conservatorships (RSA 464-A:13), guardianships (RSA 463–465), involuntary admission of the mentally ill (RSA 135-C:20), adoptions (RSA 170-B), termination of parental rights (RSA 170-C), change of name (RSA 547:7), partition of real estate (RSA 538:18), custodianship of the property of minors (RSA 463:1), the continued commitment of person committed to the state hospital (RSA 135-C:46), apportionment of federal estate taxes (RSA 88-A), finding conduct which constitutes cause for divorce (RSA 460:8, RSA 560:19), waiver of certain marriage requirements (RSA 457:6, 457:27), and general equity jurisdiction over any accounting by an executor, administrator, trustee, guardian, or other fiduciary (RSA 547:11-a).

---

13 *Id.*

14 In re Estate of Gay, 97 N.H. 102, 81 A.2d 841 (1951), overruled in part. See In re Estate of Byrne, 98 N.H. 300, 100 A.2d 157 (1953).

15 In re Estate of Gay, 97 N.H. 102, 81 A.2d 841 (1951). See also Hayes v. Hayes, 48 N.H. 219 (1868).

16 In re Estate of Gay, 97 N.H. 102, 81 A.2d 841 (1951). See also Protective Check Writer Co. v. Collins, 92 N.H. 27, 23 A.2d 770 (1942); Lisbon Savings Bank & Trust Co. v. Estate of Moulton, 91 N.H. 477, 82 A.2d 331 (1941); Robinson v. Dana's Estate, 87 N.H. 114, 174 A. 772 (1934); Wentworth v. Waldron, 86 N.H. 559, 172 A. 247 (1934); Rockwell v. Dow, 85 N.H. 58, 154 A. 229 (1931); Patten v. Patten, 79 N.H. 388, 109 A. 415 (1920); Judge of Probate v. Lane, 51 N.H. 342 (1871).

17 Wood v. Stone, 39 N.H. 572, 574–75 (1859).

18 Rockwell v. Dow, 85 N.H. 58, 154 A. 229 (1931); Kimball v. Fisk, 39 N.H. 110 (1859).

Thus, the general trend in this state, as in other states, has been to gradually enlarge the probate court's jurisdiction so that it is fully coordinated with other courts of general jurisdiction.[19]

It has also been held that while the probate courts exercise many powers solely by virtue of the statutes, they have a very extensive jurisdiction not conferred by statute, but by a general reference to the existing law of the land—to that branch of the common law known and acted upon for ages, the probate and ecclesiastical law.[20] This jurisdiction is conferred and recognized by the New Hampshire Constitution, Part 2, Art. 80, which provides that

> [a]ll matters relating to the probate of wills and granting of letters of administration, shall be exercised by the judges of probate, in such manner as the legislature have directed.

The legislature exercised the discretion granted it by this constitutional provision in enacting RSA 547:3.[21] *In re Estate of Ward*[22] describes how the statute establishes the basic parameters of probate court jurisdiction:

> The probate court shall have exclusive jurisdiction over the following . . . jurisdiction of the probate of wills; the granting of administration of all matters and things of probate jurisdiction relating to the composition, administration, sale, settlement and final distribution of estates of deceased persons, including the assignment of homestead rights and claims against the executor or administrator for those services related to the prior care and maintenance of the decedent and the administration of insolvent estates and appeals therefrom; the exclusive jurisdiction to interpret and construct wills and to interpret, modify, and terminate testamentary and express trusts as that term is defined in RSA 564-A:1, I, and as to the appointment of and administration by trustees, in the cases prescribed by law. . . ..[23]

---

[19] See Uniform Probate Code, § –302.

[20] Morgan v. Dodge, 44 N.H. 255 (1862).

[21] As amended by the Omnibus Justice Act, effective January 1, 1993. P.L., 1992, c. 284; further amended by the Technical Changes Act of 1993, P.L., 1993, c. 190.

[22] In re Estate of Ward, 129 N.H. 4, 523 A.2d 28 (1986).

[23] *Id.*

The probate court is entitled to all the presumptions in favor of its proceedings the same as if it were a court of general jurisdiction.[24] Furthermore, once it is established that the probate court has jurisdiction of the subject matter, the court's decree will not be void for mere error of form or an irregularity,[25] and the probate court has the same authority to amend, modify, or vacate its judgment for sufficient cause as does a court of general jurisdiction.[26] The decisions of a probate court acting within its jurisdiction are binding and conclusive upon all parties interested.[27] However, as is the case in other judicial proceedings, want of jurisdiction of the subject matter will render the probate proceeding void, and want of jurisdiction of the person of a party, by the service of process or notice, will render the probate proceeding voidable.[28] As an incident of its general jurisdiction, the probate court has authority to try all questions of fraud arising in the settlement of estates.[29]

Library References

Am Jur 2d Courts §§ 14, 69

CJS Courts §§ 76, 82, 204

§ 5-3. Subject Matter Jurisdiction

In 1993 the legislature enacted Chapter 284,[30] entitled an "Act Implementing the Recommendations of the New Hampshire Supreme Court's Long-Range Planning Task Force Regarding the Judicial Branch" and commonly known as the Omnibus Justice Act. This Act was part of an effort by the supreme, superior, and probate courts to transfer many areas of jurisdiction from the superior courts to the probate and district courts. The result is that, while the superior court ceded jurisdiction, the probate courts have been granted vastly increased jurisdiction over many entirely new areas related to wills, trusts, conservatorships, and guardianships.

---

[24] Knight v. Hollings, 73 N.H. 495, 63 A. 38 (1906); Kimball v. Fisk, 39 N.H. 110 (1859).

[25] Kimball v. Fisk, 39 N.H. 110 (1859).

[26] Raymond v. Goodrich, 80 N.H. 215, 116 A. 38 (1921).

[27] Tebbets v. Tilton, 24 N.H. 120 (1851).

[28] Kimball v. Fisk, 39 N.H. 110 (1859).

[29] Judge of Probate v. Lane, 51 N.H. 342 (1871).

[30] P.L., 1992, c. 284.

Because there were some errors and gaps perceived in the Omnibus Justice Act, the drafters of the Act proposed an act "making technical changes to the laws governing the courts."[31] This legislation was enacted and was made effective January 1, 1994. In the text of this treatise, the Omnibus Justice Act shall be read to include the Omnibus Justice Act with the changes made by the Technical Changes Act of 1993.

The jurisdiction of the probate courts was increased in three ways: (1) by giving the probate courts exclusive jurisdiction of matters over which they previously had no jurisdiction, (2) by giving the probate courts exclusive jurisdiction of matters over which they had previously shared jurisdiction with the superior courts, and (3) by giving the probate courts concurrent jurisdiction with the superior court of matters over which they previously had no jurisdiction. The changes are so significant that, beginning in 1993, any reference to jurisdictional issues of the probate court must take into account the changes made by the Omnibus Justice Act.

The Omnibus Justice Act repealed the basic jurisdictional provision of the probate courts found in RSA 547:3 and re-enacted it in its entirety to read as follows:

547:3 Jurisdiction.

I. The probate court shall have exclusive jurisdiction over the following:

(a) The probate of wills.

(b) The granting of administration of all matters and things of probate jurisdiction relating to the composition, administration, sale, settlement, and final distribution of estates of deceased persons, including the assignment of homestead and claims against the executor or administrator for those services related to the prior care and maintenance of the decedent and the administration of insolvent estates and appeals therefrom.

(c) The interpretation and construction of wills and the interpretation, construction, modification, and termination of trusts as that term is defined in RSA 564-A:1, I.

---

[31] P.L., 1993, c. 190.

(d) The appointment, removal, surcharge and administration of trustees of trusts as that term is defined in RSA 564-A:1, I.

(e) The appointment and removal of conservators, and of the guardians of minors, mentally incompetent persons and spendthrifts, and in relation to the duties imposed by law on such conservators and guardians, and the management and disposition of the estates of their wards.

(f) The adoption of children.

(g) The change of names of persons who apply therefor.

(h) The termination of parental rights.

(i) Durable powers of attorney for health care under RSA 137-J.

(j) The interpretation and effect of living wills under RSA 137-H.

(k) Petitions for partition pursuant to RSA 547-C.

(l) Petitions to quiet title of real estate pursuant to RSA 547:11-c.

(m) Declaratory judgment actions pursuant to RSA 547:11-b.

(n) Any other jurisdiction as may be granted by statute.

II. The probate court shall have concurrent jurisdiction with the superior court over the following:

(a) Cases involving charitable uses and trusts, and other express trusts, as that term is defined in RSA 564-A:1, I.

(b) Durable powers of attorney under RSA 506:6 and 506:7.

(c) Waivers for marriage of minors pursuant to RSA 457:6, 457:7.

III. Nothing in this section shall be construed to confer upon the probate court any additional authority over inter vivos trusts beyond that authority exercised by the superior court prior to the adoption of this section.

§ 5-3(a). Grant of Equity Jurisdiction

The 1993 Omnibus Justice Act[32] gave the probate courts broadly expanded equity jurisdiction:

547:3-a Issues to Court. In any proceeding before a probate court involving material facts which are in dispute, the probate court shall have jurisdiction to try such factual issues to court after due notice to all interested parties. However, the probate court may, if the interests of an estate require it, appoint a special administrator under RSA 553:20.

547:3-b Equity Jurisdiction. The probate court shall have the powers of a court of equity in cases in which there is not a plain, adequate and complete remedy at law involving partition, guardianships, conservatorships and the probate of an estate and in all other like cases cognizable in a court of equity arising under RSA 547, RSA 547-C and RSA 552:7. The probate court shall have concurrent jurisdiction with the superior court in cases involving charitable uses and trusts other than express trusts as that term is defined in RSA 564-A:1, I. The court may hear and determine such cases according to the course of equity, and may grant writs of injunction whenever the same are necessary to prevent fraud or injustice.

Thus, it appears that the probate courts have been fully empowered with all of the equity powers necessary to fully hear and determine any case before them over which they have subject matter jurisdiction. This power specifically includes the power to grant "writs of injunction whenever the same are necessary to prevent fraud or injustice." RSA 547:3-b. This injunction power is entirely new and was considered by the framers of the legislation necessary to enable the probate courts to fully determine and conclude cases properly before them.

---

[32] P.L., 1992, c. 284.

§ 5-3(b). Concurrent Jurisdiction Over Charitable Trusts

The jurisdictional provision of the probate courts, RSA 547:3, II(a) provides that probate courts shall have concurrent jurisdiction with the superior court over "[c]ases involving charitable uses and trusts other than express trusts, as that term is defined in RSA 564-A:1, I.[33] This power is reiterated in the statute giving the probate court equity jurisdiction, RSA 547:3-b, and is further amplified in a series of specific grants of authority in connection with charitable trusts:

> **547:3-c Deviation From Terms of Trust.** In all cases where by reason of a change of circumstances which has occurred, shall occur, or is reasonably foreseeable, subsequent to the creation, heretofore or hereafter, of a trust by any deed, will or other instrument, compliance by the trustee or trustees with the terms of the trust relating to the property or the kinds of classes of property which may be held under the trust would defeat or substantially impair the accomplishment of the purposes of the trust, the court may, upon the filing by the trustee of a bill in equity for instructions and upon notice to all parties in interest, enter a decree permitting the trustee to deviate from such terms of the trust and directing the trustee, if necessary to carry out the purposes of the trust, to sell all or any part of the property held under the trust and to invest the proceeds of such sale in kinds or classes of property which are lawful investments for trustees of estates. No such decree, after its entry, shall thereafter operate to relieve any trustee of any duty imposed by law relating to the investment of trust funds and the exercise of reasonable care for the preservation thereof. This section shall not be construed to limit or restrict the general equitable jurisdiction of the court over the trustees, trusts or trust funds.

> **547:3-d Cy Pres Doctrine.** If property is or has been given in trust to be applied to a charitable purpose, and said purpose or its application is or becomes impossible or impracticable or illegal or obsolete or ineffective or prejudicial to the public interest to carry out, the trust shall not fail. Upon petition by the trustee or trustees or the attorney general, the probate court

---

[33] See also the 1992 revision of RSA 498:1.

may direct the application of the property to some charitable purpose which is useful to the community, and which charitable purpose fulfills as nearly as possible the general charitable intent of the settlor or testator. In applying the doctrine of cy pres, the court may order the distribution of the trust assets to another charitable trust or to a charitable corporation to be held and administered by it in accordance with the terms of the governing instrument as said terms may be modified by the application of cy pres under this section and RSA 547:3-e.

547:3-e Federal Taxation. Whenever it shall be made to appear to the court that the intention of the testator or settlor of a charitable trust will be frustrated in whole or in part by reason of a tax imposed under the United States Internal Revenue Code on the income or principal of the trust, or by reason of administrative burden or disproportionate cost of administration, then the court, in order to prevent the diversion of funds from the charitable purpose by federal taxation, may enter a decree:

I. Modifying or enlarging the powers granted the trustee, or declaring that a trustee does not have certain powers under New Hampshire law to the extent necessary in order to bring the terms of the governing instrument into compliance with the tax exemption requirements of federal law.

II. Authorizing the trustee to make charitable distributions from principal.

III. Terminating the trust and directing the distribution of the trust assets to another charitable trust or to a charitable corporation, to be held and administered in accordance with the terms of the governing instrument as said terms may be modified by the application of cy pres under RSA 547:3-d and this section.

IV. Removing the trustee or trustees, or directing the appointment of new or additional trustees.

V. Reducing or limiting the charitable organizations or classes of charitable organizations or charitable objects which may be benefited under the trust instrument.

547:3-f Inapplicability of Cy Pres. Whenever it shall appear to the court that any proposed cy pres application would not be proper because it is in violation of New Hampshire law, the court shall enter a decree denying said proposed cy pres application and stating the reason therefor.

547:3-g Definitions. For the purposes of RSA 547:3-h and for the purposes of any petition for deviation under RSA 547:3-c or under common law equity powers the following words shall have the meanings ascribed here unless the context indicates otherwise:

I. "Charitable trust" means any fiduciary relationship with respect to property arising as a result of a manifestation of an intention to create it and subjecting the person by whom the property is held to equitable duties to deal with the property for charitable or community purposes.

II. "Trustee" means:

(a) Any individual, group of individuals, corporation or other legal entity holding property in trust pursuant to any charitable trust or charitable purpose.

(b) A corporation formed for the administration of a charitable trust pursuant to the directions of the settlor or at the instance of the trustee.

547:3-h Termination of Charitable Trusts. If the probate court, upon application by the trustee or trustees, finds that the continuance of a charitable trust is impracticable or unfeasible, and that the charitable purpose of the settlor or testator can be accomplished by a transfer of the trust assets to another charitable trust or corporation, or to the beneficiaries of said trust, the trust is subject to termination by the court upon such terms and conditions as it may impose. This section shall not be construed to limit or restrict the general equitable jurisdiction of the court over trustees, trusts or trust funds.

In addition to this jurisdiction over charitable trusts, the probate court was given concurrent jurisdiction with the superior court to order cy pres over cemetery trust funds. RSA 31:22-a.

§ 5-3(c). Petitions To Quiet Title

By virtue of the provisions of the Omnibus Justice Act, [34] the probate courts have been given an entirely new area of exclusive jurisdiction "to quiet title of real estate." RSA 547:3. This grant of jurisdiction is set forth at some length in RSA 547:11-c as follows:

> **547:11-c Quiet Title.** An action may be brought in probate court by any person claiming title to, or any interest in, real or personal property, or both, listed in the estate of a deceased person or listed as guardianship, conservatorship, or trust assets over which the probate court has jurisdiction, against the estate, guardian, conservator, or trustee who may claim to own the same, either in fee, for years, for life or in reversion or remainder, or to have any interest in the same, or any lien or encumbrance thereon, adverse to the plaintiff, or in whom the land records disclose any interest, whether or not the plaintiff is entitled to the immediate or exclusive possession of such property, for the purpose of determining such adverse estate, interest or claim, and to clear up all doubts and disputes and to quiet and settle the title to the same. In any action brought under this provision, where applicable, the procedure set forth in RSA 498:5-b through 5-d shall be followed.

It appears from this statute that the necessary link or keystone to the grant of jurisdiction to the probate courts to entertain petitions to quiet title is that it relates to any interest in real or personal property "listed in the estate of a deceased person or listed as guardianship, conservatorship or trust assets over which the probate court has jurisdiction." Furthermore, the statute makes clear that the procedure for probate courts established in RSA 498:5-b through 5-d shall be followed in such proceedings.

RSA 547:11-d protects the right to a jury trial by providing that any person who wishes to assert such right in any "cases where a right to jury trial is guaranteed by the constitution or granted by statute," may appeal within fifteen days to the superior court. The superior court is directed to expedite the request for jury trial. The intent of the statute is that the right to jury trial is preserved, but only after an initial hearing

---

[34] P.L., 1992, c. 284.

in the probate court. Thus, when a party asserts a right to jury trial, as for example where the title to real estate is involved, which is protected by the constitution, the person must first try the case in the probate court, and then is permitted to appeal for a trial de novo in the superior court.

§ 5-3(d). Jurisdiction Over the Dissolution of Voluntary Corporations

In 1993, the probate court was given concurrent jurisdiction with the superior court in the case of voluntary corporations (charitable corporations) to order their dissolution and such other relief as may be appropriate. RSA 284:5; RSA 284:6.

§ 5-4. Venue—Actions Unrelated to Estate Administration

As a consequence of the expansion of exclusive probate court jurisdiction authorized by the Omnibus Justice Act,[35] the probate court has exclusive jurisdiction in several types of actions that may not be related directly to a decedent's estate. In such instances, the venue of these actions is determined by virtue of the provision of RSA 507:9, which provides as follows:

507:9 Transitory.

Transitory actions, in which any one of the parties is an inhabitant of the state, shall be brought in the county or judicial district thereof where some one of them resides. If no one of the parties is an inhabitant of the state, the action may be brought in any county or judicial district.

An action by or against an administrator shall be brought "in the same county or judicial district thereof or in one of the counties or judicial districts thereof in which it might have been brought or against the testator or intestate at the time of his death." RSA 507:10. However, an executor or administrator has the right to maintain an action in the county or judicial district in which he or she is appointed. RSA 507:10.

---

[35] P.L., 1992, c. 284.

§ 5-5.   Uniform Probate Code Provisions

The jurisdiction of the New Hampshire probate court contrasts with the simply stated grant of jurisdiction found in the Uniform Probate Code. Section 1-302 of the Code provides that the probate court shall have the following subject matter jurisdiction:

> (a) To the full extent permitted by the constitution, the Court has jurisdiction over all subject matter relating to (1) estates of decedents, including construction of wills and determination of heirs and successors of decedents, and estates of protected persons; (2) protection of minors and incapacitated persons; and (3) trusts.

> (b) The court has full power to make orders, judgments and decrees and take all other action necessary and proper to administer justice in the matters which come before it.

> (c) The Court has jurisdiction over protective proceedings and guardianship proceedings.

> (d) If both guardianship and protective proceedings as to the same person are commenced or pending in the same court, the proceedings may be consolidated.

Library References

Am Jur 2d Executors and Administrators § 96

Am Jur 2d Wills § 850

§ 5-6.   Wills and Administration of Estates—In General

By virtue of the New Hampshire Constitution, Part 2, Art. 80, probate courts are given jurisdiction over "all matters relating to probate of wills and granting of Letters of Administration in such manner as the legislature" has directed. The legislature has so directed by enacting RSA 547:3,[36] which specifically provides that the probate court shall have exclusive jurisdiction over "the probate of wills"[37] and "the granting of administration of all matters and things of probate jurisdiction relating

---

[36] As amended by the Technical Changes Act, effective January 1, 1994. P.L., 1993, c. 190.

[37] RSA 547:3, I(a).

to the composition, administration, sale, settlement, and final distribution of estates of deceased persons, including the assignment of homestead and claims against the executor or administrator for those services related to the prior care and maintenance of the decedent and the administration of insolvent estates and appeals therefrom."[38]

In *Morgan v. Dodge*,[39] it was held that the broad language of RSA 547:3 recognized that the probate court has jurisdiction over matters not expressly set out by statute, but reference must be made to the existing law of the land, that is, the probate or ecclesiastical law.

Library References

Am Jur 2d Wills §§ 850–59

CJS Wills §§ 351–54, 433, 1074–80

§ 5-6(a). Venue

RSA 547:8 provides that the probate of the will and granting of administration on the estate of the deceased shall belong to the judge for the county in which the deceased was last an inhabitant. If that person was not an inhabitant of this state, venue lies in the county in which such person had estate or in which the personal representative or kin of such person has a cause of action. In *Knight v. Hollings*,[40] the Supreme Court ruled that the situs of decedent's property in this state gives the New Hampshire probate judge jurisdiction over the probate of the will even though the decedent's domicile was out of state. Since neither the statutes nor the common law require that the will be probated in the state of domicile first, it may be probated in this state first and the state of domicile later.

The probate court has authority to determine whether the decedent was last an inhabitant of the county, or if he had an estate in the county at the time of his death, thereby conferring jurisdiction on the court.[41] With respect to the settlement of an estate, RSA 547:9 provides that "[a]ll proceedings in relation to the settlement of the estate of a deceased person shall be had in the probate court of the county in which his will was proved or administration on his estate was granted."

---

[38] RSA 547:3, I(b).

[39] Morgan v. Dodge, 44 N.H. 255 (1862).

[40] Knight v. Hollings, 73 N.H. 495, 63 A. 38 (1906).

[41] *Id.*

It should be noted that the power of the probate court of the county in which a deceased was last an inhabitant to appoint an administrator of his estate is not affected by pendency of proceedings in another county for the appointment of an administrator there.[42]

Jurisdiction of the probate courts with respect to the probate of wills and the settlement and distribution of decedents' estates,[43] as well as the settlement of administration accounts has historically been within the exclusive jurisdiction of the probate courts.[44] As a consequence of the provisions of the Omnibus Justice Act,[45] there will be many instances where the title to assets involved in an estate or trust are in question over which the probate court now has exclusive jurisdiction, at least until a claim of the person's constitutional right to a jury trial is made.[46]

Library References

Am Jur 2d Executors and Administrators §§ 103–11, 1303–05
CJS Wills §§ 355, 1081

§ 5-6(b). Creditor Claims

Confusion often arises out of claims by alleged creditors. In *Hayes v. Hayes*,[47] it was held that the probate court had no jurisdiction to settle a dispute between a fiduciary and one who may stand in the position of debtor or creditor to the estate. On the other hand, RSA 554:11 clearly requires the administrator to account for "all debts due to the estate" and in *In re Estate of Ward*,[48] the Supreme Court gave an expansive reading to this statutory provision and found that the probate court had jurisdiction to determine the amount that an administrator owed an estate arising out of his own wrongdoing. Perhaps the difference lies in the fact that in *Ward*, the debtor was the administrator himself and, therefore, RSA 554:14 gave the probate court specific authority and power over debts of administrators to estates.

---

[42] Tilton v. O'Connor, 68 N.H. 215, 44 A. 303 (1895).

[43] Glover v. Baker, 76 N.H. 393, 83 A. 916 (1912); Knight v. Hollings, 73 N.H. 495, 63 A. 38 (1906).

[44] Judge of Probate v. Lane, 51 N.H. 342 (1871).

[45] P.L., 1992, c. 284.

[46] See RSA 498:5-a; RSA 547:3; RSA 547:3-b; RSA 547:11-b; RSA 547:11-c; RSA 547-C.

[47] Hayes v. Hayes, 48 N.H. 219 (1868).

[48] In re Estate of Ward, 129 N.H. 4, 523 A.2d 28 (1986).

In *In re Estate of Ward,*[49] the Supreme Court had before it two jurisdictional questions: (1) whether the probate court had jurisdiction to determine whether or not an attorney who acted as administrator had misappropriated funds from the decedent, and (2) whether the probate court had jurisdiction to order the administrator to reimburse the decedent's estate for legal fees improperly charged the decedent while living. The Supreme Court answered both questions affirmatively. The Court equated the administrator's misappropriation of funds to a fiduciary's embezzlement debt and held that RSA 554:14 specifically granted probate courts jurisdiction over debts due from administrators to their decedent's estate. As to the issue of the reimbursement of improperly charged legal fees, the Court held that:

> Fees obtained for worthless services are no more than the improper disposition of funds under a certain pretense of legitimacy. . . . Once the probate judge had properly determined that the services were of no value or benefit to [the decedent], the specific extent of [the administrator's] debt was readily ascertainable. We hold that RSA 554:14 applies to the attorney's fees charged by [the administrator] prior to [the decedent's] death. Accordingly, the probate court judge was correct in ordering [the administrator] to account for those sums.[50]

In 1993, the Omnibus Justice Act[51] expanded the power of the probate court considerably in the area of creditor claims against assets of an estate. Thus, RSA 554:1 now provides that if "any person claims a presently legal or equitable right of title to real or personal property in the estate of the deceased, the administrator may petition the probate court pursuant to RSA 547:11-b [the declaratory judgment statute] to determine the question as between the parties."

Additionally, the probate court is given jurisdiction to hear cases in which title to or any interest in any real or personal property listed in the estate of the deceased person or trust is in issue by a petition to quiet title. RSA 547:11-c.

---

[49] *Id.*

[50] In re Estate of Ward, 129 N.H. 4, 10, 523 A.2d 28, 33 (1986).

[51] P.L., 1992, c. 284.

The intent of the Omnibus Justice Act's drafters was to give to the probate court the power to determine all questions relating to the title of assets in a trust or an estate, whereas previously the superior court had exclusive jurisdiction to handle title questions. Because a constitutional claim for a jury trial may be invoked, such as where title to real estate is involved, the parties must first try the case in the probate court and then appeal for a trial de novo to the superior court. RSA 547:11-d.

Library References

Am Jur 2d Executors and Administrators §§ 671, 1301

CJS Executors and Administrators §§ 411, 840

Appealability of order of court possessing probate jurisdiction allowing or denying tardy presentation of claim to personal representative. 66 ALR2d 659.

§ 5-6(c). Collateral Matters

The probate court has jurisdiction to pass upon matters considered to be collateral, such as the question of title to property that is to be administered. See § 5-6(g) below. In addition, RSA 460:8 and 560:19 grant jurisdiction to the probate court to make findings determining conduct which constitutes cause for divorce under very limited circumstances.

Library References

Am Jur 2d Executors and Administrators § 518

CJS Courts §§ 76, 82

Jurisdiction of probate court to determine title to property which personal representative claims. 90 ALR 434.

§ 5-6(d). Actions Involving Joint Bank Accounts

Where a surviving joint tenant initially returns joint survivorship property to the estate of his decedent co-tenant but later makes a claim for all of the joint property, the appropriate forum for trial of this type of claim is the superior court, not the probate court.[52] However, with the passage of the Omnibus Justice Act, the administrator presumably has the authority to petition the probate court to determine title between the claimants to the joint property under RSA 554-1.

---

[52] Rice v. Connelly, 71 N.H. 382, 52 A. 446 (1902). See Blanchard v. Calderwood, 110 N.H. 29, 266 A.2d 118 (1969).

§ 5-6(e). Oral Contracts To Make a Will

Another example of a controversy involving an administrator where jurisdiction over an administrator lay with the superior court instead of with the probate court was where a claimant sought to enforce an oral contract to make a will. In *Blanchard v. Calderwood*,[53] the proper forum for the contract action was held to be the superior court, not the probate court.[54]

Library References

CJS Executors and Administrators § 700

§ 5-6(f). Actions Against Administrators

To the extent that the claim in issue is title to an asset in an estate, the 1993 Omnibus Justice Act[55] gives the probate court jurisdiction to hear the claim if the real or personal property is "in the estate of the deceased." RSA 554:1.

Formerly, an action against an administrator relating to property within the estate could be brought against the administrator individually and outside the administration of the estate. In *Rice v. Connelly*,[56] the petitioner brought an action against the defendant who had been the administrator of the decedent's estate. The petitioner claimed the ownership of a gold necklace she purportedly had loaned the decedent, which the decedent had in her possession at her death. The administrator had treated the necklace as part of the decedent's estate and the plaintiff brought suit against the administrator in the superior court within the six-year statute of limitations but after the administration of the decedent's estate was closed. The Supreme Court upheld the action, stating that the "gist of the action is the defendant's wrongful detainer of the beads, not an act or omission of the decedent. . . .. The action is against the defendant and not the estate."[57]

The prior law in this area governed the case of *Frost v. Frost*,[58] where

---

[53] Blanchard v. Calderwood, 110 N.H. 29, 261 A.2d 118 (1969).

[54] Blanchard v. Calderwood, 110 N.H. 29, 261 A.2d 118 (1969). See also C. DeGRANDPRE, 7 New Hampshire Practice: Wills, Trusts and Gifts (3d ed. 1997) Chapter 24.

[55] P.L., 1992, c. 284.

[56] Rice v. Connelly, 71 N.H. 382, 52 A. 446 (1902).

[57] Rice v. Connelly, 71 N.H. 382, 383, 52 A. 446, 447 (1902).

[58] Frost v. Frost, 100 N.H. 326, 125 A.2d 656 (1956).

the Supreme Court upheld an action brought by the plaintiff in superior court seeking the value of certain property belonging to her in the possession of an administrator who refused to return it. Even though the claimant had not complied with the time restrictions imposed by RSA 556:1–5, the Court held that "[s]uch a claim is against the defendant but not against the estate."[59]

Library References

CJS Executors and Administrators § 725 et seq.

§ 5-6(g). Real Estate Matters

The probate court has the jurisdiction to resolve issues involving real estate of the decedent if the property is "in" the estate of the decedent. RSA 554:1. To carry out this jurisdiction, the probate courts have the power to hear declaratory judgments (RSA 547: 11-b) and petitions to quiet title (RSA 547:11-c).

Furthermore, the probate court has the jurisdiction to partition real estate in disputed or undisputed situations. RSA 547-C. The grant of the power to partition to the probate courts was accompanied by the repeal of the superior court's power to hear petition actions, except upon appeal after a hearing in the probate court. RSA 547-C:3.

RSA 547:11-b provides that "[a]ny person claiming a present legal or equitable right or title to real or personal property in the estate of deceased persons or to guardianship, conservatorship, or trust assets, may maintain a petition against the estate, guardian, conservator, or trustee to determine the question as between the parties."

Additionally, the probate court has the jurisdiction to hear petitions to quiet title in which title to, or any interest in, any real or personal property or both, which is listed in the estate of a deceased person or in a guardianship, conservatorship or trust, is in issue. RSA 547:11-c.

The intent of these 1993 changes in jurisdiction was to give to the probate court the power to determine all questions relating to the title of assets in a trust or an estate, whereas previously the superior court had exclusive jurisdiction to handle title questions. Because a constitutional claim for a jury trial may be invoked, such as where title to real estate is involved, it is provided by statute that the parties must first try

---

[59] Frost v. Frost, 100 N.H. 326, 329, 125 A.2d 656, 658 (1956).

the case in the probate court and, if dissatisfied, then appeal for a trial de novo to the superior court. RSA 547:11-d.[60]

The prior law was that the probate court was generally not the proper forum for the resolution of issues involving the real estate of the decedent. In *Fleming v. Aiken*,[61] the issue before the Supreme Court was whether the probate court or the superior court had jurisdiction to hear a controversy over title to certain land where the probate court proceedings were still open, and an accounting had not been filed for over twenty-five years. The Court held that the title to the contested real estate passed directly to the devisee, subject to being divested due to insufficient personal assets in the estate or insolvency of the estate. "In the absence of the necessity of the executor seeking a license to sell the real estate, the probate court has no jurisdiction of the real estate of a decedent. . .. The passage of over three decades in this estate with no petition for license to sell the real estate precludes any possibility of jurisdiction in the probate court of the real estate of the decedent."[62]

Library References

CJS Courts §§ 22, 76, 82

§ 5-6(h). Appointment of Administrators

Probate courts have jurisdiction in granting administration,[63] to be exercised in such manner as the legislature may direct,[64] and its jurisdiction over such appointment is exclusive.[65] Thus, the superior court has no jurisdiction over the appointment of administrators, except that under RSA 553:21 the superior court has jurisdiction concurrent with the probate court to appoint a special administrator.

In *Morgan v. Dodge*,[66] the Supreme Court held that the probate court had the power to revoke a grant of administration where it had been granted without jurisdiction, irregularly or illegally, or issued for special courts which no longer exists.

---

[60] P.L., 1992, c. 284.

[61] Fleming v. Aiken, 114 N.H. 687, 327 A.2d 725 (1974).

[62] Fleming v. Aiken, 114 N.H. 687, 690, 327 A.2d 725, 726–27 (1974).

[63] Robinson v. Dana's Estate, 87 N.H. 114, 174 A. 772 (1934).

[64] *Id.*

[65] *Id.*

[66] Morgan v. Dodge, 44 N.H. 255 (1862).

Under RSA 553:13, "no person shall intermeddle with the estate of any person deceased, or act as an executor or administrator thereof, or be considered as having that trust," until he shall have given bond to the judge of probate.[67]

RSA 547:8 contains no requirement as to the amount of the estate that a decedent must have left in order to justify the appointment of an administrator in this state.[68] It has been held that the ownership of an auto which remained in the state following the death of the decedent was a sufficient estate within the meaning of the statute to justify the appointment of an administrator.[69] Similarly, a guardian nominated in a will may be appointed in a probate proceeding even if the decedent has no probate estate.[70]

Library References

Am Jur 2d Executors and Administrators § 157 et seq.

CJS Executors and Administrators § 13 et seq.

§ 5-7. Children

The probate court has exclusive jurisdiction over certain issues involving children. Although the 1993 Omnibus Justice Act[71] gave the probate court exclusive jurisdiction over the adoption of children, which is governed by RSA Chapter 170-B, and the termination of parental rights, governed by RSA Chapter 170-C, the legislature has since directed that pilot family court divisions in certain counties be given exclusive jurisdiction over these matters.[72] The creation of family division courts does not affect the jurisdiction of the probate court over guardianships over the estate of a minor, or guardianships over the person and estate of a minor. The legislature has provided specifically that jurisdiction over these issues remains with the probate court.[73] The probate court has

---

[67] See Kittredge v. Folsom, 8 N.H. 98 (1835).

[68] Power v. Plummer, 93 N.H. 37, 35 A.2d 230 (1943).

[69] Power v. Plummer, 93 N.H. 37, 35 A.2d 230 (1943). See also Boston & Maine R.R. v. Hurd, 108 F. 116 (1st Cir. 1901), where it was held that a claim for negligence causing the death in N.H. of a non-resident is sufficient basis for appointment of an administrator.

[70] Morey v. Sohier, 63 N.H. 507, 3 A. 636 (1885).

[71] RSA 547:3, I(f) and 547:3, I(h).

[72] P.L., 1995 152:2.

[73] P.L., 1996 265:13 amending P.L., 1995 152:2, VIII.

exclusive jurisdiction over the guardianship of minors,[74] governed by RSA Chapter 463.[75] and proceedings under the Uniform Transfers to Minors Act.[76] Thus, in *McLaughlin v. Mullin*,[77] where grandparents of a minor child sought custody and guardianship of a child, the Court held that the superior court had no jurisdiction to appoint a custodian of a minor.[78]

In some instances, the probate court may share jurisdiction with another court over certain aspects of a child-related matter, but retain final jurisdiction. For example, the initial stages of a termination of parental rights case often arise in district court, which has jurisdiction to make findings of fact relating to the abuse and/or neglect of a child. While the district courts may determine whether certain grounds for termination of parental rights exist,[79] it is only the probate court which has jurisdiction to decide the ultimate question and to terminate parental rights.[80]

In other areas relating to children, the probate court has concurrent jurisdiction with the superior court. For example, where a minor within the statutorily restricted age group seeks judicial consent to marry,[81] the waiver may be granted by either the probate court or the superior court.[82] In addition, it has been held that "[a]lthough no statute specifically mentions the power of the superior court to determine custody issues in the absence of a divorce . . .", the superior court's subject matter jurisdiction may be based on the court's authority, independent of statutory grants of authority, to protect constitutional rights.[83] The superior court's subject matter jurisdiction, where unwed parents were seeking custody, was based on the right recognized under the New Hampshire Constitution of a parent to the custody of his or her child.[84]

---

[74] RSA 547:3 I (e). See Chapter 70 *infra*.

[75] Recodified by P.L. 1995, c. 222, effective January 1, 1996.

[76] RSA 463-A. See also Prob. Ct. Proc. Bul. 12 (revised).

[77] McLaughlin v. Mullin, 139 N.H. 262, 651 A.2d 934 (1994).

[78] *Id.*

[79] RSA 170-C:5, III. See Chapter 77 *infra*.

[80] RSA 170-C:3.

[81] RSA 457:5–457:7.

[82] RSA 547:3.

[83] Ellsworth v. Heath, 678 A.2d 138 (1996).

[84] Ellsworth v. Heath, 678 A.2d 138 (1996). See N.H. CONST. pt. I, art. 2.

There are certain child-related areas over which the probate court has no jurisdiction. The superior court has jurisdiction over matters relating to child custody which arise out of a divorce or separation proceeding.[85] Additionally, the district courts have jurisdiction over children who are accused of offenses under the juvenile delinquency statutes.

§ 5-8. Guardianship

The probate court has exclusive jurisdiction over "[t]he appointment and removal of conservators, and of the guardians of minors, mentally incompetent persons and spendthrifts, and in relation to the duties imposed by law on such conservators and guardians, and the management and disposition of the estates of their wards."[86] With respect to venue, all proceedings in relation to the property or estate of a person under guardianship shall be had in the court of probate of the county in which the guardian was appointed.[87] This jurisdiction of the probate court with reference to the appointment of guardians is exclusive, and original.[88] Also, the judge of probate in each county may appoint a guardian of the person or of the estate of any minor or of both.[89]

The judge of probate has the authority to appoint a guardian for a minor, whenever there is need for such in his county, whether or not the minor is a resident,[90] and may appoint as guardian a person who is not a member of the ward's family.[91] In such proceedings the probate court has wide discretion which will not be disturbed except upon a clear showing that their discretion has been abused.[92]

Case law under a prior version of the statute suggested a clear legislative intent existed to commit the whole subject of guardianship to the jurisdiction of the probate court,[93] and that the superior court under

---

[85] RSA 491:7. See McLaughlin v. Mullin, 139 N.H. 262, 651 A.2d 934 (1994).

[86] RSA 547:3, I(e).

[87] RSA 547:4.

[88] RSA 547:10. See also Leclerc v. Leclerc, 85 N.H. 121, 155 A. 249 (1931).

[89] Leclerc v. Leclerc, 85 N.H. 121, 155 A. 249 (1931).

[90] RSA 463:1.

[91] Judge of Probate v. Hinds, 4 N.H. 464 (1828).

[92] In re Sabolevski, 107 N.H. 256, 220 A.2d 745 (1966).

[93] In re Sabolevski, 107 N.H. 256, 220 A.2d 745 (1966). See also Leclerc v. Leclerc, 85 N.H. 121, 155 A. 249 (1931).

its equity powers did not have concurrent jurisdiction with the probate court with respect to appointment and removal of guardians.[94] While it is true that in the absence of pending or possible divorce proceedings, the superior court has no jurisdiction to appoint a permanent custodian of minors,[95] a superior court can make temporary orders of custody incidental to its powers to administer the remedy of habeas corpus.[96] In *McLaughlin v. Mullin*[97] where grandparents of a minor child sought custody and guardianship of a child, the Court held that the superior court had no jurisdiction to appoint a custodian of a minor.[98] However, the Court held in *Ellsworth v. Heath*[99] that the superior court had exclusive jurisdiction over deciding the custody of the child of unwed parents where there was no guardianship issue. By operation of RSA 463:3, I the unwed parents were automatically the joint guardians of the minor, and thus there was no appointment of guardian issue as a basis for probate court jurisdiction.[100] The Court noted that "Although no statute specifically mentions the power of the superior court to determine custody issues in the absence of a divorce. . .", the superior court's subject matter jurisdiction was based on the court's authority, independent of statutory grants of authority, to protect constitutional rights.[101] The superior court's subject matter jurisdiction in this case was based on the right, recognized under the New Hampshire Constitution, of a parent to the custody of his or her child.[102]

The creation of family division courts does not affect the jurisdiction of the probate court over guardianships over the estate of a minor, or guardianships over the person and estate of a minor. The legislature has

---

[94] Leclerc v. Leclerc, 85 N.H. 121, 155 A. 249 (1931).

[95] Leclerc v. Leclerc, 85 N.H. 121, 155 A. 249 (1931). *Dicta* in following cases to the contrary must be regarded as erroneous according to above case: State v. Richardson, 40 N.H. 272 (1860); Prime v. Foote, 63 N.H. 52 (1884).

[96] Sheehy v. Sheehy, 88 N.H. 223, 186 A. 1 (1936), *citing* Leclerc v. Leclerc, 85 N.H. 121, 144 A. 249 (1931).

[97] McLaughlin v. Mullin, 139 N.H. 262, 651 A.2d 934 (1994).

[98] *Id.*

[99] Ellsworth v. Heath, 678 A.2d 183 (1996).

[100] Ellsworth v. Heath, 678 A.2d 138 (1996). See Brauch v. Shaw, 121 N.H. 562, 432 A.2d 1 (1981).

[101] Ellsworth v. Heath, 678 A.2d 138 (1996).

[102] Ellsworth v. Heath, 678 A.2d 138 (1996). See N.H. Const. pt. I, art. 2.

specifically provided that jurisdiction over these issues remains with the probate court in counties having family court divisions.[103]

RSA 464-A:41 provides that a guardian ad litem may be appointed by any court, when necessary, to prosecute or defend a suit pending before it for or against the minor or mentally ill person, or to appear for and protect the rights of the minor or other person interested in any matter pending before the court. A guardian ad litem must be appointed by the probate court pursuant to that statute in order to give a decree in the settlement of a guardian's account the full force and effect of a final judgment.[104]

Library References

Am Jur 2d Courts §§ 14, 69

§ 5-9. Mentally Ill Persons

Under RSA 135-C, the probate judge has the authority to commit a mentally ill person to the state hospital if that person is in such a condition as to render it dangerous that he be at large. Upon petition by any person, after notice to the person sought to be admitted, and after a hearing to be held within ten days of the date of petition, the probate judge may order commitment or issue such other order as may be appropriate.[105]

RSA 460:6 also provides that "[a] married man or woman, whose wife or husband is [mentally ill], and has continued insane for one year, and who wishes to convey real estate, may apply by petition to the judge of probate for the county in which the real estate lies for a license to convey the same in such manner as to bar all rights which the insane wife or husband has therein." The procedure to be followed is set out in RSA 460:7.

Library References

Am Jur 2d Incompetent Persons § 1 et seq.
CJS Mental Health § 108 et seq.

§ 5-10. Trusts and Trustees

The probate courts have exclusive jurisdiction over "[t]he interpretation, construction, modification and termination of trusts, as that term

---

[103] P.L., 1996 265:13 amending P.L., 1995 152:2, VIII.
[104] Hollis v. Tilton, 90 N.H. 119, 5 A.2d 29 (1939).
[105] RSA 135-C:45.

is defined in RSA 564-A:1, I,"[106] and "[t]he appointment, removal, surcharge and administration of trustees of trusts as that term is defined in RSA 564-A:1, I."[107] This 1993 legislation represents a major change in probate court jurisdiction. The intent of the legislation is that the probate court, not the superior court, shall have "exclusive" jurisdiction over express trusts as defined in the Uniform Trustees' Powers Act. Express trusts are defined in the Uniform Trustees' Powers Act, RSA 564-A:1, I as follows:

> I. "Trust" means an express trust created by a trust instrument, including a will, whereby a trustee has the duty to administer a trust asset for the benefit of a named or otherwise described income or principal beneficiary, or both; "trust" does not include a resulting or constructive trust, a business trust which provides for certificates to be issued to the beneficiary, an investment trust, a voting trust, a security instrument, a trust created by the judgment or decree of a court, a liquidation trust, or a trust for the primary purpose of paying dividends, interest, interest coupons, salaries, wages, pensions or profits, or employee benefits of any kind, an instrument wherein a person is nominee or escrowee for another, a trust created in deposits in any financial institution, or other trust, the nature of which does not admit of general trust administration.

The probate court's exclusive jurisdiction over inter vivos trusts is further expanded in RSA 547:3-c, which gives the probate court the power to deviate from the terms of the trust, and RSA 547:3-d, which gives the power to order cy pres where the trust's "purpose or its application is or becomes impossible or impractical or illegal or obsolete or ineffective or prejudicial to the public interest to carry out."

Concurrently with the granting of the exclusive jurisdiction to the probate courts over express trusts, the jurisdictional provision relating to the superior court, RSA 498:1, was amended to delete any reference to jurisdiction over express trusts as that term is defined in the Uniform Trustees' Powers Act.

It was not the intent of the drafters of the Omnibus Justice Act to give the probate court the power to subject revocable or inter vivos or express

---

[106] RSA 547:3, I(c).
[107] RSA 547:3, I(d).

trusts to the everyday administrative jurisdiction of the probate courts, such as the probate courts exercise over testamentary trusts. The probate courts would be overwhelmed with the administrative burden of such a requirement.

Because of the unhappiness of practicing attorneys with the vagueness of the Omnibus Justice Act as to the ability of the probate courts to administer express trusts on a day-to-day, continuous basis, the Technical Changes Act of 1993[108] added the following section to the legislative grant of jurisdiction to the probate courts:

> Nothing in this section shall be construed to confer upon the probate court any additional authority over inter vivos trusts beyond that authority exercised by the superior court prior to the adoption of this section. RSA 547:3 III.

The legislative history of the Technical Changes Act confirms that the purpose of this additional provision was to ensure that the probate courts did not have the power to administer inter vivos and other express trusts in the same manner as the probate courts presently administer testamentary trusts, by requiring annual accountings, regulating fiduciary compensation, and so on.[109]

It has been held that the probate court was intended to have jurisdiction over trusts comparable to that over estates of deceased persons,[110] and that to this extent the jurisdiction of the superior court was taken away, except for cases on appeal from the probate court.[111] The duty of the probate court to administer trusts created by will necessarily carried with it that of appointing the trustees needed to execute such testamentary trusts.[112]

The judge of probate is empowered to appoint "a suitable person as public trustee to hold office during the court's pleasure whose duty shall be to administer all such small charitable trusts as the court may assign to him, where it is found that practical difficulties or unreasonable expense involved in each trust would tend to defeat its purpose, provided,

---

[108] P.L., 1993, c. 190.

[109] P.L., 1993, c. 190.

[110] Rockwell v. Dow, 85 N.H. 58, 154 A. 229 (1931).

[111] Id.

[112] Petition of Straw, 78 N.H. 506, 102 A. 628 (1917).

however, that in each instance the trustee of the fund assigned shall give his consent." RSA 564:2-a. The probate court does not have jurisdiction to advise a fiduciary concerning questions arising out of the administration of property held in a fiduciary capacity.[113]

Historically, attempting to determine the jurisdictional boundaries in the testamentary and inter vivos trust areas has always been somewhat confusing. Insofar as testamentary trusts are concerned, the prior version of RSA 547:3 granted jurisdiction to both the superior and probate courts. However, the prior version of RSA 498:1 granted jurisdiction over inter vivos trusts exclusively to the superior court and not the probate court. RSA 498:1; *Parsons v. Parsons*.[114] The jurisdictional line was discussed extensively in *Rockwell v. Dow*,[115] where the Supreme Court ruled that the probate court's jurisdiction over testamentary trusts was exclusive in those areas that are "incident to the business of conducting an administration."[116]

Library References

Am Jur 2d Trusts § 281

CJS Trusts §§ 217, 261

§ 5-11. Custody of Remains

The court of probate for the residence of the deceased may award custody and control of the deceased's remains to the person determined by the court, applying statutory guidelines, to be most fit and appropriate to carry out the responsibilities of custody and control.[117] The probate court may make decisions regarding the subject's remains if those having custody and control cannot agree.[118]

---

[113] In re Estate of Gay, 97 N.H. 102, 81 A.2d 841 (1951), overruled in part; In re Estate of Byrne, 98 N.H. 300, 100 A.2d 157 (1953) (holding that petitions by fiduciaries for advice or instructions are within the jurisdiction of the superior court rather than the probate court). *Cf.* In re Estate of Lathrop, 100 N.H. 393, 128 A.2d 199 (1956), holding that the probate court may certify questions of interpretation of wills to the supreme court for ruling; noting that this method is more expeditious and inexpensive than application to the superior court for the interpretation of a will.

[114] Parsons v. Parsons, 9 N.H. 309 (1838).

[115] Rockwell v. Dow, 85 N.H. 58, 154 A. 229 (1931).

[116] Rockwell v. Dow, 85 N.H. 58, 66, 154 A. 229, 233 (1931).

[117] RSA 290:19.

[118] RSA 290:19. See also Section 33-23, this volume.

§ 5-12. Other Particular Matters

The judge of probate has jurisdiction of the management of a trust created by superior court for the sale, mortgage, or conveyance of real estate subject to a future interest;[119] change of name;[120] placing a transferee in an institution in another party state under the interstate compact on mental health;[121] the inventory of a surviving partner of a partnership, as well as the authority to have an appraisal or examination made of the estate;[122] appointment of conservators;[123] advancements;[124] certain insolvency proceedings;[125] assignment of homestead;[126] license to sell real estate;[127] certain proceedings under the Uniform Common Trust Fund Act;[128] durable powers of attorney for health care;[129] claims against the executor or administrator for services related to the prior care and maintenance of the decedent;[130] the interpretation and effect of living wills;[131] petitions for partition;[132] petitions to quiet title of real estate;[133] declaratory judgment actions;[134] proceedings to authorize and validate surrogacy contracts under the Surrogacy Act,[135] and "any other jurisdiction as may be granted by statute."[136]

---

[119] RSA 477:43.

[120] RSA 547:3, I(g).

[121] RSA 135-A:5.

[122] RSA 304-A.

[123] RSA 547:3, I(e); RSA 464-A:13.

[124] Locke v. Hancock, 59 N.H. 85 (1879).

[125] RSA 568:1. However, it should be noted that this statute is now largely superseded by the Federal Bankruptcy Act, thus diminishing the scope of the probate court's jurisdiction with respect to insolvency proceedings. 4th Report Judicial Council, p. 40 (1952).

[126] RSA 547:3, I(f).

[127] RSA 559:1; RSA 460:8, 9.

[128] RSA 391:2.

[129] RSA 547:3, I(i).

[130] RSA 547:3, I(i).

[131] RSA 547:3, I(j).

[132] RSA 547:3, I(k).

[133] RSA 547:3, I(l).

[134] RSA 547:3, I(m).

[135] RSA 168-B:20.

[136] RSA 547:3, I(n).

Library References

Am Jur 2d Courts §§ 14, 69

Cross References

See C. DeGrandpre, 7 New Hampshire Practice: Wills, Trusts and Gifts (3d ed. 1997) Chapter 26, Jurisdiction Over Trusts.

CHAPTER 6. REGISTERS OF PROBATE

§ 6-1. Introduction

The office of the register of probate dates back to 1694.[1] The constitutional and statutory provisions relating to registers of probate are some of the more archaic and anachronistic of New Hampshire probate law. Since many of the provisions are embedded in the New Hampshire Constitution, they have been difficult to change.

There is a register of probate for each of the ten counties of New Hampshire. By virtue of Part 2, Article 71 of the New Hampshire Constitution, registers of probate are constitutional officers who are elected on a county-wide basis.

The duties of the registers of probate are mainly administrative and clerical. It is an anomaly of our modern judicial system that such officials are elected. In comparison, the clerks of the superior court, whose functions are most closely analogous to those of the registers of probate, are appointed by the judges of the superior court and serve at the pleasure of the judges.[2] However, the constitutional provision which establishes this arrangement in the superior courts specifically excepts the probate courts from its provisions.[3] The fact that the registers of probate are

---

[1] Manuscript Treatise on Probate Law, Smith's Reports p. 514 (1879).

[2] N.H. Const. pt. II, art. 82.

[3] N.H. Const. pt. II, art. 82.

elected officials while the judges are appointed sometimes results in practical difficulties in the operation of a probate court. It is not unusual for a register of probate to be a member of one political party and the probate judge, who is appointed by the Governor with the consent of the Council, to be a member of another political party. As a result, the judges of probate and the registers of probate sometimes work completely independently of each other. This leads to many administrative problems which could easily be avoided by statutory and constitutional revision in this area.

Library References

　　Am Jur 2d Clerks of Court § 1 et seq.
　　CJS Courts § 236 et seq.

§ 6-2.　Qualifications; Office; Seal; Compensation

Registers of probate are salaried officials[4] who are chosen at biennial elections under RSA 653:1, V. Pursuant to the Technical Changes Act of 1993[5] it is a requirement that the register of probate shall "dwell in the county in which the probate records are required to be kept" and if the register "shall dwell in any other county and continue so dwelling for 30 consecutive days, the office shall be deemed vacant." RSA 548:1. Also, this section provides that the register of probate shall "be present at the probate office on all days when that office shall be required to be kept open or, in lieu of such presence, shall employ a competent clerk who shall dwell in said county and shall be present in the place of the register."

Probate offices are required by RSA 548:2 to be open on all days except Sundays, legal holidays and, if not incompatible with public business, on Saturdays. Under RSA 548:2, the register may have the office open on Saturday mornings, in the care of a custodian, when he deems it necessary.

The annual salaries of the registers of probate shall be established by the supreme court in accordance with the compensation system established by the supreme court. RSA 548:17. The register of probate is responsible for appointing deputy registers, RSA 548:14, and setting salaries for deputy registers and all nonjudicial court support staff under

---

[4] RSA 94:1, 94:1-a (superseding RSA 548:17).

[5] P.L., 1993, c. 190.

his or her supervision, consistent with the personnel procedures and compensation system established by the supreme court. RSA 548:17.

The register of probate is responsible under RSA 548:3 for keeping the seal of the probate court in his personal custody at the office where the probate records are kept, except when the seal is in use at some other place during a stated term of the probate court.

Registers of probate were formerly required to post a bond and were subject to a fine for failing to do so.[6] Under present law,[7] the register of probate, along with all other court employees, is bonded by the state and is indemnified against errors and omissions committed in his capacity as an employee of the court under RSA 93-B:1-a. The bond form and amount are approved under RSA 93-B:1-b by a board consisting of the attorney general, the commissioner of revenue administration and the banking commissioner.

Library References

Am Jur 2d Clerks of Court § 4

CJS Courts § 236 et seq.

§ 6-3. Duties Generally

Probate Court Rule 3 provides that all communications relating to estates and other probate matters must be sent to the register of probate, with copies to counsel of record or persons beneficially interested in the estate. RSA 548:4 makes it the responsibility of the register to keep a docket of all probate matters with a short memorandum of all proceedings and papers filed, a reference to the places where such proceedings and papers are recorded, and an index. The docket and index are to be open for public inspection at all reasonable times pursuant to RSA 548:4. Probate Court Rule 3 provides that no petition, motion or other pleading may be heard by the court until entered on the docket and the entry fee, if any, paid. Under Probate Court Rule 3, the register may refuse to accept any petition, motion or pleading that he determines does not comply with the rules or with statutory procedure, but, upon written motion, the register's refusal may be appealed to the probate judge for a ruling.

---

[6] RSA 548:27. This statute has not been repealed as of this writing, but appears to be without effect in light of the amendment of RSA 27:1.

[7] RSA 27:1, as amended effective January 1, 1984.

In addition to the docketing of individual matters, the register is required by RSA 548:5 to maintain a record of inventories by the amount of footing of each class of property, of all wills and their probate, of all proceedings regarding real estate, of all accounts settled, and of all orders, decisions, and appointments from which an appeal may be claimed. RSA 548:5 provides that the originals of documents filed with the register may be preserved on microfilm.

RSA 548:9 provides that the register is responsible for overseeing the filing of inventories and, in doing so, for forwarding to appraisers blanks on which to classify the property of estates. It is the register's responsibility under RSA 548:5-a to notify fiduciaries appointed by the probate court of failure to file required inventories and accounts, and the register is entitled to a fee as established under RSA 490:27, to be paid by the fiduciary, for providing such notice. When an inventory or any other instrument filed in connection with the administration of an estate lists real estate located in another county of the state the register must so notify the register of deeds of that county within fifteen days pursuant to RSA 548:7-a. The notice must state the name and date of death of the owner of the real estate. The costs of filing such notice are assessed to the estate.

The register is responsible for the safekeeping of all records, files and papers belonging to the register's office and is required by RSA 548:6 to keep them in a safe when they are not in use. RSA 548:6 provides further that such items are not to be removed from the office except when needed at the probate court or when the register is required to produce them as evidence in some other court. In *Fortier v. Grafton County*,[8] it was held that, due to this safekeeping requirement, the county commissioners could be forced to relocate the register's safe door so that it could be seen at all times from the register's office.

RSA 548:8 requires the register to provide all blanks and stationery necessary for the conduct of business of the probate court. This mandate is further expressed in Probate Court Rule 22, which requires the register to furnish approved forms and blanks to be used in all proceedings. In addition, computer generated form reproductions are acceptable under Rule 22A as modified by Probate Court Administrative Order 98-04 (rescinded effective 8/1/01). Form reproductions are acceptable for use in the probate courts if the reproduction contains the identical wording, format, and pagination as an original court-furnished form.

---

8 Fortier v. Grafton County, 112 N.H. 208, 292 A.2d 853 (1972).

In a contested matter, it is the duty of the register under Probate Court Rule 40 to furnish copies of the decree of the probate judge to all interested parties or their counsel. In uncontested matters, however, the Register of Probate shall send a notice of the Probate Judge's decision on Interim and Final Accounts (in Estates over $ 10,000) and Annual Accounts (in Guardianships) to the Attorney for the Fiduciary or to the Fiduciary if not represented by counsel. In uncontested matters, the Register of Probate shall not send a notice or copy of the Probate Judge's decision on Inventories to all interested parties or their counsel. Probate Court Administrative Order 98-07 (revised 1999)(rescinded effective 8/1/01).

Library References

Am Jur 2d Clerks of Court § 21 et seq.

CJS Courts §§ 249–255

§ 6-4. Reports

RSA 548:7 provides that each year, between the first and fifth day of April, the register of probate is required to furnish the selectmen of each town with a list of deceased persons who either resided or owned real estate in the town and whose estates were entered for probate during the preceding tax year.

Under RSA 548:7-a, a report of real estate which is the subject of the administration of an estate and which is located in another county within the state must be made to the register of deeds of the county in which the real estate lies.

Additionally, RSA 548:13 requires the register of probate to report all changes of names which have been made by the judge of probate since the date of the last such report to the register of vital statistics. Under this statute these reports are made during the months of January and July of each year.

Library References

Am Jur 2d Clerks of Court § 23

CJS Courts § 252

§ 6-5. Deputies and Clerks

If a register of probate is unable to perform the duties of office due to sickness, absence or some other cause, a deputy register may perform such duties under RSA 548:16 until the register is again able to perform the duties or until a new register is chosen. Deputy registers are appointed in writing by the register pursuant to RSA 548:14 in the event of such absence or illness and serve for a length of time not to exceed two years. The deputy register is a salaried employee and receives from the state the salary specified by the register of probate, in accordance with the personnel procedures and compensation system established by the supreme court under RSA 548:17.

RSA 548:17 also authorizes the register of probate to set salaries of nonjudicial court support staffs by supervisors, within the supreme court personnel procedures and compensation system.

Library References

Am Jur 2d Clerks of Court §§ 39–45

CJS Courts § 260 et seq.

§ 6-6. Prohibited Acts

Part 2, Article 81 of the New Hampshire Constitution prohibits any register of probate from acting as counsel or advocate, or receiving any fee as counsel or advocate, in any probate business which is pending or may be brought before the court of probate in the county in which the register serves. RSA 548:24 prohibits the register from acting as counsel or advocate in any proceeding brought in the court in which the register serves or from receiving any fee for such service. Further, RSA 548:25 prohibits the register from acting as appraiser or commissioner on any estate under administration in the court in which the register serves.

Library References

Am Jur 2d Clerks of Court § 28

CJS Courts § 256

§ 6-7. Committee on Judicial Conduct

"[R]egisters of probate and any person performing the duties of a clerk or register" are subject to disciplinary proceedings of the Committee On Judicial Conduct. Supreme Court Rule 40(1)(B)(1). Similarly, probate court stenographers or reporters and clerks and deputy clerks of any probate court are subject to the same proceedings.[9]

---

[9] Sup. Ct. R. 40(1)(B)(1).

CHAPTER 7. JUDGES OF PROBATE

§ 7-1. Introduction

The office of probate judge is an ancient one, dating back to 1694 in provincial New Hampshire.[1] There is one probate judge for each county, for a total of ten. The probate judges do not ride circuit, as do the judges of the superior court. Rather, each is appointed to fill a particular county seat. As a result, unlike the superior court, the probate courts tend to be insular, with practice and procedure varying markedly from county to county.

Unlike the registers of probate for each county, probate judges are not elected by popular vote. The New Hampshire Constitution provides for their appointment by the Governor with the advice and consent of the Council.[2] The Governor has the exclusive power to nominate and the

---

[1] MANUSCRIPT TREATISE ON PROBATE LAW, SMITH'S REPORTS p. 514 (1878).

[2] N.H. CONST. pt. II, art. 46.

power of appointment rests exclusively with the Governor's Council.[3] This method of selection of probate judges provided by the Constitution may not be altered by the legislature.[4]

It is not unusual for the probate judge for a particular county to be a member of one political party and the register of probate to be a member of another. Moreover, the probate judge for each county does not control the clerical and administrative functions of his court, which are delegated to the register of probate, who is an elected constitutional official. As a result, probate administrative and clerical procedures are sometimes haphazard at best.

Library References

Am Jur 2d Judges §§ 1–10
CJS Judges § 8

§ 7-2. Number; General Powers and Duties

The probate judge in each of the ten counties in New Hampshire holds regular sessions of the probate court at the times and places designated under RSA 549. It was held in *In re Estate of Gay*[5] that the probate court will not be deprived of jurisdiction merely because the proceeding is held at a time other than that prescribed by statute.

RSA 547:21 allows a probate judge to adjourn the court for the transaction of any business to any convenient time and place. A probate judge has the discretion of holding court at the residence of any person who, due to sickness or other sufficient cause, is unable to attend court if the attendance of such person is required.[6]

A probate judge may enforce any order or decree made by the judge in the exercise of his lawful authority, and punish for contempt under RSA 547:11. A probate judge's jurisdiction is granted by RSA 547:3. Where the judge is prohibited by statute from sitting or lacks jurisdiction under RSA 547:3, the acts of the judge are void.[7]

Probate Court Rule 46 provides for the continuing education of probate judges by requiring them to attend at least one judicial conference, approved by a majority of probate judges, biennially.

---

[3] Opinion of the Justices, 117 N.H. 398, 374 A.2d 638 (1977).

[4] Opinion of the Justices, 115 N.H. 159, 335 A.2d 642 (1975).

[5] In re Estate of Gay, 97 N.H. 102, 81 A.2d 841 (1951).

[6] RSA 547:20

[7] Stearns v. Wright, 51 N.H. 600 (1872).

It is mandatory that judicial robes "be worn by the judge during regular terms and at such other times when the nature of the hearing and the courtroom facilities command the practice." Probate Court Rule 47.

Library References

Am Jur 2d Judges §§ 22–43

CJS Judges § 58

§ 7-3. Compensation—In General

The salaries of judges of probate are established by the legislature. The compensation of a probate judge for acting in an official capacity is fixed by RSA 491-A:1. The salary of full-time probate judges is the same as that of superior court judges and full-time district court judges.[8] The salaries for part-time judges of probate vary from county to county depending upon caseload, ranging from a low of $2,500.00 to a high of $43,733.00.[9] RSA 547:24 states that the compensation provided for in these statutes is the only compensation which the judge is entitled to receive for the discharge of his official duties.[10] As a result of the court revision plan of the 1980's, which unified the New Hampshire court system, a probate judge's annual salary is paid by the state and not by the county, as was the case previously.

Library References

Am Jur 2d Judges §§ 54–67

CJS Judges § 75 et seq.

Forms

See Appendix for Form AOC 44 Inventory of Fiduciary.

§ 7-3(a). Special Session Fees Abolished

In 1986, the Supreme Court, in a split decision, overturned the practice of compensating probate judges in large part by the special session fee method. In *In re Estate of Dionne*,[11] the Court held that "the current method of compensating probate judges for special sessions smacks of the purchase of justice."[12] The Court, with one dissent, found the practice

---

[8] RSA 491-A:1.

[9] RSA 491-A:4.

[10] See also Gilmore v. Dodge, 58 N.H. 93 (1877); RSA 547:24.

[11] In re Estate of Dionne, 128 N.H. 682, 518 A.2d 178 (1986).

[12] In re Estate of Dionne, 128 N.H. 682, 684, 518 A.2d 178, 179 (1986).

an unconstitutional violation of part I, article 14 of the New Hampshire Constitution which grants citizens the right "to obtain right and justice freely." The dissent found authority for the 200-year-old practice in the Magna Carta and would approve the continuance of such a practice as being a justifiable response by the legislature to the problem of compensating part-time judges.

In 1987, in response to this decision, the New Hampshire legislature created a new system of compensation for probate judges; the manner of compensation is dependent upon whether a judge is a full-time or part-time judge. Full-time probate judges are to receive compensation equal to that of the superior court justices and fulltime district court judges [13] while part-time probate judges are compensated on a caseload system: the heavier the caseload, the greater the compensation. [14]

Prior to 1987, it was customary for probate judges to receive a substantial portion of their compensation from the charging of so-called special session fees. These fees were based upon the concept that a probate judge should be entitled to extra compensation whenever the nature of the hearing required his attention on days other than regular session days. Thus, if a probate judge sat at a contested hearing, RSA 547:23 allowed the probate judge an amount equal to the per diem allowed to masters by the superior court plus expenses. These fees were paid by the party applying for the hearing unless the court, in its discretion, determined the party to be indigent and charged the allowance to the state. [15]

In addition to his salary, a probate judge was formerly allowed a special session fee of $20.00, plus expenses by RSA 547:23 for attending an uncontested hearing on days other than those set by statute. This provision gave rise to the development of a large practice of probate law by in-chamber hearings of uncontested matters, at times convenient to the parties, the attorneys and the judges. This legislative compensation scheme had the advantage of roughly tailoring the compensation of the part-time probate judge to his workload—the busier a judge was, the more compensation he received from special session fees. Also, although parties paid for the hearing, the cost was usually far less than the cost

---

[13] RSA 491-A:1.

[14] RSA 591-A:4.

[15] Former RSA 547:23.

and expense of the delay occasioned by long waits for hearings scheduled on regular session days.

Library References

Am Jur 2d Judges § 54

CJS Judges § 82

§ 7-4. Full-Time Probate Judges

The 1987 revisions to the probate court structure, which were made in response to the Supreme Court's discussion in the *Dionne* case[16] contemplate the creation of a system staffed by full-time probate judges who will be prohibited from practicing law altogether. Pursuant to RSA 547:2-a, the full-time judges are required to assist probate courts in other counties whenever the probate judges in such counties are disqualified, disabled or otherwise unable to sit. Full-time probate judges are entitled to the same disability and retirement benefits as full-time district court judges.[17]

Under RSA 491-A:4, IV, when a part-time probate judge's caseload equals 70% of the caseload of a full-time district court justice, "the Supreme Court . . . may determine that said probate judge become full-time." In December 1990, the Supreme Court appointed John R. Maher, the judge of the Rockingham County Superior Court, to act as Administrative Justice of the probate courts.

Full-time probate judges are "prohibited from the practice of law to any degree." RSA 547:13.

In 1994, pursuant to the caseload formula, the supreme court appointed the probate judge of Belknap County as a full-time judge.

Library References

Am Jur 2d Judges §§ 48–52

CJS Judges § 14

§ 7-5. Disqualification—In General

Part 2, Article 81 of the New Hampshire Constitution states that:

---

[16] In re Estate of Dionne, 128 N.H. 682, 618 A.2d 178 (1986).

[17] RSA 547:2-a.

No judge, or register of probate, shall be of counsel, act as advocate, or receive any fees as advocate or counsel, in any probate business which is pending, or may be brought into any court of probate in the county of which he is judge or register.

In addition to this constitutional prohibition, RSA 547:12 prohibits a probate judge from drawing a will, RSA 547:13 prohibits a probate judge from acting as counsel in any business before any probate court, and RSA 547:14 prohibits a probate judge from acting as a judge on a matter in which he is interested. RSA 547:2-a prohibits a full-time judge to engage in the practice of law to any degree. A probate judge who violates any of these prohibitions is guilty of a misdemeanor under RSA 547:28.

In *Moses v. Julian,*[18] it was held that a probate judge "who is satisfied that he is legally disqualified to act in a case, ought not to wait until the parties object to him, but should refuse to hear the case." The *Moses* court stated further that any party who believes that a probate judge should be disqualified has "the right and duty . . . to object to, or recuse a judge."[19] The objecting party bears the burden of proof in establishing the disqualification.[20]

If a judge disqualifies himself or herself to sit in any case, by reason of a conflict of interest or otherwise, the judge is required to cause a record of his or her disqualification to be made and shall adjourn the case to another time and place. RSA 547:15. The administrative judge of the probate court, a full-time judge, or, if such is unavailable, another probate or district court judge, shall have the power to hear the case at issue and give appropriate decrees or orders. RSA 547:15.

Library References

Am Jur 2d Judges §§ 86–97

CJS Judges § 98 et seq.

§ 7-5(a). Drawing a Will

Although early New Hampshire case law allowed a will written by a judge of probate to be proved in court,[21] this rule was modified by

---

[18] Moses v. Julian, 45 N.H. 52, 53 (1863).

[19] *Id.*

[20] *Id.*

[21] Moses v. Julian, 45 N.H. 52, 60 (1863).

the legislative enactment of what is now RSA 547:12. RSA 547:12 provides that a probate judge may not draft a will for any other person and that any will drafted by a probate judge is void. Therefore, if a probate judge drafts a will, he is guilty of a misdemeanor under RSA 547:28, and the will is void.

Library References

Am Jur 2d Judges § 185

CJS Judges § 97

§ 7-5(b). Acting as Counsel

Part 2, Article 81 of the New Hampshire Constitution, and RSA 547:13, prohibit a probate judge from acting as counsel in any matter which may be brought before his court. RSA 547:13 further prohibits an attorney from practicing before any probate judge who is related to the attorney as partner, associate, employer, employee, or co-stockholder in a professional corporation in the practice of law.

RSA 547:15 requires a probate judge who has acted as counsel on a matter which comes before his court to disqualify himself, causing a record of his disqualification to be made, and to adjourn the proceedings to a convenient time and place. Under this statute, the case is then to be heard by the judge of any adjoining county, who will then be vested with all of the jurisdiction and authority that the disqualified judge would have had but for the disqualification.

Early case law provided that the acts of a probate judge in a case in which the judge had served as counsel were not void but, rather, were voidable on appeal.[22] However, at that time there was no statutory prohibition to the judge's sitting on the case. While the present statute, RSA 547:13, is still couched in terms of acts of the judge as counsel, rather than as a judge, RSA 547:15 now provides that a probate judge who is disqualified for any reason must transfer the case to a judge in an adjoining county.[23] Thus, the disqualified judge would lack jurisdiction over the case.[24] It is therefore arguable that under the present statutory framework the acts of a probate judge in a case in which he has served as counsel are void.

---

[22] Perkins v. George, 45 N.H. 453 (1864).

[23] Presumably, under the 1987 compensation revisions, such matters may also be heard by full-time probate judges from other counties. RSA 547:2-a.

[24] See Stearns v. Wright, 51 N.H. 600 (1872).

Library References

Am Jur 2d Judges § 185
CJS Judges § 114

§ 7-5(c). Conflict of Interest

RSA 547:14 provides that a probate judge is prohibited from acting in a case in which he has an interest as heir, legatee, executor, administrator, or as guardian or trustee of any person. However, in *Perkins v. George*,[25] such an interest was not imputed to the judge from his spouse and the court found no disqualification existed.

If the probate judge has one of the disqualifying interests in a case, RSA 547:15 requires him to state the interest on the record and adjourn the case to an adjoining county. The acts of a probate judge in a case in which he has such an interest are void.[26]

Library References

Am Jur 2d Judges §§ 98–22
CJS Judges § 125

§ 7-6. Absence or Inability To Attend

Whenever a judge of probate in any county shall be absent or unable to attend a session of the probate court, the administrative justice of the probate court is empowered to call upon a judge of some other county who shall act during such absence or inability. RSA 547:18-a. This statute also provides that any judge acting in such capacity shall receive per diem compensation as determined by the Supreme Court, plus reasonable expenses.

§ 7-7. Acting Judges

When a probate judge is disqualified by RSA 547:15, unable to attend court under RSA 547:18-a, or when there is a vacancy in the office of judge of probate in any county pursuant to RSA 547:18, a full-time judge or a probate judge from any other county may be called upon to serve as an acting judge. Furthermore, under RSA 547:2-a, a full-time probate judge from any other county is authorized to hear cases in other counties

---

[25] Perkins v. George, 45 N.H. 453, 454 (1864).
[26] Stearns v. Wright, 51 N.H. 600 (1872).

in such situations. RSA 547:19 provides that any such acting judge is authorized to transact any business that the disqualified or disabled judge could lawfully transact.

An acting judge serving due to disqualification of another judge is entitled to the same per diem compensation as is allowed masters by the superior court plus his reasonable expenses under RSA 547:16. An acting judge who serves due to the disability or inability of the regular judge is entitled to be compensated in the same manner as a superior court master pursuant to RSA 547:18-a. If the acting judge is serving due to a vacancy in the office of judge of probate, RSA 547:18 entitles the acting judge to be compensated in the same manner as a superior court master.

Library References

Am Jur 2d Judges §§ 248–267

CJS Judges § 66

§ 7-8. Disability

RSA 547:19-a governs the disability of probate judges. Under this statute, a probate judge who becomes disabled so that he cannot perform his duties may certify to the Governor and Council his inability to perform, and, if they find him unable to perform, they shall order his retirement. If a disabled judge is unwilling or unable to certify such disability, any three probate judges may do so and the Governor and Council may, after due notice and hearing, order the retirement of the judge. Upon the retirement of a probate judge, a successor is appointed by the Governor and Council to serve out the remainder of the judge's term.

RSA 547:19-a provides further that a probate judge who retires after ten years of service is entitled to be paid one-half of his salary over the remainder of his term unless he is a member of the state employees' retirement system or the New Hampshire retirement system and elects to take benefits under either of those systems instead.

Library References

Am Jur 2d Judges § 15

CJS Judges § 85

§ 7-9.   Retirement

RSA 547:19-b provides that when a probate judge reaches the age of seventy, his office becomes vacated and he is required to retire.[27] A probate judge may elect to retire at age sixty-five under RSA 547:19-d and be eligible for statutory retirement benefits. Under both of these statutes, a probate judge who retires and who has served as judge for at least twenty years is eligible to receive retirement pay equal to three-quarters of his current salary at the time of his retirement, unless he is a member of the state employees' retirement system or the New Hampshire retirement system. Both of these statutes provide that the retirement pay for judges is in lieu of other retirement benefits and require that membership in the retirement system be terminated prior to receiving the statutory retirement benefits.

Library References

Am Jur 2d Judges §§ 14–16

CJS Judges § 27

§ 7-9(a).   Referees and Masters

A judge of probate who is retired after meeting the statutory age limitation becomes a referee under RSA 547:19-c. As referees, the probate judges shall be allowed their expenses and per diem compensation as determined by the Supreme Court. Probate Court Rule 46. This rule gives referees authority in uncontested matters to appoint fiduciaries, approve wills in common form, approve inventories, licenses, and name changes, and to recommend approval or disapproval of the final account of fiduciaries to the judge of probate.

RSA 547:37, I allows a probate judge to appoint a former judge who has been retired due to the statutory age limitation as a master in any contested case where doing so will expedite the business of the court. These masters are authorized by Probate Court Rule 45 to set hearing dates, grant continuances, rule on the inclusion of evidence, make interlocutory orders, appoint guardians ad litem, attorneys and commissioners, and approve bills submitted by guardians ad litem, attorneys for indigent clients and commissioners. Under the rule, however, contempt citations issued for failing to comply with the master's orders must be ruled on by the presiding judge and fees of fiduciaries or attorneys and

---

[27] See also RSA 493:2.

all final orders and decrees must be approved by the presiding judge. Under RSA 547:37, II, a retired probate judge sitting as a master is compensated at the same rate as masters in the superior court and receive expenses. Under this statute, the compensation is paid by the party applying for the hearing unless the party is indigent, in which case the probate judge approves submission of the charge to the state.

Library References

Am Jur 2d Judges §§ 14–16
CJS Judges § 27

§ 7-10. Special Masters

The Omnibus Justice Act[28] expanded the power of a probate judge who is unable for any cause to sit in any case to appoint from a broader group of individuals other than just other probate judges, instead providing that

"a member of the Bar of New Hampshire who is a disinterested justice of the peace or a disinterested justice or special justice from a district to act as a special master, upon approval of the administrative judge of the probate court may serve in place of the regular probate judge." Special masters may hear any case as a master and make recommendations as to the disposition of the case. RSA 547:37, I. Special masters are required to keep a record of the case, which is to be kept with and constitute a part of the records of said court, all of which "shall be approved by the judge of said court before the order is issued." RSA 547:37, I.

A special master when sitting shall be allowed per diem compensation as determined by the Supreme Court, plus reasonable expenses. RSA 547:37, II.

---

[28] P.L., 1992, c. 284.

CHAPTER 8. RULES OF COURT

§ 8-1. Development of Rules

Until the 1950s, there were no unified probate court rules that applied to all counties. However, in 1959, upon recommendation of the Judicial Council,[1] the New Hampshire Supreme Court was given supervisory powers of all of the probate courts of the state. RSA 547:33–35. The Court promulgated the first set of probate court rules initially drafted by the judges of probate and made them applicable to the probate courts of all counties.[2] These rules, although a great improvement, were very basic and left many issues, such as the extent of discovery process, unresolved.

These rules remained essentially unchanged until 1983, when the probate judges formed a committee to study the rules and to recommend changes to the Supreme Court. It "had become increasingly apparent that the former Rules of Probate were outdated and inadequate."[3] The Committee, consisting of probate judges Cloutier (Hillsborough County), Murphy (Belknap County), Cassavechia (Strafford County) and Espiefs (Cheshire County) submitted proposed rules changes to the Supreme Court in 1985. These proposed changes underwent various revisions and drafts and completely revised New Rules were adopted by the Supreme Court effective September 1, 1987. Probate Judge Cassavechia of

---

[1] 6th Report Judicial Council, p. 12 (1956).

[2] 9th Report Judicial Council, p. 51 (1962).

[3] Cassavechia, *Supreme Court Rules Changes Aimed at Bringing Uniformity to Probate Court Procedures*, 14 N.H. LAW WEEKLY 111 (1987).

Strafford County, who served on the Rules Committee, has provided some insight into the thinking that lay behind the adoption of the new rules in an article in the "New Hampshire Law Weekly."[4] It should be noted that while it "was the consensus of the probate judges that, it would best serve the judges, courts and the practicing Bar not to establish substantially different practice and procedures"[5] from the district and superior court rules, subsequent changes to those rules "have resulted in a slight variance"[6] between the probate rules and the superior and district court rules.

The 1987 revisions to the probate code were a substantial step forward in narrowing the difference between the superior and probate courts, particularly in the areas of discovery and trial procedure.

Another important consideration underlying the rules is a recognition of differences in activity and geography among the probate courts, and the "rules were proposed and have been adopted consistent with the proposition that those counties having less present need may grow into them while those with the current need are not deprived of their immediate benefit."[7]

§ 8-2. Content

The probate rules provide a comprehensive set of procedures for practice in the probate courts. Unlike prior practice, under the new rules, practitioners will have occasion to refer to them often.

The rules are broken down into groups. The first major group, General Practice and Procedure, consisting of Rules 1–22 "apply to every form of proceeding before the Probate Court unless expressly or patently inapplicable." The second group, Wills, consisting of Rules 23–26 apply to specific will proceedings and the remaining groups, Bonds and Sureties, etc., consisting of Rules 27–30 apply to specific matters.

The Rules address for the first time certain areas such as discovery (Rule 10), admission of relevant facts, genuineness of documents and signatures (Rule 11), pre-trial procedures (Rule 12), etc.

---

[4] *Id.*

[5] *Id.*

[6] *Id.*

[7] *Id.*

An important new breakthrough in the rules lies in the handling of contested matters, an area of growing volume in the probate courts. Rule 12 provides a comprehensive pre-trial procedure which can be invoked by the court or by any litigant in "any pending contested matter." Rule 13 establishes certain standing pre-trial orders which apply in all matters to be heard by the court.

Of great importance in the pre-trial area is the so-called "contested hearing" form found in Appendix A of the Probate Rules. The use of this form is prescribed by Rule 12, which provides that a contested hearing form shall be filed whenever the court orders or whenever any litigant to a pending contested matter requests. Present experience shows that some probate courts are using this form and some are not. Some courts require it to be filed in all contested cases.

The form itself is less than adequate for its purposes and needs revision. It is not made clear, for example, whether the "simple and concise statement of the issues or matters to be heard" required by the form is meant to be exhaustive and meant to preclude the later raising of different or new issues.

Library References

Am Jur 2d Courts §§ 48–53
CJS Courts §§ 124–134

§ 8-3.   Rules of Evidence

The Rules of Evidence adopted in 1985 apply to practice before the probate courts.[8]

§ 8-4.   Administrative Orders

The administrative justice of the probate court has begun the practice of issuing consecutively numbered administrative orders which establish guidelines and rules for lawyers and the public who have business before the probate courts. These administrative orders are of great practical use to attorneys practicing in the probate courts. Because of the recent implementation of this procedure, it is unclear exactly how these orders should be cited, but the author suggests the orders be cited as follows: Prob. Ct. Adm. Order _____.

---

[8] N.H. Rules of Evidence, Rule 1101(a).

Because the contents of the administrative orders have not been approved by the Supreme Court and its rules committee, the value of these orders as precedent will be less than a probate court rule. These administrative orders are published in New Hampshire Bar News.

Administrative orders are issued in order to create uniform standards among the various probate courts on particular procedural or evidentiary matters. Some examples of recent administrative orders include creating standards relating to sound recordings of probate court proceedings[9] and setting guidelines for the use of computer-generated probate forms.[10]

§ 8-5. Procedure Bulletins

The administrative justice of the probate court has begun to issue consecutively numbered (by year) bulletins which are designed mostly for the use of the probate judges and registers of probate and which establish procedures for the conduct of business in the probate courts. However, they will be of very significant help to practicing attorneys as well. These orders should be cited as follows: Prob. Ct. Proc. Bul._____.

---

[9] Prob. Ct. Adm. Orders 94–01 (rescinded effective 3/31/96) and 95–01 (rescinded effective 8/1/01).

[10] Prob. Ct. Adm. Order 95-02 (rescinded effective 3/1/96).

CHAPTER 9. APPROVED FORMS AND BLANKS

---

§ 9-1.　Generally

In the 1950's, at the time of the adoption of unified probate court rules, the probate courts established a set of preprinted, approved forms for use before the probate courts.

All probate courts must use forms released by the Forms Committee, and, after the effective date for implementation of the new and revised form, the probate courts must use the form as mandated by the Forms Committee.[1]

By administrative order, probate courts have been forbidden to create any new forms for use only at that particular court.[2] If a judge or register of a particular county wishes to utilize a form for that particular county only, it must first be submitted to the Forms Committee.[3]

Probate Court Procedure Bulletin 1996-11 (rescinded effective 8/1/01) provided that if there is no approved petition form applicable to the proceeding, then the petition and motions practice for superior court should be followed. The use of the probate court all-purpose petition form (Approved Form 77) may also be used, but is not encouraged. Motions and petitions procedure in probate court is also discussed in Probate Court Procedure Bulletin 1996-01 (rescinded effective 8/1/01).

---

[1] Prob. Ct. Pro. Bul. 1996-8 (rescinded effective 8/1/01).

[2] Prob. Ct. Pro. Bul. 1.

[3] *Id.*

§ 9-2. Use of Forms

RSA 548:8 provides that the registers of probate shall provide all blanks and stationery necessary for the conduct of the business of the probate court. The use of official forms is governed by Probate Court Rule 22, Rule 22A and Probate Court Administrative Order 98-04 (rescinded effective 8/1/01). If there is insufficient space on the approved form or blank, additions or riders must "be attached on schedule pages of the same size." Rule 22.

Probate practitioners may obtain a limited supply of the probate forms from the register of probate upon request and without cost. Most probate practitioners maintain an adequate supply of the commonly used forms for use in their probate practice.

§ 9-2(a). Computer Generated Forms

Probate Rule 22A provides that practitioners "may produce forms for use in the probate courts that are either computer-generated replicas or photocopies of form furnished by the Registers of Probate." A computer-generated replica is defined as "a document containing the identical wording, in the identical format, and with the identical pagination as in the original, but font size or style may be different from the font size or style of the original form." In addition, reproductions of multi-pages probate forms may be single-sided. Although Rule 22A requires a certification that computer-generated forms are replicas of the forms approved by the Register of Probate, Probate Court Administrative Order 98-04, effective December 7, 1998 (rescinded), provided that a separate certification is no longer necessary for any acceptable probate court form reproductions, including computer generated replicas. Rather, all probate courts shall consider that the party who signs and/or files the form reproduction has agreed that the document is a reproduction of an approved form. The administrative order provides that discrepancies between a form reproduction and a court-furnished original may subject the party who signs and/or files the reproduction to court-imposed sanctions or penalties, including removal as fiduciary. Although Rule 22A provides that facsimile or mimeograph forms, or photocopies of a facsimile or mimeograph form shall not be accepted by any probate court, under administrative order 98-04 (rescinded) reproductions from a variety of sources were acceptable. However, the order further states that facsimile or photocopied signatures are not acceptable for any probate court. Notice should be taken of RSA 506:9 that provides that digital signatures may be used to sign a writing and shall have the same force and effect as a written signature.

§ 9-3. List of Forms

The registers of probate do not provide or maintain a comprehensive listing of the available approved forms but all probate practitioners should maintain such a list. The Appendix contains a listing of the available and commonly used approved forms. Commonly used New Hampshire Department of Revenue Administration Forms are included in this listing.

Forms

See Appendix for a list of currently used Approved Probate Forms.

CHAPTER 10. PROCEDURE IN GENERAL

---

§ 10-1.   Time and Place of Holding Court

Probate judges, being part-time, do not hold court every day of the week as do the superior courts. RSA 549:1 establishes "regular sessions" of the probate court for each of the counties, which generally provide for the courts to sit on a bimonthly basis. The times differ from county to county, and the judges are required to hold regular sessions in the various population centers of each county. RSA 549:1.

In addition to the regular sessions of probate court, the probate judges, in order to accommodate parties and attorneys and to meet the press of business, often meet at other than the required statutorily-prescribed regular sessions. These sessions are established at the direction and preference of each particular probate judge, and the frequency varies from county to county. The register of probate for each county must be contacted to ascertain "special session" days.

Because regular session days often required attorneys and parties to appear and wait for long hours, the scheduling of special sessions at hours and times convenient to parties and attorneys was commonplace until 1987. Prior to 1987, judges were directly compensated by the parties for special sessions, but the practice was declared unconstitutional by the Supreme Court in *In re Estate of Dionne*.[1] Now, probate judges receive a statutorily-established salary based on caseload factors, which results in salaries which vary from county to county.[2] Unless a probate judge becomes fulltime, the probate judges are free to determine the frequency and duration of special sessions. As a result of these changes, most special session days resemble regular session days of yore, with long lines and delays at the busy probate courts.

Each probate court handles the matter of docket lists and scheduling in a different manner. Many courts simply use a "first come, first served" basis, with the result that there is a race to "sign-up" early on the court list each court day. Other counties use different systems, sometimes preferring local county attorneys. It is always best to check with a local practitioner before assuming that the practice of one county will apply to another.

All counties treat contested matters differently than non-contested cases. It is seldom that a probate judge will hear a contested matter on

---

[1] In re Estate of Dionne, 128 N.H. 682, 518 A.2d 178 (1986).

[2] RSA 491-A:4, IV.

a regular session day, and almost never, even on a special session day, will a contested matter be heard without advance notice to the court of the nature of the contest, etc.

RSA 547:20 also provides the judge may hold court at the dwelling house or in the neighborhood of the residence of an administrator, guardian, trustee or other person who shall be unable, by reason of sickness or other sufficient cause, to attend the court of probate at the time and place appointed by law, whenever the personal attendance of such person is required. This statute is used most frequently in guardianship proceedings when the attendance of the ward may be required by law.

Library References

Am Jur 2d Courts §§ 16–24

§ 10-1(a). Filing of Appearance

Probate Court Rule 4 requires that any party appearing before the probate court shall file a written appearance notice with the register of probate. Rule 4 further states: "No attorney or party appearing pro se will be heard until his appearance is properly entered." However, Probate Court Procedure Bulletin 11 does allow exceptions. A written appearance is not required for any "Will Filed with No Administration," or for pro se parties who file "Change of Name" or "Marriage Waiver" cases. If any party submits a written appearance for a "Will Filed with No Administration," "Change of Name," or "Marriage Waiver" case, however, the written appearance shall be filed and not returned. Bulletin 11 sets out in detail when attorneys must file new appearance and withdrawal forms. It is incumbent upon attorneys and their law firms to file prompt and accurate Appearance/Withdrawal forms whenever there are changes in the representation of parties to ensure that probate courts and all parties appearing of record mail to the correct attorneys at the correct law firm addresses.

Forms

See Form 007 in Appendix for an Appearance and Withdrawal Form.

§ 10-2. Adjournment

By common law, probate courts are always considered open for the transaction of business. There is no language in the New Hampshire

Constitution that indicates any intention to limit and confine the jurisdiction of the probate courts, so that they would have no authority to act except on the days fixed by law. *Kimball v. Fisk.* [3]

RSA 547:21 provides that the judge of probate may adjourn his court for the transaction of any business to any convenient time and place.

Courts of probate have, as incident to their character as courts, the power of adjourning whenever they deem it necessary for the transaction of their business. [4] The fact that the legislature has conferred the same power by statute, in some qualified form, is not an indication of an intention to limit the general power ordinarily incident to courts of justice. [5]

If business before the probate court requires an adjournment, the court may adjourn, [6] and when the court is open pursuant to an adjournment it is open for the transaction of any business, as on the regular days appointed for its sitting. [7] The argument that the court may adjourn only for the trial of cases pending before it has been dismissed as placing too rigid and narrow a construction upon RSA 547:21. [8]

If it should be regarded as irregular that business should be done by the judge of probate on days not appointed by the law, such a matter does not affect the jurisdiction of the court over the subject matter. [9] The defect is not necessarily fatal as it may be waived or released; and so long as the proceedings remain, and are not set aside on motion or appeal, all parties are bound by them, and they cannot be treated as nullities, when they are incidentally brought in question. [10]

Library References

Am Jur 2d Courts § 22

---

[3] Kimball v. Fisk, 39 N.H. 110 (1859).

[4] *Id.*

[5] *Id.*

[6] *Id.*

[7] *Id.*

[8] *Id.*

[9] *Id.*

[10] *Id.*

§ 10-3.　Notice of Proceedings—In General

Revised Statutes has an entire chapter, Chapter 550, Citation and Notice, which deals with when notice is required and when it is not, the form of notice, the matter of citations, etc.

The judge of probate is authorized to act in certain cases without notice, in his discretion, but this provision should not be misunderstood.[11] The discretion to be exercised is not a capricious discretion, to be exercised according to the whim, caprice, or favor of the judge, rather it is a legal discretion, to be exercised only upon a careful consideration of the facts of the case, and with an anxious regard to the rights and interests of the parties to be affected by the proceedings. *Cummings v. Allen.*[12] It cannot be regarded as a legal or judicious exercise of such discretion to make decrees affecting the rights of others without inquiry whether those persons are aware of the proceeding, or are known to have objections to the application, whether the design to apply has been in any way studiously concealed, and whether there exist any reasons of haste or urgency which render it unsuitable that the case should be delayed.[13] As a general rule, the judge should be satisfied that the parties affected, or some of those most interested, are aware of the proceeding, or that good reasons exist against any delay.[14] If such is not the case the judge should require some notice to be given, not necessarily the formal notice required by the statute, but some notice sufficient to put the party upon the alert.[15]

The object of notice is to inform a party of the pendency of the proceedings in the probate court in order that he might appear and defend; thus, where by mistake the original petition and notice were left at a party's abode, they gave him the same information that copies would, and as no possible harm was done, justice would not require that the petition be dismissed because the originals instead of copies were left. *Adams v. Adams.*[16]

Within fifteen days of the appointment of an administrator or executor, the register of probate shall publish notice of the appointment in

---

[11] Cummings v. Allen, 34 N.H. 194 (1856).

[12] *Id.*

[13] *Id.*

[14] *Id.*

[15] *Id.*

[16] Adams v. Adams, 64 N.H. 224, 9 A. 100 (1887).

accordance with the provisions of RSA 550:10.[17] However, this publication notice is not required in the administration of small estates under RSA 553:31.

In *King v. Mosher*, it was held to be improper for a court, in an action involving cross-claims over the title to certain assets in the possession of a third party on the date of death but claimed to be owned by the estate, to involuntarily dismiss the third-party action claiming ownership where the notice of the hearing did not include notice that the third party's claims would be considered.[18] "[T]he fundamental requirements of due process require that a party be provided with such notice and opportunity to be heard as will adequately safeguard the rights for which constitutional protection is invoked."

Library References

Am Jur 2d Process § 1 et seq.

§ 10-3(a). Citations

RSA 550:2 provides that the judge of probate may, on his own motion, issue a citation directed to any fiduciary appointed by or responsible to the probate court, requiring such fiduciary to appear before him to inform the court concerning any matters related to his trust over which the court has jurisdiction. Upon due notice and hearing, the judge may make such order or decree as appears proper.

RSA 550:3 provides that service of a citation issued under RSA 550:2 shall be sufficient if made by registered mail, return receipt requested, at the address of record of the fiduciary. Any expenses incidental to carrying out the provisions of this or the preceding section shall be charged against the estate, and may, in the discretion of the judge of probate, be deducted from any fee or other compensation due the fiduciary.

§ 10-3(b). Notice Not Required

RSA 550:4 provides that the probate judge may, at his discretion, proceed without notice in the following cases:

I. In the probate of wills in common form.

---

[17] RSA 553:16, as amended by P.L., 1996, c. 199.

[18] King v. Mosher, 137 N.H. 453, 456 (1993).

II. In the appointment of the person entitled to such trust, or of the person by him nominated, as administrator.

III. In the appointment of appraisers of estates.

IV. In licensing the sale of personal estate.

V. In licensing the sale of real estate whenever the heirs at law or devisees consent thereto in writing, or it is of less than five hundred dollars in value.

VI. In the appointment of commissioners of insolvent estates.

VII. In the appointment of guardians of minors.

VIII. In granting allowances to widows.

IX. In the assignment of the homestead right.

X. In making orders for suits upon probate bonds.

XI. In changing the names of persons.

XII. In the appointment of trustees named in wills.

XIII. In licensing the mortgage of real estate pursuant to RSA 554:30–35.[19]

XIV. In allowing the payment of a sum not exceeding five hundred dollars for the perpetual care of a cemetery lot and the monuments thereon where the decedent is buried.

XV. When an accounting is filed by a guardian who is a parent of or a person standing in loco parentis to a minor having his home with such guardian.

---

[19] The judicial council has stated that there is no conflict between subparagraph XIII of this section and RSA 554:30 which provides that the mortgage of real estate requires the assent of the heirs or devisees or, if minors or under disability, their guardians or conservators. However it is advised that attorneys refer to RSA 554:30 before acting under this section. 9th Report Judicial Council, p. 43 (1962).

Library References

Am Jur 2d Executors and Administrators § 406

Am Jur 2d Wills § 840

CJS Executors and Administrators §§ 70, 352

CJS Wills §§ 369, 370

§ 10-3(c). Particular Persons

RSA 550:5 provides that in all cases in which notice is required a citation shall be issued, or an order of notice made to the parties interested, to appear at the court at a day and place therein appointed, that they may be heard if they see cause. Every citation or order of court to an individual, requiring him to perform a particular duty, is required to be served by giving to him in person or leaving at his abode a certified copy thereof, if he resides in this state, twelve days at least before the day of hearing. RSA 550:6.

Every citation or order of notice to a person residing out of the state, or to the widow, heirs, devisees, legatees, creditors or persons interested in an estate, in general terms, to be present at a proceeding relative to the estate, shall be served by giving to each person to whom it is directed or leaving at his abode, twelve days at least before the day appointed for such proceedings, a certified copy of the citation or order of notice or by publication. RSA 550:7.

In addition to the notice prescribed in the preceding sections, the judge may order personal notice, or notice sent by mail, to any person interested, or notice by publication in a newspaper printed elsewhere, as he shall deem proper in the case. RSA 550:8.

Library References

Am Jur 2d Wills §§ 933, 1512

CJS Executors and Administrators §§ 752–54

Rules of res judicata as applied to judicial construction of will. 136 ALR 1180.

§ 10-3(d). Appearances

However, RSA 550:9 provides that notice is not required to a party who has filed an appearance in writing:

> Notwithstanding any other provisions of this chapter, no publication or service of any petition, motion, pleading, or other proceeding, shall be required as to any party or person who has

filed, or for whom there has been filed, in the probate registry, an appearance in writing, and notice shall be sufficient if a copy of such petition, motion, or other proceeding, together with notice of the time and place of hearing, shall be mailed to such party or person, or the attorney of record for such party or person, at the address specified in the appearance.

Library References

Am Jur 2d Executors and Administrators § 252

CJS Executors and Administrators §§ 755, 848

CJS Wills §§ 371, 1003

Objection before judgment to jurisdiction of court over subject matter as constituting general appearance. 25 ALR2d 833.

General appearance as avoiding otherwise effective bar of statute of limitations. 82 ALR2d 1200.

§ 10-3(e). Notice By Publication

RSA 550:10 specifies the details of notice by publication:

I. Notwithstanding any other provision of law, whenever notice is required to be published in a newspaper by any provision of this title, the register of probate shall cause such notice to be published 2 weeks successively in a newspaper which circulates in the town or city in which the person whose estate is involved last resided, or in the county whose court has jurisdiction, or otherwise as ordered by the judge.

II. The register of probate may select the newspaper for publication, provided only that it is a newspaper in the English language, unless the judge shall otherwise order. The register may publish a notice in a newspaper in other than the English language, provided that he also publishes the same notice in a newspaper in the English language at the same time. The first such publication shall be at least 2 weeks before the day or thing of which notice is given and the second publication shall be at least 7 days before the day or thing of which notice is given, unless otherwise ordered by the judge.

III. The register of probate may publish in one notice the necessary information pertaining to more than one estate, provided, however, that each separate subject matter such as the appointment of a fiduciary, a hearing on an account, a hearing on a license to sell real estate, or any other designated subject matter shall have a specific designation within each such notice.

IV. Prior to such publication, the fiduciary of the estate concerned shall advance and pay to the register of probate the cost of such publication as determined by the register, and a fee to the register as established by the supreme court under RSA 490:27. The fiduciary shall be allowed said sums so paid to the register in his account.

Library References

Am Jur 2d Wills § 933

CJS Executors and Administrators §§ 53, 411, 592, 784, 846, 848

CJS Wills § 369

§ 10-3(f). Notice to Persons Beneficially Interested

RSA 550:11 provides that whenever any executor, administrator, or trustee files an account in the probate court, the fiduciary shall contemporaneously forward the following to all persons beneficially interested as defined in RSA 550:12, and all parties appearing of record:

(a) A copy of the account; and

(b) A notice that the account may be approved unless a written objection, containing the specific factual or legal basis for the objection, is filed within 30 days after the date the account is filed in the probate court. This notice requirement is waived if all assents are filed pursuant to paragraph IV.

Further, RSA 550:11 provides that the fiduciary shall certify to the probate court that the requirements of paragraph II have been complied with.

If the fiduciary files, pursuant to RSA 550:13, assents to the account from all persons beneficially interested as defined in RSA 550:12, and all parties appearing of record, the account may be approved earlier than 30 days after the date the account is filed in the probate court, at the discretion of the court. RSA 550:11 and Probate Court Procedure Bulletin 12.

RSA 550:12 defines a person beneficially interested in an estate as follows:

A person shall be deemed to be beneficially interested in an account within the meaning of RSA 550:11 if he is an heir or distributee of an intestate estate, a residuary legatee under a will, a specific legatee under a will, but has not received the legacy, a beneficiary having a vested interest in a trust, the attorney general in estates involving charitable trusts, a ward, or a minor under guardianship who is 14 years of age or older, an heir, or legatee under a will of a deceased ward, or a creditor who is known to the fiduciary and has not been paid.

Whenever a fiduciary who is either a custodian of a minor under RSA 463-A or a guardian of a veteran under RSA 465 files an account in the probate court, the fiduciary shall contemporaneously forward a copy of the account to all persons beneficially interested as defined in RSA 550:12 and all parties appearing of record. Probate Court Procedure Bulletin 12 (revised).

When a copy of an account or inventory is sent out pursuant to RSA 550:11 a failure to object to the account or inventory will act as a waiver of the right to object to the account or inventory and the right to any further notice concerning any hearing on the account or inventory. Probate Court Administrative Order 98-06 (rescinded effective 8/1/01).

Library References

Am Jur 2d Executors and Administrators §§ 655–58, 1057, 1073, 1086
Am Jur 2d Wills §§ 932–36
CJS Executors and Administrators §§ 411, 496, 519, 528–29, 784, 786, 846

Forms

See Form 011 in Forms Appendix for Assent.
See Form 011A in Forms Appendix for Assent for Summary Administration.

§ 10-3(g). Waiver

The citation and notice required to be given to any person in any proceeding may be dispensed with upon written assent by such person to such proceeding or upon his written waiver of such citation and notice. RSA 550:13. A duly-appointed guardian ad litem may give assent or waive citation or notice as aforesaid. RSA 550:13.[20] This statutory

---

[20] Since enactment of RSA 550:13, an administrator's or executor's account to which the interested parties have assented or agreed in writing may be allowed without the delay and expense incidental to notice by publication and personal service by mail or otherwise upon the interested parties. 9th Report Judicial Council, p. 43 (1962).

provision is frequently used to avoid the expense of notice by publication where the parties are in agreement and the estate is being settled amicably.

Library References

Am Jur 2d Executors and Administrators §§ 156, 252

CJS Executors and Administrators §§ 411, 839, 840, 844, 910

CJS Wills §§ 325, 370–71, 422, 488, 517, 1090

§ 10-4. Computation and Extension of Time

Probate Court Rule 1A provides a specific and clear procedure for computing time periods in the probate courts:

(1) In computing any period prescribed or allowed by these rules, by order of court, or by applicable law, the day of the act, event, or default after which the designated period of time begins to run shall not be included. The last day of the period so computed shall be included, unless it is a Saturday, Sunday, or a legal holiday, in which event the period shall extend until the end of the next day that is not a Saturday, Sunday, or a legal holiday as specified in RSA ch. 288, as amended.

(2) Motions to enlarge the time prescribed by these rules or by court order for doing any act are not favored.

The administrative judge of the probate court by administrative decree has established that the "effective date of any court order is the date of the Judge's signature. For determining the time period for filing any subsequent motion or appeal,[21] the time for filing shall run from the date of the mailing of the order or notice by the Register of Probate."[22]

§ 10-5. Pleadings, Motions and Petitions

Rule 3 of the Probate Rules addresses the issue of petitions, motions and pleadings. This rule requires all pleadings and petitions be filed with the Register of Probate. All pleadings, motions and petitions must contain both the street and mail address of the party filing the document. Notice

---

[21] Prob. Ct. Proc. Bul. 1996-03.

[22] *Id.*

to the last mail address on file shall be deemed notice to, and binding on, the party.

Copies of all pleadings filed with, and communications addressed to the court shall be furnished forthwith to all parties appearing of record or beneficially interested. All such pleadings or communications shall contain a statement of compliance with Probate Court Rule 3. Practitioners have frequently failed to comply with the so-called certification requirement of this rule. As a result, probate courts often reject pleadings when first presented for action unless a certification of compliance with the rule is contained in the pleadings or communications. Many petitions and motions and other pleadings are being returned to the filer for failure to include a statement of compliance, so great care must be taken in this area. It may be several weeks before an attorney realizes that the petition that he thought was filed has not been accepted by the court.

Probate Court Rule 3 makes clear that it is improper to address pleadings or any communications such as writs, etc., directly to the probate judge, although the practice in some counties in the past has been quite informal in this regard.

The issue of motions and petitions was addressed in Probate Court Procedure Bulletin 1996-01 (rescinded effective 8/1/01) where it was provided that "a petition initiates a new case, while a motion is a pleading in an existing case." The Bulletin also provided that a petition, unlike a motion, may require orders of notice, a return date, etc.

The Bulletin also provides that Form 77, the general purpose form, may be a either petition or motion, depending upon what relief is sought.[23] Procedure Bulletin 1996-11 (rescinded effective 8/1/01) added that when no approved probate court form is specifically applicable, persons may file petitions and motions in the probate court in accordance with superior court practice. The bulletin also said that Probate Court Rule 22 concerning the use of Form 77 is not deemed to be mandatory and parties are encouraged **not** to use Probate Court Form 77 as a cover form for petitions and motions, **but may do so if they desire.**

Probate Court Procedure Bulletin 20 (Revised), effective July 1, 2000 provides that all petitions shall be signed by the petitioner, and all bonds, inventories and accounts shall be signed by the fiduciary. Motions and other pleadings may be signed by the party, the attorney of record or

---

[23] Prob. Ct. Proc. Bul. 1996-01 (rescinded effective 8/1/01).

the attorney's associate, or by the party's attorney-in-fact. Names shall be typed, stamped or printed beneath all signatures on papers to be filed or served.

The signature of any person to a petition, motion, or other pleading constitutes a certification that the signatory has read the pleading; that to the best of his or her knowledge, information and belief there is a good ground to support the pleading; and that it is not interposed for delay. Probate Court Procedure Bulletin 20 (Revised), effective July 1, 2000. If a petition, motion, or other pleading is not signed, it may be stricken and the action may proceed as though it had not been filed.

There is a 30-day grace period following the notice of failure to pay the required initial filing fee. If the required filing fee is not paid in full by the end of the 30-day waiting period, the probate court shall dismiss the petition without notice to the sender. Any partial filing fee payment is forfeited. Probate Court Procedure Bulletin 3.

Library References

Am Jur 2d Executors and Administrators §§ 150, 1072, 1089, 1343–50

Am Jur 2d Wills § 937 et seq.

CJS Executors and Administrators §§ 91, 136, 161, 424, 428, 520, 848, 918, 992–96

§ 10-6. Discovery—In General

Rule 10 of the probate court rules provides that all of the rules of the superior courts regarding discovery (Superior Court Rules 35–45A) shall apply in the probate courts. This is a substantial and welcome change and brings to the probate courts the liberal philosophy of discovery embraced in the superior court rules.

§ 10-6(a). Interrogatories

Discovery by written interrogatory is available in the probate courts, by virtue of the incorporation of Superior Court Rules 36 and 36-A by Probate Court Rule 10.

Library References

CJS Wills §§ 430, 441, 481

§ 10-6(b).

§ 10-6(b). Depositions

The probate courts have available the deposition procedure provided by Superior Court Rules 37–44, by virtue of the incorporation of these rules by Rule 10 of the Probate Court Rules.

Library References

Am Jur 2d Wills §§ 949–50

CJS Executors and Administrators §§ 571, 890

CJS Wills §§ 311, 444, 451, 531

§ 10-6(c). Admission of Relevant Facts, Genuineness of Documentation and Signatures

Superior Court Rules 53 and 54 providing for the Admission of Relevant Facts and the Genuineness of Documentation and Signatures have been adopted for the probate courts by virtue of Rule 11 of the Probate Court Rules. This rule provides a discovery tool which is particularly useful in probate court matters which often involve a myriad of paper. By means of filing original documents with the register of probate with copies to the opposing party, together with a request for admission, a party can facilitate the preparation of his case and the pre-hearing proof and admission of his documentary evidence.

Library References

Am Jur 2d Executors and Administrators §§ 860, 1351–52

Am Jur 2d Wills § 990 et seq.

CJS Executors and Administrators §§ 167, 417, 451–52, 763–64, 774, 781, 786–87

CJS Wills §§ 378, 404

§ 10-7. Pre-Trial Procedures

Probate Court Rules 12 and 13 establish a useful pre-trial hearing and/or written procedure for simplifying issues prior to trial. This procedure may be invoked by either party or by the court. Although there has been little experience with this new concept in most counties to date, it should lead to a substantial savings of time, effort and expense in contested probate proceedings.

§ 10-8. Procedure During Trial

The procedure in probate court during trial has been made identical to the superior court procedure governed by Rules 64–72 of the superior court. Probate Court Rule 14.

These procedures include a wide variety of matters, including the handling of exhibits and the examination of witnesses.

Probate Court Administrative Order 98-01 (rescinded effective 8/1/01) provided that a probate judge or probate master may receive evidence by an Offer of Proof, whenever appropriate and within the discretion of the court. The order lays out the procedure that must be followed for an Offer of Proof.

Library References

Am Jur 2d Wills §§ 1024–31

CJS Executors and Administrators §§ 62, 603, 627, 645, 787–90, 849, 983

CJS Wills §§ 422–89

§ 10-9. Photography and Broadcasting of Proceedings

The procedure in probate court governing photography and broadcasting of proceedings has been made identical to the superior court procedure governed by Rule 78 of the Superior Court. Probate Court Rule 15.

These procedures provide that, except by order of the presiding probate judge, no person shall within the courtroom take any photograph, make any recording, or make any broadcast by radio, television or other means in the course of any proceeding.[24] The superior court has established guidelines concerning the broadcasting by television or radio for court proceedings. The experience in the superior court has shown that broadcasting and televising of court proceedings is becoming a more common practice. On an appropriate occasion, the same trend might also be seen in the probate courts.

§ 10-10. Transcripts of Proceedings

When a sound recording of a probate proceeding is made for the purposes of preserving the record, the cassette audio tapes of those recordings are the sole formal record of the proceedings and duplicate

---

[24] Superior Court Rule 78.

copies of cassette audio tapes cannot be made.[25] However, any individual may obtain a written transcript of the audio tape, at their own expense, by contacting the Register of Probate.[26]

When a party wishes to have a sound recording made of a probate court proceeding, it must be requested in writing two weeks prior to the scheduled hearing date.[27]

Probate Court Procedure Bulletin 14 provides that all hearings held ex parte shall be recorded, unless waived by the Court. Hearings considered ex parte are only those held without notice to the adverse Party or his or her Attorney. In emergency or expedited hearings when the adverse party has been provided with notice, the hearing is not considered an ex parte hearing notwithstanding the adverse party's failure to appear. In these hearings, a recording may be advisable but not required.

§ 10-11. Motion Procedure

Rule 9 of the revised Probate Rules establishes a comprehensive motion procedure which is quite similar to that of the superior courts. However, check the rule carefully, particularly in the area of time deadlines.

All motions and other pleadings must contain both the mail address and the street address of the party filing it. Probate Court Rule 3. Notice to the last mail address on file is deemed to be notice to, and binding on, the party. Probate Court Rule 3.

The probate court is required to hold any motion for ten days before acting on it.[28] A motion that is assented to does not need to be held for ten days.[29]

§ 10-12. Change of Venue and Forum Non Conveniens

Probate Court Rule 21 governs the procedures in the probate court for change of venue and forum non conveniens. This rule provides a

---

[25] Prob. Ct. Admin. Order 94-02 (rescinded effective 8/1/01).

[26] *Id.*

[27] Prob. Ct. Admin. Order 95-01 (rescinded effective 8/1/01).

[28] Prob. Ct. Proc. Bul. 1996-01 (rescinded effective 8/1/01).

[29] *Id.*

broad avenue for a change of venue "upon petition or motion and sufficient proof of inconvenience, change of residence of principal party to the proceeding, or other good cause shown."

It is in the discretion of the transferring court to grant or deny such petition, subject only to the acceptance of the receiving court.

The rule specifies in some detail the procedures required for the proper transfer of bonds, etc., which a change of venue in a complicated matter entail.

Library References

Am Jur 2d Executors and Administrators §§ 103–09

CJS Executors and Administrators §§ 15, 157, 727, 841, 980

CJS Trusts §§ 218, 234, 455

CJS Venue §§ 1 et seq., 5, 27, 37, 39, 130

CJS Wills §§ 355, 1018

§ 10-13. Reopening Decrees

The authority of courts to vacate, modify or amend their judgments for sufficient cause, has been upheld many times in New Hampshire,[30] and this power is possessed by the probate courts, as well as by courts of general jurisdiction.[31] Whether sufficient cause is shown for the action of the court is a question of fact.[32] Thus the probate court may amend, or permit to be amended, according to the facts, its own files and records. However, such an amendment is binding only upon the parties duly notified and their privies.[33]

As a general rule every application for an amendment should show who are the parties having rights which may be affected by it, and due notice of the proceedings should be given them.[34] If the notice is entirely omitted, or is given to a part only of those whose rights may be affected,

---

[30] Raymond v. Goodrich, 80 N.H. 215, 116 A. 38 (1921) *citing* Knight v. Hollings, 73 N.H. 495, 63 A. 38 (1906); Hood v. Montgomery, 73 N.H. 405, 62 A. 651 (1905); Reed v. Prescott, 70 N.H. 88, 46 A. 457 (1900); McDermott v. Hayes, 60 N.H. 9 (1880); Ayer v. Messer, 59 N.H. 279 (1879).

[31] Raymond v. Goodrich, 80 N.H. 215, 116 A. 38 (1921).

[32] Remick v. Butterfield, 31 N.H. 70 (1855).

[33] *Id.*

[34] *Id.*

the amendment will be made at the risk of being held ineffectual, and as if not made, as to those interested who had no notice. [35]

In a probate court case in Cheshire County, *Estate of Marion D. O'Brien*, docket number 32913, the probate court vacated a decree, allowing a will to be proved in common form upon a petition filed after nine years from the original decree where the court found that the will was the product of a mistake by the testator's attorney. The probate court held that "the magnitude of the estate was tantamount to a want of testamentary intent, and that it would be unconscionable to uphold a decree opposing her will." [36]

Library References

Am Jur 2d Executors and Administrators §§ 998, 1128–30
Am Jur 2d Wills §§ 1063–67
CJS Executors and Administrators § 849
CJS Wills §§ 502 et seq., 584

§ 10-14. Declaratory Judgment Petitions

Probate courts have limited jurisdiction over certain declaratory judgment actions: [37]

> **RSA 547:11-b:Declaratory Judgments.** Any person claiming a present legal or equitable right or title to real or personal property in the estate of deceased persons or to guardianship, conservatorship, or trust assets may maintain a petition against the estate, guardian, conservator, or trustee to determine the question as between the parties, and the probate court's judgment or decree thereon shall be conclusive. The existence of an adequate remedy at law or in equity shall not preclude any person from obtaining such declaratory relief.

As indicated by the statute, the touchstone of whether or not the probate court has the power to issue a declaratory judgment is based upon the fact that the property is part of or "listed" as an asset of the estate or guardianship or trust.

---

[35] *Id.*

[36] Order of the court dated September 13, 1985, p. 6, Estate of Marion D. O'Brien, Cheshire County Probate Court, Docket No. 32913.

[37] Pursuant to the provisions of the Omnibus Justice Act, as amended by the Technical Changes Act of 1993, and as amended effective January 1, 1997.

Declaratory judgment actions as authorized by RSA 491:22 are not available in the probate courts as the statute only authorizes their use in the superior court. However, matters related to probate issues are often the subject of declaratory judgment actions in the superior court.

For example, a petition for declaratory judgment in the superior court has been allowed to beneficiaries of a trust created by will asking for advice as to the validity of the trust, as to their right and title in and to the trust and for an order requiring the trustee to distribute the fund. [39] Similarly, such petitions have been allowed to determine the rights of an assignee for the benefit of creditors in certain bank accounts which were in name of assignor's decedent, [40] and as to a daughter's interest in the residue of her father's estate. [41]

On the other hand, petitions for declaratory judgment have not been allowed to determine the liability on a probate bond for losses arising or caused by the acts of an executor, [42] or on a petition to declare inheritance, [43] as the parties had a plain adequate remedy at law. [44] In *Judge of Probate v. National Surety Corp.*, [45] it was held that a petition for declaratory judgment could not be maintained to determine whether a surety is liable upon a probate bond in the event of a fiduciary breach. In a petition for construction of a will where an executrix was not entitled to advice, and neither was the widow, in her capacity as non-fiduciary beneficiary, and no adverse claim appeared to have been made, it was held that it was not a proper case for amendment into a petition for a declaratory judgment. [46]

RSA 547:11-d protects the right to jury trial by providing that any person who wishes to assert such right in any "cases where a right to jury trial is guaranteed by the constitution or granted by statute," may appeal within fifteen days to the superior court. The superior court is directed to expedite the request for jury trial. The theory of the statute

[39] Grant v. Nelson, 100 N.H. 220, 122 A.2d 925 (1956).
[40] Grant v. Nelson, 100 N.H. 220, 122 A.2d 925 (1956).
[41] Bedell v. Colby, 94 N.H. 384, 54 A.2d 161 (1947).
[42] Judge of Probate v. National Surety Corp., 94 N.H. 177, 49 A.2d 635 (1946).
[43] Young v. Bridges, 86 N.H. 135, 165 A. 272 (1933).
[44] Judge of Probate v. National Surety Corp., 94 N.H. 177, 49 A.2d 635 (1946); Young v. Bridges, 86 N.H. 135, 165 A. 272 (1933) (RSA 565:6 and RSA 547:3 respectively).
[45] Judge of Probate v. National Surety Corp., 94 N.H. 177, 49 A.2d 635 (1946).
[46] Wallace v. Brown, 89 N.H. 561, 3 A.2d 95 (1938).

is that the right to jury trial is preserved, but only after an initial hearing in the probate court. Thus, when a party asserts a right to jury trial, as for example where the title to real estate is involved, which is protected by the constitution, the person must first try the case in the probate court, and then is permitted to appeal for a trial de novo in the superior court.

Forms

See Form 007 in Forms Appendix for an Appearance and Withdrawal Form.

§ 10-15. Stenographers

Stenographers are not provided as a general rule in the probate courts. Some probate courts have electronic recording devices, and some do not. Although a judge is authorized by statute to employ a stenographer to make a stenographic record of any contested proceeding (RSA 547:31), probate judges seldom exercise this power. It is therefore incumbent for parties wishing a stenographic record in a probate court proceeding, contested or otherwise, to provide their own stenographer at their own expense.

In uncontested cases, even in courts where electronic recording devices are available, such devices are rarely used in the usual accounting procedures before the court.

If a judge does appoint a stenographer to record a contested case, the stenographer is allowed the same compensation as a stenographer in the superior court who is not on salary. In addition, the stenographer shall be reimbursed for actual expenses when away from home. RSA 547:32. The probate court has the power in its discretion to charge such stenographic expense to the parties involved or may apportion such stenographic expense among the state and the parties involved "if, in the judgment of the court, the financial circumstances of the parties warrant such a change [sic] or apportionment." RSA 547:32.

§ 10-16. Motion for Summary Judgment

The probate court is given the power to grant summary judgments in RSA 547:11-f:

> In any proceeding in the probate court, summary judgment may be granted in accordance with procedures established by supreme court rule.

§ 10-17. Exceptions

Under Superior Court Rule 77-A, formal exceptions to non-evidentiary rulings or orders of the court are unnecessary and it is sufficient that a party, at or before the time of the ruling or order of the court is made or sought, makes known to the court by a pleading or orally on the record the action which he desires the court to take or his objection to the action requested by a party opponent, provided that the party informs the court of the specific factual or legal basis for his position. This rule applies in the probate court by virtue of Probate Court Rule 14 which provides that procedure during trial shall be governed by the same rules as apply in the superior court.

CHAPTER 11. JURY TRIALS

§ 11-1. History

The common law did not provide for jury trials in probate matters and the New Hampshire Constitution does not guarantee a right to a jury trial in probate matters. As the New Hampshire Supreme Court made clear in a 1985 case, *Petition of Atkins*,[1] the right of an individual to request a jury trial in a probate matter is purely statutory and may be granted and limited as the legislature sees fit:

> Since there is no constitutional right to a jury trial [in probate appeals], the legislature may grant the right to trial by jury to the same extent as such right exists at common law; or it may grant it with restrictions, either as to the nature and extent of the right, or as to the circumstances under which it may be had, or it may make the verdict purely advisory, or it may not grant the right at all.[2]

At one time, New Hampshire law provided for advisory juries in probate matters, but this is no longer the case.[3]

Library References

Am Jur 2d Executors and Administrators § 1240

Am Jur 2d Wills §§ 743, 1026

CJS Executors and Administrators §§ 85, 163, 453, 568, 679, 787, 891

CJS Wills §§ 430, 431

---

[1] Petition of Atkins, 126 N.H. 577, 493 A.2d 1203 (1985).

[2] Petition of Atkins, 126 N.H. 577, 579, 493 A.2d 1203, 1204 (1985) (quoting James v. Staples, 87 N.H. 49, 54, 174 A. 59, 67 (1934)).

[3] Former RSA 567-A:10 and former 567-A:11 (repealed 1993).

§ 11-2.　Right to Jury

There is no provision or right to a jury trial in the probate court and the courts are not equipped for jury trial procedure. However, since 1993, the probate court has had jurisdiction to hear cases that previously had been heard in the superior courts, such as petitions to quiet title (RSA 547:11-c), declaratory judgment petitions (RSA 547:11-b), and petitions to partition (RSA 547-C). As a result, there will be many instances where a party will be forced to proceed in probate court even though the party has a constitutional right under the New Hampshire Constitution to a jury trial on the issue. For example, there is a constitutional right to a jury trial where the title to real estate is involved or because it is a case traditionally heard before a jury.[4] In order to protect the right to trial by jury, RSA 547:11-d provides for a right to appeal to the superior court for a trial de novo after a hearing in the probate court:

> **547:11-d Appeals.** In cases where a right to a jury trial is guaranteed by the constitution or granted by statute, a person may, at the time judgment by the probate court is declared, appeal therefrom to the superior court. The appeal shall be entered 15 days from the date of the register's issuance of the notice of decision unless for good cause shown the time is extended by the superior court. If such an appeal is taken, the superior court shall expedite such requests and schedule the case for trial in as timely a manner as possible. In all cases which are so appealed, it shall be the duty of the superior court to transmit to the judge of the probate court, within 10 days after the case is finally disposed of, a certificate showing the final disposition of the case.

> **547:11-e Failure to Prosecute Appeal.** If the appellant fails to enter an appeal within the time limited and prosecute such appeal, a record thereof shall be made, and, within 10 days, the clerk of court shall transmit a certificate of such forfeiture to the probate court from which the matter was appealed.

Forms

See Form 77 in Forms Appendix for a Petition/Motion.

---

[4] N.H. Const. art. 20.

CHAPTER 12. TRANSFER OF QUESTIONS OF LAW TO THE SUPREME COURT

§ 12-1. Generally; History

There are three ways by which questions of law arising in the probate court are heard by the Supreme Court for determination. The first is by the transfer of legal issues to the Supreme Court for determination pursuant to RSA 547:30. The second is by appeal of a party to the Supreme Court pursuant to RSA 567-A:1 after a decision of the probate court.[1] The third method is by way of an interlocutory appeal pursuant to RSA 567-A:1 during a proceeding in the probate court.[2] This chapter will deal with the first method; the second and third methods are discussed in Chapter 13.

In proceedings before the probate court, the determination of a question of law frequently becomes a matter of controlling importance.[3] In 1946 the Judicial Council asked the legislature to empower a probate judge to certify questions of law directly to the Supreme Court.[4] RSA 547:30, subsequently enacted, provided that:

> In any case, matter or proceeding in a court of probate, the court at any time may certify to the Supreme Court any

---

[1] See Chapter 13 for a discussion of Appeals.

[2] *Id.*

[3] 1st Report Judicial Council, p. 19 (1946).

[4] *Id.*

> questions or propositions of law concerning which instructions
> are desired for the proper decision of any matter before it and
> thereupon the Supreme Court may give binding instructions on
> the questions and propositions certified.

When the statute was enacted, an appeal from any probate matter to the
superior court also existed and the statute was designed to "expedite the
litigation at a savings of expense to the parties" where no facts were
in dispute, but only questions of law.[5] With the abolition of the appeal
route to the superior court in 1976, the need for RSA 547:30 has
decreased. However, this method of transfer is still frequently utilized
to gain answers to questions of first impression. For example, where the
executor of a will and the probate court are in justifiable doubt as to
the proper construction of a clause in a will and it is impossible to make
a legal distribution of the proceeds of the probate estate or to file an
account, the question may be certified to the Supreme Court for resolution. *In re Estate of Peterson.*[6]

Originally, the drafters of the statute envisioned that the situations for
transfer of questions to the Supreme Court would be "comparatively few"
and would be used only in
"exceptional situations."[7] This was the view of the Court in an early
case, *In re Estate of Gay,*[8] where a divided Supreme Court dismissed
petitions for instructions transferred pursuant to the statute for the reason
that the:

> authority of the probate court under [RSA 547:30], is limited
> to the certification of questions of law upon which the court
> desires instructions for the proper decision of matters duly
> before it in proceedings coming within its statutory jurisdiction.

> Since the administrator may choose to file petitions for advice
> and instructions in the Superior Court and ask the same ques-
> tions that were certified in the present proceedings, it should
> be noted that the power of that court to advise *is limited to
> questions arising out of the administration of property held in*

---

[5] *Id.*

[6] In re Estate of Peterson, 104 N.H. 508, 190 A.2d 418 (1963).

[7] *Id.*

[8] In re Estate of Gay, 97 N.H. 102, 81 A.2d 841 (1951).

a fiduciary capacity. It does not include advising a legatee or devisee concerning his private rights and duties, although such beneficiary may also be a fiduciary. The purpose of the remedy is the protection of fiduciaries. (Emphasis added.)[9]

This view was quickly reversed in *In re Estate of Byrne*,[10] where a broad interpretation was given to the statute, allowing for the transfer of questions to the Supreme Court under RSA 547:30 on matters "duly before" the probate court. Matters being duly before the probate court include:

> not only when a final account or a petition for a decree of distribution has been filed but also when it appears that a proper decision by that court will presently be required in regard thereto which cannot be made without instructions from this court.[11]

A broad and sweeping view of this statutory process is found in *In re Estate of Morey*,[12] where the Court had before it questions transferred under RSA 547:30 from the probate court which were "not model forms of unimpeachable clarity." The Supreme Court took jurisdiction, holding that where

> the parties concerned are before the court and the facts agreed to, though meager, appear sufficient to determine the questions of law transferred under RSA 547:30. Accordingly we do not propose to inquire further into the question of jurisdiction but deem it expedient to treat the probate court here as a convenient conduit for the certified questions of law.[13]

Insofar as questions certified for transfer seek instructions as to the numerous matters which may arise in "the settlement and final distribution of estates of deceased persons" (RSA 547:3),[14] which is an essential and integral part of the probate court's statutory jurisdiction,[15] or are

---

[9] In re Estate of Gay, 97 N.H. 102, 105, 81 A.2d 841, 843 (1951).

[10] In re Estate of Byrne, 98 N.H. 300, 100 A.2d 157 (1953).

[11] In re Estate of Byrne, 98 N.H. 300, 302, 100 A.2d 157, 159 (1953).

[12] In re Estate of Morey, 113 N.H. 84, 301 A.2d 333 (1973).

[13] In re Estate of Morey, 113 N.H. 84, 85, 301 A.2d 333, 334 (1973).

[14] In re Estate of Byrne, 98 N.H. 300, 100 A.2d 157 (1953).

[15] In re Estate of Harrington, 97 N.H. 184, 84 A.2d 173 (1951).

concerned with such specific matters as the distribution of personal estate bequeathed by a testator (RSA 561:7),[16] they are certifiable as they involve matters within the statutory jurisdiction of probate courts.[17] For example, where both an executor and the probate court are in doubt as to the incidence of state inheritance taxes on legacies and devises in a will, and it is impossible to make an accurate distribution of the estate, partial or final, until the will has been construed, the probate court has jurisdiction to certify the question to the Supreme Court. *In re Estate of Grondin.*[18]

It is for the probate judge to determine whether or not to certify questions to the Supreme Court. Parties have no right to demand that issues be so certified, although if a probate judge refuses, a discretionary interlocutory appeal pursuant to RSA 547-A:1 may be possible. However, it is not unusual for an administrator, or one or both of the parties, to urge the certification of questions by the probate judge.

Library References

CJS Courts §§ 502–21
CJS Wills § 437

§ 12-2. Nature of Remedy

Although an administrator or executor may be given advice concerning the construction of a will prior to a filing of a final account and a petition for a decree of distribution, the Supreme Court in *Duncan v. Bigelow*[19] has held that RSA 547:30 provides an alternative remedy which in certain cases may be more expeditious for ascertaining requested instructions.

In seeking construction of a will under RSA 547:30, a will construction question is properly certified if the executor and court are in justifiable doubt,[20] and such doubt makes it impossible to make a legal distribution of the proceeds of the probate estate or to file an account.[21] Generally, if the lawful distribution of the proceeds of the probate estate necessarily

---

[16] In re Estate of Byrne, 98 N.H. 300, 100 A.2d 157 (1953).

[17] *Id.*

[18] In re Estate of Grondin, 98 N.H. 313, 100 A.2d 160 (1953).

[19] Duncan v. Bigelow, 96 N.H. 216, 72 A.2d 497 (1950).

[20] In re Estate of Peterson, 104 N.H. 508, 190 A.2d 418 (1963).

[21] In re Estate of Peterson, 104 N.H. 508, 190 A.2d 418 (1963); In re Estate of Harrington, 97 N.H. 184, 84 A.2d 173 (1951).

depends on the construction of a will, trust instrument or deed, then questions may be certified to the Supreme Court.[22] In brief, the statute provides an alternative method which in some cases is more expeditious and inexpensive than an application to the superior court for an interpretation of the will followed by transfer to the Supreme Court. *In re Estate of Peterson*.[23] However, if a question sought to be certified under the statute would involve advice or instructions to a fiduciary, the Supreme Court will not answer it, as such a question must be addressed to the superior court within whose jurisdiction it falls. *In re Estate of Simard*.[24]

Library References

CJS Appeal and Error §§ 389–90
CJS Wills § 437

§ 12-3.   Particular Matters

The probate court may certify, among other questions, inquiries concerning the proper decision to be made in the distribution of personal estate bequeathed,[25] assets of an estate,[26] the incidence of legacy and succession taxes,[27] questions concerning trustees,[28] questions arising out of a petition for appointment of a trustee,[29] questions concerning reopening of accounts,[30] testamentary gifts in trust,[31] termination and distribution of a testamentary trust,[32] instructions to trustees as to the proper distribution of income under a will,[33] and construction and proper

---

[22] In re Estate of Allaire, 103 N.H. 318, 171 A.2d 191 (1961).

[23] In re Estate of Peterson, 104 N.H. 508, 190 A.2d 418 (1963).

[24] In re Estate of Simard, 98 N.H. 454, 102 A.2d 508 (1953).

[25] In re Estate of Harrington, 97 N.H. 184, 84 A.2d 173 (1951).

[26] In re Estate of Massey, 105 N.H. 181, 196 A.2d 46 (1963).

[27] In re Estate of Burtman, 95 N.H. 383, 63 A.2d 798, *cert. denied*, 338 U.S. 820, 94 L. Ed. 497, 70 S. Ct. 64 (1949). See In re Estate of Crozier, 105 N.H. 440, 201 A.2d 895 (1964); In re Estate of Whitelaw, 104 N.H. 307, 185 A.2d 65 (1962); In re Estate of Barnhart, 102 N.H. 519, 162 A.2d 169 (1960); Bradley v. State, 100 N.H. 232, 123 A.2d 148 (1956); In re Estate of Grondin, 98 N.H. 313, 100 A.2d 160 (1953).

[28] In re Estate of York, 95 N.H. 435, 65 A.2d 282 (1949).

[29] In re Estate of Gile, 95 N.H. 270, 61 A.2d 798 (1948).

[30] Rogers v. Munsey, 103 N.H. 37, 164 A.2d 554 (1960).

[31] In re Estate of Simard, 98 N.H. 454, 102 A.2d 508 (1954).

[32] In re Estate of Bassett, 104 N.H. 504, 190 A.2d 415 (1963).

[33] In re Estate of Merrill, 106 N.H. 99, 205 A.2d 851 (1964).

distribution of income of residuary trust.[34] The court may also certify questions concerning the validity of a will,[35] the interpretation of wills,[36] determination of the meaning of a residuary clause in a will,[37] duties of coexecutrices,[38] the construction of a will, trust instrument[39] or where the lawful distribution of the proceeds of the probate estate necessarily depends on the proper construction of a deed,[40] distribution of the remainder of an estate,[41] determination of legal heirs of decedent,[42] and questions relating to the distribution of the residue of an estate.[43]

Library References

Am Jur 2d Wills § 847

CJS Wills § 437

§ 12-4. Uncertifiable Questions

Not all questions may be certified to the Supreme Court by the probate court. Thus, in *In re Estate of Bliss*,[44] the Supreme Court refused to decide certified questions where the resolution of the questions would not affect distribution of the decedent's estate and resolution was not necessary to aid the executor in the performance of his fiduciary duties or to resolve matters in contention.

The probate court is not the proper tribunal to finally determine the validity of the title of third persons claiming to hold property by deed or gift from an intestate. The rights of the administrator, as against such

[34] In re Estate of Morrison, 106 N.H. 388, 211 A.2d 904 (1965).

[35] In re Estate of Amor, 99 N.H. 417, 112 A.2d 665 (1955).

[36] In re Estate of Rose, 95 N.H. 208, 60 A.2d 116 (1948). See In re Estate of Peterson, 104 N.H. 508, 190 A.2d 418 (1963); In re Estate of Lathrop, 100 N.H. 393, 128 A.2d 199 (1956); In re Mooney Estate, 97 N.H. 187, 84 A.2d 175 (1951); Amoskeag Trust Co. v. Haskell, 96 N.H. 89, 70 A.2d 210 (1950).

[37] In re Estate of Wood, 102 N.H. 59, 149 A.2d 865 (1959).

[38] In re Estate of Lawrence, 104 N.H. 457, 189 A.2d 491 (1963).

[39] In re Estate of Allaire, 103 N.H. 318, 171 A.2d 191 (1961). See In re Estate of Peterson, 104 N.H. 508, 190 A.2d 418 (1963).

[40] In re Estate of Allaire, 103 N.H. 318, 171 A.2d 191 (1961). See In re Estate of Peterson, 104 N.H. 508, 190 A.2d 418 (1963).

[41] In re Estate of Farwell, 106 N.H. 61, 204 A.2d 239 (1964).

[42] In re Estate of Bunker, 106 N.H. 391, 211 A.2d 902 (1965).

[43] In re Estate of Mooney, 97 N.H. 187, 84 A.2d 175 (1951).

[44] In re Estate of Bliss, 117 N.H. 914, 379 A.2d 839 (1977).

third persons, can only be determined in a court of common law or equity, and such a question cannot be certified by the probate court to the Supreme Court. *In re Estate of Bunker.*[45]

Library References

Am Jur 2d Wills §§ 847, 860

CJS Wills § 437

§ 12-5. Procedures

Probate Court Rule 16 and Supreme Court Rule 9 provide the framework for carrying out a transfer under RSA 547:30.

Such a transfer may be requested by a party but the approval of the probate court must be obtained and evidenced by the signature of the probate court in the interlocutory transfer statement pursuant to Supreme Court Rule 9 and Probate Court Rule 16. The probate judge has discretion to deny a request to transfer.

Under the terms of Rule 9 the interlocutory transfer statement is of substantially the same form as an interlocutory appeal statement under Rule 8. It must contain a statement of the transferred question, a statement of facts necessary for an understanding of the question, a statement of reasons why a substantial basis for a difference of opinion on the question exists and why the interlocutory transfer would either advance the termination of the litigation, clarify further proceedings, protect a party from substantial and irreparable injury or clarify an issue of importance in the administration of justice. As is the case with Rule 8, the Supreme Court has the discretion to decline to accept an interlocutory transfer without ruling under the terms of Rule 9.

The moving party has ten days from the date that the probate court supplies written notice to the parties that it has signed the interlocutory transfer statement to file the original and fifteen copies of the interlocutory transfer statement with the clerk of the Supreme Court, together with the appropriate filing fee, pursuant to Rule 9. This statement must contain copies of the pertinent text of all constitutions, statutes, rules, contracts and other documents involved in the case. However, Rule 9 states that where such copies exceed five pages in length, the movant will include them as a separate appendix and need only file eight copies.

---

[45] In re Estate of Bunker, 110 N.H. 285, 266 A.2d 114 (1970).

The Supreme Court recognized its power to accept interlocutory transfers from the probate court without ruling prior to the 1983 amendment to RSA 567-A:1. In *In re Penny N.*,[46] the Court for the first time allowed an interlocutory appeal and accepted the transfer of a question of law from the probate court concerning the probate court's jurisdiction over the sterilization of a minor incompetent. There is no doubt as to the Supreme Court's power to accept such transfers from the probate court.

§ 12-6. Fiduciary's Brief

Although an executor has no right under RSA 547:30 to seek any particular construction of a will, he may submit a brief in the Supreme Court citing cases on both sides of the question presented.[47] If this is done, the Court will not disregard it, but rather it will be treated as a brief of amicus curiae whose function is merely to make useful suggestions to the Court.[48] On questions certified to the Court, a fiduciary is encouraged to submit a brief as amicus curiae, *In re Estate of Allaire*,[49] and has "the privilege of making useful suggestions to the court."[50] The Court "is not averse to wisdom in any form, from any source, and does not hesitate to accept the benefit of briefs by amicus curiae in the proper construction of deeds or wills."[51] Where the proceeding is adversary, though, and there are contesting parties who will present the issues on both sides, the executor often will not file a brief in the Supreme Court.

---

[46] In re Penny N., 120 N.H. 269, 414 A.2d 541 (1980).

[47] In re Estate of Grondin, 98 N.H. 313, 100 A.2d 160 (1953).

[48] *Id.*

[49] In re Estate of Allaire, 103 N.H. 318, 171 A.2d 191 (1961).

[50] In re Estate of Allaire, 103 N.H. 318, 320, 171 A.2d 191, 192 (1961).

[51] *Id.*

CHAPTER 13. APPEALS

§ 13-1. Probate Appeals Generally

This chapter will discuss two of the three methods by which issues arising in the probate courts can be reviewed in the Supreme Court. These are (1) appeals from a final order of a probate court and (2) interlocutory appeals from interlocutory orders of a probate court during a trial. The third method, transfer of questions to Supreme Court pursuant to RSA 547:30, is discussed in Chapter 12.

The statutory method for appeals from a decision of the probate court was completely revised in 1975 by the enactment of Chapter 567-A of the New Hampshire Revised Statutes Annotated (effective January 1, 1976) and by the 1983 repeal of certain pertinent sections of Chapter 567-A. A party is no longer entitled to a trial de novo in the superior court, but must present his entire case in the probate court. The present statutory framework provides for appeals directly to the Supreme Court on questions of law and for a petition to the superior court for a jury trial on certified issues of fact.[1] An erroneous probate decree can only be corrected by appeal.[2] Assuming proper jurisdiction, a judgment of the probate court is conclusive to the same extent as a judgment of a court of common law.[3]

---

[1] RSA 567-A:1; RSA 567-A:10.

[2] Simmons v. Goodell, 63 N.H. 458, 2 A. 897 (1885); Judge of Probate v. Lane, 51 N.H. 342 (1871); Kimball v. Fisk, 39 N.H. 110 (1859); Bryant v. Allen, 6 N.H. 116 (1833); Judge of Probate v. Robins, 5 N.H. 246 (1830).

[3] Morgan v. Dodge, 44 N.H. 255 (1862).

It is clear that "[t]he right to trial by jury in probate appeals is statutory rather than constitutional." *Sylvain v. Henderson.* [4]

Prior to these revisions, the superior court was the probate court of appeal. [5] It was common to have a second full trial, de novo, in the superior court. [6] The decision of the superior court could then be appealed to the Supreme Court. [7] The Supreme Court sat as "the Supreme Court of Probate." [8]

Library References

CJS Appeal and Error §§ 39, 41, 337, 1817, 1835

CJS Wills §§ 514 et seq.

§ 13-2. Review of Prior Law

Chapter 567-A governs all appeals from decisions of the probate court brought on or after January 1, 1976. [9] Most of what follows in this section is of only historical significance since the enactment of Chapter 567-A of the New Hampshire Revised Statutes Annotated has dramatically changed the process of appeals from decisions of the probate court. However, because several of the cases decided under the old appeals statute are of some relevance to the present procedure, it is helpful to briefly review that process.

Prior to 1976, the applicable statute, former RSA 567:1, provided that "Any person aggrieved by a decree, order, appointment, grant or denial of a judge, which may conclude his interest and which is not strictly interlocutory, may appeal therefrom to the superior court." Former RSA 567:2 stated that all such appeals had to be brought within thirty days from the time of the decision, in a writing signed by the appellant or his attorney, and stating the appellant's interest and the reason for the

---

[4] Sylvain v. Henderson, 116 N.H. 10, 11, 354 A.2d 135, 136 (1976); Gauthier v. Gosselin, 94 N.H. 496, 56 A.2d 13 (1947).

[5] Fellows v. Normandin, 96 N.H. 260, 74 A.2d 548 (1950); Applin v. Knowlton, 85 N.H. 320, 158 A. 131 (1932).

[6] Fellows v. Normandin, 96 N.H. 260, 74 A.2d 548 (1950).

[7] Patten v. Cilley, 67 N.H. 520, 42 A. 47 (1894).

[8] *Id.*

[9] Chesley v. Estate of Chesley, 117 N.H. 280, 372 A.2d 281 (1977).

appeal.[10] The timeliness of the appeal was determined by the date of the filing of the appeal.[11]

Where an appeal was not filed within thirty days, the former statutes provided some redress if the appellant failed to make a timely filing due to accident, mistake or misfortune, and not from his own neglect.[12] The aggrieved party could petition the superior court within two years of the expiration of the time allowed for taking his appeal under the statute, setting forth his interest, the reasons for his appeal and the causes of his delay.[13] To prevail on the petition for late appeal, the appellant had to show that he was prevented from taking a timely appeal through accident, mistake or misfortune, that he did not unreasonably neglect the appeal, and that injustice has been done to him by the decision of the judge of probate.[14] The question of what constitutes accident, mistake or misfortune was left to the discretion of the superior court.[15] Cases dealing with this issue generally found unreasonable neglect where counsel took needless chances, and a known course of prudent action was available.[16] Injustice could be established by a showing that there were important questions at issue which the petitioner, in good faith, desired and intended to try and that there was some evidence which could be offered to sustain the reasons for appeal.[17]

The statement of reasons for appeal had to specify the legal reasons why the decision of the probate court was erroneous in order to avoid unfair surprise on the appellee. The appellant was restricted to the

---

[10] A 1959 amendment to RSA 567:2 shortened the allowable time for appeal from 60 days to 30 days. See N.H. Session Laws ch. 114 (1959).

[11] Larochelle v. Birch, 98 N.H. 190, 96 A.2d 572 (1953).

[12] Former RSA 567:7.

[13] Former RSA 567:7; Holt v. Smart, 46 N.H. 9 (1865).

[14] Beaudin v. Couture, 98 N.H. 272, 98 A.2d 148 (1953); Buffum v. Sparhawk, 20 N.H. 81 (1849).

[15] Sullivan v. Indian Head Nat'l Bank, 99 N.H. 262, 109 A.2d 572 (1954); Beaudin v. Couture, 98 N.H. 272, 98 A.2d 148 (1953); Broderick v. Smith, 92 N.H. 33, 23 A.2d 74 (1942). See Mercer v. Merchant's National Bank, 108 N.H. 199, 230 A.2d 745 (1967); Naum v. Naum, 101 N.H. 367, 143 A.2d 424 (1958).

[16] Mercer v. Merchant's National Bank, 108 N.H. 199, 230 A.2d 745 (1967); Naum v. Naum, 101 N.H. 367, 143 A.2d 424 (1958); Sullivan v. Indian Head National Bank, 99 N.H. 262, 109 A.2d 572 (1954); Broderick v. Smith, 92 N.H. 33, 23 A.2d 74 (1942); Parker's Appeal, 15 N.H. 24 (1844).

[17] Holton v. Olcott, 58 N.H. 598 (1879); Parker's Appeal, 15 N.H. 24 (1844).

specified issues and waived all questions not stated in the appeal,[18] but could amend the statement of reasons if a reason was insufficiently or defectively stated, and if the nature of the claim was unchanged.[19] The appellee, on the other hand, could raise any issue on appeal, and any errors which he pointed out could be corrected by the superior court.[20]

Persons filing appeals prior to August 21, 1983, were required to post a bond as a prerequisite to prosecuting the appeal,[21] and to pay all costs awarded against them by the superior court. The purpose of this bonding requirement was to furnish indemnity for costs taxed against the party appealing in the event that his appeal was not successful.[22]

The law prior to 1976 also placed the burden of notice on the appellant.[23] Notice of the appeal, of the return date and of the court appealed to, had to be given immediately by publication or by such personal notice as the judge of probate would order.[24] Such notice was generally required to be given personally to all parties whose rights might have been affected on appeal.[25] The order of notice was contingent upon compliance with the appeal and bond provisions discussed above,[26] and failure to comply with the notice requirement could lead to the dismissal of the appeal where there was no valid reason for the failure of notice.[27]

Appeals to the superior court could embrace either errors of fact or errors of law.[28] The review of the issues properly raised in the superior

---

[18] Mercer v. Merchant's National Bank, 108 N.H. 199, 230 A.2d 745 (1967).

[19] Rowell v. Connor, 57 N.H. 323 (1876).

[20] Patten v. Cilley, 67 N.H. 520, 42 A. 47 (1894); Simmons v. Goodell, 63 N.H. 458, 2 A. 897 (1885).

[21] Parker's Appeal, 15 N.H. 24 (1844). See Larochelle v. Birch, 98 N.H. 190, 96 A.2d 572 (1953); RSA 567:3; RSA 567-A:3. See also 7th Report N.H. Judicial Council, p. 8 (1958).

[22] Naum v. Naum, 101 N.H. 367, 143 A.2d 424 (1958); Dane v. Dane, 67 N.H. 552, 39 A. 433 (1894).

[23] Parker's Appeal, 15 N.H. 24 (1844). See Arnold v. Hay, 95 N.H. 499, 66 A.2d 705 (1949).

[24] Former RSA 567:4.

[25] Hook v. Simes, 98 N.H. 280, 98 A.2d 165 (1953); Tilton v. Tilton, 35 N.H. 430 (1857).

[26] Broderick v. Smith, 92 N.H. 33, 23 A.2d 774 (1942).

[27] Arnold v. Hay, 95 N.H. 499, 66 A.2d 705 (1949); Clough v. Sanders, 53 N.H. 618 (1873); Clark v. Courser, 29 N.H. 170 (1854); Parker's Appeal, 15 N.H. 24 (1844).

[28] Lane v. Hill, 68 N.H. 398, 44 A. 597 (1896).

court was de novo, although the superior court had no power to change the form of the proceedings or to join new parties of record.[29] The statutes also provided that particular questions of material fact could be submitted to a jury upon the direction of the court,[30] although the jury's verdict was advisory and could be modified or set aside by the court if not a satisfactory basis for a decree.[31] Under the pre-1976 framework, the dismissal of a probate appeal by the superior court worked to reinstate the order of the probate court but did not affirm any findings or rulings supporting the order.[32] An appeal to the superior court did not vacate the probate court's decree; however, the decree of the probate court remained in force until reversed in the appellate court. Appeals from decisions of the superior court to the Supreme Court were limited in scope to matters specified in the appeal or to matters properly excepted to in the superior court.[33]

Costs assessed under the law existing prior to the 1983 repeal of RSA 567-A:9 were awarded to the prevailing party. Where the decision of the probate court was affirmed in part and reversed in part, the awarding of costs was left to the discretion of the superior court. Where neither party was entirely in the right, the court would generally leave each party to pay its own costs.[34]

§ 13-3. Appeals to the Supreme Court

The procedure for appealing decisions of the probate court underwent a sweeping revision in 1976 when RSA 567-A went into effect. The procedure was further altered by various amendments and the repeal of certain provisions of Chapter 567-A in 1983.

The most dramatic change occurred in the 1975 legislation, which mandated that appeals from decisions of the probate court be made directly to the Supreme Court pursuant to RSA 567-A:1. It was held in

---

[29] Fellows v. Normandin, 96 N.H. 260, 74 A.2d 548 (1950); Applin v. Knowlton, 85 N.H. 320, 158 A. 131 (1932).

[30] Former RSA 567:11; Lane v. Hill, 68 N.H. 398, 44 A. 597 (1896).

[31] RSA 491:16; Gauthier v. Gosselin, 94 N.H. 496, 56 A.2d 13 (1947).

[32] Brown v. Jewell, 86 N.H. 190, 165 A.2d 713 (1933).

[33] Fellows v. Normandin, 96 N.H. 260, 74 A.2d 548 (1950); McDonough v. Haskell, 84 N.H. 229, 149 A. 72 (1930).

[34] Griswold v. Chandler, 6 N.H. 61 (1832). See Leavitt v. Wooster, 14 N.H. 550 (1844); Former RSA 567:10.

Chesley v. Estate of Chesley[35] that RSA 567-A:1 required all appeals of decisions of the probate court brought after January 1, 1976 be brought directly to the Supreme Court.

The purpose of enacting RSA 567-A was to streamline the appeals procedure. As was stated by the Judicial Council in recommending the passage of Chapter 567-A:

> [T]here is no sound reason, in our opinion, why the Probate Court should not be empowered to decide and rule on factual issues before it. . . . We are of the opinion that the passage of this legislation would greatly improve the administration of justice in this jurisdiction and would greatly facilitate and expedite the settlement of all matters coming within the scope of the Probate Court jurisdiction. It would relieve the congested case load in the Superior Court.[36]

RSA 567-A sought to place greater fact finding responsibility on the probate court and eliminated the second de novo trial in the superior court upon appeal. This provision was designed to prevent the proverbial "two bites out of the apple" that seasoned trial practitioners attempted to take under the old procedure. While the new appeals chapter did provide for a petition to the superior court for a jury trial on certified questions of fact, it was held in *Gray v. Gray*[37] that "[u]nder RSA 567-A:10, factual disputes are decided by the superior court or the probate court, but not by both." The statutory framework of Chapter 567-A therefore provided for one trial at the probate court level, with the option of certifying certain questions of fact to the superior court, followed by one appeal directly to the Supreme Court if so desired.

Probate Court Rules 42 through 45 provide the probate court procedure for carrying out the provisions of RSA 567-A:10.

§ 13-3(a). Persons Who May Appeal

While much of the appeal procedure has been altered as a result of the 1975 and 1983 changes, these acts did not affect the basic question

---

[35] Chesley v. Estate of Chesley, 117 N.H. 280, 372 A.2d 281 (1977).

[36] The 15th Report of the Judicial Council of the State of New Hampshire, at 21–22 (1974).

[37] Gray v. Gray, 117 N.H. 826, 379 A.2d 442 (1977).

of who may appeal from a decision of the probate court. Although Supreme Court Rule 7(4) states that all parties to the probate court action are deemed to be interested parties on appeal, the language of RSA 567-A:1 regarding appeals to the Supreme Court, states that "A person who is aggrieved by a decree, order, appointment, grant or denial of a judge of probate which may conclude that person's interest in a matter before the court may appeal therefrom to the Supreme Court on questions of law in accordance with the rules of the Supreme Court." The relevant language, that of "a person who is aggrieved," is identical to that of former RSA 567:1, which governed appeals prior to the enactment of RSA 567-A:1. Therefore, an examination of cases under the earlier statute is necessary.

A person named as executor in an instrument which was refused admission to probate is entitled to appeal. The fact that the will contains provisions for the benefit of the widow is sufficient to give her standing under RSA 557:1 as it shows that she could claim an interest under it.[38] But a legatee who is not an heir but the sister-in-law of the testator, cannot appeal from the probate of the testator's will which affirmed her legacy.[39] Where the appellant's rights are independent of the will and are not affected by it, he may not maintain an appeal.[40] Where the complainant was not a beneficiary under a former will,[41] nor one of the testator's heirs but rather was merely an heir presumptive to one of the testator's sons, he is not entitled to appeal because it is "the general rule that during the lifetime of the testator's heir, one who stands in relation of heir to him has no interest as such to contest the will." *Swan v. Bailey.*[42]

The general rule is that an aggrieved person is defined as someone who has a direct pecuniary interest in the estate of the alleged testator which will be impaired if the instrument in question is held to be a valid will. *Green v. Foster.*[43] That is, a contestant of a will must have some direct legal or equitable interest in the decedent's estate, in privity with him, whether as heir, purchaser, or beneficiary under another will, which

---

[38] Merrill v. Putnam, 76 N.H. 390, 83 A. 94 (1912); Richardson v. Martin, 55 N.H. 45 (1874); Shirley v. Healds, 34 N.H. 407 (1857).

[39] Green v. Foster, 104 N.H. 287, 184 A.2d 448 (1962).

[40] McIntire v. McIntire, 64 N.H. 609, 15 A. 218 (1888).

[41] See Morey v. Sohier, 63 N.H. 507, 3 A. 636 (1885).

[42] Swan v. Bailey, 84 N.H. 73, 74, 146 A. 89, 90 (1929).

[43] Green v. Foster, 104 N.H. 287, 184 A.2d 448 (1962).

would be destroyed or injuriously affected by the establishment of a contested will.[44] The interest which a person must possess to enable him to attack the validity of a will is such that if he prevails in the contest he will be entitled to a distributive share in the testator's estate.[45]

But this general definition is neither complete nor comprehensive since there are other parties who may be allowed to appeal providing they have an official or public duty to do so, even though they may not have any direct or pecuniary interest in the estate as such.[46] Thus, in order to appeal under RSA 567-A:1, the person appealing must be aggrieved; that is, he is an heir or creditor, or a legatee under a prior will, or he has an official or public duty in connection with the administration of the estate.[47] If a contestant does not bring himself within this rule he cannot appeal.[48]

An appellant must clearly and distinctly set forth the nature of his interest in the petition claiming the appeal so that the interest may be readily seen and understood.[49] The question of whether the appellant has a sufficient interest to entitle him to an appeal is a question for the court, and if the appellant is not aggrieved by the decree of the probate court, his appeal must be dismissed.[50]

A person is aggrieved when he has some private right which is affected by the decision of the probate court, and this private right may be held in a representative capacity.[51] A person who is so aggrieved may appeal the decision even if he did not appear in the proceedings in the probate court.[52]

The private right which is affected by the decree must be either of a pecuniary nature or must rest upon some personal right in order to

---

[44] Swan v. Bailey, 84 N.H. 73, 146 A. 89 (1929).

[45] Id.

[46] Green v. Foster, 104 N.H. 287, 184 A.2d 448 (1962).

[47] Id.

[48] Swan v. Bailey, 84 N.H. 73, 146 A. 89 (1929). See Gray v. Gray, 117 N.H. 826, 829, 379 A.2d 442, 445 (1977).

[49] Shirley v. Healds, 34 N.H. 407 (1857). See Hughes v. Smith, 59 N.H. 311 (1879).

[50] Morey v. Sohier, 63 N.H. 507, 3 A. 636 (1885). See Swan v. Bailey, 84 N.H. 73, 146 A. 89 (1929).

[51] Hutchins v. Brown, 77 N.H. 105, 88 A. 706 (1913).

[52] Sawyer v. Copp, 6 N.H. 42 (1832).

entitle the party to an appeal.[53] For example, in *Durivage v. Vincent*,[54] the parties, who had stood in loco parentis for several years, had acquired the necessary personal rights to entitle them to appeal from a dismissal of a petition for custody of an illegitimate child. Some parties who do not have a direct or pecuniary interest in an estate may also be entitled to an appeal where they have an official or public duty to do so.[55] A person is generally not aggrieved for purposes of an appeal from the allowance of a will, unless he has some interest which would be concluded by the allowance of the will, such as that of an heir, creditor or legatee under a prior will.[56]

As a person may have a right to appeal by virtue of his representative capacity for another person or entity which holds the right directly, so may a creditor of one who has a direct interest. Thus, in *Protective Check Writer Co. v. Collins*,[57] the plaintiff was able to appeal from a decision of the probate court limiting the administrators' chargeability, in trustee process, where the principal debtor was an heir of the estate.

Persons having certain interests in land under the jurisdiction of the probate court may also have a sufficient interest to appeal from a decree of the court.[58]

Library References

Am Jur 2d Appeal and Error §§ 194, 206, 210–12

CJS Wills § 550

§ 13-3(b). Appeals from Final Decisions

The present appeals procedure from probate court decisions is contained in Chapter 567-A of the New Hampshire Revised Statutes Annotated, in the Rules of Practice and Procedure in the Probate Courts of the State of New Hampshire and in the Supreme Court Rules for the State of New Hampshire. There has been little case law interpreting these statutes and rules since their adoption in 1975 and amendment in 1983.

---

[53] Hutchins v. Brown, 77 N.H. 105, 88 A. 706 (1913).

[54] Durivage v. Vincent, 102 N.H. 481, 161 A.2d 175 (1960).

[55] Green v. Foster, 104 N.H. 287, 184 A.2d 448 (1962); Welch v. Adams, 63 N.H. 344, 1 A. 1 (1885); Richardson v. Martin, 55 N.H. 45 (1874).

[56] Green v. Foster, 104 N.H. 287, 184 A.2d 448 (1962).

[57] Protective Check Writer Co. v. Collins, 92 N.H. 27, 23 A.2d 770 (1942).

[58] Bryant v. Allen, 6 N.H. 116 (1833). See Tilton v. Tilton, 41 N.H. 479 (1860); Leavitt v. Wooster, 14 N.H. 550 (1844).

RSA 567-A:1 states that appeals from the probate court are to be directed to the Supreme Court "in accordance with the rules of the Supreme Court." Much of the procedure for an appeal from a probate decision is therefore the same as an appeal from any lower court decision. It is necessary to reference the Supreme Court rules.

Under Supreme Court Rule 7(1), the Court may decline to accept an appeal from a probate court after a decision on the merits or may summarily dispose of such an appeal.

Supreme Court Rule 7(1) states that appeals from a decision on the merits by the probate court must be submitted on a notice of appeal, which is substantially in the form approved by the Supreme Court, within thirty days of the written notice of decision. Under Supreme Court Rule 7(2) an appeal is considered to be filed when the original and fifteen copies of the notice of appeal are received by the Clerk of Court in proper form and with the appropriate filing fee. The thirty-day period may be extended by filing a motion to enlarge the time under Supreme Court Rule 27(2), but such motions are treated with disfavor. If the appeal is not brought in a timely manner or fails to meet the requirements of the Rules, the matter is not properly before the court and it shall be dismissed pursuant to Supreme Court Rule 5(4).

Although both the probate court rules and the Supreme Court rules are unclear on the matter, the Supreme Court has interpreted the thirty-day appeal period in a probate appeal[59] as beginning after a decision on a motion for reconsideration is filed. A motion for reconsideration in the superior court must be filed within ten days of the decision[60] and under the interpretation of the rules by the Supreme Court, a party aggrieved by the decision on the motion for reconsideration will have thirty days from the date of the decision on the motion for reconsideration to file an appeal with the Supreme Court.

All parties to the decision of the probate court are deemed to be parties before the Supreme Court upon appeal under Supreme Court Rule 7(4). However, under Supreme Court Rule 7(4) the appellant may notify the Clerk of Court of his belief that a party to the probate court's decision has no interest in the outcome of the appeal, in which case the Clerk will notify such persons and these persons may remain party to the appeal

---

[59] Probate Court Rule 43.

[60] Superior Court Rule 73.

by notifying the Clerk that they do have an interest in the appeal. Any appellee may file a notice of cross-appeal within ten days of the filing of the original notice of appeal.

In addition to the fifteen copies of the notice of appeal which are filed with the Clerk of the Supreme Court under Supreme Court Rule 5(1), the appellant must send a copy of such notice to each of the other parties by registered or certified mail, or to their attorneys of record by regular mail simultaneously with the filing of such notice pursuant to Probate Court Rule 35. Supreme Court Rule 5(1) also provides that the appellant must provide two copies of the notice of appeal to the probate court at this time.

Once the notice of appeal has been filed it will be reviewed by the Supreme Court in order to determine if the appeal has merit. The Court may decline to accept the appeal under Rule 7(1) or if the Court determines that the appeal has no merit, it may summarily affirm the probate court's decision in accordance with Supreme Court Rule 25. If the Court determines that the appeal does have merit, the clerk of the Supreme Court will schedule a prehearing evaluation conference or set forth a scheduling order, as provided for in Supreme Court Rule 12-B. The conference or order will then determine whether a transcript of the lower court proceedings is necessary, and what the briefing schedule and anticipated month of hearing will be.

If a transcript is necessary, the Clerk will direct the appellant to pay to the Court an amount to defray the cost of reproducing the record of the probate court and, upon receipt of this amount, will direct the probate court to reproduce the record of its proceedings and forward the same to the Supreme Court pursuant to Supreme Court Rule 15. Rule 15 states that the failure of the appellant to pay this cost operates as a waiver of the appeal. This rule also states a preference by the Supreme Court that the parties attempt to enter into stipulations which would reduce the size of the transcript or eliminate the need for the transcript, and if such a stipulation can be arrived at, fifteen copies of the stipulation must be filed with the Clerk of the Court.

RSA 567-A:1 states that the aggrieved party may appeal "questions of law" to the Supreme Court. Under RSA 567-A:14 the Supreme Court's review of the determinations of fact of the probate court will only be to determine if they are plainly erroneous as a matter of law.[61]

---

[61] In the Matter of Doe, 118 N.H. 226, 385 A.2d 221 (1978).

As in other proceedings, it is the responsibility of the parties to make the record in the probate court. Any party to the probate proceeding may request that the judge issue findings of fact and rulings of law and may propose the same pursuant to RSA 567-A:4. Under Supreme Court Rule 6(5) any requested findings of fact and rulings of law must be set forth in the notice of appeal with an indication as to each finding or ruling whether it was granted, denied or not ruled upon.

Once an appeal to the Supreme Court is pending, the decision of the probate court is stayed under RSA 567-A:7 pending the outcome of the appeal. RSA 567-A:8 empowers the Supreme Court to affirm or reverse the probate court's decision in whole or in part, to remand the cause for further proceedings in the probate court, or to make any other order as is required. If the decision of the probate court is affirmed or unaltered, RSA 567-A:7 states that it will be considered to have been in force from the time it was made.

Failure to follow the rules and procedure in filing an appeal can lead to various monetary sanctions or to dismissal of the appeal. Failure to follow the mechanics of filing the proper number of copies of the appeal, failing to send the proper number of copies to the proper parties or filing papers or briefs which do not conform with the Supreme Court Rules will lead to various assessments under Supreme Court Rule 5(5). Failure to cause timely docketing, to transmit the record of the probate court proceedings or to pay the entry fee can lead to dismissal of the appeal under Supreme Court Rule 5(4). In such a case the party's only relief will be if the failure to act was due to accident, mistake or misfortune. Neglect of the party is not a valid excuse, since RSA 567-A:5 and 567-A:6 (allowing for late appeals) were repealed in 1983. Motions to enlarge or extend the time prescribed by the Supreme Court Rules are not favored. Rule 27(2).

§ 13-4. Interlocutory Appeals

Although the pre-1983 laws did not allow appeals which were "strictly interlocutory," the amendment to RSA 567-A:1 which took effect August 21, 1983, deleted the "strictly interlocutory" prohibition. The fact that an appeal is interlocutory is no longer a consideration in determining the propriety of an appeal.

RSA 567-A:1 still requires a "decree, order, appointment, grant or denial of a judge of probate which may conclude [a party's] interest," however. Therefore, an interlocutory appeal to the Supreme Court from the probate court must be from a ruling, pursuant to Supreme Court Rule 8, and cannot be a transfer without a ruling, as is allowed in appeals from other courts under Supreme Court Rule 9. Rule 8(1) makes clear that the Supreme Court may decline to accept an interlocutory appeal.

The interlocutory appeal statement is of a different form than a notice of appeal from a decision on the merits. The interlocutory appeal statement must contain a statement of the question on appeal, and a statement of the facts necessary to an understanding of the question. Supreme Court Rule 8(1) also provides that it must contain a statement of reasons why a substantial basis for differences of opinion on the question exists and how the appeal will either advance the termination or clarify further proceedings of the litigation, protect a party from substantial and irreparable injury, or clarify an issue of importance in the administration of justice.

Under Rule 8(1) the interlocutory appeal must be approved by the probate court prior to its transfer and the appeal statement must be signed by the probate court. Therefore, the consent of the probate judge is a prerequisite to an interlocutory appeal. The Supreme Court may accept the interlocutory appeal or may refuse the appeal, but Supreme Court Rule 8(4) states that the refusal of an appeal will be without prejudice to the party's right to challenge the ruling of the probate court in a subsequent appeal pursuant to Supreme Court Rule 7.

Under Supreme Court Rule 8(3), an interlocutory appeal from a ruling of the probate court must be taken within ten days from the date of the probate court's written notice to the parties that it has signed the interlocutory appeal statement. As with other appeals to the Supreme Court, an original and fifteen copies of the appeal statement must be filed with the clerk of the Supreme Court along with the appropriate filing fee. The moving party must simultaneously file two copies of the appeal statement with the probate court and deliver a copy either to each party by registered or certified mail or to a party's attorney of record by regular mail.[62]

The scope of review in an interlocutory appeal is the same as that for an appeal from a judgment on the merits. RSA 567-A:4 will limit the inquiry to errors of law unless the factual findings of the probate court

---

[62] Sup. Ct. Rs. 8(3) and 5(1); Prob. Ct. R. 35.

are plainly erroneous. As with an appeal from a decision on the merits, an interlocutory appeal stays all proceedings pursuant to RSA 567-A:7 pending the determination of the appeal. The Supreme Court has the discretion under RSA 567-A:8 to reverse, affirm, remand, modify or make any other order as law and justice require. Since an interlocutory appeal is discretionary with both the probate court and the Supreme Court, the failure to comply with the rules and procedure in making such an appeal will probably lead to the dismissal of the appeal rather than an inquiry into whether the failure to comply was due to accident, mistake or misfortune.

Library References

CJS Appeal and Error § 146

PART III

ADMINISTRATION OF ESTATES

CHAPTER 14. PROBATE COURT PROCEDURE IN A NUTSHELL

§ 14-1. Introduction

This chapter provides a brief description of the customary procedures followed by the probate courts in the administration of estates that will aid the reader in understanding the more detailed treatment that follows. This synopsis is only intended to give the reader an overview of this area of the law and should not be considered comprehensive.

§ 14-2. Purpose

The purposes of probate procedures in New Hampshire as they apply to the settlement of estates has been concisely stated as:

1. the protection and payment of creditors.

2. the protection and proper distribution to legatees or heirs.

3. the payment and distribution within as short a time after death of the testator or intestate as such protection will permit.[1]

---

[1] Hardwick, *Administration of Small Estates*, 1 N.H.B.J. 40 (1958).

§ 14-3. Generally

Usually, the probate court proceedings in the administration of a noncontroversial estate are informal and simple. They are con ducted casually, either in open court at a regular session, at the bench, or in the judge's chambers, in special session. These proceedings are without a record and usually without sworn witnesses, thus differing greatly from more formal superior court procedures.

§ 14-4. Appointment of Fiduciary and Proof of Will

The first formal step in the administration of a decedent's estate begins by petition to the probate court for the appointment of a fiduciary. If the decedent dies with a will (testate), the fiduciary who is named in the will if he is competent must first probate or prove the will. Proof of the will accompanies the request for appointment as executor. If the decedent dies without a will (intestate), the petition for appointment of a fiduciary as administrator is made by an interested party.

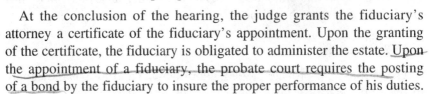

The hearing before the probate court is without notice to affected parties and is informal. The named fiduciary is customarily not present at the hearing. The hearing is conducted by the fiduciary's attorney, who presents the petition and will, if any, to the probate judge for his approval. If the will is self-proving under RSA 551:2-a, no witness to the will is necessary. If the will is not self-proving, one of the subscribing witnesses must be present. The witness will be put under oath by the judge who will ask him several simple questions concerning the will.[2]

At the conclusion of the hearing, the judge grants the fiduciary's attorney a certificate of the fiduciary's appointment. Upon the granting of the certificate, the fiduciary is obligated to administer the estate. Upon the appointment of a fiduciary, the probate court requires the posting of a bond by the fiduciary to insure the proper performance of his duties.

Library References

Am Jur 2d Executors and Administrators §§ 157–270

Am Jur 2d Wills § 822 et seq.

CJS Executors and Administrators §§ 22–94

---

[2] (1) "Is this your signature?"

(2) "Is this the signature of the testator?"

(3) "Did the testator sign in your presence and in the presence of the other witnesses?"

CJS Wills § 307 et seq.

§ 14-5. Post-Appointment Procedure

The probate of the will, the appointment of the fiduciary, and the posting of the bond are customarily accomplished by an informal hearing before the probate judge. However, where the will is self proving, a hearing to prove the will may not be necessary. Once the will is proved, the matter then comes under the general supervision of the probate court. The register of probate arranges for notice of the fiduciary's appointment by publication in newspapers of general circulation, which is designed to give heirs, creditors and interested parties notice of the commencement of proceedings.

From this point on, the settlement of the estate is normally accomplished by the fiduciary without his, or his attorney's, attendance at further hearings before the probate court until the presentation of the final account before the court. If settlement of the estate is not completed within a year of appointment, the presentation for allowance of annual accounts is required. Of course, in contested estates and in many other situations, hearings may be required on various steps taken by the fiduciary. Furthermore, although attendance at a hearing may not be required, permission of the Probate Court is required for many contemplated actions by the fiduciary; e.g., a request to sell real estate, a request to sell personal property, a compromise of claims.

Library References

Am Jur 2d Executors and Administrators §§ 94–99, 256–61, 367 et seq., 960 et seq.

CJS Executors and Administrators §§ 13–21, 69–71, 141 et seq., 827 et seq.

§ 14-6. Collection of the Estate and Filing of the Inventory

Following his appointment and publication by the register of probate, the fiduciary gives notice by mail of his appointment to interested parties,[3] and begins the administrative phase of his duties. His first task is to undertake to inventory a list of all of the assets of the estate and return the inventory to the probate court within three months from the date of his appointment.[4] The inventory assumes great importance

---

[3] RSA 553:16; RSA 552:15.

[4] RSA 554:1.

because it is the basis for subsequent accountings by the fiduciary. The valuations contained in the inventory also have inheritance and estate tax consequences. It must be filed within three months of appointment.

It is the task of the fiduciary, often with the aid of an attorney, to ascertain the assets of the estate and determine the debts and expenses of the decedent. Over the period of administration, the fiduciary usually converts certain assets to cash (e.g., by sale of securities or sale of unwanted personal property) and pays those debts and expenses which are valid obligations of the estate. Distribution of assets to heirs and legatees may also be made from time to time when appropriate.

Library References

Am Jur 2d Executors and Administrators §§ 407–08, 516–21, 1012 et seq.

CJS Executors and Administrators §§ 129–40, 153–83, 482 et seq.

§ 14-7. First and Final Accounting

Usually within a year but no sooner than six months after appointment, the fiduciary arrives at a position in which all of the debts and expenses of the estate are either paid or provided for and the assets of the estate have been sifted down to those assets which are to be distributed to heirs and legatees (e.g., cash, securities, personal property, etc.). The fiduciary, through his attorney, then files with the probate court an accounting, setting forth in itemized form the details of what he has done. The accounting is based upon the inventory of the estate and shows the debts paid, distributions made to heirs and legatees, estate expenses, including legal fees, and the proposed final distribution of any assets still remaining in the estate. Notice of the filing of the account is given by newspaper publication and by notice mailed to heirs and legatees.

The probate court will then hold a hearing, at which time the final account, if proper, will be allowed. If the account is allowed or approved, the fiduciary then undertakes to make final distribution in accordance with the provisions of the final account. The probate court has exclusive jurisdiction over the settlement and final distribution of the estate and may exercise its supervision over attorney's fees, executor's commission, or other similar matters.

In complicated estates, there may be several accounts (labeled first, second, third, etc.) filed over a period of years before the last and final account closing the estate is filed.

Upon allowance of the final account and distribution in accordance therewith, the fiduciary is discharged from further responsibility and his bond is cancelled.

Library References

Am Jur 2d Executors and Administrators § 960 et seq.

CJS Executors and Administrators § 827 et seq.

Appendix

See Appendix for a listing of the time deadlines applicable to estate administration.

CHAPTER 15. ATTORNEY FOR ESTATE

§ 15-1. Generally

The only statutory provision relating to employing or compensating estate attorneys is the probate court's supervisory jurisdiction in RSA 547:3. The choice of an attorney for an estate lies with the administrator. Although it is common for an executor named in a will and appointed after the death of the testator to choose the draftsman of the will as the attorney for the estate, he need not do so. The executor need not choose the decedent's attorney but may select anyone he wishes to represent himself in his capacity as administrator of an estate.

The testator may choose to name his attorney as administrator and it is not improper for the lawyer drafting the will to include a provision in the will naming himself as administrator.[1] Once appointed administrator, the attorney may appoint himself or his law firm as attorney for himself as executor.[2] However, the attorney must not engage in activities constituting a conflict of interest when holding these dual positions. If

[1] New Hampshire Bar Association Ethics Committee, Formal Opinion 1987-819 (1988).
[2] In re Estate of McCool, 131 N.H. 340, 553 A.2d 761 (1988).

he does so, he will be barred from collecting both attorney's and executor's fees.[3]

An administrator does not need to employ counsel to assist him and, until recent times, it was not unusual for administrators to act without an attorney. If the administrator does employ counsel, he does it subject to the control of the probate court:

If an administrator finds it necessary to employ counsel in the probate court, he must be understood to do it, subject to the control and supervision of the tribunal whose duty it is to determine in the first instance what are the just expenses of administration, with, of course, a right to appeal from the decision. *Johnson v. Tuttle.*[4]

It is not necessary to obtain the prior approval of the probate court to employ an attorney. Nor is an administrator prohibited from choosing a partner or associate or someone closely related to him as his attorney.

The employment of an attorney creates an expense for the fiduciary. Thus, the compensation of an attorney is subject to probate court approval. Probate Court Rule 36 provides that the "fees and expenses of fiduciaries shall be subject to the approval of the Court." In *In re Estate of Bergeron*,[5] the Supreme Court articulated the general rule that the "determination of reasonable compensation for the attorney was a matter resting within the sound discretion of the probate court."

In addition, for all estates, every executor and administrator must file a Statement Concerning Fees combined with the Inventory of Fiduciary (Form AOC 44) with the Register of Probate when the inventory is filed.

Library References

Am Jur 2d Executors and Administrators § 438 et seq.

CJS Executors and Administrators § 146

Necessity that executor or administrator be represented by counsel in presenting matters in probate court. 19 ALR3d 1104.

Forms

See Forms Appendix, Form AOC 44 Statement Concerning Fees included in Inventory of Fiduciary.

---

[3] *Id.*

[4] Johnson v. Tuttle, 33 N.H. 104, 118–19 (1856).

[5] In re Estate of Bergeron, 117 N.H. 963, 967, 380 A.2d 678, 681 (1977).

§ 15-2.   Uniform Probate Code Provision

The Uniform Probate Code specifically empowers a personal representative to "employ persons, including attorneys, auditors, investment
advisors, or agents, even if they are associated with the personal
representative in the performance of his administrative duties." U.P.C.
§ 3-715(21).

Library References

Am Jur 2d Executors and Administrators § 443

§ 15-3.   Will Clauses

Occasionally, in New Hampshire, the decedent testator directs by will
that his nominated fiduciary employ a particular attorney as the fiduciary's attorney; i.e., as attorney for the estate. Often such a will provision
contains an explanation that the designated attorney is particularly suited
for the task because of his intimate knowledge of the testator's financial
and family affairs.

Since, in most instances, the nominated executor voluntarily carries
out the decedent's wishes, there have been no New Hampshire Supreme
Court decisions on the question of the enforceability of such a provision.
The majority rule in the United States is that even where the testator
uses such words as *direct, command* or *appoint* in a will provision
directing the employment of specified attorneys for the executors of the
testator's estate, the provision is not deemed to be testamentary in
character and the executor is not bound to employ the attorney named
by the testator.[6] The theory behind the majority rule is that such a
provision is merely advisory,[7] or that it is the inherent right of the
fiduciary to select his own attorney to protect and advise him in the
management of the estate.[8] The majority rule has been stated as follows:

---

[6] Annotation, *Right of attorney whose selection is directed or suggested by will, against
Estate or Personal Representative*, 166 ALR 491; 31 Am Jur 2d, Executors &
Administrators § 168; Comment, *Testamentary Directives to Employ*, 41 HARV, L. REV.
709 (1928); 1 BOWE-PARKER: PAGE ON WILLS § 5.5 (1960).

[7] In re Ogier, 10 Cal. 381, 35 P. 900, 901–02 (1894); Pickett's Will, 49 Ore. 127,
89 P. 377, 380 (1907).

[8] In re Ogier, 10 Cal. 381, 35 P. 900, 901–02 (1894); Matter of Coldwell, 188 N.Y.
115, 80 N.E. 663, 664 (1907); Young v. Alexander, 84 Tenn. (16 Lea) 108, 110 (1885).

In the United States, a provision in the will selecting a certain person as attorney is generally held not to be binding. This result is generally reached on the theory that the provision is merely advisory, although the language which is used in the will frequently sounds quite mandatory. In some of the cases stress is laid on the fact that the executor is personally liable for the management of the estate; and that he ought not be bound to accept an attorney whom he does not select. It has also been said that there is "no testamentary power to control executors in the choice of . . . attorneys." (Footnotes omitted).[9]

The Louisiana Supreme Court has held that it is the administrator, rather than the testator, who is the client in a probate matter and as such, the administrator is entitled to discharge a lawyer named in the will of the decedent. *Succession of Wallace.*[10]

While the matter has never been decided by the New Hampshire Supreme Court, the issue has been raised and determined in probate court proceedings.[11] A strong argument can be made that in New Hampshire such a provision should be enforced, assuming that the attorney is otherwise suitable. This argument rests upon the unique emphasis that New Hampshire places upon carrying out the intention of the testator:

The law is too well settled in this jurisdiction to require extended citation, that the testator's intent is the sovereign guide in the interpretation of a will and this intent being ascertained, the court must enforce it unless it is illegal or impossible to do so. Amoskeag Trust Co. v. Haskell.[12]

This principle was restated in *Burtman v. Burtman,*[13] where the Court enforced a provision prohibiting will contests, stating that "[p]robably no jurisdiction has stood more steadfastly for giving effect to the intention of the testator rather than to arbitrary rules of law." The unique polestar emphasis placed by the New Hampshire Supreme Court on the intention of the testator is perhaps best summed up as:

---

[9] 1 BOWE-PARKER: PAGE ON WILLS § 5.5 (1960).

[10] Succession of Wallace, 574 So. 2d 348 (La. 1991).

[11] See In re Estate of Anna J. Broadhurst, Cheshire County Probate Court, No. 5812 (1985).

[12] Amoskeag Trust Co. v. Haskell, 96 N.H. 89, 91, 70 A.2d 210, 213 (1950).

[13] Burtman v. Burtman, 97 N.H. 254, 258, 85 A.2d 892, 896 (1952).

In this state the right of an individual to dispose of his property by will to individuals, public and private corporations, charities and public entities, including the State of New Hampshire, is singularly free from restrictions or limitations, constitutional, statutory or judicial. . . .. In the construction of wills, form is not to be exalted over substance, and there is an overriding constructional preference for the maximum validity of the testator's dispositive plan.[14]

On the other hand, the force behind the majority rule, that it is the inherent right of the fiduciary to select his own attorney, has persuaded at least one New Hampshire probate court to hold that a will clause directing the employment of a particular attorney is unenforceable. *In re Estate of Broadhurst.*[15]

A testator who wishes to assure that a particular attorney be employed in settling his estate should name the attorney as executor or co-executor. In this fashion, the attorney, once appointed administrator or co-administrator, can appoint himself or his law firm as attorney for the estate.

Library References

Am Jur 2d Executors and Administrators § 444

Right of attorney whose selection is directed or suggested by will against estate or personal representative. 166 ALR 491.

Construction and operation of will or trust provision appointing advisors to trustee or executor. 56 ALR3d 1249.

§ 15-4. Compensation—Modern Perspective v. Common Law

While at common law an administrator was not allowed compensation,[16] most American states, including New Hampshire, allow an administrator compensation for executing the duties of his office. *Tuttle v. Robinson.*[17] This idea of reasonable compensation for an administrator included the allowance of his reasonable expenses, including reasonable

---

[14] Opinion of the Justices, 109 N.H. 335, 251 A.2d 330 (1969) (citation omitted).

[15] In re Estate of Broadhurst, Cheshire County Probate Court, Estate No. 5812 (1985).

[16] See generally 31 Am Jur 2d § 922 Executors & Administrators.

[17] Tuttle v. Robinson, 33 N.H. 104 (1856). See also HOYT'S PROBATE PRACTICE at 177.

attorney's fees. *Wendell v. French.*[18] An administrator, in his final account, is allowed to charge against his receipts the reasonable legal expenses necessarily incurred by the administrator.

A New Hampshire Bar Association Ethics Committee Formal Opinion[19] discussed the ethical considerations when an attorney serves both as administrator and as attorney for an estate. The opinion found that nothing in the New Hampshire Rules of Professional Conduct prohibited an attorney who is appointed an administrator of an estate from employing himself or his law firm as attorneys for the estate. As the opinion carefully points out, the attorney, at the time of drafting the will, must "explain to the client the various duties of the fiduciary, the fees that can be generated by a fiduciary, and how that prospective attorney-fiduciary intends to charge for legal and non-legal services."[20]

In *In re Estate of Bergeron,*[21] the lay executor hired the estate's attorney to collect an estate debt by an action brought in the superior court. After the successful conclusion of the superior court action and the collection of the proceeds, the executor sought approval in his first account for a contingent legal fee of a percentage of the amount collected. The probate court approved a lower contingent fee than claimed and the matter was brought to the Supreme Court. The Court first made clear that the probate court was the proper jurisdiction to determine the fee claimed, even though the collection matter was brought in the superior court. The Court then went on to consider the reasonableness of the fee claimed. Asserting that the reasonableness of the attorney's fee was "within the sound discretion of the probate court," the Supreme Court upheld the lower fee:

> The determination of reasonable compensation for the attorney was a matter resting within the sound discretion of the probate court. . . .. Among the factors to be considered are the amount involved, the nature, novelty, and difficulty of the litigation, the attorney's standing and the skill employed, the time devoted, the customary fees in the area, the extent to which

---

[18] Wendell v. French, 19 N.H. 205 (1848). See also Tuttle v. Robinson, 33 N.H. 104 (1856); HOYT'S PROBATE PRACTICE at 178.

[19] N.H. Bar Association Ethics Committee, Formal Opinion 1987-819 (1988).

[20] *Id.*

[21] In re Estate of Bergeron, 117 N.H. 963, 380 A.2d 678 (1977).

the attorney prevailed, and the benefit thereby bestowed on his client. . . . Although the risk involved in the case may not have been great, it was nevertheless necessary that [the attorney] devote his time and skills in order to recover for the estate the balance due on the note. The responsibility on the attorney in undertaking the action should also be viewed in light of the fact that the balance due on the note was by far the most substantial asset of the estate. After reviewing the record as well as the probate court's lengthy and thoughtful decision, we are of the opinion that the probate court did not abuse its discretion in ruling that [the attorney] was entitled to a fee of twenty percent of the amount recovered on the note and we affirm the court's decision. [22]

The National Probate Court Standards as adopted by the Commission on National Probate Court Standards [23] establishes the following standard for attorneys' and fiduciaries' compensation:

Standard 3.1.5 Attorneys and Fiduciaries Compensation

(a) Attorneys and fiduciaries should receive reasonable compensation for the services performed.

(b) The probate court should determine the reasonableness of fees when a dispute arises that cannot be settled by the parties directly or by means of alternate dispute resolution. When appropriate, the court should review and determine the reasonableness of attorneys and fiduciaries compensation on its own motion. [24]

The commentary to this provision provides that there are seven factors that should be considered in determining reasonable compensation for both fiduciaries and attorneys:

- the usual and customary fees charged within that community;

---

[22] *Id.*

[23] National Center for State Courts, 300 Newport Avenue, P.O. Box 8798, Williamsburg, Virginia 23187-8798 (1993).

[24] COMMISSION ON NATIONAL PROBATE COURT STANDARDS, NATIONAL PROBATE COURT STANDARDS p. 46.

- responsibilities and risks (including exposure to liability) associated with the services provided;

- the size of the estate or the character of the services required, including the complexity of the matters involved;

- the amount of time required to perform the services provided;

- the skill and expertise required to perform the services;

- the experience, reputation, and ability of the person providing the services; and

- the benefit of the services provided.[25]

Library References

Am Jur 2d Executors and Administrators §§ 473–86

CJS Executors and Administrators §§ 840, 845, 848–49

Personal liability of executor or administrator for fees of attorney employed by him for the benefit of the estate. 13 ALR3d 578.

§ 15-4(a). Procedure For Approval

Since the compensation of attorneys for the estate is an administrator's expense, it is subject to the review and the ultimate approval of the probate court in the same way as the compensation of administrators. Probate Court Rule 36.

Probate judges, in their review of accounts, customarily and almost invariably inquire into the amount of legal fees, and administrators and their attorneys should be prepared to address any questions raised in order to substantiate their claimed legal bills. For all estates, every executor and administrator must file a Statement Concerning Fees (included in Form AOC 44) with the Register of Probate when the inventory is filed.

The usual practice is to prepare an account with the amount of the legal fees claimed entered into the account, to balance the account and present it to the probate court for approval. After approval of the amount as claimed, the account is ready to be allowed. Normally the court will

---

[25] COMMISSION ON NATIONAL PROBATE COURT STANDARDS, NATIONAL PROBATE COURT STANDARDS pp. 46, 47.

immediately allow the account at the hearing, with the result that the legal fees can then be paid following the approval.

The practice as to payment of interim legal fees varies from county to county and the local procedure should be inquired into prior to any payment of legal fees. The most conservative practice is not to pay any legal fees until an accounting is allowed by the judge. However, in large estates, it is not unusual to incur substantial fees in connection with the preparation and filing of the federal estate tax return due nine months from the date of death. Some amount of legal fees can be paid at that point, so long as the amount does not exceed the probate court guidelines. Of course, the fees are subject to later approval by the probate court and if not approved, must be repaid.

A better procedure though, is to petition the probate court for approval of interim legal fees. The problem with this procedure is that it is time-consuming and expensive and to be avoided in all but the most complex situations.

In *In re Estate of Rolfe*,[26] the Supreme Court has indicated that the probate court must hold a hearing upon the issue of the appropriateness of attorneys' and administrators' fees, presumably at the time an account claiming such fees is settled. Under *Rolfe*, it was held to be:

> fundamentally unfair to the heirs and beneficiaries to require them to contest the requested executors' fees in order to obtain court determination of their reasonableness. The court's role is not merely to "rubber stamp" the requested fees, but rather to exercise its discretion in each case to determine what fees are reasonable.

The probate court has promulgated a series of forms to be completed and submitted to the probate court for consideration whenever an account is filed asking for attorneys' or administrator's fees. These forms are found in the Appendix of Forms. Because the use of these forms is relatively new, and the forms have already been revised from the original drafts, it is expected that the probate court will continue to experiment with methods and forms to comply with the *Rolfe* decision.

---

[26] In re Estate of Rolfe, 136 N.H. 294, 615 A.2d 625 (1992). See also McDonald, *The Rolfe Decision: Its Practical Implications for Probate Attorneys, Vol. 3, No. 20, N.H. BAR NEWS 5 (1993). See the Fees Appendix for the Rolfe decision on remand to the Merrimack County Probate Court and the 1981 Probate Court Fee Guidelines.*

Library References

Am Jur 2d Executors and Administrators §§ 473–86

CJS Executors and Administrators §§ 223, 225, 788, 840, 848–49

Forms

See Appendix for Form AOC 44 Statement Concerning Fees included in Inventory of Fiduciary.

§ 15-4(b). Amount of Attorneys' Fees

In 1992, the Supreme Court handed down a case of paramount importance on the issue of administrators' and attorneys' fees, *In re Estate of Rolfe.*[27] *Rolfe* established a completely new basis for the establishment of the fees of attorneys and administrators in the administration of estates. The Court threw out the probate judges' guidelines for the calculation of total fees for the executor and attorney based on the value of the estate because "these guidelines, which we never formally approved, now appear to be the cornerstone of all estate executor and attorney fee evaluations." The Court went on to point out that the use of the fee schedule guidelines tended "to make the maximal fee under the guidelines actually the average fee for settling an estate." In place of the guidelines, the Court, in the case of attorneys' fees, adopted

> [t]he same factors used to determine "reasonable fees" as are ". . . embodied in Rule 1.5(a) of the New Hampshire Code of Professional Responsibility . . .."

> (1) the time and labor required, the novelty and difficulty of the questions involved, and the skill requisite to perform the legal service properly;

> (2) the likelihood, if apparent to the client, that the acceptance of the particular employment will preclude other employment by the lawyer;

> (3) the fee customarily charged in the locality for similar legal service;

> (4) the amount involved and the results obtained;

---

[27] In re Estate of Rolfe, 136 N.H. 294, 615 A.2d 625 (1992).

(5) the time limitations imposed by the client or by the circumstances;

(6) the nature and length of the professional relationship with the client;

(7) the experience, reputation, and ability of the lawyer or lawyers performing the services; and

(8) whether the fee is fixed or contingent.

The Supreme Court made clear that these factors, "along with any other appropriate circumstances, must be considered by the probate court in its determination of the appropriate fee to be awarded the attorney."

The Court admonished attorneys that they "should keep accurate, detailed records to the best of their ability evidencing the work performed and the time expended."

Furthermore, the Court recommended that attorneys and executors enter into a written fee agreement at the commencement of their work:

> The better practice is for executors, attorneys, and those having an interest in estates, at the inception of their relationship, to openly discuss the options and terms for payment of services to be rendered the estate and attempt to reach a fee agreement. Although such an agreement is not binding on the probate court, it is certainly an important factor to be considered when determining the final fee.

It will be some years before the full effect of the *Rolfe* case is determined. Furthermore, Probate Court Administrative Judge John R. Maher of the Rockingham County Probate Court is engaged in an effort to bring some uniformity into the procedure by which various probate courts will hear and determine fees under the *Rolfe* guidelines. One author has predicted that the *Rolfe* case will produce economic loss for attorneys when probate judges are asked to become economists:

> *Rolfe* will create uncertainty for probate attorneys. No amount of record building and logic will completely insulate the attorney from an arbitrary disallowance of fees by an overworked probate judge. Probate judges are not economists. Yet they are being

asked to make the same kinds of pricing decisions that Fortune 500 companies hire microeconomists with MBAs to make. The prevailing "abuse of discretion" standard of appellate review makes a probate judge's factual reasonableness determination virtually irreversible on appeal.[28]

In concluding its decision in *Rolfe*, the Supreme Court remanded the case to the Merrimack County Probate Court for proceedings in accordance with its decision. Upon a further hearing, the probate court for Merrimack County issued an extraordinary decision, which because of its importance is found in the Appendix. Interestingly, the probate court resolved the issue by setting fees for the administrator and his attorney in almost exactly the same amount as had been ordered earlier by the probate court using the probate fee guidelines.

Another interesting aspect of the *Rolfe* case on remand was that the probate court allowed the attorney to collect interest on his legal fees from the date of the probate court's original decree.

The remand decision of the probate court in *Rolfe* was appealed again to the Supreme Court, but the Court declined the appeal.

A formal written fee agreement that conforms with the recommendations of the court in the *Rolfe* case can be found in the Appendix.

§ 15-4(c). Pre-*Rolfe* Decisions and Former Guidelines

The succeeding sections on the issue of compensation should be read in light of the *Rolfe* case in the preceding section. Pre-*Rolfe* cases remain important to the discussion of the reasonableness of the compensation, and provide a useful historical perspective.

In the 1991 *Kelley's Case*,[29] attorneys in a will contest had a contingency fee agreement but were discharged prior to the conclusion of the case. The attorneys were not entitled to be compensated on a contingency basis, but rather, they were "entitled to recover the reasonable value of their services under a claim of quantum meruit."[30] However, the discharged attorneys were not subject to disciplinary

---

[28] McDonald, *The Rolfe Case: Its Practical Implications for Probate Attorneys, Vol. 3, No. 20, N.H. Bar News 5, 7 (1991).*

[29] Kelley's Case, 137 N.H. 314, 319 (1991).

[30] *Id.*

proceedings by the Professional Conduct Committee for violation of Professional Conduct Committee Rule 1.5(a) prohibiting illegal or clearly excessive fees, unless the committee presented evidence establishing a generally accepted, reasonable fee for the services in question.[31]

The New Hampshire courts have allowed an administrator to charge reasonable attorney's fees. *Wendell v. French.*[32]

Attorneys' fees are subject to the supervision of the probate court which may reduce the amount claimed for attorneys' fees. *Tuttle v. Robinson.*[33] Thus, in *Tuttle* the Supreme Court stated: "The remarks already made in relation to compensation for the personal services of the administrator, apply with equal force to that of counsel. If an administrator finds it necessary to employ counsel in the probate court, he must be understood to do it subject to the control and supervision of the tribunal whose duty it is to determine in the first instance what are just expenses of administration, with, of course, a right to appeal from the decision. In the present instance, all the services whose compensation is reduced were rendered before the probate court, and the fair presumption is, that, in the opinion of the judge, some portion of them was not needed, or did not answer any useful purpose to the estate."

Before the *Rolfe*[34] case, there were few Supreme Court decisions on the reasonableness of attorneys' fees. In 1973, at a meeting of the probate judges, a standard maximum fee schedule was established for administrators and attorneys. This schedule was updated in 1981 and is set forth in the Fees Appendix.

The fee guidelines were entitled "Probate Fee Guidelines for Maximum Fees" and were based upon the value of the estate and thus, were in the nature of a commission. Also, it should be noted that attorneys' fees were not established separately from fiduciary fees but "combined fees" of fiduciary and attorney were established.

The guidelines set forth the following maximum fees for the administration of an estate:

MAXIMUM FEES

---

[31] *Id.*

[32] Wendell v. French, 19 N.H. 205 (1858). See also Tuttle v. Robinson, 33 N.H. 104 (1856); HOYT'S PROBATE PRACTICE, at 178.

[33] Tuttle v. Robinson, 33 N.H. 104 (1856). See McInnes v. Goldthwaite, 94 N.H. 331, 52 A.2d 795 (1947).

[34] In re Estate of Rolfe, 136 N.H. 294, 615 A.2d 625 (1992).

Value of Estate	Combined Fees of Fiduciary and Attorney
$0–10,000	Reasonable compensation for work involved
10,000–100,000	Not to exceed 5%
100,000–500,000	4% of excess over $100,000.
500,000–1,000,000	3% of excess over $500,000.
	2% on balance over $1,000,000.[35]

If an attorney or administrator claimed fees in excess of the guidelines, the attorney had the burden of showing that fees were reasonable under the circumstances, and had to furnish an itemized statement of his fees and expenses.[36]

In computing the value of the estate, the value of a decedent's real estate was not included in the computation unless sold by the administrator. If the real estate was sold by the executor, the amount of the proceeds was included in the calculation. The value of non-probate assets, such as jointly-held property, was not included in the computation of the value of the estate in determining fees, presumably because the administrator's duties as to real estate were minimal since title to real property was considered to devolve upon the heirs immediately upon the decedent's death.[37] However, fees in addition to the prescribed maximums were allowed "if the non-probate assets require[d] additional services such as a Federal Estate Tax Return."[38]

Fiduciaries and attorneys were required to justify any fees submitted, either within the maximum fee schedule or in excess of the schedule.[39]

Massachusetts, like New Hampshire, does not specify a fixed rate of compensation for administrators or attorneys. Their Supreme Judicial Court has set forth factors to be considered in determining an attorney's fees in an estate in this oft-quoted language:

In determining what is a fair and reasonable charge to be made by an attorney for his services many considerations are pertinent, including the ability and reputation of the attorney,

---

[35] See Fees Appendix.

[36] Id.

[37] See Chapter 35 infra.

[38] See the Fees Appendix for the 1981 Probate Court Fee Guidelines.

[39] Id.

the demand for his services by others, the amount and importance of the matter involved, the time spent, the prices usually charged for similar services by other attorneys in the same neighborhood, the amount of money or the value of the property affected by controversy and the results secured. Neither the time spent nor any other single factor is to be considered as a fair and reasonable charge for such services. Cummings v. National Shawmut Bank of Boston.[40]

The reasonableness of attorneys' fees will always vary from case to case, since each fee depends upon the particular facts then before the court.

Library References

Am Jur 2d Executors and Administrators §§ 473–86

CJS Executors and Administrators § 788

CJS Wills § 568

Amount of attorneys' compensation in proceedings involving wills and administration of decedents' estates. 58 ALR3d 317.

Forms

See Appendix for Form AOC 44 Statement Concerning Fees included in Inventory of Fiduciary.

§ 15-4(d). Disallowance of Compensation

If the fees for services to the estate for which the attorney seeks to charge were of no value to the estate, they will not be allowed by the probate court. *In re Estate of Ward.*[41] The probate court may refuse any fees to an attorney where he abuses his fiduciary duties and responsibilities or there is no benefit conferred on the client.[42] "One consideration in determining the reasonableness of attorney's fees is the benefit bestowed in the client."[43]

If the attorney has already had fees paid to himself, the probate court may order the attorney to account for the fees, plus interest, by reimbursement to the estate or as a credit against other sums due the attorney.[44]

---

[40] *Id.*

[41] In re Estate of Ward, 284 Mass. 563, 188 N.E. 489, 492 (1934).

[42] In re Estate of Ward, 129 N.H. 4, 523 A.2d 28 (1986).

[43] *Id.*

[44] In re Estate of Ward, 129 N.H. 4, 10, 523 A.2d 28, 33 (1986).

Where legal fees are incurred due to the improper intransigence of the attorney claiming the fees in connection with discovery process, they may be disallowed even though the attorney prevailed on some of the claims in question.[45]

In *In re Estate of McCool*,[46] the Supreme Court addressed the issue of attorney's fees where an attorney for an estate, also acting as executor, engaged in conflicts of interest. The unanimous Court took a very strong position, disallowing the recovery of fees:

> [W]e hold that an attorney who violates our rules of professional conduct by engaging in clear conflicts of interest, of whose existence he either knew or should have known, may receive neither executor's nor legal fees for services he renders an estate. The attorney who acts for parties whose interests conflict may well be unable to provide the disinterested advice and zealous representation that he owes every one of his clients.

The requirement that an attorney shall not represent conflicting interests, at least without full disclosure to the client both of the facts and their significance, is designed to preclude the honest practitioner from putting himself in a position where he may be required to choose between conflicting duties, or be led to an attempt to reconcile conflicting interests rather than to enforce to their full extent the rights of the interest which he should alone represent.[47]

Furthermore, the attorney cannot rely upon disclosure of his conflict to the parties involved who then consent to his continuing to act unless he clearly explains "the nature and possible ramifications of these conflicts."[48] "It is the attorney who bears the burden of fully disclosing relevant facts and making their ramifications clear."[49]

An attorney who is also executor of an estate and who engages in conflicts of interest can never be found to have waived the estate's objection to his own conflict of interest and thus is absolutely barred from compensation in such a situation.[50]

---

[45] *Id.*

[46] In re Estate of McCool, 131 N.H. 340, 553 A.2d 761 (1988).

[47] *Id.*

[48] *Id.*

[49] *Id.*

[50] *Id.*

Library References

Am Jur 2d Executors and Administrators §§ 475–80

Amount of attorneys' compensation in proceedings involving wills and administration of decedents' estates. 58 ALR3d 317.

§ 15-4(e). Amount of Administrator's Fees

Under the *Rolfe* decision, attorneys' fees and administrators' fees must be separately determined by the probate court "because the standards to be applied to executors and attorneys, as well as the work performed by each, differ, the probate court must make separate findings and determine the fees separately."

Under the probate courts' maximum fee guidelines, attorneys' fees and administrators' fees were commonly lumped together by the probate judge and an award of a lump sum was made, which the executor and the administrator divided. Under *Rolfe*, this practice is no longer valid.

The remainder of the text of this section should be regarded as historical background only.

In most states, the administrator is allowed fees by the probate court and is not expected to pay attorneys' fees from this amount.[51] Attorneys' fees are allowed as a separate item. The former New Hampshire rule, at least as established by the probate judges' fee schedule, was that an administrator and his attorney were allowed reasonable fees not to exceed certain maximum fees based upon a percentage of the estate, each party sharing the combined fee, although the fee of each was accounted for separately.

The exact percentage between the administrator and the attorney varied from case to case, and attorney to attorney. For example, in Manchester it was common practice to share the fee between administrators 50-50, where the fiduciary was an active participant in the work of the estate. Where the attorney performed substantially all of the work, a 25-75 split between administrator and attorney was common. However, even if the administrator and attorney jointly shared the duties of administration, where the attorney's fees, at his customary hourly rates, were not covered by a 50-50 split, the practice was to reimburse the attorney at least at his usual hourly rates. Where an attorney was both administrator and attorney, he was customarily allowed the total maximum prescribed by the former schedule.

---

[51] In re Estate of McCool, 131 N.H. 340, 553 A.2d 761 (1988).

It is strongly recommended that fiduciaries maintain a time and expense journal, particularly where an estate is subject to federal estate taxes. Federal estate tax auditors have become increasingly aggressive in this area and often take the position that unless the executor or administrator has kept a detailed time journal, they will disallow any request by the executor or administrator for compensation. Attorneys should strongly recommend to their fiduciary clients that they keep a simple spiral-bound notebook in which are entered, by date and time, all work (including telephone calls, conferences, meetings, etc.) and expenses that they expend in connection with the administration of the estate.

Library References

Am Jur 2d Executors and Administrators §§ 475–80

Amount of attorneys' compensation in proceedings involving wills and administration of decedents' estates. 58 ALR3d 317.

Forms

See Appendix for Form AOC 44 Statement Concerning Fees included in Inventory of Fiduciary.

§ 15-4(f). Uniform Probate Code Provisions

The Uniform Probate Code's approach to this area is based on an underlying theory that personal representatives may fix and agree upon their own fees and those of the estate attorneys.[52] This is an important departure from current practices in many states,[53] but the Code builds in a specific protective section which clearly and specifically provides that the issue of the selection and compensation of attorneys for an estate may be raised by the court or by any interested person:

Section 3-721. Proceedings for Review of Employment of Agents and Compensation of Personal Representatives and Employees of Estate.

After notice to all interested persons or on petition of an interested person or on appropriate motion if administration is supervised, the propriety of employment of any person by a

---

[52] Study of Executor's and Administrator's Fees, AMERICAN COLLEGE OF PROBATE COUNSEL (October, 1984).

[53] Uniform Probate Code § 3-721, Comment.

personal representative including any attorney, auditor, investment advisor or other specialized agent or assistant, the reasonableness of the compensation of any person so employed, or the reasonableness of the compensation determined by the personal representative for his own services, may be reviewed by the Court. Any person who has received excessive compensation from an estate for services rendered may be ordered to make appropriate refunds.

As the Comment to this section indicates, the probate courts' broad jurisdiction would encompass such a power anyway, but the drafters felt it was "wise to emphasize that any interested person can get judicial review of fees if he desires it."[54]

Library References

Am Jur 2d Executors and Administrators § 483–85

§ 15-4(g). Prohibition Against Attorney-Beneficiary Drafting Will

Rule 1.8(c) of the New Hampshire Rules of Professional Conduct prohibits an attorney from preparing an instrument such as a will from which he or she would benefit. This rule was interpreted in *Kalled's Case*[55] to justify disbarment of an attorney who violated the rule, even though his defense was that he was not aware of the rule until it was brought to his attention by the Professional Conduct Committee.

Forms

See Fees Appendix, 1981 Probate Fee Guidelines.

See Forms Appendix, AOC-44 Statement Concerning Fees included in Inventory of Fiduciary.

---

[54] *Id.*

[55] Kalled's Case, 135 N.H. 557, 607 A.2d 613 (1992).

CHAPTER 16. USE OF LEGAL ASSISTANTS IN PROBATE PRACTICE

---

§ 16-1. Introduction

Probate practice is an ideal area of the law for an attorney to effectively utilize the services of legal assistants or paralegals. A fairly large segment of probate practice involves law that has been relatively stable and unchanged over a period of a great many years. Since the unification of Forms and Rules which occurred in the 1950's, little has changed. This stability of law and procedure lends itself to the use of legal assistants. A great amount of the day-to-day work of the probate lawyer can be done by a legal assistant who has a solid basic training, because much of the work is similar or repetitive.

Library References

CJS Executors and Administrators § 146

§ 16-2. Supreme Court Guidelines

The New Hampshire Supreme Court has adopted "Guidelines For the Utilization By Lawyers of the Services of Legal Assistants" as Supreme Court Rule 35. These rules were completely rewritten and readopted in 1987 as a result of a joint bench-bar effort.

Rule 5.3 of the Rules of Professional Conduct makes clear that an attorney employing a legal assistant must use reasonable care "to ensure that [the legal assistant's] conduct is compatible with the professional obligations of the lawyer." An attorney can be held responsible for a failure to meet his responsibilities with regard to the use of legal assistants.[1] A lawyer is responsible for the conduct of the legal assistant that would be a violation of the Rules of Professional Conduct if engaged in by a lawyer if:

(1) the lawyer orders or, with the knowledge of the specific conduct, ratifies the conduct involved; or

(2) the lawyer is a partner in a law firm in which the person is employed, or has direct supervisory authority over the person, and knows of the conduct at a time when it consequences can be avoided or mitigated but fails to take reasonable remedial action.[2]

Particular care should be taken to assure that legal assistants are used properly and in conformity with the Court's guidelines. In particular, legal assistants may not give legal advice to clients or to any persons involved in an estate. Supreme Court Rule 35(1). Furthermore, all work prepared by an assistant must be carefully reviewed by the attorney. It is improper for a legal assistant to represent his employer before the Probate Court in any adversary proceeding. Supreme Court Rule 35(2).

Some probate judges, but not all, allow the proof of a will in common form by a legal assistant without the presence of the lawyer, where the legal assistant was a subscribing witness. Similarly, some probate courts allow the presentation of accounts by a legal assistant, while other courts do not allow this procedure.

A probate legal assistant will often deal directly with the client and the general public. Direct client contact, in and of itself, is not improper. However, the legal assistant must carefully
"disclose at the outset that he or she is not a lawyer." Supreme Court Rule 35(8). The supervisory attorney should inform the client that the legal assistant is not an attorney or, at the least, carefully ascertain that the assistant has made the requisite disclosure. Both the attorney and the assistant should be sure that the client understood the disclosure.

Library References

Am Jur 2d Attorneys §§ 51, 62, 115

---

[1] Sup. Ct. R. 35(9).

[2] N.H. Rules of Prof. Conduct 5.3.

Am Jur 2d Contempt § 32

§ 16-3. Tasks Which May Be Performed by a Legal Assistant

A well-trained and well-informed legal assistant may be utilized to perform the following tasks, under the supervision of the attorney:[3]

1. Obtain the information and complete the "first papers" for probate.

2. Assemble the information necessary to file an inventory and prepare an initial draft of the inventory.

3. Depending upon his knowledge of and relationship with the client, the legal assistant can receive phone calls throughout the period of administration, answer administrative questions, and provide copies of documents requested by the client.

4. Write letters to banks, insurance companies, or post office in connection with gathering necessary information. The attorney needs to decide which letters to sign and which may appropriately be signed by the paralegal or legal assistant.

5. Assemble information for and prepare drafts of all tax returns including the federal estate tax return Form 706 and income tax returns, both federal and state.

6. Obtain information for and write letters to transfer agents where the transfer of securities is involved.

7. Obtain information concerning real estate, including searching the title if necessary.

8. Complete New Hampshire Inheritance Tax computations and prepare statement required by the Division of Inheritance Taxes.

9. Prepare a proposed decree of distribution.

10. Prepare administrator's accounts and related papers, such as notices to heirs, affidavit of notice and receipts from beneficiaries.

---

[3] Sup. Ct. R. 35(3).

Library References

Am Jur 2d Attorneys § 115

§ 16-4. Tasks Which Should Not Be Performed by a Legal Assistant

Even a well-trained legal assistant should not be permitted to perform certain tasks, even if under the supervision of an attorney.[4] For example, a legal assistant should not:

1. Give legal advice of any sort to anyone.

2. Render an opinion as to the effect or scope of the contents of a will or on the legal effect of any document.

3. Attend to the execution of a will without the presence of a lawyer.

4. Answer questions of clients which in any way involve legal interpretations of facts, events or documents.

5. Represent an estate at probate court hearings without the presence of an attorney.

6. Directly address letters to the probate court or judge.

7. Sign documents of any sort intended to be submitted to court.

8. Sign letters on the attorney's letterhead without "an appropriate designation so that there can be no connotation that the person so signing is a lawyer."[5]

9. Conduct any conference or oral communication relating to legal matters without making clear that he or she is not a member of the Bar.[6]

10. Sign writs, motions or pleadings of any kind.[7]

---

[4] Sup. Ct. R. 35(4).

[5] Comment, Sup. Ct. R. 35(8).

[6] *Id.*

[7] Comment, Sup. Ct. R. 35(2).

11. Engage in the unauthorized practice of law.[8]

Library References

Am Jur 2d Attorneys §§ 51, 62, 115

§ 16-5. Relationship to the New Hampshire Bar Association

A multidisciplinary task force was appointed by the New Hampshire Bar Association in 1990 to assess the use of legal assistants by attorneys and their relationship to the Bar Association. That task force issued a report dated June 12, 1991, which contained several recommendations concerning the use of legal assistants by attorneys. The task force recommended that the title "paralegal" be used rather than "legal assistant," thereby adopting the definition previously adopted by the American Bar Association. A paralegal was defined as follows:

> A paralegal is a person, qualified through education, training, or work experience, who is employed or retained by a lawyer, law office, governmental agency, or other entity in a capacity or function which involves the performance, under the ultimate direction and supervision of an attorney, of specifically delegated substantive legal work, which work, for the most part, requires a sufficient knowledge of legal concepts that, absent such paralegal, the attorney would perform the task.

The task force report was approved by the Board of Governors of the Bar Association on June 27, 1991. Subsequently, the members of the Bar Association, on June 27, 1992, voted to allow paralegals to associate themselves with the Bar Association by becoming Associate Members of the New Hampshire Bar Association, and the matter has been sent to the Supreme Court for consideration.

---

[8] *Id.*

CHAPTER 17. ROLE OF ATTORNEY AT INITIATION OF ADMINISTRATION OF ESTATE

§ 17-1. Pre-Death Matters

If the attorney has advance notice of a client's impending death, the attorney should consider whether a need exists for "death-bed estate planning." Typically, such planning might involve the testator's making gifts up to the amount of his unused federal gift tax annual exclusion or purchasing treasury "flower" or "deep discount" bonds if the estate will be large enough to occasion federal estate tax. Attorneys with notice of an impending death may also notify appropriate parties of a client's expressed intentions regarding the disposition of his organs, for examples, eyes to the eye bank, and other organs to an organ bank under the Uniform Anatomical Gifts Act.[1]

Library References

CJS Dead Bodies § 2

Power of parent, guardian or committee to consent to surgical invasion of ward's person to benefit of another. 35 ALR3d 692.

Tort liability of physician or hospital in connection with organ or tissue transplant procedure. 76 ALR3d 890.

Tests of death for organ transplant purposes. 76 ALR3d 913.

[1] RSA 291-A. See also C. DeGrandpre, 7 New Hampshire Practice: Wills, Trusts and Gifts (3d. ed. 1997) Chapter 40.

§ 17-2. Preliminary Matters

When employed to assist with estate administration after a decedent's death, the attorney should immediately advise a responsible family member (or members) about the importance of the following preliminary matters:

1. To immediately protect the decedent's valuables such as cash, jewelry, silver and collections.

2. To provide security for any unoccupied real estate, particularly if it contains valuable personal property such as jewelry, silver and antique furniture.

3. To preserve the decedent's books and records, including income tax files, bank statements and checkbooks.

4. To notify any attorney-in-fact that authority to draw against decedent's funds through any power of attorney has expired.

5. To obtain immediate authorization from the probate court (upon the appointment of an administrator) to continue the operation of any business conducted by decedent, unless the business is carried on in corporate form.

Library References

CJS Attorney and Client § 191
CJS Executors and Administrators §§ 223, 410, 519

§ 17-3. Reading of the Will

It is a common myth that there is a formal procedure after the death of a testator in which the will of the testator is read to the assembled heirs and would-be heirs. This "reading of the will" myth bears little relation to the reality. Although clients often ask when the will is going to be "read," the common procedure is simply to give copies of the will to the interested members of the family. There is no formal procedure for reading the will or disclosing its contents. Usually, the attorney distributes copies of the will at the initial conference between the attorney and the concerned family members.

RSA 552:15 requires that all interested parties to the proceedings receive notice of the formal proceedings. A copy of the will provision in their favor is usually sent to each beneficiary.

§ 17-4. Estate Checklist

Many attorneys use a checklist to help remind them of the various information which they need to start gathering at the initial conference. It is also important to have a checklist to serve as a reminder of the various steps that need to be taken during the administration of an estate, and the time-frame for doing so.

Attorney George Hanna of Keene has prepared an estate checklist which, with minor revisions, is included in the Appendix of this treatise.[2]

Attorney Malcolm McLane of Concord has devised a checklist which has received wide distribution within the State and it is found in 7 N.H.B.J. 296 (1965), as an appendix to his article entitled "New Hampshire Probate Procedure."[3]

All attorneys who do any substantial practice before the probate courts need to develop some type of checklist as an aid to the efficient handling of their estate administration practice. A checklist is particularly valuable for legal assistants who can use it to prepare the necessary forms and returns, and to alert the attorney to filing deadlines.

§ 17-5. Filing Deadlines

There are many important filing deadlines at all stages of the probate process. Attorneys have an ethical obligation to proceed expeditiously in the administration of the estate. The Appendix contains a list of the more important filing deadlines and time standards applicable to a typical New Hampshire estate.

§ 17-6. The Initial Conference

The attorney should set a reasonably prompt date for a conference with interested family members or other residuary beneficiaries to discuss plans to begin the administration of the estate. If the executor is a non-family member or a bank, that person or representative should also attend.

There are three major purposes for the initial conference: (1) reassure the family beneficiaries that the decedent's estate will be handled efficiently and that his wishes will be carried out with sensitivity to the

---

[2] N.H. Bar Association, CLE, Fundamentals of Probate Administration (1983).

[3] 7 N.H.B.J. 294 (1965).

family's needs and interests; (2) obtain all necessary information to complete the forms required to open administration, and (3) introduce the probate process to the family members or estate beneficiaries so that they will understand its purpose and their role in the estate administration.

The following documents and other materials and items need to be assembled and available at or shortly after the preliminary conference:

a. Death certificate

b. Decedent's will and copies of any trusts of which he was grantor, trustee, or beneficiary.

c. Records of the decedent's support obligations under divorce settlements with which estate may be charged; any antenuptial agreements with the surviving spouse.

d. Schedule of names and addresses of the surviving spouse, children (including dates of birth of minors or other beneficiaries if there is a life estate involved), parents or other next-of-kin. Family members should designate one or more of above persons to be the family representative(s) which the attorney will contact, and provide the attorney with appropriate telephone numbers.

e. Life insurance policies on decedent's life and payable to family, estate, or any family trust, or a schedule thereof.

f. Data as to status of decedent's income tax filings for current year.

g. Copies of the deed or deeds to any real estate owned by decedent or of which he was co-tenant, and schedule of approximate values of subject property, as well as information as to mortgages.

h. Status of insurance and of security of any real estate, including any second home.

i. Information on any income owed to the decedent, outstanding salary, pending lawsuits, pensions, debts owed to decedent, etc.; status of last Social Security check.

j. Rough schedule of decedent's other assets and form of ownership thereof (i.e., sole name, joint names, trust, etc.) including any partnership interests and expected employee death benefits; names, addresses and/or telephone numbers of parties to contact for information.

k. Information as to major debts, including any installment obligations. Any repayment obligations for institutional care of decedent under RSA 126-A:47.

l. Information as to major gifts of decedent during his lifetime; copies of any gift tax returns.

m. If decedent's residence is empty, a set of keys.

n. Safe deposit box keys.

At the conference, the attorney should deal with the following topics:

1. Immediate problems of personal concern to dependents, involving their immediate needs for support and maintenance, the protection and security of the decedent's property (including recovery of possessions in custody of others), insurance, alarm systems, authority to operate the decedent's automobile, etc. The attorney should make himself available and respond sympathetically to any questions and concerns which family or beneficiaries may have.

2. If there is a will, the attorney should review it carefully in advance, and should ascertain the circumstances of its execution. At the conference, he should endeavor to give its beneficiaries a general understanding of the estate plan which it expresses, or of which it is a part. It is this aspect of the conference that comes closest to the venerable "reading of the will." If there is no will, he should explain the relevant principles of the law of intestate succession. The attorney should be sure to inquire about and discuss any related trust, life insurance, jointly-held property, or other non-probate property which are important aspects of decedent's estate plan.

3. The conference should also give the beneficiaries an introduction to the probate function. The attorney should not

assume any of the family or beneficiaries are familiar with the decedent's estate plan or its relation to the probate process governing the transfer of all of decedent's property rights and interests.

It is sometimes useful to provide a written explanation of the New Hampshire probate and settlement process. You will find in the Appendix a client information sheet entitled *Explanation of the New Hampshire Estate Settlement Process (For Clients)*. This can be given to clients at the initial conference or forwarded by mail to interested beneficiaries. Consider discussing the following major topics, either at the initial conference or shortly thereafter:

a. The crucial importance of complete and accurate book-keeping, due to the nature of probate accounting as the underlying structure of probate administration.

(1) The role of the estate checkbook or other master record of estate receipts and distributions.

(2) The necessity for bills and receipts.

b. Valuation principles governing the inventory and the future role of estate values as federal income tax cost bases.

c. The relative roles of the fiduciary and the attorney, and selection of the person to serve as fiduciary. Explain that the estate is your ultimate client, not any individual or individuals. This is particularly important if there is any prospect of conflict among the beneficiaries.

d. The relation of the fiduciary to non-probate property and his authority or lack of authority with respect to it.

e. Development of a rough time schedule for the major steps in administration.

f. Identification of tax returns which will need to be filed on behalf of the decedent or by the estate in various jurisdictions. Work out a preliminary plan as to who will be responsible for information gathering and who will prepare the returns.

g. An introduction to major income tax aspects of estate administration and the importance of planning and conducting administration accordingly.

(1) Factors governing the choice of the accounting period and the estate fiscal year.

(2) Importance of timing the distributions from residue.

h. Where relevant, discuss various elections which may be appropriate to consider early in the course of administration. These range from various traditional protective elections reserved to a widow or surviving spouse under New Hampshire law, to disclaimers which may be extremely valuable in the context of modern postmortem estate planning, particularly where there has been skillful drafting of estate documents in anticipation of disclaimers. See RSA 563-B, the Uniform Disclaimer of Property Interests Act, and Probate Court Procedure Bulletin 16.

It is not realistic to believe that all of the foregoing topics can be dealt with effectively in a single conference with a family group which has just lost an important member. The attorney must gauge, with some sensitivity, how much to try to accomplish at the initial meeting and how much must be deferred and dealt with later.

The attorney's task will be far easier if a realistic effort is made at the outset to inform the beneficiaries of the topics noted. As the administration proceeds, it is important for the beneficiaries to recognize that there are valid reasons, sometimes for their own protection, for procedures which otherwise might seem to them to involve wasted motion, needless delay, and red tape.

4. A discussion concerning legal fees for both the personal representative (executor or administrator) and the attorney should be had at this meeting. However, it is sometimes best to not finalize a discussion of legal fees until the full nature and complexity of the estate is determined, which may be several weeks later. In any event, the beneficiaries will want to know at this first meeting something about fees and the attorney should be prepared to discuss the general nature of both executor's fees and attorney's fees.

It is recommended that a written fee agreement be used and the general nature of a written fee agreement, even if not finalized, can be discussed at the initial conference. See the Appendix for a sample fee agreement.

5. At some point during the conference, the attorney should see that the appropriate party or parties execute the necessary probate forms to open administration.

a. For testate administration, the necessary forms are:

Required

Form 220	Petition for Executor, Administrator, Administrators D.B.N. and W.W.A., Special Administrator and Waiver of Administration	RSA 550:1, 553:32
Combined Form 12-22	Fiduciary Bond	RSA 553:13
Form 101	Legacy & Succession Tax Statement of Heirs & Legatees (to be filed in duplicate)	RSA 552: 4-a RSA 86: 18-a

To be filed if appropriate

	Petition for Authority to Continue Business	RSA 553:30; N.H. Prob. Ct. Rules 12; Prob. Ct. Proc. Bul: 1996-11
Form 9	Appointment of Agent (if fiduciary is non-resident)	RSA 553:25
Form 42	Declination (if named executor declines to serve)	RSA 552:3

b. For Intestate Administration:

Required

Form 220	Petition for Administration With Real Estate Report	RSA 550:1
Combined Form AOC-001	Fiduciary Bond Executor's/Administrator's Accounting	RSA 553:13
Form 101-A	Legacy and Succession Tax Statement of Heirs and Legatees *To be filed if appropriate*	RSA 552:5a

	Motion or petition in accordance with superior court practice.	
	Petition for Authority to Continue	RSA:30; N.H. Prob. Ct. Rule 12; Prob. Ct. Proc Bul: 1996-11
Form 9	Appointment of Agent (if Fiduciary is non-resident)	RSA 553:25

c. In addition to the forms required to be filed at the Registry of Probate at the opening of administration, the attorney should also obtain execution of Form SS-4, Application for Employee's Identification Number (to be filed with IRS at its Andover, Massachusetts regional office) and Form 101-B, Report of Gifts, Transfers and Joint Tenancies, to be filed in duplicate, one copy at Registry of Probate and one at Department of Revenue Administration. (RSA 86:22).

(1) Form 101-B is not required at the outset of administration and data for its proper completion may not be immediately available, but when possible, it is wise to complete and file it promptly. It is due six months after the Administrator's appointment.

(2) Form 101-C, a report of assets passing in trust, is filed the same time as Form 101B.

d. Within fifteen days after appointment of the fiduciary, the Register of Probate is required to see to the publication of notice of the appointment, and prior to such publication, the fiduciary must advance to the Register its cost as determined by the Register. RSA 553:16. The attorney may wish to obtain funds to cover this charge from his clients at the time of the opening conference.

§ 17-7. Preliminary Steps To Be Taken by Attorney After Allowance of Petition for Administration

1. Notify client, and review by telephone any matters requiring immediate attention.

2. Obtain completed probate bond in amount required and file it.

3. Issue notices to heirs and legatees immediately and file Return of such notice with Probate Court. Consider including brief letter of explanation or extract from will if appropriate.

4. Schedule further meeting with the fiduciary to lay out work to be done, priorities, and to develop rough time schedule. Discuss fiscal year for fiduciary income tax returns.

5. Discuss with office probate paralegal, add to office estate docket control, etc.

Forms

See Appendix for New Hampshire probate procedure checklist that is a useful device for the efficient handling of estates.

See Appendix for a list of the deadlines involved in the administration of an estate in New Hampshire.

See Appendix for a client information sheet.

See Appendix for a sample fee agreement.

CHAPTER 18. SETTLEMENT OF ESTATES WITHOUT ADMINISTRATION

§ 18-1. Generally

It is now rare for an estate to be settled without an administration. This is probably due in major part to the complexity of modern life: more people own more and different types of assets (e.g., stocks, bonds, certificates of deposit) which require the appointment of an administrator before they can be transferred to the heirs. Formerly, it was a common practice for an estate to be settled by the heirs without the formal appointment of an administrator or the assistance of an attorney:

> [H]eirs frequently settle the estates of their ancestors by themselves, without the intervention of administrators. Stevens v. Meserve.[1]

§ 18-2. Joint Tenancy Between Spouses

In one particular circumstance, however, settlement without administration is still relatively common and, in such cases, an attorney should

---

[1] Stevens v. Meserve, 73 N.H. 293, 61 A. 420 (1905).

assist his client in avoiding an unnecessarily expensive administration if the estate can be settled without administration. This circumstance is where a husband or wife dies, leaving a surviving spouse, and all of the property (except for tangible personal property which can be transferred without any formality) is held in joint tenancy between the spouses. In this situation, even if there is a will, a full administration can be avoided by taking a few easy steps. However, the same procedure usually cannot be followed upon the death of the survivor, unless at that time, (1) only one heir of full age is involved and (2) all property requiring formality of transfer (e.g., real estate, bank accounts, stocks and bonds) is held in joint tenancy between the deceased spouse and the heirs.

§ 18-3. Transfer of Property to Heir

Another frequently encountered situation is when a surviving spouse and his or her children, during the old age of the surviving spouse, asks the attorney to create an arrangement to avoid probate. This is done either by (1) transferring property to one heir as joint tenant with the parent upon the promise of the surviving joint tenant to share the property with other heirs upon the death of the parent, or (2) transferring complete title to the real estate, bank books, stocks, etc. of the parent to an heir in return for the heir's promise to take care of the parent.

Both of these requests, although heart-felt and reasonable, create great risks, and the attorney should avoid them if possible. In the first example, if one heir promises to hold jointly-held real property for the benefit of others, the promise is probably unenforceable against the promisor under the statute of frauds, RSA 506:1. Even if the promise is enforceable against an heir who refuses to share the property, there will be litigation because a surviving joint tenant is considered to succeed to absolute title to the property upon the death of the joint tenant.[2]

In the second example, there is a substantial risk that the person to whom absolute title to property is transferred will not take care of the transferor, and will disagree about the maintenance of the property or its continued use by the transferor, especially where the question of a move to a nursing home arises.

It is generally better in these circumstances to leave assets in the name of the parent even if that will involve administration of his estate upon

---

[2] See RSA 384:28 relating to joint bank accounts and C. DeGrandpre, 7 New Hampshire Practice: Wills, Trusts and Gifts (2d ed. 1992) §§ 19.05, 19.06, 19.07, 19.08.

his death. This is a small cost to pay when compared to the grief of a family fight over inheritance rights as a result of attempting to save administrative costs by pre-death transfers of the nature discussed above.

Library References

Am Jur 2d Executors and Administrators §§ 321–30

CJS Executors and Administrators §§ 5–9

CJS Wills § 310

§ 18-4. Procedure

There are many small and simple estates which can be settled without administration, a procedure which should be encouraged when possible.

Even if there is a will, there is no need to resort to the administration of an estate in every instance where the decedent dies testate. In a situation where the surviving spouse takes all property of the deceased spouse and all difficult-to-transfer property is held in joint tenancy, the estate may be a suitable candidate for settlement without administration.

First of all, the will should be filed in the appropriate probate court, with a request that it be filed without administration. The reason for filing the will where administration is not contemplated is, first of all, the statutory requirement of RSA 552:2 and 552:3 that anyone having custody of a decedent's will shall deliver it to the probate court within thirty days of the testator's death, or within thirty days after the person has knowledge of being named executor of a will, whichever is later. See Probate Court Procedure Bulletin 1999-01 (rescinded effective 8/1/01). Secondly, the filing of the will serves to protect the parties by safeguarding the will if it is later needed. It is not uncommon for an asset to be discovered later which requires administration of the estate. Also, filing of the will allows anyone (e.g., a creditor) who takes issue with the proposed procedure of settling the estate without administration to move to protect his rights.

In the past, filing the will was all that was required in such instances. Now, however, Probate Court Rule 23 provides that where no administration is taken out, the will must be proved and a certified copy of the death certificate filed with the Register of Probate. Probate Court Procedure Bulletin 1999-01 (rescinded) provides the following details on filing. The counties shall not require a filing fee, nor the filing of an appearance. The county does not send a copy of the will to the

Department of Revenue Administration and does not require Forms 101/ 101B. Bulletin 1999-01 (rescinded) provided that neither self-proved nor non self-proving wills can be submitted to the court for signing and/or proving. All counties accept the testator's will from an attorney with only a cover letter. However, if the attorney is named the executor, a certified copy of the death certificate must also be provided to the court. Upon receipt of a will to be filed with no administration, the register staff will first check for any prior filings under the same name. If none are found a file will be opened, then immediately closed. If assets are found later, the file will be reopened at that time. Probate Court Procedure Bulletin 1999-01 (rescinded).

These requirements place a premium on having a self-proved will, since no hearing or subscribing witness attendance will be required. If the will is not self-proving, a hearing and the attendance of a subscribing witness will be required, costing time and expense that a settlement without administration seeks to avoid.

The next step is to record a copy of the death certificate in the registry of deeds of all counties where the decedent died owning jointly-held real estate. This step confirms title of jointly-held real estate in the surviving joint tenant.

Next, a search for all assets of the decedent should be made. The title to all accounts should be changed to the surviving joint tenant. This can be done by presenting the bank book or stock certificate to the appropriate authority for transfer. Possession of the bank book or stock certificate by the surviving joint tenant is usually sufficient to effectuate transfer of title.

Automobiles present a different situation. By the provisions of the Title Certificate Act, RSA 261:17, the transfer of title from one spouse to another is simplified so that a transfer can be made from the name of a deceased spouse to a surviving spouse, even where the title is not in the joint names of the spouse. However, the provision applies to a spouse only. In all other instances, unless the title is held jointly (RSA 261:17, III), an administration is required to transfer good title to a motor vehicle. RSA 261:14.

Wages owed a deceased employee, up to the amount of $500.00, may be paid to the deceased employee's spouse without the necessity of an administration of the employee's estate pursuant to the provisions of RSA 560:20 and 560:21.

If there is no will, and an estate is settled without administration, there is no need to file anything with the register of probate, although it is common for a death certificate to be filed. This is apparently done for the purpose of notifying the public of the decedent's death, although the Register of Probate does not actually advertise or publish the fact of death. Even when a will is filed without an administration, the register of probate does not publish the proving of the will. The only notice to the public in either situation is the notice one gets by inquiry at the registry of probate.

Several probate courts require the named executor of a will to file an affidavit in which he attests under oath "that there are no assets in the above estate upon which said will may operate." There is an official form that has been printed for this use by several courts.

When there is no administration, all debts of the decedent should be paid after all of the assets have been located and title transferred. A failure to pay all creditors leaves open the possibility that the settlement arrangement can be overturned during the two-year period after the decedent's death, by a creditor who brings action pursuant to RSA 556:29, asserting a claim against the heirs. This is due to the fact that the provisions of RSA 556:1, 556:3 and 556:5, establishing statutes of limitation for bringing actions against a decedent's estate, begin running only after a grant of administration of an estate. If there has been no grant of administration, creditors have two years from the date of death to bring actions "to appropriate the real estate or interests therein of which the deceased died seized, to the payment or satisfaction in whole or in part of his claim against the estate." RSA 556:29.

Library References

Am Jur 2d Executors and Administrators § 21

CJS Executors and Administrators §§ 5–9

CJS Wills § 310

§ 18-5. Settlement of Estate by Consent — Judicial Authority

Those in interest may validly settle an estate without the intervention of an administrator so as to bind all who consent to the settlement.[3]

---

[3] Pochitt v. Farley, 86 N.H. 79, 163 A. 399 (1932).

"[W]here the heirs of an estate being of full age and agreeable, undertake to settle the estate between themselves without administration, a court will endeavor to enforce those agreements." *Clarke v. Clay.* [4]

An administrator generally cannot later maintain an action against the consenting heirs. [5] Where one of the heirs is under age the estate cannot be settled without administration, [6] unless the minor heir is represented by a guardian, then such a settlement may be made. [7]

Settlements made between heirs without an administration should be distinguished from situations where an administration is undertaken and a settlement is reached with the administrator. In the latter case, the settlement is subject to the approval of the probate court pursuant to RSA 556:27. Thus, where an "administration is taken, or a guardian appointed over a ward, and a settlement is made with the administrator or guardian, such settlement will not be conclusive upon the parties, but will be evidence for the consideration of the court in deciding whether a further settlement should be ordered or the accounts examined." *Clarke v. Clay.* [8]

Generally, where a testator's estate has been settled, and the property has gone to those who were entitled to it and who would have received it if all the requirements of the law had been complied with, the settlement cannot be disturbed. [9] Thus, where an estate has been properly settled without administration and an attempt is made to defeat that settlement, the party who attacks it must present very strong evidence that positive injustice has been inflicted upon him, [10] as such a settlement should not be disturbed unless the necessity for it is imperative. [11]

If the heir's interests are adjusted and settled, without mistake or fraud, the settlement is binding, and none of the heirs, by procuring administration, can be permitted to defeat it. [12] The question of whether a mistake

---

[4] Clarke v. Clay, 31 N.H. 393, 401 (1855). See also Hibbard v. Kent, 15 N.H. 516 (1844); Kittredge v. Betton, 14 N.H. 401 (1843); Giles v. Churchill, 5 N.H. 337 (1831).

[5] Atherton v. McQuesten, 46 N.H. 205 (1865).

[6] Bean v. Bean, 33 N.H. 279 (1856).

[7] Woodman v. Rowe, 59 N.H. 453 (1879).

[8] Clarke v. Clay, 31 N.H. 393, 401 (1855).

[9] Mercer v. Pike, 58 N.H. 286 (1878). See Langley v. Farmington, 66 N.H. 431, 27 A. 224 (1891).

[10] George v. Johnson, 45 N.H. 456 (1864).

[11] Mercer v. Pike, 58 N.H. 286 (1878).

[12] Woodman v. Rowe, 59 N.H. 453 (1879); Hibbard v. Kent, 15 N.H. 516 (1844).

would avoid the whole settlement, or whether it would merely furnish ground for an equity proceeding to correct the mistake will not be considered where a mistake was not alleged.[13] A party who voluntarily accepts the amount awarded to him, although he did not sign the original submission of a settlement to arbitration, is bound by that act and cannot contest it, unless there is evidence of manifest mistake or fraud.[14]

If fraud exists in such a settlement, the party defrauded may avoid all that has been done, and the administrator will be entitled to administer upon the estate as if no settlement had been made. *Hibbard v. Kent.*[15] In such a case, the proper course would be for the party defrauded first to deliver the property received to the administrator.[16] Of course, an objection to such a settlement on the grounds of mistake or fraud must be brought before the lapse of too great a period of time.[17] If a settlement is made through the use of arbitrators, it can also possibly be attacked on the grounds of their misconduct or undue partiality.[18]

When an estate has been practically, although irregularly, settled, further administration will not be granted when it has not been requested by one having some interest in the estate.[19]

Library References

Am Jur 2d Executors and Administrators § 21

CJS Executors and Administrators §§ 5–9

CJS Wills § 310

§ 18-6. Wages of Deceased Employees

RSA 275:47 provides that wages due a deceased employee, if they do not exceed $300, may be paid to those who will take the decedent's estate under the intestacy laws "upon proper demand" and "in the absence of actual notice of the impendency of probate proceedings" without requiring the administration of an estate. RSA 275:47, I. Any payment

---

[13] Hibbard v. Kent, 15 N.H. 516 (1844).

[14] George v. Johnson, 45 N.H. 456 (1864).

[15] Hibbard v. Kent, 15 N.H. 516 (1844).

[16] *Id.*

[17] George v. Johnson, 45 N.H. 456 (1864).

[18] *Id.*

[19] Mercer v. Pike, 58 N.H. 286 (1878).

pursuant to the statute shall act as a release and discharge of the employer in the amount of such payment. RSA 275:47, II.

§ 18-7. Motor Vehicles

The transfer of an automobile, ownership of which is confirmed in New Hampshire by a title certificate under the title certificate law,[20] normally requires probate administration to effectively transfer title to another party. However, there is a special exception found in RSA 261:17, I, which provides that the title may be transferred to a surviving spouse without taking out administration.

§ 18-8. Wearing Apparel and Personal Effects

RSA 554:4 provides that the wearing apparel of the widow and her ornaments . . . and the wearing apparel, Bibles and school books of the minor children are not regarded as probate assets. Furthermore, the wearing apparel, Bibles, family pictures, photographs, albums and any other personal trinkets of sentimental rather than intrinsic value belonging to the deceased shall be delivered by the administrator to the surviving spouse or divided amongst the children and are not to be inventoried as probate assets. RSA 554:5.

§ 18-9. Real Estate

Although the executor is required to inventory the real estate of the decedent (RSA 554:1) under the New Hampshire rule, real estate of a decedent is not considered an asset of the decedent for purposes of the administration of the estate. The title to real estate passes upon death instantaneously to the heirs of the property, subject to divestment by the administrator only where there are insufficient estate assets to pay debts. This is a most misunderstood rule and the failure to follow it often creates confusion between the heirs and the administrator.

Therefore, the administrator does not normally get involved with the handling of real estate nor need he account for its rents or profits. However, if an administrator undertakes to collect the rents from property, he is bound to exercise reasonable care in the manner in which he handles the real estate. *McInnes v. Goldthwaite, 96 N.H. 413, 77 A.2d 849 (1951).* Similarly, if the estate is insolvent, the administrator has the

---

[20] RSA 261.

duty to account for the rents and profits of any real estate and to keep the same in repair. RSA 554:15.

Additionally, the probate court is given jurisdiction to hear cases in which title to or any interest in any real or personal property listed in the estate of the deceased person or trust is in issue by a petition to quiet title. RSA 547:11-c.

See Chapter 35, Real Estate, *infra*.

§ 18-10. Assets of Another in the Possession of Decedent at Time of Death

The assets of another person in the possession of the decedent at the time of death are not probate assets and, as they do not belong to the decedent, should not be inventoried as assets of the decedent's estate. Many disagreements can arise between persons claiming title to property and the decedent's administrator where the decedent had actual physical possession of the property at the time of death. See *Rice v. Connolly, 71 N.H. 382, 52 A. 446 (1902)* and *Blanchard v. Calderwood, 110 N.H. 29, 260 A.2d 118 (1969)*. Under the Omnibus Justice Act, the administrator may petition the probate court pursuant to RSA 547:11-b (the declaratory judgment statute) to determine the question as between the parties. Formerly, it was necessary to go to the superior court to contest title to assets claimed by an administrator as assets of an estate.

Additionally, the probate court is now given jurisdiction to hear cases in which title to or any interest in any real or personal property listed in the estate of the deceased person or trust is in issue by a petition of quiet title. RSA 547:11-c.

A claimant of property in his possession at the time of the decedent's death, but which is claimed by the estate, is entitled to notice of a hearing before his notice of the purpose of the hearing before his claim may be involuntarily dismissed. *King v. Mosher.*[21]

§ 18-11. Uniform Probate Code Provisions

The Uniform Probate Code provides for proceedings known as informal probate and succession without administration, which are alternatives to full probate or intestate proceedings, known as supervised

---

[21] King v. Mosher, 137 N.H. 453 (1993).

administration and formal testacy. § 3-301-322. These alternative proceedings further the Uniform Probate Code's objective of simplifying
all probate proceedings.

Library References

Am Jur 2d Executors and Administrators § 22–29

CHAPTER 19. SMALL ESTATES: VOLUNTARY ADMINISTRATION

§ 19-1. Introduction

New Hampshire has had some form of simplified administration since the first enactment of RSA 553:31 in 1961. This procedure is referred to as "voluntary administration," and is designed for small estates which meet certain statutory requirements. Through the years, the legislature has expanded the scope of voluntary administration. The procedure for administration of small estates has been substantially changed in 1997 and January 1, 2002 amendments. Currently, small estates in New Hampshire are defined as either testate or intestate estates consisting entirely of personal property of a gross value not exceeding $10,000. RSA 553:31, I.

The initial legislation came about as a result of a study by the New Hampshire Judicial Council whose goal was to draft "legislation which would provide for the informal and inexpensive administration of small estates in the probate court."[2] The need for such legislation had been pointed out by experienced probate practitioners. For example, former probate judge Leonard Hardwick, in a 1958 article entitled "Administration of Small Estates,"[3] pointed out that New Hampshire "has not

---

[2] 8th Report Judicial Council, p. 31 (1960).

[3] 1 N.H.B.J. 40 (1958).

adequately provided for [small estates'] administration so as to give proper protection within a limited time and at a limited cost."[4] The proposed legislation, which later became law, had as a primary purpose a desire "to avoid unnecessary expense where the assets of the estate are of small value and the costs of administering it is disproportionate to the amount involved."[5] However, the rights of creditors were recognized since the Judicial Council also stressed that the proposed legislation should be "without prejudice to creditors or to the public."[6]

§ 19-2. Requisites—In General

Voluntary administration is available for either testate or intestate estates that consist entirely of personal property.[7] Effective January 1, 1997, RSA 553:31 no longer provides for two types of voluntary administration, depending upon the size of the estate as was the case under repealed versions of RSA 553:31 and RSA 553:31-a. Currently, RSA 553:31 provides one means of administering any estate under $10,000. Financial contributions, from either trust or personal funds which are not a part of the estate, may be made for the purpose of paying estate bills. These contributions are not taken into account when determining the overall size of the estate relative to the jurisdictional limit found in RSA 553:31. Probate Court Administrative Order 99-02 (rescinded effective 8/1/01).

Another type of administration is available under RSA 151-A:15, which governs the disposition of certain nursing home residents' estate. If the requirements of RSA 151-A.15 are met, the nursing home administrator is not subject to the provisions of RSA 553:31 (Administration of Small Estates) and may file an Affidavit of Nursing Home Administrator (AOC 226-003) for the purpose of disposing of a deceased resident's estate. Of primary importance is the requirement that no petition for probate has been previously field under any section of RSA 553. See Probate Court Procedure Bulletin 13.

Additionally, a waiver of full administration is available under RSA 553:32 when a deceased dies, either testate or intestate, and the surviving

---

[4] 1 N.H.B.J. 40, 45 (1958).

[5] 8th Report Judicial Council, p. 31 (1960).

[6] 8th Report Judicial Council, p. 31, 33 (1960).

[7] RSA 553:31; RSA 151-A:15. See also In re Estate of Magoon, 109 N.H. 211, 247 A.2d 188 (1968).

spouse, or if no spouse, an only child, serves as fiduciary. If both that section and RSA 553:31 are applicable to an estate, the fiduciary may elect under which section to proceed. RSA 553:32, VII.

§ 19-2(a). Estates of $10,000 Value or Less

Under the provisions of RSA 553:31 effective January 1, 2002, a petition relating to voluntary administration may be filed with no waiting period if the will has been allowed. If there is no will, the petition may not be filed until thirty days following the decedent's death. In any case, the petition may only be filed in the absence of the filing of a petition under RSA 552:7 or 552:8 or for the appointment of a personal representative under any other section of RSA 553. The right to administer shall be in the executor named in the will, if any. RSA 553:31 To qualify, the petitioner must be of legal age and capacity, must be an inhabitant of New Hampshire, and either must be a surviving spouse, parent, lineal descendant, brother or sister of the decedent, or "such other person as the judge may think proper." RSA 553:2.

The qualified party must file a petition indicating that the petitioner has undertaken to act as executor or voluntary administrator of such estate and will administer the same according to law.

Such executor or voluntary administrator shall, as required by RSA 553:31, I, at the time of filing such petition, also file:

(a) A personal bond without sureties;

(b) A list of heirs or list of legatees or devisees as required under RSA 86:18;

(c) A report of gifts and transfers in accordance with RSA 86:22 with the register of probate and the department of revenue administration;

(d) An appointment of some person residing in New Hampshire as an agent pursuant to RSA 553:25 for every nonresident executor or voluntary administrator;

(e) A list of assets owned by the deceased, sufficiently described, along with a list of the value of each. RSA 547:33; and

(f) As of January 1, 2002, a certification that a copy of the petition has been forwarded to all persons beneficially interested, as defined in RSA 550:12.

After payment of the filing fee, the register of probate then issues an attested copy of the petition, specifying estate assets, as evidence of the administrator's authority.

After collecting all the assets, the administrator is directed to pay debts and expenses in accordance with RSA 167:13, 554:19, or 557:34, as applicable. Any balance remaining is to be distributed according to the will, or if there is no will, to the surviving spouse, or if none, in accordance with the provisions of RSA 561. No fee or commission may be taken by the voluntary administrator for his services. RSA 553:31, II.

If additional personal property is discovered after the filing of the original petition, and the aggregate assets still do not exceed $10,000, the voluntary administrator must file an amended petition listing the total value of the personal estate reported on the original petition and itemizing each additional asset to be administered.

The voluntary administrator has historically been liable as an executor *de son tort* under RSA 553:17 to those aggrieved by his administration, and was, moreover, liable to a personal representative later appointed. This liability is continued under RSA 553:31, III. In any event, all powers of a voluntary administrator cease whenever a personal representative is appointed under any other sections of RSA 553.[8]

A voluntary administrator is required to render a statement of administration and the estate shall be closed no earlier than 60 days nor later than 90 days from the date of the administrator's appointment.[9] No disbursement from the estate shall be made until the account is approved.[10]

§ 19-2(b). Nursing Home Patient with Estate of Less Than $2,500 Value

RSA 151-A:15, I provides that if 30 days after the date of a testate or intestate patient's death in any nursing home no petition for probate has yet been filed under any section of RSA 553 and the gross value of the personal property remaining at the nursing home belonging to the

---

[8] RSA 553:31, III. See also In re Estate of Magoon, 109 N.H. 211, 247 A.2d 188 (1968).

[9] RSA 553:31, IV.

[10] *Id.*

deceased, including any amount left in a patient account, is no more than $2,500, the nursing home administrator may file in the probate court an affidavit for the purpose of disposing of such deceased patient's estate. In such cases, the nursing home administrator shall not be subject to the provisions of RSA 553:31. The form of the affidavit, and the rules governing proceedings under this section are set out in Probate Court Procedure Bulletin 13.

The nursing home administrator shall not file a death certificate with the probate court, but shall attest to the death in the affidavit. If the nursing home patient died testate, the nursing home administrator shall file the will in the probate court. However, Probate Court Procedure Bulletin 13 provides that the Nursing Home Administrator needs to file the will only if the Administrator is in possession of it, or knows that a will exists and is able to obtain it. The Register of Probate shall not delay the filing or processing of the affidavit due to the absence of a will. The probate court shall waive all filing fees.

Under RSA 151-A:15, II, notwithstanding the provisions of RSA 561, if all just debts of the deceased have been paid and a balance remains in the deceased's estate 60 days after the filing required under paragraph I, and the nursing home administrator is unable to ascertain any heir or legatee, the probate court shall order the administrator to pay the balance into the treasury of the county where the deceased was domiciled, where it shall be subject to the claims of persons entitled to it, through application to the county commissioners. Probate Court Procedure Bulletin 13 notes that in completing the affidavit concerning a deceased Medicaid recipient, Nursing Home Administrators should be aware that the deceased resident's estate may owe reimbursement to the State of New Hampshire for Medicaid payments. The Medicaid amount should be listed on the affidavit.

§ 19-3. Suits By and Against Voluntary Administrators

It is not clear whether the limitations of RSA 556 with respect to actions against administrators apply equally to voluntary administrators. At any rate, RSA 556 limitations cannot apply to bar claims against property not administrable under the voluntary administration statutes. Thus, in *In re Estate of Magoon*,[11] it was held that a State claim against

---

[11] In re Estate of Magoon, 109 N.H. 211, 247 A.2d 188 (1968).

the real estate of the deceased was not barred by the State's failure to present a claim or to bring suit against the voluntary administrator of her estate since real estate cannot constitute an asset of an estate so administered.

A lawsuit may be instituted by a voluntary administrator. In *Owen v. Owen*,[12] the New Hampshire Supreme Court held:

> A voluntary administrator ought to be allowed to turn over to a regular administrator any rights or assets without jeopardy or abatement. . ..

The *Owen* Court found that the ability to maintain suit is one such transferable right. Accordingly, a wrongful death suit instituted by a voluntary administrator should not be abated because the plaintiff was not a regular administrator. Instead, he should be permitted to amend the writ to reflect the regular administrator of the estate as plaintiff.

§ 19-4. Deferral of Legacy

When it appears that a "legatee, distributee, cestui or beneficiary not residing within the territorial limits of the United States of America or any territorial possession thereof, would not have the benefit or use or control of property due him in that special circumstances make it desirable that delivery to him be deferred," the probate court is authorized to order that the legatee's property be converted into available funds and paid to the state treasurer to be invested by him. RSA 561:12-a. Further disposition of these monies is subject to further order of the probate court. RSA 561:12-a.

§ 19-5. Estates Opened Solely To Pursue a Cause of Action

By Administrative Order 2000-01, the administrative judge of the probate court has established a procedure where an estate is opened solely to pursue a cause of action and the estate otherwise contains no other assets than the underlying legal action. Under such circumstances, an administrator is authorized to file a motion to postpone the filing of annual accounts in lieu of which the administrator is required to file "an annual status report of the underlying action."

---

[12] Owen v. Owen, 109 N.H. 534, 537, 257 A.2d 24, 26 (1969).

The status report shall be required until the underlying cause of action is concluded and an account becomes due. The Administrative Order goes on to provide that a court may order status reports more frequently than annually.

If the underlying legal action is dismissed, the administrator is required to file a motion to close the estate that must include an explanation for the dismissal of the action. When acting upon such motion, the court may waive the filing of any account.

§ 19-6.   Uniform Probate Code Provisions

The Uniform Probate Code provides comprehensive procedures for the handling of small estates entitled "Summary Administration Procedures for Small Estates." § 3-1201-1204. There are two procedures allowed. The first, "collection of personal property by affidavit," involves estates which have only personal property, and the value is less than $5,000. §3-1201. Section 3-1201 also indicates that an application may not be filed until thirty days after the decedent's death, and denies voluntary administrator status if a petition for appointment of a personal representative is pending or has been granted.

The second procedure for summary administration of small estates involves estates of less than $5,000, but which may involve real estate (e.g., homestead). § 3-1203. The Code provides that the administrator may file a "closing statement" with the probate court at any time, unless this practice is prohibited by the court. If no actions or proceedings involving the administrator are pending in court one year following the filing of the closing statement, the administrator's appointment terminates.

Library References

Am Jur 2d Executors and Administrators §§ 21–30

CJS Executors and Administrators §§ 5–9

CJS Wills § 310

Forms

See Form 148 of Appendix for a Voluntary Administration Affidavit.

CHAPTER 20. WAIVER OF ADMINISTRATION

§ 20-1. Waiver of Administration by Surviving Spouse or Only Child

The legislature has provided for a streamlined administration of an estate in where a deceased dies testate and the surviving spouse, or if no spouse, an only child, is named in the will as the sole beneficiary of the deceased's estate and the surviving spouse, or if no spouse, an only child, has also been nominated and appointed to serve as fiduciary. RSA 553:32, II. In such a case there is no requirement for an inventory of the estate, no requirement for a bond, and no requirement for an accounting of assets.

Similarly, whenever a deceased dies intestate and the surviving spouse, or, if no spouse, an only child is the sole heir of the deceased's estate and is appointed to serve as fiduciary, there shall be no requirement for an inventory of the estate, no requirement for a bond, and no requirement for an accounting for assets. RSA 553:32, II.

However, the statute provides that any interested person may petition for full administration of the estate at any time from the original grant of the administration to the filing of the affidavit of administration, and such petition may be granted by the probate court for "good cause shown."[13]

Administration of the estate is required to be completed by the fiduciary filing and the probate court's approval of an affidavit of administration with the court no less than six months nor more than one year from the date of appointment of the fiduciary. RSA 553:32, II. The affidavit of administration must include a statement that "to the best of the knowledge and belief of the fiduciary there are no outstanding debts

---

[13] RSA 553:32, III.

or obligations attributable to the deceased's estate and shall list all real estate owned by the decedent at the time of death, including the location, book and page."[14]

The administrative justice of the probate court has promulgated a procedure for implementing RSA 553:32 which expands upon the statutory framework. The procedure specifies the supporting documents which are required to accompany the petition for appointment, sets the filing fee, and provides that any interested creditor may petition for full administration within six months after the original grant of the administration. The probate court will provide for publication of the appointment. Interestingly, the term *spouse* is interpreted to include a common-law spouse.

If the fiduciary fails to file the required affidavit within the required filing date, the fiduciary is considered to be in default.[15] The register of probate is required to give notice of the default to the fiduciary by first class mail within ten days after the default.[16] The register of probate shall issue a citation notice in accordance with RSA 548:5-a. RSA 553:32, II.

Disclaimer, ademption of legacies, or declination to serve as executor may be effectively used to cause the estate to conform to the requirements of paragraph II. RSA 553:32, IV. A guardian may be appointed as fiduciary if the ward qualifies. RSA 553:32, V. If the fiduciary is unable to complete the administration of the estate, the administration may be completed in accordance with section 553:32 by the successor fiduciary. RSA 553:32, VI. If both RSA 553:32 and RSA 553:31 are applicable to an estate, the fiduciary may elect under which section to proceed. RSA 553:32, VII.

---

[14] RSA 553:32, II.

[15] *Id.*

[16] *Id.*

CHAPTER 21. SUMMARY ADMINISTRATION OF ESTATES

---

§ 21-1.   Motion for Summary Administration

§ 21-1(a).   Nature and Purpose—Streamlined Filing Requirements

Under RSA 553:33, summary administration is available to expedite the closing of an estate when further court supervision of the administration of the estate is no longer necessary. The approval of a motion for summary administration of the court will eliminate the requirement of filing a final account and receipts for the balance of the estate. All other documents required by statute shall be filed. In those estates in which there is federal estate tax liability, the court shall not require the administrator to file a closing letter from the Internal Revenue Service. RSA 553:33, II.

§ 21-2.   Time for Filing

An administrator may file a motion for summary administration to close an estate not less than 6 months after the date of appointment of the administrator. RSA 553:33, II.

§ 21-3.   Requirements for Court Approval of Motion

A motion for summary administration shall contain a statement of the administrator under oath that

(1)   The estate of the decedent has been open for at least 6 months.

(2)   To the best of the knowledge and belief of the administrator there are no outstanding debts, obligations, or unpaid or unresolved claims attributable to the deceased's estate.

(3)   No New Hampshire estate or inheritance taxes are due, or all applicable New Hampshire estate and inheritance taxes have been paid, and a certificate from the department of revenue administration under RSA 86.32 has been filed with the court.

(4)   No federal estate tax is due, or the federal estate tax return has been filed and all taxes reported thereon have been paid.

(5)   Court supervision of the administration of the estate is no longer necessary.

(6)   The administration of the estate will be completed without further court supervision in accordance with the decedent's will and applicable law. RSA 553:33, III(a).

§ 21-4. Assents from All Persons Beneficially Interested

The administrator shall attach to the motion either receipts or assents from all specific legatees and assents from all other persons beneficially interested, as defined in RSA 550:12. The assents shall state that the beneficially interested person:

(1)   Agrees that further court supervision of the administration of the estate is no long necessary;

(2)   Does not request a final accounting; and

(3)   Requests that the motion for summary administration be granted. RSA 553:33, III(b).

§ 21-5. Required Certification of Tax Payments

Under RSA 86:31, no final account of motion for summary administration of an executor, administrator, or trustee shall be allowed by the probate court until the certificate of the department of revenue administration has been filed in said court, stating that all tax returns have been paid, and that provision has been made for any taxes which may become due on aid property or interest or that the payment thereof to the state is assumed by the legatee receiving such property or interest secured by deposit, or by lien on real estate.

§ 21-6. Effect of Approval of Summary Administration

Upon granting of a motion for summary administration, the court shall close the estate and release the bond. The administrator shall then be obligated to complete the administration of the estate without further court supervision in accordance with the decedent's will and applicable law. RSA 553:33, IV.

CHAPTER 22. LOST PERSONS

§ 22-1. Administration of Estates of Lost Persons

RSA 553:18 and 553:19 provide for the administration of estates of lost persons under the title "Administration of Estate of Person Not Heard Of."[1] The appointment of an administrator by the probate judge is permitted by RSA 553:18:

> upon the estate of a person who has left his home, and has not been heard of or from, directly or indirectly, for one year and whom he [the judge] believes to be dead, upon proof that notice has been published and given, as provided in the following section; but no distribution of his estate shall be made until five years after the granting of administration.

Before he may be appointed, the petitioner must provide proof that he has given notice as required by RSA 553:19 which provides that the notice must contain a description of the absentee, including his name, age and other identifying characteristics, and must call for information concerning him. Both publication and posting of the notice are necessary. The notice must be published in a newspaper printed in Concord, as well as in a newspaper printed in the county in which the absentee lived for one year. Posting is required for one month in at least three public places in the town the absentee formerly inhabited for one year. The judge may order that further notice be given to the absentee's relatives and heirs.

---

[1] The original statute, N.H. Session Laws ch. 22 (1872), was entitled "An act relating to the appointment of administrators to protect and care for property." Hanley v. Wadleigh, 88 N.H. 174, 186 A. 505 (1936).

A proceeding is begun under these statutes by filing with the probate court in the county where the lost or disappeared person last resided on Approved Form 81, Petition for Administration Upon the Estate of a Person Not Heard Of, or From, For One Year or More.

A leading case interpreting this statute is *Hanley v. Wadleigh*,[2] which involved the issue of title to certain real estate which was subject to a life estate of a disappeared person. The plaintiffs were the remaindermen of the underlying estate. Describing the statute as "in some respects anomalous," the Supreme Court held that despite the statute's postponement of distribution until five years after the appointment of an administrator, "[t]he law is not one for administering an estate of an absentee regarding as living, but provides for administration upon an estate of one believed to be dead."[3] Belief in the absentee's death is a specific requirement, and no appointment can be made without it. The "requirement of death is positive. It is not meaningless or surplusage. It is a stated condition."[4]

Belief of death "implies a finding of the fact believed."[5] The statute in effect provides that if the circumstances of the absentee's departure and absence reasonably lead to the inference of death, the inference may be adopted and the appointment follows.[6]

Since the statute operates only upon the estates of absentees believed dead, the New Hampshire Supreme Court held in *Hanley* that an administrator acting under the statute has no authority to press the absentee's continuing right to a life estate. Instead, the administrator must act upon the assumption that the life estate terminated as of the date of his appointment.

However, although the administrator is compelled to regard the absentee as dead, the "finding of death is provisional and tentative, and has no universal application."[7] In *Hanley*, for example, the Court held that the remaindermen interested in the real estate to which the absentee had held a life estate, could not regard his death as established by the

---

[2] Hanley v. Wadleigh, 88 N.H. 174, 186 A. 505 (1936).

[3] Hanley v. Wadleigh, 88 N.H. 174, 175, 186 A. 505, 506 (1936).

[4] *Id.*

[5] *Id.*

[6] *Id.*

[7] *Id.*

probate proceedings, since they were neither parties nor privies to those proceedings.[8] If the life tenant were to return, or the time of his death were later established, therefore, the remaindermen would be accountable for their use and occupation of the property during his life estate.[9] The finding of death is not res judicata as to the absentee himself, just as it is not to the remaindermen.

This holding should not apply to assets administered in accordance with the statutes. Because the absentee is treated as a decedent, it should follow that his estate consists of the same assets as that of a decedent, and the administrator should possess the same authority with respect to the absentee's estate as an administrator of a decedent's estate would possess, subject to the delay in distribution mandated by RSA 553:18. This appears to be the rule established in *Moore v. Eastman*[10] where the Court held that the interest of an absentee co-tenant could be dealt with under RSA 538 and under RSA 553:18 and 553:19, so that the whole premises could be sold pursuant to proceedings instituted under RSA 538.

Library References

Am Jur 2d Absentees §§ 1–17

CJS Absentees §§ 1–15

Administration of estate of one the fact of whose death rests upon presumption or circumstantial evidence. 140 ALR 1403.

§ 22-2. Presumption of Death

In addition to the procedures and protection afforded by RSA 553:18 and 553:19, New Hampshire common law recognizes a "legal presumption" that "[e]vidence that a party has not been heard of for seven years

---

[8] Hanley v. Wadleigh, 88 N.H. 174, 176, 186 A. 505, 506 (1936).

[9] Hanley v. Wadleigh, 88 N.H. 174, 176, 186 A. 505, 506 (1936). The remainder-men would be entitled to actual possession of the property after the life tenant's departure as against the administrator of the absentee's estate. *Hanley* offers a possible solution to the remaindermen's difficulty in dealing with the property in the event the life tenant is missing. The Court found that the absentee's abandonment constitutes waste; the remaindermen might obtain "such relief as will compensate them for injury done and protect them against further injury" through suit against the absentee with service upon him by publication and may protect their interest by suit against others who prejudice their remainder interest as well. Hanley v. Wadleigh, 88 N.H. 174, 177, 186 A. 505, 507 (1936).

[10] Moore v. Eastman, 98 N.H. 28, 93 A.2d 671 (1953).

rebuts the presumption of the duration of life." *Bennett v. Sloman*,[11] Or, put another way, there is a recognized common law "presumption that one not heard of for seven years by those who would naturally hear from or about him has died at the end of the period." *Volitas v. Ventoura*.[12] However, there "must be competent evidence to prove the supporting facts" in order for the presumption to be invoked, and the party seeking to rely upon the presumption must introduce that evidence.[13] Competent evidence does not include affidavits, because they are neither depositions nor testimony.[14] If the presumption is properly invoked, it may be used in a probate estate to support a finding that the absent person is dead and not entitled to a share of an intestate estate,[15] or to establish the fact of an absent person's death as life beneficiary of a trust.[16]

Where a bequest to an heir is dependent upon a prior beneficiary not surviving for a period of years, the seven-year presumption applies and the contingent beneficiary takes the bequest after such a period has elapsed.[17]

This seven-year presumption appears to be inconsistent with RSA 553:18 and 19. Under RSA 553:18, once a person has been missing for one year, an administrator may be appointed over his estate. The administrator may then distribute assets five years after the granting of the administration. Therefore, it is possible that after a person has been missing six years, his assets may be distributed under RSA 553:18, before the person is presumed dead under the common law rule.

Library References

Am Jur 2d Absentees §§ 1–2

Am Jur 2d Death §§ 551–69

CJS Absentees § 1 et seq.

CJS Death §§ 5–12

---

[11] Bennett v. Sloman, 70 N.H. 289, 291, 48 A. 283, 283 (1900).

[12] Volitas v. Ventoura, 86 N.H. 52, 162 A. 922 (1932).

[13] *Id.*

[14] *Id.*

[15] *Id.*

[16] Bennett v. Sloman, 70 N.H. 289, 48 A. 283 (1900).

[17] *Id.*

§ 22-3.   Payment of Legacy or Intestate Share of Lost Person

RSA 561:10 provides that upon the closing of an estate, any sum of money over $25.00
"belonging to any heir, legatee, beneficiary, creditor, or other person whose place of residence is unknown and cannot be found" shall be paid, upon order of the probate court to the state treasurer. Any person entitled to receive said sum may petition the probate court "at any time before the fund disposition thereof under the Chapter" and receive payment. RSA 561:10.

If the sum is less than $25.00, the procedure is altered to provide for distribution as if the lost person had no interest in the estate. RSA 561:10. This greatly simplifies the procedure of closing an estate in which small amounts are involved.

After the expiration of three years after payment to the state treasurer, the probate court, upon petition, is required to distribute the assets to those interested in the estate as if the lost person had had no interest therein. RSA 561:12. This provision prevents the general escheat statute (RSA 471-A) from operating to cut off the remaining parties to the estate from sharing in the portion set aside for the lost or absent person.

Library References

Am Jur 2d Absentees §§ 11–13
CJS Absentees §§ 5–6

§ 22-4.   Uniform Probate Code Provisions

The Uniform Probate Code provides that a person "absent for a continuous period of five years, during which he has not been heard from, and whose absence is not satisfactorily explained after diligent search or inquiry is presumed to be dead." § 1-107(3). The property of a person who has disappeared may be protected by the appointment of a conservator if "the person has property that will be wasted or dissipated unless property management is provided." § 5-401. However, the administration of an absent person's estate, whether testate or intestate, cannot "be maintained in relation to the estate of an absent, disappeared or missing person for whose estate a conservator has been appointed at anytime within three years after the conservator becomes able to establish the death of the protected person." § 3-108.

Forms

See Form 115 in Appendix for a Petition to Pay Money to State Treasurer.

CHAPTER 23. PROBATE OF WILLS

§ 23-1. Introduction

This chapter will concentrate on the process through which wills must pass in order for the court to determine the will was effective to pass property; i.e., the process by which wills are "allowed" or "proved." A discussion of the various types of wills, the formalities of execution or other areas pertaining to the construction or interpretation of wills in detail, are omitted as these areas are covered in the volume entitled *Wills, Trusts and Gifts* (3d ed. 1997) of the New Hampshire Practice Series.

§ 23-2. Probate of Wills Generally

Probate refers to the process of proving before a court that the document offered is the last will of a decedent. The probate of a will is the statutory method of establishing the proper execution of the instrument as a will and of giving notice of its contents.[1] A will is not brought into legal existence by the judgment admitting it to probate. Nonetheless, the will will not be admissible in evidence as the foundation of a right in title to real or personal property unless it has been duly probated.[2]

The phrase *probate of a will* is generally broadly used to include not only the process by which a will is allowed, but also proceedings involving contests of wills and proceedings to set aside the probate of wills.[3]

In New Hampshire, as in most other states, the probate of a will is statutorily governed. RSA 552:1 provides that:

> No will shall be effectual to pass either real or personal estate unless duly proved and allowed in the court of probate; and the probate of a will devising real estate shall be conclusive as to its due execution, as in the case of a will of personal estate.

Thus, a will may not pass real or personal property unless it is first proved and allowed in probate court.

In the early case of *Barstow v. Sprague*,[4] it was held that in New Hampshire a will would not be effective to pass either real or personal property "unless it has been duly proved and allowed in a probate court of this State, or something equivalent to such approval and allowance has taken place."[5] The Court went on to hold that:

> [I]t was clearly competent for the legislature to provide that property here, real or personal, should not pass by any will unless proved here. In relation to all property within their

---

[1] 79 Am. Jur. 2d, Wills, § 826. See Chapter 3, *supra* for a discussion of the historical antecedents of the term.

[2] 79 Am. Jur. 2d, Wills, § 826.

[3] *Id.*

[4] Barstow v. Sprague, 40 N.H. 27 (1859).

[5] Barstow v. Sprague, 40 N.H. 27, 31 (1859).

territorial jurisdiction, the sovereignty of the State legislature is indisputable; and, by the well recognized principles of the laws of all nations, real property can pass only according to the provisions of the local laws of the country in which it is situate.[6]

The terms executor and administrator mean the personal representative of the deceased.[7] Although at one time it was held that an executor, as distinguished from an administrator, derived his authority from the testator and not the probate court,[8] the Court in the case of *Crosby v. Charlestown*,[9] clearly established that an executor derives his right and authority from the probate court. As such, he is forbidden to intermeddle with the estate of the decedent until he has given bond to the judge of probate and is not considered as having the trust until after the filing of such bond.

It is no defense to the offered probate of a will that the will is unreasonable or vindictive. The probate of a will does not depend upon an explanation as to why the testator made it as he did. *Whitman v. Morey*.[10] "The statutory right of every person to dispose of his estate by will does not depend upon the condition that its provisions shall be reasonable, or consistent with his duties to his family."[11] The fact that the will is unreasonable may have weight in determining issues such as sanity or undue influence, but it is not the test by which a will is admitted to probate. Thus, a will will not be set aside merely because the motives of the testator cannot be explained.[12] In *Whitman*, the parties contesting the probate of a will requested that the jury be given instructions which, in effect, would have required the proponent of the will to explain why the testator had made it as he did. In denying the requested jury instruction, the Court stated that:

> The instruction requested is equivalent to the proposition that unless the provisions of the will are reasonable, or if unreasonable unless the proponents present a reasonable explanation of

---

[6] *Id.*

[7] Crosby v. Charlestown, 78 N.H. 39, 95 A. 1043 (1915).

[8] Storey v. Perkins, 3 N.H. 517 (1826).

[9] Crosby v. Charlestown, 78 N.H. 39, 95 A. 1043 (1915).

[10] Whitman v. Morey, 63 N.H. 448, 2 A. 899 (1885).

[11] Whitman v. Morey, 63 N.H. 448, 485, 2 A. 899, 906 (1885).

[12] *Id.*

its unreasonable provisions, it cannot be admitted to probate. Such is not the law.[13]

In addition, even though a will contains provisions that may be indefinite and thus void for uncertainty, it may be properly proved by the probate court if any part may take effect. *George v. George.*[14]

In *Morey v. Sohier,*[15] the Court held that "the question whether a will is entitled to probate does not depend upon the question of whether, at the time of the testator's death, or at any previous or subsequent time, there was any property which it could dispose of."[16] This is similar to the rule by which the execution and delivery of a deed may be proved in a real action prior to the adjudication of its legal affects. Thus a will may be proved in probate court without the necessity of a trial on the question of whether it will be inoperative for want of title in the testator.[17] In addition, for the purposes of probate, it is not material, as a matter of law, whether a deed purporting to convey all of the testator's property was made before or after the will.[18]

Library References

Am Jur 2d Wills §§ 822, 826–31

CJS Wills §§ 307–10

§ 23-3. Jurisdiction

The New Hampshire Constitution at Part 2, Article 80 grants to the judges of probate jurisdiction over "[a]ll matters relating to the probate of wills, and granting of letters of administration," as the legislature shall direct. In accordance with this power, the legislature, in RSA 547:3, has granted to judges of probate exclusive jurisdiction over the probate of wills. *Glover v. Baker.*[19]

It is well settled in New Hampshire that the probate courts, although there is no jury and the proceedings are not rooted in the common law,

---

[13] *Id.*

[14] George v. George, 47 N.H. 27 (1866).

[15] Morey v. Sohier, 63 N.H. 507, 3 A. 636 (1885).

[16] *Id.*

[17] *Id.*

[18] *Id.*

[19] Glover v. Baker, 76 N.H. 393, 83 A. 916 (1912). See Chapter 5 *supra* for a discussion of jurisdiction generally.

"are to be regarded as courts of general jurisdiction on the subjects to which they relate, and are entitled to all the presumptions in favor of their proceedings which are allowed in the case of the tribunals of general jurisdiction." *Stearns v. Wright.*[20] Thus, until the settlement of the executor's account, the probate court has the entire jurisdiction of the necessary procedure of administering an estate.[21]

Library References

Am Jur 2d Wills §§ 850–59

CJS Wills §§ 351–54, 433, 1074–80

§ 23-4. Venue

Pursuant to RSA 547:8, the judge of probate of the county in which the decedent was last an inhabitant has "jurisdiction" (more properly, "venue") over the probate of the will. However, if the deceased was not an inhabitant of this state, jurisdiction belongs to the judge for any county in which the decedent's property was located or in which the personal representative or relative of the deceased has a cause of action. A claim for negligently causing the death in New Hampshire of a non-resident has been recognized as a sufficient basis for the appointment of an administrator.[22]

The early case of *Knight v. Hollings,*[23] illustrates how probate venue is determined. Here the decedent's will was presented, accompanied by a petition signed by the nominated executor asking for probate and alleging that the decedent was last an inhabitant of that county and had estate in that county at the time of his death. The Court held that the probate judge of that county had jurisdiction of the probate of the will both by reason of the decedent's residence and by reason of his ownership of property in the county at the time of death. As such, "[t]he judge could not decline nor neglect to act upon the petition without violating the duty imposed upon him by law and disregarding his official oath."[24] In acting

---

[20] Stearns v. Wright, 51 N.H. 600, 609 (1872). See also Knight v. Hollings, 73 N.H. 495, 498, 63 A. 38, 40 (1906); Kimball v. Fisk, 39 N.H. 110, 119 (1859).

[21] Glover v. Baker, 76 N.H. 393, 83 A. 916 (1912).

[22] Boston & Maine R.R. Co. v. Hurd, 108 F. 116 (1st Cir. 1901), *cert, denied,* 184 U.S. 700, 46 L. Ed. 765, 22 S. Ct. 939 (1912).

[23] Knight v. Hollings, 73 N.H. 495, 63 A. 38 (1906).

[24] Knight v. Hollings, 73 N.H. 495, 498, 63 A. 38, 40 (1906).

upon a petition for probate, the judge of a probate court has the "authority to determine, and must determine, the jurisdictional questions of fact."[25] The fact that a judge assumes jurisdiction of the probate of a will and proceeds to approve and allow it in common form creates the presumption that he or she found the decedent to last be an inhabitant of the county, or that the decedent had estate in the county, or both.[26]

Library References

CJS Wills §§ 355, 1081

§ 23-5. Conclusiveness of Judgment

While at common law the probate of a will was conclusive as to its execution only in regard to personal property, now the probate of a will is conclusive as to its execution for both personal and real property.[27] RSA 552:1 provides that: "No will shall be effectual to pass either real or personal estate unless duly proved and allowed in the court of probate; and the probate of a will devising real estate shall be conclusive as to its due execution, as in the case of a will of personal estate."

A will cannot be used as evidence in any court of common law until it has been proved and allowed in probate court. However, once it has been duly proved and allowed it becomes conclusive evidence in all other courts. *Strong v. Perkins.*[28] Once proved and allowed, neither the valid execution of the instrument, nor the capacity of the testator can be called into question.[29] In other words, the proof and allowance of a will in probate conclusively settles that the instrument is the will of the testator and is to be considered as such from the time of his death.[30]

In addition, the admittance of a will to probate determines conclusively that the will was not induced by fraud or undue influence,[31] "[a]nd the issue thus adjudicated is not removed from the operation of the rule of res judicata by an 'allegation that several conspired to unduly influence' the testator." *Langley v. Langley.*[32] The decree of the probate court is

---

[25] *Id.*

[26] *Id.*

[27] Barstow v. Sprague, 40 N.H. 27 (1859).

[28] Strong v. Perkins, 3 N.H. 517 (1826).

[29] *Id.*

[30] *Id.*

[31] Glover v. Baker, 76 N.H. 393, 401, 83 A. 916, 923 (1912).

[32] Langley v. Langley, 84 N.H. 515, 516, 153 A. 9, 9 (1934).

in the nature of a proceeding in rem, and like a common law judgment, it cannot be impeached collaterally except for lack of jurisdiction.[33]

Library References

Am Jur 2d Wills §§ 1035–62

CJS Wills §§ 577

§ 23-6. Delivery of Will

RSA 552:2 requires every person having custody of a will to deliver it to the probate court or to the executor named in the will, within thirty days after learning of the decease of the testator. In addition, RSA 552:3 requires that the person named as executor of a will shall, within 30 days after the decease of the testator, or within 30 days after the person has knowledge of being so named, whichever is later, file the will in the probate court. If the estate contains any assets, the named executor shall cause the will to be proved or shall file a written refusal to accept the trust. If the estate contains no assets, the named executor shall provide a certificate of death for the decedent and shall file the will with no administration.

Unless there is a satisfactory excuse, refusal to perform as required by these two provisions may result in the imposition of a $20.00 penalty for each month of neglect after the thirty-day period, recoverable by any person having an interest in the will. RSA 552:4. Failure to deliver a will to probate court after being cited for that purpose can result in imprisonment until delivery is made. RSA 552:5.

It is a serious failure for an executor to be careless about meeting the thirty-day deadline of RSA 552:3. However, it is not uncommon for an executor to fail to act within the thirty-day period. If the failure is due to his neglect (e.g., he had possession of the will for the entire period), the executor runs a substantial risk that another will be appointed administrator in his place, if another contests the executor's appointment.[34] RSA 552:10 specifically provides that if an executor fails to present a will for probate in a timely manner, the probate court may prove the will upon application of the widow or any heir, and may appoint

---

[33] Langley v. Langley, 84 N.H. 515, 516, 153 A. 9, 9 (1934). See also Scammon v. Pearson, 79 N.H. 213, 107 A. 605 (1919); Starkey v. Kingley, 69 N.H. 293 (1897); Stearns v. Wright, 51 N.H. 600 (1872).

[34] 3 BOWE-PARKER: PAGE ON WILLS § 26.30.

such applicant as administrator in place of the neglectful executor. RSA 553:3.

Unlike some states, New Hampshire does not have a statutory provision calling for loss of one's interest under the will where a beneficiary who has possession of a will fails to present it for probate.[35]

Library References

Am Jur 2d Wills § 832 et seq.

CJS Wills § 311

Constitutionality, construction, and application of statute requiring production of wills for probate or declaring consequences of failure or delay in that regard. 119 ALR 1259.

§ 23-7. Common and Solemn Forms of Probate Distinguished

Chapter 552 of the Revised Statutes, entitled "Probate of Wills," provides for two different methods for the proving of wills, referred to by the antiquated terms of *proof in common form and proof in solemn form*:

> Wills may be proved in this State by two procedures, probate in common form (RSA 552:6), or probate in solemn form (RSA 552:7 (Supp. 1977)). Both forms are borrowed from the early common law, and neither has suffered substantial change in the interim.[36]

Although a person offering a will for probate may, in the first instance, choose to prove a will under either method, the usual course is first to offer a will for probate in common form. Common form provides for a simplified procedure and is appropriate when there is no contest concerning the probate. If the probate of a will is contested, any party may, within six months of the original probate, request that the will be proved in solemn form pursuant to RSA 552:7. This second procedure is more elaborate and requires public notice and the examination of all witnesses to the will.

Although solemn form probate most often follows a common law probate, the common law of New Hampshire allows the will to be first

---

[35] 3 Bowe-Parker: Page on Wills § 26.30. For discussion of Lost Wills, C. DeGrandpre, 7 New Hampshire Practice: Wills, Trusts and Gifts (2d ed. 1992) § 4.10.

[36] Ross v. Carlino, 119 N.H. 126, 399 A.2d 292 (1979).

offered in solemn form. *In re Estate of Pafelis.*[37] Selecting solemn form probate in the first instance is done most often when a will contest is expected from the beginning. By beginning in solemn form, the time periods of RSA 556:1 and 556:3 begin running earlier, avoiding the potential problem of a disruption of administration.

However, it should be remembered that solemn form probate is relatively rare. By far the greatest number of will probates are undertaken in common form only.

Library References

Am Jur 2d Wills §§ 840, 932, 1048, 1063
CJS Wills §§ 318, 577

§ 23-7(a). Probate in Common Form—In General

New Hampshire's early statutes did not contain special provisions relating to the form of probate, leaving the matter to be controlled by common law.[38] "Probate of wills in common form was customary at common law, and has been practiced in this state ever since the beginning of organized government here." *Knight v. Hollings.*[39] In 1842, statutory provisions were added providing that a will might be proved in common form upon the testimony of one of the subscribing witnesses if its probate was not contested, and that it might be done without previous citation and notice to the parties interested.[40] As such, "[T]hese provisions do not materially change the common law on the subject, and, in substance, they are still a part of the statute law of the state."[41]

The current statute relating to the probate of a will in common form, RSA 552:6, provides as follows:

> If the probate of a will is not contested the judge may allow and approve it in common form, upon the testimony of one of the subscribing witnesses, though the others are living and within the process of the court.

---

[37] In re Estate of Pafelis, 108 N.H. 265, 233 A.2d 825 (1967).

[38] Knight v. Hollings, 73 N.H. 495, 63 A. 38 (1906).

[39] *Id.*

[40] R.S., ch. 157, § 6; ch. 155, § 1.

[41] Knight v. Hollings, 73 N.H. 495, 499, 63 A. 38, 40 (1906). See also In re Estate of Pafelis, 108 N.H. 265, 233 A.2d 825 (1967).

A list of the names of the surviving spouse and known heirs at law of the testator, their relationships and their addresses, if known, must be filed by the executor named in the will, or any person presenting the will for probate along with the petition for appointment. RSA 552:5-a.

Where a will is self-proving, no witness testimony is required to prove the will. RSA 552:5-b.[42]

Proof of a will in common form may be made without notice to the decedent's heirs.[43] The Court in *Knight v. Hollings* held that:

> [t]he omission of notice does not appear to be unreasonable when it is considered that ordinarily the heirs learn of the decease of the person very soon after it occurs, and that their interests naturally and strongly urge them to promptly ascertain the nature, extent, situation, and disposition of his estate. They are put upon inquiry by the death of the party, and are reasonably charged with notice of all facts concerning their rights that they would learn upon diligent inquiry.[44]

Library References

Am Jur 2d Wills §§ 840, 1048

CJS Wills §§ 318, 577

§ 23-8. Probate in Solemn Form—In General

If a party wishes to have a will proved in solemn form, after a common form proceeding, RSA 552:7 and 552:8 provide for the following procedure:

> **RSA 552:7** Any party interested may have the probate of a will which has been proved without notice reexamined, and the will proved in solemn form before the court of probate at any time within six months of such probate.

> **RSA 552:8** A petition for that purpose may be presented to the judge, and notice thereof shall be given to the executor personally, if practicable, and shall be published. If, upon

---

[42] See the discussion of self-proved wills at § 23-12 *infra*.

[43] Knight v. Hollings, 73 N.H. 495, 63 A. 38 (1906).

[44] Knight v. Hollings, 73 N.H. 495, 500, 63 A. 38, 41 (1906).

hearing and reexamination, the probate shall not be confirmed, the will and probate shall be void.

A proceeding under RSA 552:7 has been held not to have abrogated the common law on the subject but to be only a statute of limitations upon the common law right to reexamination after a will has been proved without notice. *In re Estate of Pafelis.* [45] As such, the section is "designed to secure the final probate of wills while the facts are within the knowledge of living persons, and to promote the public policy looking to the speedy settlement of the estate of deceased persons." *Knight v. Hollings.* [46]

There is an untested, but broad-ranging provision found in RSA 552:9 which provides that a minor, an insane person or a person who was out of the country may have the probate of a will proved without notice reexamined at any time within one year after the removal of the disability. Because of the dangers inherent in this statute, when minors are beneficiaries of a will and a solemn form probate is petitioned for, a guardian ad litem for these interested parties should be appointed so that the proceeding can be conclusive and binding upon all parties. RSA 552:11 provides for the appointment of guardians ad litem in such situations.

Library References

Am Jur 2d Wills §§ 840, 932, 1063

CJS Wills §§ 318, 577

§ 23-8(a). Request by Interested Parties for Reexamination

The question of who may request a reexamination of a will in solemn form pursuant to RSA 552:7 is often confused with the issue of who may appeal under RSA 567-A:1 from an adverse decision in a solemn form proceeding. The courts have often mixed the issues, especially in cases involving the former probate appeal statute. [47]

Although the issues are different, they do raise similar concerns and therefore cases involving appeals to the Supreme Court under RSA

---

[45] In re Estate of Pafelis, 108 N.H. 265, 233 A. 825 (1967); Noyes v. Barber, 4 N.H. 406 (1828).

[46] Knight v. Hollings, 73 N.H. 495, 502, 63 A. 38, 42 (1906).

[47] See Chapter 13 *supra* for a discussion of who may appeal to the Supreme Court from a decision of a probate court.

567-A:1 should also be reviewed.[48] RSA 552:7 provides that "[a]ny interested party" may petition for solemn form probate while RSA 567-A:1 provides that any "person who is aggrieved" may appeal a conclusive decision of the probate court to the Supreme Court.[49] Under Supreme Court Rule 7(4), all parties to a probate court action are deemed to be interested parties on appeal.

Probably due to the broad statutory language, "any person interested," there has been very little judicial interpretation of RSA 552:7 relating solely to the narrow issue of the right to have a will proved in solemn form. The phrase has been interpreted broadly by the court. In *Morey v. Sohier*,[50] persons who were named as legatees under a prior will were held to have standing to contest the will.

In a complicated will contest case which twice went on appeal to the Supreme Court, *In re Estate of Kelly*,[51] the Supreme Court held that in a will contest "the focus of the standing issue is. . . the rights of the heirs in contesting an issue that effects their inheritance" and "not the relationship between the petitioner's attorney and his client."[52] "[A] will contestant must generally have some direct or equitable interest in the decedent's estate. . . . Generally, persons who have a direct legal or equitable interest in the estate are heirs, creditors or legatees under a prior will."[53] The term heir "applies to those who take by reason of blood relationship or persons who would take the estate under the statute of distribution."[54]

Under the appellate *aggrieved person* standard, a "contestant of a will must have some direct legal or equitable interest in the decedent's estate, in privity with him, whether as heir, purchaser or beneficiary under another will, which would be destroyed or injuriously affected by the establishment of the contested will." *Swan v. Bailey*.[55] Under this standard, a presumptive heir was not considered a person aggrieved.[56]

---

[48] *Id.*

[49] See the discussion of aggrieved parties in present and prior law in Chapters 12 and 13 *supra*.

[50] Morey v. Sohier, 63 N.H. 507, 513, 3 A. 636 (1885).

[51] In re Estate of Kelly, 130 N.H. 773, 547 A.2d 284 (1988).

[52] In re Estate of Kelly, 130 N.H. 773, 777, 547 A.2d 284, 286 (1988).

[53] In re Estate of Kelly, 130 N.H. 773, 778, 547 A.2d 284, 286 (1988).

[54] Richardson v. Martin, 55 N.H. 45, 46 (1874).

[55] Swan v. Bailey, 84 N.H. 73, 74, 146 A. 89, 89 (1929).

[56] Rogers v. Estate of Whitney, 105 N.H. 95, 193 A.2d 10, 13 (1963).

In *Rogers v. Estate of Whitney*, the Supreme Court ruled the complainant was a "party interested" under RSA 552:7, where the complainant was named a beneficiary in an inter vivos trust, and the testator provided in his will that any amendment to the trust after the execution of the will would be inoperative, but later, by codicil and by amendment of the trust agreement, eliminated the complainant as beneficiary.[57] The Court ruled the complainant was entitled to have the will proved in solemn form because "the factual situation here raises questions of law sufficient to constitute the appellant a *party interested* within the meaning of RSA 552:7."[58]

Cross References

See Chapter 44, Will Contests, *infra*

Library References

Am Jur 2d Wills § 887

CJS Wills § 315

§ 23-8(b). Return of the Legacy

Ordinarily, when a party seeks to repudiate a will as invalid, he must do so wholly and entirely, by refusing to receive the benefit of it, or, if property has been received, by returning it to the executor or the court in case the judgment should be against the validity of the will. *Hamblett v. Hamblett.*[59] In *Holt v. Rice,*[60] the Supreme Court held that a party who has received a legacy under the will will not be permitted to contest the validity of the will without repaying the amount of the legacy; and that such is the rule even if the party was a minor when the legacy was received.

Cross References

See Chapter 44, Will Contests, *infra*.

Library References

Am Jur 2d Wills §§ 897–99

CJS Wills §§ 1147–51

---

[57] *Id.*

[58] Rogers v. Estate of Whitney, 105 N.H. 95, 99, 193 A.2d 10, 13 (1963).

[59] Hamblett v. Hamblett, 6 N.H. 333 (1833).

[60] Holt v. Rice, 54 N.H. 398 (1874). See also Hamblett v. Hamblett, 6 N.H. 333 (1833).

§ 23-8(c). Procedure on Reexamination

RSA 552:7 provides only the mechanics for proof of a will in solemn form except after it has been proved in common form.[61] RSA 552:7 states that any party interested may have the probate of a will which has been proved without notice reexamined, and the will proved in solemn form before the court of probate at any time within six months of such probate. A petition for that purpose may be presented to the judge, and notice thereof shall be given to the executor, personally, if practicable, and shall be published. If, upon hearing and reexamination, the probate shall not be confirmed, the will and probate is void.

The Court in the early case of *Noyes v. Barber*,[62] defined probate in solemn form as "a probate made by the judge, after all persons whose interests may be effected by the will have been notified, and have had an opportunity to be heard on the subject."[63]

The statute requires notice to the executor, if practicable, and by publication to all persons interested. However, the heirs may waive the requirement of notice.[64]

In addition to the notice requirements, probate in solemn form requires the production of all witnesses to the will, as opposed to the common form requirement that only one witness be offered.[65] Thus in *Ross v. Carlino*,[66] the court required all three witnesses to the will to appear.

No decree approving and allowing or disallowing a will shall be made in solemn form until guardians have been appointed for all minors and others interested therein who are incapacitated to take care of their estates, and until agents have been appointed by the judge for all persons interested who reside out of the state or are unknown. RSA 552:11.

Generally the party who affirms that a will was made has the primary burden of proof.[67] In such cases, the proper order of procedure at trial is to have that party first call the witnesses to the stand, or account for

---

[61] In re Estate of Pafelis, 108 N.H. 265, 233 A.2d 825 (1967).

[62] Noyes v. Barber, 4 N.H. 406 (1828).

[63] Noyes v. Barber, 4 N.H. 406, 409 (1828).

[64] Gray v. Gray, 60 N.H. 28 (1880).

[65] Ross v. Carlino, 119 N.H. 126, 399 A.2d 292 (1979).

[66] *Id.*

[67] Hardy v. Merrill, 56 N.H. 227 (1875).

their absence. *Daley v. Judge of Probate.*[68] If a witness has died, evidence should be introduced to prove the authenticity of the deceased witness' signature.[69] That proof, coupled with the appearance of the instrument as having been executed with the formalities required by law, is competent to be submitted to the jury on the issue of the due execution of the will.[70]

Regardless of who brings the petition for a solemn form proceeding, the proponent of the will, usually the executor, must produce the witnesses to the will and prove its due execution:

> The object of the proceeding is to prove the due execution of a written instrument. In most cases such proof is offered in order to [sic] the admission of the instrument in evidence, but in the case of the proof of a will, the evidence is offered to lay the foundation of a decree that the will has been proved.

> The instrument itself must be produced, unless, in a few excepted cases, where secondary evidence is admitted; and the attesting witnesses must be produced and examined, if they are living and within reach of the process of the court. They are to be produced by the party who offers the instrument in evidence, or who seeks a decree that it has been proved. *Perkins v. Perkins.*[71]

"It is not necessary for the witness to recollect the fact of his attestation, and can state it within his memory, for if this were so the validity of a will would depend upon the fact whether the testator had secured witnesses of retentive memories, rather than upon the fact that the witness did in fact properly attest it."[72]

Where an attesting witness does not confirm the execution of the will, he may be contradicted by another attesting witness or by other competent evidence.[73]

The procedure regarding attesting witnesses is well illustrated in *Perkins v. Perkins*[74] as follows:

---

[68] Daley v. Judge of Probate, 90 N.H. 381, 10 A.2d 239 (1939).

[69] *Id.*

[70] *Id.*

[71] Perkins v. Perkins, 39 N.H. 163 (1859).

[72] HOYT, PROBATE PRACTICE 19 (1902).

[73] *Id.*

[74] Perkins v. Perkins, 39 N.H. 163 (1859).

The witness usually testifies that he was present, and saw the grantor sign, seal and deliver the instrument, or the like, and there, ordinarily, the proof closes. It is not required that the witness should be asked if the party was of sound mind, or that he was free from intoxication, duress, or any of the disabilities which invalidate the execution of a deed. The usual formal proof being offered, the law comes in with its presumption that the party is sane, and free from disability; that the instrument was properly read, and the like; and this presumption stands until evidence is offered tending to raise a different belief. Being presumptions of fact only, they are open to be repelled by proof of the contrary. Evidence being introduced, the issue is to be determined by the preponderance of the whole evidence, as in other cases, though the party offering the proof of execution continues to have the legal presumption of sanity and capacity in his favor till the end.

Though ordinarily no question need be asked of the witness who testifies to the execution of an instrument, relative to the capacity of the grantor, yet, owing to the nature of the proceedings in the case of wills, that the probate of the will is the foundation of the grant of power to the executor to take possession of the estate and the charge of administration, it is, in that case, the long settled practice of courts of probate to require that the witnesses to wills should be examined as to the fact of the sanity of the testator, before the will is established. Its object is, that if it appears that there is either doubt or suspicion on the question, that doubt may be removed before the estate is placed in the hands of a man who may prove to have no title to it. This practice is equally binding as the law in such cases, upon the Supreme Court, as on the ordinary courts of probate.

The attesting witnesses being produced and examined, it is not essential that they should sustain the legal presumption of sanity. They may all deny the sanity of a testator, and yet, if the proof of a sound condition of mind is shown by the whole evidence, the will must be established.[75]

---

[75] Perkins v. Perkins, 39 N.H. 163, 167–69 (1859).

The Court, in *Ross v. Carlino*,[76] also reviewed the procedure for reexamination in the event a witness is incompetent or unavailable. In such a case, the proponent need not produce the witness, but there must be a hearing on, and a finding of, incompetence or unavailability, and the proponent must prove incompetence or unavailability to the satisfaction of the court. Moreover, if there is a finding of incompetence or unavailability, the will must still be proved upon other satisfactory evidence. Proving the signature of an unavailable witness raises a presumption of the witness' competency at the time of execution of the will, but it makes only a prima facie case; the presumption is rebuttable and subject to challenge. In the end, the judge must still find that the will was attested and subscribed by three or more credible witnesses.

Cross References

See Chapter 44, Will Contests, *infra*

Library References

Am Jur 2d Wills §§ 842, 932–36, 951–69, 992, 1008, 1011

CJS Wills §§ 316–21, 326 et seq., 356–58, 372 et seq., 383 et seq., 409 et seq.

§ 23-8(d). Probate in Solemn Form by Original Petition

RSA 552:6 provides that "any party interested may have the probate of a will which has been proved without notice reexamined, and the will proved in solemn form before the court of probate at any time within six months of such probate." Note that the statutory language pertains only to proof in solemn form and a reexamination of a will that has first been proved in common form. However, the Supreme Court has held that since the statute is silent on proof of a will in solemn form except after it has been proved without notice, the common law in existence prior to the statute is controlling. *In re Estate of Pafelis.*[77] This ancient common law provides that "the will may in the first instance be proved in solemn form after notice to all interested parties."[78] Thus, a party may choose in the first instance to proceed directly to a solemn form probate by original petition, thereby by-passing the common form probate route altogether.

---

[76] Ross v. Carlino, 119 N.H. 126, 399 A.2d 292 (1979).

[77] In re Estate of Pafelis, 108 N.H. 265, 233 A.2d 825 (1967).

[78] In re Estate of Pafelis, 108 N.H. 265, 233 A.2d 825 (1967); Noyes v. Barber, 4 N.H. 406 (1828).

Library References

Am Jur 2d Wills §§ 840, 932, 1063
CJS Wills §§ 318, 577

§ 23-9. Timing of Petition To Set Aside Probate of Will

Petitions to reexamine the will and its probate in solemn form must be timely made. The right to reexamine will be deemed waived if not asserted within the statutory deadlines, and the probate of a will which is not directly attacked or contested, cannot be overthrown by a collateral attack. *In re Estate of Lund.*[79]

However, under certain conditions, a will that has been previously allowed, either in common or solemn form, may be set aside upon petition of a party made after the expiration of the six-month deadline for reexamination of RSA 552:7. The proper form for such a proceeding is a petition to set aside the probate of a will. There are no specific statutory provisions relating to this procedure, therefore reliance must be placed upon judicial decisions.

Knight v. Hollings,[80] is the leading case on this issue. In this case, a petition to set aside a will was commenced in the probate court twelve years after the will had been proven and nine years after the estate had been settled by the allowance of a final account. The petition claimed that the decedent was not a resident of New Hampshire at his death and that therefore the New Hampshire probate court did not have jurisdiction. The Supreme Court ruled that the probate court had the power under common law principles to set aside the probate but that this power was to be strictly construed:

> [T]he plaintiffs have petitioned the probate court to set aside the decree. There is no doubt of the court's power to do this, provided sufficient cause is shown. But the power is equitable in nature. It is not exercised upon the mere asking, nor for the sole purpose of overriding rules of law that stand in the way of maintaining proceedings at law. To entitle the plaintiffs to the relief they seek, there must be some substantial ground, such as fraud, accident, or mistake, which renders it against conscience to execute the decree they attack, and of which they

---

[79] In re Estate of Lund, 118 N.H. 180, 385 A.2d 111 (1978).
[80] Knight v. Hollings, 73 N.H. 495, 63 A. 38 (1906).

were prevented from availing themselves by fraud, accident, or mistake, unmixed with any fraud or negligence on their part.[81]

The Court went on to hold that the equitable principle of laches barred the petition to set aside the will.

In a later case, *In re Estate of Lund*,[82] the will had been proved in common form only and the petition to set aside the probate came two years after the decedent's death. All of the parties had knowledge of the document that formed the basis for the attack on the already-proved will soon after its probate in common form. The Supreme Court upheld the probate court's refusal to set aside the probate of the will as originally filed even though it appeared that the document relied upon operated to amend the decedent's will, because the petitioners had been chargeably neglectful:

> In the instant case, all appealing parties had actual notice by the end of 1975; two, shortly after July 1, 1975; and the third shortly after December 23, 1975. It was incumbent upon them to take immediate action to protect their interest; not to do so was neglect chargeable against them.[83]

Library References

Am Jur 2d Wills §§ 1063–67

CJS Wills § 502 et seq.

§ 23-10. Unavailability of Witnesses

RSA 552:12 provides that if the attesting witnesses, after execution of a will, becomes incompetent from any cause, or if the probate court determines that the testimony of such witnesses is unavailable under the circumstances, the will may be proved or allowed "upon other satisfactory evidence."

The unavailability of a witness is not an infrequent occurrence since an attesting witness to a will may predecease the testator, may have moved far away, may have become incompetent or his whereabouts may simply be unknown.

---

[81] Knight v. Hollings, 73 N.H. 495, 502, 63 A. 38, 42 (1906). (Citations omitted.)

[82] In re Estate of Lund, 118 N.H. 180, 385 A.2d 111 (1978).

[83] In re Estate of Lund, 118 N.H. 180, 186, 385 A.2d 111, 114 (1978).

Where all of the witnesses have died, the administrator must provide the probate court with proof of their death, most easily accomplished by the filing of death certificates. The will may then be proved by evidence that the signatures on the will are the decedent's and the witnesses'.

> "Where all the witnesses are dead, and the handwriting of none can be proved, the will may be established by proof of the testator's handwriting. Where a witness signs by making a mark, the mark must be shown to be his, and for this purpose evidence has been received that the witness lived in the neighborhood of the testator and that he could not write, and that no other person of the same name lived near."[84]

If a witness is incompetent, the requirement of his testimony may be waived and the will allowed upon satisfactory proof of his incompetency.

Where a witness is alive and competent, but unavailable (e.g., moved far away) the executor is required to follow a standard procedure prescribed by the probate courts in this situation. The executor must file a "Dedimus" petition which is probate court Approved Form 94, entitled "Motion to Prove Will By Deposition".[85] This petition is more properly entitled a Petition For Dedimus Potestatum in Proof of Will, which means literally "we have given power"[86] and refers to the ancient English writ by which a court empowers an individual to perform certain acts on its behalf.

In the instance of an unavailable witness, the probate court is asked to empower an oath-taking official in another state (usually an attorney or notary public) to question the witness as to the proper execution of the will. The filing of a Dedimus petition results in a probate court order empowering a specified individual (whose name is supplied by the administrator) to question the absent witness for the purpose of ascertaining the validity of the will.

Library References

Am Jur 2d Wills §§ 1008–15

CJS Wills § 411

---

[84] HOYT, PROBATE PRACTICE 19 (1982).

[85] Forms Appendix, Form 94.

[86] BLACK'S LAW DICTIONARY 372 (Fifth Edition 1979).

§ 23-11. Notice to Legatees and Heirs at Law

RSA 552:15 provides that:

> Every executor shall, within sixty days after his appointment notify each legatee specifically named in the will of the fact that such legatee appears to be interested therein, and shall notify the surviving spouse and heirs at law, if known, that the will has been proved, and shall, within ninety days after his appointment, certify to the judge that notice as herein required has been given, stating in what manner and to whom.

The notice must be in the form prescribed by the probate court and must be delivered to the legatees, surviving spouse and heirs in person or by mail to the last known place of residence or business. RSA 552:16.

This notice to legatees and heirs is not a jurisdictional requirement which will affect a decree admitting a will to probate. *Langley v. Langley.*[87] A failure of an administrator to give the notice required by the statute will not cause the probate to be set aside where the contesting parties had actual knowledge of the probate of the will.[88]

The failure of an administrator to file a return of notice of his appointment does not create a defect in the title to real estate owned by the decedent.[89]

Library References

Am Jur 2d Wills §§ 932–36

CJS Wills §§ 369–70

§ 23-12. Self-proved Wills

RSA 552:5-b, effective January 1, 1986, provides that "Any will meeting the requirements of RSA 551:2-a is self-proved and shall be allowed by the probate court." The initial statute allowing self-proved wills was RSA 552:6-a, but in 1985, the legislature repealed it because of confusion due to the mandatory nature of its language.

---

[87] Langley v. Langley, 84 N.H. 515, 153 A. 9 (1931).

[88] *Id.*

[89] See the discussion in C. DeGrandpre, 7 New Hampshire Practice: Wills, Trusts and Gifts (2d ed. 1992) § 13.33.

RSA 551:2-a provides that a will may, at the time of its execution, or at any subsequent date, be made self-proved by the acknowledgment thereof by the testator, and the affidavits of the witnesses, each made before a notary public or justice of the peace. A self-proved will need not be presented for allowance in common form (where the testimony of one witness would be required) but is "proved" or allowed upon its filing with the probate court. RSA 552:5-b.

Although the statute is not crystal clear because of the language of RSA 552:7 which speaks of wills having been proved "without notice," self-proved wills are subject to reexamination in solemn form pursuant to RSA 552:7 and 552:8.

§ 23-13. Foreign Wills

The legislature may require that a will be proved here in order for real or personal property located in this state to pass pursuant to the will.[90] The general rule of RSA 552:1 requires that a will be proved and allowed in probate court in order to be effectual to pass either real or personal estate.

While until 1868 a foreign will had to satisfy the requirements of New Hampshire law in order to be effective to pass property located here,[91] RSA 552:13 now provides that a foreign will, proved and allowed in a foreign probate court, will be given the same effect in New Hampshire as if executed with the formalities required by New Hampshire law. Thus a duly authenticated copy of a will made out of state, which has been proved and allowed in that state or foreign country, may be submitted in New Hampshire upon the application of a party in interest, and upon notice ordered by probate court may be filed and recorded in probate court and will thereafter have the same effect as if it were a duly proved and allowed New Hampshire will.[92]

RSA 552:14 provides that the executor or any person interested in the estate may present copies of the duly authenticated will and probate decree to the judge of probate in any county in which there is estate of the decedent. If upon notice there is no objection to the request that such copies be filed and recorded, a decree may be issued to that effect. RSA 552:14.

---

[90] Barstow v. Sprague, 40 N.H. 27 (1859).

[91] Kennard v. Kennard, 63 N.H. 303 (1885).

[92] RSA 552:13; Kennard v. Kennard, 63 N.H. 303 (1885).

No defect in title to real estate of the decedent is created where an authenticated copy of the will and the probate thereof is filed in New Hampshire and the executor, under the will, makes a conveyance, pursuant to a power to convey real estate, even though there has been no appointment of a real administrator and no license to sell is granted by a New Hampshire probate court.[93]

However, where a foreign will leaves cash bequests and the residue includes real estate, filing of an authenticated copy of the will may not be sufficient. Proof in New Hampshire of payment of the bequests may be necessary to clear the title to the decedent's real estate.[94]

Library References

Am Jur 2d Wills § 833

CJS Wills §§ 340–50

§ 23-14.   Uniform Probate Code Provisions

The Uniform Probate Code provides for two different types of probate proceedings, somewhat similar to common form and solemn form probate proceedings. There is an "informal probate" in Article III, Part 3, which provides for a streamlined administration of an estate without all the rigmarole of the alternative procedure. In the informal probate, there can be no will contest.

The alternative proceeding, in Article III, Part 4, is known as "formal testacy" and is designed to cope with a will contest, although one is not required to involve the formal proceedings.

In addition to these alternative procedures, an estate may be handled "without administration" (§ 3-312-322), or as a "supervised administration" (§ 3-501-505).

Library References

Am Jur 2d Wills § 841–42

§ 23-15.   Uniform Law

The National Conference of Commissioners on Uniform State Laws has adopted a Uniform International Wills Act. The Act is designed to

---

[93] New Hampshire Title Examination Standards, Standard 7–9 (1988).

[94] New Hampshire Title Examination Standards, Standards 7–8, 7–9 (1988).

be adopted separately or as part of the Uniform Probate Code. New Hampshire has not adopted this Act.

Forms

See Form 94 in Appendix for a Motion to Prove Will By Deposition.

See Form 100 in Appendix for a Petition to File Authenticated Copies of Will and Probate.

See Form 116 in Appendix for a Motion to Re-Examine Probate Will.

CHAPTER 24. APPOINTMENT OF ADMINISTRATOR

§ 24-1. Generally

As a general rule, administrators will be appointed only when there is occasion for their appointment.[1] No administration is granted by the probate court, however, unless the fact of the death of the individual whose estate is to be administered upon is first shown, or appears to the satisfaction of the court.[2] RSA 553: 1-a provides that a death certificate is required for the appointment of an administrator. This requirement can be waived by the judge upon petition.

The granting of letters of administration on the estate of an individual is prima facie evidence of the death of the person whose estate is being administered.[3] However, death alone is not enough to justify the court's exercise of its appointive authority.[4] For both resident and nonresident

[1] Haven v. Haven, 69 N.H. 204, 30 A. 972 (1898).

[2] Jeffers v. Radcliff, 10 N.H. 242 (1839).

[3] Id.

[4] Robinson v. Estate of Dana, 87 N.H. 114, 174 A. 772 (1934).

decedents, there must be "estate" within the legislative meaning of the word.[5]

The judge of probate has jurisdiction to allow a will if one is presented, or if not, to grant administration.[6] The presence of assets gives jurisdiction for the grant of administration.[7] However, there is no race to the courthouse, and priority in filing a petition for appointment does not determine the question of jurisdiction under the statute.[8] The controlling question is in which county was the decedent last an inhabitant,[9] since the judge of probate of that county is authorized to appoint an administrator.[10] RSA 547:8 specifies that the granting of administration on the estate of a person deceased shall belong to the judge for the county in which such person was last an inhabitant; but if such person was not an inhabitant of this state the same shall belong to the judge for any county in which such person had estate, or in which the personal representative or kin of such person has a cause of action.

A will may name or nominate, but cannot appoint, an executor.[11] Unlike the law of some states, under the law of New Hampshire there is no difference between the appointment of an administrator and that of an executor. An administrator and executor alike are required to be appointed by a probate court.[12]

The dual roles of an individual as both a person and as an executor or administrator are distinguishable. An individual as executor or administrator is one person and, as an individual, another.[13] The legal concept involved is analogous to that of a corporation.[14] An administrator

---

[5] Id.

[6] Kittredge v. Folsom, 8 N.H. 98 (1835). See also C. DeGrandpre, 7 New Hampshire Practice: Wills, Trusts and Gifts (3d ed. 1997) Chapter 19.

[7] Crosby v. Charlestown, 78 N.H. 39, 95 A. 1043 (1915).

[8] Tilton v. O'Conner, 68 N.H. 215, 44 A. 303 (1895).

[9] Id.

[10] Id.

[11] Lisbon Sav. Bank & Trust Co. v. Estate of Moulton, 91 N.H. 477, 22 A.2d 331 (1941); Tappan v. Tappan, 24 N.H. 400 (1852).

[12] Lisbon Sav. Bank & Trust Co. v. Estate of Moulton, 91 N.H. 477, 22 A.2d 331 (1941).

[13] Lisbon Sav. Bank & Trust Co. v. Estate of Moulton, 91 N.H. 477, 22 A.2d 331 (1941); Cross v. Brown, 51 N.H. 486 (1871); Saltmarsh v. Candia, 51 N.H. 71 (1871).

[14] Lisbon Sav. Bank & Trust Co. v. Estate of Moulton, 91 N.H. 477, 22 A.2d 331 (1941).

is a creation of the law of the state of his appointment, at all times subject to its jurisdiction, with no legal residence elsewhere.[15] While as administrator he is where he may be in person, his status as administrator is local.[16]

The acts of an administrator appointed by a court having jurisdiction are valid as to third parties interested in them and the regularity of the appointment cannot be questioned in a suit on another matter.[17]

The general rule is that a grant of letters of administration obtained irregularly or illegally is valid until revoked and that persons dealing with a court-appointed administrator are entitled to rely upon the validity of the appointment until it is revoked.[18] Consequently, the acts done by a court-appointed administrator prior to revocation of his appointment are valid and bind the estate, at least to the extent that third parties with whom the administrator has dealt would otherwise be prejudiced.[19]

For example, where a release of a wrongful death claim, in consideration of $7,500 paid by the insurer, was executed on behalf of decedent's estate by an attorney who procured his appointment as administrator of the estate through fraud, the release was set aside. The estate's ultimate recovery, however, was reduced by the $7,500 already paid prior to the revocation of the court appointment. *Kelley v. Peerless Insurance Co.*[20]

Library References

Am Jur 2d Executors and Administrators §§ 157–270

CJS Executors and Administrators §§ 22–94

Necessity and sufficiency of assets to justify appointment of administrator at domicile of decedent. 59 ALR 87.

Brevity of period after death of decedent as affecting propriety of grant of letters testamentary or of administration. 133 ALR 1483.

§ 24-2. Nature of Office

In the execution of an administrator's trust it appears to be immaterial whether he calls himself executor or administrator.[21] Either term means

---

[15] *Id.*

[16] *Id.*

[17] Boody v. Emerson, 17 N.H. 577 (1845).

[18] Kelley v. Peerless Ins. Co., 121 N.H. 253, 428 A.2d 491 (1981).

[19] *Id.*

[20] *Id.*

[21] Crosby v. Charlestown, 78 N.H. 39, 95 A. 1043 (1915).

the personal representative of the deceased.[22] RSA 553:1 provides that the word *administrator* may include every person to whom the administration of an estate or the execution of a will may be granted.

The administrator is a trustee for the heirs and creditors of the deceased.[23] In bringing an action, the administrator is sole trustee for all of the beneficiaries of the estate and his actions bind them.[24] Before probate of the will, the person named as executor is vested with legal title to all the personal estate of the deceased as trustee of the legatees and others.[25] He is also the sole representative of the whole estate disposed of by the will.[26] As such it is his duty to cause the will to be proved.[27]

Upon the decease of an intestate and the granting of administration, his personal estate, and all contingent as well as absolute interests therein vest in his administrator.[28]

Before the grant of administration, the administrator has no control over the estate and the courts are forbidden to consider him as having the trust. *Crosby v. Charlestown.*[29] The administrator, by force of the statutes, obtains his title from the grant of administration.[30] The personal estate of a deceased intestate having vested in his administrator can be divested only by operation of law, or by some act of the administrator.[31]

Letters of administration are, *prima facie*, sufficient evidence for the due appointment of an administrator.[32] The granting of letters of administration on the estate of an individual is also *prima facie* evidence of the death of the person whose estate is being administered.[33] Letters

---

[22] *Id.*

[23] Parsons v. Parsons, 9 N.H. 309 (1838).

[24] McGrath v. McGrath, 109 N.H. 312, 251 A.2d 336 (1969).

[25] Shirley v. Healds, 34 N.H. 407 (1857).

[26] *Id.*

[27] *Id.*

[28] Ladd v. Wiggin, 35 N.H. 421 (1857).

[29] Crosby v. Charlestown, 78 N.H. 39, 95 A. 1043 (1915).

[30] Crosby v. Charlestown, 78 N.H. 39, 95 A. 1043 (1915); Kent v. Exeter, 68 N.H. 469, 44 A. 607 (1896); Ladd v. Wiggin, 35 N.H. 421 (1857); Parsons v. Parsons, 9 N.H. 309 (1838).

[31] Ladd v. Wiggin, 35 N.H. 421 (1857).

[32] Remick v. Butterfield, 31 N.H. 70 (1855).

[33] Jeffers v. Radcliff, 10 N.H. 242 (1839).

of administration are in the nature of an exemplification of the record of the appointment and as such are received without further proof. [34] Such commissions constitute an exception to the ordinary rule that the best evidence must be produced, since they presuppose and depend on an appointment as much as an execution does upon a judgment. [35] However, a certificate of a register of probate is not competent evidence of a grant of administration. [36] The proper evidence of a grant of administration is a copy of the record of the grant, [37] and a copy of a record is both admissible and the best evidence. The letters of administration, which are only a copy of the record in the probate court drawn up in a more formal manner, are no better evidence. [38]

Library References

Am Jur 2d Executors and Administrators §§ 375–76, 398 et seq., 525 et seq.

CJS Executors and Administrators §§ 184, 252, 299

§ 24-3.   Compensation—In General

In most states, statutes prescribe the fee chargeable by an administrator. These statutes generally allow administrators "commissions" based upon a certain percentage of the estate. The base upon which this percentage is calculated depends upon the wording of each statute but usually applies only to assets actually administered. [39]

New Hampshire has no statute establishing the fees of administrators, but from an early date our courts have allowed reasonable fees depending upon the facts in the particular estate. In *Wendell v. French,* [40] the Supreme Court stated that

> [t]he only rule is that which gives him a reasonable compensation for his services. If the services of one administrator be actually worth more than those of another—if, for instance, in addition to the naked duties of an administrator, he brings in aid the services, the experience and the counsel of an attorney

---

[34] Remick v. Butterfield, 31 N.H. 70 (1855).

[35] *Id.*

[36] Morse v. Bellows, 7 N.H. 549 (1835).

[37] *Id.*

[38] Farnsworth v. Briggs, 6 N.H. 561 (1834).

[39] 34 C.J.S., Executors and Administrators § 863.

[40] Wendell v. French, 19 N.H. 205 (1848).

of the court, there is no reason why his compensation should not be regulated accordingly, and why he should not be paid for the discharge of services which an administrator, not qualified to render them, would have found it his duty to procure at the expense of the estate.[41]

In addition to this judicial acceptance of the reasonable fee rule, Probate Court Rule 36 specially provides that the "[f]ees and expenses of fiduciaries shall be subject to the approval of the Court."

Library References

Am Jur 2d Executors and Administrators §§ 922–59
CJS Executors and Administrators §§ 858–81

Forms

See Appendix for Form AOC 44 Statement Concerning Fees included in Inventory of Fiduciary.

§ 24-3(a). Amount

In 1992, the Supreme Court, in the significant case of *In re Estate of Rolfe*,[42] established a completely new system for the determination of administrators' fees in the administration of an estate. The probate courts' prior use of fee guidelines based on the value of the estate to set both executors' and attorneys' fees was disapproved by the Supreme Court. The probate courts were ordered to establish attorneys' fees separately from administrators' fees. As to administrators' fees, the Court expressly disapproved of the use of a commission based on the value of the estate as a starting point for determination of compensation. Rather, the Court relied on the factors discussed in *McInnes v. Goldthwaite*[43] and stated that the probate court should look to the following factors in establishing administrators' compensation: (1) the complexity of the estate, (2) the administrator's responsibilities in light of the services rendered, (3) the time involved, (4) the risk, (5) the care, and (6) the responsibility involved.

---

[41] Wendell v. French, 19 N.H. 205, 210 (1848).

[42] In re Estate of Rolfe, 136 N.H. 294, 615 A.2d 625 (1992). See also McDonald, The Rolfe Decision: Its Practical Implications for Probate Attorneys, Vol. 3, No. 20, N.H. BAR NEWS 5 (1993).

[43] McInnes v. Goldthwaite, 94 N.H. 331, 52 A.2d 795 (1947).

The Supreme Court noted that the size of the estate may be considered by the probate court as a factor in setting a proper fee:

> [T]he size of the estate is but one factor to be considered, with the final executor's fee determination being based on the actual work performed and the concomitant particular risks and responsibilities in a particular case.[44]

The Court strongly advised administrators to keep detailed time records even though they might be bothersome to keep, pointing out that knowledge of the "time expended in work performed on the estate" would "aid the probate court in the determination of the appropriate fee." The Supreme Court went out of its way, however, to point out that the probate court should not base its determination of fees simply on the time records submitted but rather "the goal is to give the probate court a clearer picture of the time and nature of the work involved instead of just a bottom-line statement of the size of the estate."

The *Rolfe* case was remanded to the probate court for further consideration in accordance with the rulings of the Supreme Court. On remand, the probate court conducted an evidentiary hearing on both administrator's fees and attorneys' fees and rendered a decision which established fees for the administrator at almost exactly the same level as the probate court had established under the prior probate fee guidelines. See the Appendix of Forms for a copy of that decision.

Interestingly, the issue was a corporate fiduciary's request for fees where the corporate fiduciary had no time records and had, as did most corporate fiduciaries, in the past charged solely on a percentage basis. The probate court reviewed the history and reputations of the two bank officers who actually rendered the services on behalf of the corporate fiduciary. The court weighed heavily the experience of the officers and accepted the officers' testimony that their time had a value of $135 and $100 per hour, respectively, based on time records compiled by the bank retroactively after the Supreme Court decision.

The heirs in this estate appealed the second *Rolfe* case, objecting to the amount of the fees and the award of interest to the attorney, but the Supreme Court declined the appeal.

---

[44] In re Estate of Rolfe, 136 N.H. 294, 615 A.2d 625 (1992). See also McDonald, The Rolfe Decision: Its Practical Implications for Probate Attorneys, Vol. 3, No. 20, N.H. BAR NEWS 5 (1993).

The National Probate Court Standards, [45] as promulgated by the Commission on National Probate Court Standards, further provides that fiduciaries are entitled to reasonable compensation. [46] The Standards provide that seven factors should be considered in determining reasonable compensation:

the usual and customary fees charged within that community; responsibilities and risks (including exposure to liability) associated with the services provided;

- the size of the estate or the character of the services required, including the complexity of the matters involved;

- the amount of time required to perform the services provided; the skill and expertise required to perform the services;

- the experience, reputation, and ability of the person providing the services; and

- the benefit of the services provided. [47]

Library References

Am Jur 2d Executors and Administrators §§ 923, 925, 928–50

CJS Executors and Administrators §§ 867–70

§ 24-3(b). Prior Rule

Before *Rolfe*, the rule in this state was that an administrator was allowed reasonable compensation for his services depending upon the facts of the particular estate but that the compensation could take the form of a commission calculated as a percentage of the value of the gross estate. In 1973, the probate judges adopted a fee schedule to govern fees allowed by administrators on the administration of estates. [48] This schedule was followed by all of the probate judges and provided

---

[45] National Center for State Courts, 300 Newport Avenue, P.O. Box 8798, Williamsburg, Virginia 23187-8798, Library of Congress Catalog No. 93-87566, p. 46 (1993).

[46] NATIONAL PROBATE COURT STANDARDS, STANDARD 3.1.5.

[47] COMMISSION ON NATIONAL PROBATE COURT STANDARDS, NATIONAL PROBATE COURT STANDARDS pp. 46, 47.

[48] Gordon v. West, 8 N.H. 444 (1837).

"maximum" combined fees for administrators and attorneys, based upon a commission approach, allowing as reasonable fees a certain specified percentage of the value of the estate, depending upon its size.[49]

In many instances the amount charged for the administrator's services was graduated according to the amount of the funds involved, but in others the amount received and paid reflected no certain criterion.[50] Some general criteria were: how many sums had been received, the risk involved, and the amount of trouble involved in the disbursement of the sums.[51] Courts considered the time, care, risk, and responsibility necessarily involved in the administration of the estate.[52]

The determination of the amount allowed always rested in the sound discretion of the court.[53] Two and one-half percent of the amount of the money collected and accounted for was held to be the normal commission for an administrator.[54] A commission of 2% was held sufficient where the activities involved in handling the estate's money were slight.[55]

A commission was also allowed on money loaned, services rendered in loaning and collecting and guaranteeing payment.[56] In particular, a 1% commission on money loaned to the estate was ruled to be sufficient.[57] Once the commission was arrived at it became a charge upon the estate.[58]

Executors were allowed to charge for their services in accordance with the law of another state where the will provided for entitlement to full commissions as provided for by the law of that state.[59]

---

[49] Gordon v. West, 8 N.H. 444, 451 (1837).

[50] Lucy v. Lucy, 55 N.H. 9 (1874).

[51] Lucy v. Lucy, 55 N.H. 9, 10, 11 (1874).

[52] Wendell v. French, 19 N.H. 205 (1848).

[53] McInnes v. Goldthwaite, 94 N.H. 331, 52 A.2d 795 (1947).

[54] McInnes v. Goldthwaite, 94 N.H. 331, 337, 52 A.2d 795, 800 (1947).

[55] See Fees Appendix.

[56] See § 15-4(e) supra for a further discussion of this schedule, which is relevant to the amount of administrative fees allowable in the probate courts. Edward's Estate, 312 Ill. App. 645, 39 N.E. 72 (1942).

[57] McInnes v. Goldthwaite, 94 N.H. 331, 52 A.2d 795 (1947); Lucy v. Lucy, 55 N.H. 9 (1874); Gordon v. West, 8 N.H. 444 (1837).

[58] McInnes v. Goldthwaite, 94 N.H. 331, 52 A.2d 795 (1947).

[59] Id.

Library References

Am Jur 2d Executors and Administrators §§ 923, 925, 928–50

CJS Executors and Administrators §§ 967–70

Loss or depreciation of assets for which executor, administrator, or trustee is not responsible, as affecting the amount of his compensation. 110 ALR 994.

Validity and effect of provision in will limiting amount of fees of executor or trustee. 34 ALR 918, supplemented 161 ALR 870, superseded 19 ALR3d 520.

Authority of probate court to depart from statutory fee schedule fixing amount of executor's commissions and attorneys' fees. 40 ALR4th 1189.

Right to double compensation where same person (natural or corporate) acts as executor and trustee. 85 ALR2d 597.

§ 24-3(c). Disallowance of Compensation

The probate court may reduce or deny a request for compensation for an administrator. Where an executor's compensation is reduced or denied by a probate court, it is not done for the purpose of imposing a penalty upon him for committing a breach of trust, but on the ground that he has not properly performed the services for which compensation is given.[60] RSA 547:2-a provides that a probate judge designated to be full-time is not permitted to engage in the practice of law to any degree.

In *In re Estate of McCool*,[61] the Supreme Court wholly denied an executor any compensation for his services as administrator where he engaged in conflicts of interest as both attorney for the estate and as administrator. Indeed, the Court in this case held further that the administrator could be surcharged where loss to the estate occurred because of his failure to liquidate assets of the estate in a quick and expeditious manner.

Library References

Am Jur 2d Executors and Administrators §§ 951–59

CJS Executors and Administrators § 876

§ 24-3(d). Procedure for Approval

According to Probate Court Rule 36, an administrator should not pay himself compensation without the prior approval of the probate court. If an administrator "takes his fee" or some portion of it prior to probate

---

[60] Gordon v. West, 8 N.H. 444 (1837).

[61] In re Estate of McCool, 131 N.H. 340, 553 A.2d 761 (1988).

court approval, he runs the risk of subsequent disapproval causing him to be obliged to return the funds with interest.

Under the *Rolfe* case,[62] the Supreme Court directed that the probate courts hold a hearing in each case "to determine what fees are reasonable." Furthermore, the Court stated that "it is fundamentally unfair to the heirs and beneficiaries to require them to contest the requested executors' fees in order to obtain court determination of their reasonableness. The probate court's role is not merely to 'rubber stamp' the requested fees, but rather to exercise its discretion in each case to determine what fees are reasonable."[63]

Pursuant to the direction of the Supreme Court in *Rolfe*, the probate court has promulgated and required the use of forms to be submitted to the probate court for approval whenever an account is filed requesting attorneys' or administrators' fees. In addition Probate Court Administrative Order 97-01 (rescinded effective 8/1/01) required that for all estates, every executor and administrator must file a Statement Concerning Fees (included in Form AOC 44) with the Register of Probate when the inventory is filed.

Library References

Am Jur 2d Executors and Administrators §§ 922–59

CJS Executors and Administrators §§ 877–80

Library References

See section Chapter 15, *supra*, on the issue of reasonable attorneys' fees.

Forms

See Appendix for Form AOC 44 Statement Concerning Fees included in Inventory of Fiduciary.

§ 24-3(e). Uniform Probate Code Provisions

Section 3-719 of the Uniform Probate Code provides that an administrator is entitled to "reasonable compensation." The compensation claimed by an administrator is reviewable by the probate court, after

---

[62] In re Estate of Rolfe, 136 N.H. 294, 615 A.2d 625 (1992). See also McDonald, *The Rolfe Decision: Its Practical Implications for Probate Attorneys*, Vol. 3, No. 20, N.H. BAR NEWS 5 (1993).

[63] In re Estate of Rolfe, 136 N.H. 294, 615 A.2d 625 (1992). See also McDonald, *The Rolfe Decision: Its Practical Implications for Probate Attorneys*, Vol. 3, No. 20, N.H. BAR NEWS 5 (1993).

notice to all parties, only upon the "petition of an interested party and any compensation found by the court to be excessive, will be ordered to be refunded. U.P.C. § 3-721. It is the Code's "theory that personal representatives may fix their own fees" and this "works an important departure from existing practice under which fees are determined by the court in the first instance."[64]

Library References

Am Jur 2d Executors and Administrators §§ 922, 924

§ 24-4. Necessity of "Estate"

Administration should be granted on the estate of a decedent, resident or nonresident, in the county where he had estate.[65] Death alone is not enough to justify the exercise of the appointive authority:

> Administration is thus to be granted 'on the estate' of a decedent resident, and as to a decedent non-resident, in any county where he 'had estate.' Death alone is not enough to justify the exercise of the appointive authority, nor is it permitted by any reason or occasion other than estate. For both resident and non-resident decedents there must be estate within the legislative meaning of the word. By the constitution . . . probate courts have jurisdiction in granting administration, to be exercised in such manner as the legislature may direct. Their jurisdiction is exclusive . . . but they "have such powers and only such as the legislature gives them". . ..

> Confirmation of the need of estate is found in the amendatory act . . . by which the authority to appoint was extended to cases where the administrator or kin have a cause of action with a statutory survival in favor of certain designated beneficiaries exists. (Citations omitted.) Robinson v. Dana's Estate.[66]

The statute contains no requirement as to the amount of the estate which the deceased must have left in order to justify the appointment of a personal representative.[67] The prerequisite of proof of estate in an

---

[64] Comment, § 3-721, Uniform Probate Code.

[65] Robinson v. Dana's Estate, 87 N.H. 114, 174 A. 772 (1934); RSA 547:8.

[66] Robinson v. Dana's Estate, 87 N.H. 114, 115, 174 A. 772, 773, 774 (1934).

[67] Power v. Plummer, 93 N.H. 37, 35 A.2d 230 (1943). See also RSA 553:1 et seq.

appointment is often satisfied by a claim of estate,[68] and the right to prosecute a claim having value if finally proved meritorious is in itself sufficient.[69]

However, an appointment or refusal to appoint does not depend upon the probable merits of a decedent's title or claim.[70] If a claim is thought to be too doubtful to have an appraisal value, but someone having a proper interest demonstrates that it is worthwhile to be asserted, an appointment should be made.[71] Where a petitioner asserts that the estate has a claim against a third party, the probate court cannot deny an appointment on a ground that the claim is without merit, because the court has no jurisdiction to pass on a claim determinable in another tribunal.[72]

While assets of an estate brought into this state after the death of the owner confers jurisdiction upon the probate court and authorizes it to charge an administrator with the property,[73] if an individual dies possessed of estate in different states, it is generally necessary that an administration be granted in each state where the property is situated.[74] The principal administration is granted in the state of the domicile of the deceased.[75]

Library References

Am Jur 2d Executors and Administrators §§ 11–15, 91, 92, 157, 1185, 1187, 1193–94, 1204–08

CJS Executors and Administrators §§ 5–9, 990

Necessity and sufficiency of assets to justify appointment of administrator at domicile of decedent. 59 ALR 87.

---

[68] Robinson v. Dana's Estate, 87 N.H. 114, 174 A. 772 (1934).

[69] Robinson v. Dana's Estate, 87 N.H. 114, 174 A. 772 (1934); Boston & Maine R.R. v. Hurd, 108 F. 116 (1st Cir. 1901), cert. denied, 22 S. Ct. 939, 184 U.S. 700, 47 L. Ed 765; Cogswell v. Concord & Montreal R.R., 68 N.H. 192, 44 A. 293 (1895); Stearns v. Wright, 51 N.H. 600(1872).

[70] Robinson v. Dana's Estate, 87 N.H. 114, 174 A. 772 (1934).

[71] Id.

[72] Id.

[73] Power v. Plummer, 93 N.H. 37, 35 A.2d 230 (1943); Ela's Appeal, 68 N.H. 35, 38 A. 501 (1894); Stearns v. Wright, 51 N.H. 600 (1872).

[74] Clark v. Clement, 33 N.H. 563 (1856).

[75] Id.

§ 24-5. Petition for Appointment

The administration of an estate begins with the filing in the probate court of a petition requesting that administration of a decedent's estate be granted to the petitioner. The probate court has established Form 220 for this petition, which replaces Forms 79, 80 and 98.

The petition for appointment will not be heard in the probate court until accompanying forms required by the probate court are completed and filed.

The petition is customarily granted a few days after filing, without prior notice to the public. The probate court usually requires the attendance of an attorney for the petitioner, but not the petitioner himself.

§ 24-6. Letters of Administration

Upon appointment, the probate court issues a "letter of administration" to the petitioner. This is usually issued by the register of probate to the petitioner by mail, a few days after the petition for administration is granted.

The letter of administration is the formal notice to the world of the appointment of the petitioner as administrator. It is often referred to as the certificate of appointment.

An administrator may be required to purchase from the register of probate several certified copies of the letter of administration because stock registrars, banks, and many others dealing with the administrator will require that he prove his appointment by the production of the letter of appointment.

Library References

Am Jur 2d Executors and Administrators §§ 256–61

CJS Executors and Administrators §§ 69–71

§ 24-7. Notice of Appointment

Pursuant to RSA 553:16, notice by publication is required within fifteen days of an administrator's or executor's appointment. RSA 550:10 provides that it is the duty of the register of probate (not the administrator as previously required) to provide for publication, at the expense of the estate, in a newspaper of general circulation in the town or city where the decedent last resided. The publication must be for two successive weeks. RSA 553:16 also provides that no publication of notice is required in the administration of small estates under RSA 553:31.

RSA 552:15 requires all executors to give notice, within sixty days of his appointment, to the beneficiaries of a testate decedent or to the heirs at law of an intestate decedent. This notice is made by first class mail.[76] The executor must certify to the probate court his compliance with the statute within ninety days of his appointment.[77]

If an interested party has actual and reasonable notice of an administrator's appointment, he cannot object to the form and manner of the notice of appointment.[78]

Prior to 1973, it was the duty of the appointed administrator, after his give formal notice of his appointment to the public at large. This was done by causing an official legal notice of his appointment to be published in a newspaper of general circulation in the county where the decedent was an inhabitant and by posting notice of his appointment in some public place, usually the court house.

Library References

CJS Executors and Administrators § 70

Failure of personal representative to file proof of publication of notice of appointment or notice to creditors within specified time as tolling statute of limitations. 42 ALR2d 1218.

Forms

See Form 9 in Appendix for Appointment of Resident Agent.

See Form 10 in Appendix for Affidavit of Notice of Filing Account.

See Form 42 in Appendix for Declination.

See Form 73A in Appendix for Notice to Surviving Spouse, Legatees, Heirs at Law.

See Form 220 in Appendix for Petition for Estate Administration

---

[76] RSA 552:16.

[77] RSA 552:15.

[78] Davis v. Smith, 58 N.H. 16 (1876).

CHAPTER 25. CHOICE OF ADMINISTRATOR

§ 25-1. Right to Administer

At common law, administration of the estate of a person dying intestate belonged to no particular person.[1] At present, however, RSA 553:2 establishes the right to administer the estate of a decedent in the following persons:

I. To the executor named in his will.

II. To the widow, husband or any of the next of kin, or to such suitable person as they or any of them may nominate.

III. To one of the devisees or creditors.

IV. To such other person as the judge may think proper.

---

[1] Judge of Probate v. Chamberlain, 3 N.H. 129 (1824).

239

RSA 553:3 provides that this listing shall be in the order of descending priority:

> No person shall be appointed to administer an estate until the several persons previously entitled thereto shall have either voluntarily renounced the trust in writing, or neglected, for thirty days after the decease of the person upon whose estate administration is to be granted, to apply for administration.

The probate court, therefore, has no power to appoint anyone as administrator in a lower class if individuals in a higher class timely seek appointment. *Munsey v. Webster.*[2] The Supreme Court has held that a voluntary renunciation of a person named as a coexecutor in a will may be withdrawn and that letters of administration may be issued to one who has declined to serve if there is a vacancy in the office before someone of a lower class will be named.[3]

Library References

Am Jur 2d Executors and Administrators §§ 163–94

CJS Executors and Administrators §§ 30–45

§ 25-2. Declination

An individual may decline to serve as administrator for any reason, even though he falls into one of the priority classes. Someone in a lower class will not be appointed administrator until others in higher classes have "voluntarily renounced the trust" or have failed for thirty days after the death of a decedent to apply for administration. RSA 553:3.

Approved Form 42 found in Appendix must be filed with the Petition for Administration when someone with a lower priority seeks appointment as administrator.

In *In re Estate of Pafelis*,[4] it was held that a declination may be withdrawn in circumstances where the named executor had declined appointment due to ill health, but, because of an unexpected delay, recovered before another administrator had been appointed.

---

[2] Munsey v. Webster, 24 N.H. 126 (1851).

[3] In re Estate of Pafelis, 108 N.H. 265, 233 A.2d 825(1967).

[4] *Id.*

Library References

Am Jur 2d Executors and Administrators §§ 186, 225–31

CJS Executors and Administrators §§ 29, 47

§ 25-3. Suitability—In General

Although RSA 553:2 appears to speak in terms of an absolute right to become an administrator of an estate if an individual is included within the first three specific statutory categories ("shall be granted administration"), RSA 553:4 modifies this provision, by adding that no person "deemed by the judge [of probate] unsuitable" shall be appointed to administer an estate. Furthermore, by the language of RSA 553:2, II, if the decedent's spouse or next of kin cannot serve, administration should be granted "to such suitable person" as they may nominate.

In *In re Estate of Quirin*,[5] the Supreme Court propounded the standard for suitability:

> In determining whether a person is suitable to be an executor or trustee, the court should
> 'inquire carefully as to his character, integrity, soundness of judgment and general capacity . . ..' Also, certain conflicts of interest might render a person unsuitable. (Citations omitted.)[6]

The Supreme Court in the *Quirin* case also provided the probate practitioner with an excellent listing of the various factors influencing the choice of the administrator by a probate court: (1) substantial experience in managing finances, which is important in the administration of large estates," (2) being "a financial advisor and intimate family friend" of the decedent's family for many years, (3) being an attorney who "specializes in trust and estate matters," (4) "being a longtime personal friend of the family," (5) being the family "legal advisor" for many years, (6) being "personally acquainted with the family and its financial status," (7) "being able to perform the responsibilities of fiduciaries better than strangers could," (8) having already been appointed fiduciary of the decedent spouse's estate, (9) the consent of a majority of the beneficiaries of the estate to the appointment, (10) familiarity with New Hampshire probate procedure as a result of appointment as administrator in the decedent spouse's estate and (11) the fact that the petitioner

---

[5] In re Estate of Quirin, 116 N.H. 845, 367 A.2d 594 (1976).

[6] In re Estate of Quirin, 116 N.H. 845, 846, 367 A.2d 594, 595 (1976).

administrators have more familiarity with the decedent's estate than others.[7]

In *Drews' Appeals*,[8] the Supreme Court, in interpreting the suitability provision of RSA 553:2, II, held that no one should be appointed who is "incapable," and that the concept of incapability was not to be given a limited or narrow interpretation:

> The word "incapable" cannot be limited in its application to the mere case of mental or physical incapacity, but must be understood to include the idea of unfitness, unsuitableness. The use of the word "suitable" in the second section of the statute referred to, . . . favors this construction. An interest that disqualifies one from fairly considering the interest and claims of another in the same matter, renders him unsuitable to be intrusted with its management; and a feeling of hostility, so intense as to cause one to resist with personal violence the claims and rights of others held in common with him, not only renders him unfit for, but also practically incapable of, managing the common interest. The claim of [the petitioning administrator] against the estate is seriously disputed by the other heirs. The interest which the claim gives her in the settlement of the estate, and the feeling engendered by the dispute, render her incapable of properly executing the trust of administrator. The feelings of bitter hostility on the part of [another claimant] made him equally unfit for the place. The law does not encourage a private or family feud. Neither of the contending parties should be entrusted with the power of administration, because there is reason to fear their animosity would lead to an abuse of the trust.[9]

Where there are several persons of the same degree of kindred, the judge of probate should appoint the most suitable one.[10] An unsuitable person should not be appointed because any one aggrieved by the administrator's abuse of trust would have a remedy by petition for his removal and suit

---

[7] In re Estate of Quirin, 116 N.H. 845, 846–47, 367 A.2d 594, 595 (1976).

[8] Drews' Appeals, 58 N.H. 319 (1878).

[9] *Id.*

[10] Pickering v. Pendexter, 46 N.H. 69 (1865).

on his bond.[11] Such litigation should be avoided by a proper appointment in the first instance.[12]

Generally, an interest that disqualifies one from fairly considering the interest and claims of another in the same matter, renders him unsuitable to be entrusted with its management.[13] One whose interest is clearly opposed to that of persons for whom he acts should not be appointed to the trust.[14] Thus the power to administer an estate should not be conferred upon an adherent of any contending party who would be likely to use it wrongfully. *Graves v. Tilton.*[15] If the person appointed, in defending a suit or otherwise administering the estate, would act as an agent of certain claimants, or with any degree of illegal favoritism, some other person should be appointed who would understand the disinterested and equitable character of his fiduciary duty, and perform it without fear or favor.[16] Nor should administration be conferred upon one whose feeling of hostility is so intense as to cause him to resist with personal violence the claims and rights of others held in common with him.[17] Thus, brothers' and sisters' feelings of bitter hostility toward each other precluded their being appointed to administer their deceased parent's estate.[18]

Library References

Am Jur 2d Executors and Administrators §§ 195–210

CJS Executors and Administrators §§ 28, 46

Physical condition as affecting competency to act as executors and administrators. 71 ALR3d 675.

Adverse interest or position as disqualification for appointment of administrator, executor, or other personal representative. 11 ALR4th 638.

§ 25-3(a). Executor Named in the Will

RSA 553:2 places an executor who has been nominated by a testator in the first class of those who are entitled to administration. In *Carr v.*

---

[11] Graves v. Tilton, 63 N.H. 192 (1884).

[12] *Id.*

[13] Drews' Appeals, 58 N.H. 319 (1878); Pickering v. Pendexter, 46 N.H. 69 (1865).

[14] Pickering v. Pendexter, 46 N.H. 69 (1865).

[15] Graves v. Tilton, 63 N.H. 192 (1884).

[16] *Id.*

[17] Drews' Appeals, 58 N.H. 319 (1878).

[18] *Id.*

Corning, the Supreme Court emphasized that although a testator may nominate a particular individual to act as his executor or testamentary trustee, the choice could be rejected by the probate court if it found the person nominated unsuitable, thus establishing the general rule that "the probate court must decide that the person named in the will is a suitable person" to administer the estate as executor.[19] Therefore, the person nominated as executor by a decedent's will is not entitled to be appointed executor of the estate as a matter of right.

The Supreme Court promulgated the more modern view of the discretion of the probate court in *In re Estate of Quirin*:[20] The

> testatrix specifically nominated the plaintiffs in her will. Although her choice is not necessarily controlling, it is entitled to great weight, and the court's objection to suitability must be strong to justify refusing the appointment.[21]

Where a will nominates a spouse or lineal descendant to represent the interests of unborn or unascertained persons, the court, unless good cause is shown, should comply with the expressed desire of the decedent even though those nominated may be personally interested in the estate.[22]

It is not unusual for a testator to request that his attorney serve as administrator of his estate, either alone or with others. There is nothing improper about this practice, but the attorney must use care not to "consciously influence a client to name him as executor, trustee, or lawyer in an instrument."[23]

Likewise, the New Hampshire Bar Association's Ethics Committee has issued a Formal Opinion, 1987-819 which concluded that nothing in the Rules of Professional Conduct adopted by the Supreme Court February 1, 1986 prohibits a lawyer from being named as a fiduciary in a will which he has drafted.[24]

---

[19] Carr v. Corning, 73 N.H. 362, 62 A. 168 (1905).

[20] In re Estate of Quirin, 116 N.H. 845, 367 A.2d 594 (1976).

[21] In re Estate of Quirin, 116 N.H. 845, 367 A.2d 594 (1976); RSA 553:4.

[22] RSA 553:12-a.

[23] Ethical Consideration (EC) 5–6, Code of Professional Responsibility (adopted in N.H. on February 1, 1986).

[24] *Id.*

Library References

Am Jur 2d Executors and Administrators §§ 159, 162

CJS Executors and Administrators §§ 22

Construction and operation of will or trust provision appointing advisors to trustee or executor. 56 ALR3d 1249.

§ 25-3(b). Widows, Husbands, and Next of Kin

The judge of probate has no power to appoint a stranger as administrator until the widow or husband and next of kin have severally renounced the administration,[25] in writing,[26] or have neglected to apply for it in thirty days,[27] or have nominated some suitable person for the trust.[28] For instance, where decedent's mother neglected for some twenty-two months to apply for administration, she lost any preference she may have had to be appointed.[29]

Within the second priority class created by RSA 553:2, II, widows or husbands have no preference over the next of kin.[30] This rule is founded upon dicta in the ancient case of *Munsey v. Webster*,[31] which involved that portion of what is now RSA 553:2, II relating to the nomination of a suitable person by the widow or husband and the next of kin.

In these modern times, however, it would be very surprising if the surviving spouse of a decedent would not, as a practical matter, have a preference of appointment over the next of kin of a decedent.

Munsey v. Webster,[32] though, does stand for the proposition that a spouse may not nominate an administrator to the exclusion of the right which is given to the next of kin by RSA 553:2, II. The spouse and the next of kin must severally decline to administer the estate or have all agreed to the nomination of another administrator.[33] The provision of

---

[25] Munsey v. Webster, 24 N.H. 126 (1851).

[26] *Id.*

[27] Drews' Appeals, 58 N.H. 319 (1878).

[28] Drews' Appeals, 58 N.H. 319 (1878); Munsey v. Webster, 24 N.H. 126 (1851).

[29] Munsey v. Webster, 24 N.H. 126 (1851).

[30] Saurman v. Liberty, 116 N.H. 73, 354 A.2d 132 (1976).

[31] Munsey v. Webster, 24 N.H. 126, 127 (1851).

[32] *Id.*

[33] RSA 553:3; Munsey v. Webster, 24 N.H. 126 (1851).

RSA 553:2, II for the nomination of the administrator by the next of kin was not intended to take from those persons any right they had before, but to give them the additional right to agree in the nomination of another person, whom the judge would be bound to appoint.[34] A stranger is not appointed.[35] The judge of probate, when any one of the next of kin is a suitable person, has no power to appoint another unless that person has been nominated by the widow and next of kin, who all must concur in it.[36]

If there are persons of kin to the deceased who are residents of New Hampshire and suitable for the trust, they would be entitled as a matter of right to administer as against one who does not reside in this state.[37]

Prior to 1860, it had been held that a husband who survived his wife was entitled to her personal estate and choses in action and had a right to administer her estate.[38] If he died before he had completed administration, his right to administer the property would go to his heirs.[39] Currently, however, RSA 553:2 unequivocally places widows and surviving husbands in the second class of those who are entitled to administration. The subsequent remarriage of the widow does not, as was previously true,[40] extinguish her right to administer her former husband's estate. RSA 553:9.

The surviving spouse and the next of kin are in the second class of those who are entitled to administration under RSA 553:2, II.[41] Judge Smith has observed that in New Hampshire pre-revolutionary era, the eldest son of a decedent was considered to have a superior claim to be administrator over other children.[42] But by 1743, it was established that no child had a preference over another.[43]

---

[34] Munsey v. Webster, 24 N.H. 126 (1851).

[35] See § 23-3(d).

[36] Munsey v. Webster, 24 N.H. 126 (1851).

[37] Pickering v. Pendexter, 46 N.H. 69 (1865).

[38] Weeks v. Jewitt, 45 N.H. 540 (1864).

[39] Hayes v. Seavey, 69 N.H. 308, 46 A. 189 (1898); Weeks v. Jewett, 45 N.H. 540 (1864); Judge of Probate v. Chamberlain, 3 N.H. 129 (1824).

[40] Hayes v. Seavey, 69 N.H. 308, 46 A. 189 (1898); Atherton v. McQuesten, 46 N.H. 205 (1865); Weeks v. Jewett, 45 N.H. 540 (1864); Judge of Probate v. Chamberlain, 3 N.H. 129 (1824).

[41] Roberts v. Place, 18 N.H. 183 (1846).

[42] Smith, *Manuscript Treatise on Probate Law*, SMITH'S REPORTS p. 518 (1879).

[43] Id.

Library References
Am Jur 2d Executors and Administrators §§ 169–79
CJS Executors and Administrators §§ 35–36

§ 25-3(c). Devisees and Creditors

RSA 553:2, III places devisees and creditors of the decedent in the third priority class of those who are entitled to administer an estate. Presumably, using the reasoning of *Munsey v. Webster*,[44] the statutory provision creates no preference between devisees and creditors.[45]

Subject to the rights of individuals with a higher priority, a creditor, under RSA 553:2, III, may petition for an appointment of an administrator.[46] This provision aids citizens of this state in collecting debts from property within this jurisdiction, belonging to the estates of their debtors.[47] Creditors are entitled to administration thirty days after the debtor's death if others entitled to administration have not applied for it within that time.[48] A person chosen by a creditor may be appointed administrator, as in a case where a creditor-plaintiff had the secretary of the plaintiff's attorney appointed.[49]

Generally, if there is property of the decedent which a creditor is entitled to, and the creditor finds the property in a certain county of the state, he may properly be appointed administrator of the estate in that county.[50] Since the debtor's death does not defeat the creditor's rights to reach the assets, their right to have an administrator appointed is a necessary incident of their right to reach the assets.[51]

If a creditor wishes to exercise the right to administer, he must act within a reasonable time after he learns of the death of the debtor.[52] If action is not attempted within a reasonable time, the creditor may be

---

[44] Munsey v. Webster, 24 N.H. 126 (1851).

[45] RSA 553:3. See also Munsey v. Webster, 24 N.H. 126 (1851) and the discussion *supra* at § 23-3(c).

[46] Robinson v. Estate of Dana, 87 N.H. 114, 174 A. 772 (1934).

[47] Stearns v. Wright, 51 N.H. 600 (1872).

[48] Hatch v. Kelly, 63 N.H. 29 (1884); RSA 553:3.

[49] Saurman v. Liberty, 116 N.H. 73, 354 A.2d 132 (1976).

[50] Stearns v. Wright, 51 N.H. 600 (1872).

[51] Robinson v. Estate of Dana, 87 N.H. 114, 174 A. 772 (1934).

[52] RSA 553:2, 553:3.

barred by laches.[53] Delays of seven years,[54] nine years[55] and forty-seven years[56] have been deemed unreasonable.

There is no requirement that a petitioning creditor prove his claim to be valid before the petition is granted.[57] It is enough if he claims honestly and seasonably to be a creditor.[58] This rule is illustrated in *Robinson v. Estate of Dana*,[59] where the Supreme Court held that:

> [T]he prerequisite of proof of estate in an appointment is often satisfied by a claim of estate. This follows from the nature of things. When the decedent's title to his only property is in dispute, the probate court does not try the issue as determinative whether an administrator shall be appointed, but appoints one so that the rights of the decedent's estate may not be lost through non-assertion. Appointment or refusal to appoint does not depend upon the probable merits of the decedent's title or claim. It may be thought too doubtful to have appraisal value, but if anyone having a proper interest deems it worth while to be asserted, an appointment should be made. The right to prosecute a claim having value if finally proved meritorious is in itself sufficient to meet the statutory test of estate.[60]

Library References

Am Jur 2d Executors and Administrators §§ 180–81

CJS Executors and Administrators § 41

§ 25-3(d). Strangers

RSA 553:2, IV provides that a fourth and last priority of those entitled to administer an estate are "such other persons as the judge may think proper." No relationship by blood, acquaintance or otherwise, is required of individuals in this class, although, no one unsuitable may be appointed

---

[53] Jones v. Herbert, 77 N.H. 282, 90 A. 854 (1914); Whidden v. Whidden, 67 N.H. 303, 32 A. 152 (1893).

[54] Hatch v. Kelly, 63 N.H. 29 (1884).

[55] Whidden v. Whidden, 67 N.H. 303, 32 A. 152 (1893).

[56] Jones v. Herbert, 77 N.H. 282, 90 A. 584 (1914).

[57] Robinson v. Estate of Dana, 87 N.H. 114, 174 A. 772 (1934).

[58] *Id.*

[59] *Id.*

[60] Robinson v. Estate of Dana, 87 N.H. 114, 116, 174 A. 772, 774 (1934).

pursuant to RSA 553:4. Complete strangers to the decedent or the heirs may be appointed administrator. However, the "judge of probate has no power to appoint a stranger administrator" until individuals in higher classes of priority have failed to apply for administration within thirty days of the decedent's death. RSA 553:3; *Munsey v. Webster.*[61]

Library References

Am Jur 2d Executors and Administrators §§ 182–89

CJS Executors and Administrators § 42

Propriety of court's appointment, as administrator of decedent's estate, of stranger rather than person having statutory preference. 84 ALR3d 707.

§ 25-3(e). Executor of an Executor

RSA 553:8 provides that the executor of an executor does not automatically become the executor of the first testator upon the death of the first executor. Of course, the second executor may, under RSA 553:2, be granted administration of the first testator, if he qualifies under that statute.

Library References

Am Jur 2d Executors and Administrators §§ 167, 190–94

CJS Executors and Administrators § 44

§ 25-3(f). Marriage of Female Administrator

It was previously held that the marriage of an administratrix, who was a feme sole, extinguished her authority as an administratrix.[62] RSA 553:9 currently provides that if an executrix or administratrix marries, her husband shall not thereby become executor or administrator in her right, but she may continue to exercise the trust as before.

Library References

CJS Executors and Administrators § 46

§ 25-3(g). Minors

RSA 553:4 precludes persons under the age of majority (18) from serving as administrators. If a minor is nominated as executor by a decedent, he may, upon coming of age, request that administration of

---

[61] Munsey v. Webster, 24 N.H. 126 (1851).

[62] Roberts v. Place, 18 N.H. 183 (1846).

the estate, if not already administered, be granted to him. RSA 553:6. His appointment revokes the prior administration unless the minor is nominated as a coexecutor, in which case, the minor (now having reached majority) becomes a joint executor. RSA 553:6.

Library References

Am Jur 2d Executors and Administrators §§ 177–78

CJS Executors and Administrators §§ 37, 39

Right of guardian of infant or incompetent to appointment as executor or administrator as representative or substitute for infant or incompetent. 135 ALR 585.

Right of minor next of kin to apply through next friend for appointment of administrator. 161 ALR 1389.

Capacity of infant to act as executor or administrator, and effect of improper appointment. 8 ALR3d 590.

§ 25-3(h). Nonresidents

RSA 553:5 provides that:

No person not an inhabitant of this state shall be so appointed [to administer an estate of a New Hampshire decedent] by reason of a right to such trust, unless other circumstances, in the opinion of the judge, render the same proper.[63]

The Supreme Court has interpreted this to mean:

A person not a resident of this State cannot claim appointment as a matter of right (Crosby v. Charlestown, 78 N.H. 39, 95 A. 1043 (1915)) but he is not disqualified simply because he is a nonresident. Pickering v. Pendexter, 46 N.H. 69 (1865). The probate court must find that the nonresident is suitable and that "other circumstances" within the meaning of the statute render the appointment proper. In re Estate of Quirin.[64]

However, a probate judge is not free under this statute arbitrarily to reject nonresident petitioners.[65] Great weight will be given to the

---

[63] See RSA 21:6 for a definition of inhabitant for purposes of statutory construction.

[64] In re Estate of Quirin, 116 N.H. 845, 367 A.2d 594 (1976).

[65] Id.

testator's choice of nonresident individuals and a probate "court's objection to suitability must be strong to justify refusing appointment."[66]

In *In re Estate of Quirin*,[67] the Supreme Court overturned a probate court's refusal to appoint as executors nonresident individuals nominated by the testator, finding that:

> "Other circumstances," within meaning of RSA 553:5, justified appointment of coexecutors and cotrustees, New York residents, where will named them, one was a retired bank executive with substantial financial management experience and had been a financial advisor and intimate friend of the family for over forty years and the other was a member of the New York bar specializing in trusts and estates and a longtime friend of the family and legal advisor for over twenty years, the stock constituting most of the estate was in New York and they managed the stock, they were the nonresident coexecutors and cotrustees under the will of the estate of the spouse of decedent, there were no family members living in New Hampshire, the majority of the beneficiaries had consented to their appointment, they were familiar with New Hampshire law on estates, and no New Hampshire resident was as familiar with the family's fortunes and personal lives as they were.[68]

The Supreme Court also cited to an earlier *Opinion of the Justices*,[69] in which the Court had emphasized the principle that in New Hampshire:

> [t]he right of an individual to dispose of his property by will to individuals, public and private corporations, charities and public entities . . . is singularly free from restrictions or limitations, constitutional, statutory or judicial."[70]

In *Pickering v. Pendexter*, it was held that "other circumstances" which justified the appointment of a nonresident sister of the decedent as administrator, instead of the resident brother, were the fact that his

---

[66] In re Estate of Quirin, 116 N.H. 845, 847, 367 A.2d 594, 595 (1976).

[67] *Id.*

[68] In re Estate of Quirin, 116 N.H. 845, 847, 367 A.2d 594, 595–96 (1976).

[69] Opinion of the Justices, 109 N.H. 335, 251 A.2d 330 (1969).

[70] Opinion of the Justices, 109 N.H. 335, 335–36, 251 A.2d 330 (1969).

interests were clearly opposed to that of the persons for whom he would act.[71]

If a nonresident is appointed to administer the estate of a New Hampshire decedent, RSA 553:25 requires him to appoint a person residing in this state as his agent "to receive notice of claims against the estate" and to receive service of process against him as administrator or executor. This person is customarily referred to as the "resident agent." It is customary that the New Hampshire attorney for the nonresident administrator be appointed resident agent.

This same rule requiring an agent for notice and service of process applies to resident administrators who, after appointment, move from the state with the intention of being absent for more than one year. RSA 553:5.

RSA 553:25, requiring the appointment of an agent by a nonresident administrator, was enacted to facilitate the due, expeditious and convenient administration of estates, and not to prevent the loss of jurisdiction.[72] It does not apply to nonresident testamentary trustees and there is no requirement that a nonresident testamentary trustee appointed by a New Hampshire probate court appoint a resident agent. *Arnold v. Hay.*[73]

A registered agent of a nonresident administrator is the proper party to receive service of process, not only against the estate itself but also against the nonresident administrator as administrator or executor. *Hall v. Koch.*[74] While a nonresident as executor is not personally present in the state, his status as executor is local and he is considered to be present here and subject to the courts of this state.[75]

A nonresident administrator cannot defend against a lawsuit brought against him in his capacity as duly appointed administrator of the estate of a New Hampshire decedent by asserting that he is a nonresident and

---

[71] Pickering v. Pendexter, 46 N.H. 69 (1865).

[72] Lisbon Sav. Bank & Trust Co. v. Estate of Moulton, 91 N.H. 477, 22 A.2d 331 (1941).

[73] Arnold v. Hay, 95 N.H. 499, 66 A.2d 705 (1949).

[74] Hall v. Koch, 119 N.H. 639, 406 A.2d 962 (1979).

[75] Lisbon Sav. Bank & Trust Co. v. Estate of Moulton, 91 N.H. 477, 22 A.2d 331 (1941).

not subject to suit. *Lisbon Savings Bank & Trust Co. v. Estate of Moulton.*[76]

> The legal concept is analogous to that of a corporation. As an artificial person distinct from himself as an individual, an executor is a creation of the law, belonging in the state of his appointment and at all times subject to its jurisdiction, with no legal residence elsewhere. Accepting the appointment, he accepts the doctrine that he shall be regarded in his capacity as executor as a subject of the State, and not as an alien or nonresident. While as executor he is where he may be in person, his status as executor is local.[77]

The appointment of a nonresident administrator agent must be in writing, must state the agent's full name and post office address, and must be filed in the register of probate's office. RSA 553:26. Furthermore, the notice of the administrator's appointment must include the name and post office address of the resident agent, and failure to comply with these provisions is cause for a nonresident's removal as administrator. RSA 553:28.

If the resident agent leaves the state, becomes incapacitated, or if there is a vacancy in the position for any reason, the nonresident administrator must immediately appoint another agent. RSA 553:27.

A resident agent is appointed by simply filing with the probate court, at the time of filing the nonresident's Petition for Administration, Approved Probate Court Form 9.

Library References

Am Jur 2d Executors and Administrators §§ 218–24

CJS Executors and Administrators §§ 28, 46

Who is a resident within meaning of statute prohibiting appointment of nonresident executor or administrator. 4 ALR4th 1223.

§ 25-3(i). Multiple Fiduciary Appointments

Although it is not forbidden by statute to occupy more than one appointed fiduciary position (e.g., conservator, guardian, executor,

---

[76] Lisbon Sav. Bank & Trust Co. v. Estate of Moulton, 91 N.H. 477, 22 A.2d 331 (1941).

[77] Id.

testamentary trustee) and it is common for individuals to be appointed to successive fiduciary positions, there are hazards involved in such multiple appointments. A fiduciary may more easily conceal breaches of trust by embezzlement or other improper conduct.[78] Or, an attorney for an estate who also serves as administrator, may be involved in conflicts of interest which will taint his service as administrator.[79]

Library References

Am Jur 2d Executors and Administrators § 1097 et seq.

CJS Executors and Administrators §§ 1041–47

§ 25-3(j). Corporate Fiduciaries

Effective June 2, 1994, the prohibition against foreign corporations acting as trustees and executors in New Hampshire was repealed in a limited provision as follows:

> Any trust company or similar corporation incorporated under the laws of any other state or any national bank having its principal place of business in any other state may be appointed trustee or executor as provided in this section if the state in which such trust company or similar corporation incorporated under the laws of that state or any national bank duly authorized and having its principal place of business in that state similarly allows any trust company or similar corporation incorporated under the laws of this state and any national bank duly authorized and located within this state to serve as appointed trustees or executors in that state. RSA 390:13 II.

Until 1935, a corporate institution such as a bank or trust company was statutorily prohibited from acting as an administrator of an estate in New Hampshire.[80] However, in 1935, the legislature enacted the predecessor of RSA 390:13, which specifically authorized:

---

[78] American Fidelity Co. v. Barnard, 104 N.H. 146, 181 A.2d 628 (1962); American Fidelity Co. v. Barnard, 104 N.H. 155, 182 A.2d 471 (1962); Barnard's Case, 101 N.H. 33, 131 A.2d 630 (1957); 101 N.H. 141, 135 A.2d 902 (1957). See also In re Estate of Ward, 129 N.H. 4, 523 A.2d 28 (1986).

[79] In re Estate of McCool, 131 N.H. 340, 553 A.2d 761 (1988).

[80] N.H. Session Laws ch. 109 § 34 (1915); Appeal of Woodbury, 78 N.H. 50, 96 A. 299 (1915).

> Any trust company or similar corporation, incorporated under the laws of this state, or any national bank duly authorized and located within the state, may be appointed trustee or executor in any case where an individual can be appointed, upon the same conditions and subject to the same control, requirements, and penalties.

This statute, found in the banking laws and not the probate statutes, also empowers New Hampshire banks and trust companies to act as resident agents or as "receiver, assignee or agent for any person, firm, association or corporation, public or private; and in all proceedings in court or elsewhere in relation to such trusts or agencies, all accounts and other papers may be signed and sworn to in behalf of the corporation by any officer duly authorized."

It should be noted that the bank administrator statute applies only to New Hampshire banks and trust companies. RSA 390:15. It was held that the statute did not authorize foreign banking corporations to act as fiduciaries in New Hampshire. *Bank of New York and Trust Co. v. Tilton*;[85] *In re Estate of Farnsworth*.[86] However, as the Supreme Court in the *Farnsworth* case makes clear, a New Hampshire decedent may provide for a foreign bank to act as fiduciary of her estate (here a testamentary trustee) where: the will is drafted and executed in a foreign state, the substantial majority of the New Hampshire decedent's assets are located there, and the New Hampshire decedent provides in her will that the testamentary trusts created therein are to be administered by the laws of that foreign state.

Until 1979, the corporate fiduciary statute contained an additional provision which prohibited banks and trust companies from advertising or circulating the fact that they were authorized to act as executor.[81] New Hampshire commercial banks tried to overturn this advertising prohibition, which it argued conflicted with federal law in *New Hampshire Bankers Association v. Nelson*.[82] Both the United States District Court for the District of New Hampshire and the United States Court of Appeals

---

[85] Bank of New York & Trust Co. v. Tilton, 82 N.H. 81, 120 A. 492 (1925).

[86] In re Estate of Farnsworth, 109 N.H. 15, 241 A.2d 204 (1968).

[81] R.L. 1935, 312:13.

[82] New Hampshire Bankers Ass'n v. Nelson, 336 F. Supp. 1330 (D.N.H. 1972), *aff'd*, 460 F.2d 307 (1st Cir. 1972), *cert. denied*, 409 U.S. 1001, 13 S. Ct. 320 (1972).

for the First Circuit upheld the New Hampshire prohibition and the United States Supreme Court denied a petition for a writ of certiorari filed by the Bankers Association.[83] The bankers finally won in the legislative field when the New Hampshire legislature repealed the advertising prohibition in 1979.[84]

Library References

Am Jur 2d Executors and Administrators § 199

CJS Executors and Administrators § 46

Eligibility of foreign corporation to appoint as executor, administrator, or testamentary trustee. 26 ALR3d 1019.

§ 25-3(k). Department of Revenue Administration

The inheritance tax statute, RSA 86:35, contains a provision which allows the Department of Revenue Administration to apply to the probate court to appoint an administrator for an estate liable for inheritance taxes if no one seeks administration for four months after the decedent's death. Any administrator so appointed shall be entitled to recover expenses of administration, including reasonable compensation, and expenses of necessary litigation or expenses of recovering property subject to the inheritance tax. RSA 86:36. Such expenses are to be paid in the first instance from the state treasury but are a charge upon any property of the estate for ultimate recovery. The provisions of RSA 86:36 and RSA 86:37 make clear that the personal liability of any such administrator is limited "to such taxes as he may, by the exercise of reasonable diligence, recover."

Forms

See Approved Probate Court Form 9 in Appendix for a Appointment of Resident Agent.

See Approved Probate Court Form 42 in Appendix for a Declination.

See Approved Probate Court Form 220 in Appendix for a Petition for Estate Administration.

---

[83] *Id.*

[84] See Opinion of the Justices, 99 N.H. 524, 113 A.2d 542 (1955) where the New Hampshire Supreme Court declined a request to issue an advisory opinion on the advertising prohibition contained in the former statute.

CHAPTER 26. REOPENING ESTATES FOR NEWLY DISCOVERED ASSETS

§ 26-1. Generally
§ 26-2. Required Procedures

§ 26-1. Generally

The administrative judge of the probate court in Probate Court Procedure Bulletin 17 has provided a required procedure to be followed "if newly discovered assets require a closed estate to be reopened." The effective date of this new procedure is August 1, 2000.

§ 26-2. Required Procedures

The procedure to be followed depends upon whether the same fiduciary who was appointed in the initial petition seeks to reopen the estate or whether a new fiduciary seeks to be appointed. In the case of an identical fiduciary seeking to reopen the estate, the fiduciary simply files a motion to "bring forward (reopen)" the estate. In the case of a new fiduciary, a petition for administration (Form 220) or a voluntary administration affidavit (Form 148) and an appearance or withdrawal form (Form 007) must be filed with the motion.

The motion to bring forward must include the appropriate list of heirs or legatees (Forms 101/101A) and, if necessary, a resident agent form (Form 009). If the estate is taxable, the Department of Revenue Administration must be included as an interested party. Furthermore, a **Rule 3** Certification is required for all motions to bring forward.

The motion to bring forward requires a $50.00 filing fee and a bond, if it is ordered by the court. In a motion to bring forward, no new letters of appointment are issued, unless a new fiduciary is appointed.

If the newly discovered asset is cash, stock or other item of certain value, an inventory is not required. But if the newly discovered asset is an item of real or personal property of uncertain value, an inventory shall be required and filed within ninety (90) days of the granting of the motion to bring forward.

The procedure substitutes a motion for distribution in lieu of an account which shall be filed within sixty (60) days of the granting of the motion to bring forward. Where an inventory is required, the motion for distribution is required to be filed within sixty (60) days of the acceptance of the inventory.

In taxable estates, a motion for distribution will not be granted until the court receives the required certification from the Department of Revenue Administration.

Upon the filing of receipts for the distribution within thirty (30) days of the granting of the motion for distribution, the estate will be closed when all receipts are filed.

Forms

See Form 007, Appendix for an Appearance or Withdrawal form.

See Form 009, Appendix for Resident Agent form.

See Form 148, Appendix for a Voluntary Administration Affidavit.

See Forms 101/101A, Appendix for List of Heirs or Legatees

See Form 220, Appendix for a Petition for Estate Administration.

CHAPTER 27. TERMINATION OF ADMINISTRATION

§ 27-1. Death

The death of an administrator terminates the administration of an estate. It is said that the administration "becomes vacant." RSA 553:7.

The personal representative of a deceased administrator does not become administrator of the first estate (RSA 553:8) but has the duty of completing the deceased administrator's accounting up to the administrator's death.

Library References

Am Jur 2d Executors and Administrators § 275

CJS Executors and Administrators § 81

§ 27-2. Resignation

An administrator may voluntarily resign his trust upon request "whenever it appears to the judge to be proper to allow him to do so." RSA 553:12.

With the consent of the administrator, an administration "may be revoked under any circumstances . . . when it shall appear to the judge to be proper." RSA 553:11.

Library References

Am Jur 2d Executors and Administrators §§ 304–05

CJS Executors and Administrators § 82

Right of executor or administrator to resign. 91 ALR 712.

§ 27-3. Absence

An administrator may be removed from office by the probate judge by reason of absence. RSA 553:10.

Library References

Am Jur 2d Executors and Administrators § 285

CJS Executors and Administrators § 90

§ 27-4. Revocation for Cause—In General

An administrator cannot be removed against his will "without legal cause."[1] The statutory provision providing for the revocation of an administration for cause is archaic and inadequate for modern day circumstances. RSA 553:10 provides for revocation of administration for cause as follows:

> If an executor or administrator, by reason of absence, or infirmity of body or mind, or by wasteful or fraudulent management in his trust, becomes unfit for the discharge thereof, or unsafe to be trusted therewith, the judge, upon due notice, may revoke the administration.

However, it has been held that the probate court has inherent power to revoke an administration of an estate, independent of this statutory provision. *Morgan v. Dodge.*[2] In this case the Supreme Court gave several examples in which it held that an administration could be revoked without reference to the statute:

> [T]here are many cases where the courts of probate may remove such executors or administrators, beside those enumerated in the statute; and in these enumerated cases it is believed they had the same power at common law which the statute aims to confer. . ..
>
> These cases fall into three classes. First, where the probate court has no jurisdiction, and consequently its proceedings are

---

[1] Morgan v. Dodge, 44 N.H. 255, 261 (1862).

[2] Morgan v. Dodge, 44 N.H. 255 (1862).

absolutely void . . . but where it is nevertheless proper that the probate, or letters of administration, should be revoked before a new appointment is made, to prevent abuses and preserve order in the records. . ..

Of this class are the cases where the deceased was not "last an inhabitant of the county" in and for which the court is held, or if not being last an inhabitant of this State, he had no estate in the county. . . .

Analogous cases in England would be the grant of letters testamentary, or of administration, by a bishop, where there were none. . ..

Or where the judge is interested as heir or legatee, executor or administrator, or as guardian, or trustee of any person. . ..

So where a will is proved, or letters of administration are granted, where the person supposed to be dead is still living, the powers of the court being limited to the estates of deceased persons . . ..

Of the second class are the cases where the judge of probate has jurisdiction, but, by mistake or otherwise, the probate, or letters of administration, are issued irregularly, or illegally. In these cases the proceedings are not void, though they may be avoided, and the letters revoked. . ..

Such are the cases where a will has been proved and letters testamentary issued, and a subsequent will has been produced and proved.

Where letters of administration have been granted, and there is a will then unknown. . ..

Where a will offered for probate in common form has been adjudged not proved, letters of administration have been issued, and the will is, upon appeal, subsequently proved in solemn form. . ..

In these cases it was formerly held that the probate or administration was wholly void. . ..

So where a will has been proved in common form, and letters testamentary issued, and upon proceedings in solemn form it is not proved. . ..

Where there is an executor duly appointed and acting, with powers not limited by the will, and an administrator is appointed *de bonis non*; . . . though it is said that in these cases the appointment is a nullity.

Where administration is granted without such notice as the law requires, *non vocatis jure vocandis*. . ..

Where administration is granted without notice, to a person not entitled, upon false suggestion as to the facts or by fraud or surprise. . ..

Where administration is granted to creditors, or remote kindred before those previously entitled by law have voluntarily renounced their trust, or have neglected for thirty days to apply for administration. . ..

Where letters testamentary, or of administration, have been granted to a minor, or other person legally incompetent. . ..

The third class consists of cases where a qualified or limited administration has been granted upon a special occasion, and the cause of such special grant has ceased; as, if administration is granted during minority of an executor, and he has arrived at full age, and applies for letters testamentary; . . . or *pendente lite*, during a suit about a will, and the will is established, and the suit otherwise terminated; . . . or *durante absentia*, during the executor's absence, and he has returned; . . . or because of incapacity, and the executor or next of kin is restored to competency; . . . or until a will, supposed to exist in a foreign country, shall be produced, and such a will is proved. (Citations omitted.)[3]

Library References

Am Jur 2d Executors and Administrators § 276 et seq.

---

[3] Morgan v. Dodge, 44 N.H. 255, 259–61 (1862).

CJS Executors and Administrators §§ 89–94

What effects removal of executor or administrator. 8 ALR 175.

§ 27-4(a). Disability or Incompetency

Someone who is incompetent or suffers from a disability preventing him from carrying out his responsibilities is obviously not a suitable person to administer an estate even if he is entitled to a preference under the statutes. RSA 553:4.

If, after being appointed, an administrator becomes unable to act because "of infirmity of body or mind" which renders him "unfit for the discharge" of his duties or "unsafe to be trusted therewith," his appointment may be revoked by the probate judge. RSA 553:10.

Library References

Am Jur 2d Executors and Administrators §§ 277–94

CJS Executors and Administrators § 90

§ 27-4(b). Misconduct

In the archaic words of the removal statute, RSA 553:10, an administrator may be removed for "wasteful or fraudulent management of his trust" thereby becoming "unfit for the discharge thereof, or unsafe to be trusted therewith."

The removal powers of the probate judge were extensively reviewed by the Supreme Court and given a broad interpretation in *In re Estate of Crowley*.[4] In this case a son was appointed executor of his father's estate, pursuant to his nomination in the father's will. The executor had a substantial interest in a corporation which was owed money by the decedent. Furthermore, there were other children of the decedent who claimed that the executor had failed to manage and care for certain real estate of the decedent which was devised to all of the decedent's children. The other children also claimed that the executor had taken other actions which benefited the executor personally.

The Supreme Court held that, under the statute (RSA 553:13), it was not necessary that the probate court find that the administrator had acted fraudulently in order to justify the administrator's removal. Waste of the estate, mismanagement, and self-dealing are sufficient reasons to remove an administrator. The Court found sufficient support for the probate

---

[4] In re Estate of Crowley, 129 N.H. 557, 529 A.2d 960 (1987).

court's removal of the executor in (1) the waste and mismanagement of property "held in a fiduciary character" and (2) "apparent self-dealing on the part of the [executor which was] inconsistent with his role as executor,"[5] and (3) by "paying the 'debt' owing to his own corporation out of the assets of the estate, without compliance with procedure outlined in Probate Court Rule 17 [requiring the executor to properly designate the claim as a private claim of the fiduciary], the executor misappropriated assets of the estate. Certainly misappropriation falls within the common law meaning of waste."[6]

The proper way to question the fitness of an administrator to execute his trust is to petition the probate court on Probate Court Approved Form 118, Petition to Remove Fiduciary, to revoke the administration of the estate under RSA 553:10.[7]

Library References

Am Jur 2d Executors and Administrators §§ 277–94

CJS Executors and Administrators § 90

Dilatoriness of executor or administrator in filing inventory, or making reports, as ground for removal. 72 ALR 956.

Personal interest of executor or administrator adverse to or conflicting with those of other persons interested in estate as ground for revocation of letters or removal. 119 ALR 306.

§ 27-5. Effect of Appointment Later Vacated

An administrator, appointed by the decree of a probate court having jurisdiction of the cause, derives from that decree the power to perform official acts. The official acts of an administrator are entitled to consideration at least equal to that that is accorded acts of officers performed under the color of an election.[8] Where administration has been granted, an individual who is named executor in a document purporting to be a will cannot control the acts of the administrator except by the probate of the true will.[9]

Acts in which third parties have an interest, done by an administrator whose appointment is afterward vacated in consequence of the discovery

---

[5] Id.

[6] Id.

[7] Id.

[8] Clancy v. Pike, 94 N.H. 33, 45 A.2d 658 (1946).

[9] Boody v. Emerson, 17 N.H. 577 (1845).

of a will, are generally valid and bind the executor.[10] The mere existence of a will does not affect the validity of the acts of a duly-appointed administrator prior to the probate of such will.[11]

An administrator appointed prior to the probate of the will is an administrator *de facto*, and his acts done in due course of administration must be valid so far as third persons are concerned.[12] The grant of administration in such a case confers an existing authority, which cannot be resisted or disregarded until the will is proved.[13] Thus the acts of such an administrator are quite as valid as those of an executor under a will which has been revoked by a testator.[14]

Library References

Am Jur 2d Executors and Administrators §§ 307–08

CJS Executors and Administrators §§ 87, 92

§ 27-6. Uniform Probate Code Provisions

The strained interpretation of RSA 553:10 required by the Supreme Court in *In re Estate of Crowley*,[15] in order to justify removal of an administrator should not be necessary. Since an administrator is a fiduciary, strict fiduciary standards should be required and a unified statutory framework established to govern the whole area of removal. For example, § 3-610, 3-611 and 3-612 of the Uniform Probate Code contain a useful and practical statutory removal structure which makes clear that removal is justified "when removal would be in the best interest of the estate" or if the administrator commits certain clearly specified prohibited acts. § 3-611(b).

Forms

See Form 118, Appendix for a Petition to Remove Fiduciary.

See Form 138, Appendix for a Resignation of Fiduciary.

---

[10] Kittredge v. Folsom, 8 N.H. 98 (1835).

[11] Boody v. Emerson, 17 N.H. 577 (1845); Kittredge v. Folsom, 8 N.H. 98 (1835).

[12] Kittredge v. Folsom, 8 N.H. 98 (1835).

[13] Boody v. Emerson, 17 N.H. 577 (1845).

[14] Kittredge v. Folsom, 8 N.H. 98 (1835).

[15] In re Estate of Crowley, 129 N.H. 557, 529 A.2d 960 (1987).

CHAPTER 28. PROBATE BONDS

§ 28-1. Generally

Bonding of administrators and executors of estates is intended to protect estate assets, similar to the supervisory procedures before the probate court requiring inventories, approval before certain sales, accountings and the like.[1] This reasoning also applies when other fiduciaries, such as trustees or guardians, are required to furnish bonds in probate proceedings.

In *Davis v. Davis*, the Supreme Court held that an administrator or executor is not considered as having that trust and is forbidden to intermeddle with the decedent's estate until he has filed a bond with the court.[2] Even if the court issues letters of administration, and its order contains no express condition that it shall not take effect until bond is given, the condition is considered implied by force of the principal statute

---

[1] Hardwick, *Administration of Small Estates*, 1 N.H.B.J. 40 (1958).

[2] Davis v. Davis, 72 N.H. 326, 329, 56 A. 747, 749 (1903). See also Crosby v. Charlestown, 78 N.H. 39, 42, 95 A. 1043, 1044 (1915); Heydock v. Duncan, 43 N.H. 95, 99 (1861).

relating to estate bonds, RSA 553:13.[3] A testamentary trustee is similarly restricted; he must give bond as well as be appointed before he may act.[4]

Nevertheless, despite the absolute language of *Davis*, there are statutory exceptions to the bond requirement relating to decedent's estates, and circumstances under which a limited form of bond may be adequate.[5]

RSA 553:13 provides that:

I. No person shall intermeddle with the estate of a person deceased, or act as administrator thereof, or be considered as having that trust, except as provided in RSA 553:14 and 15, until he has given bond to the judge, with sufficient sureties, in such reasonable sum as he shall approve, or, in lieu of a bond, other forms of security acceptable to the judge, upon condition:

(a) To return to the judge a true and perfect inventory of the estate of the deceased, upon oath, within 3 months from the date of the bond.

(b) To administer the estate according to law.

(c) To render to the judge an account of administration, upon oath, within one year, and annually thereafter unless excused by the judge of probate as provided by law, until a final account is filed and allowed.

(d) To pay all taxes for which he may be or become liable under RSA 86, RSA 87, and RSA 89.

(e) To pay and deliver the rest and residue of the estate which shall be found remaining upon the account of the administrator to such person or persons respectively as the judge, by his decree, according to law, shall limit and appoint.

---

[3] Davis v. Davis, 72 N.H. at 329, 56 A. at 749 (1903) (and *citing* other cases finding appointment of an executor conditional until bond is given: Morgan v. Dodge, 44 N.H. 255, 261, 263 (1862); Kittredge v. Folsom, 8 N.H. 98, 111 (1835).

[4] Rockwell v. Dow, 85 N.H. 58, 64, 154 A. 229, 232 (1931); RSA 564:1.

[5] See Chapter 28 *infra*.

(f) To deliver the letters of administration into the court of probate, in case a will of the deceased shall thereafter be approved and allowed.

II. [Repealed]

III. In the discretion of the judge of probate, the requirements for the giving of bond and sureties or other forms of security may be waived:

(a) When the administrator of the deceased person's estate is the sole heir of the deceased person.

(b) When the estate has a gross value of less than $50,000 exclusive of property specified in RSA 554:5.

IV. To pay all taxes for which he may be or become liable under RSA 86, RSA 87, and RSA 89.

V. To pay and deliver the rest and residue of the estate which shall be found remaining upon the account of the administrator to such person or persons respectively as the judge, by his decree, according to law, shall limit and appoint.

VI. To deliver the letters of administration into the court of probate, in case a will of the deceased shall thereafter be approved and allowed.

In the discretion of the judge of probate the requirements for sureties may be waived when the estate has a gross value of less than twenty-five hundred dollars exclusive of property specified in RSA 554:5, and for the administration of such estate a bond may be given to the judge without sureties.

This statute is generally meant to secure the faithful performance of all the duties of the administrator or executor.[6]

Without a proper bond, the authority of an executor, inchoate by the will, remains in suspense until such bond is given. *Tappan v. Tappan.*[7]

---

[6] Perkins v. Perkins, 46 N.H. 110, 112 (1865).

[7] Tappan v. Tappan, 24 N.H. 400, 404 (1852).

Any decree, appointment, or letters testamentary until bond is provided are merely void, and the executor or administrator has no authority to act by virtue of any proceedings in the probate court.[8] Similarly, prior to appointment and giving bond, an executor named in a will cannot be regarded as the owner of the testator's estate for taxation purposes.[9]

Once an administrator has been appointed and has given the appropriate bond he is subject to the control of the probate court and may have his account allowed if proper.[10] Out-of-court settlement agreements also fall within the jurisdiction of the court if the administrator has fully qualified by providing bond after appointment. The judge may review such agreements.[11]

The reasonable and necessary expense of procuring a bond when the judge of probate requires bond is an allowable expense of administration.[12] But, if the executor himself unduly delays settlement of the estate, he is not entitled to credit in his account for premiums paid on the bond resulting from the delay. *McInnes v. Goldthwaite.*[13]

Library References

Am Jur 2d Executors and Administrators § 310 et seq.

CJS Executors and Administrators § 944 et seq.

§ 28-2. Uniform Probate Code Provisions

In keeping with its stated purpose of simplifying probate procedures, the Uniform Probate Code "move[s] away from the idea that bond always should be required of a probate fiduciary, or required unless a will excuses it. . . .. The point is that the court and registrar are not responsible for seeing that personal representatives perform as they are supposed to perform. Rather, performance is coerced by the remedies available to interested persons."[14]

---

[8] Heydock v. Duncan, 43 N.H. 95, 99 (1861). But see Morgan v. Dodge, 44 N.H. at 261 (1862) (appointment without proper bond being given not void but subject to revocation).

[9] Tappan v. Tappan, 24 N.H. at 404 (1855).

[10] Crosby v. Charlestown, 78 N.H. at 42–43, 95 A. at 1044–45 (1915).

[11] Tappan v. Tappan, 24 N.H. at 404 (1852).

[12] Clarke v. Clay, 31 N.H. 393, 402–03 (1855).

[13] McInnes v. Goldthwaite, 96 N.H. 413, 418, 77 A.2d 849, 852 (1951).

[14] Comment, UPC § 3-603.

Consequently, § 3-603 of the Code does not require a bond in informal proceedings. In a formal proceeding, a bond is required only upon a specific order of the court. Even if the will requires a bond, it may be dispensed with by order of the court. UPC § 3-603. Sections 3-604 to 3-606 of the Code deal with the provisions of bonds when they are required.

Library References

Am Jur 2d Executors and Administrators § 314

§ 28-3. Form

RSA 565:1 indicates that all bonds given to the judge should be made to the judge for the appropriate county without naming the incumbent of that office. The Probate Court Rules implement the bond requirement.

No particular form for an executor's or administrator's bond is set forth by RSA 553:13. A bond containing the same substantive conditions as those found in RSA 553:13 was found sufficient in *Judge of Probate v. Claggett*.[15] The New Hampshire Supreme Court has now approved uniform probate rules and forms for use in this state. The current form for fiduciary bonds appears as Approved Form 12–222. Note that when personal surety bonds are used, Rule 30 requires the sureties to complete an affidavit upon which the sureties certify that they own real estate in New Hampshire, the net value of which, over and above any encumbrance upon it, will enable them to honor their obligations under the bond. Probate Court Procedure Bulletin 4 requires that whenever any petition for administration under RSA Chapter 553 is filed, no probate court shall require the petitioner to provide a list of debts and/or taxes before submitting the petition to the court for setting the bond.

Library References

Am Jur 2d Executors and Administrators § 310
CJS Executors and Administrators § 944

§ 28-4. Sureties

RSA 553:13 expressly speaks in terms of "sureties" for the executor's or administrator's bond. In *Tappan v. Tappan*, the Court held that a single surety will not suffice.[16]

---

[15] Judge of Probate v. Claggett, 36 N.H. 381 (1858).

[16] Tappan v. Tappan, 24 N.H. 400, 404 (1852). See also Heydock v. Duncan, 43 N.H. at 99 (1861).

Sureties are also required for a conservator's bond under RSA 464-A:15, for a guardian's bond under RSA 464-A:21, for the bond of a guardian for a veteran under RSA 465:8 (a corporate surety only is permitted) and for most trustee's bonds under RSA 564:1.

RSA 565:2 provides, however, that for any probate bond a corporation may be sufficient surety if the corporation is established by the laws of this state or authorized to transact business here, and the judge is satisfied with its ability as surety. Probate Court Rule 28 provides that when a surety company is offered as the surety, no bond shall be approved unless the name of the person executing the bond for the company has been certified to the register of probate by the insurance commissioner, or unless the surety company has filed with the register a power of attorney or certified copy of such a power authorizing execution of the bond. The court may require proof, by affidavit or otherwise, that the person is an officer of the surety company. In practice, this rule is usually only invoked when the surety company is located in a county different from the one in which the estate is being administered, since the register is familiar with surety companies in his or her county.

The current law provide occasions when no surety at all is required for an estate representative's bond. RSA 553:13, II allows the judge to waive the necessity of providing a bond and sureties at all, if the administrator is also the sole heir of the decedent and the gross value of the estate is less than $50,000, exclusive of property specified in RSA 554:5.[17]

A bond without sureties does not leave the interested parties without protection, as any person aggrieved by the administration of the estate may have recourse to the bond to recover any loss or damage suffered through default of the administrator or executor.[18]

Two other Probate Court rules apply to sureties. Rule 27 provides that neither the sureties nor the penal sum of any bond shall be changed except upon petition and for good cause shown. Under Rule 29, sureties on the bonds of executors, administrators, trustees, guardians or conservators are barred from appointment as appraisers or commissioners of the same estate, as are individuals beneficially interested in the estate.

---

[17] RSA 553:13, III. (Note: RSA 554:5 concerns certain tangible personal property not to be inventoried).

[18] 5th Report Judicial Council, p. 26 (1954).

Library References

Am Jur 2d Executors and Administrators § 349

CJS Executors and Administrators § 957

§ 28-5. Limited Estate Bonds—In General

In certain decedents' estates, the judge may approve a bond intended to assure the performance of fewer duties than are listed in RSA 553:13. Statutory approval of such limited bonds is accorded under RSA 553:14 and 553:15, discussed separately below.

Library References

Am Jur 2d Executors and Administrators § 310

CJS Executors and Administrators § 950

§ 28-5(a). Bond of Residuary Legatee

RSA 553:14 provides:

> If the executor to whom administration is granted is residuary legatee, and there is no widow, or if, there being a widow, she informs the judge in writing that she accepts the provisions of the will, a bond, with sufficient sureties, may be taken from him, with condition only to pay the funeral charges, debts, legacies and all legacy and succession taxes, and to render upon oath an account of his proceedings, when required.

Note that there is no dollar limit to the size of the estate as there is in a similar provision in RSA 553:13, III, which, as noted above, may result in an administrator-sole heir's ability to serve without sureties on his bond or without any bond.[19]

A cautious approach to the limited "debts and legacies" bond of RSA 553:14 appears in *Morgan v. Dodge*.[20] The Court noted that "many persons have been ruined by giving bonds in this form," and urged probate judges to discourage their use, and to take special care not to permit residuary legatee bonds whenever there is any doubt concerning the solvency of the estate or that the conditions of the statute have been met.[21]

---

[19] See Chapter 28.

[20] Morgan v. Dodge, 44 N.H. 255 (1862).

[21] Morgan v. Dodge, 44 N.H. 255, 262 (1862).

It must appear from the will, or the applicant must show, that the applicant is the legatee of the whole residue. *Morgan v. Dodge* defines a residuary legatee as one to whom all the property not disposed of by the will, whether real or personal, is given.[22] In *Tappan v. Tappan*, the Court held that a bequest of "all the rest, residue and remainder of my estate, whether real or personal, in Claremont, aforesaid, wheresoever being," did not render the legatee eligible for a residuary legatee bond because the Court could not know whether the description encompassed all the residue or whether some other undevised property of the decedent existed outside Claremont.[23] Faced with a similar problem in *Morgan v. Dodge*, however, the Court held that extrinsic evidence is admissible to show that there is no such other property, enabling the legatee to prove he does in fact qualify for a debts and legacies bond under RSA 553:14.[24]

A conditional bequest of the residue should not entitle the legatee to a debts and legacies bond.[25] It is not necessary, however, that everything the residuary legatee may receive vest in him absolutely at the time he gives bond. That a specific bequest, made on condition, may become a part of the residue upon failure of the condition will not preclude the residuary legatee from qualifying for the bond.[26]

A residuary legatee who is not named executor in the decedent's will but who is appointed by the court as administrator w.w.a. will not qualify for a debts and legacies bond.[27] The bond is also not available where only one of the acting executors is a residuary legatee,[28] but if it can be found that the other "executors" were merely sureties, not executors, then such a bond is valid.[29]

The requirement of RSA 553:14 that the decedent's widow must inform the probate judge in writing of her acceptance of the will is

---

[22] *Id.*

[23] Tappan v. Tappan, 24 N.H. 400 (1852). See also Tappan v. Tappan, 30 N.H. 50 (1855) (the fact that legatee will succeed to property not a part of the residue as the heir of the intestate does not render him any more eligible for a bond under RSA 553:14).

[24] Morgan v. Dodge, 44 N.H. 255, 263 (1862).

[25] Emery v. Judge of Probate, 7 N.H. 142 (1834) (condition not implied as to residue).

[26] Emery v. Judge of Probate, 7 N.H. 142, 153–154 (1834).

[27] Mercer v. Pike, 58 N.H. 286, 287 (1878).

[28] Tappan v. Tappan, 24 N.H. 400, 403 (1852). See Heydock v. Duncan, 43 N.H. 95, 99 (1861).

[29] Heydock v. Duncan, 43 N.H. at 99–100 (1861).

intended for her benefit, which she may be able to waive.[30] She may be estopped from denying acceptance if she petitions to have the will proved, petitions for her own appointment as executrix, files a bond as RSA 553:14 provides and never files an inventory or account.[31] A widow who is the named executrix and residuary legatee may not be bonded under RSA 553:14 if she refuses to accept the provisions of the will.[32]

The effect of the widow's acceptance may be that she is precluded from asserting any rights to property of the decedent on which his will does not operate. Although one case, *Brown v. Brown*,[33] holds that an acceptance of the provisions of the will goes only to the widow's distributive share of the estate and does not result in waiver or release of her rights of dower and homestead, the subsequent passage of RSA 560:17 appears to overrule *Brown*.[34]

The 1838 case of *Batchelder v. Russell* found that the statute (now RSA 553:13) had always been construed to excuse the executorresiduary legatee from filing an inventory, and that he was usually also not required to render an account.[35] The reason behind this exemption was that "[t]he policy of the law in such case seems to be to surrender to the residuary legatee all the property of the testator, and to rest solely on the bond for the security of claimants upon the estate."[36] Upon providing a bond pursuant to RSA 553:14, the residuary legatee would automatically be vested with title to property constituting the residue of decedent's estate, without the necessity for any further probate proceedings.[37]

Were this the case, there would obviously be more advantages to be gained from qualifying under RSA 553:14 than simply the limited size

---

[30] Davis v. Smith, 58 N.H. 16, 18 (1876).

[31] Heydock v. Duncan, 43 N.H. 95, 102 (1861). *Cf.* Morgan v. Dodge, 44 N.H. at 264 (1862) (application for probate of decedent's will by widow who is herself executrix and residuary legatee is sufficient writing to inform judge of her acceptance of the provisions of the will).

[32] Heydock v. Duncan, 43 N.H. 95, 101–02 (1861) (this suggests the condition is not intended entirely for the widow's benefit).

[33] Brown v. Brown, 55 N.H. 106 (1875).

[34] See also Trafton v. Trafton, 96 N.H. 188, 189, 72 A.2d 457, 458 (1950) and Chapter 52 *infra*.

[35] Batchelder v. Russell, 10 N.H. 39, 40 (1838).

[36] *Id.*

[37] See Heydock v. Duncan, 43 N.H. at 101 (1861) (*citing* Batchelder v. Russell and Tarbell v. Whiting, 5 N.H. 63 (1829)).

of the bond required. Unfortunately, later cases have questioned whether vesting really does occur as described in *Batchelder*, and the question has not been resolved.[38] All that can be said with any certainty is that RSA 553:14, unlike RSA 553:13, does not provide that the executor's return of an inventory and an account are conditions of his bond. RSA 553:14 includes no mention of an inventory, and indicates that the executor's duty as to accounts is "to render upon oath an account of his proceedings, when required." The bond may, however, contain language which will result in the duty to file an inventory and account.[39]

The bond to pay debts and legacies is not a promise to pay any specific debt, but only such debts as the executor should be legally bound to pay.[40] If the executor files only the limited bond of RSA 553:14 when he should have obtained and filed a full bond pursuant to RSA 553:13, a creditor of the estate is nevertheless protected by the debts and legacies bond.[41] As far as the creditor is concerned, administration is not suspended because of the irregularity, and the statute of limitations continues to run against his claim.[42]

An unfulfilled devise of bequest is a charge against the estate of a residuary legatee-executor who has provided a bond to cover debts and legacies pursuant to RSA 553:14.[43]

Library References

Am Jur 2d Executors and Administrators § 310

CJS Executors and Administrators § 950

---

[38] Heydock v. Duncan, 43 N.H. at 101 (1861). See Moody v. Davis, 67 N.H. 300, 301, 38 A. 464, 464 (1892); Brown v. Brown, 55 N.H. at 109 (1875). But see Richardson v. Bailey, 69 N.H. 384, 385, 41 A. 263, 263 (1898), which further muddies the water by holding that by filing of an RSA 553:14 bond, title passed to the executor-residuary legatee as an individual (*citing* the earlier cases collected at footnote above, as well as Mercer v. Pike, 58 N.H. 286 (1878)).

[39] Emery v. Judge of Probate, 7 N.H. at 156 (1833) (direction to executor "to discharge the trust of an executor" in debts and legacy bond could obligate executor-residuary legatee to file inventory).

[40] Walker v. Cheever, 39 N.H. 420 (1859).

[41] Davis v. Smith, 58 N.H. 16 (1876).

[42] *Id.*

[43] Copp v. Hersey, 31 N.H. 317, 329 (1855).

§ 27-5(b). Exemption Under the Will

It is quite common for a testator to direct in his will that his executor or his trustee be exempt from the requirement of giving a bond. Many testators die thinking that they have saved the expense of a bond but a probate court almost always requires a bond (occasionally, without sureties) in every estate as a consequence of RSA 553:15. RSA 553:15 provides that the executor or trustee will not be wholly exempt but is permitted to give only a limited bond "for the payment of debts, and legacy and succession taxes." RSA 553:15 does not guarantee that this is the only bond that the fiduciary will ever be required to file; instead the judge may at any time, upon petition of an heir, devisee or creditor, require a further bond, with sufficient sureties, if he is of opinion that it is made requisite by a change in the situation or circumstances of the executor or trustee, or by other sufficient cause.

As is the case with the residuary legatee-executor's limited bond under RSA 553:14, the executor's bond under RSA 553:15 contains no express condition that he settle an account.[44]

Library References

Am Jur 2d Executors and Administrators § 311

CJS Executors and Administrators § 944

§ 27-5(c). Waiver By Judge

RSA 553:13, III permits the probate judge to waive the bond and sureties requirement entirely if the administrator is also the sole heir of the decedent's estate or the gross value of the estate is less than $50,000, exclusive of items not required to be inventoried under RSA 554:5.

Library References

Am Jur 2d Executors and Administrators § 310

CJS Executors and Administrators § 944

§ 28-6. Trustee's Bonds

The general bonding requirement for trustees appears at RSA 564:1:

---

[44] Tilton v. Tilton, 70 N.H. 325, 327, 47 A. 256, 257 (1900). (There was no reason to require the widow-executrix who filed a RSA 553:15 bond to file an account since there was no showing she was attempting to divert property of which she was life tenant from the remaindermen by fraudulent or unauthorized mismanagement or appropriation.)

Every trustee to whom any estate, real or personal, is devised in trust for any person shall give bond to the judge of probate, with sufficient sureties, or without sureties in estates of five thousand dollars or less where the judge finds it in the interest of the estate, in such sum as the judge may order, except as provided in the following section and in RSA Chapter 553, Section 15, conditioned:

I. That he will make and file in the probate office a true inventory of the real estate, goods, chattels, rights and credits so devised, at such time as the judge shall order.

II. That he will annually render an account to the judge of the annual income and profit thereof, unless excused by the judge of probate as provided by law.

III. That at the expiration of the trust he will adjust and settle his account with the judge, and pay and deliver over all balances, money, and property with which he has been intrusted.

IV. That he will faithfully execute the trust according to the true intent of the devisor.

Note that there is an exemption, in the judge's discretion, if the trust estate is less than $5,000. Further bond relief, as already indicated, is available in the form of a limited bond, "for the payment of debts, and legacy and succession taxes," under RSA 553:15 if the testator directed in his will that his trustee be exempt from the bond requirement. RSA 564:2 also provides that if a town or city in New Hampshire is appointed trustee, it shall not be required to give a bond. A trust company or national bank appointed trustee, on the other hand, is not only under an express duty to give bond but it "shall give a surety company bond." RSA 564:4 and 564:5.

In the case of estates and/or trusts, a party may file a Motion to Reduce or Waive the bond with the assents of all residuary and/or income beneficiaries, either before or after the probate judge sets the bond amount. A Probate Court Rule 3 Certification shall not suffice as an assent in such circumstances. Probate Court Procedure Bulletin 4.

Library References

Am Jur 2d Trusts § 550 et seq.

CJS Trusts § 224

Cross References

See Chapters 63 et seq.

§ 28-7. Other Probate Bonds

Conservators are required to give bond by RSA 464-A:15:

> Such conservator shall give bond to the judge of probate, with sufficient sureties, give notice of his appointment as guardians are required to do and be subject to all provisions of law now in force as to guardians as far as they apply to estates of their wards, pursuant to this chapter; provided, however, that the court need not, but may appoint an attorney or other suitable person to review an account of a conservator and to represent the interests of the protected person.

Guardians must provide bonds, but may be excused if the value of the ward's estate is $2,500 or less or the guardianship is of limited duration. RSA 464-A:21.

> Upon appointment, the guardian of the person and estate, or the person, or the estate, shall give bond to the probate court, with sufficient sureties, in such sum as the judge shall approve. In the discretion of the judge of probate, a bond without sureties may be given if the gross value of the ward's estate does not exceed $2,500 or the guardianship is only of the person of an incapacitated person or minor. RSA 464-A:21.

Special requirements apply to a guardian for a veteran under RSA 465:8.

> If the estate of the ward consists of funds received from the United States Veterans' Administration, or earnings thereon, in excess of $1,000, the guardian shall give bond to the judge of probate in a reasonable sum, with corporate sureties, upon condition, among other things, to return an inventory, to render, upon oath, a true and just account of his guardianship, when thereto required, and to faithfully discharge his trust. RSA 465:8.

RSA 562, relating to petition of decedent's realty, contains an additional bonding provision under which bonds may be required of even nonfiduciaries.

> Every person to whom any estate whatever of a person deceased shall be decreed to be set off, assigned, paid or secured shall, if required, give bond to the judge, with sufficient sureties, to pay to the administrator, in default of other estate in his hands, his pro rata proportion of the just demands with which the estate may be chargeable. RSA 562:9.

A special administrator appointed under the provisions of RSA 553:20 is required to give bond "for the faithful performance of his duty, with sufficient sureties, to the satisfaction of the court appointing him; or, in lieu of a bond, other forms of security acceptable to the court."[45]

Library References

Am Jur 2d Guardian and Ward § 48

CJS Guardian and Ward §§ 31–33

Cross References

See Chapters 69–73, *supra.*

§ 28-8. New Bond

Probate bonds may be replaced during the course of administration. Application for change of the bond may be made by the principal (the executor, administrator, trustee or other fiduciary) pursuant to RSA 565:4, or by the surety, pursuant to RSA 565:5. In either case, after notice has been given, the judge is empowered to discharge the sureties on the old bond "from all further responsibility" on that bond. In addition to these permissive bond changes, RSA 565:3 absolutely requires a new bond, with sufficient sureties and penalty, if the sureties or the penalty on the existing bond are insufficient. Failure to comply, after notice and within a reasonable time, results in revocation of the principal's trust. Probate Court Rule 27 stresses court control over bond modifications, providing that "[n]o change of sureties or of the penal sum of any probate bond shall be made except upon petition and for good cause shown."

Bond substitution necessarily raises the question of which surety is liable for the principal's breach of his trust. According to the leading

---

[45] RSA 553:23.

case in New Hampshire, *Century Indemnity Co. v. Maryland Casualty Co.*,[46] the answer depends upon when the breach occurred and whether the breach is a continuing one. The surety on a bond later cancelled is not wholly released from liability even though he has been discharged by the court, because RSA 565:4 provides that the judge may release sureties only from further responsibility; that is, from liability for acts or omissions occurring after the surety's discharge.[47] The "discharged" surety remains liable for mismanagement and waste which occurred prior to its discharge.[48] A subsequent surety may be liable both for breaches during the effective period of its bond and for breaches which actually began before its bond issued if the breach, such as conversion of the assets of the estate, continued into its bonding period.[49] When the breach is continuing, the subsequent bond will be held to "relate back."[50] Thus, the new and old sureties may become cosureties, and if this occurs, a right of contribution exists between them.[51]

Library References

Am Jur 2d Bonds § 33 et seq.

CJS Bonds § 99 et seq.

---

[46] Century Indem. Co. v. Maryland Cas. Co., 89 N.H. 121, 193 A. 221 (1937).

[47] Century Indem. Co. v. Maryland Cas. Co., 89 N.H. 121, 124–25, 193 A. 221, 223 (1937). See also Judge of Probate v. Nudd, 107 N.H. 173, 176, 219 A.2d 454, 456 (1966).

[48] Century Indem. Co. v. Maryland Cas. Co., 89 N.H. 121, 124–25, 193 A. 221, 223 (1937).

[49] *Id.*

[50] Century Indem. Co. v. Maryland Cas. Co., 89 N.H. at 124, 193 A. at 223 (1937).

[51] *Id.*

CHAPTER 29. TYPES OF ADMINISTRATORS

§ 29-1. Introduction

This area of probate law in New Hampshire is filled with unnecessary legalisms and arcane language. While it may have been important at one time to distinguish whether a person was an administrator w.w.a. or d.b.n., it is now sufficient for all practical purposes that the person be designated as an administrator. Once so designated, he or she takes on the cloak of a fiduciary and the specific powers, duties and responsibilities given all administrators under the statutory and judicial probate law of New Hampshire.

The Uniform Probate Code uses the preferred term personal representative which sweeps away all of the baggage which terms such as *executor, administrator, administrator d.b.n., or w.w.a.*, or *d.b.n.w.w.a.* carry. Also, a successor personal representative has the same powers and duties as an originally appointed personal representative. § 3-613.

Library References

Am Jur 2d Executors and Administrators § 158

§ 29-2. Administrator De Bonis Non (d.b.n.)

The Latin phrase *de bonis non* is an abbreviation of *de bonis non administrates* and translates as of the goods not administered.[1] It refers to the appointment of a successor administrator who takes over the administration of an estate only partially settled by a prior administrator.

RSA 553:7 provides:

> If the administration of an estate becomes vacant by death, extinguishment or revocation the judge may grant administration on the estate not before administered to such person as he may think proper, having due regard to the rule prescribed in RSA 553:2.[2]

A successor administrator appointed under these circumstances is called an administrator *de bonis non* (d.b.n.).[3] Although the statute contains permissive language, *Judge of Probate v. Claggett*[4] holds that it is the duty of the judge of probate to grant administration upon the estate administered if the executor or administrator dies. However, an administrator d.b.n. will not be appointed if he can accomplish nothing through his appointment.[5]

The reference in RSA 553:7 to "having due regard" to the rule prescribed in RSA 553:2 makes clear that in choosing a successor administrator, the probate judge must have in mind the classes, and their priority, which are established by law to govern the choosing of administrators.[6]

The distinguishing characteristic of an administrator d.b.n. is that he is a successor, appointed when a previously appointed administrator or

---

[1] Black's Law Dictionary (Revised 4th Edition 1968).

[2] 2 RSA 553:2 deals with "Right to Administer" and is treated Chapter 25 *supra*.

[3] RSA 553:7; Judge of Probate v. Heydock, 8 N.H. 491 (1837).

[4] Judge of Probate v. Claggett, 36 N.H. 381 (1858).

[5] Haven v. Haven, 69 N.H. 204, 39 A. 972 (1898) (estate had no interest in the property plaintiff sought to have declared his). See also Mercer v. Pike, 58 N.H. 286 (1878) (estate was practically, although not regularly, settled, and no properly interested party sought appointment of administrator d.b.n.w.w.a.).

[6] See Chapter 25, Choice of Administrator, *supra*.

executor left the job unfinished, because of death, removal, resignation, etc.

Once appointed, the administrator d.b.n. is the official successor to the original trust.[7] He may be appointed to succeed either an administrator or an executor. An administrator appointed to succeed an executor is strictly known as administrator d.b.n.w.w.a. An administrator d.b.n. is privy to the original administrator and is liable to the same duties.[8] An administrator d.b.n.w.w.a. is also privy to the original executor.[9] In *Taylor v. Barron,*[10] it was held that the same relationship exists between the deceased or removed executor or administrator and the administrator d.b.n. as exists between parties deceased and those who represent their estates.

If there is a balance remaining in the hands of a deceased administrator which is unadministered and which constitutes either a part or the whole of the estate of the original decedent, it is the duty of the new administrator to take charge of this balance. *Judge of Probate v. Claggett.*[11] He has a legal claim to, and is entitled to receive, whatever of the estate remained in his predecessor's hands on the settlement of the predecessor's account.[12] The administrator d.b.n. may institute and prosecute to final judgment, in the names of the proper persons, all suits necessary to enable him to obtain possession of the funds committed to his charge.[13] In default of payment, he may recover the balance by a suit on the original administrator's bond.[14]

---

[7] Weston v. Second Orthodox Congregational Soc'y, 79 N.H. 245, 246, 110 A. 137, 138–39 (1919).

[8] Taylor v. Barron, 35 N.H. 484, 493 (1857), overruled on other grounds, Lomas v. Hilliard, 60 N.H. 148 (1880).

[9] Taylor v. Barron, 35 N.H. 484, 493 (1857), overruled on other grounds, Lomas v. Hilliard, 60 N.H. 148 (1880).

[10] *Id.*

[11] Judge of Probate v. Claggett, 36 N.H. 381, 386 (1868).

[12] Weston v. Second Orthodox Congregational Soc'y, 79 N.H. 245, 246, 110 A. 137, 138–39 (1919); Prescott v. Farmer, 59 N.H. 90, 91 (1879); Judge of Probate v. Heydock, 8 N.H. 491, 498 (1837).

[13] Judge of Probate v. Claggett, 36 N.H. 381, 387 (1858).

[14] Weston v. Second Orthodox Congregational Soc'y, 79 N.H. 245, 246, 110 A. 137, 138–39 (1919); Prescott v. Farmer, 59 N.H. at 91 (1879); Judge of Probate v. Claggett, 36 N.H. at 387 (1858); Judge of Probate v. Heydock, 8 N.H. at 499 (1837).

An administrator d.b.n.w.w.a. may sell real estate without a license from the probate court if the will authorizes sale by any person legally qualified to administer the estate.[15]

Library References

CJS Executors and Administrators §§ 1016–30

§ 29-3. Administrator With Will Annexed (w.w.a.)

If the testator fails to nominate an executor, or if for any reason the person nominated does not act as executor,[16] the court may appoint an administrator to perform the same functions. Such an administrator is properly referred to as an administrator "with will annexed" (w.w.a.).[17] Thus, an administrator w.w.a. is not an administrator d.b.n., which refers to a successor administrator. Rather, an administrator w.w.a. is an original administrator appointed when the person nominated as executor in a will is unwilling or unable to act as executor.

An administrator with will annexed is clothed with all the power which the laws can give him; he is thus fully authorized to take a decedent's property. *Willard v. Hammond.*[18] An administrator w.w.a. is the only person who has a right to interfere with the decedent's property, and who can maintain an action for conversion.[19]

Library References

Am Jur 2d Executors and Administrators § 161

CJS Executors and Administrators §§ 1031–34

§ 29-4. Temporary Administrators

The probate court, upon its own motion, or upon petition, has the power to appoint a temporary administrator "to determine what assets, if any, are contained within the estate." RSA 553:20-a. "An inventory

---

[15] Rollins v. Rice, 59 N.H. 493, 496 (1880).

[16] The executor may, for instance, have predeceased the testator, Parker v. Harris, 66 N.H. 324, 23 A. 81 (1890), or may simply never have qualified or administered the estate and subsequently died, leaving legacies of the testator's estate unpaid. Leavitt v. Leavitt, 65 N.H. 102, 103, 18 A. 920 (1889).

[17] Atkinson, Wills § 5 (2d ed. 1953); Parker v. Harris, 66 N.H. at 324, 23 A. at 81 (1890); Leavitt v. Leavitt, 65 N.H. at 103, 18 A. at 920 (1889).

[18] Willard v. Hammond, 21 N.H. 382, 386 (1850).

[19] *Id.*

of the assets shall be filed with the probate court within 60 days of the temporary administrator's appointment." RSA 553:20-a.

This power, given to the probate court in 1993 as a part of the Omnibus Justice Act, was designed to close a gap in jurisdiction often confronted by probate judges where a party alleges, prior to the appointment of any administrator, that certain assets of the decedent are being concealed or misappropriated in some way. Prior to the provisions of the Omnibus Justice Act, the probate court had no power to intervene. Probate Court Procedure Bulletin 1997-05 provides a procedure to implement RSA 553:20-a and provides that the "inventory of assets required by the statute is not a "formal' inventory" and it does not require the filing of Probate Court Form 44, nor does it fall within the scope of RSA 548:5-A. Rather the inventory of assets "is a simple listing of the assets found by the temporary administrator."[20]

§ 29-5. Special Administrators—In General

A special administrator may be appointed pursuant to RSA 553:20 when there is a delay in determining the final grant of administration:

> Whenever, by reason of the trial of factual issues in a proceeding involving the validity of a will, or by reason of appeal from the appointment of an administrator on questions of law, or from any other cause, there is delay in determining the final grant of administration upon the estate of a decedent, a special administrator may be appointed, if the interest of the estate requires it.

The usual purpose of this statute is to cover situations where the named executor or administrator has not yet been appointed and a need exists for an administrator to act. A special administrator, unless specifically authorized by the judge of probate court, is only a temporary custodian of the decedent's estate, and his duty is to preserve the estate intact during litigation concerning it.[21]

Towle v. Yeaton[22] held that:

---

[20] Prob. Ct. Proc. Bul. 1997-05.

[21] Ford v. Ford, 91 N.H. 161, 163, 15 A.2d 866, 867 (1940).

[22] Towle v. Yeaton, 97 N.H. 427, 90 A.2d 496 (1952).

The word *jurat* as used in the statute means "last, conclusive, not given to appeal or revision."[23]

Under RSA 553:23 the special administrator is required to give bond, with sufficient sureties, to the satisfaction of the judge or court appointing him for the performance of his duty. If an interested party alleges the bond is insufficient, RSA 553:24 provides that the court, upon summary proceedings, shall have power to order a new bond, and may order an absolute or qualified stay of proceedings until the order is complied with. Otherwise, an appeal from the appointment of a special administrator does not result in a suspension of his duties. RSA 553:24.

Library References

Am Jur 2d Executors and Administrators §§ 1147–67

CJS Executors and Administrators §§ 1035–40

§ 29-5(a). Appointment

Appointment of a special administrator is permitted under RSA 553:21 by the judge of probate court. It is clear that a special administrator may be appointed after an administrator has been appointed. The courts have a wide latitude to make an appointment either before or after the original grant of administration.[24] Thus, in *Towle v. Yeaton*,[25] the Court held proper the appointment of a special administrator pending an appeal from the proof of a will in solemn form and after the appointment of an executor under it.

A request for appointment of a special administrator in the probate court is made by petition. See Form 220 in the Appendix.

The prerequisites for appointment under RSA 553:20 are that there is a delay in determining the final grant of administration on the decedent's estate, and that the interests of the estate require it. Litigation involving the will, a delay in filling the position of a regular executor or administrator, or a situation in which the executor appointed would not be in a position to take action on behalf of the estate which a disinterested representative might consider necessary or appropriate

---

[23] Towle v. Yeaton, 97 N.H. 427, 429–30, 90 A.2d 496, 498 (1952).

[24] Towle v. Yeaton, 97 N.H. 427, 430, 90 A.2d 496, 498 (1952). See also Sargent v. Sanborn, 66 N.H. 30, 25 A. 541 (1890).

[25] Towle v. Yeaton, 97 N.H. 427, 90 A.2d 496 (1952).

because of the executor's own interests, are all examples of circumstances raising the possibility of the need for a special administrator.[26]

Under the statutory allowance for the appointment of a special administrator when there is a delay "from any other cause," it is not unusual for parties who are contesting the choice of an administrator to agree to the appointment of a special administrator while the litigation is proceeding or, in this situation, for a judge to make such an appointment even in the absence of an agreement of the parties. A special administrator and a regular executor may serve at the same time as long as their duties do not conflict. *Towle v. Yeaton.*[27]

Unlike the appointment of administrators d.b.n. and w.w.a. where the probate court is required to adhere to the classes and priorities of appointment established by RSA 553:2, 553:20 and 553:21 provide no guidelines to the court in its choice of a special administrator. In *Towle v. Yeaton*, the appointment of an experienced and competent lawyer, who was also an Internal Revenue Service collector, was upheld where he had no duty as special administrator to concern himself with tax obligations of the estate.[28] In the same case, the Court held that it is advisable when appointing counsel for the special administrator to appoint disinterested counsel, but the Court found that appointment of a law firm which also represented an alleged heir was not an abuse of discretion.[29]

A special administrator may be appointed where an administrator has been removed pursuant to RSA 553:10.

Library References

Am Jur 2d Executors and Administrators §§ 1148–49, 1153, 1161, 1163

CJS Executors and Administrators §§ 1035–38

Person to be appointed as special or temporary administrator pending will contest. 136 ALR 604.

§ 29-5(b). Duties

It is the special administrator's duty "to take care of and preserve the decedent's property and effects, and shall do all other acts which the

---

[26] RSA 553:20; Towle v. Yeaton, 97 N.H. 427, 430, 90 A.2d 496, 498 (1952).

[27] Towle v. Yeaton, 97 N.H. 427, 431, 90 A.2d 496, 498–99 (1952).

[28] Towle v. Yeaton, 97 N.H. 427, 430, 90 A.2d 496, 498 (1952).

[29] Towle v. Yeaton, 97 N.H. 427, 431, 90 A.2d 496, 499 (1952).

special administrator may be directed by the judge to perform."[30] RSA 553:22 provides that in connection with this duty, the special administrator must return an inventory of the estate. Other duties may be added by the appointing authority, and his commission may also contain directions or restrictions. RSA 553:22.

In all matters pertaining to the care and preservation of the estate, a special administrator has sole and supreme authority.[31] For all other things, however, where the court has not given the special administrator instructions, the named executor may continue to act.[32] The special administrator has no duty to sustain the decedent's will, to determine who the distributees are, or to make distribution of the estate under his charge without special authorization.[33] Money spent by a special administrator to establish the decedent's will was held not to be a proper expense of the estate and the expense was disallowed in his account in *Ford v. Ford.*[34]

Despite these restrictions upon the special administrator's authority, parties may be found to have waived their objections to actions he takes and be bound by those actions. In *Harris v. Parker,*[35] for example, the Court found parties had waived objection to administration of the decedent's estate in the insolvent course by presenting their claims to the commissioner in insolvency although the special administrator had petitioned for insolvency proceedings without their knowledge or assent (and apparently without direction from the court).

The final duty of the special administrator, upon termination of the event which led to his appointment and appointment of a regular executor or administrator, is to turn over to the latter the decedent's property and effects and render an account of his stewardship to the court which appointed him. *Ford v. Ford.*[36]

---

[30] RSA 553:22. See also In re Estate of Pafelis, 108 N.H. 265, 267, 233 A.2d 825, 827 (1967).

[31] Towle v. Yeaton, 97 N.H. 427, 431, 90 A.2d 496, 499 (1952).

[32] Towle v. Yeaton, 97 N.H. 427, 431, 90 A.2d 496, 499 (1952); In re Estate of Pafelis, 108 N.H. at 267, 233 A.2d at 827 (1967).

[33] Towle v. Yeaton, 98 N.H. at 431, 90 A.2d at 499 (1952); Ford v. Ford, 91 N.H. at 136, 15 A.2d at 867 (1940).

[34] Ford v. Ford, 91 N.H. 161, 15 A.2d 866 (1940).

[35] Harris v. Parker, 66 N.H. 324, 23 A. 81 (1890).

[36] Ford v. Ford, 91 N.H. at 163, 15 A.2d at 867 (1940).

§ 29-5(c). Taxation

RSA 553:22 provides that the place of taxation of the decedent's property shall not be changed as a result of appointment of a special administrator. The case of *Kent v. Exeter*[37] holds further that the personal estate of the decedent is not taxable to the special administrator who was appointed because of delay in determining the final grant of administration.

In fact, as the Court noted in *Towle v. Yeaton*,[38] the statute does not impose any duty upon the special administrator to concern himself with tax obligations of the estate. However, the court may impose such a duty upon him. RSA 89:16 empowers the Department of Revenue Administration to petition the court for appointment of a resident administrator or a special administrator, as the circumstances require. The property is transferred to the administrator or special administrator upon appointment, and it becomes his duty to collect and pay the tax and to account for the balance of the property.

§ 29-5(d). Uniform Probate Code Provisions

The Uniform Probate Code, in §§ 3-614-3-618 gives the register of probate in an emergency, or the probate court otherwise, the broad power to appoint special administrators whenever "necessary to preserve the estate or to secure its proper administration." § 3-614. Once appointed, a special administrator "has the power of a general personal representative except as limited in the appointment and duties" in the order appointing him. § 3-617.

---

[37] Kent v. Exeter, 68 N.H. 469, 470, 44 A. 607 (1896).

[38] Towle v. Yeaton, 97 N.H. 427, 430, 90 A.2d 496, 498 (1952).

§ 29-6.   Executor De Son Tort—In General

Although an executor *de son tort* is often considered to be a type of administrator, in reality he is not an administrator at all, in the sense of being a person appointed by law to administer a decedent's estate. Rather, the term executor *de son tort* refers to a person who wrongfully takes charge of a decedent's property and as a consequence will be charged and held to the duties of an administrator.

At common law, one who without any authority from the deceased or the probate court did such acts as belonged to the office of an executor or administrator was called an executor *de son tort* (literally, "of his wrong"). *Emery v. Berry.*[39] As such, he can be held liable for his actions by the decedent's creditors.[40] The term applies whether the decedent dies testate or intestate.[41] The action contemplated by the doctrine, and by subsequent statutes, was "intermeddl[ing] with the personal property of a deceased's estate before an administrator has been appointed." *Ela v. Ela.*[42] Since an administrator has few duties as to the decedent's real estate, intermeddling with real estate of a decedent would not constitute a person an executor *de son tort.*[43]

The present statute carries forward the same principles. RSA 553:17 makes an executor *de son tort* liable for double damages:

> If any person wrongfully intermeddles with, embezzles, alienates, wastes or destroys any of the personal estate of a deceased person he shall be liable to actions of the creditors and others aggrieved, as executor in his own wrong, to double the value of such estate.

What constitutes intermeddling? *In Emery v. Berry,*[44] the Court held that as between a creditor of the deceased and a person who intermeddles

---

[39] Emery v. Berry, 28 N.H. 473, 481 (1854).

[40] Atkinson, Wills §§ 470–571 (2d ed. 1953).

[41] Brown v. Leavitt, 26 N.H. 493, 495 (1853).

[42] Ela v. Ela, 70 N.H. 163, 164, 47 A. 414, 415 (1900); Emery v. Berry, 28 N.H. 473, 485 (1854) adds the legislative interpretation that an unlawful meddling means "all such as takes place without giving bond as administrator or executor." (Emphasis added.)

[43] Ela v. Ela, 70 N.H. 163, 164, 47 A. 414, 415 (1900). See Chapter 35 *infra*.

[44] Emery v. Berry, 28 N.H. 473 (1854).

with estate goods, "very slight acts indeed will make him liable as an executor *de son tort*."[45] Thus:

> All acts which assume any particular control over the property, without legal right shown, will make a person executor in his own wrong, as against creditors. Any act which evinces a legal control, by possession, direction or otherwise, will, unexplained, make him liable.[46]

The absence of a legal right to act will likewise render a foreign executor or administrator liable as an executor *de son tort*, if he attempts to interfere with property in a jurisdiction in which he has not been granted ancillary administration.[47]

With regard to slight or single actions, *Leach v. Pillsbury*,[48] raises, but does not answer, the question of whether a single act of receiving and paying out money of an estate can make the person so acting an executor *de son tort* as against a rightful administrator, so that the creditor may protect himself in a suit brought by the administrator.[49] However, the case of *Emery v. Berry* suggests that Leach tentatively answered the question in the affirmative.[50]

A slight action may not be enough if the actor is only a go-between, unaware that he may be wrongfully dealing with the decedent's property. In *Holden v. Farmers' & Traders' National Bank*,[51] the defendant bank had received funds for deposit from persons purporting to be executors of an estate, and subsequently paid out the funds in accordance with the depositors' instructions. The Court held that a bank is only under an obligation to ensure that once it accepts a deposit, it pays out only as the particular depositor directs. Since the depositor was not the decedent, but the alleged executors, the bank fulfilled its duty by following their

---

[45] Emery v. Berry, 28 N.H. 473, 483 (1854).

[46] *Id.*

[47] Willard v. Hammond, 21 N.H. 382, 385 (1850). See Clark v. Clement, 33 N.H. 563, 567 (1856); Chapter 32 *infra*.

[48] Leach v. Pillsbury, 15 N.H. 137 (1844).

[49] Leach v. Pillsbury, 15 N.H. 137, 139 (1844). See also Pickering v. Coleman, 12 N.H. 148 (1841).

[50] Emery v. Berry, 28 N.H. at 482 (1854).

[51] Holden v. Farmers' & Traders' Nat'l Bank, 77 N.H. 535, 93 A. 1040 (1915).

orders.[52] As to a small account the decedent held at the same bank, however, the bank was held liable for turning over the funds of that account to the alleged executors without determining whether they had qualified.[53]

Acts not intended to interfere with the decedent's property will not render the actor an executor *de son tort*. Accordingly, if he acts out of necessity or humanity—burying the corpse of the deceased, locking up his goods, or feeding his cattle—not presuming to have any more control over the property than another, he is not an executor in his own wrong, provided his benign purpose in taking possession of the decedent's goods is clearly apparent.[54]

Library References

Am Jur 2d Executors and Administrators §§ 34–51

CJS Executors and Administrators §§ 1063–68

§ 29-6(a). Effect of Acts

The Court in *Pickering v. Coleman* repeated the general proposition that payments made "in the due course of administration" by an executor *de son tort* are good.[55] The Court noted, however, one is not an executor *de son tort* through the single action of delivering goods of the decedent to a creditor in payment of a debt, with the consequence that such an action is not considered to be in the due course of administration, and the payment made can subsequently be recovered by the lawfully appointed administrator.[56]

A sale of goods of the deceased by an executor *de son tort* was thought not to give any title to the buyer as against a rightful administrator in *Giles v. Churchill*,[57] but the *Pickering* Court noted that this language in *Giles* was dicta.[58] The *Pickering* Court held that an executor could

---

[52] Holden v. Farmers' & Traders' Nat'l Bank, 77 N.H. 535, 537, 93 A. 1040, 1042 (1915) (plaintiff must show invasion of his property right).

[53] Holden v. Farmers' & Traders' Nat'l Bank, 77 N.H. 535, 538, 93 A. 1040, 1042 (1915).

[54] Emery v. Berry, 28 N.H. at 483 (1854).

[55] Pickering v. Coleman, 12 N.H. at 151 (1841).

[56] *Id.*

[57] Giles v. Churchill, 5 N.H. 337, 342 (1831).

[58] Pickering v. Coleman, 12 N.H. at 151–52 (1841).

not convey title when the act was not in the due course of administration.[59] Furthermore, if an executor *de son tort* sells goods and afterwards takes administration, the sale is good by relation.[60] And, if a buyer buys from an executor *de son tort* and the buyer later takes out administration, he cannot maintain an action in trover against the executor *de son tort* because he assented to the sale.[61] Similarly, if the executor *de son tort* is settling the solvent estate of a decedent at the request of the heirs, the heirs cannot later maintain trover against him.[62]

Library References

Am Jur 2d Executors and Administrators §§ 45–51

CJS Executors and Administrators §§ 1066–67

§ 29-6(b). Liabilities

The liability of an executor *de son tort* is founded on the tort of conversion, the liability of a duly-appointed executor is founded on consent and contract.[63] Accordingly, different rules and principles apply to each.[64]

In *Bellows v. Goodall*,[65] the Court indicated that an action against an intermeddler may be regarded as one against an administrator by estate creditors. The principle is that having found the intermeddler dealing with the assets as if he were a legal administrator, estate creditors may consider him as "having a will of the deceased in which he is appointed executor, but which he has not yet proved"[66] and therefore may treat him as holding the relation of administrator, which he has assumed, and proceed against him by suit, independently of the statute, subjecting him to the duties and troubles of executorship because he has assumed to exercise

---

[59] *Id.*

[60] Giles v. Churchill, 5 N.H. at 342 (1831).

[61] *Id.*

[62] Giles v. Churchill, 5 N.H. at 342 (1831). If the estate turns out to be insolvent, however, it is possible recovery may be had of the creditor of that which the creditor received in settlement of his debt above what he may have received beyond his just share of the estate.

[63] Brown v. Leavitt, 26 N.H. at 495 (1853).

[64] *Id.*

[65] Bellows v. Goodall, 32 N.H. 97 (1855).

[66] Bellows v. Goodall, 32 N.H. 97, 99 (1855).

its powers, and holding him to administer for their benefit all the assets in his hands, as the rightful administrator would be bound to do.[67]

On the other hand, the executor *de son tort* is not entitled to the "powers, rights or privileges of an executor, rightfully exercising that office" but is liable as the statute prescribes.[68]

At common law the liability of the executor *de son tort* was limited to the value of the assets which came into his hand.[69] This was changed by RSA 533:17, which now provides for double damages. The *Bellows* case holds that "[t]he only effect and operation of the statute are to enlarge the liability to double the amount of the common law liability."[70] This double amount is not to be recovered as a penalty by any creditor or any number of creditors but belongs to the decedent's estate as a whole.[71]

Library References

Am Jur 2d Executors and Administrators §§ 46–48

CJS Executors and Administrators §§ 1064–65

§ 29-6(c). Suits By or Against

Those who are creditors of the estate with which the executor *de son tort* has interfered may institute actions against him under the rules of law applying to recovery of their claims against the decedent's estate.[72] The form of action, properly adapted to the nature of the creditor's claim, is the same whether it is against a rightful administrator or executor or against an executor *de son tort*.[73] In either case, the object is to obtain a judgment *de bonis testatoris* (against the goods of the decedent). Under RSA 553:17, the executor *de son tort* is considered as having the goods of the estate in his hands "against which the creditors may proceed by suits for the satisfaction of their claims until [the] double value has been exhausted."[74]

---

[67] *Id.*

[68] Brown v. Leavitt, 26 N.H. at 496 (1853).

[69] Bellows v. Goodall, 32 N.H. at 99 (1855).

[70] Bellows v. Goodall, 32 N.H. at 100 (1855).

[71] *Id.*

[72] Bellows v. Goodall, 32 N.H. 97 (1855).

[73] Bellows v. Goodall, 32 N.H. 97 (1855) (an action for debt is accordingly proper against an executor *de son tort*).

[74] *Id.*

RSA 553:17 provides that an executor *de son tort* is liable to creditors of the estate "and others aggrieved." A creditor of an heir of the estate might fall within the latter category.[75] But if such a creditor can present no evidence that his debtor was an heir or heir-at-law, he cannot be considered an aggrieved party under the statute.[76]

Library References

Am Jur 2d Executors and Administrators §§ 34-1, 1252–53

CJS Executors and Administrators § 1068

§ 29-6(d). Defenses

At common law, an executor *de son tort* was held to be "liable to all the troubles of an executorship, without any of the profits or advantages."[77] Executors *de son tort* fare no better under the statutes. In *Brown v. Leavitt*, the Court examined several statutes that limit the liability of regular administrators or executors and found they did not apply to executors *de son tort* because there has been no grant of administration to them.[78] In a broader holding, *Brown v. Leavitt* asserts that none of the limitations of what is now RSA 556 can be invoked by an executor *de son tort*.[79]

An important distinction must be made here between those who are never lawfully appointed and those who, although acting initially in the role of executor *de son tort*, later do take out letters of administration. In *Emery v. Berry*, the Court found that an executor *de son tort* might be able to avoid the penalty prescribed by the statute by taking out letters of administration.[80] If he takes out such letters, "this puts him, in many respects, on the same ground as if he had been administrator before he inter-meddled; and if he is afterwards sued as executor *de son tort*, he may plead that he is administrator, and not executor, in abatement." *Clements v. Swain*.[81] But if an executor *de son tort* does not act until

---

[75] Leach v. Pillsbury, 15 N.H. at 139 (1844).

[76] *Id.*

[77] Brown v. Leavitt, 26 N.H. at 495 (1853).

[78] Brown v. Leavitt, 26 N.H. at 495–97 (1853). See RSA 554:6, RSA 556:1–3, 556:5 and 556:7.

[79] Brown v. Leavitt, 26 N.H. at 497 (1853).

[80] Emery v. Berry, 28 N.H. at 484 (1854).

[81] Clements v. Swain, 2 N.H. 475, 476 (1822).

he has been sued, he cannot escape by taking administration *pendente lite*.[82]

Even without a later grant of administration, however, an executor *de son tort* may raise some defenses. He may question whether the plaintiff truly was a creditor of the estate as of the time the plaintiff brought suit. Because a claim against a decedent's estate, "once barred, is cut off entirely,"[83] if the plaintiff's right of action has become barred, he is no longer a creditor within the meaning of RSA 553:17. Thus, if the statute of limitations provides that a claim must be brought within six years after the cause of action accrues (with an extension as against defendant decedent's estate if the statute has not run out before the defendant's death), no action can be brought even against an executor *de son tort* if the six years had passed before the decedent died.[84]

An executor *de son tort* may also defend on the ground that before the commencement of suit against him he paid over all that he held to the rightful executor or administrator.[85] Similarly, after he has himself administered to the extent of double the value of assets which came into his hands, he may defend on this ground against other creditors.[86] The strict pleading in these situations is the defensive plea of *plene administravit* ("fully administered": all assets in his hands have been fully administered and none remain out of which plaintiff's claim could be satisfied).[87] If there has been a bona fide recovery against the executor *de son tort* to double the amount he received, he will also be discharged as having paid by order of the law.[88]

The defense of voluntary payment of debts to double the amount he received is not, however, good if the estate is insolvent, because the

---

[82] Clements v. Swain, 2 N.H. 475, 476 (1822). A comparison of Emery v. Berry with Clements v. Swain raises a question because the court in Emery v. Berry found that the defendant executor *de son tort* (already the subject of a suit) might avoid the penalty of the statute by now taking out administration. Emery v. Berry, 28 N.H. at 484 (1854).

[83] Brown v. Leavitt, 26 N.H. at 497 (1853).

[84] Brown v. Leavitt, 26 N.H. at 498–99 (1853) (pleadings did not show statutory time had passed before defendant's death and accordingly suit not barred).

[85] Neal v. Baker, 2 N.H. 477 (1822).

[86] Bellows v. Goodall, 32 N.H. at 99–100 (1855). In contrast, Neal v. Baker, 2 N.H. at 478 (1822), questions whether payment of just debts to double the amount received would be a good defense.

[87] Bellows v. Goodall, 32 N.H. at 99–100 (1855); Neal v. Baker, 2 N.H. at 477 (1822).

[88] Neal v. Baker, 2 N.H. at 478 (1822).

executor *de son tort* has no right to elect whom he will pay. *Neal v. Baker*.[89] The same would be true if a recovery against him was collusive.[90]

Library References

Am Jur 2d Executors and Administrators §§ 47–51, 707, 1252–53
CJS Executors and Administrators § 1068

§ 29-6(e). Uniform Probate Code Provisions

The Uniform Probate Code has no equivalent to an executor *de son tort*. Rather, a personal representative is given strong powers to recover estate property wrongfully in the hands of another. §3-709-3-711. Specifically, the Code provides that the "request by a personal representative for dealing of any property possessed by an heir or devisee is conclusive evidence . . . that the possession of the property by the personal representative is necessary for purposes of administration. . . . He may maintain an action to recover possession of property or to determine the title thereto." § 3-709.

§ 29-7. Notice of Appointment

RSA 553:16[91] provides that the register of probate, within fifteen days of the appointment of an administrator or executor, shall cause notice to be published in accordance with the provisions of RSA 550:10. No publication of notice is required in the administration of small estates under RSA 553:31.

Forms

See Form 220 in Appendix for a Petition for Estate Administration.

---

[89] Neal v. Baker, 2 N.H. 477 (1822).
[90] *Id.*
[91] As amended by P.L., 1996, c. 199.

CHAPTER 30. CONFLICT OF LAWS

§ 30-1. Choice of Law Rules

The basic rule is that "ordinarily a will is probated and an executor appointed in the state where the decedent was domiciled at the time of his death."[1] In the case of intestacy, an administrator is customarily appointed in any state where the decedent's will would have been admitted to probate, for instance, where the decedent was domiciled at the time of his death. Restatement (Second) Conflict of Laws, § 315.

In New Hampshire, the personal estate of a New Hampshire domiciliary is governed by the laws of his domicile. *Shute v. Sargent.*[2] One spouse may have a domicile separate from the other and it is the law of the domiciled decedent spouse that governs distribution of that spouse's property.[3]

Furthermore, § 316 of the Restatement (Second) Conflict of Laws, provides that "the duties of an executor or administrator with regard to the conduct of an administration are usually determined by the civil law of the state of appointment." It is a basic principle that unless otherwise provided by statute, the devolution of personal property in both testate and intestate proceedings is determined by the law of the decedent's domicile at his death. *Eyre v. Storer.*[4] Therefore, a judgment in

---

[1] Restatement (Second) Conflict of Laws, § 314, comment e.

[2] Shute v. Sargent, 67 N.H. 305, 36 A. 282 (1892); Vandewalker v. Rollins, 63 N.H. 460, 3 A. 625 (1886).

[3] Shute v. Sargent, 67 N.H. 305, 36 A. 282 (1892).

[4] Eyre v. Storer, 37 N.H. 114 (1858). See also C. DEGRANDPRE, 7 NEW HAMPSHIRE PRACTICE: WILLS, TRUSTS AND GIFTS (3d ed. 1997) Chapter 7.

administrative proceedings by a court in the domiciliary state will usually be followed by the forum state with respect to the title to local moveables. Restatement (Second) Conflict of Laws, § 317(1).

On the other hand, succession to land is normally provided by the law of the situs state. *Eyre v. Storer*;[5] Restatement (Second) Conflict of Laws, §§ 236–243.

These somewhat mechanical rules are being gradually replaced by choice of law rules "based on the relevant policies and interests at stake in given situations,"[6] and thus must be constantly reexamined in each situation.[7] In *Royce v. Estate of Denby*,[8] the New Hampshire Supreme Court applied New York law to a will executed in New York even though the testator's domicile at her death was in New Hampshire. The Court specifically rejected mechanical application of "the usual conflict of law rule that the law of the testator's domicile at death should control distribution of his real property"[9] under the unusual facts of that case: the testator had made a will in New York while domiciled there and suffered a stroke rendering her incompetent, as a result of which her grandchildren moved her to New Hampshire to be with them. She died a domiciliary of New Hampshire, unable to change her will.

More recently, the New Hampshire Supreme Court reaffirmed the general rule that "a decedent's personal property passes according to the law of the State of domicile, while real property passes according to the law of the State where it lies." *In re Estate of Rubert*.[10] In *Rubert*, the Court distinguished the *Denby* case and held that it could "see no reason to deviate from the traditional role that the law of the situs controls the succession of the real property."[11]

Library References

Am Jur 2d Conflict of Laws § 52 et seq.

Am Jur 2d Descent and Distribution §§ 16–17

---

[5] Eyre v. Storer, 37 N.H. 114 (1858). See Chapter 53, *infra*.

[6] Royce v. Estate of Denby, 117 N.H. 893, 897, 379 A.2d 1256, 1259 (1977).

[7] C. DEGRANDPRE, 7 NEW HAMPSHIRE PRACTICE: WILLS, TRUSTS AND GIFTS (3d ed. 1997) Chapter 7.

[8] Royce v. Estate of Denby, 117 N.H. 893, 379 A.2d 1256 (1977).

[9] Royce v. Estate of Denby, 117 N.H. 893, 897, 379 A.2d 1256, 1259 (1977).

[10] In re Estate of Rubert, 139 N.H. 273, 276 (1993).

[11] In re Estate of Rubert, 139 N.H. 273, 277 (1993).

Am Jur 2d Executors and Administrators § 1171

CJS Conflict of Laws §§ 10, 13, 16(5), 16(7), 18(1)–(3), 18(10)–(12), 19(1), 19(5)–(6), 20(4)

CJS Descent and Distribution §§ 3–5

CJS Executors and Administrators § 2

CJS Wills §§ 4, 77, 96, 150, 329, 345

Conflict of laws as to legitimacy or legitimation, or as to rights of illegitimates, as affecting descent and distribution of decedents' estates. 73 ALR 941, supplemented 87 ALR2d 1274.

Nonresidence of decedent owning real property in the state as affecting application of local statute relating to descent of real property. 119 ALR 523.

Conflict of laws respecting wills as affected by statute of forum providing for will executed in accordance with law of another state. 169 ALR 554.

§ 30-2. Law Governing Property Located in Another State

When a decedent dies owns property in more than state, it may be necessary to take out administration in each state. While the principal administration is in the state in which the decedent was domiciled, administration is ancillary in all other states.[12] Insofar as ancillary administration is concerned, the general principle is that the conduct of administration is governed by the local law of the ancillary state. Restatement (Second) Conflict of Laws, § 316. Thus, the law of the state of ancillary administration governs the payment of debts and matters of administration. *Kingsbury v. Bazeley.*[13] This is so, even though the law of the decedent's domicile governs the distribution of the decedent's personal property upon his death:

> While in giving effect to a foreign will courts are governed by the law of the testator's domicile, it has never been held that in the administration of an estate the courts of the testator's domicile would be governed by the law of the situs of personal property. The estate within the control of the court is to be administered according to the law of the state. The property to

---

[12] Crosby v. Charlestown, 78 N.H. 39, 95 A. 1043 (1915).

[13] Kingsbury v. Bazeley, 75 N.H. 13, 70 A. 916 (1908).

be administered embraces all that was originally within the state, or which the executor has been able to find elsewhere and bring here. Whatever sums the executor may be obliged to pay to bring the property within the state merely reduce the amount within the control of the court.[14]

As a result of the operation of this rule, where inheritance taxes are deducted from property in an ancillary state and the balance net of the taxes is remitted to a New Hampshire primary administrator, the taxes paid in the ancillary administration will not be deducted pro-rata against the specific legacies but rather against the estate as a whole as an expense of administration in accordance with the law of New Hampshire and not the ancillary state.[15]

In *Goodall v. Marshall*,[16] New Hampshire was the ancillary state, the decedent having died with property here. There were creditors of the decedent in New Hampshire and the Supreme Court held that law of the state of ancillary administration controlled the matter of the payment to creditors:

> The ancillary administration, therefore, operating only upon the property within that jurisdiction, is, throughout its whole proceedings, so far as creditors are concerned, to be governed by the law of the place. The property which is subjected to it, notwithstanding it is moveable, no longer follows the law of the late domicile of its former possessor, except in regard to the balance which may be in the hands of the ancillary adminis-trator, after the payment of the debts; and this will be subjected to the law of that domicile, either by being transmitted to the place of the domicile; or, if special circumstances require it, by a decree of distribution, according to that law, in the forum of the ancillary administration. It seems to be settled that this latter course is within the discretion of the court. (Emphasis added.)[17]

For a full discussion of Ancillary Administration, see Chapter 32, *infra*.

---

[14] Kingsbury v. Bazeley, 75 N.H. 13, 18, 70 A. 916, 919 (1908).

[15] *Id.*

[16] Goodall v. Marshall, 11 N.H. 88 (1840).

[17] Goodall v. Marshall, 11 N.H. 88, 93 (1840).

§ 30-3. Law Governing Proof of Claims

The Restatement (Second) Conflict of Laws § 346 states the rule concerning claims as: "The manner in which a claim may be proved in a state is determined by the law of that state."

Where the entire estate is insolvent, the court in each state will, so far as possible, secure pro rata payment of all claims, irrespective of the residence, place of business, domicile or citizenship of the creditors or of the place where the claims were originally proved. Restatement (Second) Conflict of Laws, § 348; *Goodall v. Marshall.* [18]

---

[18] *Id.*

CHAPTER 31. DOMICILE

§ 31-1. Domicile—In General

Surprisingly, the New Hampshire Supreme Court has had little occasion to wrestle with a definition of the term *domicile* in the context of the administration of estates. It is, therefore, necessary to look to other authority for an understanding of the meaning of that term.

While not directly applicable to the issue of the determination of domicile under conflict of law rules, New Hampshire does define domicile for purposes of statutory construction. RSA 21:6-a provides that:

> Residence or residency shall mean a person's place of abode or domicile. The place of abode or domicile is that designated by a person as his principal place of physical presence for the indefinite future to the exclusion of all others. Such residence or residency shall not be interrupted or lost by a temporary absence from it, if there is an intent to return to such residence or residency as the principal place of physical presence.

Library References

Am Jur 2d Executors and Administrators § 1171
CJS Descent and Distribution §§ 3–5
CJS Executors and Administrators §§ 2, 18

§ 31-1(a). For Tax Purposes

For inheritance tax purposes, RSA 86:71 provides a manner of determining domicile where there is a dispute with another state over domicile. This statute is taken from the Uniform Interstate Compromise of Death Taxes Act.

For disputes over domicile in connection with federal estate taxes and the estate tax credit due New Hampshire upon the death of a New Hampshire domiciliary (the "soak-up" tax, RSA Chapter 87), New Hampshire has enacted the Uniform Estate Tax Apportionment Act. RSA 88-A.[1]

§ 31-2.   Requirements for Domicile

With regard to disputes over domicile not related to taxes, general principles of conflict of laws must be applied. Section 15 of the Restatement (Second) Conflict of Laws, provides that a person's domicile is determined by a physical presence in the state and "an attitude of mind." A person must be physically present in a state to acquire a domicile there, although this does not mean that the establishment of a home in a particular domiciliary state is necessary. Restatement (Second) Conflict of Laws, § 16.

The attitude of mind required for the establishment of a domicile is that "a person must intend to make that place his home for the time at least." Restatement (Second) Conflict of Laws, § 18.

In *Kirby v. Charlestown,*[2] the New Hampshire Supreme Court adopted a slightly different rule, holding that:

> [a] person does not acquire a new residence by merely going to another town with the intention of making it his domicile. He must not only go there with that intention but also with the intention of residing there for a more or less definite time and making it his home. . . . By home as that word is used in the law of domicile is intended what every one has in mind when he thinks of home—his principal residence, the place to which he always intends to return, or the one place he thinks of as home.[3]

The *Kirby* case followed earlier New Hampshire cases that supported the general proposition that residence plus intent to remain equals

---

[1] See Chapter 58 *infra.*

[2] Kirby v. Charlestown, 78 N.H. 301, 99 A. 835 (1916).

[3] Kirby v. Charlestown, 78 N.H. 301, 303, 99 A. 835, 836 (1916).

domicile.[4] Cases since *Kirby* have continued to so hold, adding that intention is a question of fact.[5] Furthermore, an existing domicile continues until another domicile is found.[6]

In an ancillary administration case, *Leach v. Pillsbury,*[7] the decedent died in New Orleans and his estate was settled there. The balance of funds were sent to his brother in New Hampshire who was his heir under Louisiana law. The decedent's father claimed the balance of the estate because under New Hampshire law he would be entitled to the funds. The New Hampshire Court found that the decedent was a Louisiana domiciliary, that Louisiana law applied which favored the brother, and that the father took nothing:

> There is sufficient evidence that the actual domicile of the deceased was in New Orleans at the time of his death. He was over twenty-one years of age when he went there. He lived there three years, and repeatedly declared that he should make that the place of his permanent residence. There was the fact of residence, and also the intent, and the concurrence of these constitutes the domicile. And the succession to personal property is governed exclusively by the law of the actual domicile of the intestate, at the time of his death.[8]

§ 31-3. Choice of Law

Insofar as conflict of laws is concerned, the domicile of a person is determined by the forum state according to its own standards. Restatement (Second) Conflict of Laws, § 13; *Kirby v. Charlestown.*[9] If a person is found to be domiciled here, his will cannot be filed as a will of a person not domiciled here. In the *Kirby* case, the Court held that a will of a person found by the probate judge to be domiciled here, cannot be filed under RSA 552:13 relating to the filing of foreign wills.

---

[4] Leach v. Pillsbury, 15 N.H. 137 (1844).

[5] McGee v. Bragg, 94 N.H. 349, 351, 53 A.2d 428, 430 (1947) (notary case); Bailey v. Bailey, 93 N.H. 259, 261, 40 A.2d 581, 582 (1945) (divorce case).

[6] Bailey v. Bailey, 93 N.H. 259, 261, 40 A.2d 581, 582 (1945) (divorce case); Ayer v. Weeks, 65 N.H. 248, 249, 18 A. 1108, 1109 (1889) (insolvency proceedings).

[7] Leach v. Pillsbury, 15 N.H. 137 (1844).

[8] Leach v. Pillsbury, 15 N.H. 137, 138 (1844).

[9] Kirby v. Charlestown, 78 N.H. 301, 99 A. 835 (1916).

Even where the claimant had no other avenue of appeal, New Hampshire would not allow a collateral attack on another state's finding of domicile.[10] In *In re Estate of Rubert*, the Supreme Court considered the domicile of a decedent who had moved to New Hampshire to live with his daughter but often visited with his son in another state. Shortly before death, the decedent leased a unit in a retirement facility near his son for himself and his wife. He consulted an attorney in the foreign state to prepare a new will and trust but, in the meantime, executed a handwritten will leaving everything to his son. Before the attorney could prepare the new will and trust, the decedent died in New Hampshire while visiting his daughter.

The defendant son submitted the handwritten will for probate in the foreign state. The plaintiff daughter contested the issue of domicile in the foreign court but, upon appeal, that court found that the decedent was domiciled in the foreign state. When the defendant sought to file the will in New Hampshire for ancillary probate because the decedent owned both personal and real estate property in New Hampshire, the plaintiff daughter again contested the issue of domicile. The New Hampshire probate court ruled that the decedent was domiciled in New Hampshire.

The Supreme Court reversed the probate court's finding, stating that the full faith and credit clause of the United States Constitution, article IV, section 1, requires that a "final judgment of a court of competent jurisdiction is entitled to the same faith and credit as to the parties before it as it was in the State of issuance."[11]

The Court held that the finding of domicile could not be collaterally attacked in New Hampshire even though the plaintiff's appeal in the foreign state was rejected on procedural grounds.

For a full discussion of choice of laws rules, see Chapter 30, Conflict of Laws, *infra*.

---

[10] In re Estate of Rubert, 139 N.H. 273 (1993).

[11] In re Estate of Rubert, 139 N.H. 273, 275 (1993).

CHAPTER 32. ANCILLARY ADMINISTRATION

§ 32-1. Ancillary Administration Generally

Unlike the Uniform Probate Code,[1] there is no single chapter or group of sections of the Revised Statutes dealing with ancillary administration. Rather, the principles governing this subject are primarily court-propounded, with a scattering of statutory provisions.[2]

If the decedent on the date of his death owned property in more than one state, it may be necessary to take out administration in each state. Principal administration is granted in the state in which the decedent was domiciled; in all other states, administration is ancillary. *Crosby v. Charlestown.*[3] There is no "race to the courthouse" to establish a principal administration. It is immaterial which jurisdiction grants administration first; the principal or original administration is where the decedent died domiciled.[4]

The same person may, and often does, serve as both regular administrator (also referred to interchangeably as the principal, domiciliary or

---

[1] See Article IV of the Uniform Probate Code, entitled *Foreign Personal Representatives; Ancillary Administration.*

[2] New Hampshire has not adopted the Uniform Ancillary Administration of Estates Act propounded by the Uniform Commissioners on State Laws.

[3] Crosby v. Charlestown, 78 N.H. 39, 46, 95 A. 1043, 1046 (1915); Clark v. Clement, 33 N.H. 563, 567 (1856).

[4] Crosby v. Charlestown, 78 N.H. 39, 95 A. 1043 (1915).

primary administrator) and as ancillary administrator. However, the capacity of the principal administrator to act as ancillary administrator is not automatic. The title of an administrator derived from appointment in the domicile state does not *de jure* extend beyond that jurisdiction.[5] Instead, the primary administrator may petition for appointment as ancillary administrator in the nondomicile state in accordance with the laws of that state, just as one not appointed in the domicile state must do to qualify for ancillary administration.

If an administrator appointed in one state interferes with property of the decedent in a jurisdiction where he has not been appointed, he runs the risk of liability as an executor *de son tort*.[6] Absent appointment in the foreign jurisdiction, the general rule is that an executor or administrator may not sue or be sued there.[7] Although there are circumstances under which ancillary administration can be avoided, limitations on powers often lead to a decision to seek qualification in the foreign state anyway.

The office of ancillary administrator is legally separate from the office of regular executor or administrator even when one person fills both roles.[8] Care must therefore be taken to follow the law of the jurisdiction involved, and to guard against the possibility of litigating an issue in the wrong forum. In *Keenan v. Tonry*,[9] for example, the New Hampshire Supreme Court held that the New Hampshire courts were without jurisdiction to determine the possible liability of a New Hampshire executor for maladministration because the foreclosure sale which was the subject of contention had occurred in Massachusetts and had been undertaken pursuant to a Massachusetts grant of ancillary administration to the executor.

---

[5] Heydock's Appeal, 7 N.H. 496, 503 (1835).

[6] Heydock's Appeal, 7 N.H. 496, 503 (1835). See Clark v. Clement, 33 N.H. 563, 567 (1856); Willard v. Hammond, 21 N.H. 382, 385 (1850); Leach v. Pillsbury, 15 N.H. 137 (1844).

[7] Goodall v. Marshall, 11 N.H. 88, 89 (1840). See Leonard v. Putnam, 51 N.H. 247, 249 (1871); Taylor v. Barron, 35 N.H. 484, 496 (1857), *overruled on other grounds* Lomas v. Hilliard, 60 N.H. 148 (1880); Clark v. Clement, 33 N.H. at 567 (1856); Heydock's Appeal, 7 N.H. at 503 (1835). See also Keenan v. Tonry, 91 N.H. 220, 223, 16 A.2d 705, 708 (1940); Gove v. Gove, 64 N.H. 503, 504, 15 A. 121, 122 (1888). But see Ghilain v. Couture, 84 N.H. 48, 51–53, 146 A. 395, 396–97 (1929).

[8] Keenan v. Tonry, 91 N.H. at 223, 16 A.2d at 708 (1940) (quoting Restatement Conflict of Laws, § 446).

[9] Keenan v. Tonry, 91 N.H. 220, 16 A.2d 705 (1940).

Upon the grant of administration, the ancillary representative becomes exclusively vested with title to all the assets of the decedent within the jurisdiction.[10] "But the title of the ancillary representative extends only to property of the decedent which is assets for the purpose of administration therein." *Crosby v. Charlestown.*[11] Simply because the decedent's evidence of ownership of a debt due is situated in the ancillary jurisdiction, that does not alone mean the assets are within the ancillary administrator's province. Thus, where intangibles such as stocks, bonds and notes, were found in a safe deposit box in one jurisdiction, it did not automatically follow that those assets would be administered there.[12] Similarly, an ancillary administrator is responsible in his respective state only for the assets he obtained or should have obtained as a result of his appointment by the court of that state. *Keenan v. Tonry.*[13]

The early New Hampshire case of *Goodall v. Marshall* holds that the duties of the ancillary administrator are to collect debts due the decedent in that jurisdiction, to convert the personal property into money, and upon settlement of the administrator's account to transfer the balance in his hands to the place of domicile.[14] *Crosby v. Charlestown* states the purpose of ancillary administration somewhat differently, finding an ancillary administrator's principal duty to be administration of the decedent's assets only to the extent necessary to pay decedent's debts in that jurisdiction.[15]

The court that has appointed the ancillary representative is the proper authority to review his account and to decree the balance to be paid over to the domiciliary executor or administrator.[16] Accordingly, it is error for a New Hampshire probate court with jurisdiction only over the domiciliary executor to determine what allowance shall be made to an ancillary administrator for his services and expenses, except insofar as

---

[10] Crosby v. Charlestown, 78 N.H. at 46, 94 A. at 1046 (1915).

[11] *Id.*

[12] Crosby v. Charlestown, 78 N.H. at 47–48, 94 A. at 1046, 1047 (1915) (an ancillary administrator does not acquire title to debt instruments simply because the evidences of debt fall into his hands). See also Leonard v. Putnam, 51 N.H. at 250 (1870) (administrator has no interest in debts due in state in which he has not been appointed).

[13] Keenan v. Tonry, 91 N.H. at 223, 16 A.2d at 708 (1940).

[14] Goodall v. Marshall, 11 N.H. at 90 (1840).

[15] Crosby v. Charlestown, 78 N.H. at 47, 95 A. at 1046 (1915).

[16] Keenan v. Tonry, 91 N.H. at 225, 16 A.2d at 709 (1940).

the allowance is charged against New Hampshire assets. *Keenan v. Tonry.*[17]

In *Todd v. Todd,*[18] the Supreme Court held that since there is no statute or special common law rule in this State providing for distribution of the personal estate of nonresident decedents in accordance with the laws of New Hampshire, the ancillary administrator should remit the final balance in his hands to the domiciliary executor or administrator.[19] The *Todd* case changed the prior rule, as stated in *Heydock's Appeal,*[20] that the court granting ancillary administration could, in the exercise of sound discretion, either decree distribution or remit the property to the domiciliary administrator.

The domiciliary executor or administrator is charged with the balance paid over to him by an ancillary representative, and he must account for it in the probate court overseeing the domiciliary or principal administration.[21]

Library References

Am Jur 2d Executors and Administrators §§ 1168–1213

CJS Executors and Administrators §§ 988–1015

What constitutes "estate" of non-resident decedent within statute providing for local ancillary administration where decedent died leaving an estate in jurisdiction. 34 ALR2d 1270.

§ 32-2. Appointment

The existence of an estate is a prerequisite to the appointment of an ancillary administrator.[22] However, it is enough if a creditor makes a claim against an estate; he need not prove his claim on the merits in order to apply for ancillary administration.[23]

---

[17] *Id.*

[18] Todd v. Todd, 78 N.H. 386, 103 A. 17 (1917).

[19] Todd v. Todd, 78 N.H. 386, 387, 103 A. 17, 17–18 (1917).

[20] Heydock's Appeal, 7 N.H. at 503 (1835). See also Goodall v. Marshall, 11 N.H. at 93 (1840).

[21] Keenan v. Tonry, 91 N.H. at 225, 16 A.2d at 709 (1940). See also Heydock's Appeal, 7 N.H. at 503–504 (1835) (referring to circumstance of same person serving as both principal and ancillary administrator).

[22] Robinson v. Estate of Dana, 87 N.H. 114, 174 A. 772 (1934). See Power v. Plummer, 93 N.H. 37, 39, 35 A.2d 230, 231 (1943).

[23] Robinson v. Estate of Dana, 87 N.H. 114, 174 A. 772 (1934).

As with administrators generally, any creditor may petition for ancillary administration in this state.[24]

The domiciliary administrator usually, but not always, petitions to become the ancillary administrator. Generally, the duly-appointed domiciliary administrator will be recognized as the person to whom ancillary administration will be granted in another state,[25] "and he may appeal from a decree appointing another to such office."[26] If, however, the domiciliary representative intends to use his ancillary office to give anyone an unfair advantage, then, as with any prospective administrator who holds an improper intent, he is not suitable and should not be appointed.[27]

In *Keenan v. Tonry*,[28] it was held that a determination as to whether an ancillary administrator has properly administered his trust in another jurisdiction is to be made only by the courts of that state. Nevertheless, the domiciliary administrator has the duty of exercising due diligence to hold the ancillary administrator to the performance of his duties.[29] The Supreme Court in *Keenan v. Tonry* stated that a New Hampshire probate court, that had appointed a domiciliary executor, could upon petition and proof that the executor failed in this supervisory duty, remove the executor and appoint an administrator w.w.a., whose duty it would be to take steps to have the ancillary administrator's liability determined in that jurisdiction and to have any balance turned over for administration in New Hampshire.[30]

Library References

Am Jur 2d Executors and Administrators §§ 1178–82
CJS Executors and Administrators §§ 989–97

§ 32-3. Suits By and Against Foreign Administrator

The general rule is that an executor or administrator appointed in one state may not sue or be sued in another state unless he has been appointed

---

[24] Swan v. Bill, 95 N.H. 158, 161, 59 A.2d 346, 348 (1948).

[25] Ghilain v. Couture, 84 N.H. at 51, 146 A. at 397 (1929).

[26] Ghilain v. Couture, 84 N.H. at 51, 146 A. at 397 (1929); Graves v. Tilton, 63 N.H. 192, 193 (1884).

[27] Graves v. Tilton, 63 N.H. at 194 (1884).

[28] Keenan v. Tonry, 91 N.H. 220, 16 A.2d 705 (1940).

[29] Keenan v. Tonry, 91 N.H. at 226, 16 A.2d at 709 (1940).

[30] *Id.*

there as well.[31] An early New Hampshire case, *Sabin v. Gilman*,[32] held that it is well-settled that neither an executor nor an administrator can prosecute an action in this state by virtue of letters granted him under authority of another state.

The rule presupposes that an executor or administrator "has no claim to recognition as a matter of right, beyond the bounds of the state of his appointment,"[33] but the absence of legal right is not the reason for the rule.[34] No statute or unbreakable principle of the common law forbids recognition of such a right.[35] Colonial practice was to permit administrators appointed in other jurisdictions to sue in New Hampshire as a matter of courtesy, but the practice was discontinued for lack of reciprocity.[36]

An administrator appointed in one state has no power over the property in another state,[37] unless appointed in both.[38] If one who is appointed executor or administrator leaves his jurisdiction and interferes with the decedent's property in a jurisdiction where he has not been appointed, he may become an executor *de son tort*, and as such may be sued there.[39]

If ancillary administration is undertaken, it is important to remember that the ancillary and domiciliary administrations are legally separate.[40] Litigation involving the estate may be appropriate in only one of the jurisdictions, or in both. The preclusive effect of a judgment should be considered. In *Taylor v. Barron*, the New Hampshire Supreme Court stated:

> When administrations are granted to different persons in different States, they are so far deemed independent of each

[31] See Kirby v. Charlestown, 78 N.H.301, 99 A. 835 (1916).

[32] Sabin v. Gilman, 1 N.H. 193 (1818). See also Clark v. Clement, 33 N.H. at 567 (1856).

[33] Ghilain v. Couture, 84 N.H. at 51, 146 A. at 397 (1929). (Citations omitted.)

[34] *Id.*

[35] *Id.*

[36] *Id.*

[37] Keenan v. Tonry, 91 N.H. at 223, 16 A.2d at 708 (1940); Taylor v. Barron, 35 N.H. at 496 (1857).

[38] Willard v. Hammond, 21 N.H. at 385 (1850).

[39] Willard v. Hammond, 21 N.H. at 385 (1850); Goodall v. Marshall, 11 N.H. at 89–90 (1840); Clark v. Clement, 33 N.H. at 567 (1856).

[40] Keenan v. Tonry, 91 N.H. at 223, 16 A.2d at 708 (1940).

other, that a judgment obtained against one will furnish no right of action, against the other, to affect assets received by the latter by virtue of his own administration.[41]

However, in *Lomas v. Hilliard*,[42] the Court held that when the same individual is the administrator of an estate in two states, and a judgment is entered in one state, that judgment will act as a bar against the same suit between the same parties in this state.

Library References

Am Jur 2d Executors and Administrators § 1183

CJS Executors and Administrators §§ 1007–14

§ 32-4. Exceptions to General Rule

Whether an individual should be required to procure ancillary appointment in New Hampshire will depend upon whether ancillary administration is desirable for the convenience or protection of the parties.[43] "If, upon objection to the maintenance of a suit by the foreign domiciliary administrator, it is made to appear that the interest of either party or of any beneficiary will be better protected by requiring the appointment of and the substitution of an ancillary administrator such a course will be pursued."[44]

There are situations where suit is permitted even though the executor or administrator has not been appointed in the jurisdiction in which he brings suit. For example, a domiciliary executor or administrator may appeal in another state from a decree appointing some other person ancillary administrator.[45] Also, in *Ghilain v. Couture*, the Court held that a domiciliary administratrix appointed in Massachusetts could, in the absence of local administration and without ancillary letters, maintain

---

[41] Taylor v. Barron, 35 N.H. at 498 (1857).

[42] Lomas v. Hilliard, 60 N.H. 148 (1880) (overruling Taylor v. Barron, 35 N.H. 484 (1857), to the extent that Taylor reached a conflicting conclusion; both cases involved claims denied by a commissioner of insolvency).

[43] Ghilain v. Couture, 84 N.H. 48, 58, 146 A. 395, 400 (1929).

[44] Ghilain v. Couture, 84 N.H. 48, 58, 146 A. 395, 400 (1929). But see Power v. Plummer, 93 N.H. at 39, 35 A.2d at 231 (1943); Ela's Appeal, 68 N.H. 35, 36, 38 A. 501, 502 (1894) (indicating collateral attack of ancillary administrator's appointment is not permissible).

[45] Graves v. Tilton, 63 N.H. 192, 193 (1884).

a wrongful death suit in New Hampshire.[46] Upon objection to this manner of proceeding and appointment of the administratrix as the ancillary administratrix, she would be permitted to amend the writ and continue the suit.[47]

Although an appointed executor or administrator has no authority outside his jurisdiction as a matter of right, this is "not, however, from want of title to the assets of his decedent situate in such jurisdiction, but because of his personal incapacity to enforce it."[48] Therefore, in the absence of ancillary administration or statutory prohibition, the domiciliary administrator or executor has been held to have authority to take possession of and remove the decedent's goods and effects in another jurisdiction, or to collect a debt due from a debtor residing there if voluntarily given up or paid, and the administrator or executor may give a "good acquittance and discharge therefor."[49]

New Hampshire cases find many other exceptions to the "rule" that an executor or administrator may not act outside his jurisdiction. A domiciliary administrator may make a valid assignment of a note and mortgage,[50] although to sue upon the note himself he must obtain ancillary administration first.[51] A domiciliary administrator, in the absence of ancillary administration, may also make a valid sale and assignment of stock owned by his decedent in a corporation in this state "and the corporation may voluntarily consent to its transfer by accepting the outstanding certificate and issuing a new one to the purchaser."[52]

---

[46] Ghilain v. Couture, 84 N.H. at 58, 146 A. at 400 (1929). See also Coburn v. Dyke, 103 N.H. 159, 161, 167 A.2d 223, 224 (1961).

[47] Ghilain v. Couture, 84 N.H. 48, 146 A. 395 (1929) (since suit was not being initiated by the ancillary administratrix, but merely continued, the statute of limitations did not preclude it).

[48] Luce v. Manchester & Lawrence R.R., 63 N.H. 588, 590, 3 A. 618, 620 (1886).

[49] Luce v. Manchester & Lawrence R.R., 63 N.H. 588, 590, 3 A. 618, 620 (1886) (cases from other states collected). See also Upton v. White, 92 N.H. 221, 227, 29 A.2d 126, 131 (1942) (upon distribution of assets of testamentary trust in New Hampshire, no ancillary administrator required for Michigan beneficiary, an estate, to collect estate share); Ghilain v. Couture, 84 N.H. at 51, 146 A. at 397 (1929).

[50] Coburn v. Dyke, 103 N.H. 159, 167 A.2d 233 (1961) (assignment to sole heirs at law); Keenan v. Tonry, 91 N.H. at 233, 16 A.2d at 708 (1940); Gove v. Gove, 64 N.H. 503, 15 A. 121 (1888) (assignment to legatee).

[51] Keenan v. Tonry, 91 N.H. at 223, 16 A.2d at 708 (1940).

[52] Gove v. Gove, 64 N.H. at 504, 15 A. at 121 (1888). See also Ghilain v. Couture,

Ghilain v. Couture sets forth the following other acts a domiciliary executor or administrator may perform, citing authorities in other jurisdictions: (1) vote at corporation meetings upon stock standing in the decedent's name; (2) sue on behalf of a deceased inventor in the United States Circuit Court of another state for damages for patent infringement; (3) sue in a foreign jurisdiction upon any rights which did not form part of the estate of the deceased but accrued to him after death.[53]

As the court noted in *Ghilain*, the long list of exceptions tends to show that although the executor or administrator has no legal right outside his own jurisdiction, "the acts of foreign representatives or fiduciaries, as a matter of practice, convenience and expediency, will be given effect through the exercise of a liberal comity."[54] This will not be true where such a course would conflict with public policy. Public policy usually denies a right of action in the absence of ancillary administration in order to protect resident creditors of the decedent against the withdrawal of assets on which they might equitably rely for payment of debts due them into another state.[55] In other words, "[c]omity permits the domiciliary administrator to claim the share directly when local interests are not prejudiced and no statutory demands are disregarded."[56]

Library References

Am Jur 2d Executors and Administrators §§ 1183–85
CJS Executors and Administrators §§ 1007–14

§ 32-5. Avoiding or Limiting Ancillary Administration

In addition to case law recognition of acts which a foreign administrator may perform without also qualifying as ancillary administrator, the

---

84 N.H. at 51, 146 A. at 397 (1929); Luce v. Manchester & Lawrence R.R., 63 N.H. 588, 3 A. 618 (1886) (New Hampshire ancillary administrator could not recover stock sold by Massachusetts domiciliary executor in New Hampshire corporation).

[53] Ghilain v. Couture, 84 N.H. at 51–52, 146 A. at 397 (1929). (Citations omitted.)

[54] Ghilain v. Couture, 84 N.H. at 52, 146 A. at 397 (1929) (*citing* Butler v. Butler, 83 N.H. 413, 143 A. 471 (1928)).

[55] *Id.*

[56] Upton v. White, 92 N.H. at 227, 29 A.2d at 131 (1942). See also Swan v. Bill, 95 N.H. at 161, 59 A.2d at 348 (1948) (foreign administrator could collect asset, a leasehold, and exercise option to renew, where there was no prejudice to local interests).

New Hampshire statutes provide further opportunities for avoiding the formality of ancillary administration.[57]

RSA 554:28 permits a duly-appointed foreign executor, administrator, trustee or guardian to apply for a license to sell, transfer or receive and dispose of personal property owned by the person he represents or to which that person is entitled in New Hampshire. If the property is stock, he must file his petition in the probate court in the county where the corporation has its principal place of business. As to other personal property, a petition is appropriate to the probate court in the county where the property is situated.

There are several preconditions to the granting of the license. RSA 554:28 sets two preconditions; no license will issue until notice has been given as the judge orders, and then only if "no sufficient objection appears." RSA 554:29 sets forth additional conditions:

> Such license shall not be granted until the expiration of six months after the death of the testator or intestate, nor unless it shall appear:
>
> I. That there is no executor, administrator, trustee or guardian, appointed under the laws of this state, entitled to the property;
>
> II. That such foreign executor, administrator, trustee or guardian will be liable for the avails of the property and shares in the state or country where he is appointed;
>
> III. That no creditor or person interested, who is a resident of this state, objects to such license or will be liable to be prejudiced thereby;
>
> IV. That all taxes due to the state have been paid or secured;
>
> V. That he has filed in the probate court authenticated copies of his petition, bond and appointment in such other state or country.

The New Hampshire Supreme Court, in construing the licensing statute, has held that a petition cannot be maintained if any part of the

---

[57] Noting statutory recognition of foreign representatives' ability to act without ancillary appointment. Crosby v. Charlestown, 78 N.H. 39, 95 A. 1043 (1915).

decedent's property within the jurisdiction of the state is subject to the New Hampshire inheritance tax.[58] If the license issues, the representative may sell, transfer, or receive and dispose of the property as if he were appointed in this state.[59]

There are no provisions for the issuance of a license to sell real estate by a foreign executor or administrator without the necessity for ancillary administration, as there is for sale of personal property.[60] Thus, if a sale is contemplated before the two-year period for the bringing of suits by creditors established by RSA 536:30 has expired, ancillary administration is obviously in order.[61]

If the only New Hampshire asset of the estate is real estate, the foreign executor or administrator should weigh the cost of ancillary administration against the benefit ancillary administration affords in cutting off creditors' claims. If ancillary administration is taken out, estate creditors have six months to present their claims under RSA 556:3, and one year to commence suit as set forth in RSA 556:5. In the absence of administration in New Hampshire, RSA 556:30 provides that creditors will be able to maintain suit against the real estate for two years following the date of the decedent's death.

If ancillary administration is not undertaken, the foreign representative should petition the probate court for permission pursuant to RSA 552:13 to file an authenticated copy of the decedent's will in the probate court in order to establish the legatees' title to the property. This statute provides that

> A duly authenticated copy of a will made out of this state, which has been proved and allowed by a court of probate or by a court of similar powers in one of the United States, or in a foreign country, and a duly authenticated copy of the probate of such will, upon the written application of a party in interest, and upon such citation and notice as the court shall order, may, by a decree of the court of probate, be filed and recorded in the probate office; and thereupon the will shall have the same

---

[58] Gardiner v. Carter, 74 N.H. 507, 510, 69 A. 939, 940–41 (1908).

[59] *Id.*

[60] RSA 554:28.

[61] At one time such a provision did exist, but the statute authorizing it (RSA 559:12) has been repealed.

effect as if executed with the formalities required by the laws of this state and duly proved and allowed. Regardless of whether ancillary administration is opened or not, any New Hampshire inheritance tax which is due must be paid.[62]

§ 32-6.   Uniform Probate Code Provisions

Article IV of the Uniform Probate Code provides a unified and comprehensive set of rules governing "Foreign Personal Representations; Ancillary Administration." These provisions "are designed to coerce respect for domiciliary procedures and administrative acts to the extent possible."[63] They answer many of the questions left unanswered by the sparse New Hampshire law.

The thrust of these sections is to allow the domiciliary administrator to act extensively in the foreign state upon the filing of authenticated copies of his appointment. UPC, § 4-204. Upon such filing, a domiciliary foreign personal representative "may exercise as to assets . . . all powers of a local personal representative and may maintain actions and proceedings . . . subject to any conditions imposed upon nonresident parties generally." UPC, § 4-205.

Another very important provision found in the Uniform Probate Code is § 3-202 relating to the resolution of conflicting claims regarding domicile:

> If conflicting claims as to the domicile of a decedent are made in a formal testacy or appointment proceeding commenced in this state, and in a testacy or appointment proceeding after notice pending at the same time in another state, the Court of this state must stay, dismiss, or permit suitable amendment in, the proceeding here unless it is determined that the local proceeding was commenced before the proceeding elsewhere. The determination of domicile in the proceeding first commenced must be accepted as determinative in the proceeding in this state.

This provision creates an unfortunate "race to the court house" between contesting states, which the Code recognizes but which it downplays:

---

[62] See Chapter 55 *infra*.

[63] General comment, Article IV, Uniform Probate Code (1983).

A somewhat more troublesome question is involved when one of the parties before the local court manifests a determination not to appear personally in the prior initiated proceedings so that he can preserve his ability to litigate contested points in a more friendly, or convenient, forum. But, the need to preserve all possible advantages available to particular litigants should be subordinated to the decedent's probable wish that his estate not be wasted in unnecessary litigation. Thus, the section requires that the local claimant either initiate litigation in the forum of his choice before litigation is started somewhere else, or accept the necessity of contesting unwanted views concerning the decedent's domicile offered in litigation pending elsewhere.

It is to be noted, in this connection, that the local suitor always will have a chance to contest the question of domicile in the other state. His locally initiated proceedings may proceed to a valid judgment accepting his theory of the case unless parties who would oppose him appear and defend on the theory that the domicile question is currently being litigated elsewhere. If the litigation in the other state has proceeded to judgment, Section 3-408 rather than the instant section will govern. If this section applies, it will mean that the foreign proceedings are still pending, so that the local person's contention concerning domicile can be made therein even though until the defense of litigation elsewhere is offered in the local proceedings, he may not have been notified of the foreign proceeding.[64]

Library References

Am Jur 2d Executors and Administrators §§ 1186, 1189, 1191–92, 1203

§ 32-7. Uniform Law

In 1949, the National Conference of Commissioners of Uniform State Laws adopted a Uniform Ancillary Administration of Estates Act. New Hampshire has not adopted the provisions of this Act.

Forms

See Form 100 of Appendix for a Petition to File and Record Authenticated Copies of Will and Probate.

---

[64] Comment, § 3,5302, Uniform Probate Code (1983).

PART IV

COLLECTING AND MANAGING THE ESTATE

CHAPTER 33. POWERS AND DUTIES OF ADMINISTRATORS GENERALLY

---

§ 33-1. Introduction

This chapter deals with the basic powers that administrators have in the handling of a decedent's estate and his duties and responsibilities with regard to the administration of the estate.[1]

In New Hampshire, it is a general principle, oft repeated, that it is a "known policy of the law to favor the expeditious settlement of estates . . . within a year after the executor's appointment so far as possible." *White v. Chaplin*.[2] The basic outline of procedure for the administration of estates in New Hampshire (six months to exhibit claims, one year to bring suit) leads to the generally speedy conclusion of most administrations. The substantial majority of administrations are closed between six to eighteen months after death, and most of those within six to twelve months. Unlike many states, New Hampshire probate practice has not been subject to excessive expense or delay and the administration of an estate often proceeds here so expeditiously as to sometimes confound out-of-state practitioners.

§ 33-2. Jurisdiction of Probate Court

The probate court has exclusive jurisdiction over the handling of estates by administrators. RSA 547:3.[3] It is the probate court, and no other, which regulates an administrator in the carrying out of his tasks during the administration of an estate. N.H. Const., part 2, art. 80; RSA 547:3. This area of exclusive jurisdiction has historically been one of the most unambiguous areas of probate court jurisdiction. If an administrator is to be brought to account for his actions as administrator, it must be in the probate court. As was made clear in the case of *Lisbon Savings Bank v. Estate of Moulton*:[4]

> An accounting to determine the administrator's liability must first be rendered in the probate court. "By the constitution and

---

[1] See Chapter 35 for a discussion of the powers and duties of an administrator in dealing with real estate. See Chapter 34 for a discussion of the administrator's duties as to the inventory of property. See Chapter 36 for a discussion of the administrator's payment of expenses. See Chapter 37 for a discussion of an administrator's duties as to legacies and devises.

[2] White v. Chaplin, 84 N.H. 208, 210, 148 A. 21, 22 (1929).

[3] Barrett v. Cady, 78 N.H. 60, 64, 96 A. 325, 328 (1915); Glover v. Beker, 76 N.H. 393, 398–99, 83 A. 916, 922 (1912).

[4] Lisbon Sav. Bank v. Estate of Moulton, 91 N.H. 477, 22 A.2d 331 (1941).

the statute, the probate court has exclusive, original jurisdiction of the settlement and distribution of the estates of deceased persons. The superior court has no power to require an administrator to account for his administration upon a bill in equity or to revise proceedings in the probate court except upon appeal. While the court may upon request advise the administrator as to the execution of his trust in a proper case, it has no power to advise or direct in advance the action of the probate court, or to interfere with due administration therein. While the procedure invented by the decree [here that sought by the petition] may be convenient, existing constitutional limitations preclude its adoption."[5]

By virtue of the Omnibus Justice Act of 1992, the probate court's exclusive jurisdiction has been extended to the "granting of administration and all matters and things of probate jurisdiction relation to the composition, administration, sale, settlement, and final distribution of estates of deceased persons." RSA 547:3, I(b).

Cross Reference

See § 5-3 (Jurisdiction of the Probate Court), *infra.*

Library References

Am Jur 2d Executors and Administrators §§ 94–99

CJS Executors and Administrators § 13 et seq.

§ 33-3. Administrator as Fiduciary

An administrator is a fiduciary and will be held to the high standards required of a fiduciary.[6] When dealing with assets of the estate, it is sometimes said that as to assets in his possession, he has the duties of a trustee to the estate, creditors and heirs.[7]

As a trustee, an administrator has to meet the high standard expected of trustees. This standard is now set forth in the Uniform Trustees Powers Act, RSA 564-A, which establishes the following "prudent man" standard for trustees:

---

[5] Lisbon Sav. Bank v. Estate of Moulton, 91 N.H. 477, 479, 22 A.2d 331, 334 (1941) (Citations omitted.)

[6] In re Estate of Crowley, 129 N.H. 557, 523 A.2d 960 (1987).

[7] McInnes v. Goldthwaite, 94 N.H. 331, 52 A.2d 795 (1947).

> "Prudent man" means a trustee whose exercise of trust powers is reasonable and equitable in view of the interests of income or principal beneficiaries, or both, and in view of the manner in which men of ordinary prudence, diligence, discretion, and judgment would act in the management of their own affairs. RSA 564-A:1, III.

Although this standard is more liberal than the previously judicially-recognized "prudent conservator" standard which required a trustee to "exercise the care and skill of a prudent person in conserving the property,"[8] it still requires an administrator to be mindful that he must act carefully and with prudence regarding the assets of the estate.

Library References

Am Jur 2d Executors and Administrators §§ 398–408

CJS Executors and Administrators § 184 et seq.

§ 33-4.   Standard of Care

As a general rule, administrators are held to a standard of care requiring "the exercise of all due and reasonable care" with regard to estate's assets which come into their hands in the course of administration. *Stevens v. Gage.*[9] "An executor must handle estate assets with that degree of prudence and diligence that a man of ordinary judgment would bestow on his own affairs of like nature." *In re Estate of McCool.*[10] Therefore, if he acted with care, an administrator is not held responsible for money stolen from his office safe.[11]

Furthermore, the administrator has the duty to proceed "with reasonable diligence" to carry out the provisions of the will which he is administering.[12] If he unreasonably delays, he is guilty of "breach of fidelity" due to "procrastination."[13]

The administrator has the "duty of quickly and economically executing his trust" and is under an affirmative obligation not to unreasonably

---

[8] Bartlett v. Dumaine, 128 N.H. 497, 506, 523 A.2d 1, 7 (1986).

[9] Stevens v. Gage, 55 N.H. 175, 177 (1875).

[10] In re Estate of McCool, 131 N.H. 340, 553 A.2d 761 (1988).

[11] *Id.*

[12] McInnes v. Goldthwaite, 94 N.H. at 333, 52 A.2d at 797 (1947).

[13] McInnes v. Goldthwaite, 94 N.H. at 333, 335, 52 A.2d at 797, 798 (1947).

procrastinate by requiring creditors of undisputed claims to go to court to enforce them. *Judge of Probate v. Ellis.*[14]

An administrator in possession of estate property is considered to be a trustee "and should be held to the duties of trustees in this respect."[15] However, in *McInnes v. Goldthwaite*,[16] the Supreme Court took a surprisingly lenient approach to an executor's failure to live up to the high standards of care imposed upon him. The Court overturned many items of a lower court's surcharge of a lackadaisical executor who failed to account for his administration of the estate for over eleven years, and then accounted only when forced to by petition of the beneficiaries. The Court even excused the executor's failure to liquidate securities in the estate which he held all throughout the Great Depression but some of which by chance had appreciated in value by the time they were sold some fourteen years after the decedent's death.

This should not be considered the present law of New Hampshire. As a fiduciary, an administrator is subject to a very high general standard in the administration of his estate:

> Executors are fiduciaries . . . and as such must comport with "the punctilio of an honor the most sensitive." This is a rigorous standard . . . . In re Estate of Crowley.[17]

Thus, a failure to comply with his accounting duties or to provide financial information concerning the assets of his estate to a proper party is cause for the removal of the administrator by the probate court. *In re Estate of Ward.*[18] Indeed, such conduct will be a proper and valid basis for the assessment of legal fees against the administrator personally.[19]

Where an administrator has failed to exercise common prudence, common skill and common caution, he will be required to compensate

---

[14] Judge of Probate v. Ellis, 63 N.H. 366, 367 (1885).

[15] Judge of Probate v. Ellis, 63 N.H. 366, 367 (1885); McInnes v. Goldthwaite, 94 N.H. 331, 336, 52 A.2d 795, 798 (1947).

[16] McInnes v. Goldthwaite, 94 N.H. 331, 52 A.2d. 795 (1947).

[17] In re Estate of Crowley, 129 N.H. 557, 523 A.2d 960 (1987). (Citations omitted.)

[18] In re Estate of Ward, 129 N.H. 4, 523 A.2d 28 (1986).

[19] *Id.*

beneficiaries for the losses they incur by the administrator's lack of due care. *In re Estate of McCool.*[20]

An administrator should be charged for the loss which the estate suffered through his neglect of duty.[21] In order to charge the administrator with such loss, it should be shown that he did not exercise due care and the property was lost through his negligence.[22] It has been held that whether executors are liable for the loss incurred by the decrease of the value of securities is a question for the probate court to pass on in the first instance.[23] Furthermore, it is for the probate court to determine the amount of damages sustained by an estate whose administrator has failed to act quickly enough to prevent unnecessary financial loss to the estate. *In re Estate of McCool.*[24]

Library References

Am Jur 2d Executors and Administrators § 398

CJS Executors and Administrators § 184

§ 33-5.   Uniform Probate Code Standard of Care

The Uniform Probate Code takes a much broader approach in this area by making the personal representative a fiduciary who is required to observe the standard of care applicable to trustees. Section 3-702 of the Code defines the standard of care as follows:

> [T]he trustee [personal representative] shall observe the standards in dealing with the trust assets that would be observed by a prudent man dealing with the property of another, and if the trustee [personal representative] has special skills or is named trustee on the basis of representations of special skills or expertise, he is under a duty to use those skills.

The Code throughout its provisions provides a much more "laissez-faire" approach to the supervision of the conduct of fiduciaries, placing the burden of showing lack of fair dealing upon the parties and not the probate court. However, the Code has an overriding provision which

---

[20] In re Estate of McCool, 131 N.H. 340, 553 A.2d 761 (1988).

[21] Tuttle v. Robinson, 33 N.H. 104, 120–21 (1856).

[22] Stevens v. Gage, 55 N.H. 175 (1875).

[23] Dennison v. Lilley, 83 N.H. 422, 426, 144 A. 523, 525 (1928).

[24] In re Estate of McCool, 131 N.H. 340, 553 A.2d 761 (1988).

deals with fraud in general and is applicable to the conduct of administrators:

Section 1-106. Effect of Fraud and Evasion

Whenever fraud has been perpetrated in connection with any proceeding or in any statement filed under this Code or if fraud is used to avoid or circumvent the provisions or purposes of this Code, any person injured thereby may obtain appropriate relief against the perpetrator of the fraud or restitution from any person (other than a bona fide purchaser) benefiting from the fraud, whether innocent or not. Any proceeding must be commenced within 2 years after the discovery of the fraud, but no proceeding may be brought against one not a perpetrator of the fraud later than 5 years after the time of commission of the fraud. This section has no bearing on remedies relating to fraud practiced on a decedent during his lifetime which affects the succession of his estate.

As the Comment to this section demonstrates, this section:

is an overriding provision that provides an exception to the procedures and limitations provided in the Code. The remedy of a party wronged by fraud is intended to be supplementary to other protections provided in the Code and can be maintained outside the process of settlement of the estate. Thus, if a will which is known to be a forgery is probated informally, and the forgery is not discovered until after the period for contest has run, the defrauded heirs still could bring a fraud action under this section. Or if a will is fraudulently concealed after the testator's death and its existence not discovered until after the basic three year period (section 3-108) has elapsed, there still may be an action under this section. Similarly, a closing statement normally provides binding protection for the personal representative after six months from filing (section 3-1005). However, if there is fraudulent misrepresentation or concealment in the preparation of the claim, a later suit may be brought under this section against the personal representative for damages; or restitution may be obtained from those distributees who benefit by the fraud. In any case, innocent purchasers for value are protected.

Library References

Am Jur 2d Executors and Administrators §§ 398, 403, 406, 531

§ 33-6. Duty To Act in Good Faith

"An executor or administrator has a duty to exercise the utmost good faith in all his transactions affecting the estate. He may not advance his own personal interest at the expense of the heirs, and any fraud upon the part of an executor or administrator will justify the court in declaring his acts void."[25]

An administrator must not engage in self-dealing to his own personal or private benefit. If he does, he may be removed as administrator by the probate court. *In re Estate of Crowley.*[26]

Where an administrator sells land on behalf of an estate, it is improper for him to purchase the property, directly, or indirectly through a straw person. *Hoitt v. Webb.*[27] It does not matter that the price which he pays is fair or not. The sale is voidable by any interested party or by the court itself.[28] In *Conservatorship of Bradlee,*[29] a deed by a conservator to herself only was invalidated by the probate court since the license to sell granted to the conservator by the probate court provided that the property was to be conveyed to the conservator and a third party. *Lovell v. Briggs*[30] expressed the prior rule that a sale to the administrator of a decedent's personal property makes the sale not void per se, but "merely voidable at the election of the heirs, provided, on inquiry, a greater price can be obtained for the estate."[31]

It is improper for an administrator to purchase mortgage debts of the decedent with his own means and for his own personal advantage. This practice is not to be commended, but on the contrary is to be regarded with distrust and suspicion. *Hoitt v. Webb.*[32] Although in such a situation the court will not hold a purchase illegal (the debts secured by the

---

[25] 31 Am. Jur. 2d, Executors and Administrators, §216 (1967).

[26] In re Estate of Crowley, 129 N.H. 557, 523 A.2d 960 (1987).

[27] Hoitt v. Webb, 36 N.H. 158 (1858); Remick v. Butterfield, 31 N.H. 70 (1855).

[28] Hoitt v. Webb, 36 N.H. 158 (1858).

[29] Conservatorship of Bradlee, 120 N.H. 430, 415 A.2d 1144 (1980).

[30] Lovell v. Briggs, 2 N.H. 218 (1820).

[31] Lovell v. Briggs, 2 N.H. 218, 221 (1820).

[32] Hoitt v. Webb, 36 N.H. 158 (1858).

mortgages being valid against the deceased), yet, if there is any evidence tending to show fraud upon the estate, the transfer would be treated as having been made in bad faith, and invalid.[33]

The Uniform Probate Code, § 3-713 provides that any sale or encumbrance to the personal representative is voidable unless one of two conditions is met:

> Any sale or encumbrance to the personal representative, his spouse, agent or attorney, or any corporation or trust in which he has a substantial beneficial interest, or any transaction which is affected by a substantial conflict of interest on the part of the personal representative, is voidable by any person interested in the state except one who has consented after fair disclosure, unless

(1) the will or a contract entered into by the decedent expressly authorized the transaction; or

(2) the transaction is approved by the Court after notice to interested persons.

Library References

Am Jur 2d Executors and Administrators § 528

CJS Executors and Administrators §§ 239–241

§ 33-7.   Duty of Loyalty to Estate as a Whole

An administrator is a fiduciary. *In re Estate of Crowley.*[34] Like any fiduciary, it goes without saying that an administrator must be loyal to the estate and to the creditors and beneficiaries thereof. Thus, it is improper for an administrator to advance a position that benefits one party interested in the estate over another.[35]

An administrator's duty of loyalty to the estate as a whole requires him to be neutral when a conflict occurs concerning the distribution of an intestate estate and an appeal ensues:

> The administrator, in the position of stakeholder, is properly a party, but he has only an indifferent and neutral interest in

---

[33] *Id.*

[34] In re Estate of Crowley, 129 N.H. 557, 529 A.2d 960 (1987).

[35] Tilton v. American Bible Soc'y, 60 N.H. 377 (1880).

333

the outcome of the appeal. The contest is over the inheritance, with which he is not concerned.[36]

An administrator has a duty not to engage in conflicts of interest when serving as administrator. *In re Estate of McCool.*[37] If he nevertheless engages in such conflicts, he will be prohibited from collecting any fees for his services as administrator.[38] Furthermore, if the administrator is also the attorney for the estate, there can be no waiver of the conflict of interest because the attorney cannot waive the estate's objections to his own conflict of interest.[39]

Library References

Am Jur 2d Executors and Administrators § 527

CJS Executors and Administrators §§ 239–241

§ 33-8. Duty To Locate Heirs

A New Hampshire case, *Tilton v. American Bible Society*,[40] is often cited in support of the general rule that the duty of an administrator is to use care and diligence in the discharge of his duties and to inform legatees who are unaware of the bequest to them of their right to claim the bequest.[41] In this case, even though the will was ambiguous, creating doubt as to which of several beneficiaries would benefit, Chief Justice Doe ruled that the administrator had an affirmative duty to act:

> The executors were fiduciary representatives, holding the estate in trust, and bound to exercise reasonable and impartial care in protecting the rights of all the legatees. For many years, they knew that the [legatees] were not aware of the bequests made to them; and it was their duty to give the [legatees] the information which was manifestly needed and without which . . . the will could not be executed.[42]

---

[36] Voliotes v. Ventoura, 86 N.H. 52, 53, 162 A. 192 (1932).

[37] In re Estate of McCool, 131 N.H. 340, 553 A.2d 761 (1988).

[38] *Id.*

[39] *Id.*

[40] Tilton v. American Bible Soc'y, 60 N.H. 377 (1880).

[41] See Annot., "Duty and Liability of Executor With Respect to Locating and Noticing Legatees, Devisees or Heirs," 10 ALR3d 547, 549 (1966).

[42] Tilton v. American Bible Soc'y, 60 N.H. 377, 384 (1880).

Library References

Am Jur 2d Executors and Administrators §§ 401, 402

CJS Executors and Administrators § 141

§ 33-9. Duty To Liquidate Estate

It is a cardinal rule for administrators in New Hampshire that they must move to liquidate estate assets within a reasonable time and they will be charged with losses occasioned by their failure to sell and liquidate. This particularly applies to stocks and bonds. Some probate courts will view with great disfavor the failure of an administrator to sell securities in a timely fashion.

The underlying reason for this rule is that, unless a testator otherwise directs, it is the duty of an administrator to liquidate the estate assets so that debts and estate taxes can be paid and distributions made to the beneficiaries at values approximating date of death values. Or, put another way, it is the primary duty of the administrator to make sure that the debts, expenses of administration, taxes and distributions to beneficiaries get paid, and he should not be "playing the market" with the monies needed for that purpose.

This rule was first stated in *McInnes v. Goldthwaite*,[43] (although not rigidly enforced there) when the Court, quoting a leading Pennsylvania case, stated that the "duty of an executor generally is not to retain and invest, but to liquidate and terminate."[44] Usually, therefore, an administrator should sell securities owned by the decedent at his death within a reasonable time, although there is authority to the contrary.[45] An administrator proceeds at his own risk if he retains securities which decrease in value from inventory value. For example, in *Dennison v. Lilley*,[46] the Court warned that where there is a loss in value of securities retained beyond a reasonable time, "[w]hether . . . the executors should be held personally liable for the loss is a question for the probate court to pass upon in the first instance."[47]

---

[43] McInnes v. Goldthwaite, 94 N.H. 331, 52 A.2d 795 (1947).

[44] McInnes v. Goldthwaite, 94 N.H. 331, 334, 52 A.2d 795, 798 (1947) *quoting*, In re Kohalis Estate, 348 Pa. 55, 53 A.2d 920 (1943).

[45] *Id.*

[46] Dennison v. Lilley, 83 N.H. 422, 144 A. 523 (1928).

[47] Dennison v. Lilley, 83 N.H. 422, 426, 144 A. 523, 525 (1928).

A very important case, *In re Estate of McCool*,[48] discusses this duty in some detail. In this case, the executor failed to promptly value or sell the decedent's substantial block of stock in a small, unproven company until the stock became nearly worthless. The Supreme Court found that the executor had failed to act prudently to take prompt steps to value and sell the stock and was liable to be surcharged for the loss to the estate:

> An executor must handle estate assets with that degree of prudence and diligence that a man of ordinary judgment would bestow on his own affairs of like nature. Unlike the trustee, whose responsibility is to hold assets, the executor must exercise prudence and diligence in the timely liquidation of assets. What constitutes reasonable conduct with respect to estate assets varies with the circumstances of the case. "[S]urcharge is the penalty for failure to exercise common prudence, common skill and common caution in the performance of the fiduciary's duty and is imposed to compensate beneficiaries for loss caused by the fiduciary's want of due care." (Citations omitted.)[49]

Although the burden is on the claimants to prove their damages where an executor has failed to act prudently in liquidating an estate asset and suffered loss to some degree, any uncertainty as to the extent of damage will not bar the claimants from recovery.[50] Rather, the "damages are to be closely approximated by drawing reasonable and probable inferences from the facts proved."[51]

Liquidating assets is the recommended procedure to follow in most cases. However, the will may direct otherwise. Also, there are many instances where the heirs wish to retain the securities and receive them in lieu of cash. This can generally be accomplished where all the heirs have the same desire and there are sufficient other assets to pay taxes, debts and expenses. RSA 554:9 authorizes an administrator to avoid selling any personal property including stocks and bonds "upon the

---

[48] In re Estate of McCool, 131 N.H. 340, 553 A.2d 761 (1988).

[49] *Id.*

[50] *Id.*

[51] In re Estate of McCool, 131 N.H. 340, 553 A.2d 761 (1988) (*quoting* Rippey v. Denver United States National Bank, 273 F. Supp. 718 (D. Colo. 1967)).

request of the heirs or legatees, and the administrator shall be discharged by delivery thereof to the persons entitled thereto."

It should be noted, however, that the probate court may think otherwise and the prudent practitioner should proceed with caution. In any event, the administrator should ask for and receive from the heirs a written direction authorizing him to retain securities.

These rules should be contrasted with the Uniform Probate Code's broad provision allowing administrators to "retain assets owned by the decedent pending distribution or liquidation including those in which the [personal] representative is personally interested or which are otherwise improper for trust investment." §3-715(1).

Library References

Am Jur 2d Executors and Administrators §§ 548, 549, 766 et seq.

CJS Executors and Administrators §§ 269 et seq., 305 et seq.

§ 33-10. Duty To File Will

RSA 552:3 places an affirmative duty upon the person named as the executor of a will to file the will in the probate court within thirty days of the death of the testator or within thirty days of the date the executor learns that he or she is executor, whichever is later. If the estate contains any assets, the named executor shall cause the will to be proved or shall file a written refusal to accept the trust. If the estate contains no assets, the named executor shall provide a certificate of death for the decedent and shall file the will with no administration. Under RSA 552:4, an executor who neglects to file the will can be fined $20.00 per month for each month of neglect after the thirty-day period, recoverable by any person having an interest in the will. Furthermore, an administrator who has custody of a will and fails to deliver it to court after receiving a citation to do so can be imprisoned until he delivers it. RSA 552:5.

Many other states' statutes require an administrator or other person with custody of a will to produce it promptly or incur fines, punishment, or forfeiture of rights under the will. In states without legislation, the duty to produce and file the will may be implied from the person's acceptance of the will for custody or safekeeping.[52]

Under the Uniform Probate Code, § 2-516, any person having custody of a will has a duty to deliver it after the death of the testator to a person

---

[52] 79 Am. Jur. 2d, Wills, s. 832.

able to probate it, and a failure to comply may be enforced through a contempt proceeding or, if the failure was willful, a suit for damages.[53]

§ 33-11. Duties as to Personal Property

Upon a testator's death, the legal title to all his personal estate vests in the person named as executor, who acts as trustee for the legatees, creditors and others under the will.[54] Upon the decease of an intestate and the granting of administration, his personal estate, and all contingent as well as absolute interests therein, vest in his administrator.[55] These can be divested only by operation of law, or some act of the administrator.[56] When an administrator, is appointed, his authority extends back by relation, so far as the personal property is concerned, for certain purposes, to the death of the intestate.[57]

RSA 561:7 provides that the "personal estate bequeathed by a testator shall be distributed by decree of the judge according to the will." In practice, tangible items of personal property are often distributed during administration to the specified beneficiary if it is clear that the estate is solvent and the property is not needed to pay debts or taxes. In 1975, the distribution statute was amended to allow for interim distributions upon request of the administrator or "any interested person":

> The personal estate of a person deceased which was not bequeathed or included in a bequest and which remains in the hands of the executor or administrator upon settlement of an account of such fiduciary shall be distributed according to law by decree of the judge. Upon the application of the fiduciary or any interested person, the judge may issue interim orders approving or directing partial distributions or granting other relief at any time during the pendency of administration to effect distributions as expeditiously and efficiently as may be consistent with the best interests of the estate. RSA 561:7-a.

RSA 554:7 and 554:8 require that all personal property (tangible and intangible) be accounted for by the administrator "at the appraised value"

---

[53] Id.

[54] Lane v. Thompson, 43 N.H. 320 (1861); Shirley v. Healds, 34 N.H. 407 (1857).

[55] Ladd v. Wiggin, 35 N.H. 421 (1857).

[56] Id.

[57] Lane v. Thompson, 43 N.H. 320 (1861).

(tangible personal property) or "at the prices which they shall bring at a public or private sale" (intangible personal property).

The administrator may sell both tangible and intangible personal property at public or private sale and, if he conducts the sale "with fidelity and impartiality" shall be "credited with the loss; or charged with the gain, upon the sale." RSA 554:7, 554:8.

Formerly, the administrator was required to obtain a license from the probate court to sell personal property. Since this procedure had become a needless and expensive automatic formality, the need for a license was abolished in 1977. Now, the administrator may decide how or when to sell, and generally will not be charged with any loss if he conducts the sale "with fidelity and impartiality."

RSA 554:9 provides that the administrator shall not sell personal property specifically bequeathed if such property is not needed to pay debts. Rather, the administrator should transfer such property to the persons entitled thereto. RSA 554:9. Also, the administrator, upon the heir's or legatee's request, shall not sell any personal property desired by them but may transfer such property to the heirs.

RSA 554:10 provides that instead of selling "stocks, bonds and other evidences of debt," the administrator may transfer them to the heirs "whenever he shall deem it for the interest of the heirs that the same should not be sold." However, the Supreme Court made clear in *In re Estate of Borkowski*[58] that this provision does not empower the probate judge with "the additional power to set off against his share portions of the heir's debt not yet due the estate."[59]

An administrator is bound to dispose of the decedent's personal estate in a reasonable time, and if he fails in that respect, he may be held to account for it at the value stated in the inventory.[60] It is, however, in the interest of all concerned that he be allowed a very considerable latitude of discretion as to the selection of the time of sale.[61] If an administrator sells the deceased's goods under a license from the judge

---

[58] In re Estate of Borkowski, 120 N.H. 54, 410 A.2d 1121 (1980).

[59] In re Estate of Borkowski, 120 N.H. 54, 57, 410 A.2d 1121, 1122 (1980).

[60] Griswold v. Chandler, 5 N.H. at 493–94 (1831).

[61] Griswold v. Chandler, 5 N.H. at 494 (1831). See In re Estate of McCool, 131 N.H. 340, 553 A.2d 761 (1988).

of probate, and conducts the sale in good faith, any loss upon the goods is to be the loss of those interested in the estate.[62]

A probate court's allowance of an administrator's final account does not preclude a purchaser of personal property from the administrator, who mistakenly paid more than he should have because of an arithmetical error, from proceeding to recover the overpayment from the administrator and the heirs to whom the money was distributed. *Redington Hub Co. v. Putnam.*[63]

Library References

Am Jur 2d Executors and Administrators §§ 532–537

CJS Executors and Administrators § 299 et seq.

§ 33-12. Duties with Regard to Claims Against the Estate

Unlike the area of the collection of debts due the estate, where the administrator's powers and duties are closely restricted, the administrator has much more flexibility to handle claims against the estate. RSA 556:27 specifically grants administrators the power to adjust and compromise claims against an estate:

> The probate court may authorize administrators and guardians to adjust by compromise or arbitration any controversy between them and persons making claims against the estates in their hands. The attorney general or the director of the register of charitable trusts shall be a necessary party to any agreement between an executor and creditors or legatees or heirs-at-law whenever such agreement may directly or indirectly affect a charitable interest, residuary or otherwise, created in any estate.

Indeed, an administrator is under an affirmative duty to compromise a claim if it is reasonable to do so:

> An administrator . . . should compromise a claim against the estate when that is the reasonable thing to do. *Simes v. Ward.*[64]

However, an administrator cannot compromise his own claim against the estate. RSA 554:14.

---

[62] Brackett v. Tillotson, 4 N.H. 208, 211 (1827).

[63] Redington Hub Co. v. Putnam, 76 N.H. 336, 82 A. 715 (1912).

[64] Simes v. Ward, 78 N.H. 533, 535, 103 A. 310, 311 (1918).

When deciding whether to settle a claim of the FDIC on behalf of a failed bank, administrators may want to consider the recent case of *FDIC v. Estate of Infantine*.[65] The Hillsborough Superior Court found that the state statutes (RSA 556:3 and 556:5, providing for a six-month notice of claim period and a one-year period for filing suit) were preempted by the six-year federal statute of limitations under Financial Institutions Reform, Recovery, and Enforcement Act (FIRREA) 12 U.S.C. § 1821 (d)(14). In *Infantine*, the FDIC was appointed receiver for the bank holding the decedent's promissory note after decedent's death but before the state's six-month notice of claim had expired. The court ruled the FDIC had up to six years after its appointment as receiver for the failed bank to file a claim as a creditor.

Uniform Probate Code § 3-715(3) authorizes a personal representative to "compromise or refuse performance of the decedent's contracts that continue as obligations of the estate as he may determine under the circumstances," and "to satisfy and settle claims" § 3-715(27). Also, § 3-813 provides:

> When a claim against the estate has been presented in any manner, the personal representative may, if it appears for the best interest of the estate, compromise the claim, whether due or not due, absolute or contingent, liquidated or unliquidated.

Library References

Am Jur 2d Executors and Administrators §§ 584–589

CJS Executors and Administrators § 367 et seq.

§ 33.13.   Power of Executor to Disclaim

An executor, administrator or other personal representative of a decedent has the power to disclaim a survivorship interest in joint property, jointly-owned by the decedent and another. *In re Estate of Lamson*.[66] Indeed, the rule announced by the Court in the *Lamson* case is broader than joint interests. The Court established the rule that an administrator has a broad power to renounce and disclaim any property interest based upon his fiduciary duty to the estate and to the heirs because "[v]esting the power in the executor to renounce post mortem

---

[65] FDIC v. Estate of Infantine, Docket No. 92-E-0898, Hillsborough Superior Court (1994).

[66] In re Estate of Lamson, 139 N.H. 732, 662 A.2d 287 (1995).

permits the executor to act in the best interest of the estate by renouncing interests that would otherwise burden the estate."[67]

An executor is permitted "to renounce only if renunciation benefits the estate and the beneficiaries of the estate. The executor must petition the probate court for approval of any renunciation, which could under its general equitable power refuse to approve if renunciation is not in the interest of the estate or beneficiaries . . . . Any renunciation by an executor must meet the same requirements we have established for *inter vivos* renunciations," which must be made within a reasonable time, which depends on the facts and circumstances of each case."[68]

§ 33.14. Power to Invest

An administrator should not ordinarily be investing estate assets in stocks, securities, or bonds, for example, since the administrator's duty is not to retain and invest estate property but to liquidate estate assets and distribute the proceeds in termination of the administration.[69] However, during the administration of the estate, the executor will ordinarily have large amounts of funds which are liquid. He has a duty to make these funds productive and to invest them at interest.[70]

An administrator may have funds which must be invested under some circumstances. Where, for example, it is clear that it is the testator's intention that the executors of his estate invest funds of the estate at their discretion, they may do so. *Bedell v. Colby.*[71] If there is a valid reason for the administrator to retain funds, it is incumbent upon him to invest them. *McInnes v. Goldthwaite.*[72] Indeed, if the administrator holds funds of the estate for an unreasonable time, he must invest those funds as a trustee would.[73] As such, the administrator is liable for the net loss incurred as a result of his breach of his fiduciary duty in this regard.[74]

---

[67] *Id.*

[68] *Id.*

[69] McInnes v. Goldthwaite, 94 N.H. 331, 52 A.2d 795 (1947).

[70] *Id.*

[71] Bedell v. Colby, 94 N.H. 384, 54 A.2d 161 (1947).

[72] McInnes v. Goldthwaite, 94 N.H. 331, 52 A.2d 795 (1947).

[73] *Id.*

[74] *Id.*

Executors and administrators are considered to be trustees and as such are held to the same duty of investment care as trustees are.[75] As a trustee, the administrator or executor has the duty to act in accordance with the prudent investor's standard of RSA 564-A:3-b.[76]

In *Bartlett v. Dumaine*,[79] the Supreme Court said that "under general principles of New Hampshire common law, the scope of trust investments a trustee can make is narrow."[80] This rule applies to executors in making investments because in "the management and investment of funds, [administrators] are to be regarded as trustees." *Bell v. Sawyer.*[81]

Generally, money must necessarily lie unemployed for some period of time in the administrator's hands,[82] and if this occurs without his fault or negligence, and without it being any advantage to him, the administrator will not be charged with interest.[83] Where a checking account is necessary and the yearly balances are not so large as to constitute neglect, an executor will not be liable for interest on that account,[84] although, in present times, the administrator should utilize an interest-bearing checking account to the extent possible.

An administrator will, however, be charged with interest when he retains the estate's funds in his own hands, without reason, when it ought to be paid over,[85] where he receives interest for money belonging to the estate,[86] or where he applies the estate's money to his own use.[87] If an administrator can show that his actions concerning handling of the estate's funds were done with good reason and he kept and used the funds in a reasonable manner he will not be charged with interest. Of course,

---

[75] Bell v. Sawyer, 59 N.H. 393 (1879).

[76] See Chapters 3 and 9 *infra*.

[79] Bartlett v. Dumaine, 128 N.H. 497, 523 A.2d 1 (1986).

[80] Bartlett v. Dumaine, 128 N.H. 497, 509, 523 A.2d 1, 9 (1986).

[81] Bell v. Sawyer, 59 N.H. 393 (1879).

[82] Griswold v. Chandler, 5 N.H. 492, 496–97 (1831).

[83] Bartlett v. Fitz, 59 N.H. 502, 503 (1880); Lund v. Lund, 41 N.H. 355, 359 (1860); Griswold v. Chandler, 5 N.H. at 497 (1831).

[84] McInnes v. Goldthwaite, 94 N.H. at 336, 52 A.2d at 799 (1947).

[85] Griswold v. Chandler, 5 N.H. at 497 (1831).

[86] Griswold v. Chandler, 5 N.H. at 497 (1831). See also Bartlett v. Fitz, 59 N.H. at 503 (1880); Lund v. Lund, 41 N.H. at 359 (1860); Mathes v. Bennett, 21 N.H. 188, 199 (1850); Wendell v. French, 19 N.H. 205, 213 (1848).

[87] Lund v. Lund, 41 N.H. at 359 (1860).

an administrator is chargeable with the interest which he actually receives on the estate's funds. *Bartlett v. Fitz.*[88]

The administrator may be examined upon oath as to the times when he received, and the uses to which he put, money belonging to the estate, and is bound to make a full disclosure of all the circumstances, so that it may be seen whether he is chargeable with interest.[89] If the administrator refuses or neglects, when required, to make a satisfactory disclosure of his handling of the estate's funds, it raises a strong presumption against him, and furnishes a safe ground to charge interest on all sums so long as they appear from his account to have remained in his hands.[90]

An executor as trustee should not be liable for failing to keep all the estate's funds invested unless there has been neglect on his part.[91] He may keep an amount available for the necessary expenses involved, and if there are valid reasons for keeping money uninvested he will not be charged for failure to invest it.[92]

By contrast, the Uniform Probate Code provides in § 3-715(5) that a personal representative may properly, if funds are not needed to meet debts and expenses currently payable and are not immediately distributable, deposit or invest liquid assets of the estate, including moneys received from the sale of other assets, in federally insured interest-bearing accounts, readily marketable secured loan arrangements or other prudent investments which would be reasonable for use by trustees generally. Section 7-302 of the Code additionally provides that trustees must deal with trust assets as "a prudent man dealing with the property of another" would.

Library References

Am Jur 2d Executors and Administrators §§ 538–550

CJS Executors and Administrators §§ 205–208

§ 33-15. Power To Contract on Behalf of Estate

The general rule is that, absent probate court authorization, an administrator cannot make contracts which are binding on the estate.[93]

---

[88] Bartlett v. Fitz, 59 N.H. at 503 (1880).

[89] *Id.*

[90] *Id.*

[91] McInnes v. Goldthwaite, 94 N.H. at 336, 52 A.2d at 799 (1947).

[92] *Id.*

[93] 31 Am. Jur. 2d, Executors and Administrators, §164 (1967).

An administrator who does attempt to bind his estate by a contract will be considered personally liable on the contract. An administrator cannot "bind the estate by an executory contract nor create a liability not founded upon the contract or obligation of the intestate. *Thomson v. Smith.*"[94]

The Statute of Frauds, RSA 506:2, provides that "[n]o action shall be brought to charge an executor or administrator upon a special promise to answer damages out of his own estate" unless there is an agreement in writing signed by the administrator sought to be charged. This requires anyone dealing with an administrator to use extreme caution to assure that he has an enforceable agreement with a solvent administrator.

In *E.A. Strout Farm Agency v. Worthen,*[95] the Supreme Court ruled that a real estate brokerage contract executed on behalf of the estate by an administrator was unenforceable against the estate where the parties intended that the administrator was to be personally liable. In *Livermore v. Rand,*[96] the Court held that an administrator who hires an attorney to defend a suit pending against the decedent at his death is personally liable to the attorney for the services rendered to him. In *True W. Jones Brewing Co. v. Flaherty,*[97] the Court recognized the rule that "upon a general contract of employment or purchase the administrator or guardian is personally liable. Having no power to bind the estate, and presumably intending to bind someone, the inference is that he bound himself."[98] However, the Court went on to point out that if the administrator can produce evidence that he did not intend to bind himself personally, then he will not be liable if he "made a special contract, excluding any personal liability on his part."[99]

All of which leaves a person dealing with an administrator at great risk. However, as *Thomson v. Smith,*[100] makes clear, a person who deals with an absconding administrator is not entirely without remedy. In this case, the plaintiff attorney had been hired by the administrator to provide

---

[94] Thomson v. Smith, 64 N.H. 412, 13 A. 639 (1888). See also Wait v. Holt, 58 N.H. 467 (1878).

[95] E.A. Strout Farm Agency v. Worthen, 81 N.H. 95, 122 A. 337 (1923).

[96] Livermore v. Rand, 26 N.H. 85 (1852); Wait v. Holt, 58 N.H. 467 (1878).

[97] True W. Jones Brewing Co. v. Flaherty, 80 N.H. 571, 120 A. 432 (1923).

[98] True W. Jones Brewing Co. v. Flaherty, 80 N.H. 571, 572, 120 A. 432, 433 (1923).

[99] True W. Jones Brewing Co. v. Flaherty, 80 N.H. 571, 573, 120 A. 432, 483 (1923)(*quoting* Livermore v. Rand, 26 N.H. 85, 90 (1852)).

[100] Thomson v. Smith, 64 N.H. 412, 13 A. 639 (1888).

services on behalf of an estate in connection with property of the estate located in Nova Scotia. After the services were performed, the administrator was personally bankrupt and absconded. The Supreme Court gave the plaintiff a remedy against the estate, "the case [being] an appropriate one for equity to afford relief."[101]

Of course, as the *Thomson* case makes clear, if the administrator asks for an allowance in his account to pay for the services for which he contracted on behalf of the estate, he will be allowed such charges as an expense of administration. This is how such matters are usually handled: the administrator contracts for the services without prior authorization of the probate court and is allowed the costs of the service contracted for in his account. Otherwise, he will be personally liable.

The Uniform Probate Code gives the personal representative broad powers with regard to handling the estate (§ 3-715), specifically including the power to employ persons "to advise and assist" him (§ 3-715(21)), borrow money (§ 3-715(16)), enter leases (§3-715(9)), and subdivide or develop land (§ 3-715(8)). Anyone dealing with the personal representative is specifically protected. (§3-714).

Library References

Am Jur 2d Executors and Administrators §§ 389–392

CJS Executors and Administrators §§ 198–204

§ 33-16. Powers of Fiduciaries in Environmental Matters

Because the legislature determined that "it will benefit the public health, safety, and welfare to empower fiduciaries to assess fiduciary property to determine environmental condition, to prevent and remediate contamination, and to otherwise bring fiduciary property into compliance with environmental laws,"[102] the Uniform Trustees' Powers Act was amended[103] to grant a fiduciary certain specified powers in connection with environmental matters. Under these provisions, the fiduciary is given certain discretionary powers (unless otherwise limited by instrument, judgment, decree or order establishing the fiduciary relationship) to

---

[101] Thomson v. Smith, 64 N.H. 412, 414, 13 A. 639, 641 (1888). See also Wait v. Holt, 58 N.H. 467 (1878) where Chief Justice Doe implies that an equitable remedy is available if the services were beneficial to the estate, and the executor was insolvent.

[102] RSA 564-A:3-a, I.

[103] 1995 P.L., ch. 38.

undertake the following, provided that the fiduciary shall disclose in writing to the person or persons to whom the fiduciary sends communications or statements relating to the property held in fiduciary capacity his intent to exercise any or all of the authority granted by the statute:

1. To monitor property over which he has control to determine compliance with environmental laws.[104]

2. To take any action on behalf of an estate necessary to prevent, abate or otherwise remedy a violation of environmental laws.[105]

3. To refuse to accept real or personal property in trust if such property either is or may be contaminated by hazardous substances or is being used or has been used for any activities directly or indirectly involving hazardous substances or if such property may be in violation of any environmental law.[106]

4. To settle or compromise any or all claims against the estate or trust which may be asserted by a governmental or private body involving a violation of environmental laws.[107]

5. To release or disclaim any power granted by any document or statute or rule of law, which in the sole discretion of the fiduciary, may expose the fiduciary to liability in the fiduciary's individual capacity under the environmental laws.[108]

The statute provides that the fiduciary may charge the reasonable costs of any abatement, clean-up, remediation, etc., against the income or principal of the estate or trust.[109] Most importantly, the statute provides that the fiduciary shall not be personally liable for such costs.[110]

---

[104] RSA 564-A:3-a, III(a).

[105] RSA 564-A:3-a, III(b).

[106] RSA 564-A:3-a, III(c).

[107] RSA 564-A:3-a, III(d).

[108] RSA 564-A:3-a, III(e).

[109] RSA 564-A:3-a, IV.

[110] RSA 564-A:3-a, V.

The statute goes on to offer significant protection from personal liability from environmental claims to a fiduciary in his individual capacity by providing that:

> Nothing in this section shall be construed to alter or affect a fiduciary's liability or obligations as otherwise established by environmental laws. The fiduciary's failure to exercise powers granted under this section in and of itself shall not create a cause of action against the fiduciary. A fiduciary shall not be liable in its individual capacity to any beneficiary or any other party for any action taken with the approval of a governmental agency with responsibility for environmental compliance. A fiduciary shall not be liable in its individual capacity to a beneficiary or any other party for any other action taken to:

> (1) Assess potential environmental contamination of fiduciary property; or

> (2) Bring fiduciary property into compliance with environmental laws where the fiduciary acts reasonably and prudently.

In particular, a fiduciary shall not be liable for any decrease in value or exhaustion of assets by reason of actions taken in accordance with this section.[111]

§ 33-17. Power to Continue Decedent's Business

This subject continues to be one of the most troubling areas of the law for administrators to confront. An administrator must proceed with caution before assuming that he should continue, or has the power to continue, an unincorporated business the decedent was operating at his death.

Previously, it was the rule that an administrator of an estate continued to operate a decedent's business at his own peril and the probate court had no authority to authorize an administrator to continue to operate the business. If an administrator continued a decedent's business, it was held that an administrator had the "duty to conduct it in a manner that would

---

[111] RSA 564-A:3-a, V.

lead to no preference for any of the intestate's general creditors." *Horton v. Eagle Indemnity Insurance Company.*[112]

However, the New Hampshire Judicial Council found it highly unsatisfactory that an administrator had no power to carry on a decedent's business[113] and in 1946, supported legislation which became RSA 553:30:

> Upon a showing of advantage to the estate the probate court may authorize the executor, administrator or special administrator to continue any business of the decedent for the benefit of the estate, but if the decedent died testate and his estate is solvent the decree shall be subject to the provisions of the will. The decree may be entered with or without notice, except that if entered without notice it shall be a decree nisi, in which event an order of notice shall issue within five days after the decree, and the decree shall become absolute only after notice and hearing; but the conduct of any business pursuant to such a decree nisi shall not be invalidated by failure of the court to make such decree absolute. Any decree entered hereunder may be revoked or modified for cause shown at any time. The decree may provide (a) the extent of the liability of the estate, or any part thereof, or of the executor or administrator, for obligations incurred in the continuation of the business; (b) whether liabilities incurred in the conduct of the business are to be chargeable solely to the part of the estate set aside for use in the business or to the estate as a whole; and (c) such other conditions, restrictions, regulations and requirements as may be deemed for the benefit of the estate and of creditors thereof. The authority shall not be granted for more than one year from the date of the appointment of the executor or administrator, except that for cause shown the authority may be extended from time to time, but no single extension shall be for more than one year.

An important case interpreting this statute is *Deschenes v. Estate of Deschenes.*[114] In this case, the administrator continued the decedent's

---

[112] Horton v. Eagle Indem. Ins. Co., 86 N.H. 472, 474, 171 A. 322, 323 (1934).

[113] 1st Report Judicial Council, p. 18 (1946).

[114] Deschenes v. Estate of Deschenes, 109 N.H. 389, 254 A.2d 278 (1969). See also DeGrandpre, *Lex Loci*, 11 N.H.B.J. 201, 203–04 (1969).

fuel oil business without authority of the probate court, but pursuant to an informal oral agreement among the heirs. The Court held that "[i]n the absence of permission either from the heirs or the probate court, operation of a business by an administratrix would be at her peril. She would be personally liable for losses and chargeable with all profits."[115]

Even though the *Deschenes* Court found that the heirs had informally agreed to allow the administrator to continue the business and that that agreement would be enforced, the Court held that

> [n]othing in the permission given to operate by the heirs . . . [gave the administratrix] greater rights than she would have had under permission granted under RSA 553:30. This statute requires annual accounting and limits permission to one year at a time. It was enacted to bring the operation of a decedent's business by his personal representative under judicial control and restricted such operation to protect the rights of persons interested in the estate.[116]

The Supreme Court, in *Deschenes*, went on to overturn the decree of the lower court allowing the administratrix an allowance for compensation in running the business when the allowance would result in the business operating at a loss:

> The allowance by the court of $100 weekly to the administratrix retroactively for the entire 308 weeks the business was operated defeated the purpose of the annual accounting. The annual accounting contemplated by RSA 553:30 was intended to inform the heirs whether the business was operating at a profit or loss. Even if the original consent of the heirs was considered a continuing consent, unlike the statute which is limited to one year, the heirs should have an opportunity to reconsider such consent in the light of true results shown by the accounting. The allowance of $30,800 to the administratrix for operating the business of the decedent is set aside.[117]

The moral of this story is that an administrator should continue a decedent's business only after authorization by the probate court.

---

115 Deschenes v. Estate of Deschenes, 109 N.H. 389, 391, 254 A.2d 278, 280 (1969).

116 Deschenes v. Estate of Deschenes, 109 N.H. 389, 391–92, 254 A.2d 278, 280 (1969).

117 Deschenes v. Estate of Deschenes, 109 N.H. 389, 392, 254 A.2d 278, 280 (1969).

However, obtaining probate court authorization is not the final answer. Unlike the Uniform Probate Code,[118] no provision is made to allow for the operation of the business even for a short period of time after the decedent's death. When the decedent is operating a business at his death, the administrator should gain probate court approval, even on a temporary basis, to operate a decedent's business when he files for appointment as an executor.

Secondly, annual accountings are required, and the administrator should not delay accounting but make it promptly. As the *Deschenes* case makes clear, the purpose of such accountings is to allow the court and heirs "to have an opportunity to reconsider . . . in the light of true results shown by the accounting" since the annual accounting requirement was enacted to bring the operation of a decedent's business by his personal representative under judicial control and restricted such operation to protect the rights of persons interested in the estate.[119]

Furthermore, as RSA 553:30 also makes clear, the order of the probate court may include a provision of "the extent of the liability of the estate, or any part thereof, or of the executor or administrator, for obligations incurred in the continuation of the business."

Unfortunately, RSA 553:30 does not have provisions similar to §§ 3-715(24) and 3-715(25) of the Uniform Probate Code allowing the administrator to incorporate the decedent's business and to operate it in incorporated form. The Uniform Probate Code, § 3-715(24) allows the administrator to operate a decedent's business for four months after the decedent's death if "continuation is a reasonable means of preserving the value of the business including good will." Also relevant, but not directly applicable, are the provisions of the Uniform Trustees' Powers Act which empowers trustees with the specific power "to continue or participate in the operation of any business or other enterprise, and to effect incorporation, dissolution, or other change in the form of the organization of a business or enterprise." RSA 564-A:3, III(c). Many wills empower the executor with all of the power of trustees under this Act.[120]

---

[118] § 3-715(24).

[119] Deschenes v. Estate of Deschenes, 109 N.H. at 392, 254 A.2d at 280 (1969).

[120] C. DeGrandpre, 7 New Hampshire Practice: Wills, Trusts and Gifts (3d ed. 1997) Form 45.

Library References

Am Jur 2d Executors and Administrators § 555 et seq.

CJS Executors and Administrators §§ 193–197

Preference or priority of claims arising out of continuation of decedent's business by personal representative. 83 ALR2d 1406.

Estoppel of one doing business with personal representative purporting to carry on decedent's business, to assert representative's personal liability. 83 ALR2d 1406.

§ 33-18. Discovery of Assets

An administrator has the duty to collect all of the assets of the estate and will be held chargeable for a failure to take possession and collect property of the decedent which should have been seasonably taken.

Chapter 555 of the Revised Statutes, quaintly entitled "Embezzlements," provides an administrator with an archaic remedy to pursue estate assets. This statutory scheme is designed to provide for "discovery of the [estate's] property to the end that measures may be taken in the proper court for its recovery." *Dodge v. McNeil*.[121]

RSA 555:1 provides an administrator a remedy of bringing before the probate court for questioning any person suspected of having estate assets:

> Any person suspected of having concealed, embezzled or conveyed away any of the personal estate of a deceased person may, upon complaint of the administrator, an heir, legatee or creditor of the deceased person, be cited to appear before the judge and be examined, under oath, for the discovery of the same.

"[T]he purpose of the statute is only to facilitate in reaching possible [estate] assets." *Robinson v. Estate of Dana*.[122] It provides for a method of search for estate assets. If the person cited fails to appear, or appearing, fails to answer, RSA 555:4 provides for incarceration in order to compel an answer. The cited person is granted the right to counsel by RSA 555:3. The mere citation to appear before the probate court for embezzlement

---

[121] Dodge v. McNeil, 62 N.H. 168 (1882).

[122] Robinson v. Estate of Dana, 87 N.H. 114, 116, 174 A. 772, 774 (1934).

under RSA 555 is, of course, not evidence that the person cited has committed a crime.[123]

The practicality of this statute is limited, however. After an examination, the probate court has no authority to require the delivery of any property discovered by the process.[124] The proper procedure for recovery of estate property discovered by use of RSA 555 cannot be had in the probate court.[125] Under the statute the probate court can provide for the examination of the person complained of,[126] but the judge of probate has no authority to determine the question whether the charge is or is not sustained.[127] An appeal by the administrator from a "finding" by the judge of probate that the charge of embezzlement was not sustained, will be dismissed.[128]

However, under RSA 555:4, the probate court does have the power to commit to the house of corrections a person who refuses appear or refuses to answer interrogatories concerning the assets of the estate, until such person consents to answer the interrogatories or until released by the complainant, or by order of the probate court.

Proper methods for the recovery of assets of an estate are (1) a bill in equity for discovery and disclosure of the nature, value and location of assets belonging to the decedent;[129] or (2) a bill in equity brought by the administrator to discover and recover deceased's assets;[130] or (3) an action of *assumpsit* to recover money deposited by or wrongfully obtained from the decedent.[131]

The power of an administrator to discover and collect assets is not limited to these statutory provisions. As an administrator, he is entitled

---

[123] Harvey v. Provandie, 83 N.H. at 245, 141 A. at 141 (1928).

[124] Scott v. Knight, 67 N.H. 500, 38 A. 120 (1893).

[125] Dodge v. McNeil, 62 N.H. 168 (1882).

[126] Scott v. Knight, 67 N.H. 500, 38 A. 120 (1893); Dodge v. McNeil, 62 N.H. 168 (1882).

[127] Robinson v. Estate of Dana, 87 N.H. at 116, 174 A. at 774; Dodge v. McNeil, 62 N.H. 168 (1882).

[128] Dodge v. McNeil, 62 N.H. 168 (1882).

[129] Fredette v. Foley, 98 N.H. 509, 104 A.2d 197 (1954).

[130] Stabrow v. Stabrow, 96 N.H. 74, 69 A.2d 863 (1949).

[131] Goddard v. Hazelton, 96 N.H. 231, 73 A.2d 123 (1950); Harvey v. Provandie, 83 N.H. 236, 141 A. 136 (1928).

to bring suit in the superior court, utilizing all general statutes for discovery and the recovery of property available to anyone:

> An administrator may by bill seek discovery of assets and cancellation of fraudulent conveyances by a decedent, so far as necessary to satisfy the claims of the latter's creditors.[132]

For example, in *In re Estate of Ward*,[133] the Supreme Court upheld an administrator's use of a superior court attachment action against a prior administrator to recover monies wrongfully misappropriated by him from the decedent.

In a recent case, *In re Estate of Laura*,[134] the Supreme Court discussed the issues involved when a dispute arises whether or not a particular asset belongs to the decedent's estate. The Supreme Court held that the doctrine of laches applies to a party's claim that assets in the estate belong to it, but held that evidence could be introduced to rebut the claim of laches if the party had reasonably relied on promises made by the decedent testator to return the property.

Library References

Am Jur 2d Executors and Administrators § 487 et seq.

CJS Executors and Administrators § 153 et seq.

§ 33-19.　Collection and Compromise of Debts Due to the Estate

An administrator has the duty to collect the debts of the estate. RSA 554:11. In carrying out this task, he may use the collection procedures generally available to others in the district or superior courts. A failure to proceed properly to collect debts will be a breach of duty for which he will be charged in his account. *Norris v. Towle.*[135]

However, the administrator has discretion to act reasonably in carrying out this task. Thus, an executor or administrator is not bound to enforce a doubtful claim merely because some of the heirs, or those interested, may think it well founded.[136] If any of the heirs wish to have a doubtful

---

[132] Robinson v. Estate of Dana, 87 N.H. 114, 116, 174 A. 772, 774 (1934).

[133] In re Estate of Ward, 129 N.H. 4, 11, 523 A.2d 28, 34 (1986).

[134] 141 N.H. 628, 690 A.2d 1011 (1997).

[135] Norris v. Towle, 54 N.H. 290 (1874).

[136] Sanborn v. Goodhue, 28 N.H. 48 (1853); Griswold v. Chandler, 5 N.H. at 494 (1831).

claim legally settled, they can be required to indemnify the administrator against the costs and expenses, after which it will be his duty to assert the claim.[137]

In *Cante v. Hopkins*[138] the Court held that "an administrator does not have a duty to enforce a doubtful claim merely because a party who has an interest in the estate thinks the claim is well founded."

Furthermore, RSA 554:12 allows an administrator to compromise a debt due from an insolvent person:

> A debt due from an insolvent person may be compromised and discharged on payment of such part thereof as the administrator deems proper, and the administrator shall be chargeable only for the amount received.

As can be seen, this statute is very narrow. It relates only to debts due from insolvent persons. However, prior to the passage of this statute, an administrator had the power to compromise a debt with a debtor, and receive less than the amount of the debt, if he could show that what had been done was beneficial to the estate.[139] But an administrator acted in some peril in compromising the debt; for if an objection was raised, the burden of proof lay upon him to show that he acted judiciously and that the estate had not been prejudiced by his actions. If he failed in this, he could be charged with the difference.[140] To obviate this difficulty, RSA 554:12 provides a mode whereby the administrator, by obtaining prior authority from the judge, may safely compromise with a debtor without being subjected to expense in sustaining his acts.[141] The right to compromise which existed prior to the passage of the statute was not taken away, and it may still be exercised as before, subject to the same limitations and risk.[142]

The debts due to the estate from the administrator, however, are not subject to compromise. RSA 554:14. The judge of probate has no choice.

---

[137] Cogswell v. Concord & Montreal R.R., 68 N.H. 192, 194, 44 A. 293, 294 (1895); Merrill v. Woodbury, 61 N.H. 504 (1881); Griswold v. Chandler, 5 N.H. at 494 (1831).

[138] __ N.H. __, (decided March 21, 2001).

[139] Wyman's Appeal, 13 N.H. 18 (1842).

[140] *Id.*

[141] *Id.*

[142] *Id.*

He cannot authorize an executor to compromise a debt due to the estate from himself, nor can he negotiate and compromise the debt with the executor. *Judge of Probate v. Sulloway.*[143]

The Uniform Probate Code gives an administrator broad authority to "abandon property when, in the opinion of the personal representative, it is valueless, or is so encumbered, or is in condition that it is of no benefit to the estate" (§ 3-715(11)) and to "effect a fair and reasonable compromise with any debtor or obligor" (§ 3-715(17)).

Library References

Am Jur 2d Executors and Administrators §§ 649–652

CJS Executors and Administrators §§ 442 et seq., 469

Claim due estate—compromise. 72 ALR2d 191.

§ 33-20. Redemption of Mortgage

In New Hampshire, in the absence of a will provision to the contrary, the administrator must pay all debts of his decedent, including a mortgage debt secured by property devised to others:

> The administrator, if there be sufficient assets, shall redeem all property of the deceased under mortgage, pledge or levy of execution for less than its value, or which if unredeemed would diminish the value of the estate, unless he shall by license sell it subject to the encumbrance; and neglect so to redeem shall be deemed maladministration and waste. RSA 554:16.

This is also the common law rule as it was expressed in *Tunis v. Dole*:[144]

> In the absence of a contrary intention expressed in the will, a devisee of real property in this state is entitled to have the mortgage paid out of the personal estate where there are sufficient assets. . . . The executor is bound to exonerate the New Hampshire real estate from any liability on account of any mortgages made by the testatrix since there is no statute or testamentary provision changing this common law rule.[145]

---

[143] Judge of Probate v. Sulloway, 68 N.H. 511, 44 A.2d 720 (1896).

[144] Tunis v. Dole, 97 N.H. 420, 89 A.2d 760 (1952).

[145] Tunis v. Dole, 97 N.H. 420, 426, 89 A.2d 760, 764 (1952).

This general rule has since been altered by the enactment of a proviso to RSA 554:16 which provides for an exception to the general rule as follows:

> Provided however, when real estate under mortgage is specifically devised, the devisee shall take such real estate subject to the mortgage, unless the testator in his will or by insurance has provided expressly or by necessary implication that such mortgage be otherwise paid; and if the note or obligation of the testator secured by such mortgage be paid out of other property in his estate after his decease, the executor of his will, at the request of any person interested, and by leave of the probate court shall sell such specifically devised real estate for the purpose of satisfying the estate of the testator for the amount so paid, together with the costs and expenses thereof.

The statutory language raises a question of great importance to the heirs of an estate. It may mean that the proviso rule applies only when real property is specifically mentioned in the will as being left to certain persons, or it may apply to real estate, referred to, but passing by the general residuary clause. The usual rule regarding legacies and devises would apply the statute only to real estate specifically mentioned in a will. The ultimate answer will be for the Supreme Court to decide although it appears by the use of the word *specifically* that the draftsmen intended to include only real property specifically bequeathed or devised to particular persons and not real estate passing by a residuary clause.[146]

Under RSA 554:16, an administrator must pay off the debt secured by a mortgage on the real estate which is part of the decedent's estate in all but the following four circumstances: (1) when there are not "sufficient assets";[147] (2) when the value of the debt is greater than the value of the mortgage property;[148] (3) when the administrator must sell the property, subject to the mortgage, in order to pay debts and legacies;[149] (4) when the real estate is specifically devised and there is no provision in the will indicating that the mortgage should be paid.[150]

---

[146] *Id.*

[147] RSA 554:16.

[148] RSA 554:16.

[149] RSA 554:17.

[150] RSA 554:16.

Compare the Uniform Probate Code, which reverses the common law rule exonerating specific devises from debt:

Section 2-607. Nonexoneration: A specific devise passes subject to any mortgage interest existing at the date of death, without right of exoneration, regardless of a general directive in the will to pay debts.

Library References

Am Jur 2d Executors and Administrators §§ 618, 619
CJS Executors and Administrators § 298

§ 33-21.   Mortgage of Land of the Decedent by Administrator

In certain narrow situations, RSA 554:30 authorizes an administrator to mortgage property of the estate.

> The judge, on application of the administrator or executor, with the assent of the heirs or devisees or, if minors or under disability, their guardians or conservators, may grant a license to mortgage the real estate of any person deceased, when the personal property shall be insufficient to pay the just demands by law chargeable to the estate, or to make necessary or desirable repairs to preserve such real estate, or where it is otherwise necessary to raise money to facilitate settlement of the estate.

It is important to note the three limited purposes set forth in this statute for its utilization: (1) when the personal property of the estate is insufficient to pay the debts and charges of the estate, (2) when it is necessary in order to make necessary or desirable repairs to "preserve" the property sought to be mortgaged, and (3) where it is "otherwise necessary" to raise money "to facilitate settlement" of the estate.

RSA 554:31 provides that the petition for such a license to mortgage must recite the limits of the principal amount, the interest rate, and the term of the note to secure the mortgage, and that the note and mortgage must be executed by the administrator, and the heirs or devisees, or if minors, their guardians or conservators, who must assent to the petition to mortgage. The license must include the homestead rights and any other rights, upon the consent in writing by the widow or widower of the decedent. RSA 554:32. No license shall issue later than two years after the date of the appointment of the administrator, and the mortgage must be made by the administrator under the license within ninety days from the date of the license. RSA 554:33.

The proceeds of the mortgage under license must be accounted for to the probate court. On approval of the final account, the administrator will be discharged from liability for the note and mortgage. The administrator is required to notify the mortgagee of the discharge. RSA 554:34.

Pursuant to RSA 554:35, a foreign administrator whose intestate or testator owns lands in this State, may make application for a license to the judge for the county in which the land is situated, as if appointed in this state. A foreign administrator is required to give bond with sufficient sureties, as are those who are resident of this state.

A petition to mortgage land of the decedent pursuant to RSA 554:30 is made on Approved Form 110. No general notice is required for the granting of the petition. RSA 550:4, XIII. However, this does not change the clear requirement of RSA 554:30 requiring the assent of the heirs and devisees to the mortgage petition.[151]

Section 3-715(16) of the Uniform Probate Code allows the personal representative to borrow money and give security therefor and § 3-715(23) of the Code specifically allows the personal representative to mortgage the estate's real or personal property.

Library References

Am Jur 2d Executors and Administrators §§ 394–396

CJS Executors and Administrators § 208

§ 33-22. Foreclosure by Administrator

It is clearly an administrator's duty to collect money due upon notes secured by mortgages.[152]

Money due on mortgages belongs not to the heirs, but to the personal representative of the mortgagee.[153] Thus the administrator may maintain a writ of entry to foreclose a mortgage to his decedent.[154] However, there

---

[151] 9th Report Judicial Council, p. 43 (1962).

[152] Fifield v. Sperry, 20 N.H. 338, 340 (1850).

[153] Bickford v. Daniels, 2 N.H. 71, 72 (1819).

[154] Id.

is no rule requiring an administrator to proceed with an action, if the mortgagor is willing to surrender possession, although he may foreclose in any manner in which the mortgagee could have foreclosed.[155] The administrator has a right to attempt to enforce the payment of the money, by pursuing all the remedies the law gives for foreclosure.[156] Once the mortgage has been foreclosed, the legal estate vests in the heirs, subject to the rights of the administrator as trustee.[157]

The question whether the property received by the administrator when the mortgage is foreclosed, if it is not sold, is to be distributed as personal property or as real property and distributed accordingly was addressed in *Fifield v. Sperry*:[158]

> To decide, then, whose is the land, upon the executor's foreclosure of the mortgage, we have only to inquire whose was the debt, or whose would the money have been if paid to the executor, and not used in administration? For so long as the fund, whether money or land, is not so used, the foreclosure does not change the rights of any of the parties.

Library References

Am Jur 2d Executors and Administrators § 565

CJS Executors and Administrators §§ 261–264

§ 33-23. Decedent's Burial and Disinterment

The custody and control of the remains of a decedent are governed by RSA 290:16 et seq.[159] Where a decedent leaves a written, signed document designating a person to have custody and control of his remains, custody and control will belong to that person. RSA 290:17. Without a written document, or if the named custodian refuses custody of the remains, custody and control will belong to the next of kin, as defined by RSA 290:16.

The fact of appointment as administrator of the decedent's estate does not give the administrator any greater right to the custody and control of a decedent's remains than he otherwise would have. RSA 290:22.

---

[155] Gibson v. Bailey, 9 N.H. 168, 172 (1838).

[156] Fifield v. Sperry, 20 N.H. at 340 (1850); Gibson v. Bailey, 9 N.H. at 172 (1838).

[157] Gibson v. Bailey, 9 N.H. at 173 (1838).

[158] Fifield v. Sperry, 20 N.H. 338 at 341 (1850). See also Gibson v. Bailey, 9 N.H. at 173 (1838).

[159] P.L. 1996, c. 283:18, c. 283:19.

Where a decedent leaves written and signed instructions regarding funeral arrangements and the disposal of his remains, the person having custody and control is required to abide by those wishes to the extent that the decedent paid for those arrangements in advance or left sufficient resources to carry out his wishes. RSA 290:20.

The superior court, prior to the passage of the Omnibus Justice Act, had equitable jurisdiction over controversies arising relative to the interment of the remains of the dead or their disinterment. *Lavigne v. Wilkinson.*[26] After the passage of the Omnibus Justice Act, it would seem, although it is not clear, that the superior court retains equity jurisdiction in these matters; but perhaps a statutory change should be made to put such jurisdiction in the probate courts. Regarding disinterment and reinterment, the Court has held that the trial court, in an action involving a controversy over the reinterment of the remains of a decedent, should be:

> guided in making this decree by what is fit and proper to be done taking into consideration all the special circumstances surrounding that particular case, due regard being given to the wishes of the decedent, the rights of relatives and friends, and the welfare of the public. In a case where the interment was made by the willing consent of all interested parties, and with the understanding that the place of burial should be the final sepulchre, a disinterment and removal of the remains should not be decreed except upon presentation of strong and convincing evidence showing that it would be unreasonable to refuse to make such a decree. In order to warrant such action, new and unforeseen events must have occurred since the burial, which render the exhumation and removal of the remains reasonably necessary.[27]

In *Chinberg v. Chinberg,*[28] the Supreme Court approved the trial court's disinterment order and allowed reinterment of the remains of a decedent in the Arlington National Cemetery. The Court found that the trial court had met the test of *Lavigne v. Wilkinson,* and that the

---

[26] 80 N.H. 221 (1921).

[27] 80 N.H. 221, 224 (1921).

[28] 139 N.H. 616 (1995).

decedent's wishes were clear that he wished to be cremated and buried with his wife. In *Chinberg*, the wife had, at death, consented to burial of her husband in the husband's family plot, but disagreements with the husband's family arose which made it unlikely that she would be able to be buried with her husband as he had clearly intended.

§ 33-24. Monuments

RSA 554:21 provides that:

> Administrators of estates actually solvent may erect suitable monuments at the graves of the testators or intestates, and the reasonable expense thereof shall be allowed them on settlement of their accounts.

While at one time a gift to be applied to the erection of a tomb or monument was thought to serve some public purpose,[160] it is not now of such social interest to the community as to qualify as a charitable expenditure unless the structure to be erected would confer some public benefit.[161]

The authority set out in RSA 554:21 includes a power of doing what is reasonably necessary, at the expense of the estate, to keep a monument in a proper condition during the time of administration[162] and to make the monument as durably suitable and sufficient as its purpose requires.[163]

RSA 554:21 makes a distinction between the case of a solvent, and of an insolvent estate.[164] However fit and proper it may be that monuments should be erected at the expense of heirs and legatees, there is nothing in equity or justice which will require a creditor to contribute anything for the erection of a monument at the grave of the insolvent debtor.[165] Thus the amount set out in the account of an administrator of an insolvent estate for the erection of a monument will be disallowed.[166]

---

[160] Smart v. Durham, 77 N.H. 56, 86 A. 821 (1913).

[161] In re Estate of Byrne, 98 N.H. 300, 303, 100 A.2d 157, 159 (1953).

[162] Bell v. Briggs, 63 N.H. 592, 4 A. 702 (1885).

[163] *Id.*

[164] In re Estate of Byrne, 98 N.H. 300, 100 A.2d 157 (1953).

[165] Brackett v. Tillotson, 4 N.H. 208 (1827).

[166] *Id.*

A monument will be unsuitable and its expense not subject to allowance if its cost is too expensive.[167] Whether the monument erected is suitable and the price reasonable must be determined in each case by a consideration of all the circumstances when the case is presented.[168] The principal criteria to be considered in determining a monument's suitability and reasonableness of expense are: the amount of property left by decedent at whose grave the monument is erected; his position and standing; and the location of the monument.[169] Guided by those considerations, as well as any other pertinent circumstances, an administrator may be aided in erecting a suitable monument on his decedent's lot.[170] If the trial court finds that the administrator's actions as to a suitable monument were proper, those findings of fact cannot be disturbed.[171]

If a monument is neither suitable nor sufficient, the estate is solvent, and repairs are necessary, the statute, RSA 554:21 allows an administrator to make the necessary repairs.[172]

Library References

Am Jur 2d Executors and Administrators § 594

CJS Executors and Administrators §§ 230, 385

Tombstone or monument is a proper charge against estate of decedent. 121 ALR 1103.

§ 33-25. Care of Lots

The public interest in the sightly appearance of cemeteries is served by a gift in trust for the perpetual care of a lot, and such a gift has long been recognized in this state as a charitable one.[173]

RSA 554:22 provides that

[e]xecutors, administrators and trustees may pay, upon the order of the judge, to a cemetery corporation or to the city or

---

[167] *Id.*

[168] Lund v. Lund, 41 N.H. 355 (1860).

[169] Reynolds v. Jones, 78 N.H. 84, 97 A. 557 (1916).

[170] *Id.*

[171] In re Estate of Byrne, 98 N.H. 300, 100 A.2d 157 (1953).

[172] Reynolds v. Jones, 78 N.H. 84, 97 A. 557 (1916).

[173] Bell v. Briggs, 63 N.H. 592, 4 A. 702 (1885).

town in which the decedent has a burial place, a reasonable sum of money for the perpetual care of the lot in which their decedent is buried and the monuments thereon.

It is for the probate judge to determine, after notice to all parties in interest, to whom and in what amount the costs of perpetual care shall be paid, and such sum shall be allowed in the accounts of such executor, administrator or trustee.[174] RSA 554:23.

The proper method to present these issues to the probate court is by filing Approved Form 97, entitled "Petition for Perpetual Care and Monuments."

§ 33-26. Ownership of Cemetery Plots or Burial Spaces

Chapter 289 of the Revised Statutes governs cemeteries, burials, and dead bodies. RSA 289:1, VIII, effective in April 27, 2000, attempts to clarify the ownership of cemetery plots by providing that the owner of the cemetery plot is to find as follows:

If the deceased has designated a person to assume ownership of the cemetery lot or burial space in a written and signed document, ownership passes to that person.

If the deceased has not designated a person to assume ownership of the cemetery lot or burial space in a written and signed document, ownership shall be determined under the provisions of RSA 561:1 [the law of descent and distribution].[175]

In any situation where the ownership of a cemetery plot or burial space is unclear or in dispute, the court of probate of the county where the decedent resided may, upon receipt of a petition filed by the next of kin or other interested party, render a determination regarding ownership of the cemetery plot or burial space.[176] RSA 554:1 concerning assets that must itemized in the administrator's inventory requires that cemetery plots and burial spaces be included in the schedule of decedent's assets.

---

[174] In re Estate of Byrne, 98 N.H. 300, 100 A.2d 157 (1953); Webster v. Sughrow, 69 N.H. 380, 45 A. 139 (1898).

[175] RSA 290:24.

[176] RSA 290:24, III.

Library References

Am Jur 2d Executors and Administrators § 594

CJS Executors and Administrators §§ 230, 385

Forms

See Form 110 in Appendix for a Motion and License to Mortgage Real Estate.

CHAPTER 34. INVENTORY

---

§ 34-1. Introduction

The area of probate law involving the inventory of an estate contains some of the most archaic and obsolete provisions of our probate law. There is a great need for a simple, modern, revision of the law in this area.

To the neophyte probate practitioner, these provisions are almost unintelligible without resorting to outside help. Word-of-mouth practice governs this area of probate law. Hoyt's treatise on probate practice[1] is also helpful in this area.

Judge Smith, in his Manuscript *Treatise on Probate Law* notes that from the earliest "times, there were frequent complaints against executors and administrators for not making perfect and complete inventory, and charging them with fraudulent designs in the omissions."[2]

Therefore, it will behoove all practitioners to take care that administrators they represent, or themselves as the administrator, be diligent and careful in the important task of collecting, inventorying and managing all of the assets of the decedent's estate.

---

[1] Hoyt, The Practice In Proceedings In The Probate Courts of New Hampshire (1901).

[2] Smith's Reports 518–519 (1879).

§ 34-2. Generally

After his appointment, the administrator has the duty to collect and take charge of the decedent's estate. His first major act is to file an inventory, under oath, with the probate court, no later than ninety days after his appointment:

> **RSA 554:1. Inventory.** Every administrator shall file under oath, with the court, within 90 days after the date of appointment, a full, true and itemized inventory of all the estate of the deceased which has come to the administrator's knowledge. If an administrator fails to file an inventory within 30 days after the required filing date, the administrator is in default. The register of probate shall give notice of the default to the administrator by first class mail within 10 days after the default. The register of probate shall issue a citation notice in accordance with RSA 548:5-a. The inventory shall contain a description of the real estate; a correct schedule of all goods, chattels, stocks, bonds, cemetery plots or burial spaces, and other effects of the deceased; of all notes, with their dates and terms of payment, and the date and amount of each endorsement thereon; of all deposits in savings banks, with the name and location of each bank, the number of each book, the date of the last dividend, and the whole amount then due thereon less any withdrawals since that date; and a list and description of any other written evidences of debt. If any person claims a present legal or equitable right of title to real or personal property in the estate of the deceased, the administrator may petition the probate court pursuant to RSA 547:11-b to determine the question as between the parties.

The inventory is filed using Approved Form 44, which is provided by the probate court. A 2000 amendment to RSA 554:1 adds cemetery plots or burial spaces as effects required to be itemized in the inventory. In New Hampshire's archaic scheme of probate accounting, the inventory becomes the benchmark upon which all subsequent filings and accountings are based. For example, if stock is valued at $100.00 in the inventory, and is later sold for a higher or lesser amount, the subsequent accounting must show the gain or loss using the inventory value as the basis. RSA 554:8. The subsequent accounting is generally based upon inventory values and not market values.

Similarly, an administrator is "chargeable" for the assets of the estate included in the inventory and will be required to account for all items included in the inventory. *Griswold v. Chandler.*[3]

The inventory works both for and against the administrator as Judge Hoyt makes clear:

> The inventory is equally a protection to the administrator as to the heirs, legatees, and creditors, for it shows the amount of property for which he is chargeable and limits his responsibility, and it also furnishes those interested in the estate evidence in case it becomes necessary to institute proceedings against him on account of any maladministration, it being *prima facie* evidence of the value of the property enumerated in it. Seavey v. Seavey.[4]

Although the statutes do not make it clear, assets of the estate are to be inventoried at their fair market value on the date of death.

The time and place to charge an administrator with property belonging to an estate, not inventoried by him, is in the probate court on the settlement of his administration account. *Hurlburt v. Wheeler.*[5] An action cannot be maintained upon an administrator's bond for not inventorying an intestate's estate unless a decree in the probate court has been obtained requiring the administrator to account, and he has failed to do so.[6]

For all estates, every executor and administrator shall file a Statement concerning Fees (included in Form AOC 44) with the Register of Probate when the inventory is filed.[7]

There is no inventory requirement when a surviving spouse, or if no spouse, an only child is the sole beneficiary or heir of the decedent's estate and has been appointed to serve as fiduciary, although any interested person may petition for full administration at any time from the original grant of administration to the filing of the affidavit of administration. RSA 553:32, III.[8]

---

[3] Griswold v. Chandler, 5 N.H. 492 (1831).

[4] Seavey v. Seavey, 37 N.H. 125 (1858); Hoyt, The Practice In Proceedings In The Probate Courts of New Hampshire 152 (1901).

[5] Hurlburt v. Wheeler, 40 N.H. 73 (1860).

[6] *Id.*

[7] Prob Ct. Admin. Order 97-01.

[8] As amended by P.L., 1996, c. 265:11.

Library References

Am Jur 2d Executors and Administrators § 511 et seq.

CJS Executors and Administrators § 129 et seq.

§ 34-3.　Failure to File or Delay in Filing an Inventory

An administrator must file an inventory within ninety days after the date of his appointment by the probate court or must file an account of administration within one year of appointment. RSA 548:5-a, I. The probate court can assess default fees and citation fees for an administrator who fails to file without good cause. Under RSA 548:5-a, I[9] :

> If a fiduciary fails to file an inventory within 30 days after the required filing date, or an account of administration within 90 days after the required filing date, the fiduciary is in default. The register of probate shall give notice of the default to the fiduciary by first class mail within 10 days after the default. In the case of any inventory, account, annual report, statement of voluntary administration, or waiver of administration affidavit, the fiduciary shall either file the inventory, account, annual report, statement of voluntary administration, or waiver of administration affidavit, or show good cause for the failure to file, within 30 days after notice of the default from the register. If the fiduciary fails to file or to show cause, the judge of probate shall issue a citation to the fiduciary to appear before the judge pursuant to RSA 550:2. The fiduciary shall pay default and citation fees as established by the supreme court under RSA 490:26-a to the register of probate, pursuant to RSA 490:27.

§ 34-4.　Assets Included in the Inventory

Generally, the administrator must include in the inventory all of the property owned by the decedent at his death. RSA 554:1. However, even if assets of the decedent are not inventoried, the administrator is required to account for them in the account of his administration and will be held liable for failure to do so. RSA 554:6.

RSA 554:1 contains a specific listing of assets, which must be accounted for:

---

[9] As amended by P.L., 1996, c. 265:9.

(1)   real estate;

(2)   goods;

(3)   chattels;

(4)   stocks;

(5)   bonds;

(6)   cemetery plots or burial spaces

(7)   other effects of the deceased;

(8)   all notes;

(9)   all deposits in savings banks;

(10)   other written evidence of debt.

The inclusion of real estate is curious. Although real estate must be inventoried, it is considered to be owned by the devisees and heirs,[10] and the administrator is not required to account for real estate or for the rents and profits therefrom.[11] However, Judge Smith in his *Manuscript Treatise on Probate Law* comments that the "[i]nventory has at all times contained real as well as personal estate."[12]

Other assets which should be inventoried are promissory notes of doubtful value, although the administrator is entitled to a credit in his account if he cannot, without his fault, collect all or some portion of the note.[13]

Standing trees deeded to the decedent separate from the land are assets of the estate.[14] The same rule applies to trees on land deeded by the decedent, but reserving the trees.[15] Growing crops are considered assets,[16] as is a house on land of another.[17]

It has been held that church pews, even though unsaleable, should be inventoried, as well as provisions on hand (such as food, drink, etc.).

---

[10] See Chapter 35 *infra*.

[11] *Id.*

[12] Smith's Reports 518 (1879).

[13] Hoyt, The Practice In Proceedings In The Probate Courts of New Hampshire, 152–53 (1901).

[14] Hoit v. Stratton Mills, 54 N.H. 109 (1873).

[15] Kingsley v. Holbrook, 45 N.H. 313 (1864).

[16] Cudworth v. Scott, 41 N.H. 456 (1860).

[17] Aldrich v. Parsons, 6 N.H. 555 (1834).

Griswold v. Chandler.[18] However, under modern practice, food and other items having no resale value are seldom inventoried, or if they are, they are usually included in a catchall phrase, such as "miscellaneous tangible personal property," "furniture and effects," "contents of closets," etc., and a minimal value placed upon the aggregate.

Debts due from an administrator to an estate must be inventoried. RSA 554:14. A bequest to a decedent payable upon the death of another, while not reducible to possession during the other's lifetime, nevertheless remains a property right which should be inventoried by the administrator as an uncollected item of the donee's estate:

> While this interest is not reducible to possession during Ellen's life, it nevertheless remains a property right which should have been inventoried by the appellee as an uncollected item of Lawrence's estate. If he desires to be discharged from his trust the administrator may seek authority by an order of the probate court . . . or by a decree of distribution . . ., to turn such right over to the widow and heirs of Lawrence according to their respective interests. Their recorded receipts will entitle him to be discharged of the item. Otherwise the legacy should be accounted for as an asset remaining in his hands for further administration. No disposition of the right having been made, the decree of the probate court allowing the appellee's account without charging him with this asset was error. Buber v. Buber.[19] RSA 554:1, effective in April 27, 2000, provides that the inventory shall include a description of any "cemetery plots or burial spaces" of the deceased.

Library References

Am Jur 2d Executors and Administrators § 487

CJS Executors and Administrators § 95

§ 34-4(a). Claims to Assets Included in Inventory

Under RSA 554:1, if "any person claims a present legal or equitable right of title to real or personal property in the estate of the deceased, the administrator may petition the probate court pursuant to RSA 547:11-b to determine the question as to between the parties."

---

[18] Griswold v. Chandler, 5 N.H. 492 (1831).

[19] Buber v. Buber, 85 N.H. 160, 164, 155 A. 54, 56 (1931).

This expansion of the probate court's powers was made to carry out the intent of the 1993 Omnibus Justice Act[20] to place in the probate court all actions related to claims of title to property included in the estate of a decedent. The doctrine of laches applies to claims by third parties to title to inventory included in a decedent's estate, but the doctrine may be waived if the claimant reasonably relied on the promises of the deceased testator to return the assets.[21]

§ 34-5. Assets Not Included in the Inventory

RSA 554:4 provides that the "wearing apparel, of the widow and her ornaments . . . and the wearing apparel, Bibles and school books of the minor children" are not assets of the estate. Furthermore RSA 554:5 specifically provides that

> The wearing apparel, Bibles, family pictures, photographs, albums and any other personal trinkets of sentimental rather than intrinsic value belonging to the deceased leaving a widow, husband, children or heirs surviving, shall not be inventoried or accounted for, but shall be delivered by the administrator to the surviving husband or wife, if any, otherwise shall be divided by him among the children or, if there are no surviving children, among the heirs; but the same may be otherwise disposed of by will.

Generally speaking, the articles listed in RSA 554:5 are the decedent's "personal effects."[22] The listed articles which do not need to be inventoried pass to the residuary legatees, unless otherwise disposed of. *In re Estate of Lathrop.*[23]

In addition, it is clear that property which has no value need not be inventoried. Also, although there is evidence that oftentimes notes of doubtful value are not inventoried,[24] the correct procedure is for the administrator to inventory the note (or other asset) and take a credit for

---

[20] P.L., 1992, c. 284, as amended by P.L., 1993, c. 190.

[21] In re Estate of Laura, 141 N.H. 628, 690 A.2d 1011 (1997).

[22] In re Estate of Lathrop, 100 N.H. 393, 128 A.2d 199 (1956).

[23] *Id.*

[24] Hoyt, The Practice In Proceedings In The Probate Courts of New Hampshire, 152–53 (1901).

that portion or all of it which is uncollectible without fault of the administrator.[25]

Property of third parties in the possession of the decedent at his death need not, and should not, be inventoried.[26] However, if property of others in the possession of the decedent has no earmarks and cannot be distinguished from the decedent's property, it is an asset of the estate and must be inventoried.[27]

Growing trees and crops standing on land of the decedent at his death are considered to be part of the land and not separate assets to be inventoried.[28] This same rule applies to manure and any fixtures attached to the real estate.[29]

Property in the decedent's possession at his death which has been validly given away need not be inventoried since it is no longer an asset of the decedent.[30]

The probate inventory is not coextensive with the assets which are required to be included in the "gross estate" of the decedent under the federal estate tax. That law scoops into the estate "all property [of the decedent], real or personal, tangible or intangible, wherever situated." IRC § 2031(a). The extensive range of this definition is well known. Items which are required to be included in the gross federal estate of a decedent but not in the New Hampshire probate inventory include insurance policies owned by the decedent, jointly-held property, gifts in contemplation of death, non-possessory interests in trusts, etc.

Library References

Am Jur 2d Executors and Administrators §§ 487, 493

CJS Executors and Administrators §§ 95, 97

---

[25] Stevens v. Gage, 55 N.H. 175 (1875).

[26] Hoyt, The Practice In Proceedings In The Probate Courts of New Hampshire (1901).

[27] Hoyt, The Practice In Proceedings In The Probate Courts of New Hampshire, 153 (1901).

[28] Cudworth v. Scott, 41 N.H. 456 (1860).

[29] Hoyt, The Practice in Proceedings In The Probate Courts of New Hampshire, 155 (1901).

[30] Hoyt, The Practice in Proceedings In The Probate Courts of New Hampshire, 155–61 (1901). McDonald, *Asset Protection Planning in New Hampshire*, 36 N.H.B.J. 5 (1995).

§ 34-6. The Inventory as Evidence

The inventory can be and is admissible evidence in many situations. *Seavey v. Seavey.*[31] "There is a large class of proceedings, which are not judgments, and which, in many cases, can be regarded as judicial proceedings only by a very liberal construction of that term, which are admissible in evidence."[32] Whenever "persons are appointed by the law, or under the authority of law, to investigate any matter of fact under oath, and to make a return or report upon the subject, the same being the foundation of no judgment or judicial decree between parties, the return or report is admissible in evidence between those who were in no sense parties to the proceedings."[33]

Under the New Hampshire Rules of Evidence adopted in 1985, the probate inventory is considered admissible evidence under several recognized exceptions to the hearsay rule. Rule 803.[34] Because the inventory is returned under the administrator's oath, it can be used as evidence against him.[35] It can also be used as evidence against other parties. For example, it may be used to disprove a decedent's title to land which is not inventoried.[36] Such evidence, however, is not conclusive.[37] It is, in general, *prima facie* evidence only.[38] Where an estate is not subject to an inheritance tax, the New Hampshire Title Examination Standards provide that the failure to include (or an erroneous description of real estate in the inventory) does not create a defect in title.[39]

An administrator's inventory is evidence to the world for many purposes, because it is a return of facts made under oath, by persons appointed by authority of law, to make such appraisal and return.[40]

Although the holding that an administrator's inventory is admissible as evidence has been questioned,[41] it has been pointed out that even

---

[31] Seavey v. Seavey, 37 N.H. 125 (1858).

[32] Seavey v. Seavey, 37 N.H. 125, 131 (1858).

[33] Seavey v. Seavey, 37 N.H. 125, 131–32 (1858).

[34] See also NH Rules of Evidence 1003–1015.

[35] NH Rules of Evidence 1003–1015; Morrill v. Foster, 33 N.H. 379 (1856).

[36] Morrill v. Foster, 33 N.H. 379 (1856).

[37] *Id.*

[38] Seavey v. Seavey, 37 N.H. 125 (1858).

[39] New Hampshire Title Examination Standards, Standard 7–15 (1988).

[40] Seavey v. Seavey, 37 N.H. 125 (1858).

[41] Concord Land & Water Power Co. v. Clough, 69 N.H. 609, 45 A. 565 (1899); Derry v. Rockingham County, 62 N.H. 485 (1883).

though it is considered admissible as *prima facie* evidence, it is not conclusive as to third parties. *Petition of Carlton.*[42] In that case, it was held that an administrator's inventory is not conclusive of value upon the assessment of inheritance taxes, nor upon distributees of a will in determining their several shares in the residuum. If there is a controversy as to the value then the value should be determined in some proceeding to which all interested are parties.[43]

Judge Smith in his *Manuscript Treatise on Probate Law* makes the point that "[t]he inventory is not exclusive for or against the administrator as to the value of the articles inventoried" nor does "the inventory . . . preclude the administrator from showing that the intestate did not own the property inventoried."[44]

In a condemnation proceeding, or other action where real estate value is a central issue, in the absence of a statute permitting it, the assessed valuation of property for tax purposes where value is a central issue is not admissible as evidence of value. *Holmes v. State.*[45] The appraisal in a probate inventory is seldom a more reliable index of value than a tax assessment, and the introduction of such evidence is erroneous and prejudicial unless it can be demonstrated that the error is harmless.[46] Thus, where an appraiser had not seen the property, was not familiar with market values in the town in which the property was located and did not discuss the appraisal with the heirs, and he testified that if the value was an important matter he would have engaged a real estate expert, the probate inventory and appraisal was held to be an unreliable index of the value of the property and inadmissible.[47]

Library References

Am Jur 2d Executors and Administrators § 520
CJS Executors and Administrators § 138

---

[42] Petition of Carlton, 79 N.H. 48, 104 A. 246 (1918).
[43] *Id.*
[44] Smith's Reports 477 (1879).
[45] Holmes v. State, 109 N.H. 319, 251 A.2d 320 (1969).
[46] *Id.*
[47] *Id.*

§ 34-7. Appraisers

RSA 554:2 provides that the value of the assets included in the inventory be appraised by three "suitable persons" appointed by the judge:

> The inventory, and an appraisal of the real estate, goods, chattels, stocks and bonds mentioned therein, shall be made by three suitable persons appointed by the judge and sworn to their fidelity and impartiality. The appraisers shall class the property under appropriate heads, and shall foot each class.

RSA 554:3, however, allows the judge to appoint "only one appraiser, if in his opinion the nature of the property or the size of the estate makes it advisable to do so." The statutes do not allow the probate judge to appoint only two appraisers.

It is customary for the administrator's nomination of appraisers, which is contained in the Petition for Administration,[48] to be automatically accepted by the judge and an inventory blank (Approved Form 44)[49] will be promptly issued to the appraisers, to be returned ninety days after the appointment of the administrator.

Also, in most estates, the administrator customarily nominates only one person to act as appraiser. This is generally acceptable to the probate court unless the estate is very large or very complicated. If the judge desires additional appraisers, he will generally ask for nominations from the administrator and will usually appoint the individuals nominated.

The requirement of RSA 554:2 that the appraisers be "suitable" persons was designed to produce an impartial determination of the value of the estate.[50] Any question of the disqualification of an appraiser is disposed of by a finding of the court that the property was fairly valued.[51]

However, the mere fact that an appraiser is a beneficiary of an estate or is personally familiar with the property is not sufficient to deny appointment, unless an interested party objects.[52] In Judge Smith's

---

[48] See Form 85 in Appendix.

[49] See Form 44 in Appendix.

[50] Fellows v. Normandin, 96 N.H. 260, 74 A.2d 548 (1950).

[51] Id.

[52] Id.

Manuscript Treatise on Probate Law,[53] he makes the point that, although in New Hampshire "creditors and next of kin are considered as unsuitable persons for the office of appraiser" there "does not seem to be any good reason for this premise."

Any party in interest may object to the suitability of an appraiser but this is an infrequent occurrence. The proper time to object is before the inventory is filed or seasonably thereafter. Failure to object seasonably will preclude raising of the issue of unsuitability later. *Fellows v. Normandin.*[54]

The usual procedure acceptable to most courts is for a lay administrator to nominate his attorney as appraiser. If the administrator is an attorney, he customarily nominates a partner or someone in his office to act as appraiser and no separate or independent charge is made for the work. Of course, independent appraisers are entitled to charge for their services and the administrator is allowed this charge as an expense of administration. This is an area where the practice from county to county varies considerably. For example, in at least one county,[55] the probate court will not allow someone in the employ of the attorney for the estate to act as appraiser. If real estate is involved, and it will be sold by the administrator, some counties require a written appraisal to be undertaken by someone other than the broker engaged to sell the property.

If an attorney is appointed appraiser, he should have the actual appraisal of unique items such as real estate, collections, jewelry, furniture and furnishings be made under his direction by appraisers qualified to value the particular items involved. He then may adopt their appraisals as his in the inventory. The actual appraisals need not be submitted with the inventory, but should be available if the judge or any interested party inquires.

Probate Court Procedure Bulletin 1997-03 has as its purpose "to provide guidance for the appointment of appraisers in estates of deceased persons, guardianships, or testamentary trusts." The frequency of inquiries to the Administrative Justice concerning the qualifications and appointment of appraisers underscores the need for this information, especially by probate practitioners and probate court staff. The Bulletin

---

[53] Smith's Reports 475 (1879).

[54] Fellows v. Normandin, 96 N.H. 260, 74 A.2d 548 (1950).

[55] Rockingham County.

cites the very "sparse guidance" found in the statutes concerning the qualifications for appointment as an appraiser.[56] The Bulletin states that the statutory language found refers only to an appraiser's "suitability, fidelity, and impartiality" and concludes that "any tests for these qualities or for a persons disqualification from appointment as an appraiser lies within the discretion of each probate court."

Library References

Am Jur 2d Executors and Administrators § 521

CJS Executors and Administrators § 135

§ 34-8. Amendment of Inventory

There is no statutorily prescribed procedure for handling the frequently-encountered situation where property of a decedent is found after the inventory is filed.

The proper practice is to move to amend the inventory in a separate petition. However, it is not uncommon for the matter to be handled in the final account by adding an item classified as "Property Not Previously Inventoried."

Library References

Am Jur 2d Executors and Administrators § 519

CJS Executors and Administrators § 137

§ 34-9. Uniform Probate Code Provisions

Section 3-706 of the Uniform Probate Code requires an administrator to file within three months after his appointment:

> an inventory of property owned by the decedent at the time of his death, listing it with reasonable detail, and indicating as to each listed item, its fair market value as of the date of the decedent's death, and the type and amount of any encumbrance that may exist with reference to any item.

The personal representative shall send a copy of the inventory to interested persons who request it. He may also file the original of the inventory with the court.

---

[56] RSA 542:2, 3; RSA 463:19; RSA 564-A:22; RSA 554:2, 3; RSA 548:25; RSA 126-A:34; Prob. Ct. R. 29.

Section 3-707 of the Code allows the personal representative to appoint "a qualified and disinterested appraiser" to assist him but the probate judge is not directly involved in the selection of appraisers.

If any property of the decedent is discovered after the filing of the inventory, Section 3-708 of the Code provides for the filing of a supplementary inventory.

Library References

Am Jur 2d Executors and Administrators §§ 522–524

Forms

See Form 44 in Appendix for an Inventory of Fiduciary.

See Form 85 in Appendix for a Petition for Appraisers.

CHAPTER 35. REAL ESTATE

§ 35-1. Introduction

The manner in which real estate is handled in the administration of an estate in New Hampshire is based very closely upon old and reliable common law real property principles. The general principle governing the treatment of real estate in an estate, as contrasted with treatment of personal property which passes to the administrator, is that the real estate of a decedent (unless he dies insolvent) passes not to the administrator but directly to the devisee or heir at law of the decedent. This principle was expounded at some length in the early case of *Gregg v. Currier*:[1]

> [G]enerally, in other cases, the land descends, on the death of the testator or intestate, to the devisees or heirs, with no right or duty on the part of the executor or administrator, as such, in any way to intermeddle therewith.[2]

This rule applied whether the decedent died testate or intestate.[3]

In *Lucy v. Lucy*,[4] this rule was propounded as follows:

> It is well settled that, in this state, real estate of the intestate, immediately upon his death, vests in the heirs, subject to be divested by proper proceedings for the payment of the intestate's debts. If the estate is insolvent and settled in the insolvent course, it is the duty of the administrator to take possession of it, take care of it, and take the rents and profits. But the mere fact that the estate is settled in the insolvent course does not authorize the administrator to have possession of the real estate.[5]

The general rule was set forth in *Fleming v. Aiken*,[6] as follows:

> [T]itle to the real estate passed directly to the devisees subject to the interest being divested due to insufficient personal assets in the estate . . . or insolvency of the estate. . . . In the absence

---

[1] Gregg v. Currier, 36 N.H. 200 (1858).

[2] Gregg v. Currier, 36 N.H. 200, 202 (1858).

[3] *Id.*

[4] Lucy v. Lucy, 55 N.H. 9 (1874).

[5] Lucy v. Lucy, 55 N.H. 9, 10 (1874).

[6] Fleming v. Aiken, 114 N.H. 687, 327 A.2d 724 (1974).

of the executor seeking a license to sell the real estate, the probate court has no jurisdiction of the real estate of a decedent.[7]

Most states follow New Hampshire's long-standing reliance upon the common law rule in this area. Although the basic common law rule has been altered in England, neither statutes nor decisions in America have uprooted the basic tenet of the common law that title to a decedent's realty passes at once on his death to his heirs or devisees and not to his personal representative.[8]

For title standards purposes, the failure of an administrator to file an accounting in the probate court does not create a defect in title to the decedent's real estate.[9]

The basic common law rule is a very important guidepost to keep in mind as the somewhat confusing and sometimes conflicting rules concerning real estate are explored in some detail later in this chapter.

Library References

Am Jur 2d Executors and Administrators §§ 490, 565

CJS Descent and Distribution § 8

CJS Executors and Administrators §§ 103, 252

Other References

Probate Aspects of Title Searching, unpublished paper by Richard S. Moody, Esquire.

§ 35-2. Uniform Probate Code Provisions

The Uniform Probate Code recognizes the common law rule, but alters it substantially. Thus, while § 3-101 recognizes that "[u]pon the death of a person, his real and personal property devolves to the persons to whom it is devised by his last will or to . . . his heirs."

However, § 3-709 makes clear that the Code departs from the common law rule and provides that:

> [E]very personal representative has a right to, and shall take possession or control of, the decedent's property, except that any real property or tangible personal property may be left with

---

[7] Fleming v. Aiken, 114 N.H. 687, 689 90, 327 A.2d 724 (1974).

[8] III American Law of Property § 14.7 (1952).

[9] New Hampshire Title Examination Standards, Standard 7–14 (1988).

or surrendered to the person presumptively entitled thereto
unless or until, in the judgment of the personal representative,
possession of the property by him will be necessary for purposes
of administration. The request by a personal representative for
delivery of any property possessed by an heir or devisee is
conclusive evidence, in any action against the heir or devisee
for possession thereof, that the possession of the property by
the personal representative is necessary for purposes of administration. The personal representative shall pay taxes on, and take
all steps reasonably necessary for the management, protection
and preservation of, the estate in his possession. He may
maintain an action to recover possession of property or to
determine the title thereto.

Thus, the Code treats real property owned by the decedent at his death
similar to other property of the decedent. For example, the administrator
is specifically empowered to pay taxes on the property (§ 3-709) to
"make ordinary or extraordinary repairs or alterations in buildings or
structures" (§ 3-715(7)), to enter into leases of real property (§ 3-
715(9)), insure real property (§ 3-715(15)) and sell or mortgage real
property of the decedent. (§ 3-715(23)).

Library References

Am Jur 2d Executors and Administrators § 566

§ 35-3. Administrator's Duties with Regard to Real Estate—In General

There is no direct statutory provision setting forth the administrator's
duties with regard to a decedent's real estate, except RSA 554:15 which,
in a negative fashion, reflects the common law rule that the administrator
has very little duty with regard to real estate in a solvent estate.

The administrator shall receive the rents and profits of the
real estate, in case the estate is insolvent, and keep the same
in repair, and account for the net proceeds thereof in his
administration account.

This basic rule as to an administrator's duties with regard to the
decedent's real estate was restated in *Bergin v. McFarland*,[10] as follows:

---

[10] Bergin v. McFarland, 26 N.H. 533 (1853).

At common law, the real estate of a deceased owner at once vested in the heir at law or devisee. As such, the heir or devisee was at once entitled to maintain any action, real or personal, which he might find necessary for the protection of his rights. The personal representative of the deceased had, as such, no rights whatever, connected with the real estate. His duties and his powers were entirely confined to the personal estate and choses in action of the deceased.[11]

It would appear from these statements of the rule that if a decedent dies solvent, whether testate or intestate, the administrator has "no rights whatever" in the decedent's real estate and any rights and obligations as to the decedent's real estate belong to the heirs or devisees. However, there has developed a series of confusing and conflicting rules regarding the decedent's real estate and it is not uncommon for unsophisticated administrators to further compound the situation by taking possession and control of the decedent's real property after their appointment.

Generally, an executor or administrator is authorized to receive the rents and profits of the real estate of the testator or intestate only in case where the estate is insolvent.[12] It is not an executor's duty, in his official capacity, to receive the rents and profits of a solvent estate's real estate. He has no right to intermeddle with them unless acting as agent for the heirs,[13] but even if he does act as the heirs' agent he is only personally liable; the sureties on his bond are not liable to the heirs.[14]

An intestate's real estate, immediately upon death, vests in the heirs, subject to being divested by proper proceedings for the payment of the intestate's debts.[15] Thus an administrator should not charge himself with the income from a deceased's property arising after death.[16] Nor should the administrator be credited with the expense of carrying it on,[17] the

---

[11] Bergin v. McFarland, 26 N.H. 533, 536 (1853).

[12] Clough v. Clough, 71 N.H. 412, 52 A. 449 (1902); Gregg v. Currier, 36 N.H. 200 (1858).

[13] Gregg v. Currier, 36 N.H. 200 (1858).

[14] Weston v. Second Orthodox Congregational Soc'y, 79 N.H. 245, 110 A. 137 (1919); Gregg v. Currier, 36 N.H. 200 (1858).

[15] Lucy v. Lucy, 55 N.H. 9 (1874); Gregg v. Currier, 36 N.H. 200 (1858).

[16] Weston v. Second Orthodox Congregational Soc'y, 79 N.H. 245, 110 A. 137 (1919); Perkins v. Perkins, 58 N.H. 405 (1878).

[17] Perkins v. Perkins, 58 N.H. 405 (1878); Lucy v. Lucy, 55 N.H. 9 (1874).

cost of repairs,[18] or for taxes assessed upon it.[19] Such items should be omitted from the administrator's account.[20] However, Probate Court Approved Form 001 creates more confusion by containing a Schedule E entitled "Cash Collected on Rents of Real Estate." This is applicable to insolvent estates and should not be used in solvent estates.[21]

Generally, land descends on the death of the testator or intestate to the devisees or heirs and the executor or administrator has no right or duty to intermeddle therewith.[22] The land, however, is subject to be sold by the administrator if the personal property is not sufficient to pay the debts.[23] Vesting may also be suspended by a decree of insolvency.[24]

Where an executor merely has a naked power to sell, and the land vests in the heirs or devisees, an administrator has no right to receive the rents from the land.[25] Since an administrator has no right to receive the rents of his decedent's real estate, and since he is not duty bound to take charge of or keep such real estate, the surety on his administration bond is not liable for such acts if they are performed by the administrator.[26] However, when an administrator has collected and appropriated the rents without authority, he is personally liable.[27] Also, since the estate has no beneficial interest in the property, an executor has no duty to maintain insurance on the property and payments for such insurance are not charges against the estate.[28]

The executor of a solvent estate cannot legally spend estate funds to improve the decedent's real estate.[29] Where the executor is under a decree of the probate court to sell his decedent's realty he is entitled

---

[18] Perkins v. Perkins, 58 N.H. 405 (1878).

[19] Perkins v. Perkins, 58 N.H. 405 (1878); Lucy v. Lucy, 55 N.H. 9 (1874).

[20] Perkins v. Perkins, 58 N.H. 405 (1878).

[21] Hoyt, New Hampshire Probate Practice 167 (1901).

[22] Ruel v. Hardy, 90 N.H. 240, 6 A.2d 753 (1939).

[23] Lane v. Thompson, 43 N.H. 320 (1861).

[24] Id.

[25] Gregg v. Currier, 36 N.H. 200 (1858).

[26] Ayers v. Laighton, 73 N.H. 487, 63 A. 43 (1906); Gregg v. Currier, 36 N.H. 200 (1858).

[27] Gregg v. Currier, 36 N.H. 200 (1858).

[28] Ruel v. Hardy, 90 N.H. 240, 6 A.2d 753 (1939).

[29] McInnes v. Goldthwaite, 96 N.H. 413, 77 A.2d 849 (1951).

to credit for reasonable maintenance and carrying charges for a reasonable time. [30]

Generally an administrator will not be credited for repairs made by him upon his decedent's real estate. [31] However, repairs of the decedent's real estate can be made if such a direction is contained in the decedent's will. *Ladd v. Ladd*. [32] However, the extent of repairs required is determined by the will, and the executor is bound by any directions regarding such repairs. [33]

Library References

Am Jur 2d Executors and Administrators § 565 et seq.

CJS Executors and Administrators § 252 et seq.

§ 35-3(a). Where Administrator Takes Possession

It appears that the probate court will hold the administrator accountable if he takes possession and control of the decedent's real property. In *McInnes v. Goldthwaite*, [34] the administrator took possession of certain real estate of the decedent, paying the taxes thereon, certain maintenance expenses, and insurance premiums, and sought to have those amounts allowed in his account. However, there was evidence that he had failed to seasonably sell the property and the Court disallowed certain of the expenditures, stating the rule that:

> [w]hen, however, as is the case here, the executor does in fact take over the possession and control of the real estate and seeks to have his expenditures of estate funds thereon allowed in his account he cannot complain if the corresponding duty of using reasonable care and skill to make the property productive is imposed upon him. [35]

The Court went on to say that, after the sale, the administrator "had the burden of proving not only that the price received for the property in

---

[30] *Id.*

[31] McInnes v. Goldthwaite, 96 N.H. 413, 77 A.2d 849 (1951); Lucy v. Lucy, 55 N.H. 9 (1874).

[32] Ladd v. Ladd, 74 N.H. 380, 68 A. 462 (1907).

[33] *Id.*

[34] McInnes v. Goldthwaite, 96 N.H. 413, 77 A.2d 849 (1951) (citations omitted).

[35] McInnes v. Goldthwaite, 96 N.H. 413, 416, 77 A.2d 849, 851 (1951) (citations omitted).

1941 exceeded what it would have brought . . . [earlier] but also the extent of the net benefits which the estate received . . . . This he has failed to do and for additional reasonable expenses."[36]

Prior to the *McInnes* case, it had been held that an administrator who accepted the rents and profits of his decedent's realty was accountable to the decedent's heirs but not to the judge of probate.[37]

In *In re Estate of Crowley*,[38] the probate court held an administrator accountable after he took possession of property devised to himself and several of his siblings, then failed to maintain it and it fell into disrepair. Further, it appeared that the administrator improperly rented it for a less-than-market value to one of the devisees. The Supreme Court upheld the probate court's removal of the administrator, stating surprisingly, without any discussion of the administrator's limited role as to the real estate, that "the executor committed waste in failing to maintain the . . . property."[39]

Where a testator left a life estate interest in all of his estate to his wife and devised the remainder interest in a certain dwelling house to his son, and both persons were also named executors, the son, having occupied the house during widow's life without paying rent, was not chargeable for rent as executor. *Clough v. Clough.*[40]

Where an administrator seeks an allowance for his services and expenditures, the administrator must get it by a settlement with the heirs.[41] The fact that an administrator had managed the decedent's real estate with the acquiescence of the heirs is very strong evidence of their consent that he make repairs, pay taxes, receive rents and profits, and he is bound to account to them only for the net income after deducting his charges for the care of the property.[42]

---

[36] McInnes v. Goldthwaite, 96 N.H. 413, 417, 77 A.2d 849, 852 (1951) (citations omitted).

[37] Weston v. Second Orthodox Congregational Soc'y, 79 N.H. 245, 110 A. 137 (1919); Lucy v. Lucy, 55 N.H. 9 (1874).

[38] In re Estate of Crowley, 129 N.H. 557, 529 A.2d 960 (1987).

[39] In re Estate of Crowley, 129 N.H. 557, 560, 529 A.2d 960, 962 (1987).

[40] Clough v. Clough, 71 N.H. 412, 52 A. 449 (1902).

[41] Lucy v. Lucy, 55 N.H. 9 (1874).

[42] *Id.*

Library References

Am Jur 2d Executors and Administrators § 565

CJS Executors and Administrators § 257

§ 35-3(b). Insolvency

When the estate is insolvent, RSA 554:15 clearly requires the administrator to receive the rents and profits of real property and to keep the property in repair and to account for the real property in his administration account.

Until a decree of insolvency is made, an administrator's occupation or management of a decedent's real estate and collection of rents cannot be justified as official acts in the administration of the estate. *Ayers v. Laighton*.[43] A subsequent decree of insolvency under which an administrator would ordinarily be entitled to take possession of the real estate does not have a retroactive effect. The administrator's title to possession of a decedent's realty dates only from the decree of insolvency.[44]

Library References

Am Jur 2d Executors and Administrators §§ 918, 774

CJS Executors and Administrators §§ 269, 667 et seq.

§ 35-3(c). Title Issues

Peculiarly, even though an administrator technically has very few duties with regard to the decedent's real estate, RSA 554:1 requires all real estate of the decedent to be inventoried, and Approved Form 44 provides space for the inclusion of real estate.[45] Certain forms of ownership terminate at death, such as a life estate or a joint tenancy. In those cases, ownership would pass immediately to the remainderman or to the surviving joint tenant. Where title is not terminated by death of the former owner, a transfer of title will occur in one of four ways: (1) by the laws of intestate succession; (2) by will; (3) by sale from administrator or executor; (4) by sale from testamentary trustee.

The New Hampshire Title Examination Standards provide that the failure of an administrator to file an accounting of his administration in the probate court (formerly a frequent occurrence) "does not of itself

---

[43] Ayers v. Laighton, 73 N.H. 487, 63 A. 43 (1906).

[44] *Id.*

[45] Appendix, Form 44.

invalidate title to real estate."[46] Furthermore, the payment of state and federal death taxes as shown on the probate accounting is considered to be conclusive evidence of their payment. Therefore, title to the decedent's real estate is considered valid in this situation.[47]

Library References

Am Jur 2d Executors and Administrators § 517

CJS Executors and Administrators § 133

Other References

Probate Aspects of Title Searching, unpublished paper by Richard S. Moody, Esquire.

§ 35-3(d). Payment of Real Estate Taxes

An administrator has the duty to pay real estate taxes assessed as of April 1st of a decedent who dies later in that tax year. In re Estate of Robbins.[48]

§ 35-3(e). Duty To Redeem Property Under Mortgage

RSA 554:16 provides that an "administrator, if there be sufficient assets, shall redeem all property of the deceased under mortgage, pledge or levy of execution for less than its value, or which if unredeemed would diminish the value of the estate, unless he shall by license sell it subject to the encumbrance; and neglect so to redeem shall be deemed maladministration and waste." This requirement does not operate "when the real estate under mortgage is specifically devised" since the devisee takes the real estate subject to the mortgage unless the testator in his or her will has provided otherwise. RSA 554:16.[49]

§ 35-4. Purchase of Real Estate by Administrator

In very unusual circumstances, the administrator may be obligated to purchase real estate on behalf of the estate. An example is where a mortgage note to the decedent is foreclosed and the administrator purchases at the foreclosure sale.

---

[46] New Hampshire Title Examination Standards, Standard 7–14 (1988).

[47] New Hampshire Title Examination Standards, Standard 7–18 (1988).

[48] In re Estate of Robbins, 116 N.H. 248, 356 A.2d 679 (1976).

[49] See Tunis v. Dole, 97 N.H. 420, 89 A.2d 760 (1952).

RSA 554:18 governs the powers and duties of administrators in such situations:

> Real estate purchased by, or set off to, an administrator to secure or satisfy a debt due to the estate shall vest in the heirs in the same manner as if the deceased had died seized thereof, and may be sold for the payment of debts, or divided as part of the estate.

It was formerly held that real estate acquired in this manner could be sold without a license from the probate court.[50] It is unclear whether the 1977 amendments dispensing with the need for a license in certain circumstances applies to real estate purchased by the administrator under RSA 554:18. As the statute itself makes clear, the administrator has few duties with regard to purchased real estate since title vests immediately in the heirs. *Thurston v. Kennett.*[51]

Library References

Am Jur 2d Executors and Administrators § 828 et seq.

CJS Executors and Administrators § 288

§ 35-5. Sale of Real Estate Generally

Frequently, after the death of an individual, the heirs or devisees desire to sell real property owned by the decedent at his death. Questions that often arise are (1) who are the proper parties to the deed, (2) what is the proper form of deed, and (3) can the purchaser of the property obtain good title to the property, free and clear of any liens or claims arising out of the estate.

First, the common law rule of devolution of title to the heirs and devisees must be kept in mind. Thus, by the act of probate, title to the decedent's property is confirmed in the heirs or devisees of the decedent, subject to be divested for the payment of debts and taxes only:

> [t]itle to real estate is vested in the heirs or devisees immediately upon the death of the owner, subject only to the necessities of administration such as the payment of debts, and no further action is required to perfect title in the heirs or devisees. This

---

[50] Foster v. Huntington, 5 N.H. 108 (1829).

[51] Thurston v. Kennett, 22 N.H. 151 (1850).

has been the well established common law rule for generations, and conveyancers have relied on probate titles as fully as titles recorded in the Registry of Deeds.[52]

There is no necessity for a deed from the administrator to the devisees or heirs to confirm their title.[53] Beneficiaries of real estate frequently request or expect that they will receive a deed from the administrator to the real estate in an estate but the completion of a proper administration of the estate perfects title to real property in the heirs or devisees.[54]

Therefore, if an estate has been fully settled, and a federal estate tax closing letter, if any, has been obtained, the proper parties to the deed are those persons who take the property under the will, or the intestacy laws.[55] The administrator is not a proper party. The proper form of deed is a warranty deed (or a quitclaim deed) and not a fiduciary deed. Also, in such a case, the purchasers take free and clear of any claims or liens arising out of the estate.

The next section discusses the more difficult cases—where the property is sought to be conveyed before the administration of the estate is complete.

Library References

CJS Executors and Administrators §§ 249, 270

§ 35-6. Sale of Real Estate by Consent—In General

Until 1977, real property in an estate could be sold only after obtaining the permission of the probate court (referred to as getting or obtaining a "license") and only if the sale was necessary to pay debts of the estate (RSA 559:1, 559:5) or if the will provided for sale (RSA 559:17) or with the consent of heirs or devisees (RSA 559:18).

However, this procedure was radically improved by changes in the law in 1977 which made it far easier to sell real property during the administration of an estate.

---

[52] 9th Report Judicial Council, p. 25 (1962).

[53] Id.

[54] Id.

[55] See New Hampshire Title Examination Standards, Standards 7–17 and 7–18.

§ 35-6(a). Statutory Procedure

RSA 559:18 authorizes the sale of real estate by the administrator, with the written consent of the surviving spouse and the heirs at law or devisees:

Unless the will otherwise provides, an administrator or executor with the written consent of the widow or widower and the heirs at law or devisees, or the guardians or conservators of such of them as are under disability, may sell the whole or any part of the real estate of a decedent, conducting the sale with fidelity and impartiality. The administrator, so authorized, may execute and deliver a valid conveyance of the estate to the purchaser. If there are heirs or legatees under disability, or whose whereabouts are unknown, or unknown heirs, the judge may appoint a guardian ad litem to represent their interests; said guardian ad litem to have authority to consent to a sale if, in his opinion, the best interests of his ward would be served thereby.

Any need for obtaining a license or the permission of the probate court was dispensed with in 1977. This procedure now provides for a quick and efficient manner by which real estate can be sold in the course of the administration of all estates and it is by far the most commonly-used method of sale, having almost entirely supplanted older methods provided for by law. Use of this procedure does away with potential title problems which may exist in other sale methods.[56]

In *In re Estate of McCrillis*,[57] the Supreme Court had an earlier version of RSA 559:18 before it for interpretation. The Court pointed out that this "statutory provision . . . has the obvious purpose of facilitating prompt and efficient settlement of estates where all parties in interest consent to the sale of real estate."[58]

As the statute itself makes clear, a sale by consent is authorized only if the will does not provide a procedure or distribution to the contrary. RSA 559:18. The subsequent section makes clear that a purchaser obtains

---

[56] New Hampshire Title Examination Standards, Standard 7–19 (1988).

[57] In re Estate of McCrillis, 114 N.H. 649, 325 A.2d 799 (1974).

[58] In re Estate of McCrillis, 114 N.H. 649, 650, 325 A.2d 799, 800 (1974).

"title to said real estate free from all claims of creditors of the decedent and of all other persons claiming under the decedent or under his will." RSA 559:19. The proceeds of the sale are to be accounted for by the administrator and pass, subject to debts and claims of the estate, to the "person or persons who would have been entitled to such real estate and in the proportions to which they would have been entitled had it not been sold." RSA 559:19.[59]

The statute does not make it clear what is the proper form of deed to be used in this procedure. Since the statute speaks in terms of a deed of the administrator, it would appear however, that a fiduciary deed, together with the consent of the surviving spouse and heirs is the proper form. RSA 477:30 prescribes the statutory form of a fiduciary deed.

In all cases of sale during the administration of an estate, the sale should not be made until the real property is first inventoried by the administrator, pursuant to RSA 554:1. The inclusion of the real property in the inventory is evidence of title of the decedent in the land. A failure to include in the inventory the real property to be sold is evidence that the decedent did not have title to the land. *Morrill v. Foster.*[60]

Library References

Am Jur 2d Executors and Administrators § 766

CJS Executors and Administrators § 269

§ 35-6(b). Title Issues

Under the New Hampshire Title Examination Standards, spouses of heirs or devisees need not join in the deed or instrument of consent, and no defect of title arises by their failure to join.[61] If an heir or devisee is under a disability, consent may be given by a guardian ad litem. RSA 559:18.[62]

Attorney Richard S. Moody of Claremont has written a short summary of how a title searcher can trace the ownership to real estate and

---

[59] See New Hampshire Title Examination Standards, Standard 7–19 (1988).

[60] Morrill v. Foster, 33 N.H. 379 (1856). But see Standard 7–15 of the New Hampshire Title Examination Standards (1988), which provides that a failure to include the decedent's real estate in the inventory does not create a defect in title if the estate is not subject to an inheritance tax.

[61] New Hampshire Title Examination Standards, Standard 7–12 (1988).

[62] See New Hampshire Title Examination Standards, Standard 7–13 (1988).

determine what liens and encumbrances may be attached to it, entitled "Probate Aspects of Title Searching". As Attorney Moody states:

It must be remembered that a person who receives title to real property under a will or by the laws of intestacy takes that title subject not only to any conditions, restrictions, and encumbrances to which the property was subject to in the hands of the decedent, but also to the possibility of liens arising from the following:

A. Debts, funeral expenses, and costs of administration;

B. Legacies;

C. State Inheritance and Estate Taxes;

D. Federal Estate Taxes;

E. Rights of the surviving spouse;

F. Rights of minor children;

G. Rights of pretermitted heirs.

Library References

Am Jur 2d Executors and Administrators § 766

CJS Executors and Administrators § 269

Other References

Probate Aspects of Title Searching unpublished paper by Richard S. Moody, Esquire.

§ 35-7. Sale of Real Estate to Pay Debts—In General

Until modern times, it was uncommon for real estate to be sold during the administration of an estate unless it was necessary to do so to pay debts of the estate. However, with the 1977 amendments to the sale-by-consent statute (RSA 559:18), which dispensed with the need of a license from the probate court even when the sale was necessary to pay debts, RSA 559:18 has become the usual method of sale during administration.

The license procedure of RSA 554:17 for sale to pay debts is now rarely used in an amicable estate administration, if the surviving spouse and heirs are in agreement. However, this procedure is still available. RSA 554:17 provides a sales procedure which must be strictly followed, but which is useful where the parties cannot agree and the personal estate is not sufficient to pay the debts of the decedent.

§ 35-7(a). Historical

The case of *Bergin v. McFarland*,[63] states the common law rule that all rights in the real estate of a deceased vested in the heir at law or devisee, and that the heir or devisee could maintain any action, real or personal, necessary for the protection of those rights. As the Bergin case made clear, the deceased's personal representative had no rights in the deceased's real estate at common law, but rather the rights of the personal representative were entirely confined to the personal estate and choses in action. In *Sawyer v. Jefts*,[64] the New Hampshire Supreme Court noted that the common law did not charge a person's real estate with the payment of his debts, but permitted him to do so by will, and that when a person's real estate was so charged it gave creditors an action to enforce their claims after his death.

The *Sawyer* case also noted that the charging of a person's entire estate with the payment of debts was affected by the passing of a statute in 1718 under the terms of which the administrator was under a duty to sell the real estate of the deceased to satisfy the debts of the estate where the personal estate was insufficient to satisfy these debts. The Court observed that the deceased's real estate was still deemed to vest in the heirs, subject to being divested by a proper sale under license. This statute is still in force (now RSA 554:17) and provides that:

> Every administrator shall apply for and procure license for the sale of so much of the real estate as may be necessary to pay debts and legacies, if the personal estate is insufficient; and neglect or refusal to obtain such license, to make such sale, to account for the proceeds thereof, or fraudulent conduct therein, shall be deemed maladministration and a breach of his bond.

§ 35-7(b). Grant of License

Chapter 559, License To Sell Real Estate, contains the provisions by which the administrator's duty to sell real estate to pay debts, found at RSA 554:17, are to be carried out.

---

[63] Bergin v. McFarland, 26 N.H. 533 (1853).

[64] Sawyer v. Jefts, 70 N.H. 393, 47 A. 416 (1900).

RSA 559:1 provides that:

> The judge, on application of the administrator, may grant a license for the sale of the real estate of any person deceased, or of lands purchased or set off to the administrator in payment of debts due to the estate, when the personal property shall be insufficient to pay the just demands by law chargeable to the estate.

RSA 554:18 states the rule that real estate purchased by or set off to the administrator to secure or satisfy a debt due the estate will vest in the heirs in the same manner as if the deceased had owned the property, but that such property may be sold for the payment of debts. The Court in *Sawyer v. Jefts*,[65] held accordingly that the administrator is under a duty to sell the real estate of deceased persons and to apply the proceeds to the payment of debts of the estate where the decedent's personal estate is insufficient.

The Court in *Bergin v. McFarland*,[66] held that a sale of the decedent's realty under license, if regular, divests the heir's title to the realty completely. However, a sale under a license to pay debts may be subject to the claims of a surviving spouse or orphaned minor children unless a release or waiver is obtained.[67]

It was subsequently held in *Gordon v. Gordon*,[68] that the probate court has exclusive jurisdiction over the granting of licenses to sell a decedent's realty, but in *Hatch v. Kelly*,[69] it was held that the judge of probate has no authority to grant such a license until it is shown that the decedent's personal estate is insufficient to pay the debts of the estate. The *Hatch* case stated that the decision of whether to grant a license to sell the decedent's real estate was a question of fact to be decided upon equitable principles with regard to the facts of each case. The *Gordon* Court had stated that the question of the indebtedness of the estate was a question to be tried at the hearing of the petition for a license to sell real estate, and that any interested party may appeal from the decision granting or

---

[65] Sawyer v. Jefts, 70 N.H. at 394, 47 A. at 416 (1900).

[66] Bergin v. McFarland, 26 N.H. 533 (1853).

[67] New Hampshire Title Examination Standards, Standard 7–16 (1988).

[68] Gordon v. Gordon, 55 N.H. 399 (1875).

[69] Hatch v. Kelly, 63 N.H. 29 (1884).

denying the license, although in the absence of an appeal the decision became res adjudicata.

The Court in *Hall v. Woodman*,[70] ruled that a license to sell real estate should not be granted to satisfy debts or claims which were not properly presented within the time allowed by statute except where the administration has been suspended, where the judge has ordered the administrator to hold funds in his hands for the satisfaction of contingent claims or other such circumstances.

Library References

Am Jur 2d Executors and Administrators § 860 et seq.

CJS Executors and Administrators §§ 269, 536, 537

§ 35-7(c). Notice

In *Flanders v. George*,[71] the Court held that a decree authorizing the sale of a decedent's real estate will be reversed where notice of the proceedings was not given to those interested in the land. Under RSA 550:4, V, however, such a license can be granted without notice where the heirs at law or devisees consent to the license in writing or where the value of the real estate is less than five hundred dollars.

Because the heirs at law have a right to post a bond to pay the demands against the estate under RSA 559:7, thus preventing the sale of the decedent's real estate, *Kingsbury v. Wild*[72] required that notice be given to them so that they can exercise this right.

Library References

Am Jur 2d Executors and Administrators §§ 866–869

CJS Executors and Administrators § 564

§ 35-7(d). Administrator's Rights and Duties

Under RSA 554:17, an administrator is under a duty to obtain a license to sell the deceased's real estate to pay the debts of the estate where the decedent's personal estate is insufficient to satisfy these debts, and it was held in *Willson v. Bergin*,[73] that the failure or refusal to do so is deemed maladministration.

---

[70] Hall v. Woodman, 49 N.H. 295 (1870).

[71] Flanders v. George, 55 N.H. 486 (1875).

[72] Kingsbury v. Wild, 3 N.H. 30 (1823).

[73] Willson v. Bergin, 28 N.H. 96 (1853).

In *Tilton v. Tilton*,[74] it was held to be the duty of the administrator to affirmatively show the insufficiency of the decedent's personal estate to satisfy the debts of the estate before a license to sell the decedent's realty can be granted. The *Tilton* Court stated further that where such a license is granted and it does not appear that the personal estate was insufficient to pay the debts of the estate the license has been improperly granted.

As the Court held in *Bergin v. McFarland*,[75] the special and limited estate which is created in the administrator continues until terminated by a valid sale under license by the probate court, or until the settlement of the estate if such a sale is not necessary. In *Hall v. Woodman*,[76] however, the Court held that the administrator must sell the land and appropriate it within a reasonable time after his appointment, or else his right to it ceases and the heirs may step in and assume the rights that they would have had but for the special and limited estate of the administrator.

Where a sale is declared to be void, the administrator must apply for a second license to sell the real estate as he must refund the amount paid to the purchaser in the voided sale; in such a case, it has been held that the administrator will be treated as an assignee of all creditors whose debts were mistakenly paid out of the proceeds of the voided sale.[77]

Library References

Am Jur 2d Executors and Administrators § 766

CJS Executors and Administrators § 661

§ 35-7(e). Sale by Ancillary Administrator

Where the administrator in New Hampshire is an ancillary administrator, the circumstances under which an administrator may obtain a license to sell the decedent's real estate will depend upon the relationship of the ancillary administration to the principal administration and the right of creditors to demand payment of the ancillary administration.[78]

---

[74] Tilton v. Tilton, 41 N.H. 479 (1860).

[75] Bergin v. McFarland, 26 N.H. at 537 (1853).

[76] Hall v. Woodman, 49 N.H. 295 (1870).

[77] Willson v. Bergin, 28 N.H. 96 (1853).

[78] Goodall v. Marshall, 11 N.H. 88, 90 (1840). See also New Hampshire Title Examination Standards, Standards 7–9 and 7–10 (1988).

Generally, where a person domiciled in another jurisdiction dies and ancillary administration is taken in New Hampshire and the estate is represented as insolvent, all creditors of the deceased are entitled to prove their claims in the ancillary administration and to have the assets, both personal and real, of the deceased appropriated in satisfaction of their demands.

Library References

Am Jur 2d Executors and Administrators § 1194

CJS Executors and Administrators § 1001

§ 35-7(f). Bond

RSA 559:8 provides that the judge of probate may require a bond from the administrator in an amount sufficient to account for the proceeds of the sale of the decedent's real estate. The posting of a bond protects the parties in interest and reduces the risk of disturbing sales executed according to a license by providing a remedy for the breach of the bond. *Gordon v. Gordon.*[79] RSA 559:20 provides that fraudulent conduct in the sale of the real estate, misappropriation of the proceeds of the sale, or refusal to account for the proceeds of the sale would constitute a breach of the administrator's bond.

Library References

Am Jur 2d Executors and Administrators §§ 313, 880

CJS Executors and Administrators §§ 67, 269

§ 35-7(g). Heirs' Rights and Duties

As the Court stated in *Hall v. Woodman,*[80] the heirs at law have a right in all property of the estate that is not needed to pay the estate's debts and expenses, and if the estate is solvent, the land goes to them directly, subject to divestment by the administrator for the payment of debts of the estate. The *Hall* Court stated further, however, that upon a decree of insolvency the land passes to the administrator's hands to pay the debts of the estate but will revert back to the heirs if not needed to pay the debts of the estate, as if there had been no decree of insolvency.

The heirs may oppose an administrator's petition for a license to sell the decedent's realty to satisfy a judgment against the estate. In *Nichols*

---

[79] Gordon v. Gordon, 55 N.H. 399 (1875).

[80] Hall v. Woodman, 49 N.H. 295 (1870).

v. Day,[81] it was stated that a judgment recovered against an administrator is not conclusive evidence of the estate's indebtedness as against the heirs, and that such a judgment may be attacked on the grounds that it was unfounded or fraudulently obtained. However, the *Nichols* Court observed that where the heir attempting to impeach the judgment personally defended the action and was fully heard without the interference of the administrator, he will be bound by the judgment.

In *Jenness v. Robinson*,[82] it was held that no license to sell the decedent's realty will be granted where the heirs or devisees give a bond to hold the administrator harmless from demands against the estate. The statutory provision authorizing such a bond is found at RSA 559:7. In *Judge of Probate v. Ordway*,[83] it was held further that such a bond may only be given to the judge of probate upon an application to the judge to sell the decedent's real estate for the payment of debts.

In the *Jenness* case, it was not necessary for all of the heirs or devisees to join in the making of the bond. The Court reasoned that, if some of the heirs or devisees see fit to assume the burden of paying the debts of the estate and execute a bond for that purpose, neither the remaining heirs nor devisees nor the creditors have any cause for complaint. The *Jenness* Court also stated that where some of the heirs take it upon themselves to execute such a bond and undertake responsibility for the debts of the estate, they cannot call upon the other heirs for contribution, however, the other heirs must assume the burdens of such bond in order to enjoy any of the benefits derived therefrom.

In *Judge of Probate v. Ordway*,[84] the Court held that a bond given to prevent the sale of real estate covers all of the expenses of administration regardless of the wording of the bond. In *Robinson v. Leavitt*,[85] the Court held that a bond given according to RSA 559:7 also operates to release any debts due the obligors by the estate.

Library References

Am Jur 2d Executors and Administrators § 876

CJS Executors and Administrators § 272

---

[81] Nichols v. Day, 32 N.H. 133 (1855).

[82] Jenness v. Robinson, 10 N.H. 215 (1839).

[83] Judge of Probate v. Ordway, 23 N.H. 198 (1851).

[84] *Id.*

[85] Robinson v. Leavitt, 7 N.H. 73 (1834).

§ 35-7(h). Extent of License; Other Real Property Interests

RSA 559:2 states that the license to sell real estate may extend to the reversion of a homestead right and of any interest in the land whatever, but requires any estate other than a present fee to be particularly described in the application, notice and license to sell the real estate.

RSA 559:3 allows the sale of a whole parcel of land which is situated in such a way that a part of it cannot be sold without injury to persons interested, even if the sale of the entire parcel is more than sufficient to pay the demands for which it is sold. Where the sale of timber located on a parcel of land would be beneficial to persons interested in the real estate if sold separately, the probate judge may order the sale of only the timber under RSA 559:4, and in such a case the timber will be deemed to be real estate.

Although the interest of the owner of a reversion in land may be sold under RSA 559:2, it was held in *Tilton v. Tilton*,[86] that a license for such a sale should not be granted where the need for the sale arose from the administrator's failure to properly manage the estate. The *Tilton* Court held further that the owner of a reversionary interest may appeal from a decree granting such a license.

Under RSA 559:14, a sale of real estate by the administrator must be effected within two years of the granting of the license, and sales made after that period cannot be supported by the license. In *Hall v. Woodman*,[87] it was held that sales occurring after the two-year period are void. However, where a petition for license to sell real estate to pay debts is granted later than two years from the date of appointment, a deed under such a license is valid.[88]

Library References

Am Jur 2d Executors and Administrators § 782

CJS Executors and Administrators §§ 283, 593

§ 35-7(i). Sale by Consent to Pay Debts

RSA 559:5 provides a statutory mechanism whereby the judge, upon application of the administrator and with the consent of the surviving

---

[86] Tilton v. Tilton, 41 N.H. 479 (1860).

[87] Hall v. Woodman, 49 N.H. 295 (1870).

[88] New Hampshire Title Examination Standards, Standard 7–11 (1988).

spouse or, if there is none, the guardian of any minor children, may grant a license to sell all of the decedent's real estate, including homestead rights, reversionary interests and other rights therein when such a sale is necessary to pay the debts of the estate. This procedure is little used now because of the more flexible procedure provided by RSA 559:18 which dispenses with the need of a license.

If the procedure is used, RSA 559:6 provides that the proceeds from the sale, subject to debts and claims, are to be distributed as provided in RSA 559:19: "to the person or persons who would have been entitled to such real estate and in the proportions to which they would have been entitled had it not been sold." Such a sale may be subject to claims of the surviving spouse or orphaned minor children unless their consent is obtained.[89]

Library References

Am Jur 2d Executors and Administrators § 776

CJS Executors and Administrators §§ 538–542

§ 35-8. Sale as Provided by Will

Another method of sale during administration of an estate is where the will of a decedent provides for sale. This method is set forth in RSA 559:17 which provides:

> When it shall appear by the will of a person deceased to have been his intention that his executor should dispose of his real estate for any lawful purpose, the judge may license the administrator to sell it for the purpose and in the manner intended by the testator.

This method of sale is still used but is more frequently replaced by the consent sale procedure of RSA 559:18, which avoids the need of a license altogether.

Although RSA 559:17 appears to require a license in all cases where a will shows the testator's intention to sell, no less an authority than Justice Charles Doe in *Rollins v. Rice,*[90] held that a license is not necessary where the will expressly authorizes a sale:

---

[89] New Hampshire Title Examination Standards, Standard 7–16 (1988).

[90] Rollins v. Rice, 59 N.H. 493 (1880).

This section [RSA 559:17] authorizes the probate court to give the administrator the power of sale which the will gives the executor. It does not require a license for the exercise of a power given by the will to the administrator. And a license is not necessary in this case, because the will expressly authorizes a sale by any person legally qualified to administer upon the estate and the administrator is such a person.[91]

Where the testator's intention is less clear, "it seems advisable, in view of the statutory provision on the subject in this state, that the plaintiffs should procure a license for making the sale of the land." *Harris v. Ingalls*.[92] The necessity of a license even in this situation was questioned in *Upton v. White*,[93] where the Court held that RSA 559:17 did not apply to a testamentary trustee.

In *Harris v. Ingalls*,[94] it was held that where a license to sell under a will is granted, the sale should be made without unreasonable delay. Where a sale under a power contained in the will is made during the pendency of the probate administration, the conveyance is subject to claims of creditors and a title defect may be created unless proof of payment is furnished.[95]

Library References

Am Jur 2d Executors and Administrators § 788 et seq.

CJS Executors and Administrators § 274 et seq.

§ 35-9.　Executory Sales Contract of Decedent

An infrequently-encountered situation is where the decedent dies with an unperformed or partially-performed contract for the sale of land owned by him. This situation is covered by RSA 559:16 which provides:

When a person deceased had contracted in writing to convey real estate, and the party contracted with has performed or is ready to perform the conditions of the contract, or if the contract was verbal and the party

---

[91] Rollins v. Rice, 59 N.H. 493, 496 (1880). See also New Hampshire Title Examination Standards, Standard 7–19 (1988).

[92] Harris v. Ingalls, 74 N.H. 339, 344, 68 A. 34, 37 (1907).

[93] Upton v. White, 92 N.H. 221, 29 A.2d 126 (1942), overruled on other grounds, In re Estate of Frolich, 112 N.H. 320, 295 A.2d 448 (1972).

[94] Harris v. Ingalls, 74 N.H. 339, 68 A. 34 (1907).

[95] New Hampshire Title Examination Standards, Standard 7–19 (1988).

contracted with has performed or partly performed its conditions, the judge may license the administrator to make such conveyance as the deceased if alive would be bound to make.

Under this section, it was held in *Carter v. Jackson*,[96] that the contract need not be specified in minute detail but rather if the substance of the contract is set out, the petition may be granted.

The proper method to obtain probate court approval to convey real estate in accordance with the decedent's contract is by filing Approved Form 93, Petition to Convey Real Estate According to Contract.

Library References

Am Jur 2d Executors and Administrators §§ 587, 588

CJS Executors and Administrators § 267

§ 35-10. License—In General

The permission of the probate court to conduct a sale is called a "license." If a sale is conducted pursuant to a license, care must be taken that the petition for the license describes the property accurately, for the license granted by the court will contain the exact description as provided by the administrator. Many title problems can occur where an erroneous description is used in the license which does not conform with the description of the property in the fiduciary deed which actually conveys the property.

Licenses for the sale of real estate are governed by Chapter 559 of the Revised Statutes, entitled "License To Sell Real Estate". The provisions of this chapter need to be closely examined and followed since a deviation from the terms of the license can invalidate the conveyance. *Conservatorship of Bradlee*.[97]

A license has a duration of only two years and a sale after two years from issuance is not valid. RSA 559:14.

Library References

Am Jur 2d Executors and Administrators § 774 et seq.

CJS Executors and Administrators § 536 et seq.

---

[96] Carter v. Jackson, 56 N.H. 364 (1876).

[97] Conservatorship of Bradlee, 120 N.H. 430, 415 A.2d 1144 (1980).

§ 35-10(a). Bond

RSA 559:8 empowers the probate court to order that an administrator post a bond before a license is issued, but this authority is seldom invoked.

Library References

Am Jur 2d Executors and Administrators §§ 880, 881

CJS Executors and Administrators §§ 590, 591

§ 35-10(b). Manner of Sale Generally

Under RSA 559:9, the sale of the decedent's real estate may be made either at auction or at a private sale, whichever is most beneficial to the estate. The statute requires the judge of probate to specify the manner in which the sale is to be conducted in the license, or to authorize the administrator to sell the real estate in either mode which he deems to be in the best interest of the estate.

It is improper for an administrator to buy at a sale of real estate conducted under his auspices as administrator. *Hoitt v. Webb.*[98] Such a sale is voidable by any party in interest:

> An administrator, who, under a license from the court of probate, advertises the real estate of his intestate for sale at public auction, and at the sale becomes himself the highest bidder, cannot make a valid sale and conveyance of the property to a third person; and any one whose interest is affected by such sale may avoid it. . . . And it makes no difference that the property is bid off by a third person for him, at his request. A party cannot legally purchase his own account, either by himself or by the aid of a friend, that which his duty or trust requires him to sell on account of another, nor purchase on account of another that which he sells as his own. He cannot unite the opposite characters of buyer and seller.[99]

In *Remick v. Butterfield,*[100] it was held that the election to confirm or avoid such a sale may be exercised individually by each interested party, thus any party whose interest is affected may void the transaction.

---

[98] Hoitt v. Webb, 36 N.H. 158 (1858).

[99] Hoitt v. Webb, 36 N.H. 158, 163 (1858).

[100] Remick v. Butterfield, 31 N.H. 70 (1855).

Where a license to sell real estate issued to a conservator provided for a sale of the ward's property to the conservator and another and the conservator conveyed the property to herself only, the conveyance was invalid. *Conservatorship of Bradlee.*[101]

If the administrator employs an agent to conduct the sale, the administrator is under a duty to examine the agent's conduct and compel the agent, if necessary, to make good to the estate any amounts which are lost through the agent's fraud or misconduct. *Currier v. Green.*[102] If the administrator refuses to call the agent to account, he will be deemed to have connived with the agent and may be charged with the full value of the land which was improperly sold.

RSA 559:15 requires the administrator or any other party selling real estate under license of the probate court to return an affidavit and account of the sale to the probate court stating the times, places, and manner of giving notice of the sale, within one year of the sale. The statute provides further that upon such affidavit and account being accepted by the judge of probate, the account and affidavit are to be recorded and the record is prima facie evidence that notice was given. It was held in *Hall v. Woodman,*[103] that where an administrator does not dispose of the real estate under license within a reasonable time and thus loses the right to dispose of it, the administrator would be guilty of negligence and would be liable on his bond.

Library References

Am Jur 2d Executors and Administrators § 886

CJS Executors and Administrators §§ 593–596

§ 35-10(c). Conveyance

RSA 559:11 provides that where the administrator is authorized to make a sale of the decedent's real estate and does so after the making of the oath and in accordance with the terms of his license, he may execute and deliver a valid conveyance to a purchaser. The power of the administrator to divest the legal title of the heirs must be exercised only in the manner prescribed by statute, however.

---

[101] Conservatorship of Bradlee, 120 N.H. 430, 415 A.2d 1144 (1980).

[102] Currier v. Green, 2 N.H. 225 (1820).

[103] Hall v. Woodman, 49 N.H. 295 (1870).

In *Livingston v. Pendergast*,[104] it was also held that a deed is necessary for the validity of such a sale. In *Kingsbury v. Wild*,[105] however, it was held that the deed need not state the capacity in which the administrator acted nor that the property was sold at an auction to the highest bidder. There are title standards dealing with the sale of real estate from an estate which should be reviewed before a sale is contemplated.[106]

The proper form of deed, where a sale is by a fiduciary, is by a fiduciary deed. RSA 477:30 provides a statutory form for such a deed.

Library References

Am Jur 2d Executors and Administrators § 887

CJS Executors and Administrators §§ 851, 853

§ 35-10(d). Perpetuation of Evidence

Under RSA 559:21 the administrator, purchaser, or any other interested party can petition the probate judge to perpetuate the facts set forth in the petition to sell real estate and the judge, after due notice, may decree such facts proven. Such a decree is conclusive evidence of these facts. Thus, this type of petition can provide for the protection of the parties to the sale from future factual disputes concerning the sale.

Library References

Am Jur 2d Executors and Administrators § 882 et seq.

CJS Executors and Administrators §§ 608–611

§ 35-10(e). Administrator's Expenses

In *McInnes v. Goldthwaite*,[107] the Supreme Court held that an administrator who sells a decedent's real estate under license from the probate court is entitled to charge reasonably for the maintenance of the property for a reasonable period of time. The *McInnes* Court stated that it must be determined how long, under the circumstances, it was reasonable for the administrator to keep the premises and what expenses he reasonably incurred for maintenance and carrying charges during that period. The administrator is entitled to these expenses, but keeping the

---

[104] Livingston v. Pendergast, 34 N.H. 544 (1857).

[105] Kingsbury v. Wild, 3 N.H. 30 (1823).

[106] Article VII Estates, New Hampshire Title Examination Standards (1988).

[107] McInnes v. Goldthwaite, 94 N.H. 331, 52 A.2d 795 (1947).

premises longer than reasonably necessary would be neglect and misman-agement, and the administrator would not be entitled to expenses incurred after such reasonable time.

The *McInnes* Court went on to hold, rather leniently, that if the administrator can prove that the selling price obtained exceeded that which would have been realized at the end of the reasonable period of time, he is entitled to the extra expenses to the extent of the net increase in the amount realized. Thus, if the estate benefits by the holding of the property beyond the reasonable holding period, the administrator is entitled to the additional expenses to the extent of net benefit to the estate.

Library References

Am Jur 2d Executors and Administrators § 187
CJS Executors and Administrators § 939

§ 35-11. Division of Real Property Among Heirs

It is uncommon for a probate court today to be required to divide real property among the beneficiaries who are entitled thereto. Beneficiaries of an estate take property as tenants-in-common pursuant to RSA 477:19. As such, they are entitled to maintain a partition action pursuant to RSA 547-C. The administrator "has no duty to perform as to the partition of the remaining real estate between the legatees entitled." *French v. Lawrence.* [108]

Former RSA chapter 562, entitled "Division of Real Estate Among Heirs and Devisees," which gave the probate court limited jurisdiction to divide real estate among heirs, was repealed effective January 1, 1993. [109] The probate court's jurisdiction over the division of real estate has been consolidated in RSA Chapter 547-C. See Chapter 80 for a further discussion on the partition of real estate.

Library References

Am Jur 2d Descent and Distribution § 20
CJS Descent and Distribution § 66

§ 35-12. Partition of Real Estate

Beginning January 1, 1993 [110] , the former RSA 538 relating to the

---

[108] French v. Lawrence, 75 N.H. 609, 610, 78 A. 278, 279 (1910).
[109] P.L., 1992, c. 284.
[110] P.L., 1992, c. 284.

partition of real estate was repealed and replaced with a whole new partition statute, RSA 547-C. RSA 547-C gives the probate court exclusive jurisdiction over disputed partitions, undisputed partitions, and an equal division in sale of real estate. For a full discussion of partition of real estate, see Chapter 80, *infra*.

Library References

Am Jur 2d Partition §§ 48, 103–105
CJS Partition § 20

Forms

See Form 93 in Appendix for a Petition to Convey Real Estate According to Contract.

See Form 110 in Appendix for a Motion and License to Mortgage Real Estate.

See Form 114 in Appendix for a Petition for Partition of Real Estate.

See Form 120 in Appendix for a Motion to Sell Real Estate to Pay Demands.

CHAPTER 36. PAYMENT OF CLAIMS AND EXPENSES

§ 36-1. Generally

This chapter discusses the various claims, expenses of administration and charges which are allowable as deductions against the estate and the priority of their payment.

One of the most important duties of an administrator of an estate is ascertaining the amount of claims, debts and other expenses which can be legally charged against the estate and seeing to their payment. If there are not sufficient assets to pay all legally chargeable debts and allowable expenses, then he must pay the expenses in accordance with a statutorily-prescribed priority list.

Under conflict of law rules, the priority of charges is governed by the local law under which the administrator acts and derives authority. Restatement (Second) Conflict of Laws, §§ 396, 397, 398.

Allowable charges against an estate take precedence over legacies or bequests in a testate estate or the rights of the decedent's heirs in an intestate estate. This is true even if the rights of beneficiaries are entirely defeated. In a well-turned phrase, the New Hampshire Supreme Court

411

has stated this rule as follows: "A man must be just before he is generous."[1]

Library References

Am Jur 2d Executors and Administrators § 684 et seq.

CJS Executors and Administrators § 457 et seq.

§ 36-2.　Statutory Provisions

RSA 554:19, entitled "Priority of Charges" establishes both the legally allowable claims and charges against an estate and their priority of payment.

Effective January 1, 1999, the statute provides as follows:

> 554:19 Priority of Charges. The estate of every person deceased shall be chargeable with the following. To the extent that funds are available, these charges shall be paid in the following priority:

The statute has been held to create a preference or priority by classes of charges and claims and a residuary beneficiary takes "only such of the estate that remains after the legal charges against it are paid." *Carr v. St. Paul's Parish.*[3]

Library References

Am Jur 2d Executors and Administrators § 685

CJS Executors and Administrators § 461

§ 36-3.　Expenses of Administration

The first and highest preference or priority is given by RSA 554:19,I for the "just expenses of the administration of the estate." Every estate is chargeable with the just expenses of administration. The time the administrator spends, as well as the personal expenses involved, will be allowed.[4]

However, there are limitations on the administrator's allowable expenses. In *Clarke v. Clay*,[5] a controversy arose between the administrator

---

[1] Guggenheimer v. Guggenheimer, 99 N.H. 399, 403, 112 A.2d 61, 64 (1955).

[3] Carr v. St. Paul's Parish, 71 N.H. 231, 234, 51 A. 920 (1902).

[4] Tuttle v. Robinson, 33 N.H. 104, 118 (1856).

[5] Clarke v. Clay, 31 N.H. 393 (1855).

and the heirs of the estate. The administrator charged the estate for going to see the heirs and for time spent trying to negotiate with them. The Court disallowed the charges for these items, holding that time and money expended while endeavoring to effect a private settlement with the heirs are not proper items of charge against the estate as expenses of administration.[6]

An administrator may charge his reasonable compensation as an expense of administration.[7] In settling the administrator's account, the administrator's charges for attending probate court, for defending suits commenced against him as administrator and the necessary expenses incurred on journeys for the business of administration, may be properly allowed.[8] The probate court will determine the amount of reasonable compensation for an administrator's time and expenses at each term of court, when his attendance may be required.[9]

Witness fees which must be paid to settle an estate are a proper expense of administration. If, however, fees are paid to witnesses as a method of establishing an administrator's private claim, the fees are not a proper charge against the estate.[10]

If an administrator employs an attorney to assist him in his duties, the reasonable charges for the attorney's services and expenses are an expense of administration, entitled to priority in the first class and are properly chargeable against the estate.[11]

Library References

Am Jur 2d Executors and Administrators § 701

CJS Executors and Administrators § 462

Forms

See Form 44 in the Appendix for Inventory of Fiduciary.

§ 36-4. Necessary Funeral Expenses

The second class of priority or preference of charges against an estate is the "necessary expenses of the funeral and burial of the deceased."

---

[6] Clarke v. Clay, 31 N.H. 393, 403–04 (1855).

[7] See Chapter 36 *supra* for a full discussion of administrator compensation.

[8] Wendell v. French, 19 N.H. 205, 209–10 (1848).

[9] Tuttle v. Robinson, 33 N.H. 104, 118 (1856).

[10] Lucy v. Lucy, 55 N.H. 9, 11 (1874).

[11] See Chapter 15 *supra* for a full discussion of attorney compensation.

RSA 554:19, II. At common law, the proper expenses of the funeral had priority over all debts;[12] however, the power of the state legislature to regulate priorities of claims against decedent's estates has superseded the common law rules.[13] An administrator is liable for all reasonable and necessary funeral expenses, and the law allows the administrator to retain assets for the purpose of paying the funeral expenses.[14]

An administrator must take care not to become personally liable for the funeral expenses. In an ancient case, *Trueman v. Tilden*,[15] the son of the decedent was appointed administrator. He asked Trueman to make a coffin for his father, but said nothing about the price. Trueman introduced evidence proving that the son, at the time of delivery, assumed the debts and agreed to pay for the coffin. The administrator was found personally liable. This case establishes the principle that one may be liable as an administrator, or may be personally liable.[16] When anything is furnished for a funeral, at the administrator's request, he is liable, either as administrator or personally at the election of the person who has the claim.

An administrator is not at liberty to furnish articles of mourning to a family at the expense of the estate.[17] An administrator is not allowed to charge for expenses incurred in purchasing transportation for himself and others, and expenses for his services and time incurred in attending decedent's funeral.[18] The cost of fencing a private burial place will not be allowed as a proper expense of the estate.[19] The use of a concrete burial vault has become a commonplace element in providing for a decent and permanent burial. An expenditure by an administrator for such purpose can properly be charged as a funeral expense under RSA 554:19, II. *In re Estate of Byrne*.[20] An expenditure for the necessary repair of a decedent's tomb may properly be charged as a funeral expense.[21]

---

[12] 34 C.J.S., Executors and Administrators, § 460 (1942).

[13] See 34 C.J.S., Executors and Administrators, §§ 309, 461 (1942).

[14] Trueman v. Tilden, 6 N.H. 201, 202 (1833).

[15] *Id.*

[16] *Id.*

[17] Griswold v. Chandler, 5 N.H. 492, 495 (1831).

[18] Lund v. Lund, 41 N.H. 355, 361 (1860).

[19] Tuttle v. Robinson, 33 N.H. 104, 117 (1856).

[20] In re Estate of Byrne, 98 N.H. 300, 304, 100 A.2d 157, 160 (1953).

[21] Bell v. Briggs, 63 N.H. 592, 593, 4 A. 702, 702 (1885). See In re Estate of Byrne, 98 N.H. 300, 304, 100 A.2d 157, 160 (1953).

Even if a will does not contain a provision as to the payment of funeral expenses, it is nevertheless the administrator's duty to pay for them.[22]

Probate Court Procedure Bulletin 1997-04 establishes the rule that "no probate court shall require a copy of a fully paid funeral bill as a prerequisite for acceptance of an account ("full' or "voluntary' administration or guardianships and conservatorships reporting prepayment of funeral expenses) for filing with the court." The Bulletin states that practitioners "should feel free to provide a copy of a fully paid funeral bill if it is their practice to do so, but it is not required."

The Bulletin takes great care to point out that its provisions do not preclude the statutory necessity for an administrator, executor, guardian or conservator to account for all funeral expenses, but provides that it is sufficient that the funeral bills be listed in the account of the administrator.

Library References

Am Jur 2d Executors and Administrators § 697

CJS Executors and Administrators § 230

§ 36-5. Allowance to the Widow

RSA 554:19,III establishes a third priority class for the expenses or charges of a "reasonable allowance to the surviving spouse, as by law provided." The allowance is for support of the wife, presently after the death of the husband.[23] This allowance is not a free gift to the widow, but is intended to enable her to support herself until her interest in the estate can be set out to her in some way. The allowance may be considered in the distribution of the estate as part of her share.[24] Effective January 1, 1999, the statute was amended to provide for an allowance to the surviving spouse, whether widow or widower.[25]

Library References

Am Jur 2d Executors and Administrators § 714 et seq.

CJS Executors and Administrators § 323 et seq.

---

[22] Carr v. St. Paul's Parish, 71 N.H. 231, 234, 51 A. 920, 921 (1902).

[23] Mathes v. Bennett, 21 N.H. 188, 201 (1850).

[24] Id.

[25] 1998 N.H. Laws 5.

§ 36-6. Just Debts

The fourth class of priority of charges provides for the payment of the "just debts owed by the deceased, including the necessary expenses for the last illness of the deceased."[26]

Just debts are the decedent's legal debts. They are debts due and owing at the time of decedent's death. The responsibility of the administrator to pay them will not be excused for lack of specific direction in a will to pay the just debts. The failure of an administrator to pay the decedent's just debts is breach of the condition of his bond and a creditor, if unpaid, may recover on the bond.[27]

Even without a testamentary direction to do so, the administrator has a duty to settle the decedent's just debts "for it is only out of the residue of the estate, after the satisfaction of legal charges against it, that legacies can be taken." *Carr v. St. Paul's Parish.*[28] However, the administrator must not pay debts of the decedent that are not valid and he may be held responsible to the beneficiaries if he does so.[29]

If the decedent is jointly and severally liable on a debt secured by a mortgage on real estate which is held in joint tenancy, the estate is liable for the full amount of the debt,[30] even if there is a surviving co-maker or joint tenant.[31] However, if the estate pays the entire debt it would be entitled to contribution from the surviving co-maker.[32]

The debts of the decedent include real estate taxes on the property owned by the decedent as of April 1st where the decedent dies later in the tax year. *In re Estate of Robbins.*[33]

The debts of the decedent include the mortgage indebtedness and, unless the property is specifically devised, the administrator is obligated

---

[26] RSA 554:19, IV.

[27] Hoyt's Probate Practice 39–40 (1901).

[28] Carr v. St. Paul's Parish, 71 N.H. 231, 234, 51 A. 920, 921 (1902).

[29] See 7 Bowe-Parker: Page on Wills § 51:12 (1962).

[30] RSA 554:16, 554:19, IV.

[31] RSA 382-A:3-118(e). See Pietro v. Leonetti, 26 Ohio App. 2d 221, 270 N.E.2d 660 (1971).

[32] Boardman v. Page, 11 N.H. 431 (1840). See Rice v. Snow, 116 N.H. 69, 352 A.2d 679 (1976).

[33] In re Estate of Robbins, 116 N.H. 248, 356 A.2d 679 (1976).

to redeem any property under mortgage by paying off the mortgage indebtedness. RSA 554:16.

Library References

Am Jur 2d Executors and Administrators § 684

CJS Executors and Administrators § 367 et seq.

§ 36-7. Support for Infant Children

RSA 554:19, V establishes a fifth class of priority of charges by providing that the estate of every deceased shall be chargeable for the "support and maintenance of infant children of the deceased until they arrive at the age of eighteen years, if the estate is in fact solvent." Prior to its amendment in 1975, the statute provided that a solvent estate was obligated to support infant children only until they attained the age of seven. The statute applies to the estate of every father whether married or divorced and was not intended to limit the authority of the court in divorce proceedings.[34]

The Supreme Court interpreted RSA 554:19, V in *Hurst v. Dugan*,[35] where the Court had before it the claim that a father's support obligation, which had been established under RSA 168-A, the Uniform Act of Paternity, was enforceable against the decedent father's estate. The Court held that RSA 554:19 "really establishes the priority of payment of allowable charges against the estate . . . and is not itself the source of the obligations giving rise to the charges."[36] The Court went on to interpret paragraph V of RSA 554:19 as providing:

> Only that such child support obligations as survive the father's death shall be fifth in line in priority of payment. We have consistently held that unless otherwise provided, support payments terminate upon the death of either spouse, and the estates of the spouses have no rights or responsibilities concerning these payments. . . . Thus, something more than simply the father's death is required to impose an obligation on his estate for child support. What is required is that the obligation on the estate be expressly provided for before death. If, therefore, by way of a divorce decree or support order a court "mak[es] an

---

[34] Guggenheimer v. Guggenheimer, 99 N.H. 399, 402–03, 112 A.2d 61, 63–64 (1955).

[35] Hurst v. Dugan, 136 N.H. 5, 61 A.2d 616 (1992).

[36] *Id.*

order during the life of the father binding on his estate," *Guggenheimer*, 99 N.H. at 402, 112 A.2d at 63, "the children become judgment creditors by force of the decree for support. *Id.* at 403, 112 A.2d at 64. In such circumstances, RSA 554:19, V would operate to create a charge against the estate for child support ranking fifth in priority of payment.[37]

Effective January 1, 1998, RSA 554:19,V establishes a fifth class of priority of charges by providing that the estate of every deceased shall be chargeable for the "support and maintenance of minor children of the deceased until they reach 18 years of age." Prior to its amendment in 1998, the statute provided for the maintenance of infant children only if the estate was solvent. That restriction has been removed by the 1998 amendment.

The statute applies to the estate of every father, whether married or divorced, and was not intended to limit the authority of the court in divorce proceedings.[38]

Library References

Am Jur 2d Executors and Administrators §§ 721–723

CJS Executors and Administrators §§ 323, 336

§ 36-8. Legacies

The final class of charges allowable against an estate is the "legacies given by the will of the deceased." RSA 554:19, VI. Payment of legacies, however, is precluded until after the satisfaction of the legal charges against the estate have been met.[39] It is only out of the residue of the estate, after the satisfaction of the legal charges against it, that legacies can be taken.[40]

However, as the following sections of this chapter make clear, the legislature has imposed other charges against an estate that take priority over the payment of legacies and heirs' intestate shares.

[37] Hurst v. Dugan, 136 N.H. 5, 61 A.2d 616 (1992).

[38] RSA 554:19, V.

[39] See the discussion in Chapter 37 *infra*, concerning the payment of legacies and devises.

[40] Carr v. St. Paul's Parish, 71 N.H. 231, 234, 51 A. 920, 921 (1902).

Library References

Am Jur 2d Executors and Administrators § 1015
CJS Executors and Administrators § 484

§ 36-9. Charges for Reimbursement for Institutional Care by the State

In addition to the legally established charges and claims against an estate found in the probate sections of the Revised Statutes (RSA 554:19), the legislature has created other charges against an estate which take priority over the payment of legacies and intestate shares. One such charge imposed on the estate of decedents is found in RSA 126-A:37.

This statute creates a very backward requirement that the estate of an institutional patient reimburse the state for the costs of institutional support of a deceased patient. An administrator should be alert to the provisions of this law whenever the decedent or his spouse, parents or children are under institutional care by the state at the time of the decedent's death or during the administration of his estate. As revised by a 1995 amendment, RSA 126-A:37 provides as follows:

> Except as limited in RSA 126-A:39, expenses incurred in the institutions named in RSA 126-A:34, or, at the direction of the commissioner in any public or private institution, or elsewhere, may be recovered in any action in the name of the state from the estate of the person, or the person's spouse, or mother or father, whose estate is more than sufficient to pay priorities in paragraphs I, II, III, IV, and V of RSA 554:19. The spouse and the father and mother are declared jointly and severally liable for expenses, unless otherwise ordered by the court, except that recovery of expenses against a mother or father shall be limited: I. To the expenses incurred before their child reached the age of majority. II. As provided in RSA 126-A:42, III. To the share the patient or resident is entitled to if the father or mother died intestate. IV. To the greater of the share the patient or resident is entitled to under the will or the share the patient or resident would have been entitled to if the father or mother had died intestate.

It is important to note that the statute makes a charge against the estate of a decedent, not only for the assistance provided for the decedent, but also for state assistance provided for the decedent's parents, children or spouse.

This statutory provision has been hotly contested, but found to be constitutional in *State v. Matthews*.[41] The Court found that the legally permissible purpose of this statute was "to relieve the State of part of the financial burden of caring for the mentally ill."[42] In the *Matthews* case, the Court upheld the imposition of a charge against the mother's estate for the care of her daughter, even where the charge exceeded the daughter's share of her mother's estate. The Court held that:

> [t]he legislature has determined that the estates of parents should be jointly and severally liable for the expenses incurred by the State in the care and treatment of a child in the New Hampshire hospital. We do not believe that it is unjust or unfair to hold the estate liable even if the claim exceeds the child's share of the estate.[43]

The limitation expressed in the opening phrase of RSA 126-A:37 refers to educational expenses of a patient which are recoverable against the appropriate school district rather than the estate. RSA 126-A:39. If an individual is between the ages of three and twenty-one and is capable of being benefited by instruction, the educational expenses of any resident or patient shall be recovered from the school district in which the patient's or resident's parents or legal guardian reside. The liability of the school district for such expenses shall precede that of the persons or estates named in RSA 126-A:36 and 126-A:37, which are relieved of liability for such expenses to the extent of the school district's liability.

RSA 554:19-a places a duty upon an administrator to notify office of reimbursements under the direction of the director of the division of mental health and developmental services if the administrator has knowledge of liability under RSA 126-A:37. RSA 126-A:38 imposes a further requirement upon anyone legally chargeable under this statute, including an administrator, to file financial statements upon demand of the director of the division of mental health and developmental services.

RSA 126-A:36 and 126-A:37 were revised in 1994 to limit a parent's liability, or that of the parent's estate, to reimburse the State of New

---

[41] State v. Matthews, 123 N.H. 502, 463 A.2d 889 (1983).

[42] State v. Matthews, 123 N.H. 502, 504, 463 A.2d 889, 890 (1983).

[43] *Id.*

Hampshire for expenses incurred on behalf of children in a state institution to only those expenses incurred while a child is a minor. Furthermore, the extent of liability imposed on an estate is limited to the share that the resident would be entitled to if the parent died intestate or, alternatively, to the greater of the share the resident is entitled to under the parent's will or the share he or she would have been entitled to if the parent had died intestate.

Effective January 1, 1999, the sixth class of charges allowable against the estate of a decedent is for the "total amount paid for old age assistance or aid to the permanently and totally disabled" and, under certain circumstances, charges pursuant to RSA 166:19. This latter statute provides that any county furnishing any assistance to any person within six years preceding the person's death shall be entitled to recover from the estate of such person the sum or sums paid out for such assistance. RSA 166:19 has been interpreted to mean that recovery against the estate of a decedent to whom a town has rendered assistance is limited to sums expended by the town for assistance, and recovery cannot be had for some expedient performance of a contract to furnish support. *Warren v. Weaver.*[44]

RSA 167:13 further provides that upon the death of a recipient of old age assistance or aid to the permanently and totally disabled, the total amount of assistance shall be allowed as a claim against the estate under RSA 554:19,VI.

Library References

Am Jur 2d Executors and Administrators §§ 615, 698

CJS Executors and Administrators § 229

§ 36-10. Charges for County Assistance

Another example of a legislatively-created charge against an estate not found in the probate sections of the Revised Statutes is RSA 166:19. This statute, entitled "Recovery From Estates," provides as follows:

> Any county furnishing any assistance to any person within 6 years preceding his death shall be entitled to recover from the estate of such person the sum or sums paid out for such assistance, the same to be a preferred claim against his said

---

[44] 78 N.H. 108, 97A. 748 (1916).

estate after the payment of his funeral charges, expense of last sickness and expenses of administration, provided he leaves no widow or minor children living at his decease.

Recovery against the estate of a decedent, to whom a town has rendered assistance, is limited to the amount expended by the town for assistance.[45] Conveyances of real property may be made to the town in consideration of future support.[46]

In re Estate of Harville,[47] focused on the liability of an estate for old age assistance granted to the spouse of the decedent. The state tried to recover money from decedent's deceased wife's account. The *Harville* Court held that neither the statute nor the policies which occasioned it suggest that the estate of a deceased spouse should suffer ongoing liability for loans made to the surviving spouse after the decedent's death. Therefore, an estate is not liable for old age assistance granted to the spouse of decedent after the decedent's death.

County assistance has been specifically provided for in the 1998 revisions to the priority of charges by giving such claims for assistance a sixth level priority.[48]

Library References

Am Jur 2d Executors and Administrators §§ 614, 700

CJS Executors and Administrators §§ 219, 238

§ 36-11.　Miscellaneous Expenses

In addition to the legally-established claims and charges listed in RSA 554:19, an estate is also charged by RSA 554:20 with the expenses of (1) assigning the homestead right, (2) the division and assignment of real estate and (3) the appointment of guardians for minors and others. These expenses are chargeable under the first class of charges—as expenses of administration—and thus have the highest priority. RSA 554:20.

In *Bartlett v. Fitz*,[49] the administrator made an error in setting off homestead. The administrator was allowed to charge in the administration

---

[45] Warren v. Weaver, 78 N.H. 108, 109, 97 A. 748, 748 (1916).

[46] Amazeen v. Newcastle, 76 N.H. 250, 81 A. 1079 (1911).

[47] In re Estate of Harville, 115 N.H. 480, 481, 344 A.2d 1, 2 (1975).

[48] RSA 554:19, VI.

[49] Bartlett v. Fitz, 59 N.H. 502 (1880).

account for services rendered and expenses incurred in correcting certain defects in the proceedings. Since the Court found that the error was made without the administrator being at fault, the administrator was not charged personally with the cost of correcting it and the charge was properly against the estate.[50]

Library References

Am Jur 2d Executors and Administrators § 701

CJS Executors and Administrators § 462

§ 36-12. Uniform Probate Code Provisions

The Uniform Probate Code has a similar, but much clearer, provision, entitled "Classification of Claims" regarding the payment and preferences of claims:

Section 3-805.

(a) If the applicable assets of the estate are insufficient to pay all claims in full, the personal representative shall make payment in the following order:

(1) costs and expenses of administration;

(2) reasonable funeral expenses;

(3) debts and taxes with preference under federal law;

(4) reasonable and necessary medical and hospital expenses of the last illness of the decedent, including compensation of persons attending him;

(5) debts and taxes with preference under other laws of this state;

(6) all other claims.

(b) No preference shall be given in the payment of any claim over any other claim of the same class, and a claim

---

[50] Bartlett v. Fitz, 59 N.H. 502, 503 (1880).

due and payable shall not be entitled to a preference over claims not due.

Library References

Am Jur 2d Executors and Administrators §§ 708–713

Forms

See Form 84 in Appendix for a Petition for Allowance to Widow.

PART V

LAWSUITS BY AND AGAINST ADMINISTRATORS

CHAPTER 37. LEGACIES AND DEVISES

§ 37-1. Introduction

It is the duty of an administrator to carry out the provisions of the decedent's will by making proper distribution of the assets of the estate to the beneficiaries selected by the testator. In handling this task, the administrator "is bound to act with reasonable diligence in the execution of a will." *In re Estate of Jones.*[1]

Library References

Am Jur 2d Executors and Administrators § 1012

CJS Executors and Administrators § 482

§ 37-2. Jurisdiction Over Distribution

At one time, the probate court had no jurisdiction over the distribution of personal property passing by will.[2] The present statute, RSA 561:7, however, provides that "[t]he personal estate bequeathed by a testator shall be distributed by decree of the judge according to the will." The judge of probate is the only official who can lawfully make a decree of distribution.[3] If the distribution of property is affected by the state of the domicile, or by the locus of the property, the law of distribution is derived from the state of the domicile.[4]

The general rule is that the probate court has exclusive original jurisdiction over decrees of distribution.

The probate court has sole jurisdiction over questions relating solely to a probate court decree of distribution for the personal property of a decedent. *Cobleigh v. Spring.*[5]

Where both the executor and probate court are in doubt as to the proper construction of a will, and it is impossible to make a distribution of the proceeds of the estate or to file an account, the question of construction of the will may be certified by the probate court to the Supreme Court pursuant to RSA 547:30.[6] This statute provides for the transfer of questions of law to the Supreme Court. In some cases, this alternative method is more expeditious and less expensive than an application to the superior court for an interpretation of the will.[7]

---

[1] In re Estate of Jones, 118 N.H. 504, 507, 389 A.2d 436, 438 (1978).

[2] Stark v. Winslow, 77 N.H. 599, 92 A. 733 (1914).

[3] Clancy v. Pike, 94 N.H. 33, 34, 45 A.2d 658, 659 (1946).

[4] Kingsbury v. Bazeley, 75 N.H. 13, 17, 70 A. 916, 918 (1908).

[5] Cobleigh v. Spring, 85 N.H. 560, 157 A. 886 (1932).

[6] See the discussion of the certification process in Chapter 12 *supra*.

[7] In re Peterson Estate, 104 N.H. 508, 510, 190 A.2d 418, 419 (1963).

Library References

Am Jur 2d Wills § 850 et seq.
CJS Wills § 351 et seq.

§ 37-2(a). Disclaimer of Property Interests

RSA 563-B, the Uniform Disclaimer of Property Interest Act, codifies the right of an individual, including an executor, administrator, trustee, guardian, conservator, holder of a power of attorney or any other fiduciary, to disclaim an interest in property. The statute applies where there is a will and to an intestate estate. RSA 563-B:1.

A disclaimer must be in writing, describe the property or interest disclaimed and the extent to which the property is being disclaimed, declare that it is a disclaimer, and be signed by the disclaimant. RSA 563-B:3.

The original disclaimer must be delivered, in person, or by registered or certified mail not later than nine (9) months after the date of the decedent's death to;

(a) the personal representative, or other fiduciary, of the decedent,

(b) the holder of the legal title to which the interest relates, or

(c) the person entitled to the property or interest in the event of a disclaimer. RSA 563-B:2, I.

The disclaimant must file a copy of the disclaimer in the probate court in which the administration of the estate of the deceased owner has commenced. RSA 563-B:2, I. An additional copy of the disclaimer must be recorded in the registry of deeds in the county in which the property is located, if the disclaimer involves real property or an interest in real property. RSA 563-B:2, V.

A surviving joint tenant may disclaim as a separate interest any property or interest therein devolving to a surviving joint tenant by right of survivorship. A surviving joint tenant may disclaim the entire interest in any property or interest therein that is the subject of a joint tenancy devolving to the surviving joint tenant, if the joint tenancy as created by act of a deceased joint tenant and to the extent that the survivor did not contribute to the joint tenancy. RSA 563-B:2, IV.

The disclaimer statute, not the disclaimant, controls the distribution of the disclaimed property. Probate Court Procedure Bulletin 2000-04.

Disclaimed property will pass as directed by the decedent, or, if the decedent has not provided for another disposition, the disclaimed property will pass as if the disclaimant predeceased the decedent. RSA 563-B:4. For example, an adult child may choose to disclaim his/her interest in the deceased parent's intestate estate with the intention that the surviving parent inherit the disclaimed property. Probate Court Procedure Bulletin 16. However, if the disclaimant has children, the disclaimant's children will inherit the disclaimed property, not the surviving spouse. Probate Court Procedure Bulletin 16.

Similarly, if a decedent's will provides for one-half to my spouse and one-half to my child, X, without including the limitation that X must survive the decedent and without including a provision for disclaimed property, property disclaimed by X would pass to X's children pursuant to RSA 551:12. Probate Court Procedure Bulletin 16. Further, pursuant to RSA 463:29, the guardian of the estate of a minor has the ability to disclaim inherited property only with prior court authorization and for good cause shown.

§ 37-2(b). Irrevocability of Disclaimers

Individuals disclaiming are bound by the written disclaimer and a disclaimer is not revocable under any circumstances. RSA 563-B:4, I. Therefore, in the example provided in the previous paragraph, the adult child would not be entitled to revoke the disclaimer even though the property did not pass as the disclaimant intended. Probate Court Procedure Bulletin 16.

§ 37-2(c). Waiver of Right to Disclaim

The right to disclaim property or an interest may be waived by certain acts. Specifically, a person may not disclaim after:

(1) he/she assigns, conveys, encumbers, pledges, or transfers the property or interest, or signs a contract to do any of the previous acts;

(2) he/she signs a written waiver of the right to disclaim;

(3) he/she accepts the property or interest, or accepts a benefit of the property or interest; for example, cashing a dividend check bars the right to disclaim the stock; or

(4) there is a sale of the property under a judicial sale. RSA 563-B:5.

A joint tenant may disclaim as a separate interest any property devolving by right of survivorship. RSA 563-B:2, IV. For example, assume A and B purchased property jointly with rights of survivorship and each provided one-half of the purchase price. After A dies, B automatically inherits A's half by right of survivorship. If B chooses to disclaim A's separate interest, A's half will pass as if B predeceased A and it will become part of A's estate. B cannot disclaim all interest in the property since it was created by A and B, and B contributed one-half of the purchase price. Probate Court Procedure Bulletin 16.

§ 37-2(d). Review of Disclaimers by Probate Court

Review of disclaimers in the probate court is limited to the disclaimer's execution and the proper distribution of the disclaimed property. Probate Court Procedure Bulletin 16.

Staff should confirm that the disclaimer:

(1) was signed by the disclaimant or by a person with the proper authority to disclaim on the party's behalf, i.e. power of attorney, guardian of incapacitated adult, conservator, trustee, or executor;

(2) was signed within nine months of the decedent's death; and

(3) describes the property disclaimed.

If a disclaimer does not appear to meet the above criteria, staff should immediately schedule the disclaimer for the court's review. Probate Court Procedure Bulletin 16. If the court finds the disclaimer to be invalid, notice shall be sent to the attorney for the fiduciary and the disclaimant.

Upon receipt of a motion for distribution, interim or final account, staff should confirm that the proper party(ies) are receiving the disclaimed property. If the decedent died testate, the will must be reviewed for provisions concerning the disposition of disclaimed property. If the will does not direct the disposition of disclaimed property, or the decedent died intestate, the property will pass as if the disclaimant predeceased the decedent. Probate Court Procedure Bulletin 16.

§ 37-3. Legacy and Devise

In the modern age, it is frequent to find many terms relating to the distribution of property by will to be used loosely, and often interchangeably. However, it is important to know the basic differences between the types of gifts, particularly when there may not be sufficient assets available to pay all bequests.[8]

Legacy and *devise* are terms that are frequently used interchangeably. By strict definition, however, the terms are intended to refer to different types of property. A simple definition of a legacy is a gift or bequest of personal property, left by will. *Devise*, by definition, refers to a testamentary disposition of real property. However, the word *devise* is often loosely used to define any testamentary gift, whether of real or personal property.[9]

The word *devise* is defined in *Ladd v. Harvey*,[10] as being appropriate to a gift of land. A person taking an interest in the proceeds of real estate directed to be sold by the administrator is a devisee and not a legatee. The terms, however, are often used indifferently. Legatees may inherit under a bequest to "all my devisees above named." The word *legacy* may be applied to real estate if the intent of the will shows that such was the testator's intention.[11]

Library References

Am Jur 2d Wills § 1523

CJS Wills § 1097

§ 37-3(a). Specific and General Devises

A devise of real property is not necessarily specific. A devise may be classified as general or specific. A specific devise is a gift by will of a specific piece of real property which is so described as to distinguish it from other real property.[12] A general devise passes land to another

---

[8] See also, C. DeGrandpre, 7 New Hampshire Practice: Wills, Trusts and Gifts (3d ed. 1997) Chapter 26.

[9] 1 Bowe-Parker: Page on Wills §01.3 (1960).

[10] Ladd v. Harvey, 21 N.H. 514, 522 (1850).

[11] Ladd v. Harvey, 21 N.H. 514, 528 (1850); Petition of Carlton, 79 N.H. 48, 49, 104 A. 246, 247 (1918).

[12] 6 Bowe-Parker: Page on Wills § 48.9 (1962).

without a particular description of it. A residuary devise of real property is a general devise.[13]

When the same estate is devised to the heir in the same quantity and quality as he would have taken by descent if there had been no devise, the devise is void and the heir will take by descent. This principle is referred to as the doctrine of worthier title.[14] When, by devise, a different estate is given from that which the law would give, the will prevails.[15]

Where a will bequeathed the residue of an estate to the testator's sister for so long as she shall live "with the right to use the income of [the] estate for her living expenses and for the expenses of maintaining the real estate and also with the right to invade the principal as much as necessary, in her sole discretion for the purpose of paying her living expenses and for the purposes of maintaining the real estate," the Supreme Court, in *In re Estate of Teague,*[16] held that the life tenant's right of living expenses was not limited to those expenses incurred by living on the real estate, but included the right to invade principal for the life tenant's living expenses wherever she lived.

Library References

Am Jur 2d Wills §§ 1524, 1525

CJS Wills § 1124 et seq.

§ 37-3(b). Specific and General Legacies

A specific legacy is a gift of a specific thing or of some portion of the testator's estate, which is so described by the testator as to distinguish from other articles of the same nature. *Page v. Eldredge Public Library Association.*[17]

A general legacy is one that comes out of the general assets of the testator's estate. A general legacy is different than a specific one in that it not identified as a particular item or from a certain fund.[18] A bequest of all of the testator's property is a general legacy.[19]

---

[13] *Id.*

[14] 6 Bowe-Parker: Page on Wills § 49.3 (1962).

[15] McAfee v. Gilmore, 4 N.H. 391, 394 (1828).

[16] 139 N.H. 667 (1995).

[17] Page v. Eldredge Public Library Association, 69 N.H. 575, 45 A. 411 (1889); 6 Bowe-Parker: Page on Wills § 48.3 (1962).

[18] 6 Bowe-Parker: Page on Wills § 48.2 (1962).

[19] *Id.*

Library References

Am Jur 2d Wills §§ 1524, 1525
CJS Wills § 1124 et seq.

§ 37-3(c). Pecuniary Legacy

A pecuniary legacy is a general legacy. Generally, a pecuniary legacy is a bequest of a sum of money or an annuity. A legacy may also be pecuniary if it is comprised of specific pieces of money located in a specific container.

Library References

Am Jur 2d Wills § 1534
CJS Wills § 1124 et seq.

§ 37-3(d). Demonstrative Legacy

A demonstrative legacy is a bequest of a certain sum of money that is to be paid out of a specific fund.[20]

The fund must be in existence at the time of the testator's death for the gift to be treated as a demonstrative legacy. If the fund from which the legacy is designated to be paid out of fails, the legacy is nevertheless entitled to be paid out of the estate as a general legacy.

Library References

Am Jur 2d Wills § 1526
CJS Wills § 1124

§ 37-4. Priority of Legacies

The question of priority among legacies does not arise unless there are not enough assets in the estate to satisfy all of the bequests provided for in the will. There is no need to consider an apportionment between legacies where "there is no allegation of . . . a deficiency and neither is there any probability of one."[21] The case of *Ruel v. Hardy* also makes clear that there is no priority among general legacies "and the order in which the legatees are named is immaterial."[22]

---

[20] 6 Bowe-Parker: Page on Wills § 48.7 (1962).

[21] Ruel v. Hardy, 90 N.H. 240, 245, 6 A.2d 753, 758 (1939).

[22] *Id.*

The general rule is that:

> At common law a specific bequest or devise will not be
> charged with the payment of a general pecuniary legacy, nor
> abated in favor of a general legatee, unless such appears to have
> been clearly the intention of the testator. Davenport v. Sargent.[23]

This rule was not changed by the adoption of RSA 561:17 and 561:18
establishing a priority for the payment of legacies and devises.[24]

Where, however, the testator has made clear that a beneficiary should
pay certain debts and expenses of the estate as a condition of his bequest,
the bequest will be charged with the expenses and debts even if the entire
bequest is used up. *Frost v. Wingate.*[25] Any deficiency remaining will
be apportioned among other specific legatees in the absence of a general
residuary clause.[26]

Sometimes, the directions of the testator are unclear whether he
intended to charge a bequest with the payment of debts or expenses or
not. In *Sanborn v. Clough,*[27] the testator's will provided as follows:
"After the payment of all of my just debts and funeral charges and the
expense of a proper set of gravestones, . . .", which was followed by
a specific bequest of certain stocks and bonds. The remainder of the estate
was specially devised and bequeathed to another. The Supreme Court
held that the testator did not intend to charge the specific bequest of the
stocks and bonds with the debts and expenses of the estate. Rather, the
Court held that the quoted language was "only verbiage" and that the
residuary legatee was to be charged with the expenses of administration
and certain pecuniary legacies provided for in the will.[28]

However, the assets of an estate may not be sufficient to pay all claims
against the estate and all bequests and devises provided for in the will.
In this situation, the administrator must first pay all claims of the estate
having priority over the payment of legacies and devises as provided by
RSA 554:19.[29] If, after the payment of claims having priority, there are

---

[23] Davenport v. Sargent, 63 N.H. 538, 543, 4 A. 569, 570 (1855).

[24] *Id.*

[25] Frost v. Wingatel, 73 N.H. 535, 64 A. 19 (1906).

[26] *Id.*

[27] Sanborn v. Clough, 64 N.H. 315, 10 A. 678 (1887).

[28] Sanborn v. Clough, 64 N.H. 315, 320, 10 A. 678, 680 (1887).

[29] See the discussion in Chapter 36 *supra.*

some, but not enough, assets left to pay any additional claims and legacies provided for in the testator's will, the legislature has established priorities among legacies and devises of a will. RSA 561:17 provides that:

> The estate, real and personal, not specifically devised or bequeathed, shall be first liable to the payment of the legal charges against the estate and legacies given by the will, and to be applied to make up the share of any child born after the decease of the testator, or of any child or issue of any child omitted or not provided for in the will.

It becomes necessary in such instances to look to the definition of "specifically" devised or bequeathed property to determine if a bequest or devise is to have a higher priority and therefore be protected from the payment of claims and charges. Real and personal property which is not specifically devised or bequeathed stands in the lowest class of priority and will first be used to satisfy claims against the estate and "legacies given by the will."

When legacies of money are "mere" or "common" pecuniary legacies, they contribute to the burdens of the estate, if the words relating to payment of debts can be applied to them. *Wallace v. Wallace.*[30] When they are specific legacies, they do not abate until the other devises and legacies have been exhausted.[31] This means that if the gift is specific, it should not be charged with any part of the expenses of administering the estate that may be satisfied from the residue.[32] A court, however, is not "inclined to construe a legacy as specific, unless clearly so intended."[33] A pecuniary legacy does not become a specific bequest merely because it is given for a specific purpose.[34]

A legacy is specific when it is the intention of the testator that the legatee should have the very thing bequeathed, and not merely a corresponding amount in value. This type of legacy is not liable to abatement for the payment of debts, unless the assets are insufficient for that purpose. If a legacy is given generally, with a demonstration of a

---

[30] Wallace v. Wallace, 23 N.H. 149, 153 (1851).

[31] *Id.*

[32] Duncan v. Bigelow, 96 N.H. 216, 219, 72 A.2d 497, 499 (1950).

[33] Wallace v. Wallace, 23 N.H. 149, 153 (1851).

[34] Petition of Cain, 87 N.H. 318, 319, 179 A. 347, 348 (1935).

particular fund as the source of payment, it will be a demonstrative legacy.[35] A legacy is specific when it is a bequest of a specific article of the testator's personal estate, distinguished from all others of the same kind.[36]

As RSA 561:17 makes clear, the share of a pretermitted child is taken first from real and personal property not specifically devised or bequeathed before turning to specifically devised real and personal property. The phrase, "any child . . . omitted or not provided for in the will" in RSA 561:17, is the same as "every child . . . not named or referred to in his will, and who is not a devisee or legatee" under RSA 551:10. Thus, a person who was named in the will as a legatee within the meaning of the statute, cannot, because his legacy has failed, take something else not bequeathed to him. *Davenport v. Sargent.*[37]

If, after using all property, both real and personal, there are insufficient assets to pay legal charges or specific devises and bequests, RSA 561:18 establishes that the specially devised real and personal property shall bear the expense or reduction proportionately:

> If the same is not sufficient, the property devised and bequeathed shall be liable therefor, and the judge may settle and adjust, by his decree, the amount of such liabilities, so that each devisee and legatee shall contribute in just proportion thereto. Such liabilities may be taken into consideration and allowed in the decree of distribution of the personal estate, in the division of the real estate, and in the granting of license for the sale thereof, as the case may require.

It has been held that there is nothing in the language of RSA 561:18 which shows that a specific legacy or devise is to be diminished or exhausted to satisfy a legacy that is not specific.[38]

RSA 554:19 provides for the order in which demands against the estate shall be paid. The existing and established priorities were not changed by anything in RSA 561:17 (priority of legacies), 561:18 (contribution

---

[35] *Id.*

[36] Loring v. Woodward, 41 N.H. 391, 394 (1860). See Morse v. Converse, 80 N.H. 24, 25, 113 A. 214, 215 (1921).

[37] Davenport v. Sargent, 63 N.H. 538, 4 A. 569 (1885).

[38] Davenport v. Sargent, 63 N.H. 538, 539, 4 A. 569, 570–71 (1885).

by devisees) and 554:9 (property not to be sold), providing that personal property specifically bequeathed should not be sold if not needed for payment of debts. "[S]pecific bequests and specific devises, which have not been made inferior to specific bequests of personal property, cannot be charged with the payment of general pecuniary legacies."[39]

A general legacy is chargeable with the payment of specific legacies and with the expense of administration.[40] If specifically devised real estate is changed into money by an administrator's sale, the sale does not destroy the character of the fund or impair the right of the beneficiaries beyond the payment of debts and expenses, if there is not a contrary intent in the will.[41]

Where it is unclear to the administrator how the expense and legacies should be apportioned, he should apply to the probate court for a decree of distribution because "the question of apportionment should, in the first instance, be presented to the Probate Court." *Ruel v. Hardy.*[42]

Library References

Am Jur 2d Wills §§ 1746, 1750

CJS Wills § 1311 et seq.

§ 37-5. Payment of Legacies and Devises—In General

Normally, an administrator should not pay or distribute specific legacies or devises until all debts and expenses have been paid or provisions made therefor. *Ticknor v. Harris.*[43] In the usual course of administration, where there appear to be sufficient assets to pay debts, claims and expenses of administration, and all legacies, the administrator distributes the tangible personal property during the administration of the estate, usually after the inventory is completed and filed. Pecuniary legacies are usually payable one year from the date of death of the decedent. *Ruel v. Hardy.*[44]

---

[39] Davenport v. Sargent, 63 N.H. 538, 544, 4 A. 569, 570 (1885).

[40] Sanborn v. Clough, 64 N.H. 315, 319, 10 A. 678, 680 (1887).

[41] *Id.*

[42] Ruel v. Hardy, 90 N.H. 240, 245–46, 6 A.2d 753, 758 (1939).

[43] Ticknor v. Harris, 14 N.H. 272 (1843).

[44] Ruel v. Hardy, 90 N.H. 240, 246, 6 A.2d 753, 758 (1939).

Library References

Am Jur 2d Wills § 1789 et seq.

CJS Wills § 1338 et seq.

§ 37-5(a). Receipts

RSA 561:19 requires that administrators must take a receipt from every payment of a legacy or distributive share of an estate. These must be filed in the probate court. Although a final account will usually be allowed without the filing of the final receipts of the residuary beneficiaries (whose share usually cannot be computed until the approval of the judge), the administrator will not be able to obtain a release of his letter of administration, which is necessary in order for him to obtain cancellation of his probate bond, until the receipts are filed.[45]

If the bequest is to a minor and is less than $1,000.00, payment to the parent or parents of the child and the filing of their receipt is sufficient. RSA 561:20.

RSA 561:20 provides as follows: Whenever any minor not being under legal guardianship shall be entitled to receive from any administrator or executor any distributive share as heir or next of kin, or any legacy, the full amount of which share or legacy is not more than $5,000, said administrator or executor, upon petition to and approval of the probate court, shall pay said sum to the parents of the minor, if both are living, or to the surviving parent if one parent is deceased, or to the parent or other person having custody of the minor, if the parents are divorced, or to a person standing in local parentis to the minor, if both parents are deceased. This statute goes on to provide that receipt of the parent or parents or other person provided for in the statute shall be filed with the probate court and accepted as discharge of the executor's liability for the payment of such bequest.[46] The statute goes on to provide that "[w]hen considering such a petition, the probate court shall determine the best interest of the minor."[47] If such a petition is approved by the probate court, the court is empowered to make all necessary orders for protecting the interests of the minor, even to the extent of requiring the parents to give a bond or to account for the money.[48]

---

[45] RSA 561:19.

[46] RSA 561:20.

[47] *Id.*

[48] *Id.*

Library References

Wills B (684.10(1)
Am Jur 2d Wills § 1789
CJS Wills § 1338

§ 37-5(b). Interim Distributions of Non-Specific Bequests

It is unusual for an administrator to make distribution of general residuary bequests prior to the allowance of the final account. However, where the administration is complicated and lengthy, it may be sensible or wise to make a partial distribution of the residuary amount. Often, the need (or greed) of the residuary beneficiaries creates pressure on the administrator to make early partial distributions.

Until 1975, there was no provision in the statutes for such distributions. Regardless, they were often made without prior probate court approval as circumstances dictated. Many probate courts viewed the practice adversely and adopted rules precluding partial distributions without court approval.

In 1975, the legislature specifically provided for interim partial distributions upon approval of the court of the "personal estate of a person deceased which was not bequeathed or included in a bequest."

> The personal estate of a person deceased which was not bequeathed or included in a bequest and which remains in the hands of the executor or administrator upon settlement of an account of such fiduciary shall be distributed according to law by decree of the judge. Upon the application of the fiduciary or any interested person, the judge may issue interim orders approving or directing partial distributions or granting other relief at any time during the pendency of administration to effect distributions as expeditiously and efficiently as may be consistent with the best interests of the estate. RSA 561:7-a.

With the passage of this statute, which specifically requires probate court approval for interim distributions of residuary bequests, an administrator making such distributions without court approval does so at his own risk. Many probate courts look with great disfavor upon administrators who violate this rule.

It is obviously improper for an administrator to pay some but not all pecuniary legacies at the same time. Nor is it proper for an administrator to pay some residuary beneficiaries but not others. In such a case, a beneficiary who is not paid promptly and equally is entitled to interest and the administrator may be surcharged by the probate court.

Library References

Am Jur 2d Executors and Administrators § 1086 et seq.
Am Jur 2d Wills § 1789
CJS Wills § 1343

§ 37-5(c). Interest on Legacies and Devises

There is no provision in the statutes for interest upon distributions of specific legacies and devises. However, over the years, the courts have established certain rules in this regard which are based upon an administrator's duties to diligently proceed with the settlement of the estate. *In re Estate of Jones.*[49]

"Interest, in the sense in which the word is used in connection with the payment of legacies, is the compensation allowed by law for the deprivation of a legacy or distributive share beyond the period when it is payable according to the terms of a will or statute."[50] "The right to receive interest is 'an incident to the legacy itself.'" It is incident to the principal demand and not imposed upon the executor for his neglect.[51] Whether the assets of the estate have been fruitful or unproductive does not affect the right of the legatee, for a beneficiary is considered to be in the same position as a creditor and entitled to be awarded interest at the legal rate for such time as he is unpaid beyond when he should have been paid.[52] "There is no essential connection between the obligation of an estate to pay interest on overdue legacies, and the personal liability of an executor or administrator to the estate for interest under certain circumstances." *Dennison v. Lilley.*[53]

However, where the administrator is at fault, he will be personally held responsible for the payment of interest.

---

[49] In re Estate of Jones, 118 N.H. 504, 507, 389 A.2d 436, 438 (1978).

[50] Dennison v. Lilley, 83 N.H. 422, 144 A. 523 (1928) (*quoting* Woerner, American Law of Administration).

[51] Kinghorn v. Athorne, 102 N.H. 293, 155 A.2d 805 (1959).

[52] Dennison v. Lilley, 83 N.H. 422, 144 A. 523 (1928).

[53] *Id.*

The true rule to be applied in charging administrators with interest is well settled. In all cases where the administrator, without any just reason or excuse, retains the money in his own hands unemployed, when it ought to be paid over, in all cases where he receives interest for money which belongs to the estate and in all cases where he applies money belonging to the estate to his own use, he ought to be charged with interest.[54]

In *Deschenes v. Estate of Deschenes*,[55] the Court charged an administrator with interest from one year from the date of her appointment where the administrator failed to make even partial distributions without good reason.

The rules for the allowance of interest on legacies where the will is silent on that subject, are well-settled:

(1) If a pecuniary legacy is payable generally without designation of any time of payment, it is payable at the end of the year from the death of the testator, without interest; but if not then paid, it bears interest after the expiration of the year. *Loring v. Woodward.*[56] Interest is payable at the legal rate of ten percent prescribed by RSA 336:1, for the period beginning one year after the testator's death and until payment is made. *Kinghorn v. Athorne.*[57]

(2) If such a legacy is payable at the specified time, it bears interest from that time but not before. *Loring v. Woodward.*[58]

(3) To these rules there is an exception. If the legacy is given to a child, or to an adopted child, or a child to which the testator has placed himself in the place of a parent, which is under age, and for whose support no other provision is made, it bears interest from the testator's decease. *Loring v. Woodward.*[59]

(4) In the case of a specific legacy, the income, profits, or produce of the article after the decease of the testator, goes to the legatee without

---

[54] Lund v. Lund, 41 N.H. 355, 359 (1860).

[55] Deschenes v. Estate of Deschenes, 109 N.H. 389, 254 A.2d 278 (1969).

[56] Loring v. Woodward, 41 N.H. 391 (1860).

[57] Kinghorn v. Athorne, 102 N.H. 293, 155 A.2d 805 (1959).

[58] Loring v. Woodward, 41 N.H. 391 (1860).

[59] *Id.*

regard to the time at which the article is to be delivered. *Loring v. Woodward.*[60]

(5) In the case of a bequest which provides for a gift to a person and in certain events, gift over to another, each is entitled to the income during the time he is entitled to the principal. *Loring v. Woodward.*[61]

These rules, however, do not apply where specific directions are given by the will, or where a different intention may be inferred from its provisions.[62] A legatee should not be deprived of interest without a clear expression of the intent of the testator to do so.[63] The fact that it may be inconvenient or even impossible to pay a legacy at the expiration of a one-year period is in itself no barrier to the collection of interest.[64]

For a discussion of changes made by the Uniform Principal and Income Act, which was effective from June 27, 1990 to May 18, 1992, see Chapter 39.

Library References

Am Jur 2d Wills §§ 1789-1791
CJS Wills § 1345 et seq.

§ 37-5(d). Interest on Distributive Shares in an Intestate Estate

In *Deschenes v. Estate of Deschenes,*[65] the Supreme Court established the rule that beneficiaries of an intestate estate are entitled to interest at the statutory rate on their share of the estate, beginning one year from the date of appointment of the administrator, if an administrator fails to make even partial distributions for no reason after the estate is liquidated and all taxes and claims against the estate are paid.

For a discussion of changes made by the Uniform Principal and Income Act, which was effective from June 27, 1990 to May 18, 1992, see Chapter 39.

---

[60] Loring v. Woodward, 41 N.H. 391 (1860). See also Munro v. Mullen, 100 N.H. 128, 121 A.2d 312 (1956).

[61] *Id.*

[62] Loring v. Woodward, 41 N.H. 391 (1860).

[63] Kinghorn v. Athorne, 102 N.H. 293, 155 A.2d 805 (1959).

[64] *Id.*

[65] Deschenes v. Estate of Deschenes, 109 N.H. 389, 254 A.2d 278 (1969).

Library References

Am Jur 2d Executors and Administrators § 688

CJS Executors and Administrators § 508

§ 37-6. Liability of Beneficiaries for Claims in Certain Circumstances

Usually, heirs of an estate take their share of the estate after all claims and taxes have been paid. However, early common law "held that an heir could be liable for his ancestor's debts if two conditions existed: the debts must have been of a specialty nature and they were recoverable only to the value of real estate inherited by the heir from the ancestor." *American University v. Forbes.*[66] Legatees of personal property from an estate, however, were under no similar liability.

The common law rule has undergone material changes. Heirs receiving personal estate by virtue of their inheritances and those receiving either real or personal estate under a will are subject to some liability.[67] However, the liability must be on a claim that is not provable against the representative of the estate.[68] The liability, in such cases, arises by reason of an undertaking of the decedent, the nonfulfillment of which is subsequent to his death.[69]

The legislature has provided two methods of handling this situation. RSA 558:20 provides for a creditor whose claim cannot be allowed against the estate because it depends on an unhappened contingency. The creditor shall not lose his remedy against the heirs or devisees. This provision, however, is confined to estates settled in the insolvent course. The second method is provided by RSA 556:6, which empowers the probate court to order a retention of funds for the payment of unmatured demands and demands depending on a contingency. Since a creditor may be without fault in not anticipating the contingency of the amount of his claim if the contingency should occur, the statute would not bar him from recovery from heirs, devisees, and legatees if he failed to seek retention in the representative's hands.[70] When a claim, however, is

---

[66] American Univ. v. Forbes, 88 N.H. 17, 18, 183 A. 860, 861 (1936).

[67] Hall v. Martin, 46 N.H. 337 (1865). See Russ v. Perry, 49 N.H. 547 (1870).

[68] Hall v. Martin, 46 N.H. 337 (1865). See Sawyer v. Jefts, 70 N.H. 393, 47 A. 416 (1900); Russ v. Perry, 49 N.H. 547 (1870); Ticknor v. Harris, 14 N.H. 272, 284 (1843).

[69] American Univ. v. Forbes, 88 N.H. 17, 183 A. 860 (1936).

[70] *Id.*

provable against the estate but is not presented in time and is barred, the estate goes to the heir, devisee or legatee and he is not liable to the creditor on the claim,[71] unless the claimant failed to file his claim because of fraud of the testator, his agents, or servants.[72]

Library References

Am Jur 2d Wills § 1746 et seq.

CJS Wills § 1311 et seq.

§ 37-7. General Escheat Law

New Hampshire has adopted a comprehensive escheat law entitled "Custody and Escheat of Unclaimed and Abandoned Property," RSA Chapter 471-C. This statute covers everything from unclaimed property held by police departments[73] to travelers checks and money orders[74] to bank deposits[75] and funds owing under life insurance policies.[76] Of importance to the probate area are the provisions of RSA 471-C:18, which provide that "[a]ll tangible and intangible property held in a safe deposit box . . . in this state in the ordinary course of the holder's business . . ., which remain unclaimed by the owner for more than 7 years after the lease or rental period on the box or other repository has expired, are presumed abandoned."

This New Hampshire statute is modeled on the Uniform Unclaimed Property Act promulgated by the National Conference of Uniform Commissioners on Uniform State Laws in 1981. The New Hampshire Act follows fairly closely the Uniform Act but has additional provisions not found in the Uniform Act.

This Act does not deal with the disposition of unclaimed shares of estates, which is covered by RSA 561:10-12-b. However, the Act does have a general all-purpose provision relating to property held by agents and fiduciaries which provides that "[i]ntangible property in any income or increment derived therefrom held in a fiduciary capacity for the benefit of another person is presumed abandoned unless the owner, within five

---

[71] American Univ. v. Forbes, 88 N.H. 17, 20, 183 A. 860, 862 (1936).

[72] Follett v. Ramsey, 101 N.H. 347, 349, 143 A.2d 675, 677–78 (1958).

[73] RSA 471-C:15-a.

[74] RSA 471-C:4.

[75] RSA 471-C:6.

[76] RSA 471-C:7.

years after it has become payable or distributable, has increased or decreased the principal, accepted payment of principal or income, communicated concerning the property, or otherwise indicated an interest as evidenced by a memorandum or other record on file prepared by the fiduciary."[77]

Forms

See Form 78 in Appendix for a Petition to Accept Parent's Receipt for Legacy of Minor.

See Form 115 in Appendix for a Petition to Pay Funds to State Treasurer.

See Form 136 in Appendix for a Receipt for Legacy.

---

[77] RSA 471-C:12, I.

CHAPTER 38. ADVANCEMENTS

§ 38-1. Introduction

The murky concept of advancements is another one of those ancient probate doctrines that have a kernel of truth hidden underneath a ton of redundant and confusing verbiage. The very term *advancement* adds considerably to the confusion.

The doctrine of advancements has at its heart the idea that a person during his lifetime may choose to "advance" the share a child would eventually inherit on the parent's death by a gift to the child. The reasons for which a person may wish to make an advancement are as varied as human nature. For example:

> [T]he taste, talents and constitution of one child may be of such a nature as to induce the parent to make for him a larger proportion of his property by anticipation, to advance him in the art or profession for which he evinces peculiar qualifications. This course might greatly promote his interest and happiness, while similar benefits may be ultimately secured to his other children by giving them in some other form their share of the estate. *Fellows v. Little.*[1]

Indeed, it has been stated that the "receipt of a share of a parent's estate in advance, may, in many instances, be very advantageous to a child, without being detrimental to the parent." *Nesmith v. Dinsmore.*[2]

---

[1] Fellows v. Little, 46 N.H. 27, 38 (1865).

[2] Nesmith v. Dinsmore, 17 N.H. 515 (1845).

"[T]he doctrine of advancements has for its object the furtherance of" the principle that "equality is equity among heirs." *Fellows v. Little.*[3] By this it is meant that the intention of the parent should be carried out.

> [N]o person knows so well as a parent how equity and equality may best be effected. In many families, a judicious determination in favor of one child, or against another, may work the best equity. The presumption is that the parent makes these expenditures in the discharge of his parental duties, and that all his children are treated with equality in this respect.[4]

An advancement "may be briefly defined to be a free and irrevocable gift by a parent in his lifetime to his child on account of such child's share of the estate after the decease of the parent dying intestate."[5] The doctrine of advancements provides that where an intestate decedent transfers property to a child prior to his death, the transfer will be presumed to be an advancement and the value of the property given to the child will be deducted from the child's share upon distribution of the estate.[6]

The doctrine of advancements is applicable only to intestate estates. It has no application whatsoever where an individual dies testate, unless the testator provides to the contrary.[7]

In New Hampshire, the doctrine of advancements is governed primarily by statutory law, RSA 561:13 through 561:16, supplemented by common law principles.[8]

Library References

Am Jur 2d Advancements § 1 et seq.

CJS Descent and Distribution § 91 et seq.

§ 38-2.　Historical Background

It is helpful to our understanding of the doctrine to consider its historical antecedents. In *Nesmith v. Dinsmore,*[9] the historical

---

[3] Fellows v. Little, 46 N.H. 27, 37 (1865).

[4] Fellows v. Little, 46 N.H. 27, 37–38 (1865).

[5] Fellows v. Little, 46 N.H. 27, 35 (1865).

[6] Marston v. Lord, 65 N.H. 4, 17 A. 80 (1888).

[7] Wentworth v. Wentworth, 75 N.H. 547, 78 A. 646 (1910).

[8] Fellows v. Little, 46 N.H. 27 (1865).

[9] Nesmith v. Dinsmore, 17 N.H. 515 (1845).

background of the doctrine was explored in some detail. In feudal times, the doctrine of advancements was not recognized, at least as it might apply to real estate. Even as to a person's personal estate, a share was set aside for children who could not be disinherited for cause. This share was called *orphanage*,[10] and the custom was established in London that a person could make an actual advancement to a child in return for the child's agreement to give up or release his future share in his parent's estate. This eventually became the law of England and the American common law, although it is interesting to note that the earlier law still prevails in Scotland, where the required child's share is quaintly called the *bairn's part*.[11]

Library References

Am Jur 2d Advancements § 3

CJS Descent and Distribution § 91

§ 38-3. Statutory Provisions

RSA 561:13 through 561:16 provides the basic New Hampshire statutory underpinning for the common law principles of advancements:

561:13—Advancements. If an heir of a person deceased, or any person through whom the heir claims, has been advanced by the deceased in his lifetime, such advancement shall be accounted, according to its value, as part or the whole of the share of such heir.

561:14—Adjustment of. Such advancements, or any indebtedness of an heir, the amount having been first determined by the judge, may be taken into consideration in the division of the real estate; or they may be considered and adjusted by the judge in the decree of distribution of the personal estate.

561:15—By Deed. No deed of real estate shall be deemed an advancement unless the same is expressed to be made for love or affection, or unless it is proved to be an advancement by some acknowledgment signed by the party receiving it.

---

[10] 2 Bouvier's Law Dictionary (8th ed.) p. 2431.

[11] 2 Bouvier's Law Dictionary (8th ed.) p. 1929.

561:16—Personalty. No personal property delivered shall be deemed an advancement unless proved to be such by an acknowledgment in writing, signed by the party receiving it, or by some charge or memorandum thereof in writing, made by the deceased or by his order, or unless delivered expressly as an advancement, in the presence of two witnesses who were requested to take notice thereof.

Library References

Am Jur 2d Advancements § 4

CJS Descent and Distribution § 92

§ 38-4. Statutory Interpretation

No particular form of words is required to constitute an advancement. The articles or money delivered by the parent must be charged so as not to imply the existence of a debt or an absolute gift, but rather to show the parent's intention to deliver the property and make the charges expressly as advancements towards the child's future share of the estate.[12]

According to *Nesmith v. Dinsmore*, "The transaction is one of advancement, or in the nature of advancement, to the child of its portion."[13] The intention of the parent is to govern and to be carried out.[14]

An advancement is a completed gift by the ancestor, to be accounted by the recipient as his share or part of his share in distribution, and is no part of the ancestor's estate at his death. *Wentworth v. Wentworth.*[15] It is not a loan to be repaid to the ancestor or to his representative after death, nor is it a legacy paid in advance.[16] Under the doctrine, the parties do not intend repayment, nor can it be inferred that the legislature intended the advancement should be paid as a part of the assets in distribution.[17] RSA 561:13 provides that if an heir of a person deceased, or any person through whom the heir claims, has been advanced by the

---

[12] Fellows v. Little, 46 N.H. 27 (1865).

[13] Nesmith v. Dinsmore, 17 N.H. 515, 516 (1845).

[14] Fellows v. Little, 46 N.H. 27 (1865).

[15] Wentworth v. Wentworth, 75 N.H. 547, 78 A. 646 (1910).

[16] *Id.*

[17] *Id.*

deceased in his lifetime, such advancement shall be accounted, according to its value, as part or the whole of the share of such heir.

The heir who has received an advancement, in accounting for it according to its value, as a part or the whole of his share, receives so much less of the residue of the estate than he otherwise would; it is deducting it from his share of the estate as found at the ancestor's death.[18] If the advancement exceeds what his share otherwise would be, he accounts for it as "the whole" of his share, but is not called upon to contribute something as a gift to make the other shares equal to the remainder of his advancement.[19] The advancement is accounted as part of the person's advanced share at the time of the death of the advancer.[20]

The probate court has exclusive jurisdiction of the adjustment and establishment of advancements and a party must first try such a matter in that court.[21] RSA 561:14 provides that such advancements, or any indebtedness of an heir, the amount having been first determined by the judge, may be taken into consideration in the division of the real estate; or they may be considered and adjusted by the judge in the decree of distribution of the personal estate.

New Hampshire expressly recognizes and provides for advancements as an effectual bar on the part of the child, affecting the real as well as personal estate in such cases, without any agreement on the part of the child that what is received shall be an advancement. *Nesmith v. Dinsmore.*[22] Questions of advancements are always questions of intention, and the difficulties in solving them are generally found in the kind of evidence by which such intention is to be proved.[23] No advancement shall be allowed unless it is provided in one of the ways prescribed by the statutes,[24] and the settling and allowing of advancements is for the judge of probate to determine.[25]

RSA 561:15 provides that no deed of real estate shall be deemed an advancement unless the same is expressly made for love or affection,

---

[18] *Id.*

[19] *Id.*

[20] Dixon v. Marston, 64 N.H. 433, 14 A. 728 (1888).

[21] Locke v. Hancock, 59 N.H. 85 (1879).

[22] Nesmith v. Dinsmore, 17 N.H. 515 (1845).

[23] Fellows v. Little, 46 N.H. 27 (1865).

[24] Titus v. Ash, 24 N.H. 319 (1851).

[25] *Id.*

or unless it is proved to be an advancement by some acknowledgment signed by the party receiving it.

RSA 561:15 also provides, in substance, that any deed of lands or tenements, made by a person in consideration of love or affection, to one who shall become his heir, shall be deemed and taken, if the grantor shall die intestate, to be an advancement of the share of such heir. *Comings v. Wellman.*[26] Where a deed recited that the only consideration was love and affection, but in fact part of the consideration was for the present support of the grantors, it was held that the deed did not show an advancement.[27]

RSA 561:16 defines three distinct modes of proving an advancement of personal property.[28] No personal property delivered shall be deemed an advancement unless proved to be such by an acknowledgment in writing, signed by the party receiving it, or by some charge or memorandum thereof in writing, made by the deceased or by his order, or unless delivered expressly as an advancement, in the presence of two witnesses who were requested to take notice thereof.

No particular form of words is required but it must appear that the money paid or property delivered was not paid as a loan or gift. *Cass v. Brown.*[29] It must appear that the money or property was intended as an advancement towards the child's future share of his father's estate.[30] The memorandum of the property transfer wherever and however made, or the entries of certain charges of property or money in a book, must not show a debt to be collected or paid, nor an absolute unconditional gift. Instead, the memorandum must convey to the parties interested the knowledge that a future adjustment and apportionment of the charges is intended upon settlement of the estate, as an advancement towards the final share of each child in the parent's estate.[31]

The law requires the intestate to express his intention to give an advancement in writing. No verbal evidence can be received showing subsequent parol declarations of the intestate.[32]

---

[26] Comings v. Wellman, 14 N.H. 287 (1843).

[27] *Id.*

[28] Fellows v. Little, 46 N.H. 27 (1865).

[29] Cass v. Brown, 68 N.H. 85, 44 A. 86 (1894).

[30] *Id.*

[31] Fellows v. Little, 46 N.H. 27 (1865).

[32] Fellows v. Little, 46 N.H. 27 (1865). See also Cass v. Brown, 68 N.H. 85, 44 A. 86 (1894).

Library References

Am Jur 2d Advancements § 68 et seq.

CJS Descent and Distribution § 108 et seq.

§ 38-5. Uniform Probate Code Provisions

Section 2-110 of the Uniform Probate Code provides a concise rule on advancements:

> If a person dies intestate as to all his estate, property which he gave in his lifetime to an heir is treated as an advancement against the latter's share of the estate only if declared in a contemporaneous writing by the decedent or acknowledged in writing by the heir to be an advancement. For this purpose, the property advanced is valued as of the time the heir came into possession or enjoyment of the property or as of the time of death of the decedent, whichever first occurs. If the recipient of the property fails to survive the decedent, the property is not taken into account in computing the intestate share to be received by the recipient's issue, unless the declaration or acknowledgment provides otherwise.

This section alters the common law relating to advancements by requiring written enclosure of the intent that an inter vivos gift be an advancement. Most inter vivos transfers today are intended to be absolute gifts or are carefully integrated into a total estate plan. If the donor intends that any transfer during lifetime be deducted from the donee's share of his estate, the donor may either execute a will so providing or, if he intends to die intestate, charge the gift as an advance by a writing within the present section.[33]

Library References

Am Jur 2d Advancements § 15

---

[33] Comment, Uniform Probate Code, § 110.

CHAPTER 39. ACCOUNTING

§ 39-1. Generally

An administrator, once appointed, must keep a record of his actions on behalf of the estate. These actions are reported to the judge and to interested parties annually when the administrator is required to file an account of his doings on behalf of the estate. This basic requirement is found in RSA 554:6 which requires the administrator to be accountable for all assets of the decedent's estate:

All assets, though not inventoried, shall be accounted for, and the administrator charged therewith in the account of administration.

The proper time and place to charge an administrator with property belonging to the estate, not inventoried or accounted for by him, is in the probate court on the settlement of his account.[1] If the heirs, or others interested, think anything which ought to be accounted for by the administrator has been omitted, the validity of their claim is first determined in the probate court.[2] If either party is dissatisfied with the decision of the probate court, he may appeal. Under the current appeal practice, a dissatisfied party may appeal questions of law only; the facts are determined by the probate judge.[3]

Aside from heirs, it was held in *Lisbon Savings Bank & Trust Co. v. Estate of Moulton*[4] that those who may require an accounting include a party who has obtained judgment for his claim as a creditor of the decedent. Such a creditor has the right to have the defendant executor cited into the probate court and ordered to settle his account.[5] Also, where testamentary trustees have assumed the execution of a trust, the settlor's executor, who occupies no fiduciary relation to the trust beneficiary, can be compelled to account by the trustees only.[6] In such a case, it is the rule that neither the trust beneficiary, nor his administrator, can compel an accounting.[7]

Since an administrator is not considered as having the trust to administer an estate until he has given bond under RSA 553:13[8] the judge of probate cannot settle an administrator's account until the administrator, if not excepted by the statute, has given such a bond.[9] Thus RSA 554:6 rendering an administrator accountable for assets[10] does not apply to an

---

[1] Hurlburt v. Wheeler, 40 N.H. 73 (1860).

[2] *Id.*

[3] See Chapter 13 *infra.*

[4] Lisbon Sav. Bank & Trust Co. v. Estate of Moulton, 91 N.H. 477, 22 A.2d 331 (1941).

[5] *Id.*

[6] Attwill v. Dole, 74 N.H. 300, 67 A. 403 (1907).

[7] *Id.*

[8] Tappan v. Tappan, 24 N.H. 400 (1852).

[9] *Id.*

[10] RSA 554:6.

executor *de son tort.*[11] Nor does it apply to an administrator who has been appointed by the judge of probate but who has not given bond.[12]

A judgment of the probate court upon the administrator's account determines the amount, as between the administrator and the heirs, for which the administrator should then account. Although the decree is not conclusive as to matters subsequently arising between the administrator and third persons,[13] the decree of the probate court on an administrator's account binds parties and their successors in interest but will not bind a person who was not a party nor privy to the settlement, who was not notified and who had no opportunity to appear.[14]

Where an administrator has died without filing an account, it is the duty of his own administrator to file an account for the original estate. *Weston v. Second Orthodox Congregational Society.*[15]

Library References

Am Jur 2d Executors and Administrators § 960 et seq.

CJS Executors and Administrators § 827 et seq.

§ 39-2. Jurisdiction

The probate court has original jurisdiction over the settlement of administration accounts,[16] and must decide how much an administrator is to be charged with on his account.[17] The superior court has no power to require an administrator to account for his administration upon a bill in equity or to revise proceedings in the probate court.[18] Until the settlement of the administrator's account, the probate court has entire jurisdiction of the necessary procedure.[19] The jurisdiction of the Supreme Court in such matters is simply appellate.[20]

---

[11] Brown v. Leavitt, 26 N.H. 493 (1853). See Chapter 29 *supra.*

[12] Davis v. Davis, 72 N.H. 326, 56 A. 747 (1903).

[13] Redington Hub Co. v. Putnam, 76 N.H. 336, 82 A. 715 (1912).

[14] Ham v. Ayers, 22 N.H. 412 (1851).

[15] Weston v. Second Orthodox Congregational Soc'y, 79 N.H. 245, 110 A. 137 (1919).

[16] Judge of Probate v. Lane, 51 N.H. 342 (1871).

[17] *Id.*

[18] Lisbon Sav. Bank & Trust Co. v. Estate of Moulton, 91 N.H. 477, 22 A.2d 331 (1941). But see RSA 556:22.

[19] Glover v. Baker, 76 N.H. 393, 83 A. 916 (1912).

[20] Judge of Probate v. Lane, 51 N.H. 342 (1871).

A probate accounting is settled upon equitable principles and since only the probate court has original jurisdiction over an accounting by an administrator or executor, the jurisdiction is as extensive and comprehensive as the superior court's equitable powers.[21]

Library References

Am Jur 2d Executors and Administrators §§ 960, 961

CJS Executors and Administrators §§ 839–841

§ 39-3. Form

RSA 554:25 requires every administrator to file an account of his administration:

> The account of the administrator, or the schedules filed therewith, shall contain an itemized account of every sum of money received and paid out by the administrator, with the date thereof and a statement of the source from which it was received or of the consideration for which it was paid.

The form of the annual accounting, AOC-001-003, entitled Executor's/Administrator's Accounting, was revised in 1999. It is the basic document by which the probate judge reviews the work of the administrator.

In an early case, *Allen v. Hubbard*,[22] it was held that an inadvertent omission in the settlement of an account may be corrected in a subsequent account, at any time before final settlement of the estate.

Library References

Am Jur 2d Executors and Administrators § 974

CJS Executors and Administrators § 882 et seq.

§ 39-4. Filing

RSA 554:26 requires an administrator to file an annual account of his administration:

> Every administrator and executor shall file in the probate office an annual account of administration, unless upon petition

---

[21] Lisbon Sav. Bank & Trust Co. v. Estate of Moulton, 91 N.H. 477, 22 A.2d 331 (1941).

[22] Allen v. Hubbard, 8 N.H. 487 (1837).

he is excused by the judge of probate; but in no event shall he be excused for a period longer than three years. Before giving notice to settle his final account, he shall file it in the probate office of the county where it is to be settled, and shall cause the fact of such filing to appear in the notice, and shall at the same time file a statement of the names and residences of the heirs, legatees, and beneficiaries, if known to him.

It is unusual now for an administrator to fail to file a final accounting, particularly since he will not be released from his surety bond without a certificate of settlement from the probate court. However, in the past, accounting procedures were not followed in many instances.[23] Often administrators failed to file accounts and many estates had been closed without an accounting. This often was due to the fact that the registry of probate did not keep track of due dates of accounts.[24] Consequently, in 1957, the Judicial Council recommended passage of RSA 548:5-a, which provides for an enforcement remedy against administrators who fail to file accounts.

The probate court enforcement authority is found in RSA 547:11, which provides that the probate "judge shall have power to enforce all orders and decrees made by him in the exercise of any authority or jurisdiction conferred upon him, and to punish contempts of his authority, as the superior court has in like cases;" and in RSA 547:11-a, which gives the probate court authority over a fiduciary's accounting. Under RSA 547:11-a, as amended effective January 1, 1997, an administrator who fails to file his account within ninety days after the required filing date (one year after date of appointment) the administrator is in default.[25] The register of probate is required to give notice of the default to the fiduciary by first class mail within ten days of the default.[26] If the fiduciary fails to file the account or to show good cause, the judge of probate is required to issue a citation to the fiduciary to appear before him. In such a case the fiduciary shall pay default and citation fees to the register of probate, pursuant to RSA 490:27.[27]

---

[23] 7th Report Judicial Council, p. 46 (1958).

[24] *Id.*

[25] RSA 548:5-a, I.

[26] *Id.*

[27] *Id.*

Library References

Am Jur 2d Executors and Administrators §§ 967, 968

CJS Executors and Administrators § 910

§ 39-5. Notice

Effective July 8, 1998, the legislature has provided for detailed notice to beneficiaries when an account in an estate or trust is filed as follows:

> 550:11 Accounts; Notice to Beneficiaries.

A person "Beneficially Interested" is defined in RSA 550:12 as follows:

> 550:12 Person Beneficially Interested Defined. A person is beneficially interested if the person is:

This statutory change alters current procedures in which beneficiaries are usually notified of the filing of the account by letter, but a copy of the account is not usually sent to each beneficiary. Under the prior procedure, the beneficiary was simply notified that a copy of the account was available from the court. When a copy of an account or inventory is sent out pursuant to RSA 550:11 a failure to object to the account or inventory will act as a waiver of the right to object to the account or inventory and the right to any further notice concerning any hearing on the account or inventory. Probate Court Administrative Order 98-06 (rescinded effective 8/1/01).

§ 39-6. Allowance of the Account

Accounts are approved or allowed or settled by the probate judge at a hearing, the nature of which must be given to all parties pursuant to the notice provisions of RSA 554:26.

There are two methods usually available to an administrator for establishing a hearing date for the allowance of an account. The first is to attend the regular session of the probate court at which the "account is returnable" (that is, advertised and with notice given) and to proceed to a hearing at that time at the regular session. If there is no contest of the account, this procedure usually works satisfactorily. However, a long wait for a hearing can arise since other court business sometimes takes precedence over account hearings at a regular session day. Also, if an interested party in the account shows up unexpectedly, most courts will not allow contested hearings on regular session days. As a result, another hearing date will need to be scheduled.

The second method for establishing a hearing date is to schedule a special session at a date later than the return date or to continue the account to a later regular session date. If no one appears at the advertised return date of the account, the account can be scheduled by the administrator at the later date. Special sessions are now held infrequently and are usually held at a specified time and take the form of a hearing conducted in chambers rather than in open court, without additional notice to anyone. If someone does appear on the return date (where the administrator has not appeared), a new hearing date will be established on a contested hearing calendar.

However, the practice in this regard varies widely from county to county and local rules should first be ascertained before relying upon the procedure used in another county. Indeed, the procedures for the allowance of accounts generally involve some of the greatest differences, county to county, than any other area of probate law.

The hearing concerning the account is most often conducted by the judge at the bench. However, some courts have more formal procedures than others. Whatever procedure is used, the administrator and his attorney will be questioned by the judge, who will review the account in their presence. At the conclusion of the hearing, the administrator will be put under oath by the judge, and he must swear to the accuracy of the account.

RSA 554:27 provides that the attendance of the administrator at the hearing on the account may be excused, at the discretion of the judge. In this situation, the account must be verified by the administrator before a notary or justice of the peace prior to the hearing. RSA 554:27. This rule applies to both resident and nonresident administrators. Rule 37 of the Probate Rules requires the attendance of all fiduciaries at hearings upon their accounts unless excused by the court.

Although the practice varies from court to court, the excused attendance of a person is usually easily obtainable in an uncontested case, upon a timely petition to the court.

Except in the smallest or simplest of estates, where the administrator is excused from attendance, the personal appearance of the attorney for the administrator will still be required to "present" the account for allowance, to answer any questions the court may have, and to produce documentation of any actions or transactions of the administrator.

In 1957, in order to strengthen the power of probate judges, particularly with reference to the conduct of administrators, RSA 547:11 was amended to provide that:

> Whenever it appears necessary to preserve or protect the assets of any estate, the judge, on application or upon his own motion, may impound the books, records and assets of any fiduciary or may enjoin the withdrawal of any moneys or deposits or transfers of any securities by any fiduciary, or may direct the temporary investment of the assets of any estate in securities approved by the judge or require them to be deposited in any bank or institution authorized to receive deposits.

Furthermore, in connection with an administrator's account, the probate court was authorized to require the administrator to produce the actual securities, cash or bank books or other documents relating to the investments of the estate. RSA 547:11-a. The probate court was given all the powers of an equity court to enforce its orders, including the specific powers to order an administrator to change investments or to replace monies which the administrator had improperly applied or disposed of. RSA 547:11-a.

Every probate court has different "house rules" concerning the extent required for providing documentation at the account hearing. To be safe, the probate practitioner should have available (and readily at-hand) copies of all checks, funeral bills (marked "paid"), and tax receipts.

It is often impossible to have a federal estate tax closing letter, showing that the taxes due the federal government have been paid at the time of the hearing for the final account. Most courts will allow the hearing to proceed and the account will be allowed contingent upon the later filing of the closing letter. In such a situation, in uncontested estates, a partial distribution can be made, subject to the caveat that the monies will have to be returned if the tax return is not accepted and more tax monies are required.

Probate Court Procedure Bulletin 1997-10 (Revised) (rescinded effective 8/1/01) which required a Proof of Balance has been superseded by

Probate Court Procedure Bulletin 1998-04 (rescinded effective 8/1/01), which substitutes a requirement for Proof of Assets documentation. Essentially, all requirements for Proof of Balance have been deleted in all cases. Procedure Bulletin 1998-04 (rescinded) implements new protection for a ward's finances and applies only to guardianships of minors under RSA 463, and guardianships and conservatorships of incapacitated persons under RSA 464-A. Proof of Assets documentation enables the probate court to verify that the assets comprising the reported "Balance in Hands of Fiduciary" on a guardianship or conservatorship account are established and maintained with sole ownership in the ward.

Fiduciaries shall either provide Proof of Assets documentation for all accounts (first, interim, amended, or final, including "first and final" or amended "first and final" accounts) in guardianships/conservatorships or personally appear in court at a hearing on the account. Such hearing shall be scheduled by the probate court. For each asset comprising the reported "Balance in Hands of Fiduciary," the fiduciary shall provide documentation that the ward has complete and sole ownership of the asset at the close of the current accounting period. For example, Proof of Assets documentation for savings, checking, certificates of deposit, or any other bank accounts, includes (but is not limited to) a photocopy of the current bank statement that shows the complete account title and ownership information.

Probate Court Procedure Bulletin 1998-04 further provides that the only Proof of Assets documentation required for personal property in a guardianship or conservatorship account is the inventory and account schedule, signed under oath. Probate courts shall retain Proof of Assets documentation in the case file with the account. It is not necessary to "image" the documentation, however.

Library References

Am Jur 2d Executors and Administrators § 558

CJS Executors and Administrators § 890

§ 39-7. Items Included in Account—In General

RSA 554:6 provides that all assets, even though not inventoried, shall be accounted for, and the administrator charged therewith in the account of administration.

It is the duty of an administrator to account for assets belonging to the estate.[28] An administrator's failure to account, after having been cited upon application by a creditor to appear before the judge of probate, and render an account, has been taken as an admission that there are sufficient assets to pay the debt due and judgment will be rendered against the heirs in favor of a creditor.[29]

Library References

Am Jur 2d Executors and Administrators § 989 et seq.

CJS Executors and Administrators § 882

§ 39-7(a). Tangible Personal Property

RSA 554:7 relates to tangible personal property ("goods and chattels") and provides:

All goods and chattels shall be accounted for at the appraised value, unless sold at auction or private sale; and the administrator conducting the sale with fidelity and impartiality shall be credited with the loss, or charged with the gain, upon the sale.

Library References

Am Jur 2d Executors and Administrators § 974

CJS Executors and Administrators § 882

§ 39-7(b). Intangible Personal Property

On the other hand, intangibles such as stocks and bonds are to be accounted for "at the prices which they shall bring at a public or private sale." RSA 554:8.

Library References

Am Jur 2d Executors and Administrators § 974

CJS Executors and Administrators § 882

§ 39-7(c). Real Estate

If the estate is solvent, the real property of the decedent is not an asset of the estate to be accounted for in the estate and the administrator has

---

[28] Ross v. Eaton, 90 N.H. 271, 6 A.2d 762 (1939).

[29] See the discussion at Chapter 35 *supra*, on the issue of the administrator's duties as to the real estate of the decedent.

no duty to collect and account for the rents and profits arising from said real estate. RSA 554:15.[30]

Library References

Am Jur 2d Executors and Administrators § 974

CJS Executors and Administrators § 882

§ 39-7(d). Personal Articles

RSA 554:4 provides that certain articles need not be inventoried or accounted for since they are not considered assets:

> The wearing apparel of the widow and her ornaments, according to the estate of her husband, and the wearing apparel, Bibles and school books of the minor children, are their property, and shall not be regarded as assets, or be the subject of bequest by the husband.

Similarly, certain other personal or sentimental property need not be accounted for:

> The wearing apparel, Bibles, family pictures, photographs, albums and any other personal trinkets of sentimental rather than intrinsic value belonging to the deceased leaving a widow, husband, children or heirs surviving, shall not be inventoried or accounted for, but shall be delivered by the administrator to the surviving husband or wife, if any, otherwise shall be divided by him among the children or, if there are no surviving children, among the heirs; but the same may be otherwise disposed of by will. RSA 554:5.

Library References

Am Jur 2d Executors and Administrators § 974

CJS Executors and Administrators § 882

§ 39-7(e). Debts Due the Estate

RSA 554:11 provides that the administrator is required to collect and account for all debts due to the decedent "which by due diligence might have been collected, shall be accounted for in money."

---

[30] Gookin v. Hoit, 3 N.H. 392 (1826). See Chapter 35, "Real Estate" *supra*.

However, some relief from this duty is found at RSA 554:13 which provides that:

> The judge may license an administrator to sell at auction or private sale any accounts or evidences of debt which, in his opinion, cannot be collected within a reasonable time by the exercise of due diligence; and, for such accounts and evidences of debt, the administrator shall be charged only with the proceeds of the sale if he conducts it with fidelity and impartiality.

In *In re Estate of Ward*,[31] the Supreme Court took a very broad and expansive view as to what is or is not a debt. The question can be very important because if a matter can be defined as a debt, it becomes an asset of the estate, subject to probate court jurisdiction. In the *Ward* case, the Court recognized that "[a]lthough our probate statutes do not define debt," "no automatic or mechanical test exists for determining what is or is not a debt."[32] The Court rejected a definition of a debt as "fixed, liquidated amounts created by contract."[33] The Court took a broad view of the concept of debt and held that monies which the defendant administrator had misappropriated from the decedent prior to her death were accountable by the administrator as debts to the estate. Furthermore, attorney's fees improperly charged to the decedent prior to her death were held to be debts due the estate. The Court held that these matters "involve probate court jurisdiction over fiduciary accountings for estate assets" and confirmed that the probate court had authority to order the administrator to repay these amounts to the estate.[34]

Library References

Am Jur 2d Executors and Administrators § 974

CJS Executors and Administrators § 882

§ 39-7(f). Debt of Administrator to Estate

The debt of an administrator to an estate must be treated very carefully. It is a frequent source of conflict in the administration of estates and the probate attorney must be sensitive to the problems raised in this area.

---

[31] In re Estate of Ward, 129 N.H. 4, 523 A.2d 28 (1986).

[32] In re Estate of Ward, 129 N.H. 4, 9, 523 A.2d 28, 32 (1986).

[33] In re Estate of Ward, 129 N.H. 4, 8, 523 A.2d 28, 32 (1986).

[34] In re Estate of Ward, 129 N.H. 4, 5–6, 523 A.2d 28, 33 (1986).

A debt from an administrator to an estate is an asset of the estate for which the administrator must account:

> If such debt is specifically bequeathed to him his right thereto shall be the same as that of any legatee; and the judge, after due notice, shall liquidate and adjust all debts and claims due to the administrator, or from him to the estate. RSA 554:14

This statute creates a very strict obligation on the part of an administrator who is indebted to the estate. He must proceed with great caution in these circumstances. The statute requires that debts due from the administrator to the estate are assets to be accounted for as any other debt. If such a debt is specifically bequeathed to the administrator, he has the same right to take the bequest as that of any legatee. The judge, after due notice, has the power to liquidate and adjust all debts and claims due to the administrator, or from him to the estate.

The purpose of the statute was to abolish the common law rule that, except as against creditors, an executor's indebtedness to his decedent's estate was released or extinguished. *Judge of Probate v. Sulloway.* [35] The *Sulloway* Court also held that the judge of probate cannot release an executor from his debt due the estate on the mere ground that he is unable to perform it. [36] Thus the judge or probate has only the power to determine whether the debt exists, and the extent of it, and there his authority ends. [37]

Neither the administrator nor the probate judge has any authority to compromise the debt due from an administrator to an estate:

> It is true, that [RSA 554:12] provides that a debt due from an insolvent person may be compromised and discharged on payment of such part thereof as the administrator deems proper, and the administrator shall be chargeable only for the amount received, and that [RSA 554:14] provides that the judge of probate shall liquidate and adjust all debts and claims due to the administrator, or from him to the estate. It will not be claimed that by force of [RSA 554:12] the administrator can compromise a claim against himself; and in [RSA 554:14] we

---

[35] Judge of Probate v. Sulloway, 68 N.H. 511, 44 A. 720 (1896).

[36] Judge of Probate v. Sulloway, 68 N.H. 511, 515, 44 A. 720, 721 (1896).

[37] *Id.*

think the words "liquidate and adjust" mean the same as "find or ascertain" what is due from and to the administrator, where there is a controversy as to whether there be such debt, or as to the amount, or as to the facts and circumstances attending the debt or claim. If the legislature had intended to give the judge power to compromise a claim against the administrator in case of his inability to pay in full, they would most probably have used such language as would have left no doubt upon the subject.[38]

The reason for this very strict rule is the danger of fraud in such circumstances:

If the debt is admitted or found, the judge of probate has no choice—he must charge it to the executor as a part of the assets belonging to the estate. This duty is imperative. He cannot authorize the executor to compromise with himself, nor has he any authority to negotiate and compromise with the executor. . . . It is wise that such be the law. If it were otherwise, it would open a wide door to fraud.[39]

The debt of an administrator to an estate is treated as an asset.[40] It makes no difference whether the administrator was solvent or insolvent at the time of his appointment.[41] If the administrator is solvent, he must be charged with the amount of his note as assets in his hands belonging to the estate, and his sureties will be held liable. *Yeaton v. Skillings.*[42] If the administrator is insolvent, he is equally chargeable.[43] The same rule as to absolute chargeability for his debt applies to other fiduciaries, such as conservators. *Yeaton v. Skillings.*[44]

---

[38] Norris v. Towle, 54 N.H. 290, 294–95 (1874). See Judge of Probate v. Sulloway, 68 N.H. 511, 44 A. 720 (1896).

[39] Judge of Probate v. Sulloway, 68 N.H. 511, 515, 44 A. 720, 721 (1896).

[40] Judge of Probate v. Sulloway, 68 N.H. 511, 44 A. 720 (1896); Norris v. Towle, 54 N.H. 290 (1874).

[41] Yeaton v. Skillings, 103 N.H. 352, 172 A.2d 534 (1961).

[42] Yeaton v. Skillings, 103 N.H. 352, 172 A.2d 534 (1961); Judge of Probate v. Sulloway, 68 N.H. 511, 44 A. 720 (1896).

[43] Judge of Probate v. Sulloway, 68 N.H. 511, 44 A. 720 (1896); Norris v. Towle, 54 N.H. 290 (1874).

[44] Yeaton v. Skillings, 103 N.H. 352, 172 A.2d 534 (1961).

Furthermore, as *In re Estate of Ward*[45] makes clear, an administrator may be found indebted to the estate under RSA 554:14 for funds wrongfully misappropriated from the decedent during her lifetime, and for legal services improperly charged the decedent during her lifetime. Moreover, the probate court may charge interest against the administrator on the funds wrongfully misappropriated.[46]

Library References

Am Jur 2d Executors and Administrators § 495

CJS Executors and Administrators § 100

§ 39-8. Claims by an Administrator Against an Estate—In General

Closely related to the issue of the debt of an administrator to an estate, discussed above, is the issue of a debt from an estate to an administrator. The two situations are often confused, but the differences need to be kept clearly in mind since the legal consequences of each differ markedly.

A debt of an administrator to an estate is an asset of the estate and must be accounted for as such. A debt from the estate due to an administrator is a liability of the estate which must be specifically included in the administrator's accounting, and in the notice thereof.

A debt due from an estate to an administrator is commonly referred to as a "private claim" of an administrator against an estate. The probate court has a special rule applying to the accounting for such claims, Probate Court Rule 35:

> No private claim of an administrator, executor, trustee, guardian or conservator of an estate shall be allowed in his account or otherwise, unless particularly stated in writing, and notice of such claim included in the notice on said account, or given on petition for allowance of such claim.

If a private claim is stated in an account, the heading of the account shall include the words "and private claim of" to assure its inclusion in the notice on the account.

---

[45] In re Estate of Ward, 129 N.H. 4, 523 A.2d 28 (1986).

[46] *Id.*

The reason behind this rule is the danger of fraud which can occur when the administrator is at the same time the one who is pressing the claim against the estate and the one who is charged with defending the estate. As a result, probate courts look with great disapproval on a failure to comply with Rule 35 and attorneys and administrators should proceed cautiously in this area.

In the case of *In re Estate of Crowley*,[47] a failure to comply with these rules was sufficient cause to remove an administrator from his trust where he paid a debt to himself without notice or approval of the court:

> . . . it is clear that in paying the "debt" owing to his own corporation out of the assets of the estate, without complying with procedure outlined in Probate Court Rule 35, the executor misappropriated assets of the estate. Certainly misappropriation falls within the common law meaning of waste. There was considerable controversy as to the nature of the "claim" which the executor unilaterally paid to the corporation of which he was a substantial shareholder. Such apparent self-dealing on the part of Raymond Crowley was inconsistent with his role as an executor.[48]

As the *Crowley* case makes clear, the private claim rule applies not only to claims of the administrator himself but will be broadly interpreted to include claims of a wholly or partially owned closely held corporation of the administrator. In *Crowley*, the evidence was that the administrator was only a fifty percent owner of the corporation to whom payment from the estate was made of an "open account indebtedness for cash advances to or for the account of" the decedent.[49] However, the Court found that the fifty percent owned corporation's claim was a private claim of the administrator himself and compliance with the private claim rule was required.

Furthermore, an administrator who has misappropriated funds of the decedent during his lifetime, is indebted to the estate and "the probate judge would most assuredly possess the jurisdictional capacity to force

---

[47] In re Estate of Crowley, 129 N.H. 557, 529 A.2d 960 (1987).

[48] In re Estate of Crowley, 129 N.H. 557, 560, 529 A.2d 960, 962 (1987).

[49] *Id.*

[the administrator] to account for the income as 'debt[s] due from the administrator to the estate . . . .' RSA 554:14." *In re Estate of Ward.*[50]

§ 39-8(a). Liquidation or Adjustment of Private Claims

An administrator cannot adjudicate his own claim against the estate since an "administrator claiming adversely to the estate cannot at the same time represent the estate." *Rollins v. Rollins.*[51] Unless some relief provision were made, creditors of the estate would be barred from serving as administrators of estates. However, the problem is solved by RSA 554:14 which provides "the [probate] judge, after due notice, shall liquidate and adjust all claims due to the administrator." By this statute an administrator cannot himself authorize payment of a claim he may have against the estate. This is the responsibility of the probate judge.

Any liquidation or adjustment of an administrator's private claim must be made only "after due notice" to the beneficiaries and others interested in the estate. RSA 554:14.

Although RSA 554:14 gives the probate judge the power to "liquidate and adjust all debts and claims due to the administrator," these terms in this same statute have been held not to include the power to compromise a debt of the administrator to the estate. *Norris v. Towle.*[52] "If [the rule] were otherwise, it would open a wide door to fraud." *Judge of Probate v. Sulloway.*[53] Unlike a debt of an administrator to an estate, a judge of probate may "adjust" a claim of an administrator against an estate of which he is administrator. In *Rollins v. Rollins,*[54] an administrator had incorrectly inventoried a bank deposit as assets of the decedent whereas in fact one-third of the deposit belonged to the administrator. The Supreme Court described the administrator's claim of ownership of one-third of the fund as "a claim against" the estate and held that "[p]roper notice having been given, the plaintiff's [administrator's] contention will be adjusted in the settlement of her administration account."[55]

---

[50] In re Estate of Ward, 129 N.H. 4, 8, 523 A.2d 28, 32 (1986).

[51] Rollins v. Rollins, 77 N.H. 385, 386, 92 A. 339, 341 (1914).

[52] Norris v. Towle, 54 N.H. 290 (1874).

[53] Judge of Probate v. Sulloway, 68 N.H. 511, 44 A. 720 (1896).

[54] Rollins v. Rollins, 77 N.H. 385, 52 A. 339 (1914).

[55] Rollins v. Rollins, 77 N.H. 385, 386, 52 A. 339, 339 (1914).

In *Perkins v. Perkins*,[56] it was held to be improper for a probate judge to refer the contested private claim of an administrator to an arbitration panel as provided in insolvency cases, the Court holding that "[i]t is the duty of the judge of probate to examine and adjust the private personal claim of the administrator."[57]

Previously, it had been held that an administrator could not testify in support of his own claim against the estate he was in charge of administering.[58] As a result, an administrator's private claim against an estate will be disallowed where the only evidence to support the claim is the administrator's own testimony.[59] This rule has been altered somewhat by the passage of the "dead man's statute," RSA 516:25, which permits, as an exception to the hearsay rule, the introduction of oral or written statements of the decedent in any proceeding by or against the personal representative of the decedent, provided the trial judge shall find that (1) the statement was made by the decedent, (2) was made in good faith and (3) was made in the decedent's personal knowledge. This statutory rule is now embodied in the New Hampshire Rules of Evidence as Rule 804(b)(5).

Although not directly applicable to the situation where the administrator seeks to testify in support of his private claim, the dead man's statute does provide the administrator with more latitude in proving his claim.

As to the effect of the statute of limitations upon private claims of an administrator against his estate, it has been held that where a creditor of an estate has been appointed administrator, he may waive the general statute of limitations as to his private claim. *Preston v. Cutter*.[60] However, an administrator may be estopped by his own inaction from collecting amounts due him from the estate where he has failed for many years to pay himself his debt from assets available to him.

Library References

Am Jur 2d Executors and Administrators § 612

CJS Executors and Administrators § 390

---

[56] Perkins v. Perkins, 58 N.H. 405 (1878).

[57] Perkins v. Perkins, 58 N.H. 405, 406 (1878).

[58] *Id.*

[59] *Id.*

[60] Preston v. Cutter, 64 N.H. 461, 13 A. 874 (1888). See also McLaughlin v. Newton, 53 N.H. 531 (1873).

§ 39-8(b). Uniform Probate Code Provisions

The Uniform Probate Code, in accordance with its liberal approach, does not contain any provision for dealing specifically with claims of administrators against his estate, or with debts of the estate to the administrator. Section 3-713 provides that as to "any transaction which is affected by a substantial conflict of interest on the part of the personal representative" is "voidable by any person interested in the estate" unless the transaction has been approved by the Court after notice to interested persons.

However, unless someone raises the issue, an administrator's personal claim running to or from his estate is handled under the very informal accounting procedures of the Code. §§ 3-1001 to 3-1003.

Library References

Am Jur 2d Executors and Administrators §§ 488, 604

§ 39-9. Private Accounting

Where the heirs of an estate, provided they are of legal age and capacity, undertake to settle the estate between themselves, without administration, the courts will endeavor to enforce those agreements.[61] If the heirs have adjusted and settled the estate, without mistake or fraud, with each taking his agreed share and giving the others a discharge, and all the demands against the estate are settled, a subsequently-appointed administrator, even if he is not an heir, will not be allowed to undo the arrangement.[62] In *Deschenes v. Estate of Deschenes*,[63] the Supreme Court observed that "[i]nformal agreements between the heirs to an estate relating to the administration of an estate or the settlement of the account have always been recognized by our courts."[64]

The rule is different where an informal settlement is made after an administration has been established. The distinction is that in the first class of cases, all the parties interested settle an estate without resort to the forms of law, and such a settlement, fairly and understandingly made, should be binding. *Clarke v. Clay*.[65] In the other class, the legal course

---

[61] Clarke v. Clay, 31 N.H. 393 (1855).

[62] Hibbard v. Kent, 15 N.H. 516 (1844).

[63] Deschenes v. Estate of Deschenes, 109 N.H. 389, 254 A.2d 278 (1969).

[64] Deschenes v. Estate of Deschenes, 109 N.H. 389, 391, 254 A.2d 278, 280 (1969).

[65] Clarke v. Clay, 31 N.H. 393 (1855).

is taken, a bond is given, and the estate is placed in the hands of the judge of probate for settlement. Thus, it is for the judge to say whether he will be governed by what the parties do or not.[66] If he is satisfied that a fair and honest settlement has been made, without deception or overreaching in any way, he can approve the settlement. But, if for any good cause, he thinks that the account should be fully examined, it is within his discretion so to say.[67]

If any person interested in the estate is aggrieved by a discharge between an executor under a will and the legatees he may require further administration upon application therefor to the probate court.[68] Where administration is taken, or a guardian appointed over a ward, and a settlement is made with the administrator or guardian, such settlement will not be conclusive upon the parties, but will be evidence for the consideration of the court in deciding whether a further settlement shall be ordered or the accounts examined.[69]

Library References

Am Jur 2d Executors and Administrators § 979

CJS Executors and Administrators § 830

§ 39-10. Accounting Between Co-Administrators or Between an Administrator and a Guardian

RSA 556:22, provides that a joint administrator or guardian may have an action of account or assumpsit against the other administrator or guardian who refuses to apply the estate in his hands to the discharge of the just demands against the estate, or who refuses to account therefor. The petitioning administrator may recover against his co-administrator the amount to which he is entitled.

An examination of the history and development of statutory probate law in this state shows that there never has been a time when the probate court had exclusive jurisdiction over controversies between co-executors. *Patten v. Patten.*[70] The *Patten* case, the leading decision in this area, discusses the history of RSA 556:22, illustrating that its provisions have

---

[66] *Id.*

[67] *Id.*

[68] Wentworth v. Wentworth, 75 N.H. 547, 78 A. 646 (1910).

[69] Clarke v. Clay, 31 N.H. 393 (1855).

[70] Patten v. Patten, 79 N.H. 388, 109 A. 415 (1920).

been broadened from time to time.[71] Originally, an act permitting a co-executor to recover his share as residuary legatee, this statute has been extended to include all claims of executors, administrators and guardians to possess the estate against their co-fiduciaries.[72] A proceeding under the statute, however, is not a proceeding to settle the estate as between the executors and those interested in the estate, but rather it is one between the two fiduciaries as such.[73]

The manifest intent of RSA 556:22 is to give to a co-executor a direct and efficient remedy against his delinquent associate. The remedy is not dependent upon a prior adjudication by the probate court, rather it accrues whenever the delinquent administrator has in his hands any part of the estate which he refuses to pay out as he should or refuses to account for.[74] To maintain this proceeding it is only necessary to show a refusal to administer the estate according to law in one of the particulars necessary; there is no need for a citation to account and a failure to comply therewith as prerequisites for the action.[75] The suit is not one to compel the delinquent administrator to settle in the probate court, but rather to compel him to pay over to his co-executor so that the latter may administer the estate.[76]

Under RSA 556:22, the plaintiff is entitled to recover the amount of the estate "to which he shall be entitled," that is, all the unadministered estate in the defendant's hands to which he has no personal claim.[77]

Library References

Executors and Administrators 123 et seq.
Am Jur 2d Executors and Administrators § 1104
CJS Executors and Administrators §§ 1041, 1042

§ 39-11.   Reopening an Account

The power of the probate court in this state to reopen a fiduciary's account for good cause shown was established at an early date.[78] Good

---

[71] Id.

[72] Id.

[73] Id.

[74] Id.

[75] Id.

[76] Id.

[77] Id.

[78] Massachusetts Bonding & Ins. Co. v. Keefe, 100 N.H. 361, 127 A.2d 266 (1956).

cause may consist of fraud, misrepresentation, self-dealing by the fiduciary, mistake, or any combination of these.[79]

If there has been a manifest mistake in an account settled in the probate court, it is acceptable for the judge, at any time before a final settlement of the estate, to correct it in a subsequent account, provided there does not appear to have been a particular adjudication on that subject in the record.[80] This does not mean that the mistake or error complained of should necessarily appear from the records of the probate court, for very seldom would the records themselves show it, especially where the conduct of the administrator was fraudulent. *Flanders v. Lane.*[81] When an heir or other person interested comes before the court and complains that the administrator neglected, either purposely or by accident, to charge himself with a certain sum, and the court, upon turning to the record, finds that it does not show that the error complained of was considered and adjudicated, the complainant is entitled to have the administrator called in for the purpose of correcting it if the matter complained of is established.[82]

If the record shows the matter complained of was considered and adjudicated and the time for appeal has elapsed, the complainant has no remedy, but if the record does not show that it was considered, the complainant is entitled to a hearing before the probate court.[83]

As the petition to reopen the decree is decided upon equitable grounds, in the correction of errors the court will not be confined to those of which the petitioners complain. *Scammon v. Pearson.*[84] Errors in their favor will equally be open for adjustment, for it would be manifestly inequitable to correct one error and leave standing another which may have balanced it.[85]

It is not error for a court to refuse to reopen an administrator's account due to a finding of laches.[86] However, if the petition is brought within

---

[79] *Id.*

[80] Stark v. Gamble, 43 N.H. 465 (1862).

[81] Flanders v. Lane, 54 N.H. 390 (1874).

[82] *Id.*

[83] *Id.*

[84] Scammon v. Pearson, 80 N.H. 122, 113 A. 771 (1921).

[85] *Id.*

[86] Wellington v. Wellington, 88 N.H. 482, 192 A. 153 (1937).

a reasonable time under the circumstances of the case it will be allowed.[87] The issue of laches is primarily one of fact. *Wellington v. Wellington.*[88]

Library References

Am Jur 2d Executors and Administrators § 1128 et seq.

CJS Executors and Administrators § 912 et seq.

§ 39-12. Uniform Principal and Income Act

After less than two years in existence, the Uniform Principal and Income Act, adopted effective June 27, 1990, was repealed, effective May 18, 1992. Although no longer in effect in New Hampshire, the Uniform Act is a helpful tool in answering questions which may arise in the allocation of expenses between income and principal.

In brief, the Act provides that the settlor's intent is the guiding principle which should control the disposition of income. Where that intent is unknown or unclear, the Act attempts to establish clear and uniform standards to be followed in the allocation of receipts and expenses between the income and principal of trusts and estates, as well as provide a mechanism for determining the rights of income beneficiaries and remainder beneficiaries.[89]

Forms

See Form 001 of Appendix for a Executor's/Administrator's Accounting.

See Form 096 of Appendix for a Motion for Extension of Time.

---

[87] Massachusetts Bonding & Ins. Co. v. Keefe, 100 N.H. 361, 127 A.2d 266 (1956).

[88] Wellington v. Wellington, 88 N.H. 482, 192 A. 153 (1937).

[89] Uniform Principal and Income Act, Revised 1962, U.L.A., Prefatory Note.

CHAPTER 40. UNIFORM TRANSFER ON DEATH SECURITY REGISTRATION ACT

---

§ 40-1. Introduction

Effective January 1, 1998, the legislature adopted the Uniform Transfer on Death (TOD) Security Registration Act, as RSA 563-C. This Uniform Act is also a part of the Uniform Probate Code as §§ 6-301-311.

§ 40-2. Generally

In a prefatory note to the Act, the National Conference of Commissioners on Uniform State Law made clear that the purpose of the Act is to allow the creation of "Totten Trusts" as to securities:

> The purpose of the Act is to allow the owner of securities to register the title in transfer-on-death (TOD) form. Mutual fund shares and accounts maintained by brokers and others to reflect a customer's holdings of securities (so-called "street accounts") are also covered. The legislation enables an issuer, transfer agent, broker or other such intermediary to transfer the securities directly to the designated transferee on the owner's death. Thus, TOD registration achieves for securities a certain parity with existing TOD and pay-on-death (POD) facilities for bank deposits and other assets passing at death outside the probate process.

> The TOD registration under this Act is designed to give the owner of securities who wishes to arrange for a non-probate transfer at death an alternative to the frequently troublesome joint tenancy form of title. Because joint tenancy registration of securities normally entails a sharing of lifetime entitlement

and control, it works satisfactorily only so long as the co-owners cooperate. Difficulties arise when co-owners fall into disagreement, or when one becomes afflicted or insolvent.

A security is registered in beneficiary form when the certificate contains the words "transfer-on-death" or the abbreviation "TOD", or by words "pay-on-death" or by the abbreviation "POD", after the name of the registered owner and before the name of a beneficiary.[1]

The Act makes clear that designation of a TOD beneficiary on a registration "has no effect on ownership until the owner's death."[2] The owner may cancel or change the registration at any time without the consent of the beneficiary.[3] However, on the death of the sole owner or the last to die of all the multiple owners, "ownership of securities registered in beneficiary form passes to the beneficiary or beneficiaries who survive all owners" without the necessity of probate.[4]

The Act specifically provides that a security may be registered in beneficiary form if the form is authorized by a similar statute of the state of organization of the issuer, by the state of the registering entity, by the state of the location of the registering agent's principal office, by the state of the office of the transfer agent or its office making the registration, or by a similar statute of the law of the state listed as the owner's address at the time of registration.[5]

---

[1] RSA 563-C:6.

[2] RSA 563-C:7.

[3] *Id.*

[4] RSA 563-C:8.

[5] RSA 563-C:3.

CHAPTER 41. EXHIBITION OF CLAIM AND DEMAND FOR PAYMENT

§ 41-1. Demand Generally

RSA 556:1 requires that before an action against an administrator can be commenced, it is first necessary to present the claim to the administrator and to demand payment. Unless the claim is properly exhibited and demand for payment made, the creditor is barred from bringing suit to recover his claim.[6] This statute is often referred to as the non-claim statute.[7]

The demand requirement applies to claims by legatees, heirs or creditors which are brought against the estate.[8] RSA 556:1 also applies to tort claims and to all claims involving a trust relationship.[9] In *W. A.*

---

[6] The constitutionality of this statute has been called into question by virtue of the United States Supreme Court decision in Tulsa Professional Collection Services v. Pope, 108 S. Ct. 1340, 99 L. Ed. 2d 565, 485 U.S. 478 (1988), where the Court overturned on constitutional grounds an Oklahoma statutory scheme very similar to the New Hampshire non-claim statute. See Cass v. Ray, 131 N.H. 550, 556 A.2d 1180 (1989) and Stewart v. Farrell, 131 N.H. 458, 554 A.2d 1286 (1989).

[7] Lunderville v. Morse, 112 N.H. 6, 7, 287 A.2d 612, 613 (1972).

[8] Frost v. Frost, 100 N.H. 326, 125 A.2d 656 (1956).

[9] Vanni v. Cloutier, 100 N.H. 272, 124 A.2d 204 (1956). See also *Preparation and Trial of a Tort Action in New Hampshire*, 2 N.H.B.J. 11, 16 (1959).

Emerson's Sons, Inc. v. Cloutman, it was held that the "rule also applies to unaccrued and contingent demands."[10]

Library References

Am Jur 2d Executors and Administrators § 596 et seq.

CJS Executors and Administrators § 394 et seq.

§ 41-2. Purpose

In *Saurman v. Liberty*[11] the Supreme Court set forth the purpose of the six-month demand statute as follows:

The policy of RSA 556:1 is to ensure the orderly and expeditious presentation of claims and settlement of estate. The purpose of the six-month rule is not to deprive creditors of their rights but to allow the administrator a sufficient amount of time to examine the estate, to gather the assets, and to pay just claims and thus be spared from unnecessary suits.

In *Lunderville v. Morse*,[12] it was held that "the primary purpose of this section's exhibition and demand provision is to bring a claim to the attention of the administrator so that he make further inquiry into it with a view to its orderly and expeditious adjustment and settlement."[13]

Another purpose of RSA 556:3, stated in *Little v. Little*, is:

to bring the claim to the knowledge of the administrator, that he may be enabled to judge whether or not to apply for a decree of insolvency, and also that he may make enquiry into it with a view to furnish himself with the necessary information for its proper adjustment.[14]

Library References

Am Jur 2d Executors and Administrators § 597

---

[10] W. A. Emerson's Sons v. Cloutman, 88 N.H. 59, 61, 184 A. 609, 610 (1936).

[11] Saurman v. Liberty, 116 N.H. 73, 76, 354 A.2d 132, 134 (1976) (citations omitted). See American Policyholders Ins. Co. v. Baker, 119 N.H. 958, 409 A.2d 1346 (1979).

[12] Lunderville v. Morse, 112 N.H. 6, 287 A.2d 612 (1972).

[13] Lunderville v. Morse, 112 N.H. 6, 8, 287 A.2d 612, 614 (1972). See Coffey v. Bresnahan, 127 N.H. 687, 506 A.2d 310 (1986).

[14] Little v. Little, 36 N.H. 224 (1858).

CJS Executors and Administrators § 394

§ 41-3.　Time of Exhibition

RSA 556:3 establishes the time period for the demand to be presented to the administrator and payment demanded. Exhibition of the claim and demand for payment must be made within six months after the original grant of administration, exclusive of the time the administration may have been suspended.[15] It should be noted that the six-month period does not run from the date of death but from the date an administrator is appointed. Until 1959, the period of time for the exhibition of claims was one year.

A failure by an otherwise valid creditor to demand his claim within the statutory six-month period requires the administrator to reject payment if presented later. Indeed, the payment of a claim not properly presented under RSA 556:1–556:3, will make the administrator personally liable to beneficiaries who are affected by the payment.[16]

A failure to comply with the demand requirement of RSA 556:1–556:3 will operate to extinguish the claim unless an extension of time is granted to the plaintiff under the narrow provisions of RSA 556:28.[17] A finding of such a failure will not be set aside if supported by any competent evidence. *Vanni v. Cloutier.*[18]

RSA 556:3 states that demand must be exhibited to the administrator within six months of the original grant of administration, exclusive of time that administration may have been suspended. In *Cummings v. Farnham*,[19] the Court held that the demand must be exhibited within the statutory period, even where the right of action may have existed at the time of the decedent's death and may have survived him.

Library References

Am Jur 2d Executors and Administrators § 638

CJS Executors and Administrators § 406

---

[15] RSA 556:3. See RSA 21:35 which provides that in reckoning time, the date in which such act is done is excluded in making the computation; Prob. Ct. R. 1A.

[16] See 6 Bowe-Parker: Page on Wills § 51.12 (1962).

[17] W. A. Emerson's Sons v. Cloutman, 88 N.H. 59, 184 A. 609 (1936). See Lunderville v. Morse, 112 N.H. 6, 287 A.2d 612 (1972).

[18] Vanni v. Cloutier, 100 N.H. 272, 124 A.2d 656 (1956).

[19] Cummings v. Farnham, 75 N.H. 135, 71 A. 632 (1908).

§ 41-4. Exceptions

The requirement of RSA 556:1 does not apply where the claim is against the administrator personally, rather than in his capacity as representative of the estate, such as a claim for a breach of his duty as administrator.[20] Nor will the demand requirement apply where the claim is one in recoupment in an action brought by the administrator.[21] Where the claim is for personal property which the claimant alleges an ownership interest in, the bar of RSA 556:1–556:3 does not apply since "such a claim is against the defendant [as administrator] but not against the estate."[22]

Another notable exception to the demand requirement is for claims by the federal government.[23]

In *Judge of Probate v. Heydock*,[24] it was held, however, that the failure to exhibit a claim under RSA 556:3 will not discharge a surety.

Although the demand requirement of RSA 556:1 must be complied with under most circumstances, *McInnes v. Goldthwaite*,[25] held that the statute would not be applied to deprive the rights of legatees who are ignorant, of persons who are under a disability, or of beneficiaries of a charitable trust who are not adequately represented. In *Quigg v. Kittredge*,[26] it was held further that this section would not apply where the administrator is charged as trustee on a foreign attachment.

Library References

Am Jur 2d Executors and Administrators § 603 et seq.

CJS Executors and Administrators §§ 398–403

Late filing—just cause. 57 ALR2d 1304.

§ 41-5. Waiver and Estoppel

A demand which is insufficient in itself may be made sufficient by the conduct of the person on whom it is made.[27] For example, where

---

[20] Judge of Probate v. Lane, 51 N.H. 342 (1871).

[21] Stanley v. Clark, 159 F. Supp. 65 (D.N.H. 1957).

[22] Frost v. Frost, 100 N.H. 326, 125 A.2d 656 (1956).

[23] Reconstruction Fin. Corp. v. Faulkner, 100 N.H. 192, 122 A.2d 263 (1956).

[24] Judge of Probate v. Heydock, 8 N.H. 491 (1837).

[25] McInnes v. Goldthwaite, 94 N.H. 331, 52 A.2d 795 (1947).

[26] Quigg v. Kittredge, 18 N.H. 137 (1846).

[27] Town of Jaffrey v. Smith, 76 N.H. 168, 80 A. 504 (1911).

an executor has refused to pay a claim, he will be estopped from asserting the insufficiency of the demand.[28] While the administrator has a right to be informed of a creditor's claim, he may lose that right by denying liability in advance of the presentation of the claim.[29]

As the purpose of RSA 556:1 and 556:3 is to protect the administrator, the Court in *American Policyholders Insurance Co. v. Baker*,[30] held that this purpose will not be defeated by allowing a waiver of these sections by the administrator. Therefore, an administrator can waive the demand provisions of RSA 556:1 and 556:3. Such a waiver must be knowing, intelligent and voluntary, but may be implied from the conduct of the administrator.[31]

Objections to the form in which the claim is presented are deemed waived unless taken at the time of exhibition.[32] Demand may be waived by a denial of liability by the administrator.[33] However, the administrator will not lose the right to be informed of the amount of the claim by a failure to inquire as to the amount.[34] A waiver of the time limits of RSA 556:1 and 556:3 will not operate to extend the time during which the estate may be kept open,[35] therefore the administrator waives such demand at her own peril.[36]

Library References

Am Jur 2d Executors and Administrators §§ 600, 640

CJS Executors and Administrators § 424

---

[28] Town of Jaffrey v. Smith, 76 N.H. 168, 80 A. 504 (1911); Dewey v. Noyes, 76 N.H. 493, 84 A. 935 (1912).

[29] Frost v. Frost, 100 N.H. 326, 125 A.2d 656 (1956).

[30] American Policyholders Ins. Co. v. Baker, 119 N.H. 958, 409 A.2d 1346 (1979).

[31] Dewey v. Noyes, 76 N.H. 493, 84 A. 935 (1912). See Frost v. Frost, 100 N.H. 326, 125 A.2d 656 (1956).

[32] Town of Jaffrey v. Smith, 76 N.H. 168, 80 A. 504 (1911); Ross v. Knox, 71 N.H. 249, 51 A. 910 (1902).

[33] Dewey v. Noyes, 100 N.H. 493, 84 A. 935 (1912).

[34] Watson v. Carvelle, 82 N.H. 453, 136 A. 126 (1926).

[35] Town of Jaffrey v. Smith, 76 N.H. 168, 80 A. 504 (1911); Preston v. Cutter, 64 N.H. 461, 13 A. 874 (1888).

[36] Gookin v. Sanborn, 3 N.H. 491 (1826).

§ 41-6. Notice

Proof of notice of demand is a part of the plaintiff's case which must be affirmatively established at trial.[37] The safest way to make demand in a form sufficient for easy proof in a subsequent lawsuit is to follow the provisions of RSA 556:2, which states that a notice sent to the administrator or his agent by registered mail[38] which sets forth the nature and amount of the claim and makes a demand for payment will be deemed sufficient notice. This statute was held in *Watson v. Carvelle*,[39] to serve an evidentiary function, providing a conclusive substitute for other proof that such notice was received. If proof of receipt can be established by other means, the question of whether the notice was sent by registered mail becomes irrelevant. However, proof of mailing an unregistered notice will not suffice as proof of the receipt of such notice.[40]

The question of whether notice to a person other than the administrator is sufficient depends upon proof that the person to whom notice was given is an agent of the administrator, which is a question of fact.[41] The mere hiring of counsel to appear in an action does not in itself clothe the counsel with authority to receive claims against the administrator.[42] Counsel employed to act in settling an estate, on the other hand, may be clothed with such authority.[43]

Library References

Am Jur 2d Executors and Administrators § 659 et seq.

CJS Executors and Administrators § 410

§ 41-7. Form

There is no specific or required form for an exhibition of a claim. Indeed, in *Dewey v. Noyes*,[44] the Court held that a claim against an administrator may be made orally as well as in writing. Generally, a claim may be exhibited in any form which brings the nature and amount of

---

[37] Lunderville v. Morse, 112 N.H. 6, 287 A.2d 612 (1972).

[38] See RSA 21:32-c which defines registered mail to include certified mail.

[39] Watson v. Carvelle, 82 N.H. 453, 136 A. 126 (1926).

[40] *Id.*

[41] *Id.*

[42] *Id.*

[43] *Id.*

[44] Dewey v. Noyes, 76 N.H. 493, 84 A. 935 (1912).

the claim distinctly to the notice of the administrator,[45] and demand may be implied by the exhibition of the claim except where the amount of the claim is not stated.[46] If further clarification or itemization of a claim is required, the administrator can request it.[47]

However, although a claim is often made informally or even orally, this procedure is not recommended. RSA 554:24 provides that the administrator of an estate may require that any claim against the estate be exhibited under oath in statutory form stating that the affiant is making a true statement of the claim and is unaware of any credit or offset against the claim.[48]

In determining whether the purpose of RSA 556:3 has been fulfilled, questions of form and technicality are not determinative, rather the statute should be applied according to the substance and realities of the situation.[49] Minor errors such as stating an incorrect transaction date will not serve to defeat an otherwise valid exhibition of demand.[50] Similarly, where an administrator admits an amount to be due upon being called for payment, the transaction may be deemed to be the equivalent of an exhibition of demand.[51]

Although exhibition of demand must be affirmatively established as part of the plaintiff's case,[52] the exhibition need not be pleaded.[53] The exhibition of demand must be made as a prerequisite to maintaining the action, however, and it was held in *Libby v. Hutchinson*[54] that the plaintiff must prove exhibition in order to recover under the general issue. Furthermore, no recovery can be had on any other cause of action than that stated in the demand.[55]

---

[45] Tebbetts v. Tilton, 31 N.H. 273 (1855). See Lunderville v. Morse, 112 N.H. 6, 287 A.2d 614 (1972).

[46] Watson v. Carvelle, 82 N.H. 453, 136 A. 126 (1926).

[47] Lunderville v. Morse, 112 N.H. 6, 287 A.2d 614 (1972).

[48] Frost v. Frost, 100 N.H. 326, 125 A.2d 656 (1956).

[49] Hurd v. Varney, 83 N.H. 467, 144 A. 266 (1908).

[50] *Id.*

[51] Ayer v. Chadwick, 66 N.H. 385, 23 A. 428 (1891).

[52] Hurd v. Varney, 83 N.H. 467, 144 A. 266 (1908).

[53] Watson v. Carvelle, 82 N.H. 453, 136 A. 126 (1926).

[54] Libby v. Hutchinson, 72 N.H. 190, 55 A. 547 (1903).

[55] Hurd v. Varney, 83 N.H. 467, 144 A. 266 (1908)

§ 41-8. Contingent Demands

RSA 556:6 provides that demands which are not due or which depend upon a contingency may be filed in the probate court and that the judge may require the administrator to retain a sum to satisfy such claims unless the widow, heirs or legatees post a bond for the payment of the claims. Thus, although a claim is not due or is contingent, it is still capable of presentment[56] and may be barred if not presented or exhibited within the statutory period prescribed by RSA 556:3.[57]

While contingent claims fall within the scope of RSA 556:3, it is recognized that a creditor may be without fault in not anticipating a contingency or the amount of a claim when the contingency occurs. In *American University v. Forbes*[58] the Court held that if the creditor failed to seek retention of funds in the administrator's hands, RSA 556:6 will not bar recovery from heirs, devisees or legatees. Therefore, a creditor who could not prove a claim while the estate's assets were in the hands of the administrator would not be barred as against heirs and legatees,[59] although claims against the administrator may be barred.[60]

§ 41-9. Statutory Relief from Noncompliance with the Non-Claim Statute

RSA 556:28 provides an extension of time where a party has failed to comply with the non-claim statute and has failed to exhibit his claim

---

[56] Cutter v. Emery, 37 N.H. 567 (1859).

[57] Libby v. Hutchinson, 72 N.H. 190, 55 A. 547 (1903); Walker v. Cheever, 39 N.H. 420 (1859).

[58] American University v. Forbes, 88 N.H. 17, 183 A. 860 (1936).

[59] Libby v. Hutchinson, 72 N.H. 190, 55 A. 547 (1903); Walker v. Cheever, 39 N.H. 420 (1859).

[60] Hall v. Martin, 46 N.H. 337 (1865).

and demand payment from the administrator within six months of his appointment. RSA 556:28 requires a petition "to the court having subject matter jurisdiction over the nature of the claim" and applies when the claimant is not chargeable with "culpable neglect" and "justice and equity require" relief from compliance with the statutory provision.[61]

Formerly, RSA 556:28 required a petition to the superior court. The statute was amended in 1993 to take away the right of a person to move to extend time in the superior court if "such person [is] not under the exclusive jurisdiction of the probate court."[62] In 1995, this language was deleted.[63] Currently, RSA 556:28 allows the petition to be brought in a court having subject matter jurisdiction over the nature of the claim.

The particular conduct which will constitute culpable neglect is a question of fact for the trial court and like other findings of fact, it can be set aside on appeal only if it is unsupported by the evidence or is erroneous as a matter of law.[64]

For purposes of RSA 556:28, the Supreme Court has defined culpable neglect as being less than gross carelessness, but more than a failure to use ordinary care.[65] Culpable neglect is a want of watchfulness and diligence or the unreasonable inattention and inactivity of creditors who slumber on their rights.[66] It exists if no good reason, according to the standards of ordinary conduct, for the dormancy of the claim is found.[67] It is neglect which exists where the loss can fairly be ascribed to the creditor's own carelessness, improvidence, or folly.[68]

In *Stewart v. Farrell*,[69] the Supreme Court granted relief under RSA 556:28 to a plaintiff who filed suit within one year from the date of

---

[61] The ramifications of RSA 556:28 are discussed in Chapter 45 *infra*, in connection with the relief it also affords for noncompliance with the one-year deadline for bringing suit against an administrator.

[62] P.L., 1992, c. 284:71.

[63] P.L., 1995, c. 277:24.

[64] Cass v. Ray, 131 N.H. 550, 553, 556 A.2d 1180, 1181 (1989).

[65] *Id.*

[66] *Id.*

[67] *Id.*

[68] *Id.*

[69] Stewart v. Farrell, 131 N.H. 458, 554 A.2d 1286 (1989). The constitutionality of the six-month limitation has been questioned by the decision of the U.S. Supreme Court in Tulsa Professional Collection Services v. Pope, 108 S. Ct. 1340, 99 L. Ed. 2d 565, 485 U.S. 478 (1988).

appointment, but who failed to present his claim within the six-month period. The Court held that, where the claim was a tort claim and the failure to present a claim to the executors was due to the plaintiff's ignorance of the decedent tortfeasor's death, the public policy purpose of an individual's right to recover for personal injuries outweighed the policy in favor of the speedy settlement of estates. The Court held that the tort plaintiffs were not guilty of culpable neglect under RSA 556:28, and should be allowed to proceed with their claim. In *Koziell v. Fairbanks*,[70] the Supreme Court allowed the petition for an extension of time to bring an action against the executor of an estate even though the petition was filed one month after the one-year limitation period. The plaintiff, who had great difficulty understanding English, hired an attorney who did send notice of claim four months after the granting of letters. However, the attorney did not file an action within the one-year limitation period and he was suspended from the practice of law one month after the limitation period ran out. Since the plaintiff immediately hired a new attorney upon learning of the suspension, the court determined that justice and equity required the allowance of the petition for an extension, and that the claimant was not chargeable with culpable neglect.[71] However, a contrary result was reached by the Supreme Court in *Cass v. Ray*,[72] which overturned a superior court order granting an extension of time under an earlier version of RSA 556:28. The superior court order had been based on the fact that only a three month delay had occurred in filing suit and that the delay was caused by the attorney for the creditor who made the simple mistake of missing the deadline to file suit. The Supreme Court held that the attorney's failure was chargeable to the client under general principles of agency law and held that with respect to RSA 556:28, "a client may not generally have relief from the consequences of an attorney's negligent failure to meet deadlines and other procedural requirements."[73]

It has been held that RSA 556:28 does not grant the probate court authority to extend the time for the entry of suit beyond the one year limitations period of RSA 556:5. Where the plaintiff, having a choice to bring a bill in equity for constructive trust in the superior court, chose

---

[70] Koziell v. Fairbanks, 115 N.H. 679, 348 A.2d 358 (1975).

[71] *Id.*

[72] Cass v. Ray, 131 N.H. 550, 556 A.2d 1180 (1989).

[73] Cass v. Ray, 131 N.H. 550, 554, 556 A.2d 1180, 1182 (1989).

to bring his action in the probate court, the probate court had no authority to extend the time for entry of a suit beyond a one-year statute of limitations. *Keenan v. Keenan.*[74] According to *Keenan*, there is no saving statute for a claimant in the probate court who misses the one-year statute of limitations deadline.

Library References

Am Jur 2d Executors and Administrators §§ 625 et seq., 639

CJS Executors and Administrators § 408

Late filing—just cause. 57 ALR2d 1304.

Non-claim statutes—tort claims. 22 ALR3d 493.

---

[74] Keenan v. Keenan, Strafford County Probate Court, No. 93-00021 (1994), affirmed by order of the Supreme Court after oral argument, April 25, 1996, Supreme Court case no. 94-377.

CHAPTER 42. TORTIOUS OR INTENTIONAL INTERFERENCE WITH INHERITANCE OR GIFT

§ 42-1.   Introduction

Based on the Restatement of Torts (Second), a growing number of jurisdictions have recognized the tort of interference with inheritance and gift:

§ 774B. Intentional Interference with Inheritance or Gift.

One who by fraud, duress or other tortious means intentionally prevents another from receiving from a third person an inheritance or gift that he would otherwise have received is subject to liability to the other for loss of the inheritance or gift.[1]

The theory can be traced back to cases, such as *Mitchell v. Langley*,[2] where the plaintiff alleged a fraudulent transfer of an insurance policy beneficiary. As the tort of intentional interference with prospective

---

[1] *Restatement of Torts (Second)*, § 774(b) (1982).

[2] 85 S.E. 1050 (Ga. 1915).

contractual relationships began to be accepted in many states, the tort of intentional interference with inheritance has also begun to become more widely recognized as a viable cause of action.[3]

Interference with inheritance or gift cases usually fall into three categories; (1) interference with the execution, alteration or revocation of a will[4] ; (2) the suppression, spoliation, destruction, or loss of a will; and (3) deprivation of an inheritance by inducing an inter vivos transfer.[5] The cause of action, though similar to a will contest, is distinguishable from these probate actions. In an intentional interference of inheritance or gift the plaintiff can recover punitive and compensatory damages. Also, an action based on intentional interference with inheritance or gift is against the tortfeasor personally, not the estate. Therefore, a defendant would be required to pay his/her own attorney's fees and any punitive and/or compensatory damage awarded to the plaintiff. The estate is not responsible for these expenses.[6]

§ 42-2. New Hampshire Law

While New Hampshire has not yet recognized a claim of intentional or tortious interference with inheritance, there is no reason to believe that New Hampshire courts would not do so. For example, New Hampshire has recognized claims of tortious interference with contractual relationships. *See, Tamposi Associates, Inc. v. Star Market Co., Inc.,*[7] and *Baker v. Dennis Brown Realty.*[8]

In the only known New Hampshire case involving the tort of interference with an inheritance, *Bennett-Lane v. Bennett,*[9] the Hillsborough Superior Court, speaking through Judge Dalanis, did not address the issue

---

[3] *Intentional Interference With Inheritance,* 30 Real Prop. Prob. & Tr.J. 325.

[4] *Annotation, Rights and Remedies Against One Who Induces, Prevents or Interferes in the Making, Changing, or Revoking of a Will, or Holds the Fruits Thereof,* 11 ALR 2d. 808 (__).

[5] *Liability in Damages for Interference With Expected Inheritance or Gift,* 22 A.L.R. 4th 1229 (1983).

[6] *Tortious Interference With Expectancy,* 41 OCT Res Gestae 16.

[7] 119 N.H. 630 (1979).

[8] 121 N.H. 640 (1981).

[9] Docket 99-E-0184 (Hillsborough, 1999), citing Annotation, *Action for Tortious Interference With Bequest as Precluded by Will Contest Remedy,* 18 A.L.R. 5th 211, 224–27 (1994); Minton v. Sackett, 671 N.E.2d. 160, 162 (Ind. App. 1996).

directly, holding that such an action would be barred "where the remedy in the probate court would provide the injured party with adequate relief."[10]

§ 42-3. Elements

Under the provisions of the Restatement of Torts (Second), Section 774B, a plaintiff must prove the following: (1) the existence of an expectancy; and (2) intentional interference with the expectancy through the tortious conduct; and (3) causation; and, (4) damages.[11]

§ 42-3(a). Existence of an Expectancy

To satisfy the existence of an expectancy the plaintiff has to prove that the expectancy existed.[12] A major difficulty in meeting this test is that an individual is free to change the beneficiaries of his/her estate at any time as long as he/she is competent. Each jurisdiction has separate standards in which the plaintiff must prove an existence of the expectancy. In some jurisdiction, the plaintiff has to prove that steps were taken to perfect the inheritance or gift. The plaintiff can satisfy this element by showing his name was removed from a deed, life insurance policy, etc. The plaintiff can utilize revoked documents and any drafts to show intent.[13] Other states allow reliance on the intent.[14]

§ 42-3(b). Intentional Interference

It is a requirement of the tort that the plaintiff must prove that the defendant's conduct was intentional and with intent to harm the plaintiff. The tort focuses on the defendant's conduct. It is sometimes difficult to prove that the defendant's intention was to disinherit another individual. The plaintiff has the burden of proof to show that the defendant's intentional conduct is what prevented the plaintiff from inheriting. The plaintiff has to show either fraud, duress, undue influence, or abuse of a fiduciary duty to satisfy that the defendant conduct was tortious.[15]

---

[10] See *Annotation, Actions For Tortious Interference With Bequest As Precluded By Will Contest Remedy*, 18 ALR 5th 2ll, (1994).

[11] Morrill v. Morrill, 712 A.2d 1039, 1041 (Me. 1998); See Plimpton v. Gerrard, 668 A.2d 882, 885 (Me. 1995).

[12] *Intentional Interference With Inheritance*, 30 Real Prop. Prob. & Tr.J. 325.

[13] *Tortious Interference With An Expectancy*, 41 OCT Res Gestae 16.

[14] *Intentional Interference With Inheritance*, 30 Real Prop. Prob. & Tr. J. 325.

[15] *Id.*

§ 42-3(c). Causation

As in all tort cases, the "but for" standard applies in this cause of action. The plaintiff must prove that the defendant had knowledge of the inheritance or gift and but for the defendant's actions the plaintiff would have receive the bequest. The difficulty in proving this element is that the undue influence or duress is typically done in private and outside the presence of a third party.[16]

§ 42-3(d). Damages

Damages include the value of the inheritance or gift, which was lost due to the tortious conduct, and may include compensatory or punitive damages. Other remedies are available, such as constructive trust, restitution, or other equitable remedies. The difficulty in proving damages is that the tort addresses an expectancy, not a vested interest. Therefore, the damages have an aura of speculativeness.

§ 42-4.   Statute of Limitations

Jurisdictions differ on the application of special tolling rules for a tortious interference claim. Some jurisdictions, the statute of limitation applies only during the period in which the will can be contested. The reasoning is that the tort claim is a collateral attack on the legitimacy of the will. *See, Robinson v. First National Bank,*[17] *Cyr v. Cote,*[18] and *DeWitt v. Duce.*[19] The *Duce Case* upheld a finding by the lower court that the plaintiffs had a fair opportunity to pursue their claim in the Probate Court at the time of the testator's death and so was barred from bringing the action two years later.

Plaintiffs have argued that the will contest statute of limitation should not apply because the two causes of action are not mutually exclusive. A will contest is against the estate, and the tort is against the individual tortfeasor. Moreover, the remedies are not mutually exclusive. The plaintiff in a will contest will not recover punitive or compensatory damages.[20]

---

[16] *Id.*

[17] 454 N.E. 2d. 288, 294 (Ill. 1983).

[18] 396 A.2d. 1013 (Me. 1979).

[19] 675 F.2d. 670, 671 (Fla. 1982).

[20] *Intentional Interference With Inheritance*, 30 Real Prop. Prob. & Tr.J. 325.

§ 42-5. Burden of Proof

There are separate burdens of proof depending on the allegations. If the plaintiff alleges misconduct related to a multi-party account then the burden is on the plaintiff to prove by clear and convincing evidence that it was the intention of the testator to make a gift when the account was formed. If the claim is that a fiduciary or confidential relationship existed between the defendant and the testator, then the burden shifts to the defendant to rebut the presumption by clear and convincing evidence that there was no undue influence, that he acted in good faith, he did not take advantage of his position, and the transaction was fair and equitable. In all other matters the plaintiff bears the burden of proof by a preponderance of the evidence standard.[21]

§ 42-6. Commencing Action While The Testator Is Still Alive

At this point only two jurisdictions allow filing of a tortious interference claim prior to death of a testator, Florida and Maine. *See, Carlton v. Carlton*[22] and *Harmon v. Harmon.*[23]

The policy reasons for allowing suits during the lifetime of the testator is the availability of the testator to testify, availability of other witness, the possibility of the plaintiff never obtaining adequate relief and the plaintiff can seek immediate relief. A major obstacle to bringing suit during the lifetime of the testator is proof of damages. The damages are speculative, so the claim is not for the loss of property, but for the loss of the expectancy.[24] *See, Harmon* at 1022.

Many jurisdictions have declined to follow such reasoning for allowing a suit prior to the testator's death. In *Labonte v. Giordano,*[25] the Court declined to follow *Harmon's* rational, because "it is impossible . . . to determine whether the influence allegedly exerted by the defendant will continue until the death of his mother, a necessary element in this type of claim."[26]

---

[21] *Id.*

[22] 575 So. 2d. 239 (Fla. Ct. App. 1991).

[23] 404 A.2d. 1020 (Me. 1979).

[24] See *Harmon* at 1022.

[25] 687 N.E. 2d. 1253 (Mass. 1997).

[26] *Labonte* at 1255.

§ 42-7. Res Judicata and Collateral Estoppel

Many courts follow the doctrine of claims preclusion, barring further litigation on the same matter. The parties should litigate all the claims, arising out of the claim at the same time, rather than bringing separate actions since the same evidence supports both actions.[27] Many courts consider the following factors in determining whether a subsequent action will be barred: (1) the plaintiff first sought a probate remedy; or (2) the plaintiff could have brought a probate action; or (3) the probate remedy was adequate; or (4) it was possible to litigate the suit in the probate court; or (5) the probate court has jurisdiction over the claim.[28]

Some courts have focused on the plaintiff's request for punitive damages in a tortious claim. In *Huffey v. Lea*,[29] the court relied on the difference in litigants and standards of proof for allowing a separate action for the tortious interference claim. "Stated simply, in a will contest, the testator's intent or mental state is the key issue; in an intentional interference case, the wrongdoer's unlawful intent to prevent another from receiving an inheritance is the key issue."[30]

---

[27] *Annotation, Probate of Copy of Last Will As Precluding Later Contest of Will Under Doctrine of Res Judicata*, 55 ALR 3rd 755 (1974).

[28] *Action For Tortious Interference With Bequest As Precluded By Will Contest*, 18 A.L.R. 5th 211 (1994).

[29] 491 N.W. 2d. 518 (Iowa 1992).

[30] *Id.* at 521.

CHAPTER 43. REFORMATION OF WILLS AND TRUSTS

§ 43-1. Introduction.

Reformation is a term used to refer to the equitable remedy available in courts of equity to reform or rectify written instruments whenever they fail, through mistake or fraud, to express the real agreement or intention of the parties.[31] However, it was traditionally held that a "court of equity has no jurisdiction over a suit to reform a will."[32] However, there has been a noticeable trend over the years to erode the traditional rule. In particular, the adoption of Restatement of The Law (Third), Property (Wills and Other Donative Transfers) (1998) allows extrinsic evidence to be heard in all donative documents tested by the standard that the evidence must be clear and convincing:

There is an informative article on this entire subject entitled *Reformation of Wills: The Implication of Restatement (Third) of Property Donative Transfers On Flawed But Unambiguous Testaments* by Clifton B. Cruise, of the Colorado bar, which appears at 25 Actec Notes, 299 (2000) which contains an exhaustive treatment of the current trends in

---

[31] 66 AmJur 2nd, Reformation of Instruments, § 1, p. 526 (1973).

[32] 66 AmJur 2nd, Reformation of Instruments, § 37, p. 561 (1973).

the law with regard to reformation of wills and other donative instruments. See also the article by Professors Langbein and Waggoner, *Reformation of Wills*, On the Ground of Mistake: Change of Direction in American Law? 130 U. Pa.L.Rev. 521 (1982), and the Annotation entitled "Effect of Mistakes of Draftsman (other than Testator) in Drawing Will," 90 ALR 2d 924.

Generally, New Hampshire has followed the traditional rule that provides that there is no authority given to courts of equity to reform wills:

> Intentions cannot be made part of a will unless its language shows them either on its face or in its applications to externals. What the testator has done, not what he meant but failed to do, is to be given effect. . . . External facts may be received to explain and resolve doubts, but not to create them. . . .Actual purpose may not take the place of purpose disclosed by the will. **As is often said, authority to construe includes no power to reform.** White v. Weed. (Emphasis supplied).[33]

§ 43-2. Traditional Rule.

The traditional rule, consistent with contract law, is that a will must be ambiguous before extrinsic evidence relating to the will may be introduced. The equitable remedy of reformation was not available for mistake. The underlying premise of the traditional rule was to protect the provisions of the Statute of Wills, since to allow reformation of a will after the testator's death would "give testamentary force to a mere intention regardless of the manner in which it is expressed."[34] Thus, it is stated that a primary rationale for the ambiguity rule is to avoid entertaining claims of disappointed persons who may be able to make very plausible claims of mistake after the testator is no longer able to refute them. The case of *Hills v. D'Amour*[35] is an example: "The law is too well settled to require extensive citation that the writing required by the statute of wills may not be modified, waived or supplemented by parol."[36]

---

[33] White v. Weed, 87 N.H. 153, 155–56; 175A 814 (1935).

[34] 66 AmJur 2nd, Reformation of Instruments, § 37, p. 562 (1973).

[35] 95 N.H. 130, 59 A2d 551 (1948).

[36] *Id.* at 137.

Now, however, a less restrictive view has gained ground—one that would straight forwardly allow extrinsic evidence to be heard of the donor's intent is not accurately reflected in the written instrument. This view is found in Sections 11.1 and 11.2 of the Restatement (Third) Property. The proposition that the text of a will can be reformed represents a minority but growing view. Surrounding circumstances, the skill of the drafter, and post execution statements and events are seen as relevant as they relate to probable intent. Reformation of wills is allowed for administrative purposes as opposed to dispositive provisions. Scrivener's errors still cannot generally be corrected when the effect of the change alters a beneficial interest ambiguously described in the testament.

The Restatement (Third) Property rule essentially reflects the large body of court rulings that while acknowledging the ambiguity rule, hold contrary to its dictates. The exceptions to the rule are becoming the rule, while the traditional rule is honored only in narrow circumstances such as when the effect of the change alters a beneficial interest unambiguously described in the testament.

§ 43-3. Exceptions to Traditional Ambiguity Rule.

There are many ways courts have avoided applying the ambiguity rule to avoid excluding extrinsic evidence of a testator's intent. Because the rule operates to frustrate the testator's clear intent, the argument is that the rule, which is grounded in a desire to discern the testator's intent, fails in its purpose. Included among the many court-recognized exceptions to the ambiguity rule are:

Fraud. See *Knox v. Perkins.* [37]
Lack of testamentary capacity. See *Janness v. Hazelton.* [38]
Presumption Against Inheritance. See *Jacobs v. Bean.* [39]
Lack of testator's knowledge of the will's contents when executed. See *Janness v. Hazelton.* [40]
The testator's idiosyncratic use of terms/words. See *Sylvester v. Newhall.* [41]

---

[37] 86 N.H. 66, 163A 497 (1932).
[38] 58 N.H. 423 (1878).
[39] 99 N.H. 230, 108 A2d 559 (1954).
[40] 58 N.H. 423 (1878).
[41] 97 N.H. 267, 85 A2d 378 (1952).

Corrections of punctuation and grammar. See *Reynolds v. Jones*.[42]
Corrections of the detail of identification. See *Jones v. Bennett*.[43]
Corrections of false descriptions. See *Winkley v. Kairne*.[44]
Legal impact—mistaken assumptions. See *Leonard v. Stanton*.[45]
Probable intent. See *In re Estate of Frolick*.[46]
Mistake of Draftsman. See *Simpson v. Calivas*.[47]
Construction of Will Rather Than Reforming It. See Section 46-4 infra.

§ 43-4. Construing a Will Rather Than Reforming It

The Uniform Probate Code[48] describes the Code's purposes and rules of construction and includes an obligation "[to] discover and make effective the intent of a decedent in distribution of his property."

It is in this area that New Hampshire seems to have made the greatest invasion upon the traditional rule. A recent case illustrative of this trend is *In re Lathrop Estate*[49] where Chief Justice Kenison construing a will of which he concluded "the meaning of certain parts of the will were doubtful,"[50] stated the New Hampshire rule broadly as follows:

> In this state the testator's intention as expressed in the will is carried out to the fullest extent unless it commands the illegal or the impossible. . . . Arbitrary cannons of construction give way to a single broad rule of construction that always favors rather than opposes the testamentary disposition and, whenever consistent with the terms of the will as a whole, adopts that construction that gives the maximum validity to the testamentary disposition.[51]

This is an excellent example of the exception swallowing the rule. There is no mention here of maintaining the sanctity of the statute of wills.

---

[42] 78 N.H. 84, 97A. 557 (1916).

[43] 78 N.H. 224, 99A. 18 (1916).

[44] 32 N.H. 268 (1855).

[45] 96 N.H. 113, 36 A2d. 271 (1944).

[46] 112 N.H. 320, 295 A2d 448 (1972).

[47] 139 N.H. 1 (1994).

[48] UPC § 1-102(b)(2).

[49] 100 N.H. 393 (1956).

[50] *Id.* at 394.

[51] *Id.* at 395.

Justice Kenison cites for authority for his broad statement of will construction the earlier case of *Petition of Wolcott.*[52] The *Wolcott Case* was another example of an appellate court correcting [reforming] a will which, as written, contained no provision for the use of principal for the benefit of the widow. The Court in *Wolcott* found that the testator could not have intended not to provide income for his spouse and ruled that:

> In this situation a court of equity need not hesitate to exercise its undoubted power to commit a deviation from the literal provisions of the will. A means of accomplishing the testator's purposes thereby furnished, which it may reasonably be inferred that he himself would have provided had he been able to foresee the exigency.[53]

§ 43-5. Modification of or Deviation From Wills and Reformation of Wills Contrasted

Courts have also amended wills instead of reforming them, citing public policy where wills violate perpetuity rules or where unfavorable tax consequences injurious to beneficiaries otherwise will occur. Many of the cases involve changes in tax laws after the decedent's will had been written in reliance on law then existing and after the testator's death. The term "modification" is used in cases where inartful language used by the testator adversely affects his or her probable tax objective (such as minimizing estate taxes) and does not necessarily relate back to the date of execution, because modification, unlike reformation does not give effect to the donor's original intention, but to probable intention—to what the donor's intention would probably have been had the donor known that his or her objectives could not be achieved under the donative document as formulated. A court ordered modification takes effect whenever necessary to achieve the purpose for which the modification is ordered. The standard of evidence for modification is a preponderance of the evidence. It is clear and convincing evidence standard for reformation.

The *Wolcott Case*, supra, is an example of the use of the term deviation to get around the traditional reformation rule.

---

[52] 95 N.H. 23 (1948).

[53] *Id.* at 28.

§ 43-6. Implied Gifts

The theory of gifts by implication by presumed intent is another method that a court can add provisions to a will to correct errors even though they formally reject reformation. However, direct extrinsic evidence of the testator's intent *cannot* be used. The court implies their presumption based upon the will itself and surrounding facts and circumstances. The well-regarded New Jersey Supreme Court adopted this new rule in the leading case of *Engle v. Siegel.*[54]

The doctrine of presumed or probable intent may apply where expressions in the will allow reasonable inferences to be made. Where will was silent, a court may imply a devise after examining facts and circumstances. The court not only examines the entire will but also studies competent extrinsic evidence to determine the testator's probable intent. The court attributes to the testator common human impulses and seeks to find what he or she would subjectively have desired had the testator in fact actually addressed the contingency which arose.

§ 43-7. Functional Equivalents to Wills

Furthermore, courts have applied rules from nonprobate transfers or revocable transfers such as life insurance,[55] revocable trusts, and joint accounts that are viewed as nontestamentary on the grounds that they are functional equivalents to wills. Under Restatement 3rd Property a document, including a will, which is unambiguous, may be reformed where the evidence is clear and convincing that it should be. A showing may be made that the donor's intention differs from the terms of the donative document. This doctrine may be applied both to correct mistakes and to achieve a donor's tax objectives. Where the plain meaning of will was that no trust at all would be created, courts have held that extrinsic evidence was admissible to determine the testator's true intent.

§ 43-8. Private Reformation—By Agreement

The Uniform Probate Code in § 3-1101 and § 3-1102, allows controversies to be compromised and under § 3-912, allows private agreements among successors to be entered into that are binding on the estate's personal representative. These agreements and compromises are a method

---

[54] 74 N.J. 287, 377 A2d. 892 (1977).

[55] Bosse v. Bosse, 248 Ky. 4, 57 SW2d 995 (1933).

to "reform" or change the testator's will. Although it is not explicitly required by the Uniform Probate Code, court approval has the advantage of indemnifying the personal representative. It has been held that the agreement must be made in good faith and must be just and reasonable. As such, a private reformation will be binding even if it is contrary to the testator's intent as to the disposition of his estate.

Cross Reference

DeGrandpre, *Wills, Trusts & Gifts*, (3d ed. 1997), Section 8–14 to 8–16 and Chapter 13.

CHAPTER 44. WILL CONTESTS

§ 44-1. Basis for Contest

A will contest is the term given in litigation that contests the validity of a will for any reason. The most common reasons for a will contest are claims that (1) the will did not meet the statutory requirements for proper execution, (2) the testator lacked the necessary legal competency to make a will, or (3) the testator was subject to undue influence when making the will. However, there may be other reasons forming the basis of a will contest: for example, a claim that the will offered for probate was revoked by a subsequent will; a claim that the will was the result of fraud; a claim that the will was the product of a mistake of law; or a claim that the will was the product of a mistake of fact.

§ 44-2. Hearing for Proof of Will in Solemn Form

A will contest takes place at the hearing for proof of the will in solemn form. It is during this hearing, and the litigation procedures surrounding it, that the adversaries will compete for the favor of the probate judge in determining whether the will be accepted as a valid will or not.

Beginning on January 1, 1993,[56] the probate court was specifically empowered to try all questions relating to will contests:

---

[56] P.L., 1992, c. 284.

552:7 Proof, Solemn Form; Issues to Court. Any party interested may have the probate of a will which has been proved without notice re-examined, and the will proved in solemn form before the court of probate at any time within 6 months of such probate. Any issue related to the execution of a will, testamentary capacity, or fraud, duress, or undue influence shall be tried to the court of probate, and any party interested may request the same within 6 months of such probate.

§ 44-3. Equity Powers of Probate Courts

The 1993 expansion of probate jurisdiction was accompanied by further expansion of the probate court's general equity jurisdiction as follows:

547:3-a Issues to Court. In any proceeding before a probate court involving material facts which are in dispute, the probate court shall have jurisdiction to try such factual issues to court after due notice to all interested parties. However, the probate court may, if the interests of an estate require it, appoint a special administrator under RSA 553:20.

547:3-b Equity Jurisdiction. The probate court shall have the powers of a court of equity in cases in which there is not a plain, adequate and complete remedy at law involving partition, guardianships, conservatorships and probate of an estate and in all other like cases cognizable in a court of equity arising under RSA 547, RSA 547-C and RSA 552:7. The probate court shall have concurrent jurisdiction with the superior court in cases involving charitable uses and trusts other than express trusts as that term is defined in RSA 564-A:1, I. The court may hear and determine such cases according to the course of equity, and may grant writs of injunction whenever the same are necessary to prevent fraud or injustice.

§ 44-4. Discovery

Will contests usually involve the more formal discovery procedures often utilized in the superior court, but not otherwise frequently used in probate courts. Interrogatories, admissions of fact, and depositions are common. Pursuant to Probate Court Rule 10, all of the rules of the superior court regarding discovery are deemed to apply in the probate courts.

§ 44-4(a). File of Attorney Who Prepared the Will

A party seeking to overturn a will will sometimes encounter an early obstacle when trying to obtain the file of the attorney who prepared the will. The opposing attorney, who is often the draftsman with an interest in defending its validity, takes the position that the attorney's file is work product and not discoverable. This position is groundless, since the circumstances surrounding the drafting of the will and the attorney's file itself are the very nub of the issue before the court.

Our Supreme Court has made clear that the draftsman's file relating to the preparation and execution of the will is discoverable. *Stevens v. Thurston.*[57] In this case, the trial court had denied a motion to discover "the contents of the file of the attorney who drafted the will." On appeal to the Supreme Court, the Court held that:

> [an] appeal from the probate of the will is not an adverse proceeding against the estate . . . but a contest between parties claiming through the testator. If the defendants are successful, they, rather than the plaintiff, will be the representatives of the testator. Here the privilege is being asserted not for the protection of the testator or his estate but for the protection of a claimant to his estate. The authorities uniformly hold that in this situation all reason for assertion of the privilege disappears and that the protection of the testator lies in the admission of all relevant evidence that will aid in the determination of his true will.[58]

§ 44-5. Burden of Proof

A testator is presumed to have been of sound mind.[59] An executor who offers a will to probate need not offer evidence that the testator was sane or that the testator knew the contents of the will.[60] A party opposing

---

[57] Stevens v. Thurston, 112 N.H. 118, 152 A.2d 179 (1972).

[58] Stevens v. Thurston, 112 N.H. 118, 119, 152 A.2d 179 (1972).

[59] Pettes v. Bingham, 10 N.H. 514 (1840); Perkins v. Perkins, 39 N.H. 163 (1859).

[60] Id.

the will and asserting the insanity of the testator has the burden of presenting evidence to outweigh the presumption that the testator was sane.

The case of *Ross v. Carlino*[61] discusses at length the burdens of the respective parties in a will contest proceeding, during the course of a hearing in a petition to reexamine a will in solemn form.

The burden of proof lies with the proponent of the will, usually the executor:

> It is axiomatic that the proponent of a will carries "the burden of proving its due execution." In a will contest, the propounding party has the ultimate "burden of proof as to every fact which is necessary to the validity of a will." The proponent, therefore, although aided by a host of presumptions, retains the burden of persuasion throughout the probate proceeding.[62]

However, once the executor has made out a prima facie case, the burden shifts to the will contestant to show a failure of due execution, although the ultimate burden of proof remains with the proponent:

> Thus, even though it was the contestant in the present controversy who sought the petition for reexamination, the proponent had the burden of proving in solemn form the due execution of the will.[63]

A recent case, *In re Estate of Washburn*,[64] updates the law of New Hampshire on the tricky question of the burden of proof in a will contest. In *Washburn*, the court ruled that the burden of proving testamentary capacity in will contests remains on the proponent of the will throughout the proceeding:

> In New Hampshire the burden of proving testamentary capacity in will contests remains on the proponent of the will throughout the proceeding. . . . While a substantial number of States place

---

[61] Ross v. Carlino, 119 N.H. 126, 399 A.2d 292 (1979).

[62] Ross v. Carlino, 119 N.H. 126, 129–130, 399 A.2d 292, 295 (1979). (Citations omitted.)

[63] Ross v. Carlino, 119 N.H. 126, 130, 399 A.2d 292, 295 (1979).

[64] 141 N.H. 658, 690 A.2d 1024 (1997).

the burden of showing lack of capacity on those contesting the will, we are not alone in our allocation of the evidentiary burden.[65]

In probate of a will in solemn form, RSA 552:7 (Supp. 1996), the proponent of the will has the burden of proving its due execution. . . . The proponent is aided in this task by a presumption of capacity accorded the testatrix. . . . A will proponent need not introduce any evidence upon the issue of the testatrix's capacity until a will contestant first rebuts the presumption by offering evidence of incapacity. . . . Even if the presumption is successfully rebutted, the proponent is not thereby required, as the respondent argues, to prove a negative— that the testatrix did not lack capacity. Instead, once the presumption is rebutted, the proponent merely retains the initial burden of proving due execution. The proponent must persuade the trial court, by a preponderance of all the evidence presented, that the testatrix possessed the requisite capacity to make the will.

§ 44-6. Evidentiary Rules

A statutory rule of major importance in actions by or against the representations of deceased persons "including the probate of wills" is found in RSA 516:25:

Declarations of Deceased Persons. In actions, suits or proceedings by or against the representatives of deceased persons, including proceedings for the probate of wills, any statement of the deceased, whether oral or written, shall not be excluded as hearsay provided that the trial judge shall first find as a fact that the statement was made by decedent, and that it was made in good faith and on decedent's personal knowledge.

This statute was extensively interpreted in *Sullivan v. Dumaine*[66] as follows:

---

[65] *See, e.g.*, Clardy v. National Bank of Commerce, 555 So. 2d 64, 66 (Miss. 1989); Estate of Kumstar, 487 N.E.2d 271, 272 (N.Y. 1985); Gibbs v. Gibbs, 387 S.E.2d 499, 500 (Va. 1990); 79 Am. Jur. 2d *Wills* 103 (1975).

[66] Sullivan v. Dumaine, 106 N.H. 102, 106, 205 A.2d 848 (1964).

One ". . . obvious purpose of this statute . . . was to prevent injustice to estates of deceased persons by permitting an executor in certain circumstances to give the deceased's version of a disputed transaction."[67] That is not the only purpose of the statute.[68] Under this statute the "admissibility of the evidence is based on guarantees of truthfulness in the form of preliminary findings by the Court." Yeaton v. Skillings, supra. The statute cuts both ways; it may allow evidence that is favorable to an estate or unfavorable to it. The statute allows the evidence to be admitted because it is considered trustworthy and necessary, if the conditions of the statute are met. . . .

If the Court finds the statement of the deceased (a) was not made by the decedent; (b) was not made in good faith; or (c) was not made on the decedent's personal knowledge; it is excluded. All three factors are necessary if the statement of the deceased is to be allowed in evidence and when all three factors are present, there is substantial probability that the statement is reliable.

An evidentiary rule of particular importance in will contests is Rule 804(b)(5),[69] which provides:

> **Statement of a deceased person.** In actions, suits or proceedings by or against the representatives of deceased persons, including proceedings for the probate of wills, any statement of the deceased, whether oral or written, shall not be excluded as hearsay provided the trial judge shall first find as a fact that the statement was made by decedent, and that it was made in good faith and on decedent's personal knowledge.

An evidentiary rule of lesser importance in will contests is Rule 804(b)(2) which provides an exception to the hearsay rule for dying declarations:

> **Statement under belief of impending death.** In a prosecution for homicide or in a civil action or proceeding, a statement made by a declarant while believing that his or her death was

---

[67] Yeaton v. Skillings, 100 N.H. 316, 319.

[68] McCormack, Evidence, §§ 303, 304 (1954); 5 Wigmore, Evidence (3d ed.) § 1576(2).

[69] Anctil, *New Hampshire Rule of Evidence 804(b)(5): Has the Deadman's Rule Outlived Its Usefulness?*, 16 Trial Bar News 108 (1994).

imminent, concerning the cause or circumstances of what the declarant believed to be impending death.

The comments to this rule note that the rule as promulgated in the N.H. Rules of Evidence differs from the common law dying declaration to the hearsay rule in two important respects:

> First, the declarant need not be dead, merely unavailable (his belief of impending death at the time of the statement is sufficient). Second, these declarations are not limited to use in homicide prosecutions only, but may be used in civil cases as well.[70]

In a will contest, the usual rules of evidence used in the superior courts apply to the will contest. N.H. Rules of Evidence, Rule 1101(A).

Statutory provisions allow for authenticated copies of "any certificates or other official paper" (such as death certificates, etc.) of the registrar of vital records and health statistics to be "recorded as evidence with the same effects as originals." RSA 126:5.

Similarly, a town clerk's "record of birth, marriage or death, or a duly certified copy thereof, shall be prima facie evidence of the fact, in any judicial proceedings." RSA 126:18.

§ 44-7. Attorney's Fees in Will Contests

New Hampshire has no statute which compels or governs the allowance of fees in will contests.[71] Attorney's fees are not allowed as a matter of right, and the general common law rule operates to deny them in the usual circumstance.[72]

It has been recognized that in "this jurisdiction, the allowance of attorney's fees has developed slowly and generally speaking has not been as liberal as in our neighboring states." *Concord National Bank v. Haverhill.*[73] Where the parties seeking fees take positions to defeat a

---

[70] Reporters' Notes, NH Rules of Evidence, Rule 804.

[71] Murray v. Peabody, 106 N.H. 319, 211 A.2d 855 (1965).

[72] Concord Nat'l Bank v. Haverhill, 101 N.H.416, 145 A.2d 61 (1958).

[73] Concord Nat'l Bank v. Haverhill, 101 N.H. 416, 417, 145 A.2d 61, 62 (1958).

trust (or will), they are not entitled to an allowance of fees out of the trust property.[74]

However, where the participation of the party in the litigation "can be considered a service to the trust and an aid to the Court," the trial court has discretion, to be "cautiously exercised" to grant attorney's fees.[75] The standard for the award of fees was described by Justice Oliver Wendall Holmes as being a "reasonably mean" standard.[76]

Two cases with opposite results well illustrate the principles involved. In *Murray v. Peabody*,[77] the issue of attorney's fees arose in a petition for instructions brought by the plaintiff executor. Thus, the case was not strictly a will contest over the probate of a will. The defendant advanced positions "primarily for her own benefit and not for that of either the estate or the court."[78] The Supreme Court denied the defendant's fee request, stating that:

> [w]hen [the defendant] approached the lawyer for the executor, she was advised by him that she should procure independent counsel. This advice was entirely proper and consistent with the attorney's duty not to represent what might prove to be conflicting interests. It in no way obligated the estate to pay her counsel fees. The allowance of such in this jurisdiction has always been approached in a gingerly fashion. Whether they should be allowed on a "reasonably mean" basis or not at all rests "in the cautiously exercised discretion of the court."[79]

On the other hand, in *Concord National Bank v. Haverhill*,[80] another petition for instructions case involving a testamentary trust, the party seeking attorney's fees from the trust had worked to enable the trust "to function effectively and efficiently under modern conditions."[81] Their

---

[74] Adams v. Page, 76 N.H. 270, 81 A. 1074 (1911). See Concord Nat'l Bank v. Haverhill, 101 N.H. 416, 145 A.2d 61 (1958).

[75] Concord Nat'l Bank v. Haverhill, 101 N.H. 416, 145 A.2d 61 (1958).

[76] Concord Nat'l Bank v. Haverhill, 101 N.H. 416, 419, 145 A.2d 61, 62 (1958).

[77] Murray v. Peabody, 106 N.H. 319, 211 A.2d 855 (1965).

[78] Murray v. Peabody, 106 N.H. 319, 329, 211 A.2d 855, 862 (1965).

[79] *Id.*

[80] Concord Nat'l Bank v. Haverhill, 101 N.H. 416, 145 A.2d 61 (1958).

[81] Concord Nat'l Bank v. Haverhill, 101 N.H. 416, 419, 145 A.2d 61, 63 (1958).

"participation in the litigation can be considered a service to the trust and an aid to the court."[82] As such, the Supreme Court authorized the trial court to exercise its discretion to award "reasonable counsel fees out of the trust fund."[83]

Library References

Am Jur 2d Executors and Administrators § 538
CJS Wills §§ 565–71

Forms

See Form 94 in Appendix for a Petition for Deposition .
See Form 116 in Appendix for a Petition to Re-Examine Probate Will.

---

[82] *Id.*

[83] Concord Nat'l Bank v. Haverhill, 101 N.H. 416, 419–420, 145 A.2d 61, 64 (1958).

CHAPTER 45. SUITS BY AND AGAINST ADMINISTRATORS

---

§ 45-1. Suits Generally

There are "two methods of settling estates of deceased persons, the solvent and the insolvent."[1] Fortunately for creditors and heirs, most estates are settled as solvent estates without the peculiar and special provisions relating to insolvent estates.[2]

In settling a solvent estate, the administrator is responsible for settling the debts of, and claims against, the estate.[3] If these claims are disputable, they are adjudicated in actions brought by or against the administrator.[4] The administrator has the duty of admitting all indisputable debts of the estate and paying these debts from the assets of the estate rather than "forcing creditors through the legal ceremony of suit and judgment."[5]

Library References

Am Jur 2d Executors and Administrators § 1236 et seq.

CJS Executors and Administrators § 688 et seq.

§ 45-2. Parties

"In the absence of special circumstances, it is the general rule that an executor or administrator is the only proper party to bring or defend actions relating to the personal estate of the deceased."[6] Special circumstances allowing someone other than the executor or administrator to bring an action exist "where the personal representative of the estate fails or neglects to bring or defend an action relating to the personal estate, is guilty of fraud or collusion or has a conflicting or adverse interest in the estate."[7]

Heirs and beneficiaries are not considered to be parties in interest in a proceeding by or against an administrator:

> [H]eirs and legatees are not parties in interest, in the legal sense of the term, in a proceeding by or against the representative of the estate, any more than creditors. The representative's

---

[1] Judge of Probate v. Couch, 59 N.H. 506, 507 (1880).

[2] See Chapters 49 and 50 *infra*, for a discussion of settling insolvent estates.

[3] *Id.*

[4] Parsons v. Parsons, 67 N.H. 419, 29 A. 999 (1893).

[5] Judge of Probate v. Ellis, 63 N.H. 366, 367 (1885).

[6] Scammon v. Sondheim, 97 N.H. 280, 281, 86 A.2d 329, 330 (1952).

[7] *Id.*

authority is regulated by statute, and in general he is under judicial control instead of being under the direction of the heirs and legatees. Except in cases where they in fact conduct litigation in his name, they are not parties to it through him, but are properly regarded as strangers.[8]

Although New Hampshire has a tradition of freely allowing the intervention of parties in pending litigation, the opposite is true in probate litigation, and heirs, creditors or beneficiaries of an estate have no right to intervene in a suit by or against an administrator.[9] The orderly and expeditious settlement of estates generally requires individual control of the litigation by the personal representative of the estate, and this factor is to be considered in determining whether a third party may intervene.[10]

An administrator is not required to pursue all claims made on behalf of an estate. In *Sanborn v. Goodhue*, the Supreme Court stated the rule that an administrator is not under a duty to enforce a doubtful claim merely because a party with some interest in the estate thinks the claim is well founded, unless the party indemnifies the administrator for the costs of bringing the action.[11]

Library References

Am Jur 2d Executors and Administrators §§ 1236, 1244, 1245, 1268, 1273, 1275, 1284, 1296, 1298, 1341, 1342

CJS Executors and Administrators §§ 737–751

§ 45-3. Initiation of Action by Interested Party

RSA 556:19 provides that if the administrator fails to begin an action, "[a]ny person interested in the estate of a person deceased may begin an action as administrator" and the suit may proceed and attachments made pursuant thereto continued if the administrator subsequently prosecutes the action. The purpose of this statute is that "in the interest of expediency [the legislature] wanted to allow any interested person to initiate such an action provided it is prosecuted thereafter by the administrator."[12] The Supreme Court has given this statute a liberal

---

[8] Niemi v. Boston & Maine R.R., 87 N.H. 1, 5, 173 A. 361, 364 (1934).

[9] Scammon v. Sondheim, 97 N.H. 280, 86 A.2d 329 (1952).

[10] *Id.*

[11] Sanborn v. Goodhue, 28 N.H. 48 (1853).

[12] Tanner v. King, 102 N.H. 401, 403, 157 A.2d 643, 644 (1960).

interpretation, so that the rights of those persons interested in the estate shall be protected.[13]

The statute applies to the bringing of a suit in the administrator's name for the wrongful death of the decedent.[14] Once commenced, an action for wrongful death may not be continued unless the duly-appointed administrator of the estate elects to go forward with the suit.[15]

Any action brought on behalf of an estate by a third party must be commenced in the name of the administrator. If commenced by an individual in his own name, RSA 556:19 does not apply even if the individual has an interest in the estate.[16] In *Saltmarsh v. Candia*, it was held that RSA 556:19 does not apply to a personal injury action brought by a husband and wife before the wife's death for injuries to the wife. After the wife's death, the husband has no authority to continue the suit, unless he is appointed administrator of the deceased wife's estate.[17]

Library References

Am Jur 2d Executors and Administrators §§ 1284–1286

CJS Executors and Administrators §§ 737–740, 751

§ 45-4. Time of Demand and of Suit Generally

Chapter 556 of the New Hampshire Revised Statutes Annotated establishes the statutory time framework for suits by or against administrators. This framework provides for a six-month period for the presentation and exhibition of claims against an administrator during which time suit cannot be brought, followed by a second six-month period during which suit must be brought against an administrator in order to be valid.

RSA 556:1 provides that no action may be brought against an administrator within six months of the original grant of administration to the administrator. This time limit runs not from the date of death but, rather, from the date of the grant of administration. RSA 556:2 and 556:3 together provide that notice of such claims must be given to the administrator at some time during this six-month period, exclusive of

---

[13] Halle v. Cavanaugh, 79 N.H. 418, 111 A. 76 (1920). See Owen v. Owen, 109 N.H. 534, 257 A.2d 24 (1969).

[14] Owen v. Owen, 109 N.H. 534, 257 A.2d 24 (1969).

[15] Tanner v. King, 102 N.H. 401, 157 A.2d 643 (1960).

[16] Tappan v. Tappan, 30 N.H. 50 (1855).

[17] Saltmarsh v. Candia, 51 N.H. 71 (1871).

time that administration may have been suspended, and that the notice include a demand for payment.

All suits against an administrator which are based on a cause of action against the deceased must be brought within one year of the original grant of administration, exclusive of any time that the administration may have been suspended, as required by RSA 556:5, unless a court with subject matter jurisdiction over the nature of the claim grants an extension of time pursuant to RSA 556:28.[18]

The purpose of these measures is to secure the orderly and expeditious settlement of estates.[19] The New Hampshire Judicial Council in its Seventh Report described the purpose of RSA 556:5 as being "to compress into one year the time for the presentation of claims or demands and the commencement of suits, allowing the first six months for the presentation of claims and the second six months for the commencement of suits."[20]

Earlier provisions provided for a one-year period for presentation of claims and a one-year period for suit, for a total of two years.[21]

The Supreme Court held in *Brown v. Leavitt*,[22] that RSA 556 does not apply to an executor *de son tort* as the legislature designed this chapter to apply only in cases where there is a rightful administration.

In re Estate of David R. Pratt[23] is a recent case involving the application of the statute of limitations to an action against an administrator. The petitioner, unrelated to the decedent, was the recipient of the proceeds of a joint account held with the defendant's decedent. Prior to the decedent's death, the petitioner withdrew all monies in the account which had been provided entirely by the decedent. This subjected the monies to the legacy and succession tax. RSA 86:6-a; RSA 86:8. The decedent's will had a commonly encountered tax payment clause which provided that the executor was to pay all legacy and succession taxes, whether the property was disposed of by the decedent's will or not. The

---

[18] As amended by P.L., 1995, c. 277:24.

[19] Sullivan v. Marshall, 93 N.H. 456, 44 A.2d 433 (1945). See Lunderville v. Morse, 112 N.H. 6, 287 A.2d 612 (1972).

[20] See 7th Report Judicial Council, pp. 13, 14 (1958).

[21] *Id.*

[22] Brown v. Leavitt, 26 N.H. 493 (1853).

[23] __ N.H. __, decided December 29, 1999.

Department of Revenue Administration sent the petitioner (the surviving joint tenant) a tax bill for the legacy and succession taxes and she, in turn, asked the executor to pay the taxes in accordance with the will. The executor refused and submitted his final account to the probate court for approval without providing for payment of the tax. The petitioner objected to the final accounting. The probate court dismissed the plaintiff's objection on the basis that it had not been filed within one year from the grant of administration and was time barred pursuant to RSA 556:5. The Supreme Court addressed that issue only and found that the claim of the petitioner was not a claim against the decedent that would be time barred by RSA 556:5 but rather was a claim against the defendant executor which was not time barred. The Supreme Court remanded to the probate court the issue of who is ultimately responsible for the payment of the inheritance tax on the gift.

Library References

Am Jur 2d Executors and Administrators §§ 1246–1250

CJS Executors and Administrators §§ 405–408, 729–736

Claim of government as within provision of statute fixing time for presenting claims against decedent's estate. 53 ALR 569, superseded, 34 ALR2d 1003.

Applicability of nonclaim statutes to claims arising under contract executory at the time of death. 41 ALR 144, supplemented, 47 ALR 896.

Nonclaim statute as governing claim barred, subsequent to death of obligor, by general statute of limitations. 112 ALR 289.

Unliquidated claim for damages arising out of tort as a contingent claim within statutes relating to the presentation of claims against decedent's estate or action to enforce same after rejection. 125 ALR 871.

Waiver or tolling of statute of limitations by executor or administrator. 8 ALR2d 660.

Presentation of claim to executor or administrator as prerequisite or its availability as counterclaim or setoff. 36 ALR2d 693, §§ 3, 4[a], 5.

§ 45-5. Particular Actions—Workers' Compensation Actions

A cause of action under the workers' compensation law for compensation for death belongs to the surviving dependents, as is provided in RSA 281-A:22. *Henderson v. Sherwood Motor Hotel.*[24] Hence, an action to

---

[24] Henderson v. Sherwood Motor Hotel, 105 N.H. 443, 201 A.2d 891 (1964).

recover these benefits cannot be brought by the administrator. An action to recover benefits, which erroneously names the administrator as plaintiff, may be amended to name the administrator in his capacity as guardian for a minor dependent, to whom the benefits belong, if notice of the claim is seasonably given to the employer.[25] However, if the administrator does not also serve in a representative capacity for a surviving dependent he is not a proper party.

Library References

Am Jur 2d Workmen's Compensation §§ 496–498

CJS Workmen's Compensation §§ 428, 429

Protection of interest or rights of minors in proceeding for, or award of, compensation under provisions of workmen's compensation act. 120 ALR 395.

§ 45-5(a). Claims for Services Rendered to the Decedent

The case of *Decatur v. Cooper*[26] stated the general rule that the rendition of valuable services by one to another who knowingly receives the benefit of such services is evidence of a mutual understanding that they are to be paid for. The Court recognized, however, that the mere rendition and receipt of services does not in itself establish a legal duty to pay for such services, especially where the relationship of the parties indicates that payment was not contemplated or that the labor was gratuitously performed. As a result, the rendition and acceptance of services between members of the same family will not give rise to an inference of a promise to pay.

For other reasons, it was held in *Gauthier v. Laing*[27] that the value of services cannot be recovered, even where payment for such services was mutually understood, when illicit cohabitation took place. In the *Gauthier* case, illicit cohabitation was found to be part of the agreement, and recovery was denied.

The proper remedy for the rendition of services to a decedent was stated in *Suojanen v. Tardif*[28] to be an action based upon *quantum meruit*.

---

[25] *Id.*

[26] Decatur v. Cooper, 85 N.H. 250, 157 A. 706 (1931).

[27] Gauthier v. Laing, 96 N.H. 80, 70 A.2d 207 (1950).

[28] Suojanen v. Tardif, 121 N.H. 1036, 437 A.2d 310 (1981).

In *Lemire v. Haley,*[29] it was held that in an action against an estate for *quantum meruit* for services rendered to the decedent, the value of the items promised does not fix the measure of damages where the promise is held to be unenforceable. However, it may be considered by the jury along with other evidence.

In *Blanchard v. Calderwood,*[30] the Supreme Court held that evidence of an oral contract may be received where it is contended that the services were rendered gratuitously, not for the purpose of showing the value of the services, but to establish that compensation was intended. The *Blanchard* court stated further that in some cases evidence of the oral agreement may be admissible to show the value of the services, but that such a contract should not be admitted where it is conceded that the services were not gratuitous. In *Blanchard*, the Court stressed that the purpose of quantum meruit is to allow the plaintiff to recover what equitably belongs to him, and not to compensate him for the loss of his bargain.

Lemire v. Haley[31] also held that the proper measure of damages in an action to recover the value of services to a decedent is the fair price that it would have cost to obtain the services in question from a person in the plaintiff's position. The Court stated that the value that the decedent placed on the companionship and affection of the plaintiff is not recoverable, nor is interest recoverable.

Where the statute of limitations is asserted as a defense, as in *Lawrence v. Farwell,*[32] the statute may bar recovery for services rendered outside of the time limit but will not bar recovery for services rendered within the time limit. The *Lawrence* court also held that if it can be shown that the decedent promised to pay for all of the services at a time within the statutory period, the statute will not bar recovery for all of the services rendered.

Library References

Am Jur 2d Executors and Administrators §§ 586, 1344

CJS Executors and Administrators §§ 370–373

---

[29] Lemire v. Haley, 91 N.H. 357, 19 A.2d 436 (1941).

[30] Blanchard v. Calderwood, 110 N.H. 29, 260 A.2d 118 (1969).

[31] Lemire v. Haley, 91 N.H. 357, 19 A.2d 436 (1941).

[32] Lawrence v. Farwell, 86 N.H. 59, 163 A. 115 (1932).

§ 45-5(b). Oral Promise to Bequeath Property

Many lawsuits have arisen against estates in which the claim is made that the decedent, during his lifetime, orally promised the claimant to leave him all or some portion of his estate.[33]

The general rule is that a decedent's oral promise to leave one's estate to another is unenforceable against the estate if the estate includes real property, since to enforce the promise would be to avoid the Statute of Frauds, RSA 506:2. *Blanchard v. Calderwood.*[34]

Library References

CJS Executors and Administrators § 373

§ 45-5(c). Special Promise of an Administrator

The statute of frauds provision found in RSA 506:2 provides that no action may be maintained against an executor or administrator to enforce a "special promise" of the administrator to answer for damages out of his own estate unless the promise is in writing and signed by the administrator or by someone authorized by him. The Supreme Court has held that this statute does not apply to a suit against an executor for his oral promise to pay the plaintiff one half of his share as a residuary legatee of the estate if the plaintiff would forego his claim against the estate. *Carter v. Provo.*[35] In that case, the Court characterized the defendant executor's agreement not as a "promise to pay or be answerable for a debt of the estate. His agreement was to divide his share therein with the plaintiff if she would cancel her claim against it."[36]

Library References

Am Jur 2d Executors and Administrators § 429

CJS Frauds, Statute of §§ 8–11

§ 45-6. Claims of the Federal Deposit Insurance Corporation

A federal statute which contains a preemption clause may result in the extension of the normal statute of limitations to the time provided

---

[33] For an extended discussion of the complex area of the law, see C. DeGrandpre, 7 New Hampshire Practice: Wills, Trusts and Gifts (3d ed. 1997) Chapter 13.

[34] Blanchard v. Calderwood, 110 N.H. 29, 260 A.2d 118 (1969).

[35] Carter v. Provo, 87 N.H. 369, 180 A. 258 (1935).

[36] *Id.*

for by the federal statute. For example, in *FDIC Insurance Co. v. Estate of Infantine*[37] the superior court has held that the Financial Institutions Reform, Recovery, and Enforcement Act (FIRREA)[38] preempts the state law establishing a one year estate statute of limitations in estate cases (RSA 554:5). The court held that the FDIC claims against the estate began to run from the date of the federal receivership of a failed bank, so long as the statute of limitations has not expired before the date of the federal receivership. Left unanswered was whether or not the New Hampshire estate statute of limitations provisions would be preempted for a FIRREA claim where the defendant dies after the FDIC acquires the bank's assets through receivership.

§ 45-7. Venue

RSA 507:10 requires that actions by or against an administrator must be brought in the county or counties in which it could have been brought by or against the decedent at the time of death. This section also allows an administrator to bring an action in the county in which he is appointed.

Library References

Am Jur 2d Executors and Administrators §§ 1303–1305

CJS Executors and Administrators §§ 727, 728

§ 45-8. Deadline for Bringing Suit

Chapter 556, in addition to prohibiting the bringing of suit within the first six months after the original grant of administration under RSA 556:1, also requires that suit be brought within one year of the original grant of administration. RSA 556:5. Where an action is brought after the time allowed in RSA 556:5, the action is barred[39] and must be pleaded by the administrator in bar.[40]

On the other hand, where an action is brought prematurely in violation of RSA 556:1, the statute creates a temporary disability to sue[41] and

---

[37] FDIC Ins. Co. v. Estate of Infantine, Hillsborough County Superior Court, Northern District, 92-E-0898 (1994).

[38] 12 U.S.C. § 1821(d)(14).

[39] Sullivan v. Marshall, 93 N.H. 456, 44 A.2d 433 (1945).

[40] Amoskeag Mfg. Co. v. Barnes, 48 N.H. 25 (1868).

[41] Kittredge v. Folsom, 8 N.H. 98 (1835).

the executor must plead the matter in abatement. An administrator has an affirmative duty to plead the statute and cannot, for any reason, claim not to enforce the bar of the statute.[42] In *Amoskeag Manufacturing Co. v. Barnes*, it was held that if the administrator fails to plead the failure to comply with RSA 556:5 and judgment is issued, the judgment will not bind the estate, but the administrator is personally liable as an executor *de son tort*.[43] While the administrator is required to plead such matters in bar, there is no requirement that the plaintiff show affirmatively that the suit was brought within the applicable time limits.[44]

A claim by a mortgagee of the decedent seeking payment of the balance of a promissory note executed by the decedent is barred by the failure to comply by the time limitations of RSA 556:3 and RSA 556:5, even if the executors of the decedent's estate continued to make monthly payments under the terms of the promissory note for some months beyond the statutory deadlines. *Skrizowski v. Chandler*.[45] The Court went on to hold however, that the plaintiff may be entitled to relief from the deadlines under the provisions of RSA 556:28. The view of the New Hampshire Court in the *Skrizowski* case appears to be contrary to the general rule, which holds that non-claim statutes such as RSA 556:3 and 556:5 do not cut off a mortgage holder's right to pursue his lien against the mortgage property.[46]

Library References

Am Jur 2d Executors and Administrators §§ 633–640, 1246–1250

CJS Executors and Administrators §§ 405–408, 729–736

§ 45-9. Application of Statute

RSA 556:5 applies to actions at law and in equity.[47] It has been held

---

[42] Kittredge v. Folsom, 8 N.H. 98 (1835); Amoskeag Mfg. Co. v. Barnes, 48 N.H. 25 (1868).

[43] Amoskeag Mfg. Co. v. Barnes, 48 N.H. 25 (1868).

[44] *Id.*

[45] Skrizowski v. Chandler, 133 N.H. 502, 577 A.2d 1234 (1990). But see Wheeler v. The Bedford Bank, Hillsborough County Superior Court, 91-E-121 for a contrary view.

[46] Annot., 78 ALR 1126 (1932); CJS Executors and Administrators §§ 405–408; In re Will of Skarda, 537 P.2d 1392 (N.M. 1975); Kligerman v. Union & New Haven Trust Co., 18 A.2d 683, 684 (Conn. 1941).

[47] Sullivan v. Marshall, 93 N.H. 456, 44 A.2d 433 (1945); Sugar River Bank v. Fairbank, 49 N.H. 131 (1869).

to apply to suits to enforce a constructive trust,[48] to suits based upon the decedent's negligence where no action was pending at the time of decedent's death,[49] to suits against the deceased covenantor's heir for breach of warranty occurring during the decedent's lifetime,[50] to suits against an executor who was a residuary legatee and who had given bond for debts and legacies,[51] and to suits by the state to recover expenses for the maintenance of the deceased while a patient or inmate of the New Hampshire Hospital.[52]

RSA 556:5 has been held not to apply to suits against the distributees of money paid to an administrator under a mistake of fact and distributed by him,[53] to actions against an heir or devisee on the covenants of a deed made by decedent where the claim could not be proved against the estate because it was contingent,[54] and to a suit arising out of transactions of a testator but brought against the executrix in her private capacity.[55]

The provisions of Chapter 556 do not apply to a challenge to the due execution of a will since such a challenge is not a claim against the estate.[56]

Library References

Am Jur 2d Executors and Administrators §§ 603–632

CJS Executors and Administrators §§ 398–403

§ 45-10.　Waiver by Administrator

The bar created by RSA 556:5 cannot be waived by an administrator,[57] and the executor or administrator cannot by any promise take the claim

---

[48] Sullivan v. Marshall, 93 N.H. 456, 44 A.2d 433 (1945).

[49] Perutsakos v. Tarmey, 107 N.H. 51, 217 A.2d 177 (1966).

[50] Sawyer v. Jefts, 70 N.H. 393, 47 A. 416 (1900).

[51] Walker v. Cheever, 39 N.H. 420 (1859).

[52] In re Estate of Dockham, 108 N.H. 80, 227 A.2d 774 (1967).

[53] Redington Hub Co. v. Putnam, 76 N.H. 336, 82 A. 715 (1912).

[54] Hall v. Martin, 46 N.H. 337 (1865).

[55] Perkins v. Perkins, 68 N.H. 264, 38 A. 1049 (1895).

[56] Ross v. Carlino, 119 N.H. 126, 399 A.2d 292 (1979).

[57] Amoskeag Mfg. Co. v. Barnes, 48 N.H. 25 (1868). See Preston v. Cutter, 64 N.H. 461, 13 A. 274 (1867); Hall v. Woodman, 49 N.H. 295 (1870).

out of the operation of the statute.[58] However, a new promise may be sufficient to avoid a general statute of limitations.[59]

Library References

Am Jur 2d Executors and Administrators §§ 600, 639, 640

CJS Executors and Administrators §§ 382, 424

Waiver or tolling of statute of limitations by executor or administrator. 8 ALR2d 660.

Power and responsibility of executor or administrator in respect of waiver or compromise of claim due estate. 85 ALR 176, superseded, 72 ALR2d 191.

§ 45-11. Statutory Relief from Noncompliance with the One-Year Statute—In General

In some instances, the application of RSA 556:1, 556:3 and 556:5 may work a hardship on persons who, without fault, have failed to follow the mechanics of these sections and find themselves barred from bringing an action as a result. In recognition of this, RSA 556:28 was enacted to provide an equitable remedy where the legal remedy has failed.[60] RSA 556:28 has the effect of extending the time in which a plaintiff may assert an action against the administrator where justice and equity require such a result and the plaintiff is not chargeable with culpable neglect.[61]

Though expressed in statutory form, the relief given by RSA 556:28 is equitable in that it excepts certain cases from the mechanics of the notice and limitation of actions requirements under Chapter 556.[62]

RSA 556:28 provides that:

> Whenever any person has a claim against the estate of a
> deceased person, which has not been prosecuted within the time
> limited by law, such person may apply to the court having

---

[58] Amoskeag Mfg. Co. v. Barnes, 48 N.H. 25 (1868). See Hall v. Woodman, 49 N.H. 295 (1870).

[59] Amoskeag Mfg. Co. v. Barnes, 48 N.H. 25 (1868). See Preston v. Cutter, 64 N.H. 461, 13 A. 274 (1867).

[60] Libby v. Hutchinson, 72 N.H. 190, 55 A. 547 (1903).

[61] Sullivan v. Marshall, 93 N.H. 456, 44 A.2d 433 (1945).

[62] Mitchell v. Estate of Smith, 90 N.H. 36, 4 A.2d 355 (1939); W. A. Emerson's Sons v. Cloutman, 88 N.H. 59, 184 A. 609 (1936).

subject matter jurisdiction over the nature of the claim, by petition setting forth all the facts; and if the court shall be of the opinion that justice and equity require it, and that the claimant is not chargeable with culpable neglect in not bringing or prosecuting his or her suit or claim within the time limited by law, it may extend the time for filing and prosecuting the claim to a date certain; however, no such extension or judgment entered upon the claim shall affect any payments or compromises made before the beginning of the proceedings.

The judgment does not affect any payments or compromises made before the beginning of the proceedings, however.[63] It was held in *Parsons v. Parsons*,[64] for example, that upon receipt of such judgment the creditor is at liberty to take any property of the estate which has not previously been used in making payments or compromises without reference to the claims of other creditors, except where the estate is insolvent.[65]

In *W. A. Emerson's Sons, Inc. v. Cloutman*,[66] it was held that the relief provided by an earlier version of RSA 556:28 was not limited to a situation where demand and exhibition were made pursuant to RSA 556:3, since the same cause which prevented the bringing of suit may have prevented the exhibition of the claim. Thus, this section also applied where the claim was not properly presented to the administrator in the first instance.[67]

The petition must set forth sufficient facts to constitute just reason for the delay in prosecution[68] and must state all the facts on which the plaintiff relies for relief.[69] While the petition must set forth sufficient facts to show that the failure to assert the action was not due to the culpable neglect of the plaintiff, it was held in *Lisbon Savings Bank &*

---

[63] Parsons v. Parsons, 67 N.H. 419, 29 A. 999 (1893).

[64] *Id.*

[65] See Judge of Probate v. Couch, 59 N.H. 39 (1879). See also Vanni v. Cloutier, 100 N.H. 272, 124 A.2d 204 (1956).

[66] W. A. Emerson's Sons v. Cloutman, 88 N.H. 59, 184 A. 609 (1936).

[67] Stewart v. Farrell, 131 N.H. 458, 554 A.2d 1286 (1989).

[68] Lisbon Sav. Bank & Trust Co. v. Estate of Moulton, 91 N.H. 477, 22 A.2d 331 (1941).

[69] W. A. Emerson's Sons v. Cloutman, 88 N.H. 59, 184 A. 609 (1936).

Trust Co. v. Estate of Moulton,[70] that it is not necessary to state specifically in the petition that the plaintiff was free from culpable neglect or that the delay has not prevented a proper defense to the claim. Where the petition, although showing a good excuse for failure to file the claim, fails to set forth sufficient facts to enable the court to render judgment the court may grant leave to amend.[71] It has also been held that an action against an administrator which could not be maintained due to failure to exhibit the claim to the administrator could be amended into a petition under RSA 556:28.[72]

RSA 556:28 restricts its application to unsettled portions of the estate by stating that no payments or compromises made before the commencement of the proceeding will be affected.[73] Therefore, once payment has been made from the estate to the heirs, legatees or their representatives, payment will be considered to have been made under the statute and no relief can be had. In *Follett v. Ramsey*,[74] however, it was held that where such a distribution was fraudulent, relief may be granted under RSA 556:28.

RSA 556:28 does not apply to contingent claims[75] nor to claims against insolvent estates.[76] Neither does this statute apply to claims against the administrator for maladministration, as such claims can only be determined by an accounting in the probate court.[77] Where a right to recovery has been extinguished by operation of law, no claim exists and RSA 556:28 will not apply.[78]

Library References

Am Jur 2d Executors and Administrators §§ 639, 644

CJS Executors and Administrators §§ 408, 423

---

[70] Lisbon Sav. Bank & Trust Co. v. Estate of Moulton, 91 N.H. 477, 22 A.2d 331 (1941).

[71] Sullivan v. Indian Head Nat'l Bank, 99 N.H. 226, 108 A.2d 553 (1954).

[72] Watson v. Carvelle, 82 N.H. 453, 136 A. 126 (1926).

[73] See also American Univ. v. Forbes, 88 N.H. 17, 183 A. 860 (1936).

[74] Follett v. Ramsey, 101 N.H. 347, 143 A.2d 675 (1958).

[75] Libby v. Hutchinson, 72 N.H. 190, 55 A. 547 (1903).

[76] Judge of Probate v. Couch, 59 N.H. 39 (1879). See Parsons v. Parsons, 67 N.H. 419, 29 A. 999 (1893).

[77] Lisbon Sav. Bank & Trust Co. v. Estate of Moulton, 91 N.H. 477, 22 A.2d 331 (1941).

[78] Heath v. Cleveland, 104 N.H. 451, 189 A.2d 488 (1963).

§ 45-11(a). Justice and Equity

Relief under RSA 556:28 is to be granted only where "justice and equity" require it.[79] The question of whether justice and equity so require is a question of fact to be determined by the trial court.[80] In *Sullivan v. Indian Head National Bank*,[81] it was held that the court's finding cannot be set aside upon appeal unless the finding is against the weight of the evidence, construing the facts against the moving party. Thus, if the finding that justice and equity require the granting of relief under RSA 556:28 is supported by any competent evidence, it must be upheld on appeal.[82]

Library References

Am Jur 2d Executors and Administrators §§ 639, 641–645

CJS Executors and Administrators §§ 408, 423

§ 45-11(b). Culpable Neglect

In addition to establishing that justice and equity require a remedy under RSA 556:28, the petitioner must show that the failure to prosecute the claim was not due to culpable neglect. In dealing with the question of what constitutes culpable neglect, the Supreme Court stated that:

> Culpable neglect has been defined to be that which is censorious, faulty or blameable. . . . It signifies a lack of due diligence. . . . It is less than gross carelessness, but more than the failure to use ordinary care; it is a culpable amount of want of watchfulness and diligence, the unreasonable inattention, and inactivity of creditors who slumber on their rights.[83]

The issue of culpable neglect is an issue of fact for the determination of the trial court[84] and the determination of the trial court must be

---

[79] Vanni v. Cloutier, 100 N.H. 272, 124 A.2d 204 (1956)

[80] Sullivan v. Indian Head Nat'l Bank, 99 N.H. 226, 108 A.2d 553 (1954); Page v. Whidden, 59 N.H. 507 (1880); Webster v. Webster, 58 N.H. 247 (1878).

[81] Sullivan v. Indian Head National Bank, 99 N.H. 226, 108 A.2d 553 (1954).

[82] *Id.*

[83] Sullivan v. Indian Head National Bank, 99 N.H. 226, 228, 108 A.2d 553, 555 (1954), *citing* Mitchell v. Estate of Smith, 90 N.H. 36, 38, 4 A.2d 355, 357 (1939).

[84] Sullivan v. Indian Head Nat'l Bank, 99 N.H. 226, 108 A.2d 553 (1954); W. A. Emerson's Sons v. Cloutman, 88 N.H. 59, 184 A. 609 (1936); Libby v. Hutchinson, 72 N.H. 190, 55 A. 547 (1903).

affirmed on appeal if there is any competent evidence to support it.[85]

In *Cass v. Ray*,[86] the Supreme Court ruled that where the failure to file a suit against a decedent estate within one year of the date of grant of administration is due to an attorney's slip-up by his failing to properly docket the deadline, no relief was available under RSA 556:28:

> "[T]he evidence required the conclusion that failure to bring timely suit was the consequence of the carelessness of former counsel or his firm, and that it was therefore culpable neglect as we have defined it."[87]

However, where an attorney filed a notice of claim four months after letters of administration were granted but failed to bring action against the executor of an estate and was suspended from practice, the petitioner was allowed an extension of time under RSA 556:28. *Koziell v. Fairbanks*.[88] In *Koziell*, the court found the petitioner was not chargeable with culpable neglect, since he had difficulty understanding English and hired a new attorney immediately upon learning of his attorney's suspension.

Where the failure to pursue a claim was due to a mistake of fact or law, or where the administrator is guilty of fraud, misrepresentation or deceit, and the failure to pursue the claim was due to these circumstances, culpable neglect was found not to be present.[89] But, where the administrator promised to pay a claim and failed to do so and the creditor fails to take the necessary steps for enforcement of the claim within the time limits set by law, the question of culpable neglect was less clear and will be determined at trial.[90]

Where culpable neglect is found, the action is barred regardless of whether justice and equity would otherwise sustain the petition.[91]

---

[85] Vanni v. Cloutier, 100 N.H. 272, 124 A.2d 204 (1956).

[86] Cass v. Ray, 131 N.H. 550, 556 A.2d 1180 (1989).

[87] Cass v. Ray, 131 N.H. 550, 554, 556 A.2d 1180, 1182 (1989).

[88] Koziell v. Fairbanks, 115 N.H. 679, 348 A.2d 358 (1975).

[89] W. A. Emerson's Sons v. Cloutman, 88 N.H. 59, 184 A. 609 (1936).

[90] Powers v. Holt, 62 N.H. 625 (1883).

[91] Mitchell v. Estate of Smith, 90 N.H. 36, 4 A.2d 355 (1939).

Library References

Am Jur 2d Executors and Administrators §§ 639, 641–645

CJS Executors and Administrators §§ 408, 423

§ 45-11(c). Suspension of Administration

The time allowed for bringing an action against an administrator under RSA 556:5 and for exhibition of demand under RSA 556:3 is tolled while the administration is suspended.

The suspension of administration within the meaning of these sections was defined in *Preston v. Cutter*[92] to contemplate the death, resignation, or removal of the original administrator within the period proscribed by statute. The suspension must be during the period of administration. Therefore, in *Cummings v. Farnham*,[93] where there was a failure to apply for an administration of an estate, it was held that the statutory period had not commenced and there was no suspension of it. The suspension refers to the estate of the debtor, not the creditor.[94]

The appointment of a creditor of the deceased as administrator will suspend the creditor's right of action against the estate and hence will suspend the statute of limitations with respect to his personal claim.[95] If the administrator is absent from the state and his absence prevents the presentation of a claim against the estate, the action will not be barred provided that the creditor could not have presented the claim through the exercise of reasonable diligence.[96] A payment by an executor on a claim, however, does not amount to a successive new promise which would suspend the statutory period.[97]

Where there has been no suspension of administration and the creditor fails to bring the action within the time limits set by statute, the action will be barred unless the claim has been exhibited to the administrator and has been taken out of the debtor's estate.[98]

---

[92] Preston v. Cutter, 64 N.H. 461, 13 A. 274 (1888).

[93] Cummings v. Farnham, 75 N.H. 135, 71 A. 632 (1908).

[94] *Id.*

[95] Preston v. Cutter, 64 N.H. 461, 13 A. 274 (1888).

[96] Walker v. Cheever, 39 N.H. 420 (1859).

[97] Brewster v. Brewster, 52 N.H. 52 (1872).

[98] Cummings v. Farnham, 75 N.H. 135, 71 A. 632 (1908).

Library References

Am Jur 2d Executors and Administrators §§ 596–598, 638, 639

CJS Executors and Administrators §§ 405–408

§ 45-12. Setoff and Recoupment

Setoff is a claim of the defendant, usually arising out of a transaction separate from the plaintiff's claim, which is asserted to diminish the amount of the plaintiff's claim. Setoff was unknown at common law and is regulated by statute. [99]

Recoupment arises from the same transaction as the plaintiff's action and is therefore viewed as a defense to the plaintiff's claim rather than as a separate cause of action. [100]

RSA 515:9 states that mutual debts existing between a deceased person and another may, when due, be set off in actions by or against an administrator. This statute specifically provides that contingent claims may be subject to setoff in such actions. It was held in *Shaw v. Gookin*, [101] that a debt which accrued since the death of the testator to the executor could not be set off against the estate since to do so would alter the course of distribution. RSA 515:9 applies only to actions by or against the administrator in her official capacity [102] and as was held in *McCaffrey v. Kennett*, [103] an administrator cannot set off a personal claim against a claimant of the estate as the two debts are not mutual.

When a claim is asserted as a setoff it must be presented to the administrator under RSA 556:3, unless the estate is insolvent, [104] or it will not be allowed. [105]

The setoff statute does not apply to claims which are for recoupment. [106] In *Stanley v. Clark*, [107] it was held that recoupment is allowed regardless of the statute.

---

[99] Stanley v. Clark, 159 F. Supp. 65 (D.N.H. 1957).

[100] *Id.*

[101] Shaw v. Gookin, 7 N.H. 16 (1834).

[102] Petition of Keyser, Inc., 98 N.H. 198, 96 A.2d 551 (1953).

[103] McCaffrey v. Kennett, 73 N.H. 189, 60 A. 96 (1905).

[104] Mathewson v. Strafford Bank, 45 N.H. 104 (1863).

[105] Jones v. Jones, 21 N.H. 219 (1850).

[106] Stanley v. Clark, 159 F. Supp. 65 (D.N.H. 1957).

[107] *Id.*

Library References

Am Jur 2d Executors and Administrators §§ 1238–1239

CJS Executors and Administrators §§ 429, 717–724

Persons other than personal representative or surviving spouse, paying funeral expenses as entitled to set off against debt due estate. 35 ALR2d 1405.

Personal representative's right of retainer or setoff, against debtor's distributive share of estate, of debt barred by statute of limitations. 39 ALR2d 675.

Bank's right to apply or set off deposit against debt of depositor not due at time of his death. 7 ALR3d 908.

Presentation of claim to executor or administrator as prerequisite of its availability as counterclaim or setoff. 36 ALR3d 693.

§ 45-13. Effect of Insolvency—In General

These sections will discuss only the effect of an insolvency upon the issue of actions brought by or against administrators.[108]

Once an estate has been decreed to be administered as insolvent, RSA 556:8 prohibits the bringing of an action against the administrator unless the deceased was insured for the subject matter of the action, and in such cases recovery is limited to the coverage of the policy. This section further provides that any actions pending against the deceased or the administrator at the time that the estate is decreed to be administered as insolvent cannot be further prosecuted except by leave of court, and that if judgment is rendered thereon the amount of judgment will be added to the list of claims against the insolvent estate.

The settlement of insolvent estates is dealt with in Chapter 557 of the New Hampshire statutes. RSA 557:1 allows the administrator to apply to the court to have the estate administered as insolvent and, once the estate is decreed to be so administered, this section provides for the appointment of up to three commissioners to examine the claims of creditors of the estate to determine which claims should be allowed. Once the commissioners have been appointed, the judge will prescribe a time of at least three but no more than six months for creditors to present their claims against the estate to the commissioners, pursuant to RSA

---

[108] The general law relating to insolvent estates is found in Chapters 49 and 50 *infra.*

557:7. The commissioners are then required to make a report of the claims presented and amounts allowed to the judge under RSA 557:17 and the judge, after allowing payment of certain preferred claims under RSA 557:22, will decree the amount to be distributed to each of the remaining creditors as provided for in RSA 557:24 and 557:25. Once the estate has been decreed to be settled by the insolvent course under Chapter 557, the administrator cannot adjust claims against it and no action can be commenced or prosecuted against the administrator.[109]

In *Fairfield v. Day*,[110] the Court held that once the trial court is informed of a petition to settle the estate through the insolvent course, the suit against the decedent should be continued to await the resolution of the petition. If through oversight judgment is rendered and execution is issued, further proceedings may be stayed through injunction.[111]

The effect of RSA 556:8, however, is to abate the action in the trial court and in *Lyford v. Dunn*,[112] it was held that where the administrator fails to assert the decree, the administrator cannot collaterally attack the judgment, and the deceased's property in his hands is subject to execution. Also, the administrator cannot give a preference to some of the estate's creditors by failing to exercise his right to abatement, for any levy which gives one of the creditors of an insolvent estate a preference as to other creditors of the estate is void as to the other creditors.[113]

Where a plaintiff depends wholly on the decedent's bond for satisfaction of her cause of action, disclaiming any right to the assets of the estate, she is as a matter of law entitled to receive leave of court to pursue her cause of action.[114]

Library References

Am Jur 2d Executors and Administrators §§ 918–921

CJS Executors and Administrators §§ 677, 679–687

Remedies of creditors of insolvent decedent's estate where other creditors have received excessive payments. 77 ALR 981.

---

[109] Judge of Probate v. Couch, 59 N.H. 506 (1880).

[110] Fairfield v. Day, 72 N.H. 160, 55 A. 219 (1903).

[111] *Id.*

[112] Lyford v. Dunn, 32 N.H. 81 (1855).

[113] Blaisdell v. Peavey, 79 N.H. 243, 108 A. 134 (1919).

[114] Brown v. Brockway, 87 N.H. 342, 179 A. 411 (1935).

Basis of distribution among decedent's unsecured creditors of ancillary assets where entire estate or ancillary is insolvent. 164 ALR 765.

§ 45-13(a). Attachment

RSA 511:46 states that where an estate is decreed to be administered by the insolvent course, all attachments against the decedent or his estate are dissolved as of the date of his death. This statute was interpreted in *Blaisdell v. Harris*[115] as being applicable to cases pending at the date of the decedent's death, but not to those in which judgment had been rendered prior to the decedent's death. Therefore, when a suit is pending against a deceased party and his estate is decreed to be insolvent, the suit must be discontinued and the attachment dissolved.[116]

Except where another creditor asserts a claim on the attached property, or the administrator asserts such a claim on another creditor's behalf, property may be taken by attachment and execution if the administrator does not raise the objection that the estate has been decreed insolvent.[117]

RSA 511:47 supplements 511:46 by providing that if the property attached has been sold and the attachments on the property dissolved, the money resulting from the sale will be restored to the debtor or his personal representative upon request, after deducting the expenses of sale. The effect of RSA 511:47 is to return the proceeds of sale to the estate, where the attachment was dissolved before judgment was rendered, such as when the defendant dies while suit is pending and his estate is decreed to be insolvent.[118]

Library References

Am Jur 2d Executors and Administrators §§ 918–921

CJS Executors and Administrators §§ 677, 679–687

§ 45-13(b). Trustee Process

It was held in *Hall v. Harvey*,[119] that when a trustee has answered a summons but dies before judgment is entered, the judgment may be entered against the trustee as of the term when disclosure was made. RSA

---

[115] Blaisdell v. Harris, 52 N.H. 191 (1872).

[116] Fairfield v. Day, 72 N.H. 160, 55 A. 219 (1903).

[117] Lyford v. Dunn, 32 N.H. 81 (1855).

[118] York v. Sanborn, 47 N.H. 403 (1867).

[119] Hall v. Harvey, 3 N.H. 61 (1824).

512:4 provides further that if a trustee dies pending the proceedings against him the administrator may be summoned as a party and will be liable as if the action had been brought against the administrator as trustee.

Where the administrator is sued as trustee and the estate is insolvent, however, the claim must be presented to the commissioners under RSA 557:7. If the claim is not presented to the commissioners within the time prescribed, the claims may be barred under RSA 558:22. It was held in *Chapman v. Gale*,[120] that when it appears to the court in which the trustee suit is pending that a decision cannot be reached in time to present the claim to the commissioners of an insolvent estate, it would be proper to order the proceeding stayed until the claim is presented to and considered by the commissioners.

§ 45-14. Compromise of Claims

RSA 556:27 provides that:

> The probate court may authorize administrators and guardians to adjust by compromise or arbitration any controversy between them and persons making claims against the estates in their hands. The attorney general or the director of the register of charitable trusts shall be a necessary party to any agreement between an executor and creditors or legatees or heirs-at-law whenever such agreement may directly or indirectly affect a charitable interest, residuary or otherwise, created in any estate.

In *Burtman v. Butman*,[121] the Court held that RSA 556:27 provides a means to protect the administrator from liability, but is not a prerequisite to enforcing a compromise agreement. The *Burtman* Court reasoned that when originally enacted the statute did not cut off the pre-existing power of a fiduciary to compromise a claim without prior probate court approval, subject to the chance of a surcharge.

Although it had been held earlier in *Phinney v. Cheshire County Savings Bank*[122] that probate court approval must be obtained in order

---

[120] Chapman v. Gale, 32 N.H. 141 (1855).

[121] Burtman v. Butman, 94 N.H. 412, 54 A.2d 367 (1947).

[122] Phinney v. Cheshire County Sav. Bank, 91 N.H. 184, 16 A.2d 363 (1940).

to make a compromise of a claim against the estate valid, the *Burtman* Court overruled this decision, stating that RSA 556:27 is a permissive, rather than a mandatory measure and that a compromise of a claim against the estate by an administrator would be upheld so long as the compromise was reasonable and beneficial to the estate.

The power of the probate court to approve an administrator's compromise of a claim against the estate was held to imply that no such power existed to compromise claims of the estate in *Protective Check Writer Co. v. Collins.* [123] In this case, the Court held that the question of whether the compromise of claims of the estate by an administrator was proper is a question which should properly be passed on during a hearing upon the administrator's account in settlement of the administration, and that a probate court's ruling in advance on the settlement of a claim of the estate would assume a power of judicial management which had not been granted in any specific terms.

The power of the probate court to approve the compromise of claims by the administrator applies only to claims against the estate and not to claims which arose out of a transaction with the administrator. *Redington Hub Co. v. Putnam.* [124]

Library References

Am Jur 2d Executors and Administrators §§ 650–652

CJS Executors and Administrators § 469

Power and responsibility of executor or administrator in respect of compromise of claim against estate. 85 ALR 199, superseded, 72 ALR2d 243.

§ 45-15. Actions by Interested Persons

A person who has an interest in an estate may bring an action as administrator under RSA 556:19 if the administrator who is then or afterward appointed endorses the writ and prosecutes it as plaintiff at the first or second term of the court. RSA 556:19 states that any action so begun cannot be abated, nor any such attachment lost because the person bringing the action is not the true administrator, and that the action will survive the death of the party who brings it. This statute should be

---

[123] Protective Check Writer Co. v. Collins, 92 N.H. 27, 23 A.2d 770 (1942).

[124] Redington Hub Co. v. Putnam, 76 N.H. 336, 82 A. 715 (1912).

liberally construed so as to fully protect the rights of those interested in the estate.[125]

Ordinarily, an action brought under RSA 556:19 will be abated if the true administrator does not endorse the writ at the first or second term of the court.[126] For example, in *Tanner v. King*,[127] a widower brought a wrongful death action as a "person interested in the estate." The Court held that the action could not be maintained because of the administrator's failure to endorse the writ.

The failure of an administrator to endorse the writ can work injustice where the compulsory abandonment of the suit leaves the party bringing the suit without redress. In recognition of this it was held in *Merrill v. Woodbury*[128] that in such situations, where justice requires, the person bringing the suit may be allowed to amend the writ by inserting the name of the administrator as plaintiff and may prosecute the suit in the administrator's name upon indemnification of the administrator against cost. The *Tanner* Court indicated, however, that an action for wrongful death must be brought by the administrator as a party.

RSA 556:19 does not apply to an action which is brought by a person in an individual capacity rather than as administrator,[129] although it was held in *Saltmarsh v. Candia*,[130] that where a personal injury suit was brought by a husband and wife for injuries suffered by the wife, the action could not be prosecuted by the husband alone after the wife's death but could be brought by the administrator of the wife's estate.

Library References

Am Jur 2d Executors and Administrators §§ 1284–1297

CJS Executors and Administrators §§ 737–751

§ 45-16. Administrator's Rights and Duties—In General

An administrator who becomes a party to a pending suit enjoys a right as of course to one continuance under RSA 556:24. RSA 556:21 provides

---

[125] Halle v. Cavanaugh, 79 N.H. 418, 111 A. 77 (1920). See Owen v. Owen, 109 N.H. 534, 257 A.2d 24 (1969).

[126] Merrill v. Woodbury, 61 N.H. 504 (1881).

[127] Tanner v. King, 102 N.H. 401, 157 A.2d 643 (1960).

[128] Merrill v. Woodbury, 61 N.H. 504 (1881).

[129] Tappan v. Tappan, 30 N.H. 50 (1855).

[130] Saltmarsh v. Candia, 51 N.H. 71 (1871).

that the estate and the administrator of the estate will be liable on joint or joint and several demands against the deceased and another person unless it appears that the intention of the parties was that only the survivor should be liable. An action in which the administrator is a party will not be abated by the death of the administrator, but rather RSA 556:20 provides that the action may be prosecuted or defended by the administrator succeeding the deceased administrator. The succeeding administrator may be called into court by *scire facias* under the terms of RSA 556:20.

In addition, RSA 556:22 provides for actions of account or assumpsit between co-administrators. It was held in *Patten v. Patten*[131] that such actions are not in the nature of a proceeding to settle the estate but rather are actions between two fiduciaries. The *Patten* Court stated that no citation to account or adjudication by the probate court are necessary as a prerequisite to bringing an action under RSA 556:22, but rather all that is necessary to maintain such an action is a showing that the defendant has refused to administer the estate according to law as alleged. The Court stated that the remedy in such an action is not to compel the delinquent fiduciary to settle in the probate court but rather to compel him to pay over to the co-administrator so that the latter may administer the estate. The amount which may be so recovered is all of the unadministered estate in the defendant's hands to which he has no claim.

§ 45-16(a). Summoned as Party

It was stated in *Parker v. Badger*,[132] that where a party dies in a pending suit, his death should be noted on the record and the proceedings should be stayed until the administrator should appear or be served with a writ of *scire facias*. RSA 556:23 provides that where an administrator who has been served with *scire facias* does not become a party to the suit, judgment may be rendered against the estate in the same manner as if he had become a party. The purpose of the *scire facias*, as stated in *Shea v. Starr*,[133] is to call the administrator into court. The Shea Court stated that all that is required is that the writ be issued and served, there is no requirement that it be made returnable or returned.

An administrator who has been served with *scire facias* should appear in the action and, if the estate which he represents has an interest, may

---

[131] Patten v. Patten, 79 N.H. 388, 109 A. 415 (1920).

[132] Parker v. Badger, 26 N.H. 466 (1852).

[133] Shea v. Starr, 76 N.H. 538, 85 A. 788 (1913).

plead or defend on behalf of the estate, but as was held in *Pierce v. Jaquith*,[134] if the estate has no interest, the administrator should plead nontenure or disclaim the estate's representative.

Library References

Am Jur 2d Parties §§ 217, 218, 223, 229

CJS Parties §§ 58–64

Construction of Federal Rule 25(a)(1) as permitting substitution, as a party, of personal representative of a nonresident decedent. 79 ALR2d 532.

§ 45-16(b). As Witness

RSA 516:25, known as the "dead man's statute," provides that:

> In actions, suits or proceedings by or against the representatives of deceased persons, including proceedings for the probate of wills, any statement of the deceased, whether oral or written, shall not be excluded as hearsay provided that the trial judge shall first find as a fact that the statement was made by decedent, and that it was made in good faith and on decedent's personal knowledge.

This statute allows evidence which may be either favorable or unfavorable to the estate to be admitted, although it was held in *Sullivan v. Dumaine*[135] that the preliminary findings of trustworthiness must be made before the evidence is admitted. Under RSA 516:25 and its identical counterpart, Rule 804 (b)(5) of the New Hampshire Rules of Evidence, the trial court must make three preliminary findings. "First, the trial court must find that the statement was made by the decedent. Second, the statement must have been made in good faith. Finally, the statement must be based on the decedent's personal knowledge. If the party seeking admission fails to satisfy any of these preliminary requirements, the evidence will not be admitted. . . ."[136]

In *Nute v. Blaisdell*,[137] it was stated that one obvious purpose of this rule is to prevent injustice to the estate by allowing the executor, in

---

[134] Pierce v. Jaquith. 48 N.H. 231 (1868).

[135] Sullivan v. Dumaine, 106 N.H. 102, 205 A.2d 848 (1964).

[136] Anctil, *New Hampshire Rule of Evidence 804(b)(5); Has the Deadman's Rule Outlived Its Usefulness?*, 16 Trial Bar News 108 (1994).

[137] Nute v. Blaisdell, 117 N.H. 228, 374 A.2d 923 (1977).

certain circumstances, to give the decedent's version of a disputed transaction. However, it has also been held in *Drescher v. Granite State Machine Co.*,[138] that a decedent's admission to a third party may be admitted against a party claiming the decedent's right as heir, executor or administrator.

Library References

> Am Jur 2d Witnesses §§ 303 et seq.
>
> CJS Witnesses §§ 132 et seq.

What constitutes claim or demand against estate within statute disqualifying witness. 54 ALR2d 1103.

§ 45-16(c). Appeals

RSA 556:18 provides that an appeal to which the deceased was entitled or which may be brought against him at the time of his death may be prosecuted by or against his administrator.

Library References

> Am Jur 2d Appeal and Error §§ 287, 288
>
> CJS Appeal and Error §§ 406–412

§ 45-16(d). Executions

RSA 556:25 provides that an execution issued against an administrator under a cause of action against the deceased runs only against the estate of the deceased and that the administrator cannot be arrested or have his personal estate attached or levied upon.

Where the estate is insolvent, the administrator cannot satisfy the claims of creditors according to RSA 556:8. Therefore, a creditor cannot levy on the goods of the deceased in the hands of the administrator. In *Blaisdell v. Peavey*,[139] it was held that any levy which gives one of the creditors of an insolvent estate a preference over other creditors of the estate is void as to the other creditors.

Where the estate is solvent, however, the opposite is true. Thus, in *Lisbon Savings Bank & Trust Co. v. Estate of Moulton*,[140] it was held

---

[138] Drescher v. Granite State Mach. Co., 96 N.H. 508, 79 A.2d 16 (1951).

[139] Blaisdell v. Peavey, 79 N.H. 243, 108 A. 134 (1919).

[140] Lisbon Sav. Bank & Trust Co. v. Estate of Moulton, 91 N.H. 477, 22 A.2d 331 (1941).

that a creditor of the decedent could attach the goods or estate of the deceased and may obtain a writ of execution against it upon recovering judgment. Where misconduct or mismanagement of the administrator is alleged, the creditor may also attempt to recover under the administrator's bond.[141]

Where a return of execution is made by the sheriff indicating "no goods" or "waste," an execution may be awarded on *scire facias* against the goods and estate of the administrator to the amount of such waste, if it can be ascertained, or otherwise to the amount of the debt under RSA 556:26. While this statutory remedy is available, it is often unnecessary as an action on the administrator's bond may be preferable. The retention of the statutory remedy has been viewed as showing a legislative purpose to preserve the right to proceed against a delinquent administrator independent of the proceedings in probate court.[142]

Where a plaintiff in any action in whose favor judgment is rendered dies before execution is issued, RSA 527:8 provides that the clerk of court issue execution to the administrator upon request and upon filing a certificate of his appointment from the probate court.

Library References

CJS Executors and Administrators §§ 806–812

§ 45-16(e). Trustee Process

In *Adams v. Barrett*,[143] it was held that an administrator, until he is personally liable in an action by his private promise, by the settlement of the estate, by a decree against him, or by other cause, cannot be personally liable to a writ of trustee process. However, it was held in *Walsh v. Boulanger*[144] that where the debt is liquidated and the decree of payment has passed, a writ of execution could run against the administrator's own goods.

RSA 512:4 provides that where the trustee dies pending the proceedings against him, the administrator may be summoned as a party and will be liable as if the action had been brought against her as trustee.

---

[141] *Id.*

[142] Patten v. Patten, 79 N.H. 388, 109 A. 415 (1920).

[143] Adams v. Barrett, 2 N.H. 374 (1821).

[144] Walsh v. Boulanger, 107 N.H. 458, 225 A.2d 185 (1966).

On the other hand, in *Hall v. Harvey*,[145] the Court stated that when the trustee has answered and the cause continued, and the trustee dies before judgment is entered, judgment may be entered as of the term when the trustee answered.

In *Chapman v. Gale*,[146] it was held that, absent fault or fraud, the administrator can be charged only for the property of the trustee in his hands at the time of judgment. If the process is founded on a contract or debt due the principal debtor from the deceased, no recovery can be had if the contract or debt is barred without fault of the trustee.

In *Palmer v. Noyes*,[147] the Court held that an administrator may be charged as a trustee for a legatee or heir for any sum of money in her hands, upon settlement of the estate, which belongs to the legatee or heir. Similarly, in *Protective Check Writer Co. v. Collins*,[148] it was held that where the administrator had settled a claim on behalf of the estate and payments were to be made from the debtor to the estate with the provision that they then be distributed to certain heirs, the administrator could be charged as trustee for the heirs' creditors.

Whether the administrator is summoned as trustee in the first instance or is summoned upon the death of the trustee before disclosure, the administrator's disclosure will become the disclosure of the trustee within the meaning of RSA 512:18 and 512:19, and the disclosure is competent evidence.[149]

§ 45-17. Attorney-Client Privilege in Beneficiary's Suit

When an administrator is sued by a beneficiary, problems can arise surrounding a possible limitation of the administrator's attorney-client privilege. The administrator may make many disclosures to the attorney handling the estate administration in the course of making strategic decisions. However, the attorney's true client is the estate, not the administrator. The beneficiaries of an estate have a right of access to the opinions of counsel, which may include access to otherwise privileged discussions the attorney may have with the administrator.

---

[145] Hall v. Harvey, 3 N.H. 61 (1824).

[146] Chapman v. Gale, 32 N.H. 141 (1855).

[147] Palmer v. Noyes, 45 N.H. 174 (1864).

[148] Protective Check Writer Co. v. Collins, 92 N.H. 27, 23 A.2d 770 (1942).

[149] Clark v. Robinson, 37 N.H. 579 (1859).

When the beneficiary sues the administrator, the attorney for the administrator could be subject to a motion to compel disclosure and may be forced to turn over many documents relating to the attorney-client relationship. Furthermore, the attorney could be compelled to testify or to withdraw from further representation of the administrator. "Overall, the three factors that courts use to determine whether a particular communication between a fiduciary and its counsel is protected are: (1) whether the fiduciary is paying counsel out of its individual resources or out of the trust estate; (2) whether a claim by a beneficiary exists or at least is a realistic possibility; and (3) whether the representation is aimed at protecting the fiduciary in its individual capacity. E.g., *Riggs National Bank v. Zimmer*, 355 A.2d 709 (Del. Ch. 1976)."[150]

One way to protect the attorney-client privilege is for the administrator to retain separate counsel when sued in his individual capacity by a beneficiary of the estate. "Mixing the functions, even in a nominal way, can lead to an ethical and discovery quagmire."[151]

Cross References

See Chapter 45 for a discussion of the time limitations for exhibiting claims.

---

[150] Wingfield, *Fiduciary Attorney-Client Communications: An Illusory Privilege?*, Probate and Property (July/Aug. 1994).

[151] *Id.*

CHAPTER 46. SURVIVAL OF ACTIONS

---

§ 46-1. Introduction

At common law, the rule was that all suits and causes of action, whether pending or not, died with the decedent. However, the unfairness and illogic of this rule quickly led to statutory revision. In New Hampshire, a series of statutory provisions, found in Chapter 556, entitled "Suits By and Against Administrators," change the common law by providing for the survival and continuance of actions by and against a decedent.

RSA 556:7 provides that actions not yet pending, by or against the decedent at his death may be brought by or against the decedent's administrator within one year of his appointment. RSA 556:9 provides for the survival of tort actions for physical injuries to the person. RSA 556:10 provides that pending actions by or against a decedent may be continued under certain prescribed circumstances. RSA 556:11 provides for the survival of new actions brought after the death of the deceased party. RSA 556:16 and 556:17 govern actions relating to real property. RSA 556:15 provides that all other actions and causes of action by or against the decedent survive and may be maintained. Unfortunately, this statutory framework is misleading and needlessly confusing, leading to situations where the statute of limitations as applied to decedents' estates is incorrectly interpreted by many practitioners.

In addition to these sections, the general statute of limitations found in RSA 508 must be constantly kept in mind. To increase the confusion, the statutes relating to the bringing of wrongful death actions, RSA 556:12–556:14 are interwoven within the statutes relating to the survival of actions.

In order to help understand the application of these statutes, certain general rules should be kept in mind. First of all, if the action involving the decedent is pending upon the death of the decedent, RSA 556:10 applies. If the action is a tort action (including wrongful death actions) RSA 556:9–556:14 apply. If the action is a contract action, for example, RSA 556:15 applies. If the action is a tort action not pending upon the death of the decedent, RSA 556:11 applies.

Library References

Am Jur 2d Abatement, Survival, and Revival §§ 47–48, 51–112

CJS Abatement and Revival § 117 et seq.

Constitutionality and construction of statute authorizing continuation of pending action against foreign representative of deceased nonresident driver of motor vehicle arising out of accident occurring in state. 18 ALR2d 544.

Effect of delay in appointing administrator or other representative on cause of action accruing at or after death of person in whose favor it would have accrued. 28 ALR3d 1141.

§ 46-2. Time Limitations

RSA 556:7 establishes a general rule of survival by providing that if a right of action existed in favor of or against the decedent at the time of his death and survives, an action may be brought by or against the administrator at any time within one year after the original grant of administration. In *Barrett v. Cady*,[1] the Supreme Court held that since the right of action does not accrue until after the death of the debtor, the statute does not begin to run until the grant of administration.

RSA 556:7 extends the general statute of limitations found in RSA 508 and was enacted to extend the time for suits to be brought which would otherwise be barred.[2] It is a savings statute and extends, rather

---

[1] Barrett v. Cady, 78 N.H. 60, 96 A. 325 (1915).

[2] Morse v. Whitcher, 64 N.H. 591, 15 A. 207 (1888).

than constricts, the general statute of limitations. It suspends the running of the statute of limitations in favor of the administrator as to all rights of actions existing in favor of the deceased at his death if suit is brought within the time provided. [3] It does not limit the time for bringing an action by an administrator on a claim not barred by the general statute of limitations, RSA 508:4.

The case of *Cummings v. Farnham*[4] determined that the only advantage conferred by RSA 556:7 in addition to RSA 556:5 is that if the plaintiff party is an administrator, he may begin his suit within one year after original administration is taken out on the creditor's (instead of the debtor's) estate if it will be of advantage for him to do so, with the consequent extension of time within which payment may be demanded before suit is brought.

RSA 556:5 requires that no suit shall be maintained against an administrator for any cause of action against the deceased unless it is begun within one year after the original grant of administration. The purpose of this section is to secure the speedy settlement of estates. [5]

The time for bringing suit is measured from the time of the original grant of administration on the creditor's estate. [6] In order to maintain an action against an administrator, however, a demand must be exhibited as required by RSA 556:3. RSA 556:3 provides that no action shall be sustained unless the demand was exhibited to the administrator within six months after the original grant of administration. [7]

RSA 556:5 will not bar a suit brought by the plaintiff creditor's administrator under the provisions of RSA 556:7. [8] This means that once the demand has been made, RSA 556:7 provides an exception to RSA 556:5, which requires that a suit be brought within one year, by allowing an extra year for bringing suit. The purpose of this section can be stated as follows: By RSA 556:5, a plaintiff's right of action against a defendant is limited to one year, but he has the full time of one year in which to commence an action. If the plaintiff dies a few days or weeks before

---

[3] Frye v. Hubbell, 74 N.H. 358, 68 A. 325 (1907).

[4] Cummings v. Farnham, 75 N.H. 135, 71 A. 632 (1908).

[5] Coffey v. Bresnahan, 127 N.H. 687, 506 A.2d 310 (1986).

[6] Perkins v. Perkins, 68 N.H. 264, 39 A. 1049 (1895).

[7] See the discussion in Chapter 41 concerning the questioned constitutionality of this requirement.

[8] *Id.*

the expiration of said time, the action must be prosecuted by his administrator. However, before the affairs of the decedent's estate can be investigated and administration thereupon granted, the one-year time limit may have expired and the administrator would otherwise be barred by the statute of limitations. However, the equitable provisions of RSA 556:7 are intended in such a situation to suspend RSA 556:5.

The provisions of RSA 556:28 allow, under certain circumstances, an extension of time for anyone with a claim against an estate which has not been prosecuted within the time limited by law. RSA 556:28 applies to RSA 556:7. In *Mitchell v. Estate of Smith*,[9] the Court held that if a party is culpably negligent in not bringing suit within the time provided, the suit will be barred, although otherwise, justice and equity would sustain it. See Chapter 41, section 40-9, for a discussion of RSA 556:28.

Library References

Am Jur 2d Abatement, Survival, and Revival §§ 51–60, 107–110, 113, 125

CJS Abatement and Revival §§ 118, 130–134, 155–158, 169–179

§ 46-3. Pending Actions

RSA 556:10, as its title, "Pending Actions," makes clear, governs the survival of tort actions which have been brought and which are pending in which a decedent is a party plaintiff or party defendant at the time of his death. A failure to comply with RSA 556:10 will cause the action to abate in the absence of any discretionary authority on the presiding justice.[10] RSA 556:10 states that if an action of tort for physical injuries is pending at the time of the decease of plaintiff, it shall abate and be forever barred unless the administrator shall appear and assume prosecution of the action. The administrator must appear before the end of the second term after the decease of such party.

If the deceased party was the defendant, the plaintiff must procure a scire facias to be issued to the administrator of the deceased party before the end of the second term, after the original grant of administration on decedent's estate. Also, when the decedent is defendant, his administrator must notify the adverse party or his attorney, in writing, of defendant's death and the subsequent grant of administration. After giving notice, the pending action will not be barred until the end of the second term

---

[9] Mitchell v. Estate of Smith, 90 N.H. 36, 4 A.2d 355 (1939).

[10] Costoras v. Noel, 100 N.H. 81, 119 A.2d 705 (1956).

after giving notice. Such notice shall be by registered mail, return receipt requested.

The administrator must file an affidavit in the probate court showing compliance with the probate court's provisions. A justice of the superior court may, for good cause shown, grant leave from any of the foregoing provisions as justice may require.

The Supreme Court in *Belkner v. Preston*[11] considered the requirement of RSA 556:10 that administrators must prosecute pending actions within two terms after the original plaintiff's death. A plaintiff has approximately eight months to file in counties with three terms, and twelve months to file in counties with two terms. The Court held that this violates equal protection provisions of the constitution as the difference in time has no rational relationship to the statutory purpose of providing for the survival of pending tort actions. The requirement of RSA 556:10 that the administrator assume prosecution of the action before the end of the second term after the death of the plaintiff was held to be unconstitutional to the extent that it allows administrators in counties with three terms less time to assume prosecution of actions.[12] The Court in *Belkner* held that a plaintiff should be allowed the same amount of time (one year) to file as plaintiffs with actions situated in counties with only two superior court terms.

Fairgraves v. Stark Mills[13] states that under RSA 556:10, the administrator has two full terms after decedent's death in which to appear. The term of court during which plaintiff dies cannot be deemed the first term after his decease; the succeeding term is the first term after his decease. For example, if the court holds January, May and September terms, and if the plaintiff died at anytime during the January term, the unexpired portion of that term after his death is not the first term succeeding his decease. The first term after the party's death would be the May term.

The issuance of a *scire facias* under RSA 556:10 is used to revive an action against a deceased party's administrator. It is not an institution of a new action. All that is required is that a *scire facias* is issued and served. There is no condition that in order for the action to survive, the *scire facias* should be made returnable or returned.[14] If a plaintiff fails

---

[11] Belkner v. Preston, 115 N.H. 15, 332 A.2d 168 (1975).

[12] *Id.*

[13] Fairgraves v. Stark Mills, 77 N.H. 215, 90 A. 510 (1914).

[14] Shea v. Starr, 76 N.H. 538, 85 A. 788 (1913).

to procure a *scire facias* to be issued to the defendant's administrator within one year, the suit will abate and the action of tort for physical injuries will be barred.[15] *Therrien v. Scammon*[16] stated that the limitation on the issuance of a *scire facias* against an administrator applies only to an action to recover for personal injuries and not to actions of contract.

The provisions of RSA 556:12 which designate the elements for damages for wrongful death do not apply to an action in which the party is plaintiff. RSA 556:12 also does not apply to actions the administrator is permitted to prosecute under RSA 556:10, which provides for prosecution of pending actions.[17]

In *Lundgren v. Hagen*,[18] the Supreme Court held that where the defendant is the sole beneficiary of the estate of the person who began the action, for example a wife suing her husband, the action will not be dismissed for that reason, even though the husband may be found liable to pay the estate and will ultimately receive the damage award by reason of being the sole beneficiary of the wife's estate. Additionally, RSA 514:12 provides that when one of two or more plaintiffs or defendants dies, and the right of action survives, the action may be prosecuted by or against the surviving parties.

§ 46-3(a). Tort Actions for Physical Injuries

In *Hebert v. Hebert*,[19] the Supreme Court stated that *actions of tort* for physical injuries to the person and the causes of such actions survive only to the extent specified by statute. RSA 556:9 provides that actions of tort for physical injuries to the person survive to the extent allowed by, and subject to the limitations set forth in RSA 556:10–556:14. The purpose of RSA 556:9 was to repeal, to the extent named in the following five sections (RSA 556:10–556:14), the common law rule that tort actions for physical injuries do not survive.[20]

The meaning of the term actions of tort in RSA 556:9 includes all causes of action for physical injuries to the person regardless of the

---

[15] Dubois v. Pouliot, 97 N.H. 78, 81 A.2d 305 (1951).

[16] Therrien v. Scammon, 87 N.H. 214, 176 A. 116 (1935).

[17] Piper v. Boston & Maine R.R. 75 N.H. 435, 75 A. 1041 (1910).

[18] Lundgren v. Hagen, 114 N.H. 110, 316 A.2d 177 (1974).

[19] Hebert v. Hebert, 120 N.H. 369, 415 A.2d 679 (1980).

[20] Hinman v. Director Gen. of Railroads, 79 N.H. 518, 112 A. 382 (1920).

differences in the proper remedy at common law.[21] The Supreme Court in *Cochran v. Laton*,[22] stated that a tort is ordinarily defined as "the loss or damage a person sustains by reason of the failure of others to perform a duty the law imposed on them for his benefit, apart from contract, regardless of whether the loss is the mediate or immediate result of their misconduct." Thus, a cause of action for pain and suffering caused by a physician's negligence, although not the cause of the subsequent death, when death does not result, will survive.[23] An action to recover for the death caused by a physician abandoning his patient will also survive.[24]

RSA 556:9 applies in a cause of action for death caused by a town's negligence in the maintenance of its highways.[25] An action for tort does not include an action for breach of an express warranty, although the breach causes death or physical injury. Although an action for breach of warranty may have begun as a tort act, it is now generally treated as a contract action.[26] An action for breach of warranty causing death must, therefore, be brought under RSA 556:15 which provides for survival of other actions.

The case of *Lozier v. Brown Co.*,[27] discusses the types of actions that are not barred. In *Lozier*, the decedent was injured in the course of his employment in 1966. From that date until his death in 1977, he received workers' compensation benefits for his injury. The wife of the decedent, as administratrix of the estate, was not barred from bringing a wrongful death action against the employer in 1978, since the action to recover for the decedent's loss of earning capacity could not have been brought prior to the decedent's death. It was held that RSA 556:11 limits only those claims that the decedent could have maintained during his lifetime.

In an action of tort for personal injuries, it is not necessary for the administrator either to allege or prove that the intestate left relatives surviving him.[28] The reason for this is that the administrator has the

---

[21] Cochran v. Laton, 78 N.H. 562, 103 A. 658 (1918).

[22] *Id.*

[23] Brown v. Weeks, 79 N.H. 509, 112 A. 393 (1920).

[24] *Id.*

[25] Davis v. Rumney, 66 N.H. 331, 29 A. 542 (1890).

[26] Kelley v. Volkswagenwerk Aktiengesellschaft, 110 N.H. 369, 268 A.2d 837 (1970).

[27] Lozier v. Brown Co., 121 N.H. 67, 426 A.2d 99 (1981).

[28] Niemi v. Boston & Maine R.R., 87 N.H. 1, 173 A. 361 (1934).

authority to save the rights of possible distributees. The administrator, however, will not be permitted to go to trial unless he satisfies the court that the decedent left beneficiaries as named in RSA 556:13.[29] RSA 556:13 describes the limitation of recovery and lists possible beneficiaries: widow, widower, child, father, mother or any relative dependent of the decedent.

The administrator is the agent of the statutory beneficiaries in an action of tort for personal injuries. The beneficiaries may assume full charge of the action, may settle directly with the defendant, or may affirm the administrator's unauthorized institution or prosecution of the action. RSA 556:9 permits an action for personal injury to be brought after the injured person's death, and then operates to transfer, from the decedent's estate to the beneficiaries, the interest in the action.

Although RSA 556:9 provides that actions for tort for physical injuries are subject to the limitations set forth in RSA 556:10 through 556:14, the provisions of RSA 556:1, barring suit against an administrator within six months of the original grant of administration, also apply.[30]

There are several leading cases involving the tort actions of minor and stillborn children. In *Dean v. Smith*, it was held that an unemancipated minor child may maintain an action against a parent or parent's estate for injuries sustained as a result of a parent's negligent operation of an automobile.[31] The administrator of a stillborn child who was a viable fetus when the injury was inflicted, may maintain an action for injuries and resulting death suffered by the fetus while *en ventre sa mere*.[32] *In re Estate of Fontaine*[33] held that an action for the death of a viable fetus may be maintained wholly apart from any action to recover for injury to the mother arising from the same incident. Furthermore, an infant born alive may maintain an action to recover for prenatal injuries inflicted on it by the tort of another even if it had not reached the state of a viable fetus at the time of injury.[34] If a fetus is nonviable, however, at the time of injury and dies in the womb, its representative cannot maintain an

---

[29] *Id.*

[30] Hall v. Brusseau, 100 N.H. 87, 119 A.2d 703 (1956).

[31] Dean v. Smith, 106 N.H. 314, 211 A.2d 410 (1965).

[32] Poliquin v. MacDonald, 101 N.H. 104, 135 A.2d 249 (1957).

[33] In re Estate of Fontaine, 128 N.H. 695, 519 A.2d 227 (1986).

[34] Bennett v. Hymers, 101 N.H. 483, 147 A.2d 108 (1958).

action. *Wallace v. Wallace.*[35] In *Wallace*, the Court defined viable as the ability to live outside the mother's womb. Damages may not be recovered for wrongful death of a nonviable fetus which was not born alive.

Library References

Am Jur 2d Abatement, Survival, and Revival §§ 61, 62, 66–68, 84, 85, 94, 98
CJS Abatement and Revival §§ 135, 140–143, 162

Survival of action or cause of action for wrongful death against representative of wrongdoer. 61 ALR 830, supplemented, 171 ALR 1392.

Survival of cause of action for personal injury or death against tortfeasor killed in the same accident. 70 ALR 1319.

Medical malpractice action as abating upon death of other party. 50 ALR2d 1445.

Effect of death of beneficiary upon right of action under death statute. 13 ALR4th 1060.

§ 46-4. New Actions

RSA 556:11 governs the survival of tort actions, on behalf of or against, deceased parties which have not been brought at the time of the decedent party's death. The statute is a savings statute which operates to extend the general three-year statute of limitations governing tort actions (RSA 508:4, I).

Formerly, RSA 556:11 provided only a two-year extension of time, as compared with the then six-year statute of limitations. In 1983, RSA 556:11 was amended to allow six years to bring a suit in tort for physical injuries. Questions followed as a result, concerning causes of action that arose prior to the 1983 amendment but were not pursued until after the two-year period had lapsed, although still within the amended six-year time limit. *Gould v. Concord Hospital,*[36] a leading case in this area, held that the classification created by RSA 556:11 violated the equal protection clause of the New Hampshire Constitution:

The law of torts is premised on the policy that a person who unreasonably interferes with the interests of another should be

---

[35] Wallace v. Wallace, 120 N.H. 675, 421 A.2d 134 (1980).
[36] Gould v. Concord Hosp., 126 N.H. 405, 493 A.2d 1193 (1985).

liable for the resulting injury. . . . Our constitution provides that all citizens have a right to the redress of their actionable injuries. N.H. Const. pt. I, art. 14. These principles require that the substantive rights of plaintiffs to maintain actions in tort be accorded solicitous protection.

We now find that the State's interest in the prompt administration of estates is not sufficiently important to justify discrimination against plaintiffs in survival actions, relative to plaintiffs in other tort actions. By establishing a short limitations period for survival actions, the State facilitates more seasonable distribution of estates and thereby helps prevent overcrowding of the dockets of the probate courts. Although these are entirely reasonable goals, we find that the substantive rights of survival plaintiffs merit greater deference.[37]

> RSA 556:11 permits suits to be brought within the designated period after the decedent's death on all claims not already barred at the time of death by the general statute of limitations, RSA 508.[38] Under the 1986 amendment to the general statute of limitations, all personal actions, including tort actions, must be brought within three years of the act complained of. RSA 508:4, I. If the action is not barred by the statute of limitations at the time of the decedent party's death, RSA 556:11 extends to six years the time in which an action may be brought. An action of tort for physical injuries is forever barred unless brought within six years of the date of death of a party whose death the statute permits it to survive.

In order to bring an action under RSA 556:11, the condition that there is not an action pending must be met. *Ham v. Maine-New Hampshire Interstate Bridge Authority*,[39] states that one may not amend, for example, an action for consequential injuries to health as a result of an intentional trespass, initiated by a decedent while still living, into an action after his death brought for causing death. If such an amendment is made, it will be considered only as including death as an additional

---

[37] Gould v. Concord Hosp., 126 N.H. 405, 409, 493 A.2d 1193, 1196 (1985).

[38] Perutsakos v. Tarmey, 107 N.H. 51, 217 A.2d 177 (1966).

[39] Ham v. Maine-New Hampshire Interstate Bridge Auth., 92 N.H. 268, 30 A.2d 1 (1943).

element of damage to the decedent since they "cannot be regarded as actions originally brought for causing death, since such actions depend upon the condition that no action for the injury done the decedent and brought by him be then pending."[40]

The provision of RSA 556:11 which limits the bringing of a suit within six years, controls the bringing of a new action for tort for physical injuries and thus prevents the application of RSA 556:10, which provides for the bringing of a second suit, from being applied to such an action.

The limitation of time of RSA 556:11 for bringing an action relates not only to the remedy, but also to the right to recovery that the statute creates. The right granted to the administrator to sue is not an absolute right. It is conditioned on suit being brought within the time as set out in the statute.[41]

Unlike the general statute of limitations, this special statute that creates the right and gives the remedy, does not merely confer a privilege on the defendant to interpose a definite time limitation as a bar to the enforcement of a distinct and independent liability, but it defines and limits the existence of the right itself.[42]

When bringing an action under RSA 556:11 against a deceased defendant's administrator, the plaintiff must comply with the prohibition on suits being brought within six months of the original grant of administration. If an action of tort for physical injuries is brought against an administrator within the time limit contained in RSA 556:1 (six months), the administrator's motion to dismiss will be granted.[43]

To bring an action under RSA 556:11, a writ must be served on the defendant in compliance with RSA 510 regarding service of writs. If the writ is not timely served, in compliance with the statute, the court will not have jurisdiction over the defendant and action may not be brought under RSA 556:11. *Peabody v. O'Leary*.[44] The *Peabody* Court determined that the joining of another party as defendant to a wrongful death

---

[40] Ham v. Maine-New Hampshire Interstate Bridge Auth., 92 N.H. 268, 275, 30 A.2d 1, 6 (1943).

[41] Poff v. New England Tel. and Tel. Co., 72 N.H. 164, 55 A. 891 (1903).

[42] Guerin v. New Hampshire Catholic Charities, Inc., 120 N.H. 501, 418 A.2d 224, 226 (1980); *citing* Poff v. New England Tel. and Tel. Co., 72 N.H. 164, 55 A. 891 (1903).

[43] Heath v. Cleveland, 104 N.H. 451, 189 A.2d 488 (1963).

[44] Peabody v. O'Leary, 102 N.H. 496, 161 A.2d 167 (1960).

action will not be allowed after the statute of limitations of RSA 556:11 has expired.

Library References

Am Jur 2d Abatement, Survival, and Revival §§ 54, 125
Am Jur 2d Limitation of Actions §§ 182–185
CJS Abatement and Revival §§ 130–134, 172–179
CJS Limitation of Actions §§ 243–245

§ 46-4(a). Damages for Physical Injury

RSA 556:11, which provides for the bringing of a new action "for such cause," may be either for personal injuries alone or for injuries resulting in death.[45] A declaration, therefore, based on injuries suffered by a decedent with no claim of resulting death, may be joined with one which seeks recovery for resulting death. If death resulted, recovery may be sought under RSA 556:12, which deals with wrongful death actions.[46] If death did not result, recovery is governed by the rules of damages which pertain to an action brought before death. The recoverable damages depend on whether death resulted. If the two causes of action are separable, they are alternative, rather than concurrent. If the question of whether death resulted is an issue, and an alternative submission is made, the jury's determination of the issue may be indicated by special verdict.[47]

Generally, the ordinary grounds of damages in actions of tort for physical injuries are: the expense of board, nursing, medical care, compensation for loss of time, physical and mental pain. This includes an amount the jury thinks ought to be given for distress or anxiety experienced while in imminent danger of death from the injury received, to the close of life.[48]

If a suit is brought in a decedent's lifetime and prosecuted after his death by his administrator, the damages obtainable are not limited by RSA 556:12 (Damages for Wrongful Death) and RSA 556:13 (Limitation of Recovery).[49] Death is an additional element of damage to the

---

[45] Burke v. Burnham, 97 N.H. 203, 84 A.2d 918 (1951).

[46] See Chapter 47 *infra.*

[47] *Id.*

[48] Corliss v. Worcester, Nashua & Rochester R.R., 63 N.H. 404 (1885).

[49] West v. Boston & Maine R.R., 81 N.H. 522, 129 A. 768 (1925).

decedent. The decedent's loss of life entitles his estate to recover for his loss of earning capacity for the remainder of his life, since life would have continued but for the defendant's wrong. An allowance for bodily and mental suffering may be granted, but the amount must be within the bounds of justice.[50]

If death results from causes other than personal injuries, the administrator may recover only the damages suffered by the decedent during and to the close of life.[51]

Library References

Am Jur 2d Abatement, Survival, and Revival § 68

CJS Abatement and Revival §§ 140–143

Shortening of life expectancy as element of damages recoverable in action by person injured or in action under survival statute or death statute. 131 ALR 1351.

Recovery, in action for benefit of decedent's estate in jurisdiction which has both wrongful death and survival statutes, of value of earnings decedent would have made after death. 76 ALR3d 125.

§ 46-5. Actions Relating to Real Property

The administrator, under RSA 556:17, entitled "Real Actions Pending," may prosecute and defend all real actions pending at the time of decedent's death.

RSA 556:16 permits the administrator to maintain any necessary and proper actions relative to real estate for debts that are owed to the estate. In cases of insolvency, the administrator may maintain necessary actions until the administration is closed.

If administration has not been granted to the estate of the deceased within two years, a creditor under RSA 556:29 will not be entitled to maintain an action or proceeding to appropriate real estate or interests which the deceased died seized of, for payment in whole or part of his claim against the estate.

If the estate is insolvent, then under *Benton v. Collins*,[52] the administrator is entitled to possession of any real property of which the decedent

---

[50] Ham v. Maine-New Hampshire Interstate Bridge Auth., 92 N.H. 268, 30 A.2d 1 (1943).

[51] Burke v. Burnham, 97 N.H. 203, 84 A.2d 918 (1951).

[52] Benton v. Collins, 67 N.H. 498, 39 A. 442 (1893).

was in possession at the time of death. The administrator may maintain a writ of entry to recover possession of lands belonging to the estate. *Forist v. Androscoggin River Improvement Co.*[53] held that if an administrator is to sustain an action for an injury to real estate after the death of the intestate, the facts on which the right to sue is dependent on, must be stated in the declaration. Thus, the declaration should state that plaintiff, as administrator, has a right to sue as he would have if the deceased died seized, the estate was insolvent and the administration not closed.[54]

The case of *Pierce v. Jaquith*[55] determined that if a mortgage foreclosure suit is pending, or if the estate is insolvent and the administrator has interest in the land, the administrator should appear and protect the suit. In cases where land descends to the heirs, and consequently the estate has no interest in it, the administrator should not defend the suit, as his actions could not bind the heirs.[56]

Library References

Am Jur 2d Abatement, Survival, and Revival §§ 69–71, 89, 90, 100, 104, 106

CJS Abatement and Revival § 138

Does right of grantor to maintain a suit in equity to set aside his conveyance for cause survive to his heir? 2 ALR 431, supplemented, 33 ALR 51

Revivor or other steps necessary in event of mortgagee's death after sale of property but before confirmation of sale. 150 ALR 502.

§ 46-6. Survival of Other Actions

RSA 556:15 governs the survival of other than tort or real property actions. This statute, entitled "Survival of Other Actions," abrogates the old common law rule against survival and allows an action that was

---

[53] Forist v. Androscoggin River Improvement Co., 52 N.H. 477 (1872). See also Carter v. Jackson, 56 N.H. 364 (1876).

[54] Carter v. Jackson, 56 N.H. 364 (1876) stated that an administrator of an insolvent estate may maintain an action of trespass *quare clausum fregit* (a writ of trespass) against a person who has entered the decedent's property. The plaintiff-administrator, however, must either have or be entitled to have possession of the estate on which trespass is alleged to have been committed. Carter v. Jackson, 56 N.H. 364, 368 (1876).

[55] Pierce v. Jaquith, 48 N.H. 231 (1868).

[56] See Chapter 35 *supra*.

pending at the death of the decedent to survive if the administrator revives it. The action may exist in favor of or against the decedent and may be prosecuted or defended by the administrator.

For an action to survive, however, it must not be an action for the recovery of penalties and forfeitures of money under penal statutes.

The most common actions which survive under this section are contract actions, but, under RSA 556:15, all actions of negligence survive except actions of tort for physical injuries, which survive through RSA 556:9. Actions for breach of warranty causing death must be brought under RSA 556:15.

When the legislature enacted 556:15, it made the survival of actions almost universal with the exception of penalties and forfeitures of money under penal statutes, although, *Coulombe v. Eastman*[57] held that the debt of a corporation is penal in character and does not survive the decedent.

Library References

Am Jur 2d Abatement, Survival, and Revival § 61 et seq.

CJS Abatement and Revival §§ 146–154

---

[57] Coulombe v. Eastman, 77 N.H. 368, 92 A. 168 (1914).

CHAPTER 47. WRONGFUL DEATH ACTIONS

§ 47-1. Generally

A wrongful death action is an action brought to recover damages sustained as a consequence of the death of a person. Such actions are usually founded in negligence and assert that the death of the decedent was caused by the negligence of a third party.

Actions for wrongful death were not recognized at common law because it was reasoned that any damages causing the death of a person were damages of the decedent and the action died with him. All wrongful death actions which are now recognized are statutorily-based and are usually circumscribed by carefully drawn, narrow, statutory rules. These statutes vary considerably from state to state, although all have as their common root the mid-1800s English Act known as Lord Campbell's Act[1]

---

[1] Pitman v. Merriman, 80 N.H. 295, 117 A. 18 (1922).

which has as its origin the Industrial Revolution and the vastly increased danger to life and limb which industrialization brought to Anglo-American civilization.

In New Hampshire, a wrongful death action may be brought only by the decedent's bona fide administrator. If damages are recovered, the proceeds, less expenses of recovery, pass into the decedent's estate. Such an action is brought in the superior court by the administrator of the decedent. The administrator is appointed by the probate court and after any recovery in the superior court action, the proceeds are administered and accounted for by the administrator in the probate court.

Library References

Am Jur 2d Death § 1 et seq.

CJS Death § 13 et seq.

§ 47-2. Wrongful Birth and Wrongful Life Actions Distinguished

Often confused with wrongful death actions, particularly wrongful death actions involving unborn but viable fetuses, are two types of actions which are somewhat related but which are wholly nonstatutorily-based and which seek damages for related, but different prenatal torts.

A wrongful birth claim is a claim brought by the parents of a child born with severe defects against a physician who negligently fails to inform them in a timely fashion of an increased possibility that the mother will give birth to such a child, thereby precluding an informed decision as to whether to have the child.

A wrongful life claim, on the other hand, is brought by or on behalf of the child born with birth defects. The child contends that the defendant physician negligently failed to inform the child's parents of the risk of bearing a defective infant, and hence prevented the parents from choosing to avoid the child's birth.

In the 1986 case of *Smith v. Cote*,[2] the New Hampshire Supreme Court refused to recognize an action for wrongful life but did recognize, subject to specific damage limitations, a common law action for wrongful birth.[3] However, since the child is born alive in a wrongful birth case, there is no probate court involvement.

---

[2] Smith v. Cote, 128 N.H. 231 (1986).

[3] See Lex Loci, 27 N.H.B.J. 247.

In 1957, the New Hampshire Supreme Court recognized in *Poliquin v. MacDonald*[4] for the first time that a wrongful death action can be brought to recover damages for the wrongful death of a viable fetus:

> We are of the opinion that the early orthodox views must give way to justice and logic. "Precedents are valuable so long as they do not obstruct justice or destroy progress.". . . The common law has always been most solicitous for the welfare of the fetus in connection with its inheritance rights as well as protecting it under the criminal law. If a child can live separate and apart from its mother, even though she die, it does not seem logical to say that the injury was wholly that of the mother and not of the child. Consequently recovery should be allowed on behalf of a viable child born alive.

We are also of the opinion that a fetus having reached that period of pre-natal maturity where it is capable of independent life apart from its mother is a person and if such child dies in the womb as the result of another's negligence, an action for recovery may be maintained in its behalf. . . . On the other hand if a fetus is non-viable at the time of injury and dies in the womb its representative can maintain no action.

In *In re Estate of Fontaine*[5] the Supreme Court dealt with the issue of the distribution in the probate court of the proceeds of a wrongful death award to the estate of a viable fetus and held that the mother of the decedent, a beneficiary of the estate of the decedent, could take her share of the estate even if she were comparatively or contributorily negligent in the death of the decedent.

Library References

Am Jur 2d New Topic Service Right to Die; Wrongful Life § 63 et seq.

CJS Infants § 215

Cause of action for "wrongful life." 83 ALR3d 15.

§ 47-3. Historical Antecedents

New Hampshire's wrongful death statute is found in RSA 556 entitled "Suits By and Against Administrators." The New Hampshire statute is confusing since it has some of the attributes of both a survival action

---

[4] Poliquin v. MacDonald, 101 N.H. 104, 135 A.2d 249 (1957).

[5] In re Estate of Fontaine, 128 N.H. 695, 519 A.2d 227 (1986).

(see Chapter 46, *supra*) and of a separately recognized wrongful death action. An excellent article by John T. Franklin in the New Hampshire Bar Journal entitled "Wrongful Death and Survival Actions in New Hampshire,"[6] contains a very helpful discussion of the elusive but important distinctions between survival actions and wrongful death actions.

Controversy exists as to whether New Hampshire has a survival statute or a wrongful death statute. New Hampshire RSA 556 has been interpreted to apply to both survival and wrongful death actions. "A survival statute merely allows the decedent's representative to maintain any actions that accrued to the decedent during his lifetime, while a wrongful death action creates a new cause of action in someone other than the decedent for loss caused by the decedent's death." *Lozier v. Brown Co.*[7]

The legislative history of RSA 556 is helpful for an understanding of the statute. At common law, no action for wrongful death was recognized. In the 1850 enactment of a wrongful death act,[8] the New Hampshire statute appears to have been administered after the English act, Lord Campbell's Act.[9] The purpose of the Campbell Act was to compensate specific relatives of the deceased for loss sustained by death. The intent in bringing such an action against the defendant was not punitive in nature; recovery was treated as compensatory.[10] In 1879, the earlier 1850 New Hampshire statute was repealed and a more direct antecedent of present law was enacted. It was entitled "An Act in Relation to Actions for Personal Injuries."[11] In 1885, a general survival act was adopted. In 1887, a new death act was passed.[12] In 1891, the Public Statute was revised to combine the 1887 death act and the 1885 survival act. The death act was refined by distinguishing actions pending at death from

---

[6] Franklin, *Wrongful Death and Survival Actions in New Hampshire*, 6 N.H.B.J. 305 (1964).

[7] Lozier v. Brown Co., 121 N.H. 67, 426 A.2d 29 (1981), *citing Franklin, Wrongful Death and Survival Actions in New Hampshire*, 6 N.H.B.J. 305, 305–06 (1964).

[8] For a comprehensive overview of the legislative history of New Hampshire RSA 556, see Franklin, *Wrongful Death and Survival Actions in New Hampshire*, 6 N.H.B.J. 305 (1964).

[9] Lord Campbell's Act, 6 & 7 Vict., c. 96; Pitman v. Merriman, 80 N.H. 295, 117 A. 18 (1922).

[10] *Id.*

[11] Laws 1879, ch. 35, §§ 1, 2.

[12] Laws 1887, ch. 71, §§ 1–4.

those instituted after death.[13] In 1913 an exception to the amount of recovery was instituted in instances where the decedent left a widow or widower, minor children, or dependent mother or father.[14] After 1913, the legislature from time to time increased the maximum limitation for recovery of damages and in 1973, the legislature wholly removed the damage limitation where the decedent left a widow or widower, child, mother, father or any dependent relative.[15] In all other cases, the recovery was limited to $50,000.[16] In 1971, the statute was amended to provide that wrongful death damages were to be distributed in accordance with the decedent's estate, instead of to certain specified individuals.

As a result of the 1971 changes to the wrongful death statute, by which the distribution of damages was changed from particularly specified beneficiaries to distribution as part of the decedent's estate, the statute has become much more like a survival statute rather than a pure wrongful death act. The effect of this change was recognized by the Supreme Court in *In re Estate of Fontaine*,[17] where the Court characterized the newly-revised law as permitting the "survival of the decedent's action, rather than authorizing a new and separate wrongful death action."[18]

Library References

Am Jur 2d Death § 2

CJS Death § 15

§ 47-4. Elements of Cause of Action

The elements of a cause of action for wrongful death are "damages for the injury to the person and estate" of the deceased party by the "wrongful act or neglect and consequent death." RSA 556:12.

---

[13] P.S. 1891, ch. 191, §§ 8–14.

[14] See Franklin, *Wrongful Death and Survival Actions in New Hampshire*, 6 N.H.B.J. 305 (1964).

[15] Middleton and Chiesa, *Trial of Wrongful Death Cases in New Hampshire*, 19 N.H.B.J. 69 (1977).

[16] *Id.*

[17] In re Estate of Fontaine, 128 N.H. 695, 519 A.2d 227 (1986).

[18] In re Estate of Fontaine, 128 N.H. 695, 700, 519 A.2d 227, 230 (1986).

§ 47-4(a). Contract Actions—Breach of Warranty Causing Death

Prior to *Kelley v. Volkswagenwerk Aktiengesellschaft*,[19] which was decided in 1970, wrongful death claims that were based on contract actions were barred. *Kelley*[20] overruled *Howson v. Foster Beef Co.*,[21] and *Wadleigh v. Howson*,[22] by holding that the administrator of an estate can maintain an action for a breach of warranty which allegedly caused the death of the decedent. Contract actions are now permissible in certain circumstances when they are brought prior to the expiration of the contract statute of limitations period.[23]

An action for breach of warranty causing death will not survive if brought under RSA 556:9, which specifically provides for survival of tort actions. Although an action for breach of warranty may have begun as a tort act, it is now generally treated as a contract action.[24] An action for breach of warranty causing death may be brought under RSA 556:15 which pertains to survival of other actions.

Library References

Am Jur 2d Abatement, Survival, and Revival § 65

CJS Abatement and Revival §§ 131, 147

§ 47-4(b). Liability for the Suicide of Another

New Hampshire has recognized the general rule of non-liability for the suicide of another. *Bruzga v. PMR Architects*.[25] The basis of the general non-liability rule is that if the action lies in negligence, the act of suicide is considered a deliberate, intentional and intervening act which breaks the causal connection between the wrongful or negligent act and the death.[26]

Two exceptions to the general rule recognized in other states have been recognized in New Hampshire. The first exception "recognizes a cause

---

[19] *Id.*

[20] *Id.*

[21] Howson v. Foster Beef Co., 87 N.H. 200, 177 A. 656 (1935).

[22] Wadleigh v. Howson, 88 N.H. 365, 189 A. 868 (1937).

[23] Hodgdon v. Weeks Mem. Hosp., 122 N.H. 424, 445 A.2d 1116 (1982).

[24] Kelley v. Volkswagenwerk Aktiengesellschaft, 110 N.H. 369, 268 A.2d 837 (1970).

[25] *Bruzga v. PMR Architects*, 141 N.H. 756 (1997).

[26] *Id.*

of action where the defendant actually causes the suicide." The Court had adopted that first exception in *Mayer v. Town of Hampton*.[27] Thus, based on *Mayer*, a defendant may be found liable "where the conduct of the defendant was an intentional tort and extreme and outrageous, and where this conduct caused severe emotional distress on the part of the victim which was a substantial factor in bringing about the victim's ensuing suicide."

The second exception, also recognized in New Hampshire, *McLaughlin v. Sullivan*,[28] recognizes a cause of action where the defendant "has a specific duty of care to prevent suicide arising from the defendant's special relationship with the suicidal individual."

In *Bruzga*, the Court held that neither exception applied either to the action brought by the plaintiff in negligence or to the account brought on the theory of strict liability, the Court holding that where the action was against the architect for allegedly designing a dangerous and negligent fire system for a prison in where the decedent had used the sprinkler to hang himself was not liable and the matter did not come within the two exceptions to the general rule of non-liability for suicide.[29]

§ 47-5. Elements of Damage

Early statutes provided a remedy by fining the wrongdoer, if found guilty. The fine was paid to the deceased party's widow or heirs at law.[30] In 1879, a civil form of action was substituted for the criminal form to recover damages for an injury. By an act of 1887,[31] the damages recoverable in the action were enlarged, and the elements to be considered in assessing damages were specified to an extent. To be considered were "damages for the injury to the person and estate" of the deceased party by the "wrongful act or neglect and consequent death." In assessing damages, "the mental and physical pain of the injured person, the expense occasioned to him in his life and to his estate upon his decease, his age and probable duration of life and earning capacity, but for said wrongful act or neglect" were to be considered.[32]

---

[27] Mayer v. Town of Hampton, 127 N.H. 181 (1985).

[28] McLaughlin v. Sullivan, 123 N.H. 335, 461 Atlantic 2d 123 (1983).

[29] *Id.*

[30] Burke v. Burnham, 97 N.H. 203, 84 A.2d 918 (1951).

[31] Laws 1887, ch. 71.

[32] Carney v. Concord St. Ry., 72 N.H. 364, 57 A. 218 (1903).

The present statute, RSA 556:12 entitled "Damages for Wrongful Death, Elements," incorporates elements from the early statutes and provides as follows:

> If the administrator of the deceased party is plaintiff, and the death of such party was caused by the injury complained of in the action, the mental and physical pain suffered by the deceased in consequence of the injury, the reasonable expenses occasioned to the estate by the injury, the probable duration of life but for the injury, and the capacity to earn money during the deceased party's probable working life, may be considered as elements of damage in connection with other elements allowed by law, in the same manner as if the deceased had survived. RSA 556:12, I.

In addition, the statute provides that the trier of fact may award damages to a surviving spouse of the decedent for the loss of the comfort, society, and companionship of the deceased; however, where fault on the part of the decedent or the surviving spouse is found to have caused, in whole or in part, the loss complained of, damages recoverable shall be subject to diminution to the extent and in the manner provided for in RSA 507:7-d. In no event shall damages awarded under this paragraph exceed $150,000. RSA 556:12, II.

Where the decedent is a parent of a minor child or children, the trier of fact may award damages to such child or children for the loss of familial relationship, whether caused intentionally or by negligent interference; where the decedent is a minor child with a surviving parent or parents, the trier of fact may award damages to such parent or parents for the loss of familial relationship, whether caused intentionally or by negligent interference. However, where fault on the part of the decedent or the claimant is found to have caused, in whole or in part, the loss complained of, damages recoverable shall be subject to diminution to the extent and in the manner provided for in RSA 507:7-d. For purposes of this paragraph, loss of familial relationship shall include the loss of the comfort, society, affection, guidance, and companionship of the deceased. In no event shall damages awarded under this paragraph exceed $50,000 per individual claimant.

RSA 556:12 is the only section that deals with damages that are recoverable when death results. This section does not apply to "an action pending at the time of the decease of one of the parties." RSA 556:10. Such actions are considered survival actions and governed by RSA 556:9. Damages recoverable under RSA 556:12 are exclusively limited to cases where the damages sought and recovered are for injuries resulting in death. One cannot also recover through RSA 556:12 under a separate cause of action in favor of the estate for damages to the decedent.

Recovery for damages is exclusive in cases where the damages sought and recovered are for injuries resulting in death. Damages are to be assessed from the position of the loss suffered by the deceased and his estate. Before the adoption of RSA 556:12, II and III allowing the surviving spouse and children to be awarded damages for the loss of the comfort, society, and companionship of the deceased; it was improper for surviving relatives to request a damage assessment based on the loss they have suffered personally.[33]

Burke v. Burnham[34] refers to RSA 556:12 and states that the damages recoverable in a death action include several elements of damage which might have been recovered by the decedent in his lifetime:

In the assessment of damages, the administrator is entitled to have the following considered: expenses of physical pain and injury for one already ill when injured; damages for mental pain that precluded physical injury—victim knows severe injury is unavoidable; the costs of maintenance, hospital, medical and funeral charges; decedent's capacity to earn money during life but for the injury; and other elements of damages allowed by law.

In *Emery v. Boston & Maine Railroad*,[35] it was held that damages are obtainable where one already in ill health, who is injured, suffers additional expenses from the illness which were caused by the injury complained of. In an action for wrongful death, an estate is entitled to recover damages for the mental and physical pain suffered by the deceased in consequence of the injury.[36]

In *Baker v. Salvation Army*,[37] the Court held that recovery may be granted for a wife's earnings which are in excess of the cost to her

---

[33] Siciliano v. Capital City Shows, Inc., 124 N.H. 719, 475 A.2d 19 (1984).

[34] Burke v. Burnham, 97 N.H. 203, 84 A.2d 918 (1951).

[35] Emery v. Boston & Maine R.R., 67 N.H. 434, 36 A. 367 (1893).

[36] Lees v. Nolan, 121 N.H. 680, 681, 433 A.2d 1287, 1288 (1981).

[37] Baker v. Salvation Army, 91 N.H. 1, 12 A.2d 514 (1940).

husband for her maintenance, in addition to hospital, medical, nursing and funeral charges. In *Baker*, the deceased lived for fifty days after a car accident with considerable pain and substantial mental anguish.

In *Jewell v. Colby*[38] it was held that evidence of a person's insanity is not admissible to defeat the right to recover for damages for wrongful death. If, however, greater damages are sought on account of the intent or motive of the insane defendant, insanity is a good defense to that claim, as an insane person may not have will or malice, and the measure of damages is compensation for the actual loss.

The phrase *other elements allowed by law*, (RSA 556:12) according to *Burke v. Burnham*,[39] refers to the elements of damage recoverable in actions where death is not a factor, and is sufficiently broad to include expenses occasioned to the decedent during his lifetime "where death is not a factor."[40]

In a landmark 1999 case of first impression, a split New Hampshire Supreme Court ruled that hedonic damages in wrongful death cases were allowed. *Marcotte v. Timberlane/Hampstead School District*.[41] In this case, the Court upheld the trial judge's admission of evidence of the "decedent's computer diary," highlighting "the activities the decedent enjoyed" during his life and various photographs depicting the decedent, his home, his family, and his belongings, which the Court indicated were properly admitted because such "evidence was relevant to prove damages for loss of life and helpful to the jury in assessing the amount to award for such damages."

§ 47-5(a). Earning Capacity

RSA 556:12 provides that in assessing damages in wrongful death cases, consideration may be given to the decedent's "capacity to earn money." *Dillon v. Hudson, Pelham & Salem Electric Railway*[42] states that "evidence that the decedent had never earned money, and from her station or situation in life probably never would, might be competent upon the question of capacity to earn, but would not establish its

---

[38] Jewell v. Colby, 66 N.H. 399, 24 A. 902 (1891).

[39] Burke v. Burnham, 97 N.H. 203, 84 A.2d 918 (1951).

[40] Burke v. Burnham, 97 N.H. 203, 206, 84 A.2d 918, 922 (1951).

[41] 143 N.H. 331 (1999).

[42] Dillon v. Hudson, Pelham & Salem Elec. Ry., 73 N.H. 367, 368, 62 A. 93, 93 (1905).

nonexistence." *Pierce v. Mowry*,[43] in following *Dillon*, stated that although the capacity to earn is made material, it is not declared to be the measure of the damages, rather the loss to the estate by the destruction of that capacity is the measure.

In *Golej v. Varjabedian*,[44] a twelve-year-old boy died as the result of being thrown from a horse-drawn wagon when it was hit by an automobile driven by the defendant. The issues of the boy's earning capacity and probable duration of life were considered. The *Golej* Court held that where damages are prospective, the gross amount thereof should be reduced to present worth; and that the sum given must be the present worth of future pecuniary benefits of which the beneficiary has been deprived by the wrongful act, neglect or default of the defendant.

In *Carney v. Concord Street Railway*,[45] an infant was killed by a train. The *Carney* Court considered the issue of decedent's capacity to earn money, and defined it as the capacity to earn money for his estate, and such capacity is not that which exists at the time of death but that which would exist during his life, but for the injury.

Morrell v. Gobeil[46] held that in determining a decedent's earning capacity, his disposition to earn, although not the test, is a material fact to be considered. The *Morrell* Court stated that if the decedent was a drunken loafer, who, though physically able, probably would never do a day's work, there would be no loss to his estate if his earning capacity was cut off. *Pitman v. Merriman*[47] said that when determining the amount the decedent could have earned for his estate, one should deduct his necessary living expenses.

Library References

Am Jur 2d Death § 215 et seq.

CJS Death § 95 et seq.

§ 47-5(b). Loss of Consortium

Effective January 1, 1998, a surviving spouse may be awarded damages as a result of the death of her spouse "for the loss of the comfort,

---

[43] Pierce v. Mowry, 105 N.H. 428, 201 A.2d 901 (1964).

[44] Golej v. Varjabedian, 86 N.H. 244, 166 A. 287 (1933).

[45] Carney v. Concord St. Ry., 72 N.H. 364, 57 A. 218 (1903).

[46] Morrell v. Gobeil, 84 N.H. 150, 152, 147 A. 413, 414 (1929).

[47] Pitman v. Merriman, 80 N.H. 295, 117 A. 18 (1922).

society, and companionship of the deceased."[48] However, if either the surviving spouse or the deceased spouse "is found to have caused, in whole or in part, the loss complained of, damages recoverable shall be subject to diminution to the extent and in the manner provided" under the comparative negligent provisions of RSA 507:7-d.[49] However, loss of consortium damages are limited by this provision to $150,000 or less.

Effective January 1, 1999, RSA 556:12, III provides that where the decedent is a parent of a minor child or children, the trier of fact may award damages to such child or children for the loss of familial relationship, whether caused intentionally or by negligent interference; where the decedent is a minor child with a surviving parent or parents, the trier of fact may award damages to such parent or parents for the loss of familial relationship, whether caused intentionally or by negligent interference. However, where fault on the part of the decedent or the claimant is found to have caused, in whole or in part, the loss complained of, damages recoverable shall be subject to diminution to the extent and in the manner provided for in RSA 507:7-d. For purposes of this paragraph, loss of familial relationship shall include the loss of the comfort, society, affection, guidance, and companionship of the deceased. In no event shall damages awarded under this paragraph exceed $50,000 per individual claimant.

§ 47-4(c). Hedonic Damages

Marcotte v. Timberlane/Hampstead School District[50] was a wrongful death action on behalf of a student who was killed by a soccer goal designed and paid for by a public school's independent soccer league, modified and built by a manufacturer, and subsequently donated to the school district. The student lost his life when one of the 310 lb. steel goals toppled over upon him while playing soccer. The jury awarded $925,000 to the plaintiff administrator which was abated to $150,000 by the judge's application of RSA 507-B:4.

The Court addressed the issue in the case was whether or not in a wrongful death action the plaintiff was entitled to recover "hedonic damages," defined by the Court as "the value translated into dollar figures for the purpose of compensation, of the decedent's lost life." The Court

---

[48] RSA 556:12, II.

[49] *Id.*

[50] 143 N.H. 331, (1999).

first found that the damages were not limited by RSA 412:3 which authorizes school districts to procure liability insurance and which further provides that the school district's liability shall not exceed the policy limit or the limit specified in 507-B:4, "whichever is higher." The insurance policy involved provided that liability was limited to $150,000 or $1,000,000, depending upon whether or not RSA 507-B:4, I applied or was found to be unconstitutional. RSA 507-B:4, I provides that liability of a governmental unit for bodily injury is limited to $150,000. Reading the different parts of the policy together, the majority of the Court concluded that the limitation provided for in RSA 507-B:4, I "does not apply when a governmental unit purchases liability insurance that would apply but for the statutory limit itself" and ruled that the superior court should not have abated the jury verdict.

Turning to the issue of hedonic damages, the Court, in a case of first impression in New Hampshire, focused on the language of the wrongful death statute, RSA 556:12, which provides for the recovery to a decedent's estate both for "the probable duration of [his/her] life but for the injury" and "[his/her] capacity to earn money during [his/her] probable working life." The Court ruled that these two phrases must be read separately or otherwise the additional phraseology is "mere surplusage" and the legislature "is not presumed to waste words or enact redundant provisions and whenever possible, each word of a statute should be giving effect." Thus, the Court reasoned that the phrase "the probable duration of his life but for the injury" "may include the hedonic element, which is generally compensable as lost enjoyment of life."

Having found that hedonic damages were allowed, the Court then upheld the trial judge's admission of hotly contested evidence of the "decedent's computer diary, highlighting "the activities the decedent enjoyed during his life" and various photographs depicting the decedent, his home, his family and his belongings, which the Court indicated were properly admitted since such "evidence was relevant to prove damages for loss of life and were helpful to the jury in assessing the amount to award for such damages."

§ 47-6. Defenses

In a wrongful death action, the comparative negligence or the contributory negligence of estate beneficiaries is not a relevant consideration in assessing the defendant's liability because wrongful death actions are for the benefit of the estate rather than the distributees.[51] Furthermore, the mother's comparative negligence in an action brought by the estate of the viable fetus is not imputable to the deceased fetus.[52] As a result, the mother of the decedent, even though comparatively or contributorily negligent, may still recover as a beneficiary of the estate of the decedent.[53]

§ 47-7. Limitation of Recovery

If death results from causes other than the personal injuries complained of, *Burke v. Burnham*[54] held that the administrator would be entitled to recover only the damages suffered by his decedent during and to the end of life. When a plaintiff claims that death did result from the injuries, RSA 556:12 provides a broader rule of damages, although the amount that may be recovered is limited.[55] *Welch v. Boston & Maine Railroad*[56] held that there may be instances where the actual damages may exceed the statutory limit.

RSA 556:13, which establishes a limitation on the amount of damages recoverable, states that the damages recoverable in a wrongful death action shall not exceed fifty thousand dollars if the decedent has not left either a widow, widower, child, father, mother or any relative dependent on him. In the event where the decedent has left someone from the above-stated group, there shall be no limitation on the amount of recovery. *Welch v. Boston & Maine Railroad*[57] establishes the rule that the existence of dependents is not an element of damages, but merely establishes a limit to recoverable damages.

Trovato v. Deveau,[58] presented the important issue "[w]hether RSA 556:13, which caps at $50,000 the damages recoverable in a wrongful death action, where the decedent was not survived by a spouse, child, parent or other dependant relative, violates the rights of the representative

---

[51] In re Estate of Fontaine, 128 N.H. 695, 519 A.2d 227 (1986).

[52] *Id.*

[53] *Id.*

[54] Burke v. Burnham, 97 N.H. at 206, 84 A.2d at 922 (1951).

[55] *Id.*

[56] Welch v. Boston & Maine R.R., 78 N.H. 277, 99 A. 296 (1916).

[57] *Id.*

[58] 143 N.H. 523 (1999).

of the estate under the New Hampshire or United States Constitution."[59] The Court found that the cap violated the New Hampshire Constitution, specifically, Part I, Article 14, which provides: Every subject to this state is entitled to a certain remedy by having recourse to the laws, for all injuries he may receive in his person, property, or character; to obtain right and justice freely, without being obliged to purchase it; completely, and without any denial; promptly, and without delay, conformably to the laws.

The Court found that this provision requires that litigants similarly situated should be treated with like protection and without discrimination. The Court then turned its analysis to the plaintiff's estate's two arguments, the first being that distinctions within the cap provision between decedents who are survived by dependant relatives and those who are not violated this constitutional provision. The Court agreed with the defendant on this issue, basing its decision in large part on the legislative history of the cap. The Court held that "maintaining a limitation on damages for estates without dependant relatives, while eliminating any cap for estates with dependant relatives, bears a fair and substantial relationship to the compensatory purposes of the statute."[60]

Next, carefully addressing the argument of the plaintiff that the judicial remedy provision of the constitution was violated by "distinctions outside the cap provision" [RSA 556:9–14][61] "because there was an impermissible distinction between decedents whose death is causally related to a tort injury and decedents whose death is due to unrelated causes, the Court found that the statutory cap of RSA 556:13 "restricts only the damages available in an action where the decedent's death is causally related to the injury." "Based on our review, we conclude that the statutory cap does not satisfy [our] scrutiny because the distinction between decedents whose death is causally related and decedents whose death is unrelated to the injury is arbitrary and does not have a fair and substantial relation to the object of the wrongful death statute."[62] The Court reasoned that "the cap applies to the estate's recovery of both predeath and post-death losses when the decedent's death is causally related to the injury, whereas no cap applies to pre-death losses where the

---

[59] *Id.*, 524.

[60] *Id.*, 527.

[61] *Id.*, 528.

[62] *Id.*, 528.

decedent's death is unrelated to the injury" and found that "this distinction is not justified."[63] The Court concluded "that the imposition of a cap on pre-death damages when a decedent's death is causally related to the injury but no cap when the decedent's death is unrelated to the injury violates the plaintiff's right to recover for personal injuries under Part I, Article 14 of the State Constitution."[64]

RSA 556:13 further states that in the trial of a wrongful death action, the jury shall not be informed of the limitation, if any, imposed by this section. If the jury, however, awards damages in excess of such limitation, the court shall reduce the amount of the award to conform to such limitation.

The provisions of RSA 556:13 apply only to recovery for damages for wrongful death. As *Burke v. Burnham*[65] stated, it does not apply to actions pending at the time of the decedent's death. In *Burke v. Burnham*,[66] the decedent received a settlement from one of two joint tortfeasors while she was alive. Her administrator brought suit against the other tortfeasor, asserting that the injuries sustained by the deceased caused her death. The Court determined that the cause of action which survived the decedent was a right to recover the present worth of the total damages occasioned by the injury, reduced by the amount paid to her, before death, in partial satisfaction. The credit to which a defendant is entitled on account of a settlement with the decedent in their lifetime may be effected by deducting from a general verdict returned without reference to the statutory limit, the amount of the settlement made to the decedent. Judgment may then be entered upon the remaining balance or for the statutory limit, whichever shall be less.

In 1999 the Court upheld the $50,000 limitation in recovery by non-dependent beneficiaries as constitutional. In *Trovato v. Deveau*,[67] the Court stated "[t]he statute does not restrict pre-existing rights, but rather creates them where none previously existed."[68] The Court also clarified the distinction between pre-death damages and post-death damages. The

---

[63] *Id.*, 530.

[64] *Id.*

[65] Burke v. Burnham, 97 N.H. 203, 84 A.2d 918 (1951).

[66] *Id.*

[67] Trovato v. Deveau, 143 N.H. 523, 736 A.2d 1212 (N.H. 1999).

[68] *Id.* at 526, 1216.

Court held the Statute placed a cap on an estate's recovery of post-death damages.[69]

Library References

   Am Jur 2d Death § 217
   CJS Death § 112

§ 47-8. Distribution of Proceeds

Until 1971, the statute specified the particular persons to whom the wrongful death damages were to be distributed and in what percentages.[70] However, a very significant and far-reaching change was made when the statute was amended in 1971 to provide that wrongful death damages "shall become part of the decedent's estate and be distributed in accordance with applicable provisions of law." RSA 556:14.

This change makes the statute much more akin to a survival statute as distinguished from a separate wrongful death action, the proceeds of which belong to persons other than those who would inherit the decedent's property. In *In re Estate of Fontaine*,[71] the Supreme Court stated that "the focus of New Hampshire's wrongful death action is the interest of the decedent's estate and not the distributee" and characterized the modern New Hampshire wrongful death statute as one which "permit[s] survival of the decedent's action rather than authorizing a new and separate wrongful death action."[72]

This change has been interpreted by the Supreme Court in *In re Estate of Wood*,[73] to mean that if the deceased left a will, the wrongful death proceeds are to be distributed in accordance with the provisions of the will. If the decedent dies intestate, the wrongful death proceeds pass to those who take under the statute of descent and distribution.[74]

---

[69] *See, Id.* At 528, 1217.

[70] See Hinman v. Director Gen. of Railroads, 79 N.H. 518, 112 A. 382 (1920). See also Cote v. Martel, 103 N.H. 110, 165 A.2d 590 (1960); Holland v. Morley Buttas Co., 83 N.H. 482, 145 A. 142 (1929).

[71] In re Estate of Fontaine, 128 N.H. 695, 519 A.2d 227 (1986).

[72] *Id.*

[73] In re Estate of Wood, 122 N.H. 956, 453 A.2d 1251 (1982).

[74] *Id.*

Library References

Am Jur 2d Death § 371 et seq.

CJS Death § 37(1) et seq.

§ 47-9. Conflict of Laws

The nature of the right of action in a wrongful death claim and the party in whom it is vested, was formerly held to be determined by the *lex loci delicti*: the law of the place of wrong or tort. *Ghilain v. Couture*.[75] This 1929 case recognized that a foreign administrator could sue in New Hampshire for the wrongful death of his decedent without being appointed here. The only virtue of the old rule was that it was easy for a court to apply because it was a mechanical rule.[76]

In *Clark v. Clark*,[77] the Supreme Court established a modern rule, citing five factors that may influence the application of a particular state's law in a negligence case. These considerations are: (1) predictability of results; (2) maintenance of reasonable orderliness and good relations among the fifty states; (3) simplification of the judicial task; (4) advancement of the forum state's governmental interest; and (5) application of the favored rule of law.[78]

The New Hampshire Supreme Court has favored the 1971 change in RSA 556:14, which provided that wrongful death damages became part of the decedent's estate and distributable according to the applicable law. In *In re Estate of Wood*,[79] a New Hampshire resident was killed in an automobile accident which occurred in Massachusetts, and the other driver was also a New Hampshire resident. The Supreme Court held that the New Hampshire distribution statute would apply. The decedent died with a will and the Court held that

> It is clear that New Hampshire has a strong governmental interest in resolving controversies which are closely bound up with its residents and the administration of their estates. The present case constitutes such a controversy. As noted above, both drivers involved in the accident were residents of New

---

[75] Ghilain v. Couture, 84 N.H. 48, 146 A. 395 (1929).

[76] Clark v. Clark, 107 N.H. 351, 353, 222 A.2d 205, 208 (1966).

[77] Clark v. Clark, 107 N.H. 351, 353–55, 222 A.2d 205, 208–209 (1966).

[78] In re Estate of Wood, 122 N.H. 956, 957, 453 A.2d 1251, 1252 (1982).

[79] In re Estate of Wood, 122 N.H. 956, 453 A.2d 1251 (1982).

Hampshire. Additionally, the potential wrongful death claim was listed as an asset of the decedent's estate, which was to be administered in New Hampshire. Furthermore, the record reveals that the executor intended to initiate a wrongful death action in New Hampshire; he never commenced legal action in Massachusetts. The site of the accident was the only contact with Massachusetts, and we find this contact an insufficient reason to apply Massachusetts law in this case.

In addition to recognizing New Hampshire's overriding governmental interest in this matter, we find that the New Hampshire wrongful death statute, which permits distribution of the death benefits in accordance with the provisions of the decedent's will, is the sounder rule of law because it fosters the intent of the decedent-testator. . . . As a result, we hold that the probate court correctly ruled that New Hampshire law governed the distribution of the wrongful death benefits in this case. (Citations omitted.)[80]

Cross References

Am Jur 2d Death §§ 21–23
CJS Death § 28
Lex loci—wrongful death. 77 ALR 1311.

§ 47-10. Creditor Claims

The distribution statute, RSA 556:14, provides that the damages "less the expenses of recovery, expenses of administration, taxes or other debts as approved by the probate court" shall become part of the decedent's estate. Therefore, it is clear that the net wrongful death proceeds, less attorney's fees, etc. are the starting point.[81] From this amount, the proceeds bear their proportional costs of administration and taxes, unless the will directs otherwise.

A workman's compensation carrier's lien attaches only to the net recovery of an estate in a wrongful death action. *Gelinas v. Sterling Industrial Corporation.*[82] The net recovery is the recovery in a wrongful

---

[80] In re Estate of Wood, 122 N.H. 956, 453 A.2d 1251, 1252 (1982).

[81] Martineau v. Waldman, 93 N.H. 386, 42 A.2d 735 (1945). See Gelinas v. Sterling Indus. Corp., 139 N.H. 14 (1994).

[82] Gelinas v. Sterling Indus. Corp., 139 N.H. 14 (1994).

death case from which are deducted expenses of recovery and expenses of administration; these include attorneys' fees pursuing the recovery, and administrators' and attorneys' fees and probate costs, and expenses in the administration of the probate matter, as approved by the probate court. "These expenses come off the top, before there is any res to which the lien may attach."[83]

The question has arisen whether the general creditors of the decedent have a claim against the wrongful death proceeds. Under the prior statute, under which the wrongful death damages were distributed to specified individuals, the damages were not assets which could be used to satisfy the claims of general creditors of the decedent.[84] This would appear to be the rule under RSA 556:14, since the statute does not list general creditors of the decedent's estate as a deductible expense from the wrongful death proceeds.

Library References

Am Jur 2d Death § 379

CJS Death § 37(1)

§ 47-11. Estate and Inheritance Tax Issues

The proceeds of a wrongful death action are not subject to the federal estate tax, except for those portions of the proceeds, if any, which "represent damages that the decedent could have sued for during his lifetime (pain and suffering and medical expenses)."[85]

If the proceeds of a wrongful death action pass, either under the decedent's will or under the intestacy laws, to recipients who are not exempt under the New Hampshire inheritance tax,[86] the proceeds so passing will be subject to the eighteen percent New Hampshire inheritance tax.[87]

See the informative article entitled *Taxation in Torts*, by attorney Jeffrey J. Zellers, found in Volume 33, Number 1, of the *New Hampshire Bar Journal*, at page 340.

---

[83] Gelinas v. Sterling Indus. Corp., 139 N.H. 14, 18 (1994).

[84] Davis v. Herbert, 78 N.H. 179, 97 A. 879 (1916).

[85] Middleton and Zorn, *Tax Consequences of Recoveries for Personal Injury*, 25 N.H.B.J. 137, 147 (1984).

[86] RSA 86:6, II.

[87] Middleton and Zorn, *Tax Consequences of Recoveries for Personal Injury*, 25 N.H.B.J. 137, 147 (1984). See Chapter 55 *infra*.

Library References

Am Jur 2d Inheritance, Estate, and Gift Taxes § 1 et seq.

CJS Taxation § 1111 et seq.

§ 47-12. Statute of Limitations

RSA 556:11, which governs wrongful death actions, provides that if an action is not pending, an action may be brought for wrongful death at any time within six years after the date of death of the deceased party, subject to the provisions of RSA 508. RSA 508 provides for a three-year statute of limitations period for all personal actions. For a period of time, there was confusion as to which statute applied. This was cleared up in the case of *Cheever v. Southern New Hampshire Regional Medical Center,*[88] where the Supreme Court acknowledged the conflict between the statutes but opted for application of the three-year statute of limitations provided by RSA 508. The Court made a distinction between the six-year statute of limitations in RSA 556:11 and the three-year statute of limitation in RSA 508. The Court held that since the action in the case was not brought by the administrator of the estate, the six year statute did not apply. Instead, because the parents had brought a survival action, the three-year statute of limitations applied.[89]

---

[88] 141 N.H. 589 (1997).

[89] *See Id.* at 591, 568.

CHAPTER 48. SUITS ON PROBATE BONDS

§ 48-1.   Generally

Suits upon probate bonds are relatively uncommon. However, when these lawsuits occur, the situation and potential damages are usually serious; recourse to a bond suit is a measure of last resort to a seriously damaged party.

Library References

Am Jur 2d Bonds § 33
CJS Bonds § 99

§ 48-2.   Breach of the Bond

The probate bond only becomes important if the fiduciary breaches a condition of his bond, Then suit upon the bond may be in order. A successful suit results in judgment against the surety, who forfeits the full amount of the bond penalty. Claimants may seek to recover against this amount to the extent of their claims.

What constitutes breach? The answer depends upon the type of bond given. Each statute setting forth the bond requirement generally describes the duties the fiduciary must fulfill; these are the "conditions of the bond."

An early case, *Gookin v. Hoit*,[1] without referring to any statute, held that individuals are not always entitled to judgment for their own claims upon every breach of condition, but only if the breach has been a particular prejudice to them. The Court found the following to be breaches for which suit on a probate bond may be maintained for "the particular benefit of an individual":

> 1. When an executor or administrator, having assets, and being, by law, bound to pay a debt, neglects or refuses to pay it, when demanded.

> 2. When an executor, or administrator, refuses or neglects to pay, upon demand, a dividend ordered by the judge of probate, by a decree of distribution of an insolvent estate, to be paid to a creditor.

> 3. When an executor, or administrator, neglects to pay, on demand, to an heir, a share in the estate, ordered by the judge of probate to be paid.

> 4. When an executor neglects to pay, upon demand, a legacy, which he is, by law, bound to pay.[2]

Although worded differently, these conditions appear to be implicit within the statutory conditions for estate bonds. Each of the bond forms under the statutes provides for payment of debts,[3] which should include payment of dividends from an insolvent estate. Only bonds under RSA 553:15 do not contain a duty to pay legacies.

Judge of Probate v. Briggs,[4] further clarifies the duty to administer the estate according to law, as provided by RSA 553:13, I(b), stating that it includes the administrator's duty to obtain a license to sell real

---

[1] Gookin v. Hoit, 3 N.H. 392, 393 (1826).

[2] *Id.*

[3] RSA 553:13 does not expressly mention payment of debts, but Judge of Probate v. Briggs, 5 N.H. 66, 67 (1829), finds this duty falls within the duty to administer the estate according to law.

[4] Judge of Probate v. Briggs, 5 N.H. 66, 67 (1829).

estate when the estate is insolvent, neglect of which is unfaithful administration and a breach of the bond.

Misappropriation of the assets of the estate is also clearly a breach of an RSA 553:13 bond, although it has not been linked to any particular condition.[5]

A trustee's bond provided under RSA 564:1 was breached by the trustee's failure to make demand of his predecessor-executor for the balance remaining in the executor's hands.[6] The same duty of demand would seem to apply to any successor fiduciary, such as an executor or administrator d.b.n.

In addition to the duties imposed upon the fiduciary by the express language of the bond, the failure to meet any one of which may constitute a breach of the bond, RSA 559:20 specifically describes conduct which constitutes breach of a probate bond:

> Fraudulent conduct in the sale of real estate, misappropriation of the proceeds thereof, or refusal to account for the same, shall be a breach of the administrator's bond.

For instance, self-dealing with a sale, by arranging that title to estate real estate would be conveyed to a third person in trust for the executor's own use and at a price much less than the value of the property falls within the proscription of RSA 559:20.[7]

Establishing any breach requires either the fiduciary's assent to a claim[8] or a legal demand and refusal to comply. Thus, failure to account has not been held a breach of the bond unless the probate court has taken steps to compel it and the fiduciary has still failed to account.[9] No suit

[5] Century Indem. Co. v. Maryland Cas. Co., 89 N.H. at 124, 193 A. at 222 (1937).

[6] American Fld. Co. v. Barnard, 104 N.H. 146, 152–53, 181 A.2d 628, 632 (1962).

[7] Judge of Probate v. Lane, 50 N.H. 556, 559–60 (1871). Note: if agent of administrator fraudulently deals with sale of real estate, administrator will be considered as having connived with agent unless administrator calls agent to account; Currier v. Green, 2 N.H. 225, 227 (1820).

[8] RSA 565:9; Judge of Probate v. Locke, 6 N.H. 396 (1833). See Judge of Probate v. Lee, 72 N.H. 247, 248, 56 A. 188, 189 (1903) (*discussing* Judge of Probate v. Lane, 50 N.H. 556 (1871)); Judge of Probate v. Emery, 6 N.H. 141, 142 (1833).

[9] Gookin v. Hoit, 3 N.H. at 394 (1826). See Judge of Probate v. Couch, 59 N.H. 39, 40 (1879); Hurlburt v. Wheeler, 40 N.H. 73, 75 (1860).

may be maintained on the bond for breach of the condition to pay the residue until there has been a decree of distribution and a demand,[10] and also none for a legacy until decree and demand.[11]

Since it is the duty of executors and administrators to resist claims they deem groundless, a refusal by an executor or administrator to pay a debt on the ground that nothing is due should not be a breach of the bond. *Judge of Probate v. Adams.*[12] Only if the claim is first legally established is refusal to pay a breach. A refusal to account for a particular sum of money on the ground that it was never received, or never received on account of the estate, or was accounted for in an earlier, settled account is similarly not a breach.[13] Again, the reason for refusal must be unjustified. A claim allowed by a commissioner in insolvency does not establish breach of the condition to pay it.[14] Instead, the claimant must show that the judge of probate accepted the commissioner's report, payment was ordered, and the administrator, having assets, refused to pay it. *Judge of Probate v. Couch.*[15]

Library References

Am Jur 2d Bonds §§ 31, 32

CJS Bonds § 98

§ 48-3. Maintaining Suit on the Bond

In the event of fiduciary breach, suit upon the probate bond determines whether the surety is liable. A petition for declaratory judgment cannot be entertained on this issue, since the proper remedy is at law.[16] "Suits

---

[10] Judge of Probate v. Briggs, 5 N.H. 66, 68 (1829) (no action on probate bond for the benefit of heirs at law until there has been a decree of distribution and a demand; nor for the benefit of a legatee without demand). See Judge of Probate v. Adams, 49 N.H. 150, 153 (1869) (no action for breach of residuary payment condition for the benefit of heirs at law until decree of distribution and demand and no action for the benefit of a legatee without decree of court and demand). *Cf.* Glover v. Baker, 76 N.H. 393, 399, 83 A. 916, 922 (1913) (heir at law may have remedy upon bond if executor refuses to pay him sums to which he may be entitled upon settlement of executor's account).

[11] Judge of Probate v. Adams, 49 N.H. 150, 153 (1869).

[12] Judge of Probate v. Adams, 49 N.H. 150, 153 (1869). See also Judge of Probate v. Briggs, 5 N.H. 66, 69 (1829).

[13] Judge of Probate v. Briggs, 5 N.H. 66, 70 (1829).

[14] Judge of Probate v. Couch, 59 N.H. at 40 (1879).

[15] *Id.*

[16] Judge of Probate v. National Sur. Corp., 94 N.H. 177, 179, 49 A.2d 635, 636 (1946).

upon probate bonds, can be maintained only by reason of, and in accordance with statutory provisions."[17]

RSA 565:8 provides that suit must be undertaken in the name of the judge of probate without naming the incumbent of that office.[18] Naming the judge as plaintiff is in keeping with the requirement of RSA 565:1 that the probate bond itself is to be addressed to the judge.

Suit is initiated by application to the judge for an order of suit in accordance with RSA 565:6:

> Any person interested in a bond given to a judge may apply to the judge for an order for suit thereof, setting forth the claim intended to be recovered in such suit; and the judge may make the order, upon the applicant giving bond, with sufficient sureties, to pay the costs which may be adjudged against him.[19]

The writ which issues must be indorsed by those interested in the suit pursuant to RSA 565:7:

> The name and residence of every person at whose request the order is made and suit instituted shall be indorsed on the writ before service thereof, with a brief statement of his claim.

As the statutes imply, although the probate bond and the writ are in the name of the judge of probate, the real party in interest is not the judge but the person whose name is indorsed on the writ.[20] The indorser will receive the benefit of the suit if successful, and is liable for costs if suit fails.[21]

Appropriate indorsers/claimants include a legatee or heir whose share of the estate the administrator has refused to pay, a creditor of the

---

[17] Judge of Probate v. Adams, 49 N.H. 150, 152 (1869). See also Judge of Probate v. Peerless Ins. Co., 103 N.H. 322, 323, 171 A.2d 39, 41 (1961); Judge of Probate v. National Sur. Corp., 94 N.H. at 179, 49 A.2d at 636 (1946).

[18] See also Prescott v. Farmer, 59 N.H. 90, 91–92 (1879) (amendment of declaration to make judge nominal plaintiff permitted where suit instituted before the commissioner of insolvency and judge of probate accepted the commissioner's report).

[19] A person who joins in a suit upon a bond without authority to proceed in the name of the judge is improperly joined. Judge of Probate v. National Sur. Corp., 94 N.H. at 180, 49 A.2d at 637 (1946).

[20] Judge of Probate v. Merrill, 6 N.H. 256, 260 (1833).

[21] *Id.*

decedent or of the estate, or an administrator d.b.n. who is attempting to recover the balance found in the former administrator's hands on settlement of his account.[22] There should be only one suit upon a probate bond,[23] but, upon giving security for costs, interested persons may be allowed to indorse the writ and be parties at any time during pendency of the suit.[24] Indorsement is permitted even after the action has been removed to the New Hampshire Supreme Court by appeal.[25] Any person indorsing the writ during the pendency of the suit is entitled to the same rights as if his name had been indorsed before service of the writ but subsequent to the other indorsers.[26]

The indorser's claim against the estate need not be described with any great degree of formality.[27] It is enough if its nature is ascertainable from the description, so that the judge may see that there is a legal claim enforceable by suit upon the bond, and the executor or administrator may understand what the claimant seeks to recover.[28] An objection that the statement of the indorser's claim was not as full and explicit as the statute contemplated must be raised at an early stage of the proceedings.[29] A breach of the bond should also be alleged.[30] In the usual case, stating the claim will necessarily involve reference to the breach (e.g., failure to pay debt or legacy as required by law).

Several cases indicate that there can be no action on a bond until the breach has been established and the claim liquidated.[31] Thus, if the

---

[22] See, e.g., Gookin v. Hoit, 3 N.H. 392 (1826); Judge of Probate v. Heydock, 8 N.H. 491, 497–98 (1837) (as to administrator d.b.n.); Judge of Probate v. Claggett, 36 N.H. 381, 386–87 (1858) (same); Prescott v. Farmer, 59 N.H. 90 (1879) (same).

[23] Judge of Probate v. Colcord, 2 N.H. 36 (1819).

[24] RSA 565:13; Judge of Probate v. Lane, 51 N.H. 342, 345 (1871).

[25] Judge of Probate v. Tillotson, 6 N.H. 292, 296–97 (1833).

[26] RSA 565:13.

[27] Judge of Probate v. Tillotson, 6 N.H. 292, 296 (1833).

[28] Judge of Probate v. Tillotson, 6 N.H. 292, 295–96 (1833) (*but note* that *Tillotson* requires description of claim upon the application and holds that the statutes do not require that the nature of the claim appear in the indorsement; RSA 565:7 now requires a brief statement of the claim within the indorsement in addition to the requirement of RSA 565:6 that the claim be set forth in the application).

[29] Judge of Probate v. Lane, 50 N.H. at 559 (1871).

[30] Judge of Probate v. Couch, 59 N.H. at 40 (1879).

[31] See Judge of Probate v. Briggs, 5 N.H. 66, 68 (1829) (no action upon probate bond, for the benefit of heirs at law, until there has been a decree of distribution and demand).

claimant alleges breach of the duty to account, for example, the administrator must first have been ordered to account by the court and have failed to comply. A liquidated claim can be one which the administrator has admitted, a claim which the creditor has reduced to judgment, or a legacy established by an accounting and decree of distribution.

The cases do not always definitely state the prerequisites to suit. In *Judge of Probate v. Lee*, the court disagreed with defendant-sureties' assertion that suit on behalf of heirs must be abated until after the settlement of the administrator's account and a decree of distribution in the probate court, holding that "[a]n action will lie at any time after there has been a breach of the bond, although parties in interest may not have their claims in the condition that will entitle them to the benefit of the security afforded by the bond."[32] *Lee* thus appears to suggest there is no absolute requirement for prior proof of either breach or the claim. The court went on to observe, however, that had the defendants denied the breach instead of pleading in abatement, a continuance would have been necessary to await a finding of breach by the probate court.[33] This reasoning may mean breach must be established, but it can be established through defendant's failure to deny it.

The cases of *Judge of Probate v. Lane*,[34] and *Lisbon Savings Bank & Trust Co. v. Estate of Moulton*,[35] are in accord with the finding in *Lee* that claims may be liquidated after suit on the bond has begun. The court in *Lisbon Savings Bank & Trust Co.* stated:

> While a breach of the bond may be sufficient ground for the judgment creditor to have action instituted for forfeiture of the

---

See also Prescott v. Farmer, 59 N.H. 90, 91 (1879) (generally, decree of distribution or acknowledgement of claim by administrator necessary to maintenance of suit on bond for legacy or distributive share); Judge of Probate v. Adams, 49 N.H. 150, 152, 154 (1869) (no action on bond for breach of condition to pay out residue until there has been a decree of distribution; claims must be liquidated or admitted before suit upon bond); Hurlburt v. Wheeler, 40 N.H. at 75 (1860) (no action upon bond can be maintained for failure to inventory and account without first obtaining decree of probate court ordering administrator to account and administrator's failure to do so); Judge of Probate v. Kimball, 12 N.H. 165, 170 (1841) (no remedy upon bond until failure to pay legacy established).

[32] Judge of Probate v. Lee, 72 N.H. at 248, 56 A. at 189 (1903).

[33] Judge of Probate v. Lee, 72 N.H. at 248–49, 56 A. at 189 (1903).

[34] Judge of Probate v. Lane, 51 N.H. 342 (1871).

[35] Lisbon Sav. Bank & Trust Co. v. Estate of Moulton, 91 N.H. 477, 22 A.2d 331 (1941).

bond, yet if an accounting is necessary to show the administrator's liability to pay the creditor's judgment, recovery on the bond must be withheld until the liability as shown by the accounting is established.[36]

and in *Lane*:

It must follow, as a matter of course, that persons interested may be entitled to an award of execution, even although their claims were not perfected when the suit on the bond was brought or even when the judgment was rendered, either by the proper decrees in the probate court, by judgment at law, or by assent of the executor.[37]

Permitting a claimant to perfect his claim after suit on the bond has begun is reasonable in light of the limited result of a successful suit: forfeiture of the entire penalty of the bond. This amount then stands as security for all interested parties.[38] No claimant is entitled to recover against it until the judge has thereafter examined and ascertained the claim.[39]

The penalty of the bond is the limit of the surety's liability.[40] Because judgment is rendered for the judge for the whole penalty in a successful suit, there can be no more than one such judgment.[41] Also, because the parties to suit are always the judge of probate and the surety, and the controversy is whether the fiduciary breached some condition of the bond, for which the penalty must be forfeited, there is no need for more than one suit.[42]

---

[36] *Id.*

[37] Judge of Probate v. Lane, 50 N.H. 556 (1871).

[38] RSA 565:9; Judge of Probate v. Davis, 1 N.H. 248, 249 (1818). See Judge of Probate v. Lane, 51 N.H. at 346 (1871).

[39] RSA 565:10. See also Lisbon Sav. Bank & Trust Co. v. Estate of Moulton, 91 N.H. at 479, 22 A.2d at 334 (1941) ("While a breach of the bond leads to its forfeiture, the forfeiture does not show liability to pay the judgment creditor's claim. Only to the extent the liability is proved may the creditor recover on the bond.").

[40] Lisbon Sav. Bank & Trust Co. v. Estate of Moulton, 91 N.H. at 479, 22 A.2d at 334 (1941).

[41] Judge of Probate v. Colcord, 2 N.H. 36, 38–39 (1819). See Judge of Probate v. Lane, 51 N.H. 342, 345–46 (1871).

[42] Judge of Probate v. Colcord, 2 N.H. 36, 39 (1819).

Library References

Am Jur 2d Bonds § 33

CJS Bonds § 99

§ 48-4. Notice Before Suit

RSA 550:4, X provides that the judge of probate may, at his discretion, proceed without notice in "making orders for suits upon probate bonds." Apparently, neither hearing nor notice to the obligors upon the bond has ever been required before an order for suit upon the bond issues. In *Judge of Probate v. Kimball*, the court found no notice requirement in the statutes, and observed that notice might in fact defeat the purpose of the suit: "that of procuring security upon the institution of the suit."[43] Moreover, the defendant would not be harmed by the omission, since:

> An order for a suit upon the bond does not conclude the obligors from denying a breach, or prevent them from setting up any matter which may show why judgment should not be rendered against them.[44]

Accordingly, under *Kimball*, as under the present RSA 550:4, the decision to issue notice was held to be a matter within the judge's discretion.[45]

Library References

Am Jur 2d Bonds § 33

CJS Bonds §§ 108, 125

§ 48-5. Surety's Defenses

What induced a person to sign as surety on an administration bond is immaterial so long as the obligee was not responsible therefor.[46] Accordingly, in *Judge of Probate v. Nudd*, the defendant surety's defense that he had signed the bond in blank, without reading it or knowing it to be a bond, and having been misled as to its nature, was rejected since

---

[43] Judge of Probate v. Kimball, 12 N.H. 165, 169 (1841) (referring to statute of July 2, 1822).

[44] Judge of Probate v. Kimball, 12 N.H. 165, 169 (1841).

[45] *Id.*

[46] Judge of Probate v. Nudd, 105 N.H. 311, 313, 199 A.2d 296, 297 (1964) (*quoting* Scholl v. Gilman, 263 Mass. 295, 299 (1928)).

there was no evidence that the creditor who sought recovery on the bond was aware of or responsible for any fraud practiced upon the surety.[47] The court cited with approval the reasoning of other jurisdictions that the surety was bound either on the ground of estoppel, apparent authority of the person who obtained his signature, or upon "the familiar principle that where one of two innocent parties must suffer, the loss should fall upon the one who by his misplaced confidence has made the fraud possible."[48]

The surety may raise the defense that the indorser-claimant has not brought suit in a timely manner. However, the nature of the claim must be kept in mind in determining exactly which time limitations apply. Suit upon the bond is based upon the fiduciary's breach of an administrative duty, and the focus is upon the particular duty at issue. The usual reasons for suit against an administrator, on the other hand, have their basis in actions of the decedent during his lifetime: incurring a debt or committing a tort. The result of this distinction is that the time limitations of RSA 556,[49] relating to bringing suit against an administrator, generally do not apply to a suit upon the probate bond.[50]

---

[47] Judge of Probate v. Nudd, 105 N.H. 311, 313, 199 A.2d 296, 297 (1964) (*quoting* Scholl v. Gilman, 263 Mass. 295, 299 (1928)).

[48] Judge of Probate v. Nudd, 105 N.H. 311, 313, 199 A.2d 296, 297 (1964).

[49] Principally, section RSA 556:1 (no action shall be sustained against an administrator if begun within six months of grant of administration, nor unless demand exhibited and payment demanded) and RSA 565:5 (no suit sustained unless begun within one year of grant of administration). For further discussion of this topic, see Part V of this treatise.

[50] Judge of Probate v. Lane, 51 N.H. at 349 (1871). If the claimant is pursuing a debt owed him by the decedent, however, and the claimant did not meet the time deadlines of RSA 556, then the chapter should afford the surety protection. Under those circumstances, the claimant is alleging a breach of the duty to pay estate debts; since the claim is time-barred and therefore not a legal debt of the estate, the fiduciary did not breach any duty in refusing to pay it and the surety cannot be liable. See Judge of Probate v. Heydock, 8 N.H. at 496 (1837) (to the effect that defendant sureties of Heydock, the administrator of an estate who subsequently died, were not discharged by the failure of the administrator d.b.n. to exhibit claim against Heydock as administrator to Heydock's administrator (Hadduck) because "when there is a surety a creditor is under no obligation to active diligence to enforce his claim against the estate of his deceased principal debt," but asserting in dicta that the defendants would have been discharged if they had instead been Hadduck's sureties). But see Judge of Probate v. Harris, 1 N.H. 248 (1818) (holding that suit could still be maintained for the benefit of parties not of record even if the claims of the interested parties of record were time-barred).

One question which has not been squarely addressed is whether a surety may successfully allege that an interested party who consents to the fiduciary's breach of his duty or enters into a conspiracy with the fiduciary which will lead to a breach cannot later attempt suit upon the bond. An unusual case considering this possibility is *Judge of Probate v. Cook*.[51] In *Cook*, the sureties alleged that Cook, the principal on the bond and the successor-guardian of Bemis, conspired with Bemis to remove Bemis's prior guardian with the intention of obtaining control of the guardianship property, which Cook and Bemis then squandered. The Court held that this did not bar suit on the bond.[52] The *Cook* case, of course, presents a special situation. Empowering a ward to consent to such conduct would defeat the entire purpose of a guardianship. Under other circumstances, the surety might have a better chance of successfully arguing that consent or conspiracy by the party seeking recovery under the bond (such as a creditor) precludes his claim.

The existence of multiple bonds can raise defense possibilities. When there are successive bonds for the same fiduciary, liability of any surety depends upon when the breach occurred and whether it was a continuing breach. The judge of probate may release the surety on a cancelled bond "from all further responsibility" pursuant to RSA 565:4 and RSA 565:5 when a new bond issues. The surety so released is not liable for breaches occurring only after his discharge. *Judge of Probate v. Nudd*.[53] Nevertheless, the "discharged" surety remains liable for breaches which occurred before his discharge. *Century Indemnity Co. v. Maryland Casualty Co.*[54] Also, the surety on the new bond may be liable not only for a breach which began while he was surety but for a breach which began before he became surety if the breach continued into the period of his suretyship.[55] Applying these principles can lead to overlapping liability. The new and old sureties may become co-sureties, and if this happens, a right

---

[51] Judge of Probate v. Cook, 57 N.H. 450 (1876).

[52] Judge of Probate v. Cook, 57 N.H. 450, 452–53 (1876) (three justices writing separate opinions).

[53] Judge of Probate v. Nudd, 107 N.H. 173, 219 A.2d 454 (1966) (defendant surety, who was unsuccessful in Judge of Probate v. Nudd, 105 N.H. 311, 199 A.2d 296 (1964), in maintaining he could not be bound because he had never intended to act as a surety at all successfully defended on this ground).

[54] Century Indem. Co. v. Maryland Cas. Co., 89 N.H. at 124–25, 193 A. at 223 (1937).

[55] Century Indem. Co. v. Maryland Cas. Co., 89 N.H. at 124, 193 A. at 222–23 (1937).

of contribution will exist between them.[56] The shared loss can include interest on a sum converted and reasonable expenses incurred in connection with the suit.[57]

In *American Fidelity Co. v. Barnard*,[58] the Supreme Court dealt with a related liability apportionment problem. Barnard served in three successive fiduciary capacities with respect to one individual: as his conservator, as the executor of his estate, and finally, as testamentary trustee, and in each capacity he provided a bond to the court. In each role he also converted assets to his own use. The court found the surety on the conservator's bond liable only for the amount Barnard converted as conservator, because, although Barnard never filed any inventory or account during the conservatorship, he did transfer remaining assets into the estate.[59] The full amount of the executor's bond was forfeited without dispute, Barnard having converted more than that amount during the course of estate administration.[60] As trustee, Barnard converted an amount less than the amount of the penalty of his trustee's bond, but the court held that the full penalty must be forfeited.[61] Because a trustee is bound to ensure that the executor "complied with the statutes in administering the estate, and to expeditiously secure possession of the particular estate to which he was entitled, thus prevent[ing] any defalcations or losses,"[62] which duties he breached, the surety on the trustee's bond was liable for losses during estate administration as well as for losses during Barnard's trusteeship.[63]

§ 48-6. Limits on Surety's Liability

The surety executes an administration bond for the purpose of securing to those interested in the estate whatever belongs to them by law. *Judge*

---

[56] Century Indem. Co. v. Maryland Cas. Co., 89 N.H. at 125, 193 A.2d at 223 (1937).

[57] Century Indem. Co. v. Maryland Cas. Co., 89 N.H. at 125, 193 A.2d at 223 (1937). See also American Fid. Co. v. Barnard, 104 N.H. 146, 154, 181 A.2d 628, 633 (1962).

[58] American Fid. Co. v. Barnard, 104 N.H. 146, 181 A.2d 628 (1962).

[59] American Fid. Co. v. Barnard, 104 N.H. at 151–52, 181 A.2d at 631 (1962).

[60] American Fid. Co. v. Barnard, 104 N.H. at 152, 181 A.2d at 631 (1962).

[61] American Fid. Co. v. Barnard, 104 N.H. at 152–53, 181 A.2d at 631–32 (1962).

[62] American Fid. Co. v. Barnard, 104 N.H. at 152, 181 A.2d at 632 (1962).

[63] American Fid. Co. v. Barnard, 104 N.H. at 152–53, 181 A.2d at 632 (1962). See also Judge of Probate v. Heydock, 8 N.H. at 494–96 (1837) (similar reasoning: sureties on domiciliary executor's bond liable for his failure to account for proceeds of land he sold as ancillary administrator).

of Probate v. Sulloway.[64] "The surety is liable for whatever is properly chargeable to his principal in the official capacity on account of which bond was given."[65] While this statement of liability seems only logical, it has yielded unusual results.

In *Judge of Probate v. Sulloway*, the court held that the surety is liable for payment of an executor's personal debt to the testator, even if the executor-debtor was at no time financially capable of paying the debt. The court's holding is surprising since an administrator is generally only responsible for collecting debts owed his decedent which can be collected; if the debtor cannot pay, the administrator is not liable for the debt himself. Once the administrator does collect on a debt, of course, he is liable for conversion if he fails to treat the amount collected as an asset of the estate, and the surety would be liable for the conversion, because the conversion would be a wrongful act committed by the administrator in his official capacity.

In *Sulloway*, the surety was found liable because the executor never paid a debt he owed to his decedent, a debt the executor incurred in his personal, not official capacity, and which the defendant surety claimed the debtor was at no time in a position to pay. The court viewed the executor-debtor's failure to pay as a breach of his duty as administrator on the basis of RSA 554:14, which provides that "[a] debt due from the administrator to the estate shall be assets and accounted for as other debts."

RSA 554:14, as the court observed in *Sulloway*, was enacted in order to abolish the common law rule that except as against creditors, an executor's indebtedness to the testator was released or extinguished.[66] RSA 554:14 thus provides for survival of a debt which would otherwise be extinguished. As interpreted in *Sulloway*, the statute also makes a debt due from the administrator one in his official capacity, making non-payment, regardless of his own insolvency, a breach of his administrative

---

[64] Judge of Probate v. Sulloway, 68 N.H. 511, 516, 44 A. 720, 722 (1896).

[65] Judge of Probate v. Sulloway, 68 N.H. 511, 516, 44 A. 720, 722 (1896) (*quoting* Choate v. Arrington, 116 Mass. 552, 556). Note: The surety is accordingly bound by whatever decree of the probate court binds the surety's principal. A surety is not bound, however, by a decree which binds the administrator d.b.n. who is successor to the surety's principal; neither is the administrator d.b.n. bound by that decree as against his predecessor's surety.

[66] Judge of Probate v. Sulloway, 68 N.H. 511, 513–14, 44 A. 720, 721 (1896).

duty. The problem could again be viewed as one of conversion of estate assets, except that if the executor-debtor was never personally able to pay the debt, then he is being held responsible as executor for conversion of an amount he never could have collected.

In *Yeaton v. Skillings*,[67] the court held that the principles of *Sulloway* apply to conservators and found a conservator's surety liable for the conservator's failure to account for debts he owed to his ward. In light of *Sulloway* and *Yeaton*, a prospective surety should proceed with caution if the fiduciary making application for the bond is also a debtor of his decedent or ward. Failing discovery of the fiduciary's insolvency and indebtedness before the bond is executed, *Sulloway* suggests that a surety who signed the bond in ignorance might be relieved of liability if the surety asks the court to discharge him upon discovery of the situation, or the surety may seek removal of the fiduciary and appointment of another.[68]

A surety has been held not liable for acts of an executor outside the executor's authority. In *Gregg v. Currier*,[69] the court found that the will under which an executor was named and appointed gave the executor only power to sell real estate, not to collect rents and profits. His alleged failure to account for these receipts was not a breach of his duty as executor, and his surety could not be held liable for his conduct.[70] The heirs at law, who were entitled to the rents and profits, could only sue the person who served as executor in his personal capacity.[71]

The basic liability of the surety is limited to the amount of the bond penalty.[72] In appropriate circumstances, interest and costs may also be assessed.[73] As to any claimant, "[d]amages resulting from the breach

---

[67] Yeaton v. Skillings, 103 N.H. 352, 172 A.2d 354 (1961). In fact, the executor in *Sulloway* had included the amounts of his debts in the estate account as assets of the estate.

[68] Judge of Probate v. Sulloway, 68 N.H. 511, 516, 44 A. 720 (1896).

[69] Gregg v. Currier, 36 N.H. 200 (1858).

[70] Gregg v. Currier, 36 N.H. 200, 204 (1858).

[71] *Id.*

[72] Lisbon Sav. Bank & Trust Co. v. Estate of Moulton, 91 N.H. at 479, 22 A.2d at 334 (1941).

[73] See Judge of Probate v. Heydock, 8 N.H. at 493–94 (1837). See American Fid. Co. v. Barnard, 104 N.H. at 154, 181 A.2d at 633 (1962); Century Indem. Co. v. Maryland Cas. Co., 89 N.H. at 125, 193 A. at 223 (1937).

of the bond measure the extent within the amount of the penalty of the bond for which there may be recovery."[74] If a fiduciary is liable beyond the amount of the penalty, "action besides or otherwise than on the bond may be brought against him, but with no liability of the sureties on the bond over and above its penalty."[75]

The surety is not discharged simply because the executor properly accounted for monies up to the amount of the penalty. *Judge of Probate v. Heydock.*[76] Rather, the bond serves as security for losses and defalcations to that amount.[77]

Library References

Am Jur 2d Bonds § 45

CJS Bond § 132

§ 48-7. Judgment on Probate Bond

Judgment is a term with two connotations when dealing with a suit upon a probate bond. It refers to both the surety's forfeiture of the bond penalty upon proof of fiduciary breach, and to the recovery particular claimants may have against the forfeited amount upon proof of damage to them. Thus, pursuant to RSA 565:9, the first step is forfeiture:

> When it shall appear, upon confession, verdict, demurrer or in any other way, that the penalty of the bond is forfeited judgment shall be rendered against the defendant for such penalty; and such judgment shall be security for all parties interested.

Judgment for the penalty is a formality. "No execution issues for the penalty. It is a mere mode of enforcing the rights of those interested, and those rights are enforced by separate executions." *Robinson v. Leavitt.*[78]

The second step is judgment in favor of claimants pursuant to RSA 565:10:

---

[74] Lisbon Sav. Bank & Trust Co. v. Estate of Moulton, 91 N.H. at 479, 22 A.2d at 334 (1941).

[75] *Id.*

[76] Judge of Probate v. Heydock, 8 N.H. 491, 499 (1837).

[77] *Id.*

[78] Robinson v. Leavitt, 7 N.H. 73, 78 (1834).

Upon a hearing in chancery on such forfeiture, the court shall examine and ascertain the claims of the parties whose names are indorsed on the writ; and judgment shall be rendered for such parties respectively for the amount so ascertained, "that the judge of probate for the county of . . . now have execution for . . . being part of the penalty forfeited, and for costs taxed . . ., for the use of A, B or C," with which such further description as the court may deem expedient.

The dual nature of the proceedings was early described in *Judge of Probate v. Davis*:

Before judgment [resulting in forfeiture of the penalty] the proceedings are all according to the rigid rules of law, and the object of them is to obtain judgment for the penalty. After judgment, the proceedings are an act of chancery, and the object of them is to obtain an award of execution for what is equitably due.[79]

It has been frequently stated that "[t]o obtain judgment in the suit upon the bond . . . [the] endorser must show the liability of the [fiduciary] to pay its claim."[80] The cases are not always clear as to whether the claimant must be in a position to prove both breach and his precise claim in order to obtain the initial "judgment"—forfeiture of the bond penalty. The cases do reach a consensus, however, in holding that the claimant must have a liquidated claim in order to obtain the second stage judgment—entitlement to recovery on the bond in the particular claimant's favor.[81]

Thus, in *Judge of Probate v. Davis*, the Court found that the merits of the claims are only pertinent in determining whether the claimant can recover:

The merits of particular claims for damages, by reason of breaches of the condition, are not before the court till after the

---

[79] Judge of Probate v. Davis, 1 N.H. 248, 250–51 (1818).

[80] See, e.g., Judge of Probate v. Peerless Ins. Co., 103 N.H. at 323, 171 A.2d at 41 (1961) (citation omitted).

[81] Judge of Probate v. Peerless Ins. Co., 103 N.H. at 323–24, 171 A.2d at 41 (1961) ("In general all claims, unless admitted, must be liquidated before they can be recovered upon a probate bond." Citations omitted).

judgment for the penalty, because the action may be maintained by shewing (sic) any single breach whatever. Hence whatever ground there may be for rejecting particular claims upon a hearing in chancery after judgment, still the action may be maintained for the penalty.[82]

A liquidated claim may result from proceedings in the probate court,[83] or from a judgment in the superior court.[84] In order to collect upon his judgment, a claimant must sue out execution or *scire facias*.

The preclusive effect of a judgment is described in RSA 565:16 and 565:17:

> No suit or judgment on such bond shall operate as an abatement or bar to any suit thereon against any obligor, against whom no suit has previously been commenced or judgment rendered. RSA 565:16.

A judgment in favor of the obligors shall in no case operate as a bar to any suit on such bond for the benefit of a different claimant, or of the same claimant for a different claim. RSA 565:17.

> In addition, Judge of Probate v. Lane points out that a claimant can be entitled to recovery for fiduciary misconduct which occurred and is proved subsequent to the forfeiture judgment. Simply because the penalty has been forfeited and some claimants have recovered against it, does not mean that a claimant later proving other misconduct is precluded from recovering against whatever of the forfeited penalty may remain:

The security (the penalty) is to be made available for the faithful discharge of the trust at every stage of it, whether a suit has been brought on the bond or not; and it would be absurd to say that by obtaining a judgment for the penalty of the bond, no remedy could be had upon it for subsequent cases of maladministration.[85]

---

[82] Judge of Probate v. Davis, 1 N.H. at 251 (1818).

[83] Judge of Probate v. Heydock, 8 N.H. 491 (1837). See Glover v. Baker, 76 N.H. 393, 83 A. 916 (1912) (both referring to settlement of fiduciary accounts.)

[84] Judge of Probate v. Peerless Ins. Co., 103 N.H. 322, 171 A.2d 354 (1961).

[85] Judge of Probate v. Lane, 51 N.H. at 346 (1871).

If judgment is rendered for the defendant, the parties in whose interest suit was maintained are liable for defendant's costs. RSA 565:6, 565:18.

Library References

Am Jur 2d Bonds § 43

CJS Bonds § 126

§ 48-8.   Collection on Judgment By the Interested Party

In order to be entitled to a judgment in his favor and to subsequent execution, a claimant must have indorsed the writ in the suit.[86] He may indorse the writ before it is served,[87] or at any time during pendency of the suit upon court approval of his motion to indorse.[88] He may even indorse after the suit has been removed to the New Hampshire Supreme Court on appeal.[89] Under RSA 565:13, a later indorser "shall . . . be entitled to the same rights as if his name had been so indorsed before the service of the writ but subsequent to the other indorsers, upon his giving bond, with sureties, for the payment of costs."

RSA 565:12 establishes priority among indorsers, according to the designation of the order of the writ:

> If there be more than one party for whose use such executions may be awarded, the order of priority in the attachment shall be as designated in the indorsement on the original writ; and if there be no such designation, in the order in which the names are indorsed.

Library References

Am Jur 2d Bonds § 43

CJS Bonds § 133

§ 48-9.   Damages Recoverable

A claimant may only recover upon a breach of a bond condition which is of particular harm to him, not upon a breach which is a grievance common to all creditors.[90] The surety is liable only to the extent of the

---

[86] Judge of Probate v. Tillotson, 6 N.H. 292 (1833).

[87] RSA 565:7.

[88] RSA 565:13.

[89] Judge of Probate v. Tillotson, 6 N.H. 292, 296–97 (1833).

[90] Gookin v. Hoit, 3 N.H. 392, 392–93 (1826).

bond penalty.[91] If the administrator would be liable beyond that amount, action may be brought against him, but other than on the bond and the surety will not be liable for the additional amount.[92] "Damages resulting from the breach of the bond measure the extent within the amount of the penalty of the bond for which there may be recovery."[93]

In addition, the claimant may be able to recover costs incurred in establishing the fiduciary's breach. In *American Fidelity Co. v. Barnard*, defendant sureties were held liable for paying the fees of an accountant who spent a considerable amount of time tracing fiduciary misappropriation of funds.[94] Interest may also be assessed against the surety. In *Judge of Probate v. Heydock*, the court held that "where the whole penalty has become a debt, which the obligors unjustly detain, [the obligee may] recover the penalty, and interest upon it during all the time it may have been so detained."[95] In *American Fidelity Co. v. Barnard*, American Fidelity Company was found liable for interest from the date of the probate court decree against it, and the court held that under the circumstances of that case, interest should be compounded annually.[96]

Library References

Am Jur 2d Bonds §§ 43–47

CJS Bonds § 130 et seq.

§ 48-10. Execution

Having perfected his claim,[97] indorsed the writ, and obtained a judgment in his favor from the probate court, the claimant is entitled to sue for execution under RSA 565:11:

---

[91] Lisbon Sav. Bank & Trust Co. v. Estate of Moulton, 91 N.H. at 479, 22 A.2d at 334 (1941).

[92] *Id.*

[93] Lisbon Sav. Bank & Trust Co. v. Estate of Moulton, 91 N.H. at 479, 22 A.2d at 334 (1941).

[94] American Fid. Co. v. Barnard, 104 N.H. at 154, 181 A.2d at 633 (1962).

[95] Judge of Probate v. Heydock, 8 N.H. 491, 494 (1837).

[96] American Fid. Co. v. Barnard, 104 N.H. at 154, 181 A.2d at 633 (1962). The Court in Century Indemnity Co. v. Maryland Casualty Co., 89 N.H. at 125, 193 A. at 332 (1937), held that interest and costs should be paid by the sureties, but did not discuss the issue further.

[97] A claimant may perfect his claim even after suit on the bond has been brought and judgment (forfeiture) rendered and still be entitled to execution. Judge of Probate v. Lee, 72 N.H. at 248, 56 A. at 189 (1903) (*citing* Judge of Probate v. Lane, 51 N.H. at 346).

> The party for whose use such judgment shall be rendered may sue out execution thereon, and shall be taken to be the creditor. If the execution is levied on real estate the same shall vest in such party as it would do if he were the nominal as well as the real plaintiff in the suit; and the attachment made on the original writ shall inure to his benefit in the same manner.

Execution may be awarded for money, the nonpayment of which is not a breach of the bond.[98] For example, in an action on an administration bond, execution might be awarded for money received by the administrator since the commencement of the suit.[99]

Library References

Am Jur 2d Bonds § 47

CJS Bonds § 128

§ 48-11. *Scire Facias*

"A scire facias or the statutory substitute therefor is a proceeding for the endorcement of a judgment. . . . It is generally regarded as a reanimated judgment, and not a new one."[100]

The New Hampshire statutes provide for scire facias in connection with probate bond suits:

> After judgment for the penalty of such bond any person interested, upon giving bond to the judge, with sufficient sureties, for the payment of such costs as may be adjudged against him, may sue out a *scire facias* on such judgment, to show cause why execution should not be awarded for his use out of the same. RSA 565:14.

According to RSA 565:15, in a *scire facias* for execution of judgment in a probate bond, the claim of a person is examined, judgment rendered and execution therefor awarded and he shall be taken to be the creditor.

Evidently New Hampshire treats the process as other jurisdictions do, as a continuation or form of revival of the original judgment, the court observing in *Judge of Probate v. Davis*:

---

[98] Judge of Probate v. Heydock, 8 N.H. 491, 497 (1837).

[99] Judge of Probate v. Heydock, 8 N.H. 491, 497 (1837).

[100] 46 Am. Jur. 2d Judgments § 362 (1969).

But the court awards execution only for such sum, as upon a hearing in chancery is found equitably due at the time of rendering judgment; and for such sums as upon *scire facias* brought for the purpose, may afterwards be found equitably due on account of further breaches of the condition.[101]

In *Judge of Probate v. Jackson*, scire facias was held to be a process requiring the defendants to show cause why the person suing it out should not have execution against them for another part of the judgment that was rendered for her benefit.[102] In that case, service of the *scire facias* was considered to be notice of an intent to make amendments to the original claims upon a rehearing, and defendants were found properly brought into court by the *scire facias* to show cause against such a motion for rehearing and amendment.[103]

Library References

Am Jur 2d Judgments § 1044

CJS Scire Facias § 1 et seq.

Forms

See Form 12-222 in Appendix for a Form of Fiduciary Bond.

---

[101] Judge of Probate v. Davis, 1 N.H. at 249 (1818).

[102] Judge of Probate v. Jackson, 58 N.H. 458, 460 (1878).

[103] *Id.*